A
History and Genealogy
of
BADLEY
Suffolk

Researched & compiled by

Mike Durrant

Published by Suffolk Family History Society - 2005

Dedicated to the people of
Badley
past and present.

Suffolk Family History Society

The Suffolk Family History Society is a Registered Charity (No. 1087748). It was founded at Lowestoft in 1975. Its objectives are to promote and encourage the public study of British family history, genealogy, heraldry and local history with particular reference to Suffolk and to promote the preservation, security and accessibility of archival material.

Design, typesetting and origination by Mike Durrant
Published by Suffolk Family History Society
© Michael J Durrant 2005

ISBN No 1-905111-01-0
Printed in England by Fuller-Davies, Ipswich, Suffolk 2005

INTRODUCTION

This work has taken much longer to finish than I intended and to those who have waited patiently for its completion, it is perhaps right that some explanation should be offered for the time which has passed since its first announcement. The delay has arisen principally due to the nature of the work and volume of research required, which I have only been able to pursue, often irregularly, between other projects, interests and the exacting routines of modern daily life - and - I daresay in common with other authors engaged in this type of publication, I will also admit to having been reluctant to finish, fearing there may be more worthwhile material awaiting discovery just round the corner!

In the past there has been the occasional newspaper article written about Badley. These have tended to concentrate on either the Hall, St Mary's church, or both. Also there are brief references to the parish in various gazetteers etc.

Of note are the series "Badley Hall" (Nos 4,871-4,922) written over a number of issues of *East Anglian Miscellany*' in 1917 by 'E. F. Botesdale' (alias the Rev Edmund Farrer F.S.A. of Botesdale, a very observant local antiquarian); the series *"Badley Parish Registers : Poley Entries"* (No. 6,981 - 7,023) in the same publication contributed in 1925 by 'Silly Suffolk' (alias Charles Partridge F.S.A. of Stowmarket who also wrote in the East Anglian Daily Times) (see page 32); and a six page booklet *"No 342 - Badley"* in the 'Pocket Histories of Suffolk Parishes' series by 'Yeoman' (alias R. T. Cooper), published by the Suffolk Chronicle and Mercury on 9th February 1934.

In order to present a wider history of this ancient place, I have spent the last few years collating information about the parish and the genealogy of some of the families who have lived there. Although it has not been possible to compile a 'joined-up' history, I nevertheless hope you will find the result both readable and informative.

Given the size of the parish, I was surprised as to the extent of the material available and I hope those seeking information about Badley will be able to find it here. However, although I have taken a lot of trouble to ensure that the data in this account is as accurate as possible, some of the sources of information have proved to be unreliable. In some cases this has simply been due to a lack of geographic knowledge on the part of the recorder or translator. Caution has especially proved necessary in respect of Internet genealogy where speculative and erronous entries have gone on to be adopted without question by others and duplicated in their own accounts.

Studies of this nature are invariably dependent on help from others and this work on Badley is no exception.

I am grateful to all the residents of Badley for their help and cooperation with this project and in particular to Margaret Scott for access to the Hall, Maurice Sore and Charles Morton for their help and local knowledge, Hew Stevenson for help with Columbine Hall, Anthony Breen for Latin translations, Roy Tricker for the use of his church text, Betty Barber (née Haydon), Bert Hadley, the late Millie Manning (formerly Catchpole, née Woods) and Peter Buck for family information and the use of photographs and Sue and Steve Williams for proof-reading and help with deciphering some of the wills and manuscripts.

I would also like to thank my wife Gil for enduring the countless journies along the uneven track to Badley church and Hall; the time at other places sitting in the car whilst I foraged for information and for the all the hours at home she has spent as a 'computer widow' whilst I was compiling this book.

Lastly, I am very grateful to the Suffolk Family History Society for agreeing to fund the publication of this research.

Mike Durrant
Stowmarket 2005

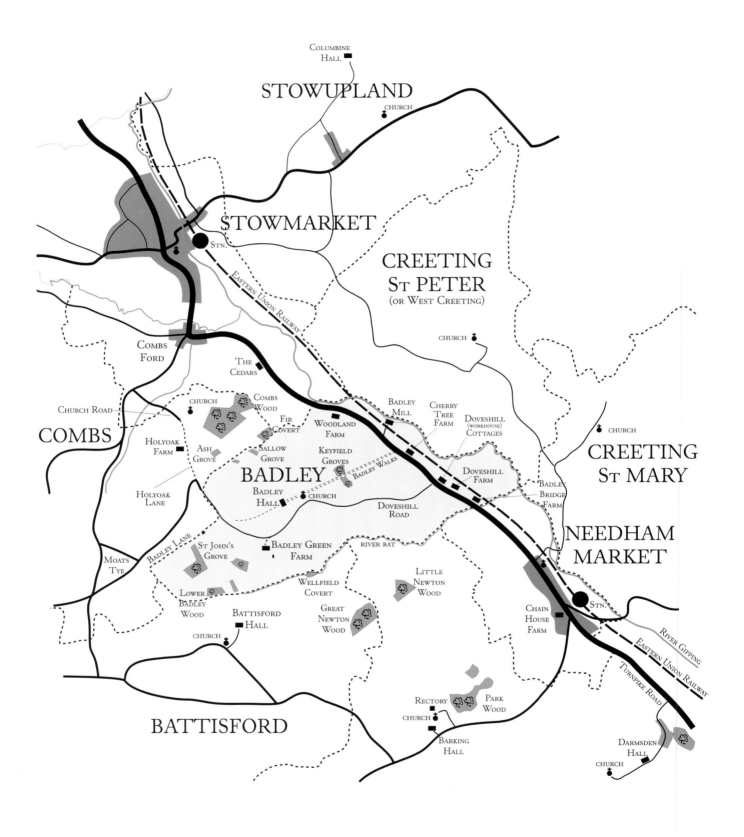

COLUMBINE HALL

STOWUPLAND

CHURCH

STOWMARKET

STN.

CREETING
St PETER
(OR WEST CREETING)

COMBS
FORD

THE
CEDARS

CHURCH

CHURCH ROAD

COMBS WOOD

COMBS

HOLYOAK
FARM

ASH
GROVE

FIR
COVERT

SALLOW
GROVE

WOODLAND
FARM

KEYFIELD
GROVES

BADLEY
MILL

CHERRY
TREE
FARM

CHURCH

DOVESHILL
(WORKHOUSE)
COTTAGES

CREETING
St MARY

HOLYOAK
LANE

BADLEY

BADLEY
HALL

CHURCH

BADLEY WALKS

DOVESHILL
FARM

DOVESHILL
ROAD

BADLEY
BRIDGE
FARM

NEEDHAM
MARKET

BADLEY LANE

MOATS
TYE

ST JOHN'S
GROVE

BADLEY GREEN
FARM

RIVER BAT

WELLFIELD
COVERT

LITTLE
NEWTON
WOOD

STN.

LOWER
BADLEY
WOOD

BATTISFORD
HALL

CHURCH

GREAT
NEWTON
WOOD

CHAIN
HOUSE
FARM

RIVER GIPPING

EASTERN UNION RAILWAY

TURNPIKE ROAD

BATTISFORD

RECTORY

CHURCH

PARK
WOOD

BARKING
HALL

DARMSDEN
HALL

CHURCH

EASTERN UNION RAILWAY

MAP OF THE PARISH OF BADLEY

DRAWN BY MIKE DURRANT

Contents

Bibliography

(for S.I.A.H. read - *Proceedings of the Suffolk Institute of Archaeology & Natural History*)

Ancient Families of Suffolk (from the notes of Sir Richard Gipps) - *Rev Francis Haselwood FSA* - *S.I.A.H. Vol VIII, Part 2, p.121-214* (1893)

Ancient Funeral Monuments Within the United Monarchie of Great Britaine, &c. - *John Weever* (1631)

Anglo-Saxon Studies in Archaeology and History - *Oxford University Committee for Archaeology* (1992)

Annals of Ipswich - *Nathaniel Bacon* (1654)

Architectural & Historical Account of the Church of St Marie Bury St Edmunds, An - *Samuel Tymms F.S.A.* (1854)

Ashburnham Family Archives - *Suffolk Record Office* (HA1)

Badley History Project (HE2) - *Roger Mayhew* (1980/81)

Badley (Needham Market) Bowl, The - *R H White* (1992)

Badley Parish Registers - *Suffolk Record Office* (FB1)

Badley Towne Booke - *Suffolk Record Office* (A2/1 and 2)

Calender of Inquisition Post Mortem Henry VII - *C Series II, Vols. 3 & 8* - *National Archives, Kew*

Epitaph from *The Castell of Courtesie* (1582)

Church Bells of Suffolk, The - *John James Raven* (1890)

Complete Peerage of England, Scotland and Ireland - *Kearsley* (1799)

Concise Description of Bury Saint Edmunds and Its Environs, A - *Public Subscription* (1827)

Dandy Pedigree, The - *F W Steer* - *(S.I.A.H.) Vol. XXVII Part 3, p.133-137* (1957)

Dictionary of Genealogy, The - *Terrick V H FitzHugh* (1985)

Domesday Book (Suffolk) - *Phillimore* (1986)

Dovecotes of Suffolk, The - *John McCann* (1998)

East Anglian Pedigrees - *Arthur Campling F.S.A.* (1939-45) (Harleian Society)

English Topography, Part VIII - *Gentleman's Magazine Library* (1896)

George Stepney, 1663-1707, Diplomat and Poet - *Susan Spens MBE* (1977)

Guide to Heraldry of Suffolk Churches - *Suffolk Heraldry Society* (1990)

Handbook to English Heraldry - *Charles Boutell* (1914)

Hartest, A Village History - *Hartest Local History Group* (1984)

Historical Atlas of Suffolk, An - *Suffolk C.C./S.I.A.H.* (1988)

History of Needham Market - *Edward Robert Hugh Paget CBE* - *Needham Market Society* (1988)

History of Parliament The Houses of Commons 1660-1690 - *Basil Duke Henning* (1983)

History of Stowmarket, The - *Rev A G H Hollingsworth* (1844)

History and Antiquities of Suffolk - Thingoe Hundred - *John Gage* (1838)

History of Suffolk, A - *David Dymond & Peter Northeast* (1985)

History of The County of Suffolk Vol. One - *William Page F.S.A.* (1911)

History, Gazetteer and Directory of Suffolk - *William White* (1855)

Horringer Parish Registers 1558-1850 - *Suffolk Green Books No IV* (1900)

Journal of Excursion Through the County of Suffolk 1832-1844 - *David Elisha Davey* - *Suffolk Records Society* (1982)

Journal of the Plague Year - *Daniel Defoe* (1722)

Journal of William Dowsing - Iconoclasm in East Anglia during the English Civil War - *edited by Trevor Cooper* - *(Boydell & Brewer)* (2001)

Kidwelly Tin Works 1737 to 1914 - *W. H. Morris*

Land Girls at the Old Rectory - *Irene Grimwood* (2000)

Manor and Woodlands of Barking - *John Vane* (1990)

Manors of Suffolk Vol 2, The - *Walter Arthur Copinger* (1905-11)

Miscellanea Genealogica et Heraldica - Vol I - *Joseph Jackson LL.D., F.S.A.* (1868)

Parish & Parish Church of All Saints Stoke Ash - *Rev W H Sewell* (1874)

P.C.C. Wills - *National Archives, Kew & Suffolk Record Office*

Pocket History of Suffolk Parishes No 342 - Badley - *Yeoman (R T Cooper)* - *Suffolk Chronicle & Mercury* (1934)

Proceedings of The Suffolk Institute of Archaeology & Natural History *(Various)*

Revolution, War & Politics 1689-1714 - Chapter 8 Stuart England - *Geoffrey Holmes* - *Phaidon Press* (1986)

Ships & Shipyards of Ipswich 1700-1970 - *Hugh Moffat* (2002)

St Mary's Church Badley - *Roy Tricker* (1966)

State Papers Domestic, Charles I, Vol 411 - *National Archives, Kew* (1638)

Suffolk Heraldic Brasses - *T M Felgate* (1978)

Suffolk Family, A - *Eric D Wolton* (1978)

Suffolk Houses - *Eric Sandon F.R.I.B.A.* (1977)

Suffolk in the XVIIth Century - The Breviary of Suffolk - *Robert Reyce* (1618)

Suffolk Limiters, - *Lilian J Redstone* - *S.I.A.H. Vol. XX, Part 1, p.36-42* (1928)

Suffolk Manorial Families - *J J Muskett* (1900)

Suffolk Returns From the Census of Religious Worship of 1851 - *Suffolk Records Society* (1997)

Suffolk Traveller, The - *John Kirby* (1764)

Supplement to the Suffolk Traveller - *Augustine Page* (1844)

Sweffling, Leather case at - *Rev E Farrer FSA* - *S.I.A.H. Vol X, Part 3, p.369-374* (1900)

The Catholic Encyclopedia, Volume XIV *(Online Edition)* - *Kevin Knight*

Tithe Records: A Detailed Examination - *National Archives, Kew* - *Domestic Information Leaflet 41*

Tithe Wars 1918-1939 The Countryside in Revolt - *Carol Twinch* (2001)

Tudor and Stuart Suffolk - *Gordon Blackwood* (2001)

Visitation of Suffolke 1561 - *William Harvy*, Clarenceux King of Arms - *Harleian Society 1981-4*

Visitation of Suffolk, 1664-68 - *Sir Edward Bysshe Knt.*, Clarenceux King of Arms - *Harleian Society 1910*

Voyage D'espagne - *Brunel* (1667)

White Friars of Ipswich, The - *Rev B Zimmerman* - *S.I.A.H. Vol. X Part 2 , p. 196-204* (1899)

Wills from the Archdeaconry of Suffolk 1637-1640 - *M E Allen & N R Evans* (1986)

the MANOR of BADLEY

Domesday and the Early Years

INTRODUCTION

BADLEY is a small Mid-Suffolk parish situated 1¾ mile W.N.W. of Needham Market and consists of a few scattered houses, farms, a manor-house and church (St Mary).

It comprises of about 1,050 acres of land bordered on two sides by rivers, the eastern boundary being formed by the River Gipping and the southern boundary by the River Bat, which flows into the River Gipping. The Bat is a small stream flowing through Battisford and is also fed by a spring in Badley (see *"Lady Well"*, page 7).

The land in Badley slopes down from the north-west to the south-east corner where the River Bat flows into the River Gipping. The highest point in Badley is in the NW corner at 66 metres (215 feet) above sea level. The lowest point is in the SE corner at the junction of the Bat and the Gipping at 21 metres (68 feet) above sea level. The soil in Badley is a slightly acid heavy loam which is suited to arable farming; generally cereal crops and sugar beet are grown.

Origins and early history

The name Badley (*Badelea*) is of Saxon origin and in some old records was spelled Badeleia. The origin of the name is the subject of speculation by historians. It is said Badley derived its name from Badelea, which means *'Bada's leah'* *(Bada's meadow)*, or alternatively, Ba(a)da's clearing.

Baðlela   Baðeleıa
Baðley

The same name and possibly the same individual features in the orgins of two other Suffolk villages - Badwell Ash and Badingham.

Birch in his Cart. Sax. 1 (1885) p.304, records *Badan-dene* or *Bada's Valley* and Kemble has *Badan-pyt* or hole.

The suffix *'ley'* is a common one and appears twenty two times in Suffolk village names, all presumably with the same vague 'meadow' meaning.

Badley's history, therefore, begins post 5th century A.D. during the time when the Saxons were raiding and settling parts of southern Britain. Whether the Saxon 'Bada' cleared and settled in what became Badley, or simply found and adopted a clearing for his settlement we shall never know.

OTHER INSTANCES OF THE NAME 'BADLEY'

The 19th century census returns list over ten other instances of 'Badley' as the place of birth. Occurring, for example, in Northamptonshire, Staffordshire and Worcestershire. However, the current Ordnance Survey Gazetteer only lists four - two other Badley halls situated within a distance of two miles of each other, within the adjoining parishes of Ardleigh and Great Bromley in North Essex and a Badley Wood and Badley Wood Common, situated adjacent in north Herefordshire, south of the hamlet of Tedstone Delemere.

As with so much local history, we have to reply on King William's 1086 Domesday Survey for the first definite evidence of Badley's existence.

The Domesday Survey 1086

WHAT WAS IT?

Twenty years after he conquered England, William the Conqueror ordered a survey and valuation of land holdings throughout England in order that he could reassess Danegeld[1] and maximise the revenue, and value of knowing, in as much detail as possible, precisely what his subjects possessed in England.

An Anglo-Saxon chronicler tells us that in 1085 -
"at Gloucester at midwinter ... the King had deep speech with his counsellors ... and sent men all over England to each shire ... to find out ... what or how much each landowner held ... in land and livestock, and what it was worth ... "

The survey was undertaken by Royal Commissioners. They visited each of the county courts in turn and cross-questioned all those with an interest in the land from the barons to the villagers. They were required to give sworn answers to their questions, for example :

- What was the name of the place. Who held it, before 1066, & now?
- How many hides? How many ploughs, both those in lordship & the men's?
- How many villagers, cottagers & slaves, how many free men & Freemen?
- How much woodland, meadow & pasture? How many mills & fishponds?
- How much has been added or taken away? What the total value was & is?
- How much each free man or Freeman had or has?
- All threefold, before 1066, when King William gave it, & now; & if more can be had than at present.

The results were collated at Winchester and within a year had been entered by a single scribe into a summarized

Note :

[1] **Danegeld**: A tax raised in the 10th & 11th centuries to buy peace from Viking raids. It continued to be raised by Anglo-Norman kings as a method of financing military and naval services. (Source: *The Dictionary of Genealogy*)

volume known as *Domesday Book Vol. I*. This considerable achievement is believed to have been accomplished by Sampson, a royal chaplain, later to become Bishop of Winchester.

However, the Commissioners' returns for the Eastern circuit (Norfolk, Suffolk and Essex), which were amongst the most populous counties of England, had not been prepared in time and were omitted from Sampson's summary. These were later copied by several writers and published unabridged as *Domesday Book Volume II*, or *Little Domesday Book*.

"In the year one thousand and eighty-six from the incarnation of our Lord, and in the twentieth year of the reign of William there was made this survey not only through these three counties, but also through others." (From Little Domesday Book)

Suffolk is therefore included in the unabridged *Little Domesday Book*, a misleading description, since the entries are in considerably more detailed than those of *Domesday Book Vol. I*.

The *Domesday Book* is written in a stylised and abbreviated 11th century clerical Latin and is therefore inaccessible to all but a few medieval scholars. The text was set and printed in English in 1783. However, recognising that a new uniformed translated was needed, in 1969, a team of 'medieval Latinists', lead by Dr. John Morris of University College London, decided to complete the task. The work, the first full translation in 900 years is printed in parallel with the corresponding Latin, the latter in the specially designed type, cut at Government expense for the 1783 edition. This translation was sponsored by specialist local history publishers Phillimores & Co. Ltd. of Chichester, and occupies 35 volumes which correspond to the county divisions of the original. A limp covered edition in two parts covering the whole of Suffolk has subsequently been published (ref. DB 34).

All land in feudal times was in the absolute ownership of the King. It was *'held'* on his behalf through grants to tenants in several forms, who in turn commonly infeuded it to subtenants. These tenants were liable to the King for their holdings be they the tenant-in-chief or an under tenant. In some cases this was an obligation of military service when required (Knights Service) although this was sometimes commuted to scutage i.e. an annual monitory payment in lieu.

Given its size, it is perhaps surprising to discover three separate assessments relating specifically to the Manor of Badley in *Little Domesday*. They show Badley was King's land *'held'* by Ralph, Earl of East Anglia *(aka Ralph Wader and Ralph Guader)*, the son of Earl Ralph the Constable and managed by Godric the Steward, the Liberty of St. Etheldreda *(at the time, this belonged to the prior and convent of Ely)* and Richard Fitzgilbert, Lord of Clare *(aka Richard of Tonbridge)*, son of Count Gilbert of Brion.

William White's '*History, Gazetteer and Directory of Suffolk*' (1855) p.36, records that 629 Suffolk manors were parcelled out by William the Conqueror to his followers. Of these, 95 were assigned to Richard of Clare, who was William's chief justice and confidant. Only two other recipients, William Mallet, Lord of Eye (221) and King William's cousin, Roger Bigod, Earl of Norfolk (117) exceeded him. King William constituted Ralph Wader as the first Norman *Earl*, or chief governor, of East Anglia. However, in 1076 Ralph was forced to flee the country, having plotted rebellion whilst celebrating his marriage at Exning, which probably explains why Godric the Steward was supervising his former holdings by 1086. The Earldom lapsed before being conferred on a later Roger Bigod by Richard I in 1189.

The assessments for Badley are reproduced below along with annotated translations.

Lands of the King

foł.m̄.xi.foł.7 iiii.đ.In æccła aut̄.xvi.ac̄.In badelea.i.lib̄ hō.xxx.acr̄.fep
.i.car̄.7.ii.ac̄r & dim̄ p̄ti. 7 uał.vii.foł.7.iiii.đ.7.i.foc̄.xx acr̄.7 uał.
tc̄ uał.xx.
iiii.foł.

Translation -
LANDS OF EARL RALPH which Godric the Steward keeps in Suffolk, in the King's hand. In BADLEY 1 free man; 30 acres. Always 1 plough. Meadow, 2½ acres. Value 7s [8] d. 1 Freeman; 20 acres. Value 4s.

Suffolk Lands of St Etheldreda's

In badeleiā tenuit . scā . A . xxx . ac in dñio . t . r . e ; hoē in p̄tio de b chingis

Translation -
In BADLEY St. Etheldreda's held 30 acres in lordship before 1066. *(This is in the assessment of Barking.)*

Lands of Richard son of Count Gilbert

BOSEMARA. *H̃*. Badeleiā teñ Afchil . t . r . e . modo . R . in dñio p̄ ii . carr terræ . 7 xx . ac . p̄ mañ . femp . iiii . uiłł . 7 . iiii . borđ . 7 . v . feru . 7 . ii . car in dominio 7 . ii . carr hominū . viii . ac p̄ti ; 7 dim moliñ . 7 . ii . runc . & xx . vi . aniat . 7 xxxii . porc . Tc̄ . lx . ous . modo . c . Ecclia . xiiii . ac . Tc̄ uał lx . fol . modo . iiii . lib . Ex hac tr̃a calūpniat Abb dim . car . tefte . h̃ . Rex & comes focā . Huic manerio additi st̃ . t . r . . . xx . vi . uiłłi Willmi libi hoes . i . car terræ 7 xl . v . ac . hos oms teñ Ricar . ad hoc maneriū quod tenuit fint . 7 ipfe phin tenebat eos p̄ acommodatione . | uicecnmit . ut ipfe uicecomes dicit. | Tc̄ 7 p̄y v . car . modo . ii . Tc̄ uał xl . fol . modo . xl . vii . Rex 7 comes focā & facā . h̃t . x . qr̃ in longo . & . v . in lato . 7 . x . deñ de gelto.

This is the main assessment. The translation opposite shows the Saxon Askell held the land under the previous King, Edward the Confessor (1042 - 5th Jan 1066) and that Richard of Clare succeeded to the land previously held by Finn the Dane.

It is interesting to note that by 1086 a church was already established at Badley with 14 acres of glebe[1] land. Whether this church occupied the same site as the present church, however, is not clear. The assessment of '½ a mill' is also intriguing. Fractions of a mill appear in many of the other assessments and almost certainly refer to water mills as the first Suffolk windmill is not thought to have been built at Bury St Edmunds until c.1191. Perhaps it is the other half of a '½ a mill' shown in the assessment for Creeting

St Peter, given they shared a river (now the *Gipping*) as a common boundary. Whether or not Burntmill Hill, Badley was the site of this mill is discussed under Badley Mill Lodge (Badley Mill) in Chapter 5, page 121.

Fig 1.1 Medieval monastic scribe.

Note :

1 glebe: land granted to a clergyman as part of his benefice.

Translation:

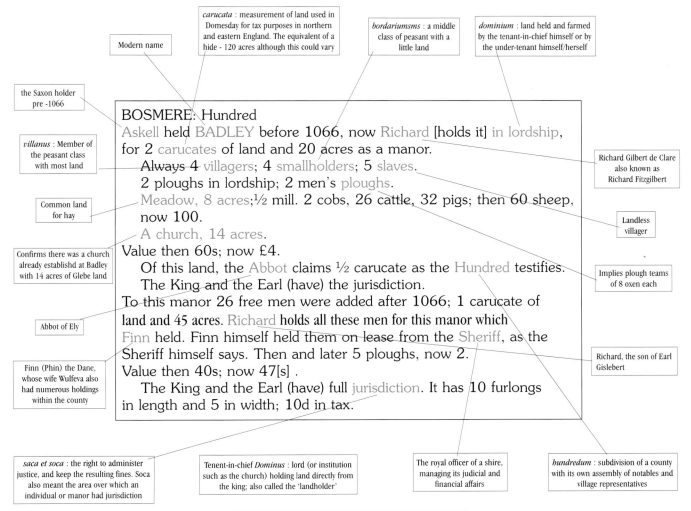

Labels around the translation box:

Modern name

carucata : measurement of land used in Domesday for tax purposes in northern and eastern England. The equivalent of a hide - 120 acres although this could vary

bordariumsms : a middle class of peasant with a little land

dominium : land held and farmed by the tenant-in-chief himself or by the under-tenant himself/herself

the Saxon holder pre -1066

villanus : Member of the peasant class with most land

Common land for hay

Confirms there was a church already establishd at Badley with 14 acres of Glebe land

Abbot of Ely

Finn (Phin) the Dane, whose wife Wulfeva also had numerous holdings within the county

Richard Gilbert de Clare also known as Richard Fitzgilbert

Landless villager

Implies plough teams of 8 oxen each

Richard, the son of Earl Gislebert

Translation text:

BOSMERE: Hundred
Askell held BADLEY before 1066, now Richard [holds it] in lordship, for 2 carucates of land and 20 acres as a manor.
   Always 4 villagers; 4 smallholders; 5 slaves.
   2 ploughs in lordship; 2 men's ploughs.
   Meadow, 8 acres;½ mill. 2 cobs, 26 cattle, 32 pigs; then 60 sheep, now 100.
   A church, 14 acres.
Value then 60s; now £4.
   Of this land, the Abbot claims ½ carucate as the Hundred testifies.
The King and the Earl (have) the jurisdiction.
To this manor 26 free men were added after 1066; 1 carucate of land and 45 acres. Richard holds all these men for this manor which Finn held. Finn himself held them on lease from the Sheriff, as the Sheriff himself says. Then and later 5 ploughs, now 2.
Value then 40s; now 47[s] .
   The King and the Earl (have) full jurisdiction. It has 10 furlongs in length and 5 in width; 10d in tax.

Bottom labels:

saca et soca : the right to administer justice, and keep the resulting fines. Soca also meant the area over which an individual or manor had jurisdiction

Tenent-in-chief *Dominus* : lord (or institution such as the church) holding land directly from the king; also called the 'landholder'

The royal officer of a shire, managing its judicial and financial affairs

hundredum : subdivision of a county with its own assembly of notables and village representatives

12th to 14th CENTURY BADLEY

LITTLE appears to be known about Badley during the years immediately following Domesday Survey, which saw the coronations of William II (1087), Henry I (1100), Stephen (1135) and Henry II (1154) and Richard I (1189).

Early Norman Lords embarked on castle building programmes at locations such as Framlingham, Haughley, Bungay, Eye, Clare and Orford during this period and the county was, as elsewhere, often the scene of tumult and bloodshed as rival factions settled old scores or fought for or against the King.

de Badley
Arg. a cross Sa.

During this time the manor passed from the Domesday tenant to Gilbert de Clare and for a long period after that, it was in the hands of a family which derived its name from the place. Dr. Copinger in his *"Manors of Suffolk"* II., 238, gives Ralfe de Badele as the first of the name, but assigns no date, and his name is not found in any fine[1].

In 1228 there is one between Hugh de Badelee against Alan de Hulm in Badele and then in 1240 another by *"Thomas, son of Geoffrey, against Geoffrey de Baddel in Buddel."*

This name occurs in the Close Rolls of the period I Edward I. (1272), *"an order to the Escheator not to intermeddle with the fees in Badley, unless Geoffrey held of the King in chief as the King learns from the Exchequer Rolls that he held of Gilbert de Clare, Earl of Gloucester,"* and then there is another record in 2 Edward I., *"to permit Gilbert, Earl of Gloucester, to hold the above, as he was in seizen of the homage of Geoffrey de Badele for the said fees until Geoffrey's death."*

This owner was succeeded by a son, Robert de Badeley, and in 1327 he is to be found the following fine: *"Robert de Badele and Meliora, his wife, against Richard de Hasting, and John Bateman, of the manor of Badele, in the town of Badele."* These people are all recorded in the Subsidy List of that same year. Under Badley we have:

De Roberto de Badele	IXs.	VIIId
De Johanne Bateman of Badele		XIId.
De Sampson de Badele	IIs.,	
De Michaele de Badele,		XIId.,

and under Ipswich we find the name of Richard de Hasting.

Writing in Volume X of the *Proceedings of the Suffolk Institute of Archæology of Natural History* in 1899, on the White Friars of Ipswich, the Rev. Benedict Zimmerman says, "About the middle of the 14th century a number of knights, attracted by the saintly lives of the friars, joined the Order, although owing to their want of learning, they were only able to occupy an inferior position. Among these we find Geoffrey Badley at Ipswich".

In the same volume there is a descriptive list of Ancient Deeds pertaining to Suffolk in the Public Record Office. A number of these early Treasury deeds *(A series)* relate to the de Badele family (alias Badelea, Badeleia, Baddele) (i.e. 'of' Badley), including Sir Geoffrey de Badele, Knt, (the son of Robert of Badele), his sons William and Roger and John the son of Hugh de Badele, for example:

A.3284 - Grant[2] by Geofrey de Badele, son of Robert of Badele, to the canons of the Apostles Peter and Paul of Ipswich, of the gift that William de Badele his uncle made them of 24s. yearly rent less ¾d, in Brokes and Turlestone, payable by the tenants named, and of land in Brokes, called "Scarboteswallelond", "Risewikelond", "Goredlond", land abutting on the meadow of Helioch, on Berewelle, and on Pingel's land, a messuage by the mill of Horsewade, pasture by Hagneford mill, and land before William Pikehorn's gate. Witnesses :- Bartholomew de Glanvill, Robert de Angervill', Baldwin de Pesehale, and others (named). Equestrian seal.

A.3305 - Grant by William son of Geoffrey de Badelea, to Robert Doi, son of Herbert de Brokes, of three acres in Brokes, paying 27d. yearly and the Services of the King and the Earl of Clare. Witnesses :- Robert son of Geoffrey de Badelea, Roger his brother, and others (named).

A.3306 - Grant by Geoffrey de Badele, knight, to Robert Joie, of Ipswich, for 34s. of land with pasture in Brokes in S. Peter's parish, between the highway and the water flowing from Horsewade mill towards Botflod, abutting Southward on Mandulveswalle, and with all "le Rettel pond," paying yearly. November, 47 Henry III (1262).

See Appendix G for the five other deeds summarised in the list.

Dr. Copinger says the manor remained in the hands of the family of Badele until 1424, when it passed from William de Badele through the hands of the de Mortimer's[3] to Edmond Alcock, and in 1436 there is a fine recorded between *"Edmund Neve, John Furbusshour, and William Bret, all chaplains, against Henry Alcock and Elizabeth, his wife, in Badley."*

Mortimer
Barry of six Or. & Az. an Inescutcheon Arg.

He records that the will of Edmond Alcock[4] (alias Edmund Rafman, gent) was proved 10th February, 1491. However, this could not have been the original purchaser in 1424, more especially as we have Henry Alcock in 1436. However, this Edmond Alcock left a daughter and heiress named Margery, who married Simon Poley of Woodhall[5] Stoke Ash.

Alcock(e)
Arg. a chevron engrailled between three
moorcocks Sa. proper, membered Gu.

Notes :

1 **fine**: derived from the Latin *finis* - an end, in this context a judgement or Final Concorde regarding a title to land after a form of legal action, nearly always collusive, and intended to provide a record of title, often after a purchase.

2 **grant**: the conveyance of property to another by deed.

3 **de Mortimer**: the notorious de Mortimers were the Earls of March, who included amongst their ranks Roger, the 1st Earl (c.1287-1330) the lover of Isabella the wife of Edward II (1307-1326) and who was at the forefront of his murder. He effectively ruled the country in the name of Edward's son Edward III (1326/7-1376/7) until the latter had him executed. Roger, the 2nd Earl (1327-60), who died commanding English troops at Rouvray, and Roger the 4th Earl was hewn to pieces in the Battle of Kells 1398. Their stronghold was Wigmore Castle, Hertfordshire. One is left to speculate whether the de Badeles sold the manor of Badley to the Mortimers or had it confiscated by Roger, the 1st Earl, during the reign of Edward III. In his will Edmund Alcock (4 below) refers to his "manor of Badley lately purchased and recovered from Robert Mortimer".

4 **Edmund Alcock's will**: reproduced Appendix D.

5 **Woodhall**: see Fig 6.2, Chapter Six, page 151.

The origins of this family of Alcock are unclear. A John Alcock, and Simon his son, of Weybread, are recorded in a fine of 6 Edward III (1333); and in the 1327 Subsidy List there is a William Alcock, at Haughley, paying *viid.*, the aforesaid John Alkok at Weyebrede paying *vis. ixd.*, and Peter Alcock at Bardwell paying *vid.*

However, in an article, *'The Ancient Families of Suffolk'*, by Revd. Francis Haslewood, F.S.A., (S.I.A.H., Vol. VIII. Part 2, p.125) cites Antiquitates Suffolciences. OR *"An Essay. Towards recovering some account of the Ancient Familys in the County of Suffolk"*, a collection compiled, but never completed, by the Suffolk antiquarian Sir Richard Gipps K^{nt} of Great Wheltham (Welnetham). Here Alock(e) is listed as ALCOTT, but appears to relate to the same family as the following reproduction shows:

"ALCOTT. This Family was ancient, and for many years seated at Shottely in Santford Hundred, till the sole Daughter and Heir marri'd to *John Felton* of the same Town. Beside their Lands in Shottely, they were possess'd of the Mann^r of Badly-Hall, with Lands in Needham and Combs.

They bare sag. a chev. between 3 Cocks Heads eras'd sab. crested g. barb'd and beak'd or."

This is the only instance of this spelling I have discovered.

The passage of the manor of Badley from the Alcocks to the Poleys is examined in more detail in Chapter Six.

Exactly what constituted the manor of Badley at this stage is unclear. I have been unable to conclude whether it was all or most of the land within the current parish boundary or just a few fields surrounding the hall? Manuscripts from the period describe land transacted but most of the names used do not correlate with the earliest surviving manuscript maps. A good example of which is John Maddison's survey of 1621, discussed in Chapter 2.

Several references to manuscripts relating to this period are recorded in Appendix G.

Poley of Badley
Or. a lion rampant Sa. (collared & chained Or.)

Lady Well

OVERGROWN in a rushy meadow on the southern boundary of Badley parish, S.E. of Badley Green, and about half-a-mile S. of Badley Church and Hall, is a spring known as "Lady Well".

It is one of the sources of a little stream called the Bat (hence possibly Badley and Battisford) which winds through a stretch of fair green meadows to join the Gipping above Needham Market. The country people have some vague traditions that this well was formerly a place of veneration and resort. (*The East Anglian 1897-98* New Series Vol II, p.32)

On William Collier's 1741 manuscript map of Badley (Fig 1.3 overleaf), the approach to the 'Lady Well' is via an avenue of trees, off Goslins (sic) Lane, perhaps a processional way, illustrating a degree of importance formerly attached to the site.

What history lies behind the Lady Well? Was it a healing well, about which rituals had to be performed in order to "activate" the power of the water on certain acknowledged days? Or perhaps a christianised or "sainted" well which almost always had to be visited on the appropriate saint's day or on such dates as Easter Sunday or Whit Sunday?

An appropriate time of day for a visit was dawn or just before sunrise. Direction of approch was important and the ceremonies often stipulatied a need for silence, if not for the entire duration of the visit, certainly during the ritual.

Fig 1.2 The Lady Well today - overgrown but still identifiable.

Although no artefacts have been found at Badley, it was not uncommon for offerings to be made at well sites. This ancient practice dates from the early Bronze Age and items such as swords, helmets, shields and other pieces

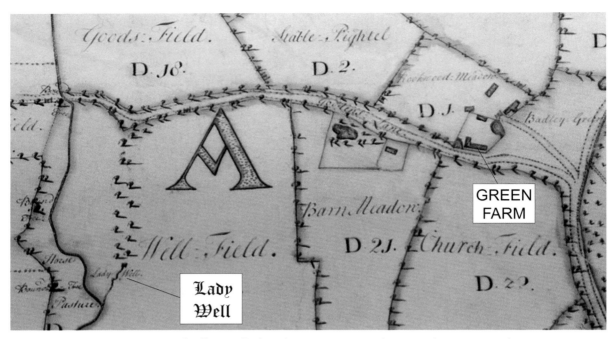

Fig 1.3 a part of William Collier's 1741 manuscript map (courtesy of Hew Stevenson).

of metalwork have been found at river and wells sites in considerable quantities. In folklore, a spring was reputed to be the entrances to the Other Worlds and, like thresholds the world over, many of them had guardians - usually in the form of one or more fish.

Invariably, the details of the rituals to be carried out were lost before being recorded. What remains, therefore, is often simply a record of a social folk gathering, or pilgrimage. Where these tradition have been upheld, those involved are often therefore unclear what they should do when they get there!

An exception to this is Well Dressing in Derbyshire. Some sources attribute this practice to the period of the Black Death in 1348-9, when probably a third of the population of England died of the disease. Those who survived attributed this to their clean water supply and gave thanks by 'dressing' the village wells. However, it seems very likely that the practice goes back much further than this - probably to pagan times - and the fact that many well dressings have a 'well queen' suggests echoes of ancient fertility rites. (Adapted from '*Peak District Multimedia Guide*' - *Cressbrook Multimedia 1997.*)

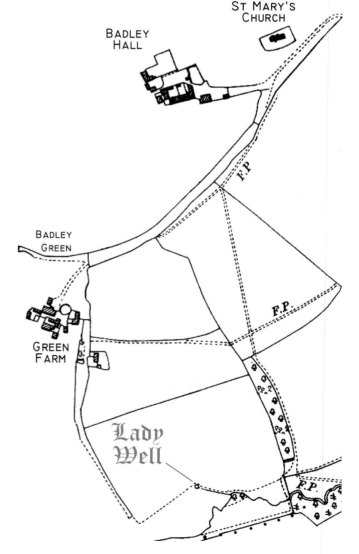

Fig 1.4 (right) Modern map showing the location of the Lady Well in relation to Green Farm, Badley Hall and St Mary's church.

the
MANOR
of
BADLEY

*Between
the two
Elizabeths*

Badly Crosse and the 1621 Survey

IN 1621 **John Maddison** was commissioned, presumably by the Poleys, to survey the Manor of Badley. This survey survives in the Suffolk Record Office (HA1/DC3/1). Part of the survey is reproduced below.

Within the survey the description the Edmund Poley's holdings contains frequent reference to the 'Kings Highway at Badly Crosse'. One is left to speculate where this was and what form it took.

As it is associated in the text with the 'Kings Highway', the most likely location would have been beside the road at the entrance to the roadway leading down to St Mary's church (Doveshill Road).

This contention is supported by an Estate Map drawn for Orlando Bridgeman of Combs in 1710 which shows Holyoak Lane, the track linking Badley Lane/Doveshill Road with Church Road, Combs via Holyoak Farm, as "A road leading from Badley Crosse to Stowmarket . . . " (see map page iv).

Was the Badley Crosse another victim of the iconoclast William Dowsing's visit to Badley on 5th February 1643, at a time when they were considered to be papist symbols and the tops of them were smashed off?

Translation
The Manor of Badlye

"A Survey of the said manor made by the inspection and scrutiny of the rolls and ancient rentals of this manor in so much as they show how much the copyholders hold and by their inquest in the court showing which tenements are customary. And also the abuttals of their lands whether customary or free are inscribed in this book. An account of the tenure, inheritance and rents from the aforesaid rolls. This survey was made by John Madison, surveyor, in the 19th year of the reign of King James etc. AD 1621

All lands in Badlye as much ploughlands and lands free and customary tenure, as plainly set forth and delineated in a geographic description or by a complete map[1] of all the Town of Badly."

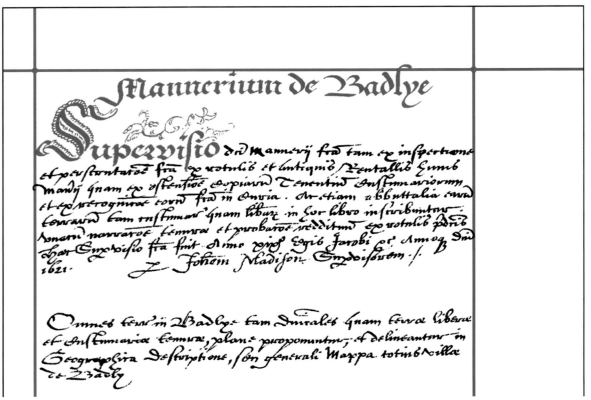

Fig 2.1 A reproduction of the front sheet to John Madison's 1621 Survey of the Manor of Badley.

Note:

[1] Unfortunately this map is missing from the surviving survey and would have helped confirm whether the Poleys' Manor of Badley included the whole of the parish of Badley.

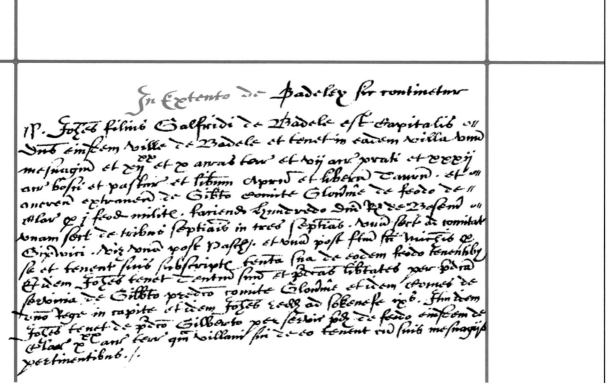

Fig 2.2 A reproduction of the second page of John Madison's 1621 Survey of the Manor of Badley,
which appears to be a commentary on the situation prevailing shortly after the Domesday survey.

Translation

In extent Badeley thus contains

I. P. John, son of Geoffrey of Badely is the chief lord of same town of Badely. And he holds in that same town, one messuage and acres of land and seven acres of meadow and 32 acres of woods and pasture and liberty of boar and liberty of bull and of stray draft beasts of Gilbert, Earl of Gloucester of the fee of Clare for one knight's fee. He must undertake a three separate suits in the Lord King's Hundred Court of Bosmere and three other suits at the County Court of Ipswich, namely once after Easter and one after the feast of St Michael for this his holdings written below which are held by him of this fee. And the same John holds his tenement and the aforesaid liberties for the said service of the said Gilbert, Earl of Gloucester and the same Earl of the Lord, the King as tenant in chief. And the same John pays for Sokenes IXs. Item the same John holds of the said Gilbert for his service of the same fee of Clare, 200 acres of land in that vill together with his messuage and other belongings.

Translation *(of Fig 2.3 overleaf)*

Edmund Polye esquire son of Richard Polye esquire brother of Edmund Polye esquire son of John Polye esquire Lord of the Manor of Badlye holds the following land namely:

Site of the Manor

The Site of the Manor with gardens, an orchard, woodyard, milkingyarde and other (yards) lying between a pasture called Cowespasture on the part of the north and Calvespytell and Barnefeld on the south and the aforesaid Cowespasture and Churchegrene on the east and Horseclose on the west and contains together 7a 2r 19p.

Calves Pytell

One pightle called Calvespitell lying in a triangle between the King's highway from the church to Badly Greene on the southeste and the site of the manor on the north and Barnefeld on the west and contains 2a 0r 16p.

Horseclose

One pightle called Horseclose lying between the aforesaid site and Cowepasture on the east and Barnefeld on the south and Woodmedowe on the northwest and contains 4a 3r 37p.

Woodemedo(we)

One meadow called Woodemedowe lying between Cowepasture and Crookefelde on the part of the east and partly on the north and Crosfeld on the west and northwest and the aforesaid Horseclose and Barnefeld on the south and contains 15a 0r 11 p.

Crosfelde

One close called Crosfelde lying between Barnefelde on the south and Crookefelde Queach on the northwest and abuts on the aforesaid Woodemedowe and in part on the said Crookefeld towards the east and partly the north and on the King's Highway at Badly Crosse towards the west and contains 17a 2r 25p.

Crookfeld Queach

One close of land called Crookefeld Queach lying between Crosfelde and Crookefeld on the south and east and land in Combes and Goslingmedowe in part on the north and abuts on the King's highway leading from Badly Crosse to [gap] towards the west and on Goslingclose towards the east and partly north and contains 24a 2r 36p.

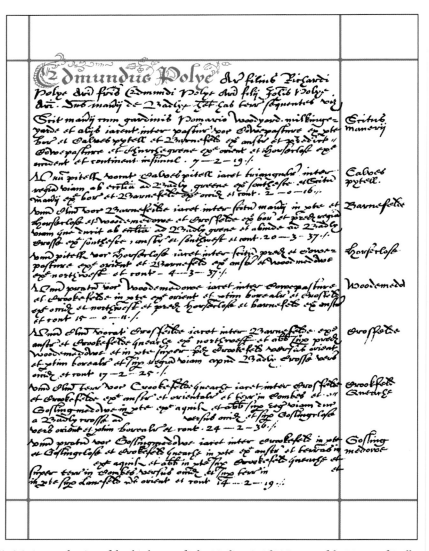

Fig 2.3 A reproduction of the third page of John Madison's 1621 Survey of the Manor of Badley, detailing part of Edmund Poley's holdings & containing the references to Badly Crosse.

Goslingmedowe

One meadow called Goslingmedowe lying between Crookefeld in part and Goslingclose and Crookefeld Queach in part to the south and lands in [gap] to the north and abuts in part on Crookefeld Queach and on land in Combes towards the west and on land in [gap] and in part on Lanefeld towards the east and contains 14a 2r 19p.

———————————————————

c) *Free land*

Badley Crosse - Edmund Lockwood holds freely two parcels of land whereof one lies at Badley Cross between the king's way there to the northwest and desmene land of this manor called Bugges Woode to the southeast and abuts upon the said king's way to the northeast and upon the said Bugges Woode in part and [upon] the other piece of the said Edmund in part to the southwest containing 4a 3r 14p. The other piece lies between the aforesaid king's highway to the northwest and Bugges Woode to the southeast and abuts upon the preceding piece to the northeast and upon land lately St(?) John's now Thomas Barker gent to the southwest containing 1a 3r 14p.

The Plight of the Poor and the Badley Towne Booke

PRIOR to the Reformation the responsilbility for the care of the poor appears to have largely rested with the Church, and one third of the parish parson's tithes were intended to be given by him to the poor. Following the dissolution of the monasteries, the problem of relieving poverty became acute and the clergy were ordered to collect alms for poor people. An Act of 1572 created Alms Collectors and Supervisors of the Labour of Rogues and Vagabonds in each parish. People who would not give alms voluntarily could be compulsorily assessed. In 1597 the two offices were combined under the title of Overseer of the Poor, an honorary parochial appointment which required the approval of the Justices of the Peace.

By the great Poor Law Act of 1601, churchwardens became ex-officio Overseers of the Poor, together with those approved by the Justices. One of their number was appointed executive officer of the Overseers and looked after the funds raised by parochial rates. From 1691, the Overseer was obliged to keep a record of his disbursements and distribution of clothing, etc. His rate books list the sums collected from parishioners according to the value of their properties.

An interesting insight into how this applied at Badley is provided by two Badley Towne Books which survive in the Suffolk Record Office (Ref A2/1 & 2). These books contain amongst other church records, the Churchwardens' and Overseers' accounts for the periods 1669 to 1690 and 1669 to 26th October 1747 respectively. The first page from the latter is reproduced at Fig 2.4, when William Holmes was the churchwarden. Notable amongst his entries is the charge of 1s. 6d. "for going to Ipswich for ye court". This was to take the oath before a Justice of the Peace prior to taking up the overseers' duties. The second book spans the years 17th May 1762-1820. Both books contain a wealth of information and two pages, one recording the collection of the poor rate and the other the payments for 1744 (see Fig 2.5 overleaf).

Fig 2.5 shows that the lord of the manor, Ambrose Crowley, was rated at £3. 16s. 6d., whereas two Badley farmers, Abraham Southgate and Thos Wolton, who were also the overseers, paid £5. 11s. 6d. and £4. 4s. 6d. respectively.

Although the Wolton family, who tenant-farmed at the Hall and at Green farm are discussed in Chapter 8 - Other Notable Badley Families, their almost continuous association with the offices of Overseer, Constable or Churchwarden at Badley between 1720 and 1782 when they relocated to Newbourn, deserves further mention here.

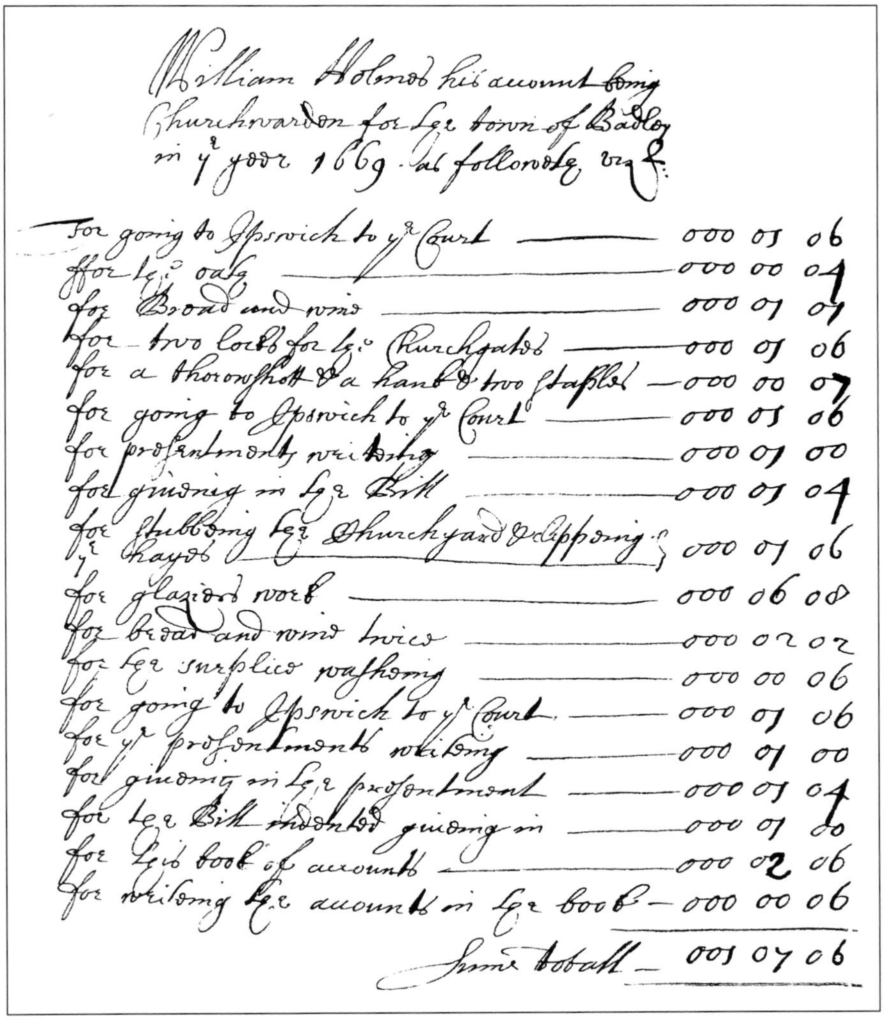

William Holmes his account being Churchwarden for the town of Badley in ye year 1669 as followeth viz

For going to Ipswich to ye Court	000 01 06
ffor the oath	000 00 04
for Bread and wine	000 01 01
for two locks for the Churchgates	000 01 06
for a thoroughshott & a hank & two staples	000 00 07
for going to Ipswich to ye Court	000 01 06
for presentments writing	000 01 00
for giving in the Bill	000 01 04
for stubbing the Churchyard & clipping ye hayes	000 01 06
for glaziers work	000 06 08
for bread and wine twice	000 02 02
for the surplice washing	000 00 06
for going to Ipswich to ye Court	000 01 06
for ye presentments writing	000 01 00
for giving in the presentment	000 01 04
for the Bill indented giving in	000 01 00
for this book of accounts	000 02 06
for writing the accounts in the book	000 00 06
Summe totall	001 07 06

Fig 2.4 The first page of the Badley Towne Book (SRO A2/1).

In his book 'A *Suffolk Family'*, Eric D Wolton devotes pages 13-18 to extracts, with notes, from the Badley Town Books in the section dealing with 'the Woltons of Wyverstone and Badley'. For example -

1672 For the Act for the Buriall in Wooling £0. 0s. 4d.
(This was the Act passed in Charles II's reign that every Englishman or woman should be buried in a woollen shroud. Its object was to stimulate the growth of the woollen manufacturing industry and it remained in force until 1815.)

1676 To ye last Churchwarden that he paid at ye court for not repairing ye Church   £0. 1s. 10d.
(It is interesting to note that the more conscientious Church authorities in those days did their best to see that the parish churches were kept in repair. Following this entry there were eleven items of expenditure on the Church including the following:)

For 5 dais work of a mason   £0. 8s. 6d.

1685
Apparill for ye poor   £0. 15s. 0d.
For wood for ye poor   £0. 19s . 6d.
For a poor mans buriall   £0. 10s. 0d.
for a Book of Hommiles *(Homilies)*   £0. 7s. 0d.
paid for a book for the day of thanksgiving £0. 0s. 7d.
(Presumably for James II's suppression of Monmouth's and Argyll's rebellions.) and

1762, May 17.
Tho. Wolton Pd at the toulgate (tollgate[1]) £0. 0s. 3d.
John Wolton as deto   £0. 5s. 0d.

1762 July 30. John Wolton Constable
for a Journey to Claydon with Hannah Porter £0. 1s. 6d.
for A Journey to ditto with Codd   £0. 1s. 6d.

for a Sumont (Summons) Warrent   £0. 2s. 0d.
for ¼ of a Day for a Man to Carry Hannah Porter
          £0. 0s. 9d.
pd for A order of Barstardy for Codd   £0. 4s. 0d.

Rcd of John Codd for Hannah Porter Lying in £2. 0s. 0d.

Oct 9 John Wolton for Close (clothes) for Tho. Danley
          £0. 15s. 0d.
1764 Aug 11.
Paid Mashol (Marshalsea) money   £0. 12s. 1d.
(An annual entry. This was a county rate. Originally each parish had to contibute towards the cost of maintaining prisoners in the Marshalsea Prison[2], whether or not any parishioners were in the prison. Later, when this was discontinued, the levy was still known as Marshalsea Money, but was applied to other purposes.)

1766 Oct ye 7.
for a man and carte horse to carrie the poore to The Industery House at Barham for ye Churchwardens and Overseers
journey with them   £0. 3s. 0d.
Expences with them   £0. 1s. 0d.
(Badley paupers were conveyed to the House of Industry (workhouse) at Barham and put to work spinning wool and making ploughs, etc.)

Doveshill Cottage (see Chapter 5, Fig 5.55) opposite the driveway leading to Badley church was originally a row of three small cottages which served as the parish workhouse.

Badley was incorporated with the other parishes in the Bosmere and Claydon Hundred for the support of their poor under Gilbert's Act in 1765. A workhouse capable of accommodating about 500 inmates was built at Barham the following year on 20½ acres of land purchased from the Rev John Bacon of Coddenham for £354.

Notes :

[1] **tollgate**: parishes were charged with the upkeep of the highways which traversed them, but as these were used for the most part by travellers from a distance, they usually scamped the work or left it undone. Consequently turnpike companies began to be established in 1728 and were granted Parliamentary powers to erect gates and toll bars and charge the actual users of the road in return for re-making and maintaining particular stretches of highway. Between 1700 and 1750 as many as four hundred Road Acts were passed and between 1751 and 1790 sixteen hundred. The white turnpike gates with their attendant pikemen were to be found on most main roads at five mile intervals and their presence was bitterly resented by the local users of the road. Cordy S. Wolton 1857-1946 used to say that when John and his descendants could avoid this payment they did so by making their horses jump the gate or the rails. This was a considerable feat but could be done by a good horse and rider. In 1864 the turnpike companies began to be abolished and the cost of the repair of the roads put on the rates. *The Claydon to Bury Turnpike Co* was established in 1771. Local tollgates were situated at Claydon, Blakenham and Stowmarket. In the Town Booke, there are frequent entries - 'Working on the Roads with a Draught'. (adapted from, *A Suffolk Family* - Eric D Wolton)

[2] **Marshalsea prison**: one of London's most important prisons pre-dating 1381, when it was attacked in the Peasants' Revolt. Mainly used for debtors, the prison was immortalised by Charles Dickens in Little Dorrit. In closed in 1842 - one of the walls still survives.

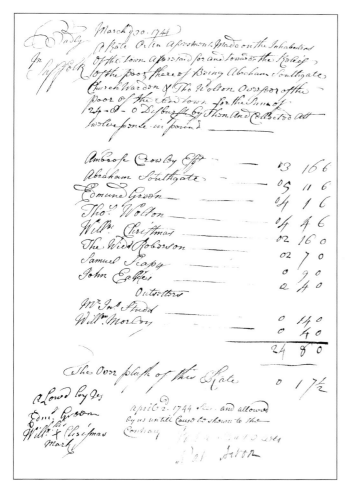
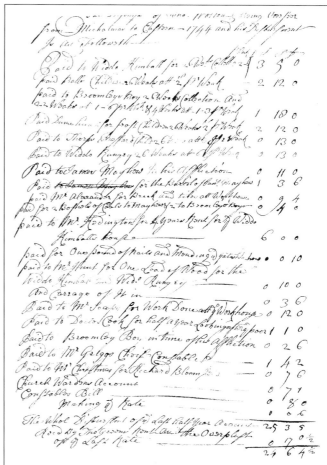

Fig 2.5 The Badley Town Book 1774 - the Overseers' account showing left - income collected under the poor rate and right -expenditure in support of the poor.

The Overseer's account contains several entries for expenses incurred conveying persons to Barham workhouse by horse and cart.

In 1834, parochial responsibility for the poor was ended. Parishes were amalgamated for such purposes into Poor Law Unions, governed by elected Poor Law Guardians. The Bosmere & Claydon workhouse was re-designated the Bosmere & Claydon union-house. On 5th April 1836, John Kirby Moore of Badley (see Chapter 8) was elected Vice-Chairman of the Board of Guardians for Bosmere Union.

The English Civil Wars 1642-51

It is sufficent to note here that throughout this period Sir Edmund Poley of Badley, a catholic, was amongst Suffolk's rich gentry who actively supported the King's (Royalist) cause. This eventually led to sequestration. The register of *"Royalist Composition Papers. Entries of Reports on Delinquents Estates and Fines Levied Thereon"*, records: "THIS delinquent that he rose in Arms against the parliament and rose in Oxfordshire at the time when it rose holden a Garrison against the parliament and at the time of the surrender and is to have the benefit of those articles as by Sir Thomas Fairfax certificate of the 24th of June 1646 doth approve." (see Chapter 6 and Appendix G)

For a more in formation about this period see *Tudor & Stuart Suffolk* by Gordon Blackwood (2001).

The Great Plague 1665

The adjacent town of Needham Market suffered very severely from the Plague of 1665, although exactly how many died is not known. In those days Needham people were buried at Barking and their burials were recorded in the Barking Parish Registers. One therefore would have expected that the registers would show a sharp rise in the number of burials in 1665, but in fact there were fewer than usual. At first sight this is surprising, but the reason for it doubtless is that, during the visitation of the plague in 1665, Needham people, being strictly confined to their own village, were unable to take their dead along the causeway to Barking Church.

In his "*Journal of the Plague Year*", Daniel Defoe (1772) explains why the records at this time were, in many cases, defective: "Now when I say that the parish officers did not give a full account, let anyone but consider how men could be exact in such a time of dreadful distress, and when many of them were taken sick themselves and perhaps died in the very time when their accounts were to be given in."

In the absence of a graveyard around St John's Church (then a chapel) it is believed that Needham's victims of the plague were buried in two Plague Pits. One on Town Lands off Ipswich Road close to the Lion Inn and the other near Badley Bridge.

'If they could, people fled from London and other infected towns into the country but, as Defoe tells us, they had to obtain certificates of health in order to do so "for without these there was no being admitted to pass through the towns upon the road, or to lodge in any inn," and eventually an order of the government was issued "to place turnpikes and barriers in the road to prevent people travelling." Despite these precautions, however, these refugees in many cases took the infection with them and it was in this way that it is said that the plague was brought to Needham. Chains

were set up as barriers across the highway at both ends of Needham, a fact commemorated in the names of the Chain House farm on the way to Ipswich and Chain Bridge (i.e Badley Bridge) on the way to Stowmarket. Chains, however, could not keep out infested rats and many people, in any case, believed that the infection was borne on the air from the south and that the only way to keep it out was to seal up the windows with a southern aspect.' Adapted from '*A History of Needham Market*' by Hugh Paget CBE.

Although Ipswich was also badly affected, Stowmarket only three miles away escaped. There is no evidence to suggest that the population of Badley suffered either. For only one burial is recorded for 1665, unless the register is defective for the same reasons given earlier.

On 11th September 1665, Thomas Whitecake of Badley married Sarah Colchester from Needham Market at St Mary's church Badley. One wonders what precautions, if any, were taken to ensure the plague did not accompany her to the church, and whether she opted to be married at Badley rather than in her home town of Needham Market because of it.

Perhaps Badley's isolated nature was its salvation on this occasion, although we know from the extracts in Samuel Pepys' diary reproduced in Chapter 6, that Sir Edmund Poley of Badley Hall was living in plague-torn London for some of this period and could so easily have brought the disease back with him to Suffolk.

> Ring a ring o' roses   A pocketful of posies.
> Atishoo! Atishoo!   We all fall down.

The song/game 'Ring-a-ring of roses' which is widely assumed to have originated from the time of the 1347 or 1665 plagues is still sung/played by children today. It is said to describe in great detail the symptoms of the plague. A ring of rose coloured spots was one of the first symptoms of the plague; popular belief prescribed posies of herbs as protection against the disease; sneezing was a sure sign that you were about to die from it and the last line ' we all fall down' omits only one word.....Dead. However, there are many who question this given the earliest known printed version of the rhyme apparently occurs in Kate Greenaway's *Mother Goose* or *The Old Nursery Rhymes* in 1881. For the "plague" explanation to be true, it is contended one has to believe that children were reciting the nursery rhyme continuously for over five centuries, yet no one during that time span found it popular enough to write down. Is it therefore credible to assert that a rhyme which didn't appear in print until 1881 actually "began in 1347 or 1665"?

William Collier's 1741 Map

Fig 2.6 William Collier's 1741 map of Ambrose Crowley's Suffolk estate (courtesy of Hew Stevenson).

Measuring in excess of six feet and covering several square miles, this large manuscript map is a credit to Collier's surveying and draughting skills given the basic measuring tools which would have been available to him at the time. Centre stage is Badley Hall (1) and Badley Walk (2) which is shown extending the Combs side of the hall as far as Badley Lane; the distinctive Key Field Groves (3); the Needham Market to Stowmarket turnpike (4) and Combs Church and Hall (5). On the lower right are two 'detached' plans showing Crowley's property in Stowupland (Columbine Hall) (6) and farms in Hitcham and Buxhall (7). Surprisingly Barking Hall, his residence, is not shown. Note also the two vignettes *(top left)* Combs Church & Hall and *(bottom left)* Badley Hall (see Chapter 4). See overleaf for a tracing of the Badley section of this map (Fig 2.7).

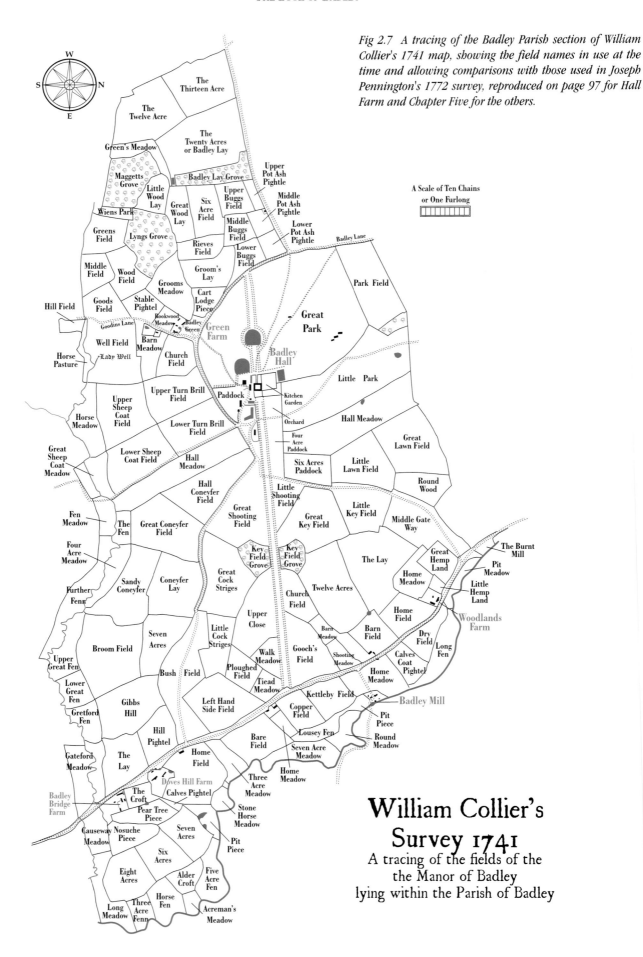

Fig 2.7 A tracing of the Badley Parish section of William Collier's 1741 map, showing the field names in use at the time and allowing comparisons with those used in Joseph Pennington's 1772 survey, reproduced on page 97 for Hall Farm and Chapter Five for the others.

A Scale of Ten Chains or One Furlong

William Collier's Survey 1741
A tracing of the fields of the
the Manor of Badley
lying within the Parish of Badley

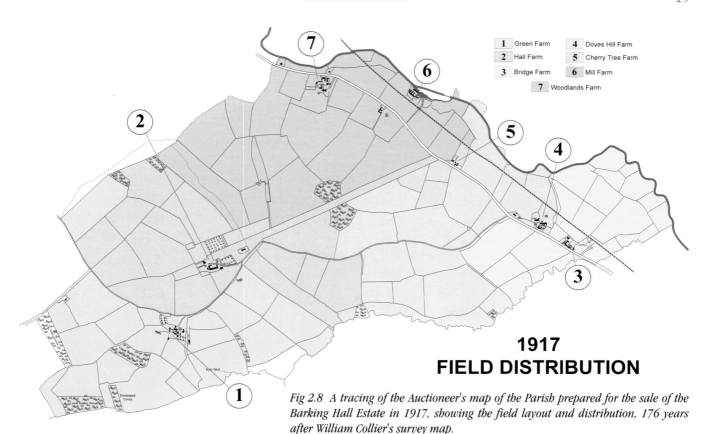

1 Green Farm   **4** Doves Hill Farm
2 Hall Farm   **5** Cherry Tree Farm
3 Bridge Farm   **6** Mill Farm
7 Woodlands Farm

1917
FIELD DISTRIBUTION

Fig 2.8 A tracing of the Auctioneer's map of the Parish prepared for the sale of the Barking Hall Estate in 1917, showing the field layout and distribution, 176 years after William Collier's survey map.

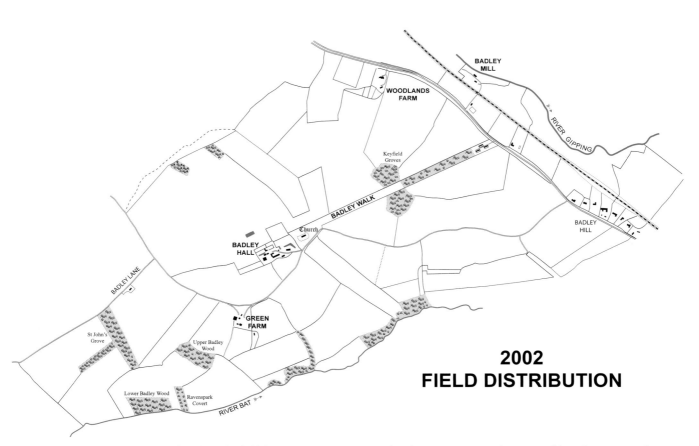

2002
FIELD DISTRIBUTION

Fig 2.9 The above tracing adjusted to show the field layout in 2002, 85 years after the 1917 Auctioneer's map and based on an aerial survey covering most of the Parish taken that year. Whilst the outlines of most of the old field patterns are still visible in the photographs, sadly, they reveal that a number of the 1917 hedgerows have been removed, presumably to facilitate modern farming methods. The aerial photograph also showed that although many of the fields had been merged, they were still being sub-divided by being planted with several different crops.

Eastern Union Railway.

The Eastern Counties Railway Company (ECR) was incorporated in 1836 to build a line from Shoreditch to Yarmouth via Colchester, Ipswich and Norwich. The first public trains ran between Mile End and Romford on 20 June 1839. Shoreditch to Brentwood opened in 1840 and Colchester was finally reached in 1843 where the line terminated.

In 1844 the Eastern Union Railway (EUR) was formed to extend the faltering ECR from Colchester to Ipswich and then to Bury St Edmunds. The chairman of the new company was John Chevallier Cobbold Esq., M.P. of Ipswich, a member of the brewing family, with John Footman, from the equally well-known family of drapers in Ipswich, as the vice-chairman and managing director.

The same year a plan of the proposed route between Ipswich and Bury St Edmunds was produced by the project engineer Joseph Locke Esq., FRS. This was based on a survey by Peter Bruff of Charlotte Street, Bloomsbury (SRO Ref: B/150/2/5.151 & B/105/2/5.239). Interestingly, on this plan the farm now known as The Woodlands, Badley is referred to as Burnt Mill Farm. No other instances of this have been discovered.

Within two years, a passenger line was established between London and Ipswich, opening on the June 15th 1846. By December the same year, Bury St Edmunds was reached via Needham Market and Stowmarket with the line passing through Badley. A considerable feat within the timescale, considering most of the work, executed by hand, required extensive earthmoving and the construction of numerous bridges - not to mention the Ipswich tunnel.

Particular difficulties were experienced on the Ipswich side of the site of Stowmarket station due to the boggy nature of the ground. To prevent the prepared trackbed and rails continually sinking into the soft surface, the line was floated across the offending area on a raft of brushwood, a techique pioneered by George Stephenson to cross Chat Moss during the construction of the Liverpool to Manchester railway.

Not surprisingly, no station was built to serve Badley, but a splendid one was constructed at Needham Market (see Fig 2.7 opposite). Badley therefore had a turnpike and an operational canal and railway, just a few hundred yards apart within its eastern boundary.

Although the latter was probably of minimal benefit to the residents of Badley, severing as it did the farmlands of Badley Bridge and Doves Hill farms in two, the construction phase certainly had an impact on both individuals and the community, as the following press cuttings illustrate -

The SUFFOLK CHRONICLE;
Or, Ipswich General Advertiser, and County Express.

30th May 1846

"FATAL ACCIDENT ON THE BURY TO IPSWICH RAILWAY -
On Saturday last, a young man, named Richard Strange of Ipswich, was carting on the railway works between Badley and Needham-Market when he unfortunately slipped, and the truck heavily laden passed over both legs, smashing them in a dreadful manner. He was conveyed to Needham-Market, and speedily attended by Mr. Pennington, Mr. H. and T. Beck, surgeons of that place, and by Mr. Bree and Mr Freeman of Stowmarket, who decided, in consultation, that the only chance of saving the poor fellow's life was by amputation of both limbs. The operations were skillfully performed by Mr. Pennington, but we regret to say that the unfortunate man died during the night. On Monday an Inquest was held at the George Inn, before J. E. Sparrow Esq. His interment took place on Wednesday, where his employers and upward of a hundred of his fellow workers testified their regard for him by following him to the grave, each of them wearing a white satin favour. The bearers were very cleanly attired in navy blue caps, white stops, white trousers and white gloves, which presented a very respectable appearance."

(N.B. Mr [Dr] Pennington was John Kirby Moore's brother-in-law)

The Barking Burial Register records that Richard Strange, aged 20 was buried on 27th May 1846. The entry is endorsed - "killed on railway Badley". The Mr. Bree and Mr. (Spencer) Freeman mentioned in the report were both Stowmarket surgeons.

The SUFFOLK CHRONICLE;
Or, Ipswich General Advertiser, and County Express.

6th June 1846

"Needham Market - This once quiet village has now become a scene of disquietude, and has continued so since the operation of the railway works commenced. A license has been granted to a temporary building as a beer-house at Badley, where on a Sunday, no matter what the time of day, you may find from 50 - 100 men seated on the ground in all directions, with their pipe and glass, until intoxicated; & proceeding from there to their lodgings at Needham insulting almost every person they may chance to meet, and using the most obscene language. We are at a loss to know why the police should go round to all the old-established houses on the Sunday and forget to walk to Badley, the short distance of a mile."

Navvies were notoriously physically fit and strong. In an intoxicated state they would have easily overwhelmed the local constable(s), which is probably why he wisely adopted a softly-softly approach to this transient workforce!

The ECR/EUR placed prominent advertisements containing a timetable in the December 1846 editions of the Suffolk Chronicle and Ipswich Journal to announce the start of their Bury St Edmunds/Ipswich passenger service from Monday 21st December 1846. This effectively linked Suffolk and London by train for the first time.

The first timetable for trains to London ('Up Trains') is reproduced at Fig 2.8 overleaf. Note the additional Suffolk stops at Bentley and Bramford.

It shows that the 'fast' train to London took 2 hours 50 minutes from Ipswich and a normal journey from Needham Market lasted between 3½ to 4 hours.

Passengers faced with crossing London, or an additional journey to reach their intended destination, was catered for, because, if they could afford it, they had the option of of taking their own horses and carriages with them.

The final entry of John Kirby Moore's Journal (see Chapter 8) reads, "Lord and Lady Ashburnham left Barking Hall for Dover Street. Mary P. and myself went to see them off from Needham station".

Given that the Ashburnhams in their horse-drawn sedans, accompanied by their footmen and attendants, would have literally processed the two miles or so from the hall to the station, this would have undoubtedly provided quite a spectacle.

FOOTNOTE:
In 1864 Parliament forced the ECR to prepare a Bill for amalgamation with the EUR and this occurred in 1862 to form the Great Eastern Railway.

Fig 2.7 Needham Market station in its heyday.

OPENING
OF THE
IPSWICH AND BURY SAINT EDMUND'S RAILWAY
FOR PASSENGERS.

Eastern Counties' and Eastern Union Railways.

LONDON, COLCHESTER, IPSWICH, AND BURY.
ON AND AFTER MONDAY, 21st DECEMBER, 1846.

UP TRAINS.

Distance from Bury	FROM	Week Days — 1st & 2d Cl. Morn. Mail.	1st & 3d Cl. Even.	1st, 2d & 3d Class. Morn.	1st, 2d & 3d Class. Quick Morn.	1st & 2d Class. Mail Mor.*	1st & 2d Class. Morning	1st, 2d & 3rd Class. Even.	1st, 2d & 3rd Class. Parlm Even.	1st, 2d and 3d Class. Even.	1st, 2d & 3d Class. Even.	Sun. 1st & 2d Cl. Morn. Mail.	1st & 3rd Class. Parlm Morn.	1st, 2d & 3rd Class. Even.	1st, 2d & 3rd Class. Even.	1st, 2d & 3rd Class. Even.	1st, 2d & 3rd Class. Even.	Fares 1st Class s.d.	2nd Class s.d.	3rd Class s.d.	Horses 1 s.d.	2 s.d.	3 s.d.	Carriages s.d.
	BURY	..	..	..	..	8 45	11 55	..	..	3 45	5 30	6 20	..	..	3 30	..	..							
4	THURSTON	..	..	..	..	8 58	..	..	..	3 58	5 43	6 33	..	..	3 45			0 10	0 6	0 4	4 0	5 0	6 0	5 0
9	ELMSWELL	..	..	..	..	9 18	12 20	..	..	4 14	5 58	6 48	..	..	3 58			1 10	1 2	0 8	5 0	6 0	8 0	5 0
11	HAUGHLEY ROAD	..	..	..	..	9 20	12 26	..	..	4 21	6 6	6 55	..	..	4 5			2 4	1 4	0 11	5 0	7 6	9 6	8 0
15	STOWMARKET	..	..	..	9 30	12 38	..	..	4 30	6 15		7 2	..	..	4 15			3 0	1 10	1 3	6 0	10 0	15 0	10 0
18	NEEDHAM	..	..	..	9 38	12 48	..	..	4 40	6 25		7 11	..	..	4 23			3 8	2 4	1 6	6 0	10 0	15 0	10 0
22	CLAYDON	..	..	..	9 48	..	..	..	4 50	6 35		7 22	..	..	4 33			4 6	2 10	1 10	8 0	12 0	18 0	12 0
24	BRAMFORD	..	..	..	9 56	..	..	..	..	6 40		7 28	..	..	4 41			5 0	3 0	2 0	8 0	12 0	18 0	15 0
27	IPSWICH	1 34	..	8 10	10 10	1 10	..	3 40	5 10	6 55	1 24	..	..	4 55			5 6	3 6	2 3	9 0	15 0	22 0	15 0
32	BENTLEY	..	..	8 24	10 24	1 24	..	3 53	5 24	7 9		7 54	..	..	5 9			6 6	4 2	2 7	12 6	21 0	30 0	19 6
38	MANNINGTREE	1 47	..	8 36	10 36	1 36	..	4 4	5 36	7 21	1 47	8 6	..	..	5 21			7 0	4 6	3 0	13 0	22 0	31 0	20 0
40	ARDLEIGH	1 57	..	8 48	10 48	1 48	..	4 15	5 45	7 32	1 57	8 18	..	..	5 33			7 0	4 6	3 4	14 0	23 0	35 0	21 6
44	COLCHESTER	2 11	N.B.	7 45	9 0	11 0	2 0	..	4 30	6 0	7 46	2 11	8 30	..	..	5 45		7 0	4 6	3 8	15 0	26 0	37 0	23 6
49	MARKS TEY	..	..	9 10	..	2 10	..	4 42	..	..		8 40	..	..	5 55			8 0	5 1	4 0	..	..	..	..
53	KELVEDON	2 39	..	8 7	9 22	11 23	2 23	..	4 57	6 20	2 37	8 52	..	..	6 7			9 0	5 9	4 5	16 0	27 0	39 6	29 6
56½	WITHAM	2 47	..	8 18	9 32	11 32	2 32	..	5 7	6 34	2 47	9 2	..	..	6 17			9 6	6 3	4 8	16 0	27 0	39 6	29 6
60	HATFIELD	..	..	8 26	9 40	..	..	..	5 15	6 45		9 12	..	..	6 27			10 6	6 10	5 0	..	..	..	..
65	CHELMSFORD	3 12	..	8 43	9 55	11 54	2 49	..	5 32	6 57	3 21	9 26	8 0	..	6 41			11 6	7 8	5 5	19 0	32 6	47 0	32 6
71½	INGATESTONE	3 30	..	8 58	..	12 8	3 6	..	5 53	7 13	3 30	9 44	8 15	..	6 50			23 2	8 6	6 0	..	..	..	..
77	BRENTWOOD	3 49	8 30	9 15	10 26	12 2	3 10	5 30	6 11	7 27	3 40	10 0	6 30	7 15	8 33			14 11	9 6	6 5	23 0	39 6	57 0	37 6
82	ROMFORD	4 6	8 36	9 30	10 35	12 39	3 34	5 45	6 29	7 42	4 6	10 18	1 17	6 46	7 33	8 51	15 6	10 3	6 11	25 0	43 0	62 0	40 0
89	ILFORD	4 16	8 46	9 42	..	12 49	3 46	5 55	6 45	7 56	4 16	10 33	1 30	6 58	9 7	8	16 8	11 0	7 0	26 6	45 0	66 0	42 0
90	FOREST GATE	..	8 51	9 47	..	..	..	6 0	6 50	8 3		10 38	1 36	7 3	9 14			17 3	11 6	7 0	..	..	..	..
91	STRATFORD	4 22	8 50	9 55	10 50	12 56	3 56	6 8	7 0	8 12	4 22	10 48	1 43	7 13	9 25			17 3	11 6	7 0	28 0	47 6	69 0	43 0
94	MILE END	..	..	..	..	†	..	..	7 10	8 22		10 57	1 50	7 20	9 35			18 0	12 0	7 0	..	..	..	..
95	LONDON	4 38	9 10	10 5	1 12	4 10	6 25	7 20	8 35		4 30	11 5	2 0	7 20	8 0	9 45	18 0	12 0	7 0	30 0	50 0	75 0	45 0

† On Wednesdays the Trains marked thus † stops at Mile End, to take up and setdown Passengers.

N.B. - This train starts at Colchester on Monday Mornings at 6.40 calling at all the intermediate Stations except Mile End.

N.B. Third Class Passengers are conveyed from all Stations on the Ipswich and Bury, and Eastern Union Railway, by the 8.45 A.M. to London.

*This train to Stop at Hatfield on Friday.   Carriages and Horses are not conveyed by the 3.0 p.m. Down Train.

A Train of 1st, 2nd, and 3rd Class Carriages will LEAVE STRATFORD FOR LONDON at 8.15 a.m., and a Train will also LEAVE (SHOREDITCH) LONDON, FOR STRATFORD, consisting of 1st and 2nd Class Carriages at 10.15 p.m. EVERY DAY, and will stop when required at Mile End Station.

Fig 2.8 A reproduction of the inaugural timetable published jointly by the Eastern Counties & Eastern Union Railway in the Ipswich Journal on Wednesday 16th Decmber 1846.

Fig 2.9 The Badley milespost situated on the B1113 road opposite the lay-by near to 'Roots & Shoots' garden centre. The milepost dates from the days when the road was a turnpike and using it was subject to a toll charge.

BADLEY HILL 1927

The following illustrations are from the publication *"The March of the 1st Bn. Suffolk Regiment through the County of Suffolk 16th to 23rd August 1927"* arranged by Lieut. W. M. Lummis. MC. The Suffolk Regiment, and printed by the East Anglian Daily Times Co. Ltd. Ipswich.

"At Badley Hill a two hours' halt was made for the mid-day meal and here the photographer secured pictures of the officers at an al fresco lunch, as well as the issue of the men's dinners, . . "

ASCENDING BADLEY HILL.
C.Coy, commanded by Major J. L. Likeman, D.S.O., followed by the Drums.

The Sergeant Cook (Sergt. Durrant) preparing dinner.

Officers at lunch.

'C' Company drawing their dinners.

Fig 2.10 Photographs of the Suffolk Battalion enjoying a dinner break on Badley Hill en route to Stowmarket. Note the stackyard in the top photograph which was on the opposite side of the road to Doveshill farm.

Miscellaneous

Buxhall & Badley SCHOOL TREAT - On Friday, the worthy Rector of these parishes invited the children of the school to their annual treat. In the course of the afternoon they received various rewards for improvement, and a bountiful supply of tea, cake &c. Games of all kinds were heartily entered into. About 100 of the inhabitants of the two parishes also partook of the kind hospitality of the Copingers, the repast being presided over by the Rev C Hill, to whom and to his family many thanks are due for their kindness and hearty welcome.

(The Stowmarket Courier No. 63 - 26 Aug 1869 Thursday page 2, col. 5.)

Newby's STOWMARKET ANNUAL *Guide and Directory 1956*

The 1956 edition of *Newby's Stowmarket Annual*, p.21, records that Badley, 1078 acres, population 92, was represented on Gipping Rural District Council (see Chapter 7, page 186) by the Rev. W. G. Hargrave-Thomas, G. S. Southgate and L. Williams. These three gentlemen also represented Needham Market, whereas the previous years edition (1955) showed Badley represented in its own right by W. F. Freshwater. In this list of parishes and their representatives, it is worth noting that there were six other less populated parishes.

1955 Edition, pages 90 to 93 (Badley related names only reproduced):
"When calling give name of Exchange - Needham Market - then Number".

281 De la Bere, Rev. S.H. Barking Rectory
253 Farrow, C. S., Doveshill, Badley
259 Freshwater, Mrs. V., Badley Mill, Badley
302 Pirkis, J. C., Green Farm, Badley
295 Scott, A. B., Hall Farm, Badley
356 Short, S. L., Cherry Tree Farm, Badley
224 Horsford Maj. T. O'b., Badley Bridge Farmr

COMBS AND BADLEY NURSING ASSOCIATION

This association was set up in 1930 and its meetings were held at the Hut, Combs and reported in the Stowmarket Recorder and Needham Market, Combs & Stowupland Advertiser. On Thursday 1st April 1937 for example it reported the retirement of Nurse Groves: "The loss of the services of a faithful servant is always a cause for regret, but when that individual has put into duty that little extra bit which takes the service greater, then the severance is the more felt. This can truthfully be said of Nurse M. Groves who for the past five years has ministered to the sick needs of the folk of Combs and Badley. During that time there is hardly a household that has not sought her advice and assistance, always given with a disposition that endeared the giver to the recipient".

Nurse Groves was presented with a handbag, travelling clock and coronation spoon at the Hut, Combs on Thursday last.

Her successor Nurse Lodge commenced duty on April the 5th and would live at 23 Edgar Avenue, Combs.
(Stowmarket Recorder & Needham Market, Combs & Stowupland Advertiser, Thursday 1st April 1937, page 1, col. 5.)

A number of parishes were served by Nursing Associations in the 1930's. Presumably these were the equivalent to District Nurses of today. The Combs and Badley Nursing Association comprised of the two ecclesiastical parishes, and was nine years old by 1939. Mrs. Freshwater of Badley Mill was the chairman of the association in the late 1930's and the newspaper carried reports of their Annual General Meetings and any personnel changes as the above excerpt illustrates.

HONOUR TO A BADLEY LADY
Irish Setter Association of England

At a recent election by ballot of Members of the above Association to fill two vacancies in their list of approved judges, Mrs E V M Freshwater of Badley Mill Irish Setter Kennels, Needham Market, had the honour of leading the poll. There were seven candidates for the two vacancies and the other successful candidate was Mrs Badenoch Nicholson. The I.S.A.E. has members in all parts of England, Scotland and Wales.
(Stowmarket Recorder & Needham Market, Combs & Stowupland Advertiser, Thursday 4th March 1937)

"OUR DOGS"
Badley Ladies Successes at Ipswich

At the Suffolk Kennel Association's Show held at Ipswich on Thursday last, the entries of Mrs E V M Freshwater (the Association's Chairman) won her very honorable distinctions in no less that five classes.
In competition (amongst members of the Association) Irish Setter (bred by exhibitor) "Jim of Badley" secured the premier trophy from amongst his class. (Open) dog or bitch (owned and led into the ring by a lady), Mrs Freshwater came 3rd with "Brenda of Badley". Veteran (over 5 years of age on date of show) "Brenda of Badley" ranked 2nd. Postgraduate dog or bitch, 2nd with "Hilaro of Badley" and open (dog or bitch) 1st with "Jim of Badley". All entries were well filled. Entries being on a record scale.
(Stowmarket Recorder & Needham Market, Combs & Stowupland Advertiser, Thursday 21st October 1937)

Chapter Three

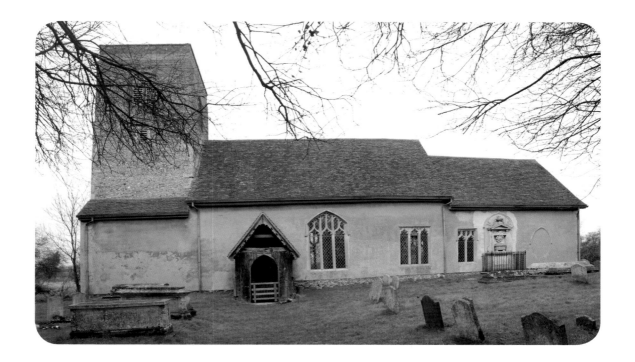

Saint Mary's Church

The technical description of the church is based on the guide to St Mary's Church, Badley (1966)
written by Roy Tricker of Ipswich and used with his permission.

"Here there are no gaudy tessellated tiles, no varnished benches of imported pitch-pine, no ugly carpets and hanging oil lamps from Birmingham, no "handsome" brass rails." (SILLY SUFFOLK)

BADLEY has one of Suffolk's most remarkable and unforgettable churches. Few of the county's 500 mediaeval churches are more remote or further from a made-up road and the situation of St Mary's is one of its most memorable features.

The visitor who perseveres along the rough track, sign-posted on the B1113 Stowmarket/Needham Market road 'Badley Church', will endure a rigorous test of his car suspension. But he will enjoy a beautiful piece of Suffolk countryside and will be rewarded at the end of a mile-long journey by an absolute gem of a church, idyllically situated in a tree-studded dip, within a hedged enclosure in the middle of a meadow, without even a footpath to the field-gate which gives access to the churchyard. This access road is known locally as Doveshill Road (see map page iv).

Time has stood still at Badley and what can be seen here was the situation of many rural churches in times past - green meadows, trees, a farm track and, apart from the 16th-century hall to the west (reduced c.1739 to a quarter

"From this church they led their brides,
From this church themselves were led
Shoulder-high; on these waysides
Sat to take their beer and bread.
Names are gone — what men they were
These their cottages declare."
"Forefathers", by Edmund Blunden.

*Fig 3.1 One of the earliest photographs know to exist of Badley Church taken by **J Nunn** of Needham Market c1870. The premises appear to be in a fine state of repair and the wooden paling enclosing the churchyard is clearly visible. (Reproduced by kind permission of Nick Balmer)*

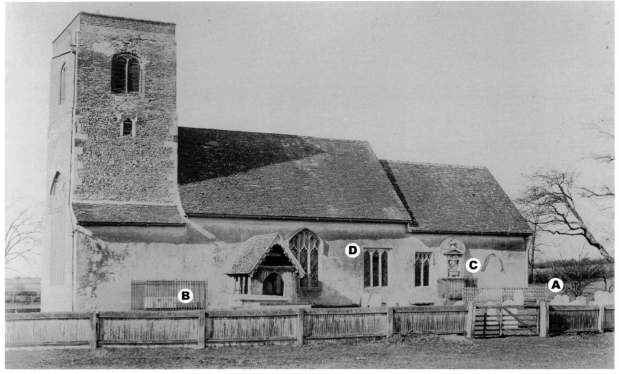

*Fig 3.2 This photograph was taken in 1906 and shows a closer view of the former fence. In the churchyard the elaborate iron railing containing the **Moore Family** vault (A) and the plainer set surrounding the grave of **William Mudd** (B) of Badley Hall are clearly visible. Both are now missing presumably removed during the quest for iron during WW II. However, those protecting a tablet memorial to **Henrietta Maria Robins** (C) on the south wall survive. Note the blocked south-east chancel window (D), and also that the Perpendicular window nearest the porch, is the only on the south side which still retains its original arch - were the others too damaged by Dowsing's men to retain? (Photo - Cole)*

of its original size), not a house in sight. Only the electricity pylons and the occasional helicopter overhead serve as reminders of the 21st century world of motorways and computers.

THE CHURCHYARD

Few visitors to St Mary's will forget their journey here, or its pastoral setting, or the charm of its country churchyard, in which a simple headstone commemorates Clark Cooper, who died in 1803, "in the service of a friend whom he voluntarily offered to assist in concluding his harvest".

All the marked graves in the churchyard lie to the south of the church. Although 448 persons are recorded buried there since 1589, there are only 66 monuments in the churchyard and a further 23 in the inside the church to commemorate them. A scale plan of the churchyard is provided on page 30 (Fig 3.12) (see Appendix C for key to grave numbers).

However, there is one on the other side of the church. This grave is unmarked as the man's name was unknown. Aged about 35 years-old, he drowned in the River Gipping on the 13th May 1911 and his body was recovered from the water in the north east corner of Badley at the bottom of New Cottage by Jack Mayhew. He placed the corpse in his wheelbarrow and carried him to the church. Since the man's name was unknown he was not allowed to be buried in the front of the church, so Jack Mayhew buried him in the church grounds to the north. A small mound was visible at the site for several years.

In 1669 the churchwarden William Holmes recorded in the Badley Towne Booke -

- *for two locks for ye churchgate 1s. 6d.*
- *for a thoroughshott & a hant & two staples 0s. 7d.*
- *for stubbing the churchyard & clipping ye hayes 1s. 6d.*

Early photographs show that the churchyard was protected from grazing animals by a low wooden paling affording good views of the church (see Figs 3.1 & 3.2). For many years however, this has been superseded by a tall deciduous hedge. Although the hedge contibutes to the tranquility of the site it does restrict overall views of the church and external photography. The maintenance of this hedge has occasionally been controversial. (see for example the East Anglian Daily Times Dec. 5th 1985, p.15). In 2005 the hedge surrounding the church was laid, see Fig 3.5 (top) opposite and the photograph on page 295.

Fig 3.3 The churchyard from the SW. The slab tomb close to the porch is that of William Mudd, who tenant farmed at Badley Hall for a number of years. The graves in the foreground are 20th century.

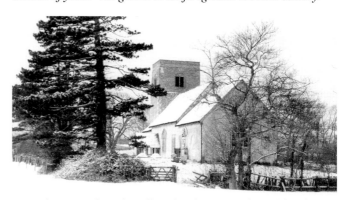

Fig 3.4 A snowbound Badley church. On Sunday 14th February 1853, John Kirby Moore recorded in his diary, "A deep snow, 14" deep" & on the 27th he wrote, "No sevice at Churh, the ways there-to being so bad in consequence of the deep snow". Note the entrance is via the SE corner of the churchyard.

Fig 3.5 (above) Badley Church from Church Green. The two large pine trees are probably those planted by John Kirby Moore in 1865 (see text next page) and (below) Badley Hall from Badley Walk, with St Mary's Church in the foreground.

Fig 3.6 The blocked lancet window (see Fig 3.12 for location).

The two tall pine trees which dominate the SW and SE corners of the churchyard are Pinus Austriacas (Austrian or Black Pine). They are almost certainly those planted by John Kirby Moore, churchwarden, on March 4th 1865 and noted in his diary (see plan Fig 3.5 & 'Other Notable Badley Families', Chapter 8).

THE EXTERIOR

The core of the present nave and chancel may contain parts of the church (with 14 acres of glebe) recorded in the Domesday Survey of 1086 (see Chapter 1, Fig 1.3). The earliest visible features (dating from c.1180-1200) are the plain south doorway and the blocked northern lancet window. The doorway, which is rebated, has tiny holes where a shutter may have been fixed. The blocked south-east chancel window may date from the 1300's, but most of the others are Perpendicular windows, added in the 1400's, including one erected through the generosity of Richard Schyrlock (a Badley man who was buried in Norwich), whose will of 1434 bequeathed 20s.8d. for this purpose.

On the south chancel wall is a handsome monument to Henrietta Robins, a lawyer's wife from Battlesden in Bedfordshire, who died in 1728 (Fig 3.11).

The south wall of the nave and chancel (which are of equal width) has been rendered and looks much the same as it did when Henry Davy made an etching of the church in 1841. (Fig 3.40) The north wall, which is supported by 18th-century buttresses, reveals its flint-rubble masonry in which can be seen whole flints (some quite large), pebbles, pieces of stone, a few chunks of brown septaria from the Suffolk coast and a block of dark-brown ironstone.

Fig 3.7 The tower and the very large Perpendicular west window, sadly now only filled with clear glass.

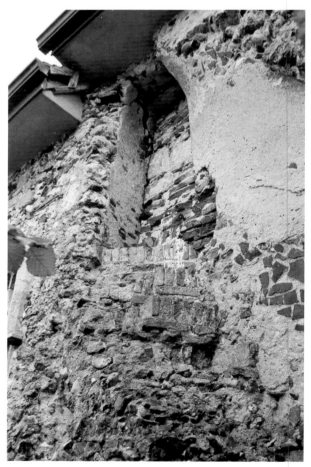

Fig 3.8 Remains of the Tudor steps leading to the former rood-loft.

*Fig 3.9 The Porch - note the rare example of a
sheep-gate stile protecting the entrance.*

*Fig 3.10 The sturdy ancient porch door - with two of the holes
made by musket shot circled for ease of identification.*

Near the division of the nave and chancel on this side are the remains of the staircase which led to the former rood-loft inside. This was built into the wall of the church and, when part of it collapsed, it seems that a quick patching-up job was done and the remains were just left. Some of the Tudor brick steps remain, leading to the blocked upper entrance; part of the lower entrance is visible behind the adjacent buttress (Fig 3.8).

The nave walls have been extended to enclose the north and south sides of the unbuttressed western tower, which is rectangular in plan and not square. In its western face is the largest and grandest window in the church - a fine five-light Perpendicular example, which appears almost too large in proportion to the tower. A staircase-vice on the north side gives access to the first stage of the tower, which is lit by a small square-headed southern window (Fig 3.13). The belfry stage, with its double windows, is a 16th-century addition, or rebuilding, in Tudor brick (Fig 3.7).

The attractive wooden porch has been restored, but some of its mediaeval timbers remain. Entry to it involves lifting aside the sheep-gate stile, a rare survival which adds to the rustic charm of the church (Fig 3.9). The sturdy south door, with its curious iron grille, was made in the 15th century (Figs 3.9, 3.10 and 3.39).

Fig 3.11 The wall memorial to Henrietta Robins (1728).

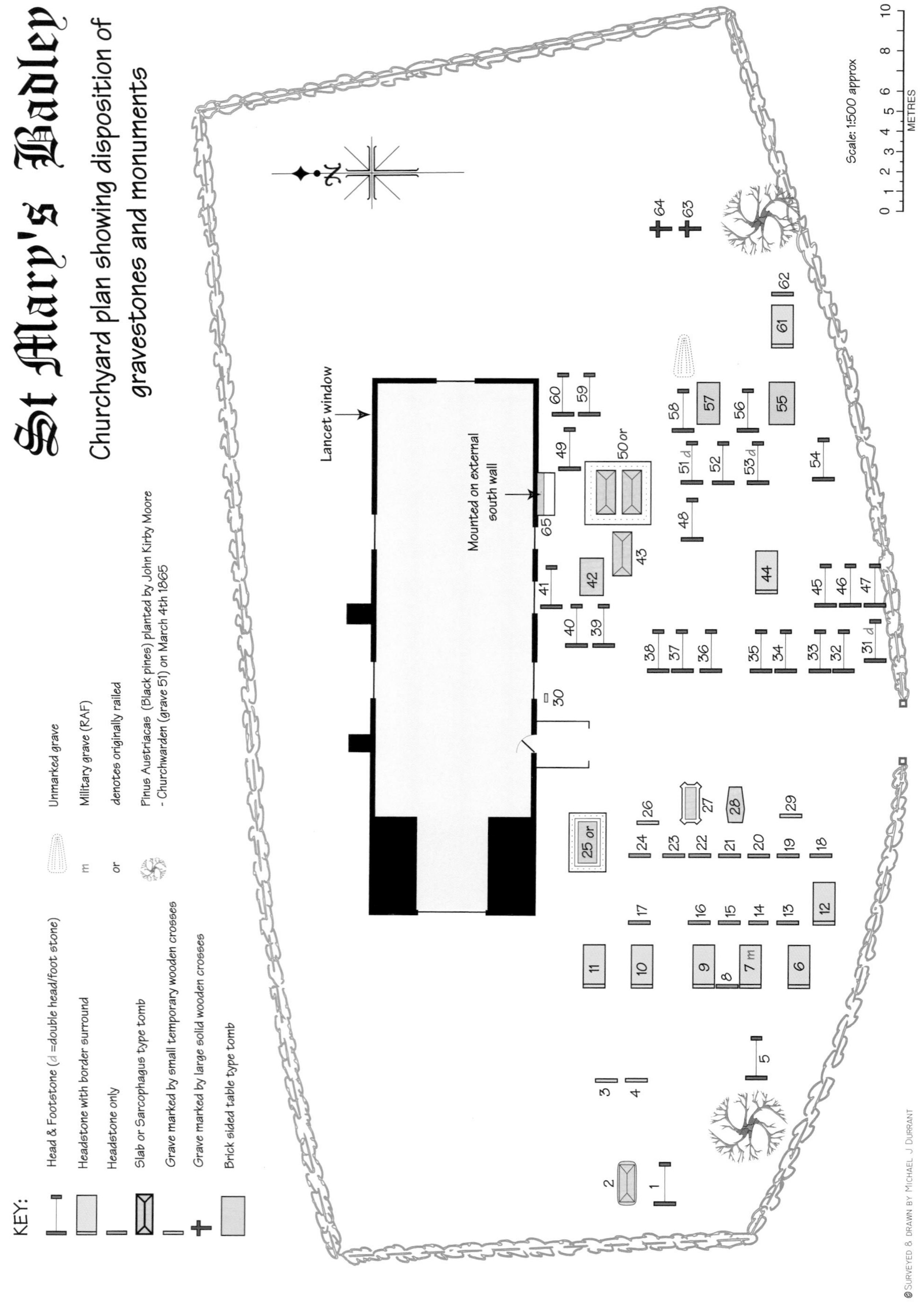

St Mary's Badley

Churchyard plan showing disposition of gravestones and monuments

Scale: 1:500 approx

0 1 2 3 4 5 6 8 10
METRES

Lancet window

Mounted on external south wall

KEY:

- Head & Footstone (d = double head/foot stone)
- Headstone with border surround
- Headstone only
- Slab or Sarcophagus type tomb
- Grave marked by small temporary wooden crosses
- Grave marked by large solid wooden crosses
- Brick sided table type tomb

- Unmarked grave
- Military grave (RAF)
- *m* denotes originally railed
- *or* Pinus Austriacas (Black pines) planted by John Kirby Moore - Churchwarden (grave 51) on March 4th 1865

© SURVEYED & DRAWN BY MICHAEL J. DURRANT

Fig 3.12 Churchyard plan showing the disposition of grave-stones - see Appendix C for the Inscriptions.

Fig 3.13 The north-west corner of the church tower showing the staircase to the first stage of the tower lit by a square-head window.

THE INTERIOR

Suffolk has many fine and enormous churches, with lofty and ornate interiors, but here, by contrast, all is simple, rustic and unpretentious. Much of the woodwork has never been treated with stain or varnish and the oak has matured to a mellow grey colour. Light pours in through the clear glass of the windows, particularly the great west window. In mediaeval times, by contrast, the interior would have been a blaze of colour and carving, but in 1643 William Dowsing inspected the building.

William Dowsing's Visit

On 5th February 1643, William Dowsing, a puritan from Suffolk and a Provost Marshall General of the Eastern Association Army, was empowered by warrant to demolish church ornaments etc., within the County of Suffolk.

"By vertue of a Warrant directed to me from the right Honourable the Earl of Manchefter I do hereby depute and appoint you ...... in my absence to execute the fayd Warrant in every particular, within the County of Suffolk according to an Ordinance of Parliament therein mentioned and power given to me by the said Warrant as fully as I myself may or might execute the same In witness whereof I have hereunto set my hand and seale."

His brief was to pull down and cast out all roods, graven images and shrines with their relicts, to which 'ignorant people came flocking in adoration, or anything else which (punctually) tended to idolatory and superstition'. In short, all things relating to the Catholic faith. Of his visit to Badley Dowsing records in his journal:-

"**BADLEY** Feb. the 5th : We brake down 34 superstitious pictures; Mr. Dove promised to take down the rest, 28 ; and to levall the Chancel. We took down 4 superstitious inscriptions with ora pro nobis, and cujus animæ propitietur Deus" (These latter were on the four mediaeval brasses here).

The antiquary Claude Morley, visiting the church in the early 20th century, discovered evidence of what appeared to be Puritan bullets in the church door (see Fig 3.10).

Translated the inscription *'ora pro nobis'* means *'pray for us'* and *'cujus animae propitietur deus'* means *'on who's soul may God have mercy'*.

In the record of his visit to Badley Church the 'pictures' mentioned by Dowsing referred to storied glass stained windows, glass figures of saints and the Virgin Mary. Dowsing's men smashed most of the Mediaeval glass including two heraldic shields in the windows. They made the chancel a little lower than the nave and tore away 'brasses' from four stones dated 1485 to 1539. Church plate, a silver covered chalice, donated by Edmund Poley (1592-1640) in 1630 and a silver communion plate and pewter jug, were mercifully saved from Dowsing and are still owned by the Church today (Figs 3.41 & 42).

Commenting on Dowsing's visit in an article published in the *Proceedings of the Suffolk Institute of Archaeology* (1888, Vol VI), the author Rev'd C. H. Evelyn White says in relation to the reference to Mr Dove, "This individual it would seem, with all the gentleness with which his name is associated, and perhaps with not a little of a distinctly opposite tendency, pleaded, at least, for a more convenient season, and thus averted to some extent the destroyers hand".

"The Journal of William Dowsing - Iconoclasm in East Anglia during the English Civil War" edited by Trevor Cooper, (Boydell & Brewer)(2001) commenting on the Badley visit says, "William Dove was the principle inhabitant of this hamlet apart from Edmund Poley Esq., at the Hall,

Fig 3.14 Badley font and organ.

the nave was a set of royal arms. The font was painted blue (a little of this 17th century colour remains) (see Fig 3.14 on this page). Davy noted that in front of the communion table were placed two very rough and slight long stools or benches for the communicants to kneel against!

This may explain the absence of the 17th century communion rails which one would expect to find here. It seems that either they disappeared very early or that there never were any - hence the make-shift apparatus mentioned by Davy, replaced by the present iron rails in the 19th century (Pevsner dates them c.1830). The only other 19th century feature is the stained glass in the east window (see Fig 3.19).

The roof is supported by octagonal crown-posts with moulded capitals which rest upon tiebeams. These may date back to the 14th century, as do several similar rooves in this part of Suffolk. The floor is paved with quarry tiles and numerous burial slabs.

The small octagonal font, standing upon its raised step, has shallow arches in its Purbeck marble bowl, indicating work of the 13th century. Its present cover may well be 18th century, but in the stonework of the bowl are traces of the device by which its mediaeval predecessor was locked to the font.

The doorway to the belfry stairway is interesting because it is about seven feet above the floor, indicating the possible use of the tower as a place of refuge or for storing valuables; gaining entry was impossible without a ladder (Fig 3.15). Beneath the west window stands the bier, upon which coffins were transported at funerals.

In the wall just east of the door is the niche for a holy water stoup, where mediaeval people dipped their fingers and made the sign of the Cross as an act of purification (Fig 3.16).

Fig 3.15 The narrow belfry access door, seven feet above floor level.

whose recent - and thus not superstitious - ancestors' brasses (1613, 1615 & 1633) were respected, while four English inscriptions to earlier forebears, recorded by William Hervy in 1561, were taken up. Darby (1827) drew the four indents".

The general belief is that William Dowsing was buried at Laxfield on 14th March 1679, although two other 'Williams' were also buried there during the relevant period. Some scholars now say it was probably at Coddenham.

During the 17th century the interior was adapted to the 'plain and Prayer Book' worship of the Established Church and the box-pews, pulpit, etc. were added. Worship was centred around the preaching of the Word and Holy Communion was celebrated four times per year at the most.

When David Elisha Davy visited the church in 1827, it looked much as it does today. He did, however, note three mediaeval coats of arms in the windows (only one now remains) and some other fragments of ancient glass in the west window. On the east wall was the frame of a hatchment (the canvas had gone) and at the west end of

Fig 3.16 The niche on the south wall, partially covered by low wooden panelling.

The recess in the north wall, opposite the pulpit, may have contained a statue or painting, but could well have been part of the entrance to the rood-loft stairs.

The seating in the church is a mixture of benches and box-pews. In the nave are some 15th century benches with poppyhead ends. One on the north side has remains of animal arm-rests and another has a wheel design. Certain bench-ends have evidence of a sloping book-desk and may have been part of the return stalls with which the chancel was furnished before the box-pews arrived. The poppy-heads are all made up of differing leaf designs. The plain benches are probably 17th century additions (see Fig 3.24 for poppy-heads).

The box-pews, dating from the 17th century, were occupied by the more wealthy families who could afford to rent them. Those east of the screen are embellished with knobs and were used by the Lords of the Manor and the important families who sat in the chancel. Characteristic Jacobean carving can be seen on the pew entrance opposite the pulpit and there is more on the entrance to the reading desk and pulpit (Fig 3.23). The reading desk is commodious, although the pulpit is remarkably small. They were both equipped with red cushions and hangings, which had rotted and were removed earlier this century.

The base of the rood screen, which separated the nave and chancel, remains in place, although now much the worse for wear. It has been painted red and studded with gold stars, but this painting may not be original. Along the horizontal beam at the top are remains of wooden brattishing decoration (Fig 3.25). The knobs surmounting it are 17th century additions. Set in the box-pews west of the screen is some traceried woodcarving which may have come from the upper parts of the screen or maybe even from the roodloft, which was approached by the now ruined staircase outside (Fig 3.57).

Two chests used to be seen in the church. One was plain and dates probably from the 17th century, whilst the other had linenfold panelling indicating 16th century work. Unfortunately these were both stolen in July 2002 (Fig 3.17 below).

Fig 3.17 The two missing Badley church chests. (Photographs courtesy of The Churches Conservation Trust.)

On the east wall of the sanctuary are the framed Lord's Prayer, Creed and Commandment boards, dating from the late 18th century (Fig 3.18). The altar itself is a carved 17th century communion table, now covered with a colourful frontal which, with the candlesticks, is comparatively modern and made by the Warham Guild.

The stained glass in the east window was donated by John Kirby Moore in 1866, in memory of his wife Henrietta. It shows the appearance of Jesus to Mary Magdalene, to his followers at Emmaus and to Thomas, after his Resurrection. It was designed by the eminent Victorian church architect Frederick Preedy of Worcester (1820-1898) (whose glass may also be seen in the Suffolk churches of Tuddenham St Martin and Little Thurlow) (Fig 3.19) (see Chapter 8 re John Kirby Moore).

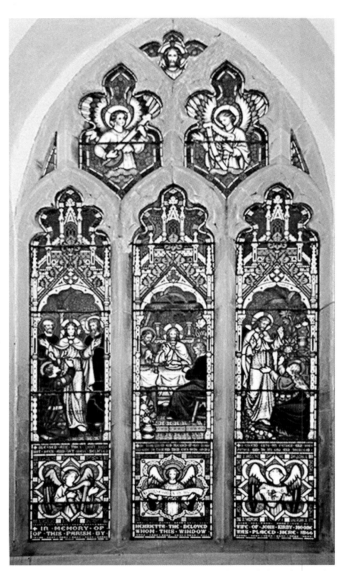

Fig 3.19 Frederick Preedy's east window donated by John Kirby Moore in memory of his wife Henrietta in 1866, which some commentators have described as 'ugly'!

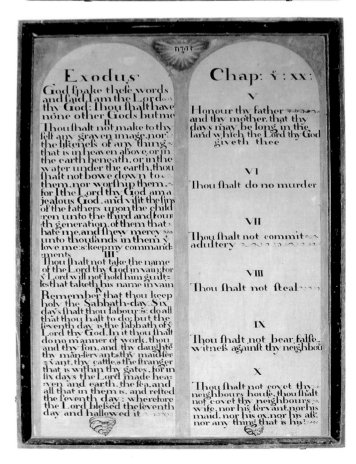

Fig 3.18 The Creed and Commandment boards which hang either side of the altar (see Fig 3.21 opposite).

Fig 3.20 The earliest surviving glass in the church situated in one of the north windows. The arms, a cross patonce Or; a border engrailed Arg., which some scholars believe belong to the de Badele family, dates from the early 1320's.

Figs 3.21/22 The unspoilt interior: above - towards the altar (east) & below - towards the tower & west window.
Note the tie beams in the roof supporting octagonal crown-posts with moulded capitals.

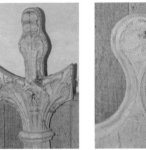
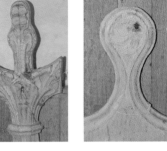

Fig 3.23 Jacobean carving on the entrance to the reading desk & pulpit.

Fig 3.24 A selection of 'poppy-heads'.

Fig 3.25 Part of the base of the rood screen showing the faded painted panels & wooden brattishing decoration.

The BADLEY BELLS

The tower at the west end of the church houses three bells. The oldest, cast by **Roger Reve** at Bury St. Edmunds in about 1530 is inscribed:

'sancte : augustine ora pro nobis' (Fig 3.26)

The other two were cast in 1702 by **John Goldsmith** of Redgrave, of whom J.J.Raven says, "no poet, but fortunately a preserver of ancient dedications, his bells being frequently inscribed "Maria", "Gabriel", etc. In tone his bells are rather sweet than powerful." Those at Badley are inscribed:

'+ John Goldsmith fecit 1702. W.R. St Maria'
and
'Ex dono Elebth Pooley + John Goldsmith fecit 1702. St Margaret' (Fig 3.27)

Only twenty of Goldsmith's bells are known to remain, most are in the Waveney Valley but one remained at Darmsden church until recently.

In 1968 the Church magazine recorded, "the repair of the damaged church bell has been suggested and we have been offered a grant of £60 by the Central Council for the Care of Churches. The work will cost a good deal more than this and it will only be possible to carry it out if sufficient funds are received during the year. *And later* - 'we have also been advised to have the cracked bell welded, by a process which has only recently been developed."

The upper part of the tower is built from early Tudor red brick and the belfry windows are boarded with wooden louvres. The tower was in need of repair as the bricks were crumbling and the louvres decaying. Since being taken over by the Churches Conservation Trust most of the repairs needed to the tower have been done and it is now in a good state. Sadly the bells can no longer be used unless and until substantial repairs are undertaken in the belfry.

A close-up of two of the Badley bells : Fig 3.26 (left) 'showing the inscription 'AUGUSTINE' and Fig 3.27 (right) showing in between the bands '.....LDSMITH : FECIT : 1702' and above 'ST. MARGARET'.

Fig 3.28 Bell-rope holes in the trapdoor situated above the belfry access door on the right, as shown in Fig 3.15.

Fig 3.29 (left) The three Badley church bells. The second & third are by Goldsmith.

Many of Preedy's original window designs are now preserved in the Royal Institute of British Architecture (RIBA) Library Drawings Collection in London. Although the RIBA has the following record in relation to the east window, sadly the drawing is not amongst those bequeathed to the library.

"Badley, Suffolk, St. Mary
Design for three light window with three figurative panels under canopies:
Incredulity of St Thomas|Supper at Emmaus|'Noli Me Tangere'; (three tracery lights) two musician angels and head of Christ. Scale : ¾ inch to 1 ft
Insc. Badley Church Suffolk, Design for east window s. & d.
F Preedy 13 York Place, Portman Square, London July 1866. Pen & ink with watercolour approx 250 x 115"

One piece of mediaeval glass remains in a north window, having been moved here from the east window. It depicts the arms of the de Badele family, who were lords of the manor here until the 15th century (Fig 3.20).

The partial replastering of the walls in 1994 revealed the blocked priest's doorway in the south chancel wall, also traces of mediaeval wall paintings which adorned the interior until the Reformers covered them over in the 16th century. Of particular interest is the simple masonry pattern painted on the south wall of the chancel, possibly as early as the 13th century. On the north wall opposite is a consecration cross, see Fig 3.85, page 67.

Repairs and Maintenance

On 22nd June 1925 the East Anglian Daily Times newspaper published a letter from the Archdeacon of Suffolk appealing for funds to repair Badley church This was accommpanied by a technical report written by Mr. A. R. Powys, secretary of the Society for the Protection of Ancient Buildings (SPAB) following a site inspection which was also attended by the Bishop. The society concluded -

"A church which has undergone no material alteration, in structure or furniture, since the time when Laud was Archbishop (beheaded in 1645) indeed deserves the attention of all interested in the building crafts of the county, whether members of the Church of England or not".

The same newspaper had published between 14th March and 10th May, six articles by *'Silly Suffolk'* on Badley, its church, squires and hall etc.

Charles Partridge F.S.A. of Stowmarket wrote these articles, and also contributed the following letter in support of the appeal.

Dear Suffolk Folk
For nearly six years, the East Anglian Daily Times has published nearly every Saturday an article written by me. In every one of them I have tried to sing, in one way or another, the praises of our fair county of Suffolk, second, of course, to no other county in England. I am always - to my huge delight - receiving kicks and curses, but some kind readers have told me that they like my articles, and to them I venture to appeal on behalf of the £350 required for the reparation - not "restoration"! - of Badley church. It is one of the half-dozen Suffolk churches to which we could proudly take our American cousins, and I do hope that Suffolk folk will send their shillings to the fund. I have it very much at heart. Believe me,
Your everlasting admirer,
SILLY SUFFOLK.

An estimate for the repair was drawn up as follows :

Stripping roof & re-tiling with old tiles	£225
Repair to tower roof	£25
Repair to south window head of tower	£15
Repair to plaster outside	£25
Repainting down pipes etc,	£10
Repair to boarding in pews	£2-0s
Architects supervision	£30
Total repair cost	**£332-10s**

Unfortunately this appeal was launched in the middle of industrial depression and money was scarce, but eventually the sum was raised and the work was carefully carried out in 1934-35 under the supevision of local expert William Wier on behalf of the SPAB. Before this reparation was carried out, Badley church had remained practically unchanged, save for the east window, since the time of Oliver Cromwell.

The Church Organ

Maintaining the church, given the tiny parish population, has been a constant struggle. As the advertisements from the Church Magazine of the day show, (Figs 3.30 & 3.33) Mrs Eva Violet Mary Freshwater who lived at Badley Mill, and Miss Lillian Key (Fig 3.31) of Stowmarket were active fundraisers.

Miss Key, who was an Associate of the Royal College of Music trained under Sir (Henry) Walford Davis, Master of the King's Musick and but for a shoulder injury would have become a concert pianist.

She was organist at Badley for 49 years and at St Mary's parish church, Combs, for 46 years where she was also choir mistress. She came from a musical family - her

BADLEY CHURCH
You are invited to a
BRING and BUY SALE
GIFT STALL, CAKES,
SWEETS and BISCUITS.
WHITE ELEPHANT STALLS
and
BOTTLE STALL
IN
BADLEY MILL HOUSE GARDEN
ON
SATURDAY JUNE 3rd.
3 p.m. to 5 p.m.
PROCEEDS TOWARDS
ORGAN FUND
Please come and bring your
friends
TEA and BISCUITS.

Fig 3.30 Fundraising Parish Magazine May 1967.

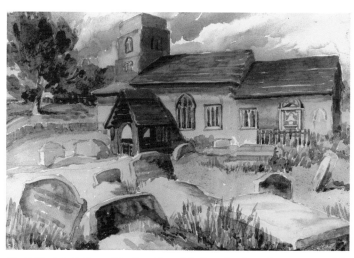

Fig 3.32 A painting of Badley Church believed to have been executed by Miss Lillian Key and given to Mrs. Elizabeth Woods of Badley. It was in possession of her daughter, the late Muriel Manning (see Chapter 4, page 99), at the time of her death in June 2005.

father was organist in Towcester for 30 years and her brother played in Newcastle for 29. She first moved to Suffolk in 1929, and served under six different rectors in her time at Combs church.

The Parish Council reported in 1968 that "the church organ has been causing some distress both to organist and congregation. 'The trumpet giving an uncertain sound' has proved unusually unreliable. The causes have been various. An unusually dry winter and the increased effectiveness of our central heating system, which have resulted in slight warping of the sound boards which now permit air to escape when the organ is being used. These leakages in turn cause the organ blower to work hard all the time it is switched on. When the organ is being played the noise of the blower is covered by the sound of the organ.

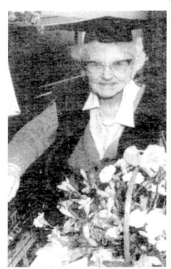

Fig 3.31 Florence Lillian Key - organist at Badley for 49 years.

Two remedies are possible: to connect the blower to the bellows by a longer wind-trunk and to rearrange the heating system so that no hot water pipes run near the organ. Meanwhile a bucket of water is to be placed strategically inside the works to provide the necessary humidity.

The congregation would not appreciate the simplest remedy of all, that is, a cold and draughty church".

A decision was therefore made that year to purchase a second-hand church organ with an electric blower. Miss Key had every incentive to double her fundraising efforts in order to ensure the church had sufficient funds to not only purchase the organ, but also cover the cost of providing an electricity supply to power it.

BRING & BUY SALE
in the
Mill House Garden
by kind invitation of
Mrs. Freshwater
and
Miss Key
at
2.30 p.m.

IF WET, IN THE CHURCH HALL,
KING WILLIAM STREET,
NEEDHAM MARKET

Fig 3.33 Fundraising - Parish Magazine June 1968.

To make room for the organ, the unsightly sentry box, which served as a vestry, was removed.

The present small refurbished organ, with five speaking stops, originally made by Bevington in the mid-19th century, was installed W & A Boggis of Roydonian Works Diss, Norfolk in March 1969. It was dedicated in a serivce attended by the Bishop of Dunwich on Sunday April 27th (see Fig 3.14).

Miss Key died on 6th Janauary 1989 aged 91, only three months after she had retired. By this time she was living at 11 Shimpling Close Combs. Her neighbour at number 15 had been fellow fundraiser Mrs Freshwater who died on 23rd September 1972, aged 79.

They are buried alonside each other in the churchyard, their graves marked by identical stout wooden crosses. There is a commemorative brass plate to Miss Key attached to the organ, viz *"Thanks for God. Florence Lillian Key, A.R.C.M., 1897-1989, who loved this church and was organist here for 49 years. For it is a good thing to sing praises unto our God"*.

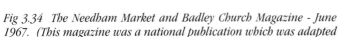

Fig 3.34 The Needham Market and Badley Church Magazine - June 1967. (This magazine was a national publication which was adapted for each participating parish by changing the top title on the front cover and in the case of Needham Market with Badley, by inserting a four-page supplement relating to the benefice - hence the unrelated illustration on the front cover.) In this edition the listed officials for Badley were - Vicar: The Revd. Paul Davidson, M.A.,Churchwardens: Mrs F. Scott, Mr A.B. Scott, Organist: Miss L. Key, A.R.C.M., Caretaker: Mr R.W. Sore, Badley Bungalow.

Needham plans take-over of 12-house hamlet

THE hamlet of Badley, which only has about 12 houses, may come under the wing of neighbouring Needham Market.

The idea has come from Needham Market Parish Council, which is now to approach representatives of the annual Badley parish meeting for members' reaction.

Mr. S. W. Watkinson, chairman of Needham Market Parish Council's boundary committee, said yesterday that Badley did not have a parish council, only an annual parish meet-

ing. Under local government reform, no allowance was made for parish meetings.

'TIDYING-UP'

Mr. Watkinson said the parish council was following the advice of the Parish Councils' Association that, where possible, parish councils should administer areas which only had parish meetings.

Mr. Watkinson said that on Gipping Rural Council, Badley was already represented by Needham Market councillors. "This is just tidying the

position up", he said.

Needham Market Parish Council also wants to take over small parts of the adjoining villages of Barking and Creeting St. Mary to "tidy up" the Needham boundaries.

It plans to take over the Brick Kilns area of Barrett's Lane, Barking.

Mr. Watkinson said that, because of the boundary, people living in the Brick Kilns area had to go through Needham Market to Barking to vote.

Fig 3.35 Ipswich Evening Star 17th March 1972.

THE PARISH COUNCIL

The demise of the parish status enjoyed by Badley for hundreds of years was no doubt prompted by a dwindling population and a change of public attitude towards church attendance.

On 14th August 1928 an *Order in Council* was published in the London Gazette. This Order amalgamated the benefices of Badley and Needham Market, but preserved their individual parish status (reproduced Appendix F(a)).

Badley holds a Parish Meeting as opposed to a Parish Council. In 1972 it was proposed that Needham Market Parish Council should take over the Badley Parish Meeting. Fortunately for Badley, Needham Market Parish Council was reorganised to form a town council. Since a town council cannot merge with a parish meeting, Badley retained its independence (see press cutting Fig 3.35).

However, Badley finally lost its independent Parish status on 5th June 1986, when HM the Queen formerly signed an Order in Council consenting to a petition by the Church Commissioners. This order (reproduced Appendix F(b) -

a) amalgamated the parochial parish of Badley with that of Needham Market;
b) declared St Mary's Badley redundant;
c) transferred the church plate, register books and records to the "new parish church of the new parish" i.e. St John Needham Market, and
d) transferred all the other church assets, and the responsibilty for maintenance to the Redundant Churches Fund (now The Churches Conservation Trust - see later in this chapter).

The Badley Parish Meeting is only convened when the need arises. In March 1997 it met to elect a new Chairman due to Mr. Ian Morton retiring after serving for more than 25 years. Also on the agenda was the question of the footpaths over the river at Badley Lock, which are not in the parish but will affect it (see also Arthur Scott in Chapter 8).

The CHURCHES CONSERVATION TRUST

The Churches Conservation Trust was set up in 1969 to care for Church of England churches no longer needed for parish use. All churches under their care are Grade I Listed as architecturally or historically important.

Ironically redundancy has partially solved the continual problem of maintenance.

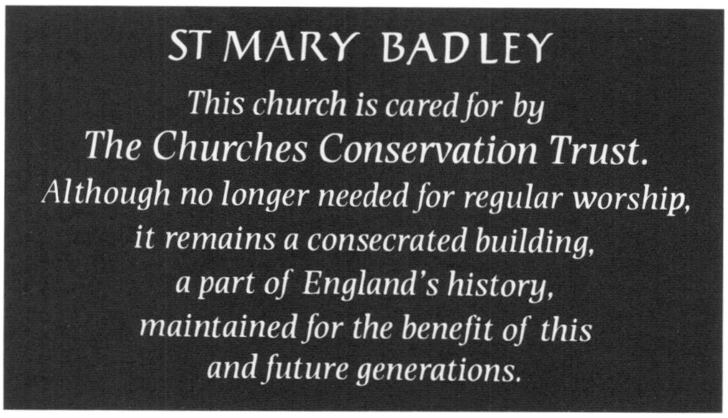

ST MARY BADLEY
This church is cared for by
The Churches Conservation Trust.
Although no longer needed for regular worship, it remains a consecrated building, a part of England's history, maintained for the benefit of this and future generations.

Fig 3.36.

Although services are no longer regularly held at St Mary, it remains consecrated.

By arrangement it is now only used for Baptisms, Funerals and Weddings. An annual 'Harvest Festival' service is usually held in late summer/ early autumn.

Fig 3.37.

Although there is an understandable desire for St Mary's to be left unlocked for visitors, especially during the summer, it's remoteness unfortunately attracts vandalism and more seriously theft.

In July 2002 the two ancient church chests were stolen along with a number of tiles from the porch roof. Consequently it is now kept locked during the week, although the key is available via the churchwardens.

Fig 3.38 The hymn-board.

Fig 3.39 White with age. The 15th century church door with its unusual iron grille and wooden slots underneath originally housing a small 'door' capable of being raised to block it off. Note the unidentified memorial stone immediately inside (No 1 on plan Fig 3.68).

Fig 3.40 Badley church drawn, etched and published by Henry Davy, Globe Street, Ipswich, September 22nd 1841.

ST MARY'S CHURCH PLATE

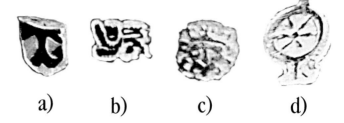

a)   b)   c)   d)

a) the date letter - this appears to be the letter 'T' or an ornamental 'J'. This is not the correct style of lettering for the alphabetical period 1618 - 37. However, it could be the 'T' used for the year 1616, but the shield design is incorrect. i.e.

1616

b) the Lion Passant - the standard, purity or sterling mark introduced in 1544;

c) the assay mark for London - a crowned leopard's head;

d) the maker's mark - despite the distinctive appearance I have been unable to identify this manufacturer.

These marks suggest the chalice was made in London but the hallmark for 1630 should be as follows:

Although the chalice was donated in 1630, we have no means of knowing whether it was specially commissioned that year, or of an earlier manufacture.

The silver plate Fig 3.42 is also hallmarked and bears a leopard's head crowned (London 1680?) with the maker's mark 'EG' (unidentified); a small Roman 'c' for 1778 and a lion passant.

The heavy pewter jug is unmarked. The celebration of Communion in a rural church was a relatively rare occasion in the 17th century and likely to have attracted more communicants than the chalice could accommodate without being refilled. It is thought the pewter jug was used for this purpose. (A return in 1603, gave the number of communicants in the parish as 50.)

Fig 3.41   The attractive hallmarked silver Badley Chalice and Cover donated by Edmund Poley in 1630. It measures height 7½ inches; diameter at top 3¾ inches; diameter at base 3⅛ inches. It is engraved -
"ex dono edmvndi polei de badley armigeri an domi 1630" *(cup) and* **"Ex dono Edmunde Poley de Badley Armigei"** *(cover). It is regularly used for Communion at St John the Baptist parish church, Needham Market.*

Fig 3.43 The Badley Church offertory plate.

The wooden church offertory plate engraved "Freely ye have received - Freely give" and "Jerusalem" painted in the centre.

Fig 3.42 (top) A hall-marked silver paten (plate). In the centre the inscription "I.H.S."(i.e. the first three letters of the name Jesus in Greek) surrounded by a circle of rays; (below) a large covered pewter jug used for replenishing the communion chalice.

Fig 3.44 The 6 feet long Badley Churchwardens' Staves purchased in 1967.

The pair of brass vases opposite, were donated to the church in memory of Frances Emmanuel Haydon of Doveshill Farm, Badley and are engraved -

In Memory of
F. E. Haydon
1879-1945

Fig 3.45 The 'Haydon vases'.

THE BADLEY BIBLES

The Badley Bibles are now safely stored in a locked container at St John, Needham Market. None are exceptionally old and some appear to have been re-bound.

The Book of Common Prayer (1845) opposite right, is inscribed on the title page, *"Presented by John Kirby Moore Churchwarden June 19th 1868".*

The oldest is probably the 1748 edition (3rd from right).

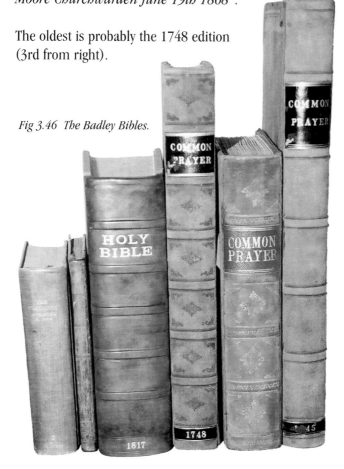

Fig 3.46 The Badley Bibles.

The BOOK of

COMMON PRAYER,

And Adminiſtration of the

SACRAMENTS,

And other

Rites and Ceremonies of the Church,

According to the Uſe of

The Church of England :

Together with the

PSALTER or PSALMS

OF

DAVID,

Pointed as they are to be ſung or ſaid in Churches;

AND THE

Form or Manner of Making, Ordaining, and Confecrating

OF

BISHOPS, PRIESTS, and DEACONS.

CAMBRIDGE :
Printed by JOSEPH BENTHAM, Pronter to the UNIVERSITY, 1748.
Sold by CHARLES BATHURST, in Fleet-ſtreet, London.

CUM PRIVILEGIO.

Price Eight Shillings unbound.

Fig 3.48 Title page from the bible dated 1748.

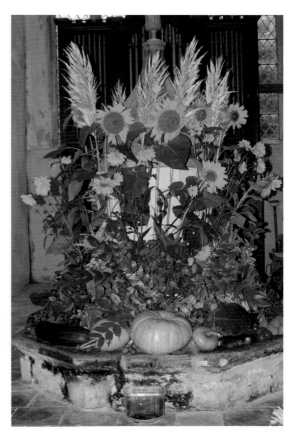

Fig 3.47 (above & right) The altar and font decorated for the (2002) Harvest festival service, held annually in September.

FROM OLD NEWSPAPERS -

PRESENTATION

6th Oct 1938 - Presentation to Mr. & Mrs. Harry Stearn of a hand painted picture of Badley Church by Miss E E Hammond, a Liverpool artist and sister of Mrs. F E Haydon of Badley, in oak frame by Archdeacon T O Wonnacott, in appreciation of their services over past 20 years. Mr. as churchwarden and Mrs. as organist mainstay over a long period.

Stowmarket Recorder, and Needham Market, Combs & Stowupland Advertiser, Thursday

HARVEST THANKSGIVING
AT BADLEY

Remote from the highway, away from the roar of road-traffic, and reposing in beautiful verdant surround, stands the unpretentious little church of St Mary's Badley, with a seating capacity for sixty worshippers. This was more than absorbed by the parishioners and visitors who trekked their way thitherwards on the glorious afternoon of Sunday last. It was the occasion of the season's thanksgiving.

Mrs. H Stearn and Mrs. Haydon had been responsible for a pretty decoration of the church and the visiting preacher was the Rector of Creeting St Mary (The Rev. H. A. Fleetwood).

Mr. H Stearn read the lessons and Mrs. Stearn officiated as organist. The villagers and friends paid wonderful tribute by the mass of choice produce in display and crowned their service by a very substantial offering of £6.4. 0. for the East Suffolk Hospital. The flowers, fruit and vegetables were afterwards sent to be divided equally between the inmates of Stow Lodge and Stowmarket Children's Home.

Stowmarket Recorder, and Needham Market, Combs & Stowupland Advertiser - Thursday October 8th 1936 page 5, col. 2

LADY CHURCHWARDEN

At a meeting of the congregation of Badley Church, presided over by Canon H. A. Fleetwood, Mrs. Carri Louise Haydon of Doveshill, Badley, was unanimously appointed Churchwarden, on the proposition of Mrs. Freshwater seconded by Mr. W. J. Cock. The duties of organist have been kindly undertaken by Miss Key, in succession to Mrs. H. Stearn.

Services are held on Sunday afternoons, by Canon Fleetwood and the Rev. R. S. Shrubbs.

Stowmarket Recorder, and Needham Market, Combs & Stowupland Advertiser - Thursday, June 15th, 1938. No. 159.

PASSING OF
MRS E. LOCKWOOD OF BADLEY

The funeral recently took place of Mrs. Emily Lockwood one of Badley's oldest residents. The deceased was the wife of Mr. W. Lockwood of the Green Farm and had reached the age of 74.

The service took place at Badley Church being conducted by the Rev. H. A. Fleetwood of Creeting St Mary. The hymns ....

The principal mourners were: the widower, Mr. C. Lockwood, Mr. G. Lockwood, Mrs. F. Lockwood, Mr. Lockwood, Mr. R. Firman, Florence, Fred and Olive Lockwood, Mrs. Hallett and Mrs. A. Mason.

Other sympathisers present were Mrs. E. Firman, Mr. and Mrs. W. Lockwood, Mr. E. Rose, Miss Rose, Mrs. Woods, Mrs. C, Hadley, Mrs. Catchpole, Miss Catchpole, Miss Prentice, Mr. and Mrs. G. Cullum, Mr. E. Wenham, Mr. H. Stearn, Mr. Mason and Mrs. A. Peters.

Among beautiful floral tributes were those from the employees at Mr. Mudd's farms.

Summarised from The Stowmarket Recorder, and Needham Market, Combs & Stowupland Advertiser - Thursday 2nd June 1938, page 5, col 3.

Key of porch door Badley ch.
Suffolk

Fig 3.49 A sketch of the old key to the porch door of Badley church by Rev James Ford of Navestock, Essex (undated). (SRO: HD/1678/4/2)

A Few Badley Related Weddings

SAUNDERS—HAYDON

The early 15th century parish church of Badley was the setting for a charming wedding (the first solemnised in this church for twelve years) when Mr. Leslie Howard Saunders, son of Mr. and Mrs. W. H. Saunders, of The Grove, Creeting St. Mary, was married to Miss Ida Mary Haydon, eldest daughter of Mr. and Mrs. F. E. Haydon, of Doveshill, Badley, on Saturday, June 20th. The Rev. H. A. Fleetwood, rector of Creeting St. Mary, officiated, and the bride's grandmother, Mrs. E. Hammond, was organist.

The bride and bridegroom are to make their future home in Chilton Avenue, Stowmarket.

Stowmarket Recorder, and Needham Market, Combs & Stowupland Advertiser—Thursday 25th June 1936 page 5, col 3. (This report was accompanied by a wedding photograph, which was a rare occurrence in this newspaper at that time and is probably the earlist newspaper photograph of a Badley wedding, see Fig 8.28, Chapter 8).

TWEED—HAYDON

WHITSUN WEDDING AT CREETING ST. MARY.
MONDAY, MAY 20th, 1937.

The quiet little church of Creeting St Mary was the theatre of much joy and splendour on Whit Monday afternoon when it was filled with relatives and friends to witness the marriage of Miss Marjorie Haydon, second daughter of Mr. and Mrs. F. E. Haydon of Doveshill, Badley, to Mr. Charles Tweed, only son of Mr. and Mrs. Alfred J. Tweed of Colchester, and a partner in the well-known catering firm of Messrs. Tweed & Son.

Glorious May sunshine favoured ..... for some time the bride has been on the teaching staff at Baylham school, and was also a member of Needham Market Ladies' Hockey Club.

Mr. and Mrs. Charles Tweed are making their home at Great Horkesley, Nr. Colchester.

Summarised from The Stowmarket Recorder, and Needham Market, Combs & Stowupland Advertiser—Thursday 20th May 1937, page 4, col. 5

See also Chapter 8 for details of a further Haydon wedding.

WEDDING CHIMES
STEEL—HADLEY

The wedding took place on Easter Saturday at Stowmarket Parish Church (the Rev. F Tucker-Harvey Officiating) of Miss Vera Kathleen Hadley, daughter of Mr & Mrs G Hadley of Badley Hill to Mr. Luis Andres Charles Steel, son of the late Mr & Mrs C Steel of Gibraltar.

The bride who was given away by her father . . . . .
Summarised from The Stowmarket Recorder, and Needham Market, Combs & Stowupland Advertiser—Thursday 21st April 1938, page 5, col 3.

WEDDING CHIMES
WOODS—ANDREWS

A wedding of considerable local interest took place on Monday last at the Congregational Church, Stowmarket (the Rev. Edgar Jones officiating).

The contracting parties were Miss Dorothy May Andrews, eldest daugher of the late Mr. and Mrs. W. May of Stowmarket and Mr. William Frederick Woods, only son of Mr. and Mrs. W. Woods of Badley.

Mr. and Mrs. Woods are making their home at 35 Regent Street, Stowmarket . . . . .
From The Stowmarket Recorder, and Needham Market, Combs & Stowupland Advertiser—Thursday August 4th 1938, page 5, col 4.

SORE—BOREHAM

On 9th June 1990, Jeremy Sore of Badley married Sally Boreham of Bury St Edmunds. This was the first marriage at Badley church since 1973 and only its eighteenth 20th century wedding.

See also photograph, Chapter 5, Fig 5.62 re wedding of Ellen Maria (Goody) Williams of Doveshill Farm, Badley.

Richard Schyrlok of Badley

"Richard Schyrlok, of Badlee, who died in 1434, and was buried before St John's image, in the College of St Mary in the Fields, at Norwich, gave £26 13s. 4d. to be entered in the martyrology and bead-roll; to the work of the new window, 26s. 8d., and £5 for a marble to be laid over him".

(Source: Page 566, "*A Supplement to the Suffolk Traveller*" by Augustine Page, 1844).

Edmund Alcocke's Chantry

One of the major reasons for church growth in the 14th and 15th centuries was the popularity of establishing chantries and chantry chapels.

A chantry was an endowment in a will for the maintenance of priests to sing masses, usually for the soul of the person making the endowment and also the body of priests or chapel so endowed. It was believed to speed their passage through Purgatory into Heaven. It led to a huge rise in the number of priests and in the richness of parish churches to the detriment of monks and monastic income.

Chantries were established not only by the wealthy, but also by guilds of devout parishioners, a form of collectivism that led to the building of many impressive guildhalls.

The abolition of chantries in 1547 was only one instance of 16th century religious 'reform' being used as a pretext to divert wealth from parishes to the state.

In his will dated 10th February 1491 (reproduced in full in Appendix D), Edmund Alcoke, lord of Badley, alias Edmund Rafman states:

"Item I bequeath to an honest priest who will sing for my soul <u>in the parish church of Badley</u> aforesaid for my soul and for the souls of my ancestors and for the soul of Richard Schyrlocke my uncle, my wives Beatrice and Isabel, and all my friends and benefactors until the end and term of 5 years immediately following after my death, 10 marks lawful money of England coming from my lands lately purchased by me as appears below and one messuage by me newly built called Prestshows with garden and orchard ajoining the same as now enclosed rendering therefore to the chief lords of the fee 12d per annum.

Item I will that if my heirs do not find an honest priest for 9 months then I will that the house bequeathed to the said priest and the said money be expended by my heirs to the repair and sustenance of my chapel there and the said priest's house. ......"

Does the Ordnance Survey therefore erroneously locate Alcocke's chantry to south of the Badley Hall barn despite the fact that the will appears to indicate it was in the church and if so, on what basis? Additionally could "my chapel there" literally have been a building no longer attached to the church?

Parish Clerks

1875 - 9	Zachariah Southgate
1908 -1916	John Mayhew
1922	Charles Firman

Ministers at Badley

From the Marriage registers, various directories and records. (It appears that after about 1900 until 1964, there was no regular minister at Badley. However, a few rectors from adjoining parishes evidently regularly returned to conduct the services and some of them are therefore included in this list).

1338	Richard of Setheheche
1629	Priest Mr Thomas Colson[1]
1664-66	Thomas Hollobrough
1677	Curate Mr Thomas Colson
1690-1704	Edward Foster A.M. d. 5 Oct 1704, aged 37 years, bur. in chancel at Horningsheath
1733/4	Curate Thomas Poke
1754	Curate Samuel Uvedale
1761	Curate Ambrose Uvedale
1773	Curate Edward Griffiths
1778	Curate Thomas Naylor
1804	Rev Ambrose Uvedale B.A.
1806	William Aldrich
1812	Curate James Wood
1817	William Kirby
1819	Curate James Wood
1818 -1836	Rev Charles Davy (also of Barking where he resided)
1834	Rev Thomas Nunn
1845 - 1870	Rev Copinger Hill[2] (also of Buxhall where he resided)
1870 - 1874	Rev John Richard Heawood, M.A. (also of Combs)
1875	Rev Henry Thomas Curry, M.A.
1884	Rev Hon. Arthur C Baillie-Hamilton, B.A., J.P (resided at Combs)
	Curate Revd Frances John Wright Girling, B.A. (resided at Stowmarket)
1895 - 1911	Rev William James Knapton (also of Creeting St Peter)
1911 - 1917	Rev Edward Dennis Rock, B.A. (also of Creeting St Peter)
1918 - 1922	Rev Samuel Hugh De la Bere, M.A. (vicar of Barking where he resided & of Creeting St Peter)
1915 - 1919	Rev H H Ashley Nash
1916 - 1952	Rev H A Fleetwood (of Creeting St Mary)
1927 - 1938	Rev Thomas Oswald Wonnacott, M.A. (died 7th Dec. 1957)
1938 - 1969	Canon R Shrapnell Shrubs (later Rural Dean)
1964 - 1986	Rev Paul Davidson, M.A. (also of Needham Market) (inducted for parish of Needham Mkt with Badley April 16th 1964)
1987 - 1997	Rev Ralph Stuart Stringer (and of Needham Market)
1998 - 2005	Rev Paul Daltry (and of Needham Market)

[1] Thomas Colson was believed to have been the Minister at Badley between about 1629 and his death in 1679. Although he probably lived at Stowmarket, where his names appears quite frequently in the parish registers, he states in his will that he was 'minister of Badley'. (Source: Robin Colson.)

[2] Commenting on the fact that the 'Return from the Census of Religious Worship of 1851' (see Appendix E) gives no information about the private income of clergy, the editor says, "There is little doubt that many Suffolk clergy were wealthy in their own right. Most villages had at least some land owned by a parson in his personal capacity . . . and his private income often exceeded what he received from his living. - It would be a mistake therefore, to assume that even perpetual curates all lived in poverty." To illustrate the point he points out that the incumbent of Badley (Copinger Hill) owned an estate of 575 acres at nearby Buxhall, where he lived at his 'seat', Buxhall Lodge.

Suffolk Limiters

If you were living in Badley about 160 years after Domesday, you might well have received a visit from a wandering monk. But who was he and what was he doing?

From about 1248, Austin friars[1] of the Order of Eremites of St Augustine, in their white habits and black cloaks, were visiting Suffolk villages from their convent at Clare. As begging friars, or 'limiters', they were confined to well-defined areas or 'limitations'.

In 1388 John of Gaunt indicated that he intended to establish a new house of their Order at Theford which would necessitate the Clare convent surrendering some of their Parishes which bordered Thetford to the newcomers. Not surprisingly this was a very unpopular decision from their point of view and in order to ensure they complied, the Provincial Chapter ordered that the two priories should draw up an agreement in writing.

The Provincial Prior, Thomas Winterton of Stamford, Lincs., commanded the friars of Clare let him have a list of the parishes and the arrangements made within eight days. Friar John, the Provincial Prior to the Convent of Clare, agreed to hand over forty-seven parishes to the newcomers. However, he was careful to ensure the surrendered parishes included no town of any size and restricted to the small villages situated between the north of Bury St Edmunds and Thetford.

The villages retained in the cartulary of Clare Priory were subsequently divided into two limitations, Bury and Lavenham. The Parish of Badley was included in the Lavenham limitation. The accompanying illustration is part of the *'Limitation of Lavynham'* held in the British Museum (Fig 3.51). Unlike the Bury list, which is arranged alphabetically, each line of the Lavenham limitation contains groups of adjoining parishes, perhaps those capable of being visited in a single day before the limiter moved on to the next group.

Based on 'Suffolk Limiters' by Lilian J Redstone p. 36-42, Proceedings of the Suffolk Institute of Archaeology & Natural History, Volume XX (1928).

Fig 3.50 An Augustinian Eremite.

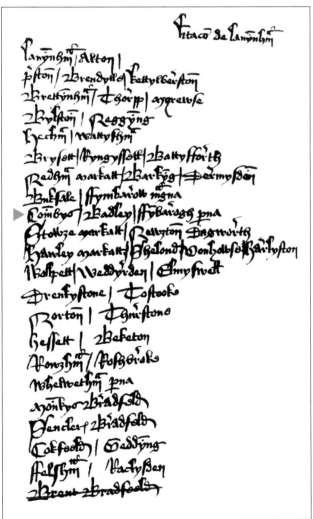

Fig 3.51 The Limitation of Lavenham (British Museum)
"Combys | Badley | ffynbor'rgh parva".

CONNECTION WITH BATTISFORD

HOUSE OF KNIGHTS HOSPITALLERS
THE PRECEPTORY OF BATTISFORD

Fig 3.52 Red maltese cross on a white field worn by the Templars.

BADLEY - "The impropriation[1] was given to the Templars[2] by Robert Fitz-Jefferey and Beatrice his wife, and confirmed to them by Richard Clare, Earl of Hertford". *(John Kirby's Suffolk Traveller (1764, p.200)*

This refers to the Knights Hospitallers of the Order of St. John of Jerusalem who had a Commandry in the adjoining parish of Battisford, the only one in Suffolk.

Although there is no record of the actual founder, there was a preceptory or hospital of the Knights of St. John at Battisford at least as early as the reign of Henry II, for that king gave lands at Bergholt to the Hospitallers of Batesford (Battisford). In 1270, Henry III granted some privileges to the prior of St. John of Jerusalem at Battisford including a market, a fair, and free warren on their lands at Battisford. At this commandry the tenants of the Knights Hospitallers in the county of Suffolk paid their rents.

In 1275 William de Batesford gave them 40 acres of land and 6 acres of wood; at the same time they had a grant from Henry Kede of Battisford of a certain messuage with the customary service pertaining thereto.

A remarkable source of information as to the Knights Hospitallers in England in the reign of Edward II, is contained in the report of Prior Philip de Thame, in 1338, to the Grand Master of the whole order, which is very explicit with regard to the Suffolk preceptory.

The bailiwick or preceptory of Battisford had two members or 'camerae' attached to it, namely those of Coddenham and Mellis. Following the abolishion of the Templars Order in 1312, Preston, Compton, Shepelee and Gysclingham were added. The total receipts for the year 1338 were £93 10s. 7d.

Half the church of Battisford was appropriated to the Hospitallers and was worth 10 marks a year, whilst the rectory of Badley produced £10 a year.

By far the largest source of income was, *'de Fraria[3] ad voluntatem contribuentium,'* which produced that year the large sum of £50.

The expenses enable us at once to see that the chief local charges on the income were those of maintenance and hospitality. Following the general rule, it is found that there was (i) a preceptor or master of the house, Richard de Bachesworth, who acted as receiver and who was himself a knight ; (2) a confrater or brother, William de Conesgrave, also a knight ; (3) a salaried chaplain at 20s. ; and (4) a corrodian, one Simon Paviner, who in return for certain benefactions had board and lodging at the house. In addition to these there were of the household a chamberlain, a steward, a cook, a baker, each receiving 6s. 8d. a year, two youths at 5s. each, and a page at 3s.

Fig 3.53 Knight Hospitaller in monastic habit.

The board for all these, in addition to the hospitality they were bound to extend to visitors, particularly the poor, caused an expenditure of £7 4s. in wheat and oats for bread; £3 4s. for barley for brewing; and £7 16s. at the rate of 3s. a week, for fish, flesh, and other necessaries for the kitchen. The robes, mantles and other necessaries for preceptor and brother cost £3 9s. 4d. The three days' visit of the prior of Clerkenwell, the mother-house of the order in England, caused an expenditure of 60s. The total outlay for the year was £33 3s. 10d., leaving the handsome balance of £60 0s. 10d., to be handed over to the general treasury.

Notes :

[1] **Impropriation**: to place ecclesiastical property, rights, etc., including the benefits of the Great Tithe, from the church into lay hands, with the vicar retaining responsibility for the care of the parish.

[2] **Templars**: *(Poor Knights of Christ and of the Temple of Solomon)* a military religious order of knight-hood founded c.1120 in Jerusalem by a group of French Knights to protect the pilgrim routes and Christian holy places in the kingdom of Jerusalem from the Moslems. The Knights Templars were, with the Knights Hospitallers, the most important military order of the Crusades. Accused of heresy and immorality by Philip IV of France, who feared their power, and envied the wealth, the Templars were eventually suppressed by the Papacy in 1312 with great cruelty. Their wealth was supposed to be passed to the Knights of St John (i.e the Hospitallers) for the continuation of their hospitaller role. It was probably no coincidence that not one penny of the Templars' great wealth in France ever reached the Knights of St John!

[3] **'Confraria', 'Fraria' or 'Collecta'**: was the regular annual collection for the needs of the order made throughout the particular district assigned to a preceptory (in this case, as in most, a whole county) by authorized clerks.

The value of the property of this bailiwick deteriorated after the Black Death. A return in 1538 gave its clear income as £52 16s. 2d.

After the dissolution of the order, Henry VIII granted this preceptory in July 1543, to Andrew Judde, alderman of London. In the following September he obtained licence to alienate it and on 18 April, 1544, it was granted to Sir Richard Gresham.

Fig 3.54 Banner of the Templars.

Fig 3.55 Costumes of the Knights Hospitaller.

terracotta panel on it with the head of St. John the Baptist lying on a charger, Fig 3.56 below.

Fig 3.56 (photo courtesy of Pip Wright).

The site, which still remains moated, is now occupied by Manor House Farm. Some re-used materials may be seen in the buildings, including a stone in one of the chimney stacks, which has a carved

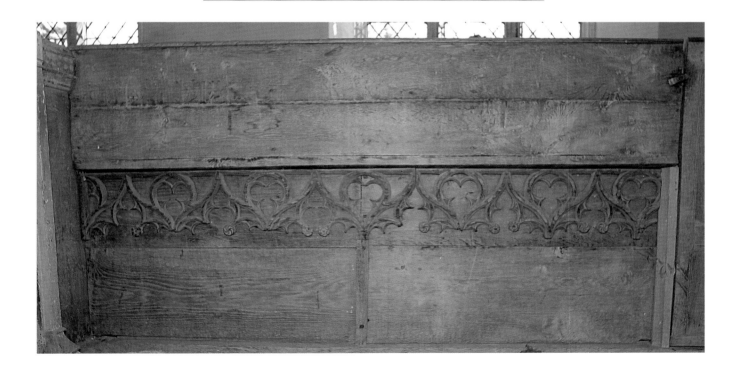

Fig 3.57 St Mary, Badley, traceried woodcarving set into the side of the box-pews which may have come from the upper parts of the rood screen or rood loft.

BADLEY TITHES

HISTORICAL NOTE:

Tithes - generally defined as "the tenth part of the increase arising from the profits of land and stock, allotted to the clergy for their support or devoted to religious or charitable uses". A more radical definition is "the tenth part of all fruits and profits justly acquired, owed to God in recognition of his supreme dominion over man, and to be paid to the ministers of the church". *(The Catholic Encyclopedia, Volume XIV.)*

At first, the tithe was payable to the bishop, but later the right passed by common law to parish priests. Abuses soon crept in. The right to receive tithes was granted to princes and nobles, even hereditarily, by ecclesiastics in return for protection or eminent services. In 1179 this unsatisfactory situation was stopped by the Pope decreeing that no alienation of tithes to laymen was permissible without his consent.

The first reference to the tithe system in England occurs in AD 747. Originally tithes were payments in kind, but from early times these began to be substituted by money payments. This arrangement was formalised by the Tithe Commutation Act 1836 when both payment methods were replaced by a single rent-charge linked to the price of grain. Until 1917 the charge was collected on a voluntary basis. In 1925 the government abandoned the link with grain, fixing the rent charge in perpetuity at £105 per £100 of nominal value, with a further £4.50 to be paid annually to ecclesiastical persons or corporations as a sinking fund for the eventual redemption of tithe in 2009. No account was taken of farmers income. Not surprisingly, tithes, which had always tended to be unpopular, became even more so and a tithe war rapidly developed, with many Suffolk activists. (see *Tithe Wars 1918-1939 The Countryside in Revolt* - Carol Twinch 2001)

The whole scheme as envisaged by the 1936 Act was wound up prematurely under the Finance Act 1977.

What was originally a voluntary giving of the first tenth to support the clergy has its origins in the Bible. For example, the third book of Moses, called Leviticus, Chapter XXVII says:

30. And all the tithe of the land, whether of the seed of the land, or of the fruit of the tree, is the Lord's: it is holy unto the Lord.
31. And if a man will at all redeem ought of his tithes, he shall add thereto the fifth part thereof.
32. And concerning the tithe of the herd or of the flock, even of whatsoever passeth under the rod, the tenth shall be holy unto the Lord.
33. He shall not search whether it be good or bad, neither shall he change it : and if he change it at all, then both it and the change thereof shall be holy ; it shall be redeemed.

The parish of Badley appears to have remained in single ownership from the Domesday Survey until 1917, when it was sold off in lots by the 6th Earl Ashburnham.

From "The Calendar of the Counterparts of the Deeds of Sale of the Monastic Fee Farms Preserved Upon Grant from the Crown" for Badley we find:

Badley	An annual rent out of the hall	Fee Farm Rent Reserved £. s. d.	Grantees of the Fee Farms Revd - No
		0. 5. 1.	Sefton 7
Badley	An annual rent issuing out of the Township	0. 2. 0.	" "

FEE FARM RENT is defined as, where an estate in fee is granted, subject to a rent in fee of at least one-fourth of the value of the lands at the time of its reservation.

A fixed annual payment. The "borough farm" or "fee-farm" *(firma burgi)* was the basic lump sum from a town which had to be paid into the Exchequer each year either by the sheriff of the county or by the town's own officials. Cite, 198.

Fee:
A fee was an estate, sublet to a knight by a baron, bishop or abbot, tenant-in-chief to the king.

Throughout this period the Lord of the Manor appears to have been responsible for paying the tithe. If I have interpreted the above Calendar correctly it appears that upon the dissolution of the monastries and post 1917 this obligation was transferred to the owner of Badley Hall.

The land within the Parish belonging to all the other premises sold at auction in 1917 is described as tithe free, whereas potential purchasers of the Hall were warned - *"Modus in lieu of Tithes payable to the Incumbent of the Living of Badley £40 0s. 0d"*.

Although the production of tithe maps was necessitated by the 1936 Tithe Commutation Act, the scheme was never successfully completed and was abandoned in the 1950's. This, however, is unlikely to be the reason why no such map exists for Badley, as they were completed for all the surrounding parishes.

"In many districts, although the tithes were commuted under the provisions of the 1836 Act, no apportionment was made. This was either because the amount involved was negligible or because there was a merger of the tithe rentcharges. By this means the expense of a formal apportionment and of the preparation of a map was avoided.

Deeds of Merger - when the landowner was also the tithe-owner, a situation was created in which an individual was effectively liable to pay tithes to himself. Such a situation was usually resolved by merging the tithes (or tithe rentcharge) in the land, that is to say, annihilating the liability to pay tithes by virtue of being also entitled to receive them". (*Tithe Records: A Detailed Examination National Archives - Domestic Information Leaflet 41.)*

The document Fig 3.58 below, appears to confirm the church was virtually a manorial chapel (donative, with the lord of the manor as patron and impropriator of tithes). That is, the church lands including any tithes due, had been transferred to them as their private property and they appointed their own parson who was not subject to the usual approval by the bishop (i.e. donative benefice). Without the benefits of further research, it is assumed a Deed of Merger applied until the auction in 1917 when responsibility for the entire Badley tithe reverted to whoever purchased the hall.

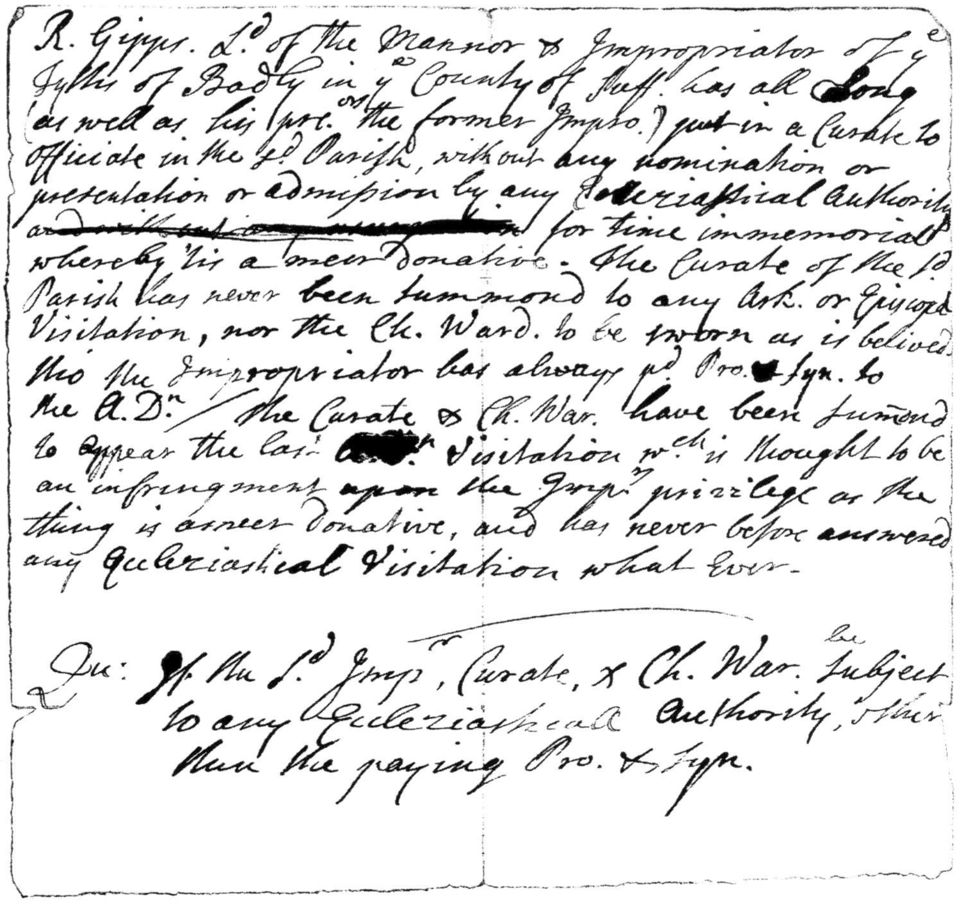

R. Gipps. Ld of the Mannor & Impropriator of ye Tythes of Badly in ye County of Suff. has all Long (as well as his preors the former Impro.) put in a Curate to Officiate in the sd Parish, without any nomination or presentation or admission by any Ecclesiastical Authority for time immemorial whereby tis a meer donative. The Curate of the sd Parish has never been summond to any Ark. or Episcopal Visitation, nor the Ch. Ward. to be sworn as is believed tho the Impropriator has always pd Pro. & Syn. to the A.Dn / the Curate & Ch. War. have been summond to appear the last Visitation wch is thought to be an infringment upon the Impr. privilege as the thing is a meer donative, and has never before answered any Ecclesiastical Visitation what Ever.

Qu: If the sd Impr, Curate, & Ch. War. be subject to any Ecclesiastical Authority, other than the paying Pro. & Syn.

Translation: "R. Gipps Lord of the Manor & Impropriator of the Tithes of Badley in ye County of Suff. has all (a)long (as well as his predecessors the former Impropriators) put in a Curate to Officiate in the said Parish, without any nomination or presentation or admission by any Ecclesiastical Authority for time immemorial whereby this a mere Donative. The Curate of the said Parish has never been summoned to any Archdeaconal or Espiscopal Visitation, nor the Church Warden to be sworn as is believed this the Impropriator has always paid Pro & Syn to the Archdeacon. The Curate and Church Warden have been summoned to appear the last Visitation which is thought to be an infringement upon the Impropriators privilege as the thing is *assess* donative, and has never before answered any Ecclesiastical Visitation what ever.
Question: If the said Impropriator, Curate & Church Warden be subject to any Ecclesiastical Authority, other than the paying Pro and Syn."

Fig 3.58 An early 18th century memo probably written by Richard Gipps' land agent, as to the advowson of Badley being a donative, the curate being nominated by the lord of the manor & impropriator of the tithes and the incumbent and churchwardens having never been summoned to Archdeaconal or Espiscopal visitations (SRO : HA1/DB/3/21).

MEMORIALS

On the walls and floors of St Mary's church there are twenty-four fascinating memorials commemorating people of the past who have been associated with it.

However, according to the Parish Burial Register (See Appendix A), many other individuals were buried in the chancel of the church, but the whereabouts of their graves are unknown. Perhaps they have been covered over by later burials.

In the floor are twenty-one burial slabs of varying descriptions, some with indents of former brasses, some with 17th century brass inscriptions and shields. Several black ledger slabs, or more properly memorials, have fine coats of arms and good lettering; others are very worn. Many of the inscriptions are in Latin and some of the epitaphs are worth pausing to read. Most commemorate members and relations of the Poley family, who directly held the Manor of Badley from about 1491 until 1714.

A plan showing the location of these memorials is provided on page 58 (Fig 3.68). Some of the fine black ledger stones are also reproduced to scale and the inscriptions are recorded for all those not illustrated along with approximate translations for some of those written in Latin.

Taking these memorials in the sequence they appear on the plan - just inside the church door there is a very worn memorial slab (1). This is believed to have been one of the three memorials orginally containing some of the four mediaeval brass indents referred to earlier, which were removed by order of William Dowsing in 1643.

These mediaeval brasses commemorated: (a) Edmund Alcock (1491) and his two wives Beatrice and Isabel; (b) Simon Poley (1485) and Margaret (nee Alcock); (c) Simon's brother Edmund (1504) and Jane his wife; (d) Elizabeth Garneys of Kenton (1539).

We can gain perhaps an insight into the wording on some of these brasses by reference to inscriptions "in the cherch of Badley" recorded on page 780 in "*Ancient Fvnerall Monvments with the Vnited Monarchie of Great Britaine, &c*" compiled by John Weever and published in 1631, i.e. twelve years ahead of Dowsing's visit and reproduced below (Fig 3.58).

All these deaths occurred before the earliest known parish burial register and therefore this is a valuable record, the only earliers sources being Inquisition Post Mortem and Wills.

780	*Ancient Funerall Monuments*
In the Cherch of Badley.	*Symon Powley* gent. and *Margery* his wife, the doughter of *Edmond Alcokes*, which dyed the xiii.of October, M. cccc. lxxx. v. *Edmond Alcock* gent. Lord of the towne of Badley, *Beatrix* and *Izabell* his wiues, which *Edmond* dyed the v. of February, M cccc.lxxxxi. *Edward Powley*, gent. which dyed the xxv. of Ianuary, M. D. iiii. and *Iane* his wife. *Elizabeth Garnes*, wedow, late wife of *Iohn Garnes* Esquire, of Kenton, which died the second of April, *an. M. D. xxxix.*

*Fig 3.58 The Badley entry from the "*ANCIENT FVNERALL MONVMENTS WITH THE VNITED MONARCHIE OF Great Britaine, &c*" compiled by John Weever and published in 1631.*

Notes :

Roman numerals - M = 1000, D = 500, C = 100, L = 50, X = 10, V = 5 and I = 1. Examples M.cccc. lxxx. v = 1485 and M.D. iiii = 1504

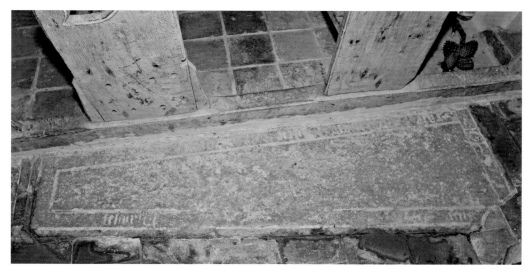

Fig 3.59 The oldest monument in the church? - and thought to relate to one of the de Badley family (No 2 on the plan).

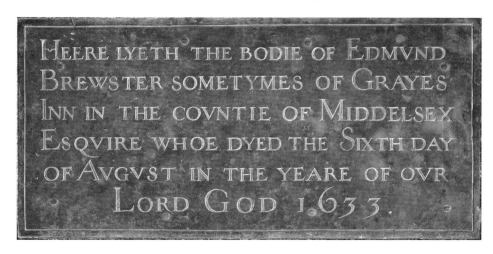

HEERE LYETH THE BODIE OF EDMVND
BREWSTER SOMETYMES OF GRAYES
INN IN THE COVNTIE OF MIDDELSEY
ESQVIRE WHOE DYED THE SIXTH DAY
OF AVGVST IN THE YEARE OF OVR
LORD GOD 1.633.

Fig 3.60 The brass plate on the memorial to Edmund Brewster who died in 1633)(3 on plan).

In the nave close to the font and illustrated at Fig 3.59, a 13th century coffin-shaped burial slab is probably the oldest monument in the church (2 on plan). With tantilising traces of an incised inscription round the border, it is thought to relate to one of the de Badele family.

Moving along the nave towards the altar, firstly, there is the memorial to Edmund Brewster (3) bearing a well preserved brass inscription which is reproduced above (Fig 3.60).

Edmund Brewster may have been the tenant at Badley Hall at the time of his death. Alternatively, he may have been buried within the church because he was related to the Poleys by marriage. Mirabel Poley was married to William Brewster of Castle Hedingham, Essex and Cicely Crofts, the daughter of Cicily Croftes (née Poley) and Sir Charles Croftes of Bardwell, was married to Francis Brewster of Wrentham (see Poley 6th Generation Family Tree, Fig 6.9, Chapter 6).

Next is the memorial to Thomas Poley (4), whose brief inscription is reproduced below (Fig 3.61).

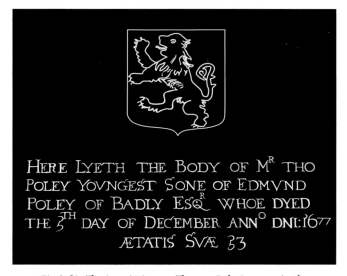

HERE LYETH THE BODY OF M[R] THO
POLEY YOVNGEST SONE OF EDMVND
POLEY OF BADLY ESQ[R] WHOE DYED
THE 5TH DAY OF DECEMBER ANN[O] DNI:1677
ÆTATIS SVÆ 33

Fig 3.61 The inscription on Thomas Poley's grave in the centre gangway (4 on plan).

In the widest part of the nave and just prior to the chancel are the three memorials abreast 5, 6 & 7. The two outer memorials 6 & 7 have indents which it is thought formerly contained the remainder of the brass inscriptions removed by Dowsing and referred to earlier. They are otherwise unreadable and in any event partially obscured by the box pews constructed over them. The centre memorial (5) marks the grave of Edmund Poley (1613) and is adorned with three well preserved brass amorial shields (Fig 3.62) viz Poley (top), Poley impaling Cockerham/Cokeram - Arg. on a bend Sa. three leopards' heads Or. (below right) and Poley impaling Seckford - Erm. on a fess GU. three escallops Or/Arg. (below left Fig 3.63) and the brass indent reproduced opposite Fig 3.64), with a translation underneath.

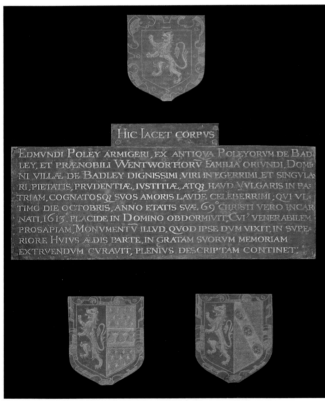

Fig 3.62 Edmund Poley 1613 - arrangement of brasses.
(central inscription has been enlarged to enable it to be read)

Fig 3.63 A close-up of the arms on the lower shields.

HIC IACET CORPVS
EDMVNDI POLEY ARMIGERI EX ANTIQVA POLEYORVUM DE BAD=
LEY, ET PRÆNOBILI WENTWORTHORV FAMILIA ORIVNDI, DOMI=
NI VILLÆ DE BADLEY DIGNISSLMI VIRI INTEGERRIMI ET SINGVLA=
RI, PIETATIS, PRVDENTIÆ, IVSTITIÆ, ATQ HAVD VVLGARIS IN PA=
TRIAM, COGNATOSQ SVOS AMORIS LAVDE CELEBERRIMI, QVI VL=
TIMO DIE OCTOBRIS, ANNO ETATIS SVÆ 69° CHRISTI VERO INCAR=
NATI, 1613° PLACIDE IN DOMINO OBDORMIVIT CVI⁹ VENERABILEM
PROSAPIAM, MONVMENTV ILLVD, QVOD IPSE DVM VIXIT, IN SVPE=
RIORE HVIVS ÆDIS PARTE, IN GRATAM SVORVM MEMORIAM
EXTRVENDVM CVRAVIT, PLENIVS DESCRIPTAM CONTINET.

Fig 3.64 The inscription on Edmund Poleys memorial, with a translation below (the * refers to the large wall monument, No 23 on the plan)

Translation of inscription :

"Here lies the Body of Edmund Poley Esquire of the Ancient Poleys of Badley and the very noble Wentworth family is descended. Lord of the town of Badley, a worthy man of integrity and singular piety, prudence, justice and known for his love of the ordinary people of the country his praise is celebrated. Who on the last day of October in the 69th year of his age of Christ's true Incarnation 1613 peacefully fell asleep in the Lord. Of which venerable family a full description continues on that monument,* which there whilst he lived in the upper part of this building with pleasure to their memory he carefully put up".

The first monument in the chancel is number 8 on the plan. Unfortunately it is in a very worn condition, but from the date 1635 and the wording which is just legible and the burial records we can surmise it relates to Miss Elizabeth Crompton one of the two unmarried daughters of Sir John Compton, Knight & Lady Frances *(nee Crofts)* his wife of Skern, Yorkshire, who was born at Toddington, co. Beds., and buried on 25th Feb 1635. By computer enhancing photographs of the memorial, I have been able to reconstruct the Crompton arms *(Gules, a fess wavy between three lions rampant Or,)* and a good deal of the inscription, the top part of which is in English, as shown in Fig 3.66 on the next page. (Sir John was M.P. for Brecknock [Brecon],Wales. He died 8th December 1623 and was buried in London).

Monument number 9 is a small (now broken) ordinary stone marking the grave of infant Henry Poley inscribed as follows:

Here lyeth the body
of Mr. Henry Poley
eldest Son of Edmund Poley, Esq
which he had by his second Wiffe
the Lady Crompton, he lived
6 Months & 10 days, and dyed
the 16th of March, Ano Domi 16.. 0.
(Effaced)

Fig 3.65.

Fig 3.66 The partially reconstructed memorial to Elizabeth Crompton (8 on plan). NB. Register gives year as 1635.

Parallel to this, the death of John Poley, another unfortunate Poley infant is marked by a brass indent (number 10 on the plan) the Latin inscription on which reads as follows:

> READE IF THOV CANST, AND MOVRNE NOT, HIS NAME & STOCKE BEING KNOWNE FOR THEY WILL TELL WHAT PITIE TWAS HE WAS BVT BORNE & SHOWNE
>
> HIC LACET PRIMO GENITVS FILIVS ET EXITVS EDMVNDI POLEY AR: ET DOROTHEE VXORIS EIVS, CVI NATVRA DEDIT ET IN MVNDVM ET EX MVNDO PREPRO PERVM TRANSITVM, IN MVNDVM ENIM VENIT. 16. DIE APRILIS ANO SALVTIS. 1615. ANTE DIES PARJENDI COMPLETAS EO DEMQ DIE MVNDVM VIDIT ET VICIT, PRIVS EX FIDE PARENTVM SVORVM IN FIDE CHRISTIANA BAPTIZATVS ET NOMINATVS JOHANNES POSTRIDIEQ HIC SEPVLTVS QVI SIC PRIMITIAS SVAS SANCTE TRINITATI DEDICA VERVNT, ET IN EIJUS MEMORIAM HVNC LAPIDEM SVPER SEPVLCHRVM SVVM PONI CVRAVERVNT.

Translation of inscription :

Reade if thou canst, and mourn not, his name and stocke being known for they will tell what pitie twas he was but born and shown
Here lies the first born son an issue of Edmund Poley Esquire and Dorothea his wife whom nature gave and in the world and from the world too hastily lost passed into the world for to come 16th day of April the year of salvation 1615 before the day of complete ruin all too brief God's world saw and overcome. Before by the faith of his parents in the Christian faith baptised and named John. And and the next day here buried which thus originally his to the Holy Trinity has been dedicated and in his memory this stone on his tomb has been carefully placed.
(NB.: The Parish Register says he was born and baptised on the 12th and buried on the 13th of April 1615. (See Appendix A, page 241)).

Fig 3.67 The Scrivener grave showing the very distinctive, almost hieroglphical nature of the border engraving, and above the two shields (grouped together for convenience) of Scrivener and Scrivener impaling Shorland (11 on plan).

The distinctive Purbeck marble slab with inscriptions and two coats of arms in white marble placed by Susanna Shoreland to commemorate her husband Peter Scrivener, son of Ralph Scrivener of Belstead Parva, who died and was buried on 17th December 1604, with an inscription beneath to their son Randolph Scrivener dated 1605 (Fig 3.67)(11 on plan), is the second oldest legible memorial in the church. It is presumed the Scriveners were tenants at Badley Hall before Edmund Brewster.

St Mary's Badley

Interior plan showing disposition of pews, box-pews and monuments

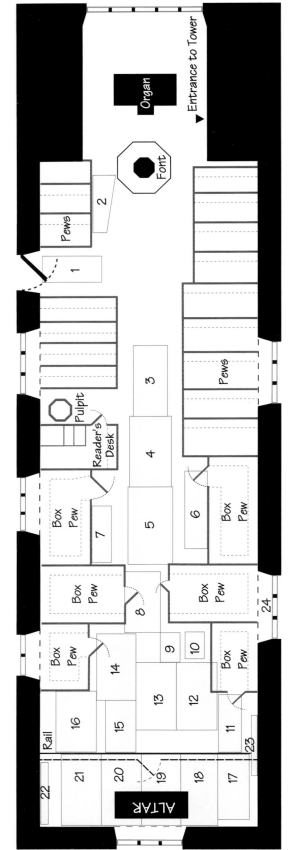

© M.J.D. 2001

KEY TO MONUMENTS :

1. unknown - unreadable - originally a brass?
2. de Badele family?
3. Edmund Brewster 1633
4. Thomas Poley 1677
5. Edmund Poley 1613
6. unknown - unreadable - originally a brass?
7. unknown - unreadable - originally a brass?
8. Elizabeth Crompton 1636
9. Henry Poley 1630 (infant)
10. John Poley 1615 (infant)
11. Peter & Randolph Scrivener 1605
12. Cecily Poley 1679
13. Mary & John Crompton 1641
14. Katherine Crofts 1685
15. Katherine Gipps 1705
16. Edmond Poley 1714
17. Dorothy Poley 1625
18. Edmond Poley 1640
19. Dame Frances Crompton 1661
20. Sir Edmund Poley 1671
21. Dame Hester Poley 1714
22. Henry Poley 1707 (wall)
23. Poley Family 1604 (wall)
24. Shield (north window) - a cross patonce Or; a bordure engrailed Arg. (de Badele?)

Fig 3.68.

The 'hieroglyphical' style of this memorial is very similar to the brass memorials to William Sydnor (1613) at Blundeston and William Doggett (1610) at Boxford. *(see Suffolk Heraldic Brasses - T M Felgate (1978) plates 7 & 8)*

Translation -

Here lies buried Peter Scrivener son and heir apparent of Radulph Scrivener of Little Belstead, Gent., who died in the Christian faith 17th day of December in the year 1604 and in the 45th year of his age who was married to Susanne Shoreland who was the daughter of John Shoreland of Winston, Gent. and Mary his wife.

And who lyes above Radulph his only born son who died on the 1st May in the year of Our Lord 1605 before completing seven months and is buried here next to his father may their souls rest with God and in their sweet memory the aforesaid Susanna placed this monument.

To the right of the Scrivener memorial Cicely Poley (12) lies buried and her monument is reproduced opposite Fig 3.69.

Next to her (13) is another very badly worn Crompton memorial which from earlier surveys we know is the final resting place of Sir John Compton's other daughter Mary (Marie) Crompton who was buried on 14th April 1641. Again I have attempted reconstruct the arms and recover some of the inscription, Fig 3.70 opposite.

Continuing to the right across the chancel is the well-preserved white marble slab memorial to Catherine Crofts (14) bearing the arms of Crofts (three bulls heads couped) in a lozenge (in heraldry a *lozenge* ie a diamond shape, takes the place of a Shield to bear the arms of Ladies) (Fig 3.71 next page). The parish register shows she was buried on 5th January 1686.

Nearer the altar the next ledger stone marks the grave of Catherine Gipps (15) reproduced Fig 3.72 next page.

Between 15 and the south wall is another finely carved black ledger stone (Fig 3.73 next page). Sadly the spot also marks the end of the Poley dynasty at Badley, for Edmund Poley, the diplomat, was the last of the male line and like his brother Henry (22) he never married. It was probably placed there by his sister Elizabeth, the wife of Sir Richard Gipps of Horringer, knt., as his mother, who survived him, died the following month, see Fig 3.78, page 63.

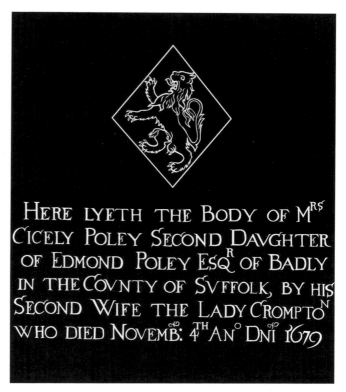

Fig 3.69 Cicely Poley's memorial, of whom the burial register states died in London and was buried at Badley on 10th November 1679 (12 on plan).

Fig 3.70 The partially reconstructed memorial to Marie Crompton, the daughter of Sir John Crompton Knt of Skerne, Yorks (13 on plan).

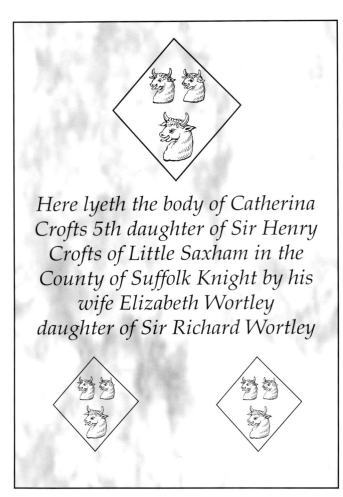

Here lyeth the body of Catherina Crofts 5th daughter of Sir Henry Crofts of Little Saxham in the County of Suffolk Knight by his wife Elizabeth Wortley daughter of Sir Richard Wortley

Fig 3.71 A reproduction of the only white marble ledger stone in the church commemorating Catherine Crofts, bearing three lozenges containing the arms of Crofts. Traces of the gold coloured paint used to highlight the lettering are still visible (14 on plan).

The penultimate group of memorials are the five within the altar rails all of which are in variety of different syles. From left to right these are -

Dorothy Poley (née Warner) 1625 (17) Edmund Poley's (18) first wife, with the frequently quoted inscription in English, reproduced Fig 3.74 next page;

EAST WINDOW				
Dorothy Poley 1625	Edmund Poley 1640	Dame Frances Crompton 1661	Sir Edmund Poley 1671	Dame Hester Poley 1714
(17 on plan)	*(18 on plan)*	*(19 on plan)*	*(20 on plan)*	*(21 on plan)*

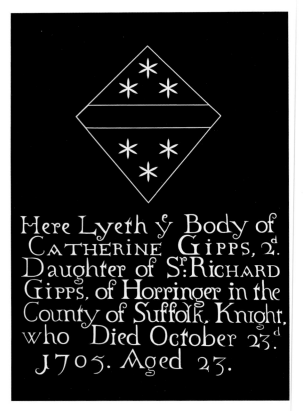

Here Lyeth yͤ Body of CATHERINE GIPPS, 2ᵈ. Daughter of Sʳ RICHARD GIPPS, of Horringer in the County of Suffolk, Knight, who Died October 23ᵈ. 1705. Aged 23.

Fig 3.72 The ledger stone covering the grave of Catherine Gipps (d.1705) with the arms of Gipps (Az a fess between six estoiles Or) (15 on plan).

Here lyes yͤ Body of EDMOND POLEY Esq; third Son of Sʳ EDMOND POLEY of *Badly* in yͤ County of *Suffolk* who departed this Life May yͤ 16.ᵗʰ 1714.

Fig 3.73 (16) Edmond Poley's memorial with fine lion carvings.

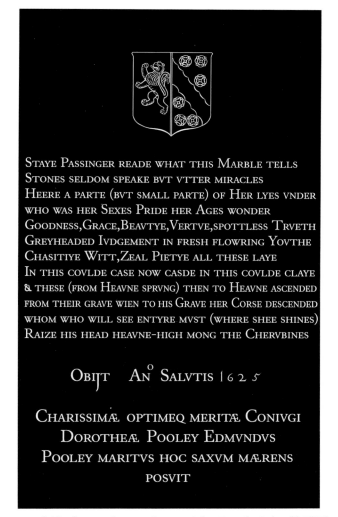

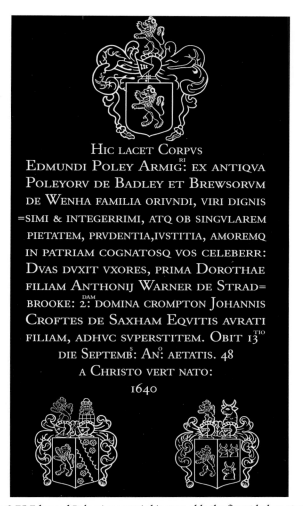

Fig 3.74 The frequently quoted memorial to Dorothy Poley (d.1625) situated to the left of the altar (No 18 on plan).

Fig 3.75 Edmund Poleys' memorial is arguably the finest ledger stone of all. The arms are lower left - Poley, impaling Warner (enlarged below left), with Poley impaling Crofts opposite (18 on plan). See below for approximate translation.

Edmond Poley 1640 (18) Fig Fig 3.75 opposite. Although the mantling and crest on the upper arms are now quite coroded despite its 'protected' position, in its heyday this must have ranked as one of the finest ledger stones in the church. Because the little Elizabethan face on the lower right arms is easily missed, an enlargement has been provided.

Dame Frances Crompton (née Crofts) 1661 (19) the widow of Sir John Crompton Knt of Skerne, Yorkshire, the second wife wife of Edmund Poley (18) and the daughter of Sir John Crofts of Little Saxham, see Fig 3.76

Sir Edmund Poley, Knt (20) see Fig 3.77.

Dame Hester Poley (née Crofts) (21) the wife of Sir Edmund Poley (20) see Fig 3.78.

Translation No 18 -
Here lies the body of Edmund Poley Esquire, descended from the ancient families of the Poleys of Badley and the Brewse of Wenham and man of dignity and integrity and for singular piety prudence justice true love in the county you were known and celebrated: He took two wives first Dorothea the daughter of Anthony Warner of Stradbroke, secondly Lady Crompton the daughter of John Croftes of Saxham, Knight still surviving. Died 13th day of September in the year of age 48 and from Christ's true birth 1640.

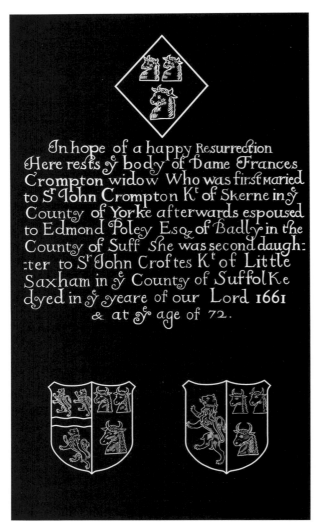

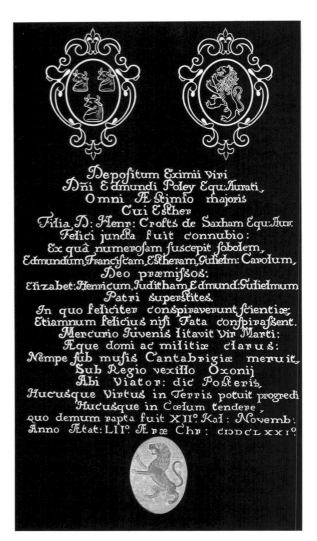

Fig 3.76 The beautifully inscribed memorial to Dame Frances Crompton (d.1661) showing the arms of Croft (top) and those of Poley impaling Croft at the foot (19 on plan).

Fig 3.77 Sir Edmund Poley's fine memorial situated under the right hand side of the altar. The inscription is enlarged below left with an approximate translation below (No 20 on plan).

Depofitum Eximii Viri
Dñi Edmundi Poley Equ : Aurati,
Omni Æ stimo majoris
Cui Esther
Flilia D : Henr : Crofts de Saxham, Equ : Aur.
Felici juncta fuit connubio :
Ex quâ numerofam fuscepit fobolem,
Edmundum, Francifcum, Estheram, Gulielm: Carolum
Dec præmifsos:
Elisabet; Henricum, Juditham Edmund: Gulielmum
Patri superstites.
In quo feliciter conspiraverunt fcientiæ;
Etiamnum felicius nifi Fata confpirafsent.
Mercurio Juvenis litavit Viri Marti :
Æque domi ac militiæ clarus :
Nempe fub mufis Cantabrigiæ meruit,
Sub Regio vexillo Oxonij
Abi Viator : dic Posteris,
Hucusque Virtus in Terris potuit progredi
Hucusque in Cœlum tendere,
quo demum rapta fuit XII°. Kal : Novemb :
Anno Ætat : LII°. Æ r æ Chr : CIƆDCLXXI°.

Translation of No 20 above -

Deposit of the distinguished man Lord Edmond Poley Knight of all in the estimation of most who with Esther the daughter of Henry Crofts of Saxham Knight in a happy union was joined.

From whom numerous offspring begot Edmund, Francis, Esther, William, Charles predeceased: Elizabeth, Henry, Judith, Edmond, William survive after the father in whose knowledge that they have happily agreed until then fortune, except the fates conspired.

Mercury, young man have offered war equally to the house as military service bright of course under the muse of Cambridge served under the King's standard of Oxford where the summoner: Day of posterity and hither strength in the world can go out and hither into heaven proceed who at last was carried away the 12th day of the calender November in the 52nd year of his age 1671.

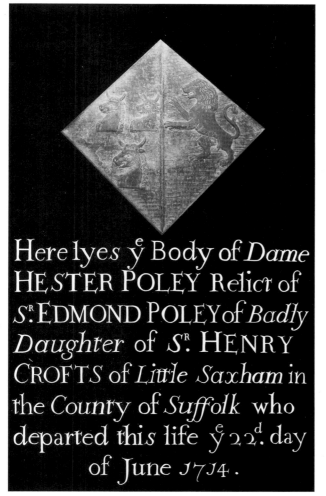

Here lyes y̎ Body of *Dame* HESTER POLEY Relict of *S*.̇EDMOND POLEY of *Badly Daughter* of *S*. HENRY CROFTS of *Little Saxham* in the *County* of *Suffolk* who departed this life y̎ 22.̇ day of June *1714*.

Fig 3.78 The memorial to Sir Edmund Poley's wife Hester who died in 1714 - chronologically the most recent memorial in the church.

Sir Edmund Poley's monument (Fig 3.77) gives the date of his death as 12th November 1671, whereas the Parish Register (Appendix A, page 251) says he "*died at Burie St Edmunds 8bris 22 & was buried in ye chancell in Badly 8bris 23 1671*". 8bris being Latin for 'octo', the month of October, as the church year began in March until 1752.

The final memorials 22 & 23, are the two large monuments situated on the wall either side of the altar.

No 22, a monumental tablet situated on the south wall (Fig 3.79), is perhaps the most impressive and probably the most expensive. It was erected by Edmund Poley (16) to the memory of his brother Henry Poley who died in 1707.

The shield above the inscription was originally painted, no doubt with the Poley arms i.e. a black lion rampant on a gold background. The outline of the lion is still just visible.

Fig 3.79 The impressive memorial to Henry Poley the lawyer and politician erected by his brother Edmund. He was probably the last Poley to actually reside at Badley. In a long Latin inscription (enlarged and translated opposite) his brother lists in detail all his merits and honours (22 on plan).

Hic Iacet
Henricus Poley Armiger
Filius et Hæres Edmundi Poley de Badley
In Comitatu Suffolciæ Militis
A Iuventute Legibus Patrijs
Felicem navavit operam,
Quas nec elegantius quifquam Expofuit,
Nec propugnavit liberius.

Inter Primos sui temporis,
Ut in fforo, ita etiam in Regni Senatu
Oratores claruit
Nee tamen ei plus ad Famam ingenii dotes
Quam Virtutis Studium, Valuere.

Et tandem ex Ærumnojâ hac vita
Omni Pietatis et Charitatis
Ornamento confpicuâ
Suis Omnibus magnum Sui
Defiderium relinquens
Placide excefsit 70 die Augusti
Anno Domini. 1707.
Ætatis suræ 540.

Edmundus Poley Armiger
Fratri Charifsimo
Hoc Monumentum moerens Pofuit.

Approximate translation :

Here Lies
Henry Poley Esquire
son and heir of Edmund Poley of Badley
in the County of Suffolk Knight
after youth to the laws of the County
He has successfully worked
which neither choice anyone had set out
nor he had to defend freedom

During his first time
as in the Forum as in the Kingdom's Parliament
He was a distinquished orator
Yet however oh more to fame nature endows
what virtues, enthusiasm to value

And finally from this wretched life
All pieties and Charities we looks at
as ornaments of all his greatness
longing left behind
Peacefully He departed 7th Day of August
The Year of the Lord 1707
of his age 54

Edmund Poley Esquire
His beloved brother
This monument mournfully put up

Erected by Edmund Poley 400 hundred years ago to his relatives and decendants on 18th September 1604, the final monument, 23 on plan (Fig 3.82 and 3.84), is the oldest legible memorial. It is also the largest - a wall monument, crowned with obelisks enclosing a large coloured heraldic shield, commemorating Edmund Poley (1548) - grandson of Simon Poley and Margaret (née Alcock) - and Myrabel his wife (1558); also their son John (1589) and his wife Anne (daughter of Thomas, Lord Wentworth) (1589), their son Richard (1592), his wife Mary (Brews) (1593) and Richard's sister-in-law Catherine (Seckford) (1601) and Alice (Cockram) (1604), who were the two wives of Edmund Poley and his family (see next column and page 66 for full inscription and translation).

Interestingly, the nine quartering of Poley, engraved by Dr Joseph Jackson Howard, Maltravers Herald, in his *'Visitation of Suffolk I'* and based on a pedigree drawn in *'Glovers Ordinary'* by Robert Glover (1544-1588), Somerset Herald in 1579, differ from those actually on the shield (see Fig 3.80 opposite). This fact was recognised by the Rev Edmund Farrer F.S.A. writing on Badley Hall in *East Anglian Miscellany (No 4,897)*. The same quarterings are also reproduced in *Visitations of Suffolk 1664-8* p.177)

Given Glover's sketch was made some 25 years before the present monument was erected, this must have either been

based on another monument torn down by Dowsing's men, or simply a shield constructed from the family's known genealogy. Eitherway, the incusion of Gardeville (Arg. a fess between three garbs Gu.) in the quartering relates to be the Poleys conections with Stoke Ash, (See Chapter 7).

Traces still visible on various parts of the monument indicate that a good deal of the detail on this fine marble memorial was originally painted.

What a sight this must have been in pristine condition in 1604.

Fig 3.80.

THE CERTEINE END OF ALL ON EARTHE THAT LIVE,
IF DEATHE THEM ONCE ARRESTE NONE CAN ESCHEWE,
BUT MUST OF FFORCE PLACE TO HIS JUDGEMENTS GIVE,
AND LEAVE THE WORLDE, AND YELDE NATURE HER DEWE ;
FFOR BY THEIRE BYRTHE, TO DETH THEY ARE MADE THRALL,
AND MUST NEEDS GOE, WHEN GOD FOR THEM DOETH CALL.
FFOR WORLDLIE WEALTHE, NOR WYTT, CANNOT PROLONGE
THE HASTINGE DAIES, WHICHE SWIFTLIE PASSE AWAYE ;
NOE MEEDE, NOE PLEA, NOE FFRINDSHIPPEIS SOE STRONGE
TO LENGTHEN LYFE, OR BYTTER DEATHE, TO STAYE,
WHICHE WITHE UNPARTIAL HANDES, SUBIECTE AND KINGE,
UNTO THE EARTHE, FROM WHENCE THEY CAME, DOTHE BRINGE.
SITHE SUCH THEN IS THE STATE OF EVERIE ONE,
THAT NONE CAN PASSE THE LIMITES THAT GOD HATH SET,
FFOLLIE WERE IT, THEIRE FFORTUNES TO BEMONE,
WHOM FROM THE EARTHE, BY DEATHE YOW SEE HEARE SETT,
FFOR TO THEMSELVES, THE CHAUNGE MOST HAPPIE IS
TO LEAVE THE WORLD, TO DWELL THROUGHE CHRISTE IN BLISSE ;
AND YOW THESE FFRINDES, WITH HEAVIE HEARTES, THAT MOURNE
THEIR LIVES BEREFETE WHOM YOW DID HOULDE MOST DEARE;
OUGHTE CEASE YOUR TEARES, AND DEATHE HIS MALICE SCORNE,
WHOSE POWRE DOETH REACHE NOE FARTHER THEN THE BEERE,
MAWGER WHICH THEIR SOWLES, THE HEAVENS HEIGHE POSESTE,
AND AYE THE EARTH, THEIR VERTUOUS WAYES CONFESSE.

Fig 3.81 The upper inscription, in English.

Missing armoral shields

Missing armoral shields

Fig 3.82 The magnificent memorial commemorating Edmund Poley (1548) and his family. The crest is reproduced on the title page of this book and discussed in Chapter 7. Unfortunately at least seven other shields are now missing from what is still a very expressive monument indicative of the wealth of the Poley family. The inscription and translation is recorded on the next page (23 on plan).

SEPELIVNTVR IN ISTA ECCLESIA, ET DORMIVNT HIC IN PACE, ET IN FIDE CHRISTIANA, RESURRECTIONEM CORPORVM SVORVM, ET EORVM BEATAM ET PERPETUAM VNIONEM, CVM ANIMIS SVIS CREDENTES ET EXPECTANTES, EDMVNDVS POLEY ARMIGER DOMINVS HVIVS VILLE, ET MIRABELLA VXOR EIVS, QVE FVIT VNA FILIARVM IOHANNIS GARNEIS DE KENTON ARMIGERI, QVI OBIJT VLTIMO DIE DE= CEMBRIS IN ANNO DOMINI 1548. ET DICTA MIRABILLA. 25 DIE FEBVARIJ. 1558. ET IOHANNES POLEY. DOMINVS TOTIVS HVIV VILLE FILIVS ET HERES PREFATI EDMVNDI, ET ANNA UXOR EIVS QVE FVIT FILIA PRIMOGENITA IOHNE WENTWORTHE MILITIS DOMINI WENTWORTHE DE NETTLE= STED, QVE OBIJT, 28 DIE AVGVSTI. 1575. ET PREDICTVS IOHANNES. 26 DIE OCTOBRIS. 1589. ET RICHARDVS POLEY FILIVS SECVNDVS, DICTI IOHANNIS ET MARIA VXOE EIVS, FILIA PRIMO= GENITA IOHANNIS BREWSE DE WENHAM MILITIS ET CICILIE VXORIS EIVS QVI HABVERVNT EXITV INTER EOS EDMVNDVM POLEY ET CICELIAM POLEY, ADHVC DEI GRACIA VIVENTES QVI QVIDEM RICHARDVS OBIJT. 14. DIE FEBRVARIJ, 1592. ET DICTA MARIA. 29. DIE IVNIJ. 1593. ET CATHERINA FILIA PRIMOGENITA, FRAVNCISCI SECKFORDE ARMIGERI ET ELLENE VXORIS EIVS, VXOR EDMVNDI POLEY, FILIJ ET HEREDIS DICTI IOHANNIS POLEY, QVE OBIJT SINE PROLE. 18. DIE IVNIJ. 1601. PREFATO EDMVNDO SVPERSTITE, QVI TAM IN MEMORIA PROGENITORV SVORVM PREDICTORV, QVA PREDICTI RICHARDI POLEY FRATRIS SVI, ET MARIE VXORIS EVIS, ET PREFATE CATHERINE NVPER VXORIS EIVS, ET SIBI DVM VIXIT CHARISIME, ET ALICIE RELICTE RICHARDI KEMP DE GYSSINGE ARMIGERI, LA VXORIS EIVS, ET SIBI NON MINVS CHARE ET DILECTE, HEC POSVIT. 18 DIE SEPTEMBRIS, ANO DOM 1604.

Fig 3.83 The lower Latin inscription, with the translation below.

No 23 Translation of lower inscription -

Buried in this church, and they sleep here in peace, and in the Christian faith believing and expecting the resurrection of their bodies and their blessed and Perpetual Union, with his soul, Edmund Poley Esquire and Lord of this town and Mirabella and his wife, who was one of the daughters of John Garneis of Kenton Esquire, who died the last day at December in the year of Our Lord 1548. And the said Mirabella 25th day of February 1558. And John Poley Lord of all this town, son and heir of the aforesaid Edmund, and Anna his wife who was the first-born daughter of John Wentworth Knight, Lord Wentworth of Nettlested, who died 28th day of August 1575 and the aforesaid John the 26th day of October 1589* and Richard Poley the second son of the said John, and Mary his wife, the first born daughter of John Brewse of Wenham Knight and Cicely his wife, who have departed between. Edmund Poley and Cisley Poley till now by the grace of God living which certain Richard died 14th day of February 1592†, and, the said Mary 29th day of June 1593. And Catherine the first-born daughter of Francis Seckford Esquire and Ellen his wife, wife of Edmond Poley son and heir of the said John Poley, who died without issue the 18th day of June 1601‡. The aforesaid Edmund survives who so much in memory of his aforesaid ancestors, of the aforesaid Richard Poley his brother and Mary his wife and the aforesaid Catherine his late wife and for himself whilst he lives for charity true love and Alice the widow of Richard Kemp of Gyssinge Esquire his wife and further and for herself with no less charity and love has put this here the 18th day of September in the year of Our Lord 1604.

Note ~ the dates on this monument differ from the entries in the Parish Register (reproduced Appendix A) as follows:
  * The date of John's death is given as 20th October 1589.
  † The register records Richard died at Little Saxham on 8th February 1592.
  ‡ The date of Katherine's death is recorded as the 19th June 1601.

1 POLEY of Badley Or. a lion rampant Sa.	2 GISLINGHAM of Stuston? Az. a fess between three birds, beaked and legged Gu.	3 ALCOCKE of Badley Arg. a chevron engrailed between three black birds proper, membered Gu.	4 BADWELL of Boxted Arg. a chevron engrailed between three pierced mullets with six points Sa.
5 de BADLEY of Badley Arg. cross Sa.	6 GEDDYNG of Icklingham Gu. a chevron Or. between three griffins' heads erased Sa.		7 ASPALL Az. three chevrons Or.
8 PECHE Arg. a fess between two chevrons Gu	9 PEVERELL Quarterly Gu. and Vair Or. and Az. overall a bend Arg.		10 WATEVILLE Arg. three chevrons Gu. in the dexter chief a mullet Sa. for difference.

Fig 3.84 (top, left), a close-up of the 'great crest' and (top, right and opposite) details of the arms on the crest and the families they relate to (see Chapter 7 for further details).

Consecration Cross

Easily missed on the north wall and just to the left of Edmund Poley's (1548) monument (Fig 3.82, page 65) is a consecration cross - the sole survivior of twelve normally placed in mediaeval churches to mark the places where the consecrating Bishop anointed the walls with holy oil either when the church was first consecrated or, more likely, after a major mediaeval restoration. This one has a central hole where a gnomon (a stick in the centre of the dial which would cast a shadow) could be fitted and one is left to wonder if it also served as a *mass dial* at some stage to regulate the times for worship. More likely it was where rush lights were pushed in, to give light on the darker days.

Fig 3.85 The Badley consecration cross, the outline of which has been electronically over-traced to improve visibilty.

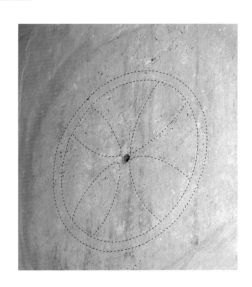

MISCELLANEOUS

From the 'Badley Towne Booke'

<u>April 25th 1671</u> - agreed by the inhabitants of Badley for
Sexton's* wages as follows:

Sr. Edmund Poley	10s	
William Wood	1s.	6d.
Thomas Banks	1s.	6d.
Edmund Smith	1s.	6d.
John Balls	1s.	
John Goodwin	1s.	
Edmund Baxton	1s.	
William Cock	1s.	
Mrs Burgesse		8d.
William Durdeon		8d.
Richard Lambert		8d.
Henry Bull		4d.
John Hall		4d.
Total £1. 1s. 2d.		

*man employed to act as a caretaker of a church and often also as a
bellringer, grave-digger, etc.

Extracts from Needham Market with Badley Parish Magazine -

"A new pair of churchwardens' staves was purchased to
mark the visit of the Diocesan Bishop on September 9th
1967 (Fig 3.44). The Communion Rail has been repainted
and a number of defective tiles on the roof has been
renewed - Two trees, a cedar and a cypress have been
planted in the church yard.

The two Austrian pines were planted in 1865 so the time
had come when we should prepare for the day when they
may become dangerous and need to be removed, even if
that day is still in the distant future".
(PPC Magazine Nov 1967) *(See Fig 3.5, page 28 and
Chapter 8 ~ Moore, re the planting of these two trees.)*

David Elisha Davey

Fri June 15th

"After breakfast this morning, we got upon the Stowmarket
Coach, which took us about 2 or 3 miles & set us down
at the avenue leading to Badley Hall. We walked to the
church; but the Clerk living at some distance, we were
detained a considerable time before we could obtain the
key. The Hall stood at a very short distance to the W. of the
church; it is now entirely pulled down; only a small part of
some of the offices remaining; a good farm house[198] stands
near the old site, occupied by Mr. Mudd, who sent for the
key for us. He told me that he remembered the church in
a very deplorable state of dilapidation; but that it had, not a
great many years ago, undergone a complete repair, when
the Steeple was raised several feet with brick. His account
reminded me much of the reported state of Letheringham
Chancel about the same time: It was fortunate however
that the Monuments did not suffer at Badley, as they did at
Letheringham.

From Badley we crossed the Navigable Cut to Creeting St.
Peter, where however we did not arrive till near 3 o'clock,
having been kept at Badley, till after two, by the number
of inscriptions we found there. Creeting St. Peter did not
detain us very long, there not being a great deal in it."

[198] William Mudd called his farmhouse Badley Hall. D.E.D. to G.B.J.:
"Mudd: We want some acct. of these dirty folks, but they have been &
are still numerous, so that it is difficult to know where to look for the
cleanest."

Source: Page 92, *"A Journal of Excusion Through the County of Suffolk 1823-
1844"* by David Elisha Davey. Published by Suffolk Record Society 1982

---

*Fig 3.86 (below) The congregation enjoying light refreshments
following the September 2003 Harvest Festival service.*

Chapter Four

BADLEY HALL
c.1520-30

BADLEY Hall is situated on higher ground just to the west of St Mary's church. The first manor house on this site is thought to have been erected towards the end of the 15th century, probably by Edmund Alcocke. Some commentators suggest an earlier building may have existed.

This house is believed to have been considerably enlarged 60 or 70 years later, probably during Edmund Poley's (d.1546) time and possibly to accommodate the marriage of his son John to Anne the daughter of the wealthy Baron, Lord Wentworth of Nettlestead.

Sadly many of Suffolk's great manor houses have been demolished over the years. In about 1756, nearby Combs Hall suffered this fate whilst in the ownership of Ambrose Crowley, who partially inflicted the the same on Badley Hall a decade or so later, which some say was pre-empted by earlier storm damage. Having seen for myself the size of the remaining oak timber frame and in the absence of serious structural failure or subsidence, I would be surprised if the weather alone could have blown it down.

What remains is therefore only the south-west quarter of the old hall which used to contain the kitchens (i.e the service range).

Perhaps a contentious issue is its original shape. Some scholars favour 'E' and others 'H'. As a layman on such issues I would prefer to rely on the evidence available from a manuscript map of Ambrose Crowley's estate drawn by William Collier albeit not until 1741 (Figs 4.1 and 4.2).

Badley Hall forms the centre-piece of this very large map. Collier was undoutedly a competent draughtsman and his very detailed survey is enclosed in a vignette which includes fine sketches of both Combs and Badley Hall.

These are significant, as they were drawn some years before the Crowleys completely demolished the hall at Combs (c.1756) and drastically reduced the size of Badley (c.1795). They appear to be the earliest and perhaps the only drawings of both halls in existence. It is perhaps important to mention that an earlier vignette of a previous Combs Hall which existed in 1710 was included in an estate map produced by William Tallemache that year (S.R.O. HA/1/EA/1/22). However, this was replaced by one of considerably more architectural grandeur by Orlando Bridgeman Esq., in 1724.

Collier's sketch of what is taken to be the front elevation of Badley Hall is shown below (Fig 4.1). One is immediately impressed by the sheer size of the place, albeit that we were already aware from the Suffolk Heath Tax returns of 1674, that The Lady Poley declared 30 heaths, only 18 other Suffolk houses having more.

Eric Sandon *(Suffolk Houses (1977), p.248)* and others, have concluded that the existing solid brick piers, capped with stonework and ornamental pineapples (Fig 4.5), must have adorned what used to be the main entrance. Were these the pair offered for sale in 1795 (see Fig 4.6), or more likely, were they the ones in Collier's sketch (Fig 4.1 & 4.3).

If the existing ornamental pineapples signifiy the main entrance, this should not be confused with the front of the hall, as nothing in Wm. Collier's sketch (Fig 4.1), except for the ornamental pineapples, remotely resembles what is now left, which is quite plain and perhaps what one would expect of a service range. As it is unlikely that Collier would have sketched anything other than the front of the hall, I have concluded that that this was the elevation that used to face Badley Walk and that ornamental pineapples adorned both entrances (see also Restoration, page 99).

Turning our attention to the centre of the map, we find the hall depicted as quadrangular. By a simple imposition of today's remains over those drawn by Collier we find there is a very close resemblance (Fig 4.8).

Surely it is inconceiveable that Collier would have recorded this or the elevation in the vignette incorrectly. If the original hall was not quadrangular, would there have been any need for the arched entrance-way, for use by carriages?

Fig 4.1 Badley Hall on the lower left of William Collier's Manuscript Map drawn in 1741 (Photographed courtesey of Hew Stevenson).

The articles mentioned in the introduction to this book and other diverse publications such as for example, the Schedule of Listed Buildings compiled by the Local Authority under Town & Country Planning Acts (SRO q 5 720), and the Suffolk Institute of Archaeology and Natural History Vol XXXVII (1992) provide technical descriptions and comment on the construction of of what remains of the hall and outbuildings.

I am not an expert in these matters; I therefore have had to rely on these sources to construct much of this chapter, supplemented by my own photographs and drawings.

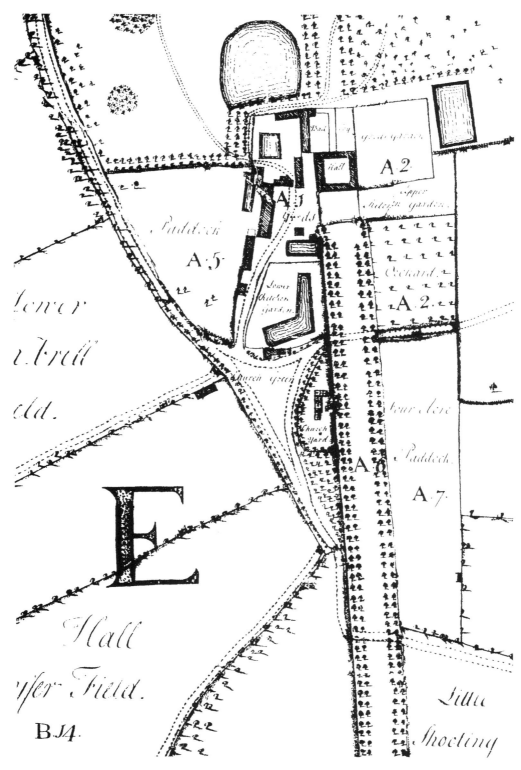

Fig 4.2 The centre section of Wm Collier's 1741 manuscript map showing the quadrangular hall, St Mary's church, a distinctive tree-lined Badley Walk and many other features which still exist today.

Perhaps I should include the technical description of the Hall from the 1955 Listed Building list at this point, viz:

Farmhouse: the surviving service range of an early C16 manor house, probably for Sir Edmund Poley (d.1548); the remainder of the house was demolished c.1759. 2 storeys and attics. Timber-framed and plastered, the upper storey is a long wall jettied along the east side; here and elsewhere are some richly-carved exposed framing members.

Plain-tiled roofs with axial chimneys of red brick, one having a massive triple-flue shaft of C16 or early C17, partly rebuilt C18. A flat roofed C18 casement dormer. Mainly C19 small-pane casements; on the west side are some C18 mullioned and transomed windows with wrought-iron casements and leaded lights. Also on the west is a fine original 2-storey entrance porch giving access to the cross-passage. It was formerly jettied at 1st floor and gable levels; carved tie-beams and an altered oriel with flanking polygonal shafts at 1st storey.

The outer doorway was remodelled in C18, but the inner doorway has an arched head with rose-carved spandrels and a C16 moulded plank door refaced with two C18 panels. On the north wall is a cambered spere beam with central shield and vinescroll in two orders, beneath which access was gained from the crosspassage to the demolished open hall. The jettied east wall has unusually fine carved pilasters and a vinescroll-enriched bressumer. Good quality internal framing with 4-centred arched doorways and plain crownpost roof. Several rooms have wainscotting of all periods from C16 to (especially) mid C18" or,

"16C Grade II two storys and attic, gable w. half-timber frame, overhanging 1st floor now plastered over. Former 'E' plan, one wing now gone, several carved external beams, shafted brackets several old 4-centred arched doorways and old doors internally. Early 18C brick gate piers with stone pineapple finials and W.I. gates, in state of dilapidation. Two storeys and attic, half-timbered cottage now plastered, plaintiles used as farm building" *(National Buildings Register)*.

"The Hall extended about twelve yards northwards towards the pond from today's building. It is said the old boundaries can still occasionally be seen during frosts and also in dry summers. The inner walls of the Hall that were exposed by the demolition were patched up and plastered to pass for an outer wall. Since then the Hall has had very little work carried out on it. The outer walls were cemented and it was converted into a pair of farmworkers' cottages in the early 1900's, although these were never physically separate,

the occupants appearing to have had to share the only remaining stairway and the kitchen.

Scaling from the map would make the sides approximately 39 yds (117ft) long and occupy a space of almost 1/3rd of an acre. The map also shows an area of water to the SW of the Hall and an avenue of trees similar to the Walk, extending westerly from the Hall to Badley Lane. There is also a line drawing of the Western face of the Hall showing a pair of iron gates (still there) in the surrounding brick wall (see Figs 4.1, 4.5 and 4.6) and what looks like an entrance for horse drawn carriages through that side of the Hall to the quadrangle inside.

The remaining part of the Hall still contains several oak beams and carvings. On the north exposed inner wall there is a large oak beam which is over a foot wide at the centre and tapers to eight inches either side. In the centre of this beam is a weather worn shield; all the other markings are now indistinguishable (see pages 75 and 76).

The Hall's main entrance was on the West side in the demolished part of the Hall via a fine pair of iron gates pillared either side leading into a walled garden and to a large panelled oak square doorway with an arched head with rose-carved spandrels (Fig 4.7). The Hall had many panelled rooms before it was reduced in size, the time when sadly for us, the most splendid part of the Hall was lost for

Fig 4.3 Badley Hall - the vignette from Wm Collier's 1741 manuscript map showing the south-west (front entrance?) elevation. Note the pineapples capping the gate pillars.

Fig 4.4 The motif from Wm Collier's 1741 map -
"A SURVEY /OF THE MANOR OF /BADLEY /WITH SEVERAL FARMS ADJOINING /LYING IN THE PARISHES OF /Barking, Battisford, Creeting St /Mary, Creeting St Peter /AND THE DEMEANS IN THE /Manor of Combs, /IN THE COUNTY OF /SUFFOLK /THE ESTATE OF /AMBROSE CROWLEY ESQR"

Fig 4.5 The same elevation today - showing the paved pathway & gate pillars capped with pineapples. The latter were offered for sale in 1795 (see Fig 4.6 below).

ever. Today the Hall's main entrance is on the south side into a unmodernised and basic kitchen".

Some of the farm's outbuildings may have been built from the wooden structural remains of the old Hall.

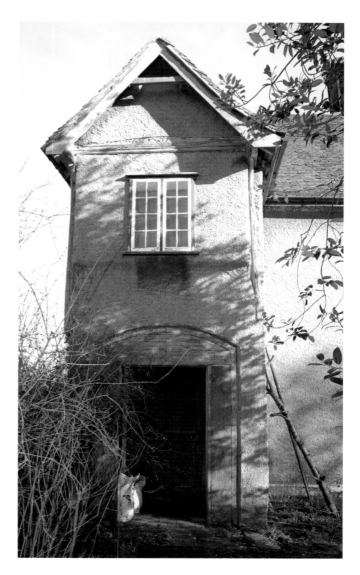

To be SOLD *at* BADLEY HALL

(*near* Needham *and* Stowmarket *in Suffolk*)

The FRAME of a BUILDING, about fixty Foot long and eighteen Foot wide ; the whole is of good found Oak Timber, and fit to be fixt up in any other Place with very little Alteration. Alfo a large Quantity of Building Materials ; confifting of good Oak Timber, in Variety of Scantlings, from three Farthings to 14d. per Foot ; Doors, Windows, Warncot, Brick, Tiles, &c. and a Quantity of Pebbles for Paving.

Likewife a Pair of Iron Gates, nine Foot six inches wide, of exceeding neat Workmanship, and in good Condition, and a Pair of Stone Caps, and Pine-Apples for Pins.

N.B. To be fold at the fame Place, a Mafh tub for about eight or nine Comb, very found and good.

Conftant Attendance will be given at the above-mentioned Place.

Fig 4.6 A reproduction of the advertisement which appeared in the Ipswich Journal during March 1795.

Fig 4.7 A close-up of (top) the west end of the hall showing the entrance porch and doorway. Note the carved beam above the bedroom window; and (below) the inner door showing the arched head with the rose-carved spandrels mentioned on the previous page.

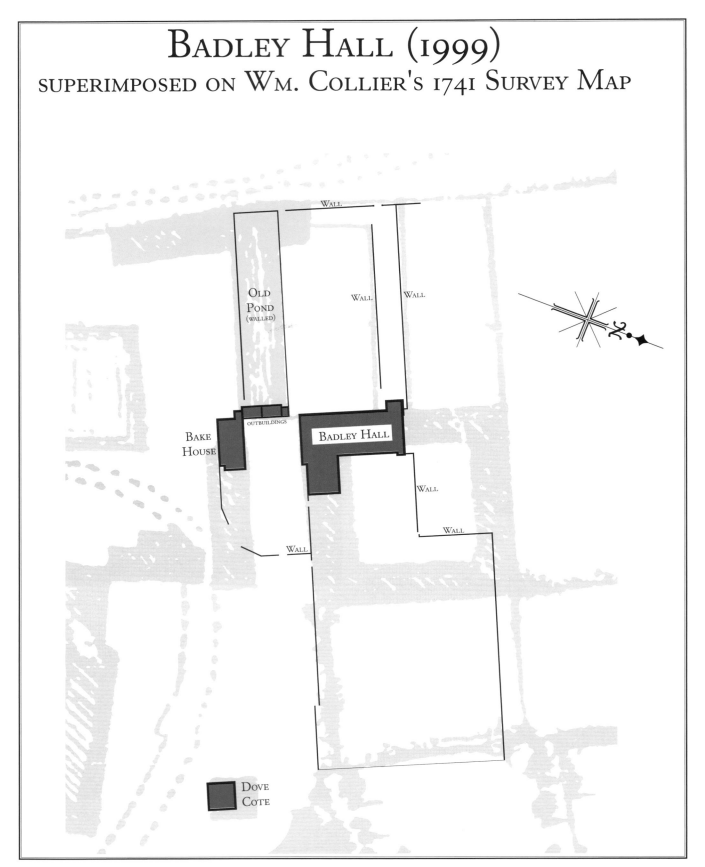

BADLEY HALL (1999)
SUPERIMPOSED ON WM. COLLIER'S 1741 SURVEY MAP

WALL

OLD
POND
(WALLED)

WALL

WALL

OUTBUILDINGS

BADLEY HALL

BAKE
HOUSE

WALL

WALL

WALL

DOVE
COTE

Fig 4.8 The outline of William Collier's 1741 Survey map in the background (coloured grey), with my 1999 survey of the hall, bakehouse, dovecote, garden boundaries and a dried-up pond superimposed in black. The fit is exact and shows that only the south-west corner of the original hall and part of the service range survive. Scaled up the each side of the original hall must have been about 38 metres with a 26 metre centre quadrangle.

Fig 4.9 *The walled pond (see Fig 4.8). The hall is visible on the left and the building on the right is the Cottage (or Bakehouse).*

Hints of Past Glory

Fig 4.10 **A**. *the north end gable showing the location of the exposed carved beam & sawn wall frame ends;* **B**. *(top right) recently discovered photographs (circa late 1940's) with the plaster removed exposing the extent of the timber framing & the existence of linen fold panelling, which has also since been discovered in the cross-passage on the other side of the partition (see Fig 4.51, page 100) and* **C**. *a conjectural reconstruction of the timber-framework and linen fold panelling based on* **A** *&* **B**. *(b & w photos courtesy of Margaret Scott)*

Fig 4.11 The north end gable showing:

(a) a close-up of some of the saw beam ends;

(b) the point where the left-hand end of the carved bressumer meets the corner post inside the house, note the bricknogging which is also visible on the east wall in Figs 4.12 and 4.13 opposite;

(c) detail of the carved crest which would have almost certainly have borne the Poleys' arms;

(d) a section of the similarly carved bressumer on the east wall (front) of the house (see Fig 4.13 next page) protected from the elements inside the hall.

(e) a close-up the exposed cambered spere beam with central shield and vinescroll carving;

Opinion:

Rev Edmund Farrer FSA, in a series on the hall in the *East Anglian Miscellany* in 1917 (Article No 4,877) says - *that the carved bressumer on the lower part of the otherwise blank plastered gable was once the support for a gallery at the lower end of the hall.*

Eric Sandon FRIBA - *Suffolk Houses* (1977) p.248 - agreed this was *a distinct possibility: the top mouldings are pierced at short regular intervals by dowel holes compatible with tenoned joints of balusters.*

With the benefit of the photographs of the exposed end, Fig 4.10(B), previous page, this now seems unlikely.

Fig 4.12 Badley Hall (1999).

Fig 4.13. A closer view of the East elevation showing the 16th century wall surface exposed by peeling plaster, the significance of which is discussed opposite.

In the record of a visit to Badley Hall by the Suffolk Institute of Archaelogy in 1997, interesting reference is made to the East elevation, as follows, "East elevation jettied with richly-moulded fascia and carved brackets at intervals beneath. In 17th century. wall otherwise clad in plaster. but this has recently begun to peel away to expose 16th-century wall surface. Technique. uncovered for first time in 300 years, of startling significance. Between closely-spaced studs is original infill of herringbone bricknogging. About fifty known examples of 16th-century bricknogging in Suffolk, far more than in any other county. A prestige material used in manor houses, inns, guildhalls etc. at first, then in best yeoman houses. Extinct in Suffolk by 1630, well before it came into use so widely in Midlands and elsewhere. Furthermore, nogging at Badley so recently exposed, still has original pale pink paint with mortar joints highlighted in thin lines pure white. Original effect. which can be seen to have been touched up soon afterwards, as bright as stage-set, quite unlike mellow bricknogged buildings familiar to us, such Aldeburgh Moot Hall. From new evidence elsewhere, clear that bricknogging intended be painted externally wherever used in Suffolk. At Badley, diaper-pattern brickwork also in front wall which may also have been highlighted with paint". *(S.I.A.H. Vol XXXVII, page 172)*

Further evidence of the former splendour of the hall is provided by E.F. Botesdale (alias Rev Edmund Farrer FSA), in a series on the hall in the *East Anglian Miscellany* Pt II April-June 1917. In article No 4,895 he says -

"It was no doubt in the house at Badley as occupied by John Poley, where were the 'heraldic shields as recorded in the Ayse Collection in the British Museum, which is thus headed: "In Mr. John Powley's house at Badley".

He then goes on to number the shields and make a few comments on each, to warrant their presence in the windows of Badley Hall. For my part, I have attempted to reconstruct each of these in Fig 4.14 below (left to right):

"(1) Argent, a chevron sable between three, mullets gules impaling Gules, on a bend or three escallops blue. The coat on the dexter side is that given by Papworth for Deneys, and it may indicate a connection between them and the Alcockes, suggested by the recorded fine in 1356: "Philip Deneys, against John Deneys and Thomas Colette with Kathrine, his wife, of two parts of the manor of Badley." I am unable to suggest any name for the impalement. The coat, though simple, is new to me.

(2) Alcoke, Argent a chevron engrailed sable between three hethcocks, impaling Argent a chevron sable between three mullets. This represents the coat of Alcock as drawn out by Robert Glover in 1579, and as appears is the engraving with the pedigree in Dr. Howard, and I expect that the impalement would represent the wife of Edmund Alcock, the purchaser of Badley.

(3) Argent, a fesse between three chess rooks sable, impaling Alcoke. This would, I think, be intended to represent the marriage of the other daughter of Edmund Alcock to Roger Rookwood; though I have never yet seen the coat used by that family, however, the charge of "chess rooks" is so rare.

(4) Or a lion rampant sable impaling Badley, Argent a cross sable. The coat on the dexter side, is intended, I think, to represent Poley. This is the only occasion on which I have seen a coat of arms attributed to the family of Badley, and it seems to point to an alliance between the family and the Poleys.

(5) Sable a cross engrailed or, quartering, Gules a cross moline argent, impaling, Ermine, three bendlets, middle one gules, the two others or. This would be, without doubt, the quartered coat of Ufford and Beke, as used by the Willoughbys, and the impalement the coat of Jenney, of Knoddishall, Ermine, a bend gules between two cotises or. Sir Christopher, Lord Willoughby, married Margery, the daughter of Sir W. Jenney, of Knoddishall.

(6) Chequy or and gules a fesse ermine. Calthorpe, of Nfk. If this shield is intended for Calthorpe it ought to be chequy or and azure, a fesse ermine, but I think it is more likely to represent Cayly, of Nfk, who used that field, and sometimes a fesse, though more often a bend.

(7) Ufford and Beke, impaling, Or a lion rampant sable biquerced. The impalement is that of Welles, of Lincolnshire, and represents a well-known marriage between that family and the Uffords.

(8 and 9) are Badley and Alcock both alone."

Fig 4.14 A mock-up of the shields described by Revd Farrer FSA, in an imaginary window at the hall! (I could not find a reference for the term 'biquerced' used in description of shield 7 and have taken this to mean 'double-queued' i.e. having two tails.)

These attractive arms must have provided quite a spectacle in the windows of the main range of the hall. At first glance it is not clear why some of the families are represented, or for that matter who placed them there. Little is known of Edmund Alcoke, who preceded the Poleys at Badley, but we know from his will (reproduced Appendix D) that he married twice and as suggested in Rev Farrer's text the unidentified impalement in shield 2 could well represent one of their families.

In the Proceedings of S.I.A.H. Vol 38 (1996), p233 reporting on an excursion to Combs Church in 1993, reference is made to The Blois MSS. This is a County-wide collection in four volumes of original heraldic drawings, family trees and church notes compiled by Sir John Blois which records lost heraldic glass - "the arms of Willoughby family of Parham (successors to Uffords as Lords of manor). – latest recorded shield of which had Willoughby impaling Jenny, commemorating Sir Christopher Willoughby (1453-1498) and wife Margaret Jenny (d.1515). Margaret seems to have retained life interest in Combs (? could Margaret's window be connected with her) and her younger son, Robert Willoughby, was Rector of Combs 1500-24."

The Willoughbys succeeded the Uffords in the manor of Combs through the marriage of Cecily one of the three sisters and co-heirs of William de Ufford who died in 3rd Richard II (1379) to John, 3rd Lord Willoughby de Eresby. It continued through their descendants until 1525, when it passed to Charles Brandon, Duke of Suffolk and later to the Daundys, one of whom, Thomas (d.1607), married Martha Poley of Badley who died in December 1625.

Given the proximity of these families at the relevant time, undocumented marriages may well have occurred between Alcoke or Poley daughters and the Willoughbys to 'justify' the inclusion of the shield of the latter in the hall windows.

Despite the Poleys having made a number of illustrious marriages their arms are only represented once (shield 4) - impaled with those of de Badley, who held the manor before the Alcokes (see Chapter 1, page 6). It is assumed this was a symbolic union only, as there is no record of any marriages between these two families. Does the greater representation of those of the Alcoke's (three) indicate they were installed by them rather than the Poleys?

Fig 4.15 The remains of elegant panelling inside the left-hand closet in bedroom B (Fig 4.17).

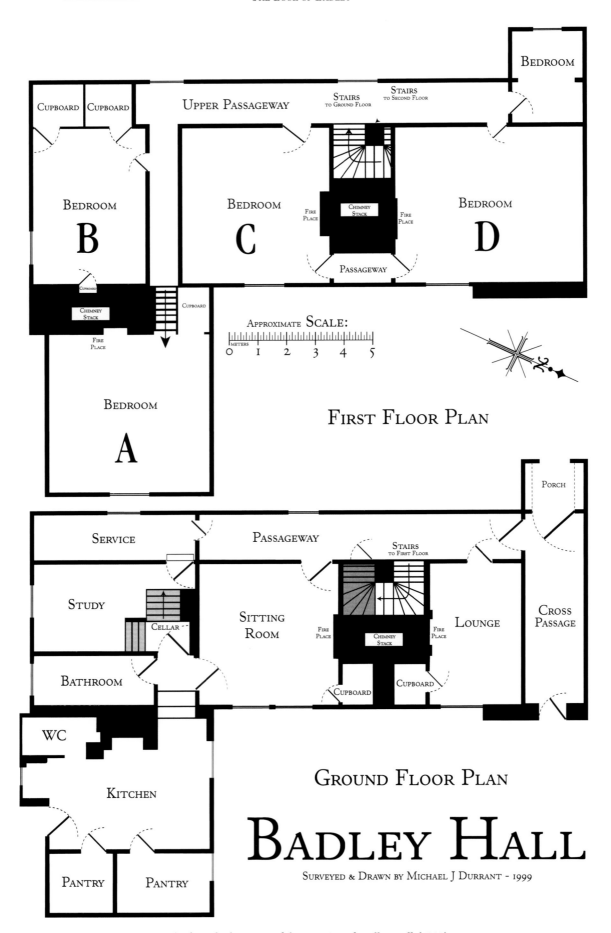

CUPBOARD CUPBOARD

UPPER PASSAGEWAY

STAIRS
to Ground Floor

STAIRS
to Second Floor

BEDROOM
B

BEDROOM
C

BEDROOM
D

BEDROOM

FIRE
PLACE

CHIMNEY
STACK

FIRE
PLACE

PASSAGEWAY

CUPBOARD
CHIMNEY
STACK

CUPBOARD

FIRE
PLACE

APPROXIMATE SCALE:

METERS
0 1 2 3 4 5

BEDROOM
A

FIRST FLOOR PLAN

PORCH

SERVICE

PASSAGEWAY

STAIRS
to First Floor

STUDY

CELLAR

SITTING
ROOM

FIRE
PLACE

CHIMNEY
STACK

FIRE
PLACE

LOUNGE

CROSS
PASSAGE

BATHROOM

CUPBOARD

CUPBOARD

WC

GROUND FLOOR PLAN

KITCHEN

BADLEY HALL

SURVEYED & DRAWN BY MICHAEL J DURRANT - 1999

PANTRY

PANTRY

Fig 4.16 Scale drawings of the remains of Badley Hall (1999).

Fig 4.17 Further examples of the strength of the timbers in the hall. These are in the passageway linking the present Kitchen and Sitting Room and situated (A) above and (B) adjacent to the sitting room door. One of the carved pilasters, see page 100 & Fig 4.54, was discovered behind plaster now temporary filled with fibreglass. Photograph C is part of the outer wall frame in the ground floor passageway (see Fig 4.16 opposite and Fig 4.18 overleaf). The upright timbers average 7 inches (17.75cm) in width and on average are set at a similar distance apart.

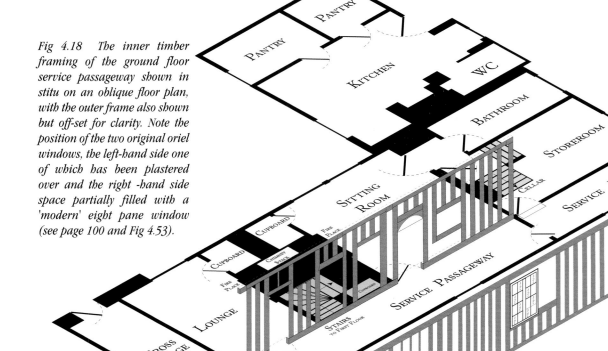

Fig 4.18 The inner timber framing of the ground floor service passageway shown in stitu on an oblique floor plan, with the outer frame also shown but off-set for clarity. Note the position of the two original oriel windows, the left-hand side one of which has been plastered over and the right -hand side space partially filled with a 'modern' eight pane window (see page 100 and Fig 4.53).

Fig 4.19 The ground floor service passageway. The frame of the former service hatch is clearly visible in the foreground in the left-hand photograph. The right-hand photograph, taken from the opposite direction, shows the entrances to the stairs, cupboard and sitting room. Note the good condition of the heavy timber framing.

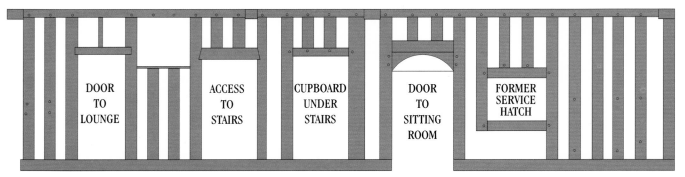

Fig 4.20 A scale drawing of the inner timber framing in the ground floor service passageway on the south-west side of the hall. Note the existence of the heavily framed service hatch which gave servants access to the main kitchen. The method of fixing the lintel above the access door to the stairs indicates that this was created at a later date.

The Attic

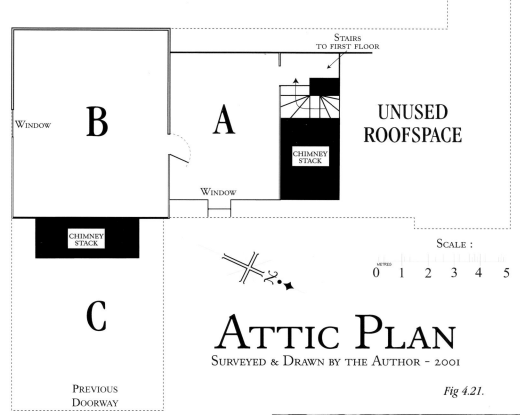

STAIRS
TO FIRST FLOOR

UNUSED
ROOFSPACE

WINDOW

B

A

CHIMNEY
STACK

WINDOW

CHIMNEY
STACK

C

SCALE :

METRES
0 1 2 3 4 5

ATTIC PLAN

SURVEYED & DRAWN BY THE AUTHOR - 2001

PREVIOUS
DOORWAY

Fig 4.21.

The third floor attic at Badley Hall, consists of two large rooms (A & B) with a third (hidden) room (C) over the bedroom directly above the kitchen (see Fig 4.21 above & Fig 4.24 overleaf). None of the other surviving roof space appears to have been used.

On the chimney stack of room C there are two pencilled messages relating to repairs viz, "New window 4th November 1895 prepared same Mr Underwood & Dorling" and "Mr Underwood, Needham Market, Suffolk Fore G Farthing June 25/85".

The remains of a bell mechanism (Figs 4.25 and 4.26 overleaf) suggests they were originally part of the servants quarters.

During the Mudd's time at the Hall they were either the children's bedrooms or occupied by the farm-servants and/ or labourers shown in the 1841-1891 Census returns.

Access is gained by a narrow stairway, part of which is illustrated in Fig 4.23 opposite. One can imagine that moving about on these creaking stairs and sleeping in this attic with the prospect of only candles for light was not for the faint-hearted.

Fig 4.22 A photograph taken in the unused roof space opposite room A, showing a crown post with one brace missing and a section of the substantial oak roof timbers which comprise the roof and the blocked-off north-east gable wall.

Fig 4.23 The attic access stairway.

Fig 4.24 The 'hidden' attic 'C' on Fig 4.22 showing evidence of a doorway opposite the chimney stack. The presence of this doorway supports the contention that it once led into the adjoining roofspace beyond the partition wall as per Fig 4.8, page 74, otherwise it would have served no purpose.

Fig 4.26 A close-up of the remains of the servants' bell mechanism.

Fig 4.25 A general view across room A, showing the access to room B, the original solid oak door, dormer window and the remains of the servants bell mechanism.

There appears to have never been a door between the stairs and the first room (A). However, the solid oak door between the rooms A & B is almost certainly the original. It is still in good condition and a gem (Fig 4.27 opposite). The wood is beautifully grained and the simple cast iron fittings are still intact.

On the attic wall in room A, there are also two messages written in pencil by Margaret Mudd, who lived at nearby Green Farm, in 1889. These are reproduced in Chapter 8.

Some of the best views of St Mary's Church and Badley Walk are obtained from the attic window.

Fig 4.27 The solid oak attic door showing the original cast iron fittings.

Fig 4.28 Easily missed, this painting is situated above the door in the poorly-lit short interconnecting passageway situated between bedrooms C & D (Fig 4.16).

The Cellars

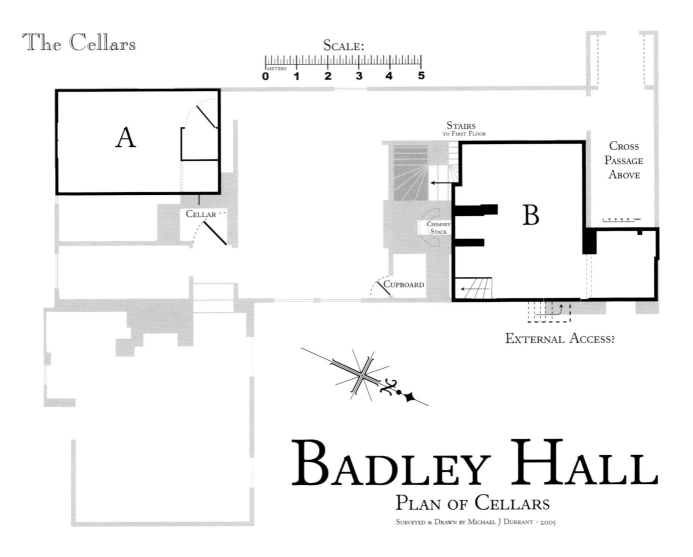

SCALE:

METERS 0 1 2 3 4 5

A

CELLAR

STAIRS
TO FIRST FLOOR

CROSS
PASSAGE
ABOVE

CHIMNEY
STACK

B

CUPBOARD

EXTERNAL ACCESS?

BADLEY HALL
PLAN OF CELLARS
SURVEYED & DRAWN BY MICHAEL J DURRANT - 2005

Fig 4.29.

There are two surviving cellars at the hall marked A & B on the above plan (Fig 4.29) for easy reference. Cellar A is still accessible via stairs close to the present kitchen (see also Floor Plan Fig 4.16).

However, access to the larger of the two, marked B on the plan has been prevented, presumably from the time the hall was partially demolished and the present building was converted into two cottages. Their existence in this part of the building strengthens the assumption that this was the service area for the original hall.

Fortunately I was able to contort myself sufficiently to gain access to the sealed cellar by removing (with permission!) one of the stair treads in the central staircase.

The room designated 'Sitting Room' on the ground floor plan (Fig 4.16) has already been indentified as the original main kitchen. Once inside cellar B, stairs indicate that it was originally accessed from the kitchen via what is now a cupboard off the present Sitting Room, adding further weight as to the original function of this part of the building.

The photographs overleaf taken inside the cellars again illustrate the hefty oak floor joists used in the original construction.

Fig 4.30 Inside cellar A showing the hefty floor joists and the ground level service access.

Fig 4.31 The sealed cellar B, showing the remains of the stairway access to/from the former kitchen. The 'fresh' brickwork alongside the staircase is at ground level and was thought to have been the position of either a window to light the stairs or a service access similar to that in cellar A above. This brickwork has since been replaced by a louvred window to provide ventilation and during this work it was discovered that the opening was in fact originally protected by a series of strong, closely-set, vertical iron railings (similar to those on a prison cell but much closer).

Fig 4.32 Cellar B looking toward the north-east foundation wall showing substantial floor joists and evidence of 'recent' repairs. Note the variation in the brickwork on the right hand foundation wall. This has since been revealed to have been the site of a door-way with steps, which emerged into the courtyard outside, just to the left of the doorway shown in Fig 4.11(A). There is also evidence that this cellar originally extended beyond the existing hall cross-passage and under the demolished open hall.

Fig 4.33   A painting of Badley Hall in the 1930s?

A :   Hall

B :   Cottage or Bakehouse

C :   Dove Cote

D :   Great Barn

E :   Woodshed

F :   Stackyard

Outbuildings

THE COTTAGE *or* BAKEHOUSE

I have heard house historians express differing opinion as to the origin and purpose of this building situated about 15 metres to the SE of the hall.   In 1955 the Listed Building Register described it as:

"Outbuilding known as 'The Cottage', built as a bake house for Badley Hall, early or mid C16. 2-cell plan. 2 storeys and attics. Timber-framed and pebble-dashed, partly underbuilt in C19 red brick. Plaintiled roof. A large gable-chimney of red brick is possibly original, but the upper section is rebuilt; at each of several offsets, the brickwork is tumbled-in. Plaintiled roof. Slatted unglazed windows, the original openings have in some cases been retained with their diamond mullions removed.   The main room is of 2 bays with a large lintelled fireplace and a cross-entry.   The single-bay end room also has accommodation above, but the attic floor is a C17/C18 insertion. Clasped-purlin roof with reduced principals. Plain   heavy   timber-framing   exposed throughout".

Was it simply a cottage used accommodate staff, or as some believe a detached kitchen to lessen the risk of fire in the main hall? As Fig 4.35 opposite shows, it certainly had a large enough fireplace.

Fig 4.34 The Cottage with the Hall in the background.

Fig 4.35 Photographs of the cottage or bakehouse, showing the heavily timbered interior and large hearth.

THE DOVECOTE

This timber-framed square plaster and plain-tiled dovecote, which has a hipped roof with gables, is another of the hall's ancient listed outbuildings in need of urgent renovation.

For a technical description of this building readers are recommended to consult *"The Dovecotes of Suffolk"* by John McCann (1998), where there are almost five pages devoted to it. Here it is described as an unusal building whose timber-frame contains "many ingenious and probably unique features". The author found dating it difficult, as there are no others with which to compare it, but concluded that, "an origin in the later sixteeth century seems most likely".

The author also tells us it contained 470 nest boxes, which he considered small for the high quality of the building and importance of the site, but concluded this was due to the the nest boxes being "unusually capacious".

Over the years, the building has been put to a variety of other uses, including a stable, farm-store and dog-kennel. Despite this, it still appears to be structurally sound given its age. However, parts of the walls have lost their plaster and this needs to be replaced as soon as possible to safguard this rare structure.

Fig 4.36 The 16th century Badley Dovecote.

Fig 4.37 Inside the dovecote, where the timber-framed wattled wall and some of the original nest boxes can be clearly seen.

Fig 4.38 The Dovecote in the late afternoon sun with the tower of St Mary's church in the background - a view unchanged for over 500 years.

THE GREAT BARN

Fig 4.39 Badley Great Barn - now a rather sorry sight externally, but 500 year-old mid Suffolk timber-framed splendour awaits inside. The west-end, i.e. furthest from the camera, is thought to be the oldest part of the structure.

The barn at Badley has been described as 'one of the largest and finest manorial barns in the Gipping Valley area'. The Great Barn, as I shall call it, is a Grade II listed, early 16th century, twelve-bay barn of timber and weatherboard construction. It was originally thatched, but is now covered with a mixture of corrugated iron and asbestos.

In the 1955 listing it was described as follows:

"Barn, C15 or early C16. In two 4-bay sections, with a single-bay stable added to the west end in C17. Timber-framed and weatherboarded; the eastern 4 bays stand upon a tall and massive plinth of flint rubble with dressings mainly of red brick. Roof partly of corrugated iron and partly of asbestos sheeting; formerly thatched.

3 bays from each original end are narrow entrance bays having boarded barn doors on each side (some missing). A large, very well built and unusually complete barn. Very fine queenpost roof of the north-east Suffolk School; arch-braced cambered tie-beams, jowled queen posts with arch-bracing up to heavy square-set purlins and to cambered square collars. In C17 or early C18, intermediate arch-braced trusses were inserted in each main bay, reversed assembly being used; the workman ship is high, and superficially appears to be original.

High quality close-studwork, with tension wind-bracing at the eastern-most bay, and arch-bracing at the west; despite this difference the two sections must be of similar dates. The flint walling has inclusions of brick rubble and one quoin of dressed limestone; some original plaster finished with random indentations still adheres to the flintwork and probably covered flint and timber-framing alike until C18/C19 when much repair was done. The barn stands upon a scheduled site (Ancient Monument No.135), believed to be of a Chantry endowed by Edmund Alcock (d.1491) of Badley Hall. However, documentary evidence suggests that the Chantry was attached to nearby St. Mary's Church".

To the visitor, the interior view is somewhat inhibited by the installation of 20th century farming paraphernalia, but one has to remember that until 1999 it was part of a working farm.

It is difficult to do justice to this wonderful old building with a camera, but in the series of photographs overleaf I have attempted to capture the atmosphere of the building for those unable to experience it for themselves.

The ravages of time are evident, but to my untrained eye

Fig 4.40 Another view of the Badley Great Barn with the oldest section nearest the camera. (The building at the end of the muddy roadway in this reverse view of the barn is the Cowhouse/ Woodshed.)

the most affected area is the plinth of the building, a high wall of flint and brick supporting the sill beam/sole plates. In some places this has required urgent restoration, for example, see the corner in Fig 4.39.

Externally the barn measures approximately 51½ yds. by 9½ yds., which is unusually wide. How long did it take to build and how many trees were consumed? Whatever the answers, I would like to think its completion gave those involved a wonderful sense of satisfaction and pride to see it standing there crowned with a gleaming thatched roof.

Architectural historians have identified it as 'one of most southerly examples of a building technique found in central and North Suffolk circa 1360-1550, but in no other county, except Norfolk'[1].

Nevertheless it seems the 'carpenter apparently over-reached himself; for no other reason than severe stress, warranting a series of massive intermediate trusses to be threaded into structure circa 1700'[2].

([1] & [2] S.I.A. Journal, Vol XXXVII, page 172)

Fig 4.41 A close-up of the Queen Post roof trusses.

Fig 4.42 Views inside the Great Barn showing the wealth of timber framing and bay partitioning.

THE STABLE

Fig 4.43 A general view of the former stable block with the Great Barn in the background.

The stable block has been modified internally for a number of farm uses over the years following the departure of the last carthorses in the 1950's. It is formally described as:

"Originally a barn north-west of larger barn, forming west side of yard. Mid C16, adapted as stable C17. Alterations of C19 and C20. Timber-framed, clad with tarred weatherboarding. Tall, C19 plinth of red brick to east elevation. C20 low-pitched roof of corrugated iron. Boarded stable doors. INTERIOR: Heavy C16 timber-framing, tension stud braced and with midrail to east and north elevation. In four bays, from the west: Bay 1 is largest, Bay 2 contains evidence for set of barn doors, later removed. Rear wall opposite has blocked pedestrian door. Bay 4 was probably partitioned off as stabling with loft above (evidence obscured). Jowled storey posts, open trusses with long archbraces (some missing). Loft floor inserted with binding beams and square-set joists (mostly removed) when barns doors removed and replaced by studding above pair of stable

doors. Plaster ceiling applied to stables C17 or C18. Further C19 remodelling phase when studwork, especially to west elevation, partly replaced. Boarded internal cladding replaces plaster and external weatherboarding applied. Brick floor and tack pegs in eastern bay indicate more recent use of stabling, but also evidence for mangers along much of west wall. 'Stabling in two divisions for ten horses' is listed in a terrier of 1830 (SRO HA1/HB4/2) and this building is most likely to be the one mentioned".

Fig 4.44 Interior view of the stable. Above left, notice the tack hooks on the left-hand wall, probably used to hang the heavy neck collars used for harnessing the heavy cart-horses. Above right, a carpenter's ingenuity - using the base of a branch to form a natural tack hook!

The COW-HOUSE

Situated to the south-east of the Great Barn is the former Cow-house, described as:

"a late C18 timber-framed building with brick infill on east face, (facing entrance to house); otherwise weather boarded. 5 bays, originally lofted, tie beams supported on massive roughly cut bolted knee braces and no sign of mortices for earlier bracing. Four jowelled corner posts to building. Roof much rebuilt with flimsy purlins and diagonal bracing nailed on.

It has been much altered and doorways are not original. Most recently it was used

In the general view of the interior ('D'), the heavy tie-beams which originally supported an upper floor and the saw-pit are visible. The far wall is a partition separating the workshop from the small cartshed and shed visible in view 'C'. About mid-way to the right of centre on this partition, there is a built-in ladder to give access to the loft.

Fig 4.45 The Cow House.

as a sawing shed and carpenter's shop with a carpenter's bench and brick lined C19 saw pit in place (a rare survival).

A "cowhouse for 12 cows" is listed in a terrier of 1830 (SRO HAl/HB4/2)" and this building is most likely to be the one mentioned".

The rusty corrugated iron roof looks unattractive, but as view 'A' in Fig 4.45 on the previous page shows, it is still in a reasonable condition and, crucially, waterproof. Only the roof timbers survive of what appears to have been a lean-to on the north side of the building - possibly used as a straw and later wood store (views 'A' & 'C' on previous page).

Fig 4.46 Various views inside the Cow-shed.

A   *The roof timbers - well protected by the corrugated iron sheets and seemingly still in good condition.*
B   *The north wall - this is the only wall infilled with brick, presumably to provide the strength to bear the additional load imposed by the lean-to (Fig 4. 'A' & 'C').*
C   *A close up of the north-west corner.*
D   *A carpenter's vice.*
E   *The saw pit - a close-up of the brick-lined saw pit, where the gruelling task of manually sawing a log into planks with a large pitsaw was undertaken by two men, one standing on top of the log and the other in the pit underneath it.*

BADLEY HALL FARM

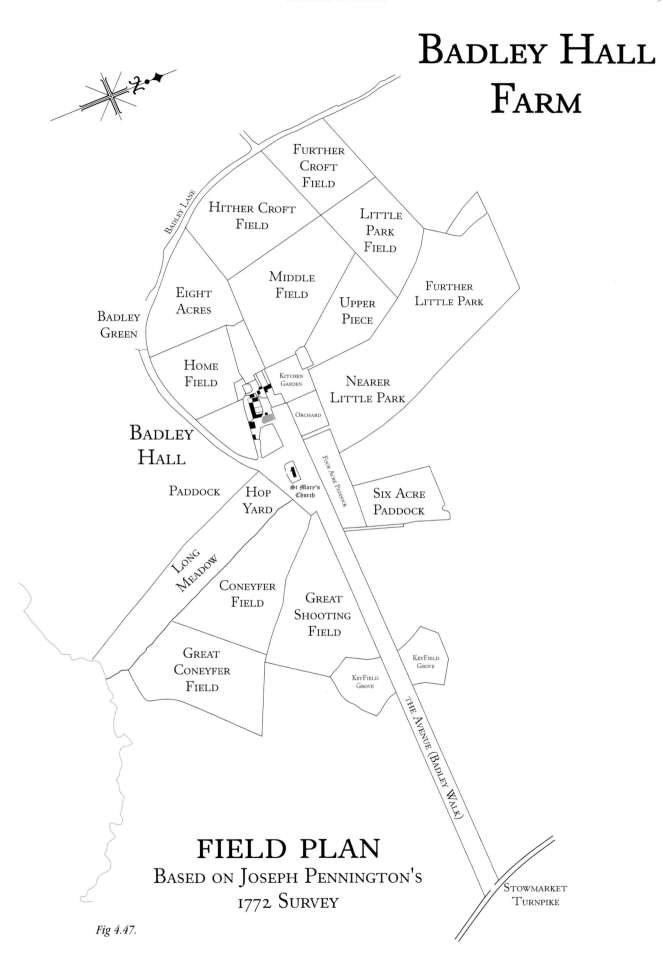

FURTHER CROFT FIELD

HITHER CROFT FIELD

BADLEY LANE

LITTLE PARK FIELD

MIDDLE FIELD

EIGHT ACRES

FURTHER LITTLE PARK

UPPER PIECE

BADLEY GREEN

HOME FIELD

KITCHEN GARDEN

NEARER LITTLE PARK

ORCHARD

BADLEY HALL

FOUR ACRE PADDOCK

St Mary's Church

PADDOCK

HOP YARD

SIX ACRE PADDOCK

LONG MEADOW

CONEYFER FIELD

GREAT SHOOTING FIELD

KEYFIELD GROVE

GREAT CONEYFER FIELD

KEYFIELD GROVE

THE AVENUE (BADLEY WALK)

FIELD PLAN
BASED ON JOSEPH PENNINGTON'S 1772 SURVEY

STOWMARKET TURNPIKE

Fig 4.47.

A farm sale was held at Badley Hall on 5th October 1901 following the death of the tenant William Mudd. The catalogue produced for the sale by the auctioneer Alfred Preston gives an insight into the range of equipment and implements in use on a typical farm at the time.

Page 5 of the catalogue reproduced opposite indicates the importance placed on the horse. A total of eighteen were offered for sale, albeit at least four belonged to William Mudd's other farm at Battisford. Applying this level of usage across the county there must have been literally hundreds of carthorses kept for farmwork, supported by an army of village blacksmiths and agricultural wheelwrights.

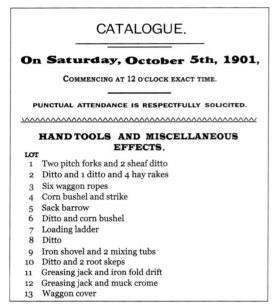

CATALOGUE.

On Saturday, October 5th, 1901,

COMMENCING AT 12 O'CLOCK EXACT TIME.

PUNCTUAL ATTENDANCE IS RESPECTFULLY SOLICITED.

HAND TOOLS AND MISCELLANEOUS EFFECTS.

LOT
1 Two pitch forks and 2 sheaf ditto
2 Ditto and 1 ditto and 4 hay rakes
3 Six waggon ropes
4 Corn bushel and strike
5 Sack barrow
6 Ditto and corn bushel
7 Loading ladder
8 Ditto
9 Iron shovel and 2 mixing tubs
10 Ditto and 2 root skeps
11 Greasing jack and iron fold drift
12 Greasing jack and muck crome
13 Waggon cover

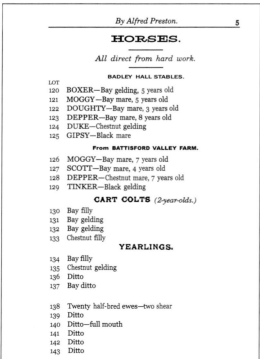

By Alfred Preston. 5

HORSES.

All direct from hard work.

BADLEY HALL STABLES.

LOT
120 BOXER—Bay gelding, 5 years old
121 MOGGY—Bay mare, 5 years old
122 DOUGHTY—Bay mare, 3 years old
123 DEPPER—Bay mare, 8 years old
124 DUKE—Chestnut gelding
125 GIPSY—Black mare

From BATTISFORD VALLEY FARM.

126 MOGGY—Bay mare, 7 years old
127 SCOTT—Bay mare, 4 years old
128 DEPPER—Chestnut mare, 7 years old
129 TINKER—Black gelding

CART COLTS *(2-year-olds.)*

130 Bay filly
131 Bay gelding
132 Bay gelding
133 Chestnut filly

YEARLINGS.

134 Bay filly
135 Chestnut gelding
136 Ditto
137 Bay ditto

138 Twenty half-bred ewes—two shear
139 Ditto
140 Ditto—full mouth
141 Ditto
142 Ditto
143 Ditto

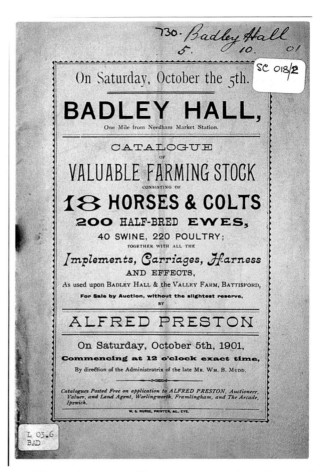

Fig 4.48 The front page of the 1901 auctioneers' catalogue and opposite pages 1 (part) & 5 (Suffolk RO Ref: L 03.6 BAD).

BADLEY HALL OWNERS & OCCUPIERS

I daresay if one checked all the old velums at the Suffolk Record Office and elsewhere, a clearer picture of who lived at Badley Hall besides the Poleys could be obtained.

Following the death of Sir Edmund Poley (1671) if not before, given that entries in Samuel Pepys' diaries (see Chapter 6, page 160) tells us he had a house in London, it seems very likely that at least a part of what was then such a vast building would not have been occupied by socially suitable tenants or relations (see page 164). For example, the Brewsters, Scriveners, Robins and Richard Pearch, who were also given 'special' burial positions at St Mary's church, presumably due to their connections with the Poley family.

Date:	Farmers/Occupants:	Owner:
- 1491	Edmund Alcocke	Edmund Alcocke
1491-1714	The Poleys of Badley	The Poleys of Badley
1714		Elizabeth Gipps (née Poley)
1715		Maj. Richard Gipps
1735	John Crowley	

1772	John Wolton	John Crowley
1830-1892	Thomas Mudd	Earl of Ashburnham
1900	William Mudd	Earl of Ashburnham
1906	J & Edgar H Mudd	Earl of Ashburnham
1910	Wm Alfred Catchpole	Edgar Mudd
	William Woods	
1918 - 38	Edgar Mudd	
1938	William Hunt	
1946 - 1968	Leonard Scott	Leonard Scott
1968 - 1997	Arthur Blake Scott	Arthur Blake Scott
1998	Margaret Scott	Margaret Scott

Fig 4.50 William Woods at Badley (photo courtesy of the late Murial Manning (see Fig 4.49 below left).

WILLIAM WOODS

In 1910 Edgar Herbert ('*Spider*') Mudd (*see Mudd's - Chapter 8*) advertised for a Farm Bailiff.

William Woods, who was working and living at Pear Tree Farm, Stradbroke for a Mr Tooley, successfully applied for the position and moved his family moved into Badley Hall (now used as two tied cottages), part of which was already occupied by William Alfred and Agnes Catchpole.

William and his wife Elizabeth Mary (née Fairweather), had three children Violet, William Frederick and Muriel (*Millie*) (then age 5).

His son, William Frederick Woods, married Dorothy Andrews at Stowmarket on 1st August 1934 (*see wedding report Chapter 3*) and his daughter Murial (*Millie*) left Badley upon her marriage in 1933.

Unfortunately William Woods suffered a servere stroke in the late 1930's and, unable to work, he was re-housed at No 6 Badley Walk. He resided there with his wife until 25th January 1947 when he died aged 80 years and was buried at Badley on the 29th.

His gravestone is No 44 on the Churchyard plan in Chapter 3 and the inscription is recorded in Appendix C.

Fig 4.49 the late Murial (Millie) Manning (formerly Catchpole, née Woods) who died in June 2005, aged 95 years.

Restoration work

Restoration work is being undertaken at the hall as funds allow. This work is enthusiastically being carried out by local historic building restorer Graham Barker, whose discoveries have already contributed a great deal of new information about the original structure of the building.

For example, the removal of plaster-work in the passageways in the course of restoration has revealed the location of several oriel windows (see Fig 4.53), raising the prospect that the front of the original house faced SW until it was extended and turned 180° so that the new front, depicted in Wm. Collier's sketch (Fig 4.3), faced NE i.e. towards Badley Walk.

In the hall-way, fine linenfold panelling has been uncovered (Fig 4.51 overleaf). It appears there may have been a doorway beneath the plasterwork to the right of the panelling which would have given access to the open hall under the carved bressumer shown in Fig 4.10(A). However, Fig 4.10 (B), taken from the otherside in the 1940's shows this area was bricked-up. However, this may have been done using recycled bricks when the hall was resized in the late 1700's.

The original door frame at the other end of the hall passageway to that shown in Fig 4.51 has also been discovered set back about 50 cm from the existing frame (Fig 4.52 overleaf).

Behind plaster and inbetween the corner-post and wall frame shown on Fig 4.17 (page 81), a carved pilaster, which along with at least five others, divide-up the jettied east wall (see Fig 4.13), has been uncovered in pristine condition after hundreds of years (Fig 4.54 overleaf).

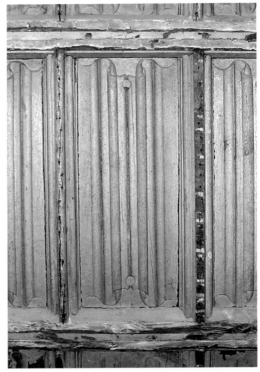

Fig 4.51 Fine linenfold panelling uncovered in the hall cross-passage with close-up (right).

Fig 4.52 The original NE door frame found in situ behind later plaster-work.

Fig 4.54 (a) A section of a richly carved pilaster recently-discovered inside the hall, with closeup (b) and external views of the tops of some of the others (c and d). Note the Tudor Rose motifs.

(Ignore temporary fibre glass and felt)

Fig 4.53 One of the blanked out oriel windows in the ground floor passageway. The three mullions are just visible. See also Fig 4.18.

Chapter Five

Badley's
Other Buildings

This section contains a photograph of all the other properties currently within the Parish of Badley, together with their description, history and **AS MANY** of the names of their owners or occupiers as possible.

WHEELING AND DEALING . . . .

In 1735 all property within the Parish probably passed into the ownership of Ambrose Crowley, Esq. when he purchased the Manor of Badley from the Poleys' heir Major Richard Gipps (see page 180). Ownership was then transferred via the Crowley heirs through marriage to the Rt. Hon. John, Earl of Ashburnham, (the 2nd Earl) in 1819, and it remained in the Ashburnhams' ownership until 1917 when the Suffolk (Barking Hall) estate was sold.

Following the death of Rt. Hon. Betram, Earl of Ashburnham (the 5th Earl) on 15th January 1913, a contract dated 4th October 1917 shows the Rt. Hon.Thomas, Earl of Ashburnham (the 6th Earl) and the other Ashburnham Trustees agreed to sell the 3,450 acre Suffolk estate to Harry Hagon Arnold, Esq. of No 9 Bank Plain, Norwich, Nfk. for £58,000. Arnold *(the first Purchaser)* subsequently sold the estate on to John William Newcombe, a estate agent, of St. Mary's Road, Market Harborough and Albert Wilkinson, a merchant, of Stopsley, Luton, *(the second Purchasers)* for £64,000. They probably were the owners at least in principle by 11th December 1917, the date the estate was sold by public auction at Ipswich.

It also transpires that several other agreements were reached prior to the auction. The Abstract of Title, a lengthy complex document, detailing the above contract also show that Newcombe & Wilkinson *(the second Purchasers)* agreed to sell Badley Bridge Farm (72a 3r 3p) (togr. with other heredicts) to Edward Albert Fenning, a farmer, of Creeting St. Mary *(of the 5th part)* for £2,600.

He promptly re-sold it to Samuel Willie, a merchant, of South Bank, Yeoville, Somerset, *(of the 7th part)*, (togr. with other heredict) for £2,750. Willie also agreed with the second purchasers to buy three fields (called Long Fen (part of), Home Meadow and Kettleby Field, situated to the east of the turnpike and totalling 19.6 acres) (togr. with other heredits) for £6,360.

On 10th December 1918, within a year of the auction, he sold Badley Bridge Farm to Robert Dykes Cooper, a miller,

Notes on the sale of the
BARKING HALL ESTATE

of Creeting St Mary for £1,700. The latter had already purchased the adjoining Raven's Farm, Creeting St Mary, on 11th October 1915 from Percy Christopher Gallimore Hayward, a solicitor and trustee of the late Thomas Maw Esq., Gent. of Needham Market, who died on 26th Jun 1891 for £510. Cooper's address on that occasion was given as Hawkes Mill House, Needham Market.

Badley Bridge Farm together with Raven's Farm were subsequently resold several times as a single entity. In 1969 this practice was broken when the Mortons separately sold Badley Bridge farmhouse to Mr. & Mrs. Beaney.

Charles Edward Creasey, a farmer from Trimley *(of the 7th part)* was sold Cherry Tree Farm and other land by the *1st, 2nd and 3rd purchasers* for £850 on 15th November 1918.

Fig 5.1 Page 2 from the 1917 Sales Catalogue.

The farm subsequently remained in the possession of the family until 4th December 1949 when the two remaining trustees/beneficiaries sold it to Frederick Charles Squire Crockford, who sold it to Sidney Lancelot Short two years later on 26th October 1951. Sidney Short remained at the farm until his death on 19th July 1971.

SALE OF BARKING HALL ESTATE.

ONLY FOUR LOTS UNSOLD

A crowded attendance of agriculturists and others interested in the Barking Hall Estate gathered at the Crown and Anchor Hotel, Ipswich, on Tuesday, when it was offered for sale in 48 lots by Messrs. Woodward and Woodward. Running into 3,450 acres, the estate, the tenure of which was freehold, was recently sold by its owner, Lord Ashburnham, to it is understood, a local syndicate.

The proceeds of the sale were over £73,000, but in addition there is the value of the six lots withdrawn, which include the mansion and park and three separate farms. The original sale price of the estate was a matter of conversation, and there was considerable discussion as to what profit would accrue to the vendors, the estate, it being understood, having changed hands since it was first sold. The figure mentioned as the first sale price was £57,000, but it is said that price was advanced by another £6,000 when it changed hands again. The estimated profit accruing to the last vendors can therefore be easily calculated.

The estate comprises Barking Hall and grounds; twenty-one mixed farms, three acres of well-timbered woodlands, a fully-licensed inn, numerous small holdings, cottages, and allotments. The farms were tenanted by well-known agriculturist, several of whom purchased their holdings, a result which was received with general applause by the company present. Very brisk competition ensured for woodlands sold in separate lots, and one bidder, who ran up the lot 89 acres of wood and 46 acres of arable and pasture land, asserted that the buyer must have paid 3s. a foot for the timber. The sale was conducted by Mr. Gordon Woodward, with the following, results:-

Enclosures or pasture, **Pincen's Pightle, Combs**, 3 acres	Mr. C. A. Creasey	£260
Badley Water Mill, with dwelling-house, premises, and 68 acres,		
let to Messrs. J. & E Mudd	Mr. Willie, Yeovil	£1,7,00
Badley Hall Farm comprising house, buildings, and 217 acres,		
let to Messrs. J. & E. Mudd	Mr. H. Capon	£3,850
Badley Green Farm *(tithe free)*, with house, agricultural premises,		
four cottages, and 230 acres, let to Messrs. J. & E. Mudd	Mr. Mudd	£3,700
The Woodlands, Badley, and Combs, comprising farm residence,		
agricultural premises, cottage, and 232¾ acres; **Combs Hall** and		
Holy Oak Farms, with farmhouse, agricultural premises, two cottages,		
& 243 acres; **Combs Wood**, of 36 acres; & double cottage, the whole		
being let to Mr. Harry Stearn	Mr. Harry Stearn	£10,200
Eleven acres arable land, Combs Ford	Mr. French	£410
20½ acres of arable land, Combs	Mr. Peecock	£600
Doveshill Farm, comprising house, premises, three cottages, & 175 acres,		
let to Mr. Fredk. Williams	Mr. Willie	£4,050
Cherry Tree Farm (tithe free), comprising double cottage &, 13 acres,		
let to Messrs. H. Stearn & J. & E. Mudd	Mr. Willie	£610
Dods Farm in Creeting St. Mary, Battisford and Badley,		
comprising residence, grounds, agricultural premises, & two cottages;		
also the Batttisford Farm, comprising thatched		
farmhouse, premises, & 465 acres, let to Mr. H. W. J. Snell	Mr. Willie	£10,600
Badley Bridge Farm, comprising farmhouse, premises, & 111¾ acres,		
in the occupation of the Exors. of Mr. A Hammond	Mr. A. E. Fenning	£2,600
3¾ acres of pasture land, Creeting St. Mary	Mr. E. R. Oxborrow	£125
Two rod garden ground, Needham Market.	Mr. French	£85
Barking Hall, with 40 acres of park land	Withdrawn at £2,800	
Home, or **Pound Farm**, Barking, comprising house,		
agricultural premises, and 92 acres; let to Mr. G. F. Woollard.	Mr. Spearman	£1,850
Chain House or **Needham Farm**, Needham Market, comprising		
residence, stabling, agricultural premises, off premises, cottage,		
and 321¾ acres; let, the residence to Mr. P. C. G. Hayward, &		
the farm to Mr. Wm. Hunt	Mr. Williamson	£9,000
Dog Kennel Farm, Barking, comprising house, premises, &		
95 acres; let to Mr. Wm. Hunt	Mr. Williamson	£1,500
22½ acres of timbered park lands, Barking; let to Mr. Wm. Hunt.		
	Mr. Spearman	£685
Home Farm, Barking, comprising house, premises, & 52 acres;		
let to Mr. Wm. Battle	Mr. Battle	£1,125
Bungeous Farm, in Barking, Battisford & Creeting, comprising		
farmhouse, premises, & 75 acres	Withdrawn at £1,075	
College Farm, Creeting St. Mary, & 47 acres	Withdrawn at £500	
3¾ acres pasture, Creeting St. Mary	Mr. P. C. G. Hayward	£76/10
Spalding Hall, Barking, comprising dwelling house & 3 acres	Mr. S. A. Notcutt	£320
Ten acres of land, Barking Tye	Mr. S. A. Notcutt	£290
7½ acres arable land, Barking Tye	Mr. S. A. Notcutt	£200
Double-fronted cottage, Barking	Mr. Spearman	£90
Walnut Tree Cottage & (a double & single) & blacksmith shop,		
Barking, with half-an-acre	Mr. S. A. Notcutt	£300
Three houses, wheelwright's and carpenter's premises, with half-acre		
of land, Barking	Withdrawn at £260	
Double-fronted cottage, Barking	Mr. Spearman	£180
Fully-licensed free house, **Fox Inn, Barking**, with 5 acres.	Colchester Brewing Co	£1,120
44 acres timbered woodland & pasture, Barking	Mr. Stacey, High Wycombe	£2,000
Swingen's Wood, comprising 14 acres, Barking	Mr. Stacey	£550
Bonny Wood, of 89 acres and 46 acres of pasture, Barking	Mr. Stacey	£5,450
Bonny Wood Farm, Barking comprising house, premises,		
& 40 acres of land; let to Mr. J. Gibbons	Withdrawn at £595	
4¾ acres, Barking.	Mr. J. Gibbons	£145
Swan Cottages (three), Needham Market		
Mr. J. B. Cullingham	£200	
2¾ acres of allotments, Barking	Mr. French	£80
5¾ acres of allotments, Barking	Mr. French	£160
17¾ acres of allotments, Barking	Messrs. Rutter, Sons, & Co.	£320
Lime Kiln Farm, comprising dwelling-house, & 28 acres,		
let to Mrs. R. T. Graves	Mrs. Graves	£635
Lion Cottages (three) Barking	Withdrawn at £110	
25 poles of land, Barking	Mr. A. Quinton	£27 10s.
Darmsden Hall, in Barking and Baylham, comprising residence,		
grounds, agricultural premises, three farmhouses, six cottages,		
& 457 acres, let to Mr. Wm. Wilson, jun.	Mr. Wm. Wilson jun.	£8,500
One acre of pasture, Barking		£27.10s.
Hungergut Hall, Creeting St. Mary, comprising farmhouse, premises		
& 35½ acres, let to Mr. E. Fuller	Mr. W. Packard	£500
Pastures and Bosmere in Barking and Creeting with acreage of 11½.		
	Mr. Wm. Wilson jun.	£310
Lion Barn, Barking, comprising barn, cattle & other		
sheds, & 17½ acres	Mr. W. Wilson jun.	£25
Sixteen acres of accommodation & pasture land, Barking	Mr. W. Wilson jun	£450
Bungeons Farm, Barking (75 acres), and		
College Grove Farm, Creeting St Mary (47 acres) were afterwards sold by private treaty		

Fig 5.2 The East Anglian Daily Times newspaper report dated Wednesday 12th Dec 1917, on the previous day's sale.

Tithe Modus

Whether there was any property left in Badley subject to the payment of tithe was raised by the sale documents. Originally a tenth part of anything, but especially that of the profits and stock generated within a parish, was due, under Canon Law, to their incumbent for his support (known as a Praedial Tithe). Hence tithe barns. However, by the 1800's most preferred to make a cash payment and this practice was formalised by the Tithe Commutation Act 1836, after which commissioners were appointed to made Tithe Awards based on professional land valuations.

The Abstract of Title stated that some of the property sold was subject to the payment of a modus in lieu of tithe amounting to £40 a year payable to the Incumbent of the living of Badley. It said it had been agreed that the forthcoming sale of Badley Hall to Edgar Herbert Mudd, a farmer of Creeting St Mary, referred to as the 'Badley Hall owner', (of the 6th part) for £3,850, (plus Badley Green Farm for £3,700) should be subject to the payment by him, his heirs and assigns, of the whole of the annual £40 payment.

Solicitors' notes state that the 'blue book' issued by the Tithe Redemption Commission (TRC) does not show Badley as having any property subject to tithe and concluded that the modus had been extinguished but had no evidence to prove it, questioning whether or not to write to a Revd. Vincent Fennie. There is no tithe map for Badley recorded at the Suffolk Record Office.

For further information on the Badley Tithes see Chapter 3, page 52.

The auction sale of the estate raised over £73,000 despite six lots being withdrawn, including Barking Hall and park together with three separate farms. Arnold, Newcombe, Wilkinson & Co appear to have profited quickly and well from their shrewd investment and it leaves one to wonder whether or not the Ashburnhams 'should have done better!'

NOTE ON LISTED BUILDINGS

All of the main buildings in Badley are 'listed', but what does this mean?

The Criteria Used

All the properties that the Department of Culture, Media and Sport inspect are judged according to a set of national standards. These standards are approved by the Departments professional advisers, English Heritage. Very broadly the Department of Culture, Media and Sport list:-

All buildings built before 1700 which survive in anything like their original condition

Most buildings of 1700 to 1840 although selection is necessary

Between 1840 and 1914 only buildings of definite quality and character and the selection is designed to include the major works of principal architects.

Between 1914 and 1939, selected buildings of high quality or historic interest

A few outstanding buildings erected after 1939.

The buildings are classified into grades to show their relevant importance. These are as follows:-

Grade I Buildings of exceptional interest (about 2% of all listed buildings)

Grade II* Particularly important of more than special interest (around 4%)

Grade II Buildings of special interest, which warrant every effort being made to preserve them

What does the Listing mean?

The lists are a register, but they do mean that if you wish to demolish, alter or extend a listed building in a way that affects its character, then Listed Building Consent (LBC) must be obtained from the local authority. Both the exterior and interior of a property are covered by the listing and LBC is required in addition to any planning permission or building regulation approval that may be needed, although these are usually considered together.

The fact that a building is listed does not necessarily mean that it must be preserved intact for all time, but it does mean that the case for its preservation can be considered quite separately from the merits of any development proposals. It is a criminal offence to demolish, alter or extend a listed building without consent and the penalties can be heavy.

(Source: Mid-Suffolk District Council - *www.mid-suffolk-dc.gov.uk)*

BADLEY COTTAGE,
Badley Lane IP14 2ET
TM: 053 556

Fig 5.3 Badley Cottage.

Description & History : Remotely situated in Badley Lane, this was originally a pair of plaster and thatched cottages, each containing two bedrooms, sitting room and kitchen and pond of water (enclosure 91 on OS map 1904 edition).

Although surrounded by land belonging to Green Farm land, they were known as Badley Hall cottages and went with Hall Farm. However, in 1917, when the Barking Hall Estate was sold, the cottages were sold with Badley Green Farm (Lot 4). When Green Farm was re-sold in June 1938 the cottages were included with Badley Green Farm (Lot 19).

In the 1940's whilst it was two cottages, the children living there had to walk along the footpaths via Badley Walk to the main road (about 1½ miles) to catch the bus to go to school in Needham Market.

In 1947 the cottages were purchased along with Badley Hall by Leonard Scott. Upon his death in 1968 they passed to their daughter Dorothy who died the following year and left the cottages to her son Geoffrey. They remained tenanted until 1973, when Geoffrey and Margaret Scott took over both cottages and whilst living there converted them into a single dwelling. They remained there until 1980 when they sold the premises to Mr & Mrs J Staddon who were connected with the world famous preservers Wikin & Sons Ltd., of Tiptree, Essex.

It remains a privately owned single cottage and has been considerably extended by its current owners.

Summary of Tenants/Owners (t/o)

Pre 1917	Poleys/Crowleys/Ashburnhams
11th Dec 1917	Edgar H Mudd, The Grange Creeting St Mary (o)
1851	Benjamin Coppin (t) *(from Census Return)*
1861	Caroline Archer (t) *(from Census Return)*
1871	George Berry (t) *(from Census Return)*
	Martha Dallenger (t)
1881	William Bloomfield (t) *(from Census Return)*
	Martha Dallenger (t)
1891	William Lockwood (t) *(from Census Return)*
	William Bloomfield (t)
18th Oct 1938	William Hunt, Hill House, Needham Mkt (o)
June 1938	G Lockwood (service tenant at a rental of £4 per annum. Adjoining cottage vacant - source June 1938 sales brochure)
1947	Leonard and Frances Scott (o)
1961	G W Brown
1965	D H Vale
1968	Dorothy Scott (o)
1969	unknown (t)
1973-80	Geoffrey & Margaret Scott (o)
1980-82	Mr & Mrs J A Staddon (o)
Oct 1982	Trefor & Sherrill Edwards (o)

BADLEY GREEN FARM
IP6 8RU
TM: 058 555

Technical Description : A two storey, Grade II listed, 16th century farmhouse, with evidence of major 17th & 19th century alterations. It is of timber-framed construction, pebble-dashed on the south side and encased in 19th century red brick (now painted) on the north.

The roof is of mainly concrete plaintiles, but some faces have old clay plaintiles. It has a 16th/17th century axial chimney of red brick and another of the 20th century. The windows are 19th and 20th century small-pane casements and there are 20th century half-glazed panelled entrance doors in gable end.

The house has a late 16th century core with plain exposed framing and a large open fireplace with a cambered lintel in the hall. Extensions in 17th/18th century enlarged the parlour at the west end and gave extra service rooms at the east. A parlour block was added early in the 19th century of red brick with a hipped plaintiled roof.

History : About 60 metres south of the farmhouse there is a double cottage (see page 108).

The farm land, which was formerly part of the Poley estate, has passed down through the Crowley and Ashburnham estates and individuals to the current owners. A 1741 map shows Ambrose Crowley Esq let/leased the land, except the woodland which he retained. This practice of leasing continued until the 1917 sale (see below).

Thomas Wolton is recorded as the tenant in Joseph Pennington's 1772 'Survey with Maps of the Suffolk Estate'. Various directories and the Census returns (see Appendix B) show that William Mudd was there in 1830 and Robert Abbott a farm baliff was living their in 1851. By 1858 he had been suceeded by William Frederick Mudd, who was still recorded there twenty-three years later in 1881 (see Chapter 8). However, by 1892, White's Directory has John M & Edgar Herbert Mudd as farming there. This was confirmed by Robert Lingwood's survey in 1906.

On 11th December 1917, the farm comprising of some 230 acres, was sold at auction (Lot 4) as part of the Barking Hall Estate to the sitting tenant Edgar Herbert Mudd of The Grange, Creeting St Mary for £3,700. On the 18th

Fig 5.4 Badley Green Farmhouse.

October 1938, he sold the farm along with Badley Hall farm, a total of over 440 acres, to William Hunt of Hill House, Needham Market for £3,300. On 12th April 1946 the latter sold the farm, less the cottage and garden in Badley Lane (see page 105), to Wilfred Hollis, of 7 Elm Close, Brackleham, Sussex.

The following year, Frederick Hollis is recorded as having died there in 9th November and is buried in Badley churchyard (grave no 9, page 30).

In 1963 'The Green' was bought by John & Kirsten Jugeborg Christensen and it is now occupied and farmed by their son Jeus Henrick Christensen and his wife Debra. It is a mixed arable farm maintaining a small sheep herd.

Summary of Tenants/Owners (t/o)

1772	Thomas Wolton (t)
1830	William Mudd (t)
1858 - 1885	Frederick William Mudd (t)
1900	John & Edgar Herbert Mudd, CSM (t)
11th Dec 1917	Edgar H Mudd, The Grange, CSM (o)
18th Oct 1938	William Hunt, Hill House, Needham Mkt (o)
12th April 1946	Wilfred Hollis (o)
1956	J C Pirkis (Tel: No 302)*
	*(*Source - Newby's 1956 Stowmarket Trade Directory)*
1961	Grant M Sokolov (o)
1963	John Christensen (o)

BADLEY GREEN FARM

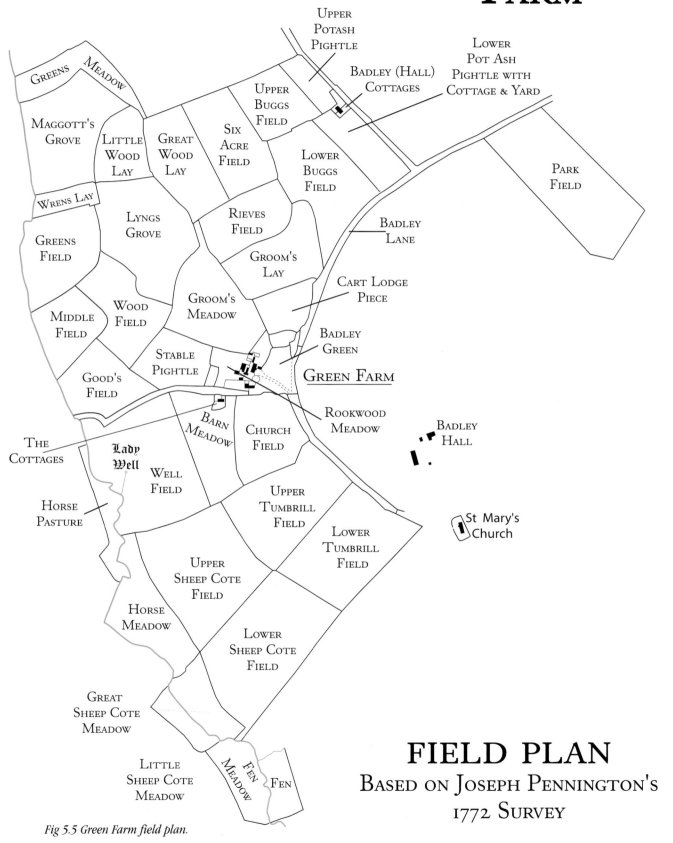

GREENS MEADOW

UPPER POTASH PIGHTLE

BADLEY (HALL) COTTAGES

LOWER POT ASH PIGHTLE WITH COTTAGE & YARD

MAGGOTT'S GROVE

LITTLE WOOD LAY

GREAT WOOD LAY

SIX ACRE FIELD

UPPER BUGGS FIELD

LOWER BUGGS FIELD

PARK FIELD

WRENS LAY

GREENS FIELD

LYNGS GROVE

RIEVES FIELD

BADLEY LANE

GROOM'S LAY

CART LODGE PIECE

WOOD FIELD

GROOM'S MEADOW

MIDDLE FIELD

BADLEY GREEN

GOOD'S FIELD

STABLE PIGHTLE

GREEN FARM

ROOKWOOD MEADOW

BADLEY HALL

THE COTTAGES

Lady Well

BARN MEADOW

CHURCH FIELD

WELL FIELD

HORSE PASTURE

UPPER TUMBRILL FIELD

LOWER TUMBRILL FIELD

St Mary's Church

UPPER SHEEP COTE FIELD

HORSE MEADOW

LOWER SHEEP COTE FIELD

GREAT SHEEP COTE MEADOW

LITTLE SHEEP COTE MEADOW

FEN MEADOW

FEN

Fig 5.5 Green Farm field plan.

FIELD PLAN
BASED ON JOSEPH PENNINGTON'S 1772 SURVEY

THE COTTAGE(S), BADLEY GREEN
TM: 059 554

Technical Description : Situated some 60 metres south of Badley Green farmhouse, this Grade II listed building appears to have been constructed in two stages, probably in the 16th or 17th century. Comprising of one storey and attics, it is a timber-framed and plastered premises which now has a corrugated iron roof, with axial chimney of red brick.

The windows are mainly 19th century casements. A lower section at the east end is probably the earlier and of two cells, with a chimney between it and the taller parlour block to the west.

History : These cottages have always been part of Green Farm. When the Barking Hall Estate was sold in 11th December 1917, they were described in the auctioneers' catalogue as each containing two bedrooms, sitting room and kitchen, gardens and pond of water. Edgar Herbert Mudd, the sitting tenant, purchased the Lot and retained the property until 13th October 1938 when it was sold to William Hunt of Hill House, Needham Market.

On 12th April 1946, William Hunt sold Green Farm to Wilfred Hollis of 7, Elm Close, Bracklesham, Sussex, an accountant. The next owner was Grant M Sokolov who retained it until 1963 when it was purchased by the current owners John and Kisten Christensen.

Like their counterparts at Hall cottages, the children that lived there had to walk along the footpaths via Badley Walk to the main road (about 1½ miles) to catch the bus to go to school in Needham Market.

The Badley Baptism register records that Frederick Arthur Hollis, born 25th Dec 1949, the son of Edwin and Eunice Hollis, a farmer, of Green Farm Cottage, was baptised on 28th May 1950.

A Frederick William Lockwood, believed to have been a farm baliff for Edgar Mudd, was evidently living there at the time of his death, aged 83 years in Nov 1950.

The cottages remain part of Green Farm and because of the restrictions of their Grade II listing will probably remain uneconomical to renovate and reuse, which seems to be rather counterproductive.

Fig 5.6 The Cottages, Badley Green.

Summary of Tenants *(for Owners see above & entry for Green Farm)*

1938	F Lockwood (a service tenant @ 2s. per week)
	T Alexander (@ 3s. per week)
	Jonas Lockwood (t) (shepherd)
1950	Edwin and Eunice Hollis (t)
1950	Frederick William Lockwood (t)
1961	G E Woolnough (t)*
1965/8	H C Mundell (t)*

(* Local Ads Directory of Stowmarket, Needham Market & Mid-Suffolk)

Fig 5.7 Ground floor interiors. Right - the taller parlour block showing substantial beams, the old oven and more recent sink & water heater Left - the plain living room of the adjoining cottage.

Fig 5.8 Farmworkers at Green Farm photographed in the 1930's.
Boy on horse: R. Manning. Standing left to right: Emerson ('Tacker'), Freddie Lockwood, (Lily Lockwood's brother) or Willy Woods, Fred Lockwood (Lily Lockwood's husband) ('Pedlar') & Charlie Lockwood (another of Lily Lockwood's brothers). Boy in foreground: Ron Hallett.

NEW COTTAGES
Burntmill Hill IP6 8RT
TM: 064 570

Technical Description : A double cottage, built c.1889 originally comprising of three bedrooms, sitting room and kitchen. Brick & tiled wash-house, timber & tiled wood-shed, garden and water pump.

History : These semi-detached cottages were built for agricultural workers employed on the Ashburnham estate and were let with the Woodlands.

Although they were auctioned separately as Lot 7 when the Barking Hall Estate was sold in 1917, they were bought by the sitting tenant Harry Stearn, along with Woodlands and Holy Oak Farms.

Their ownership remained tied to that of the Woodlands until 1976 when the No. 1 cottage (nearest Stowmarket) was sold to the sitting tenants, Peter & Margaret Mayhew. The No. 2 cottage continued to be tenanted until 1987 when it was also sold, to Richard & Alison Dawson.

Fig 5.9 New Cottages, with the River Gipping in the foreground.

Summary of Tenants/Owners (t/o)
No 1 cottage

c.1889	Earl of Ashburnham (o)
	Suiter (t)
Pre 1917	Edwin Stearn (t)
11th Dec 1917 - Oct 1938	Harry Stearn, Woodlands (o)
1961 -	Peter John Mayhew (t)
18th Oct 1938 - Nov 1976	Charles Morton, Woodlands (o)
15th Nov 1976	Peter John & Margaret Rose Mayhew (o)

No 2 cottage

c.1889	Earl of Ashburnham (o)
Pre 1917	Edwin Stearn (t)
11th Dec 1917 - Oct 1938	Harry Stearn, Woodlands (o)
18th Oct 1938 - Sep 1987	Charles Morton, Woodlands (o)
1961-70	C H Crysell (t)
30th May 1978	Mrs Anne Hathaway (t)
	Roy & Beryl Ormes (t)
	Taplin (t)
	Andy Woolard (t)
8th Sep 1987	Richard Charles & Alison Jane Dawson (o)
1999	Robert & Linda Sillett (o)

LOT 7 (Coloured Pink on Plan No. 1).—A Brick, Plaster and Tiled

DOUBLE COTTAGE

in the Parishes of Badley and Combs, situated facing the Main Road from Stowmarket to Needha containing 3 Bedrooms, Sitting Room, and Kitchen. Brick and Tiled Wash-house, and Timber Shed. Good Gardens. Pump of Water.

Area about Half an Acre.

SCHEDULE.

No. on Plan.	Description.	Area.
	In Badley.	
2A	Cottages and Gardens	·440
	In Combs.	
514	Garden	·015
		·455

As in the occupation of Mr. Harry Stearn or his Under-tenants.

Possession may be had on Completion of the Purch

Tenure - Freehold.

OUTGOINGS. Land Tax as assessed.

Fig 5.10 Lot 7, page 13 - Double Cottage.
(i.e. New Cottages, Burntmill Hill, Badley, from the auctioneer's catalogue - auction sale of the Barking Hall Estate, 11th Dec. 1917.)

The WOODLANDS
IP6 8RS
TM: 066 567

Fig 5.11 The east-elevation of The Woodlands farmhouse taken by J. Nunn of Needham Market about 1860. The persons in the photograph are probably the tenant John Kirby Moore and his wife Henrietta (née Pennington).

Description : Grade II listed, this building has a 17th century core with major alterations of circa 1840. Two storeys, partly with attics. Timber-framed and plastered; some 18th or early 19th century herringbone pargetting in large panels. Plaintiled roofs, the right-hand section pantiled. Axial chimneys of red brick, that to right is of 17th century. 19th century smallpane sashes; in the c.1840 parlour wing to left are tripartite sashes.

Pair of 19th century glazed panelled entrance doors with open porch on posts; the bargeboards have fretted and cusped soffits. Probably a 3-cell mid 17th century house of lobby-entrance type; but perhaps with earlier core at the centre, where the walls have been raised and a new roof built in 19th century. 17th century framing exposed at the service end to right, the floor joists are laid flat in one room and on edge in another, but are contemporary.

History : This two hundred and thirty acre farm was part of the Ashburnham Estate. In 1770 it was recorded that the farm had a windmill. However, apart from the fact that it was believed to have stood on high ground within the confines of what is now a depot belonging to the Eastern Energy Group, no other information is available about this windmill apart from the fact that it burnt down before 1885, and may have given the name to the hill on which it stood (Burnt Mill Hill). In his diary, John Kirby Moore recorded on 28th March 1833, "Badley Mill burnt to the ground this morning". And on 2nd July he refers to a new mill being completed. It is thought, he was referring to the water mill.

Samuel Scapey was occupying 'Woodlands' in 1772. By 1793 he appears to have been succeeded by James Moore, who in turn was succeeded in the tenancy in 1831 by his son John Kirby Moore. He was born in the farmhouse in 1794 and lived there all his life, dying in 1885 aged 91 years (see page 192). White's Directory (1892) lists Edwin Stearn as the next tenant.

Unusually the farmhouse did not appear to be known by any name, being referred to in the Census returns as 'near Turnpike' (1851), 'farmhouse' (1861), 'Badley Road' (1871) and 'Stowmarket Road' (1881).

Fig 5.12 The same elevation 140 years later in June 2000 showing how little has changed.

John K. Moore recorded on 16th Oct. 1833, "Offord completed well and pump in wash-house at Badley"; 8th July 1839, "Began to build drawing room at Badley"; 10th Nov. 1849, "Planted walnut trees in Stackyard field at Badley."; 1st Jan. 1851, "Planted vine at the back of kitchen chimney, White Grape from Barking Hall".

The farm was known as "Woodlands" by the time the Ashburnham's Suffolk estate was sold in 1917 (as Lot 5). Then 232 acres, it was sold together with Holy Oak Farm and Combs Hall (Lot 6), Combs Wood (Lot 6a) and New Cottages, Badley (Lot 7) for £10,200 to the sitting tenant Harry Stearn, who had succeeded his father, Edwin Stearn.

In 1938 Charles Morton snr and his wife Barbara bought the farm from Harry Stearn. Upon his death it passed to his son, Charles Ian Morton and his wife Eileen. On 6th Oct 1967 they purchased Badley Bridge Farm from Major Thomas O'Bryen Horsford and his wife Yvonne, eventually selling off the farmhouse (1969), land (1995), outbuildings (1996) and barn (1995) separately.

New Cottages, Badley, bought with The Woodlands, along with Woodlands Cottage and an adjacent meadow were also subsequently sold *(see individual entries for further details)*.

They now live in a modern bungalow within the grounds called 'Pomeltrees' (Fig 5.14). His son Eric occupies the farmhouse with his wife Sally (née Smith) and their children.

In 1968 Charles Ian Morton founded a vending machine business *'Morvend Ltd'* having inherited 12 milk dispensing machines with the purchase of Bridge Farm. Due to the subsequent and continuing success of this venture, the family no longer farm the land themselves. It is now share-farmed and the farm buildings are now used for their vending business, together with other commercial units.

Website: www.morvend.co.uk.

Fig 5.15 Views from the north-east corner taken in 1918 and 2001.

Fig 5.13 Morvend logo.

Fig 5.14 Pomeltrees bungalow (TM: 067 567).

Summary of Tenants/Owners (t/o)

1750	Mr. Hardwick?
1772	Samuel Scapey (t)
1793 - 1831	James Moore (t)
1831 - 1885	John Kirby Moore (t)
1892 - 1917	Edwin Stearn (t)
1917 - 1937	Harry Stearn (o)
1938 - 1948	Charles Morton snr. (o)
1948 -	Charles Ian Morton/Eileen Winifred Morton (o)

OTHER COMMERCIAL TENENTS

SAS (Sands Agricultural Services), concerned with agricultual chemical spraying, occupied part of the former dairy for about 10 years. However, they relocated to Eye in summer 2002.

DERRICK WELLS, who specialises in servicing Mercedes Benz vehicles, moved his garage business from Needham Market to the Woodlands in 1992 and occupies the site of former farm buildings.

Fig 5.16 SAS logo.

Fig 5.18 Derrick Wells logo.

LAMVA LTD., electrical and civil engineers now occupy the premises vacated by SAS and part of the adjacent former Eastern Electricity site.

Website: www.lamva.com.

Fig 5.17 Lamva Limited logo.

Fig 5.19 Derrick Wells' garage.

On SATURDAY, October 13th, 1917.
AT THE WOODLANDS FARM, BADLEY,
1½ miles from Stowmarket and 1½ miles from
Needham Market

WOODWARD and WOODWARD

Are instructed to SELL by AUCTION, the
Live and dead FARMING STOCK, comprising:—
HORSES, including 6 Active Cart Mares
and Geldings, and Bay Hackney ;
31 Head of Neat Stock, including 7 Cows and
24 Home-bred Steers and Heifers ;
21 Feeding Pigs and White Sow ;
200 Head of Poultry ;
The Dead Stock includes—2 breasted road
waggons, 3 harvest carriages, 4 Scotch carts,
spring van, turnip cart, pony carriage, 4 iron
feeding troughs, expanding beet plough, 6 gangs
of harrows, rib roll, Smythe's seed and corn
drill, Massey-Harris self-binder, McCormick's
grass cutter, root cutters, harness, ladders,
42 IRON WHEEL HURDLES,
sheep troughs, 10 iron hog troughs, standard
and hanging mangers, hand tools, 2 bean
drills, 3 stack covers, iron garden roll, garden
chair, 2 lawn mowers, 3 portable fowl-houses,
8 h.p. portable engine, and miscellaneous
effects, by direction of the Exors. of the late
Mr. Edwin Stearn.
Sale to commence at 12 o'clock.

*Fig 5.20 Reproduction of a press notice of a
Farm Auction at The Woodland on October 13th
1917, following the death of Edwin Stearn.*

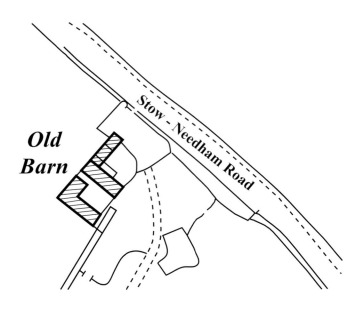

*Fig 5.21 Detail of the Woodlands Old Barn, now demolished, which
used to stand in the corner of Barn Field (see Fig 5.23). In the late
1940's the adjacent Barn Field was used by the Stowmarket ICI works
as a football pitch.*

Lots 5, 6, 6a, and 7 will first be offered as an entirety, and if not so sold will be submitted as Lotted.

LOT 5 (Coloured Green on Plan No. 1).

An Excellent Agricultural Occupation

(A large proportion being TITHE FREE)

KNOWN AS

"THE WOODLANDS"

situated in the Parishes of Badley and Combs, having a long frontage to the Main Road from Bury St. Edmunds
to Ipswich, 1½ miles from the Town and Station of Stowmarket, and about 2 Miles from Needham Market ;
comprising a Plaster, Tiled, and Thatched

FARM RESIDENCE

approached by a Carriage Drive, containing :

ON THE FIRST FLOOR—Landing and 7 Bedrooms.

ON THE GROUND FLOOR—Large Entrance Hall, Dining Room, Drawing Room, Study, Storeroom, Kitchen,
and Dairy. Pump of Water.

Flower and Kitchen Gardens and Orchard.

THE AGRICULTURAL PREMISES

include Timber and Thatched Hackney Stable, and Coach House with Loft over. Two Gig Houses. Timber and
Thatched Neat House. Loose Box and Yard. Brick, Timber and Thatched Barn. Large Chaff House. Fowls'
House and Cattle Yard with 3-Bay Open Shed. Bullock Yard with Thatched Shed. Brick, Timber and Tiled Cart
Horse Stable for 9 Horses. Chaff House. Harness House. Corn Barn. Horse Yard with 3-Bay Timber and Tiled
Open Shed and Loose Box. Brick, Timber and Tiled Granary. Mixing House and 6 Piggeries. Timber and
Tiled 4-Bay Implement Shed and 2 Faggot and Thatched Implement Sheds. Also

SET OF OFF PREMISES

viz. :—Timber and Thatched Barn. Cattle Yard with Timber and Tiled Shed, and another Cattle Yard with 5-Bay
Timber and Tiled Open Shed, and Timber and Plaster Open Shed. Also

A Plaster and Tiled Double-Fronted Cottage

Containing 3 Bedrooms, Sitting Room, Kitchen and Pantry. Good Garden. Pump of Water. Together with
several Enclosures of

Good Corn Growing Arable and Old Pasture Lands,

the whole containing by the Ordnance Survey Map

232a.   3r.   17p.

or thereabouts, as set forth in the following

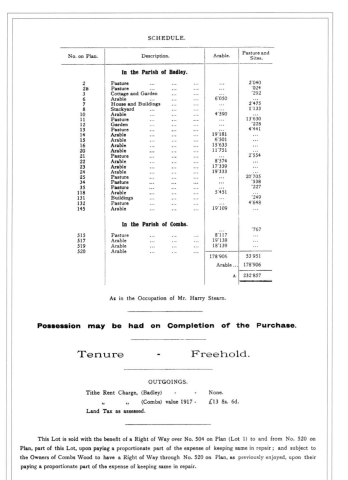

SCHEDULE.

No. on Plan.	Description.				Arable.	Pasture and Sites.
	In the Parish of Badley.					
2	Pasture	...	...	...	...	2·040
2B	Pasture	...	...	...	...	·024
3	Cottage and Garden	...	...	...	...	·292
6	Arable	...	...	...	6·050	...
7	House and Buildings	...	...	...	...	2·475
8	Stackyard	...	...	...	...	1·133
10	Arable	...	...	...	4·590	...
11	Pasture	...	...	...	...	13·630
12	Garden	...	...	...	...	·228
13	Pasture	...	...	...	...	4·441
14	Arable	...	...	...	19·181	...
15	Arable	...	...	...	6·501	...
16	Arable	...	...	...	15·633	...
20	Arable	...	...	...	11·751	...
21	Pasture	...	...	...	...	2·554
22	Arable	...	...	...	8·574	...
23	Arable	...	...	...	17·339	...
24	Arable	...	...	...	19·333	...
25	Pasture	...	...	...	...	20·705
34	Pasture	...	...	...	...	·538
35	Pasture	...	...	...	...	·227
118	Arable	...	...	...	5·451	...
131	Buildings	...	...	...	...	·249
132	Pasture	...	...	...	...	4·648
145	Arable	...	...	...	19·109	...
	In the Parish of Combs.					
						·767
515	Pasture	...	...	...	8·117	
517	Arable	...	...	...	19·138	...
519	Arable	...	...	...	18·139	...
520	Arable	...	...	...	...	...
					178·906	53·951
				Arable ...		178·906
				A.		232·857

As in the Occupation of Mr. Harry Stearn.

Possession may be had on Completion of the Purchase.

Tenure   -   Freehold.

OUTGOINGS.

Tithe Rent Charge, (Badley)   -   None.
"   "   (Combs) value 1917 -   £13 8s. 6d.
Land Tax as assessed.

This Lot is sold with the benefit of a Right of Way over No. 504 on Plan (Lot 1) to and from No. 520 on
Plan, part of this Lot, upon paying a proportionate part of the expense of keeping same in repair ; and subject to
the Owners of Combs Wood to have a Right of Way through No. 520 on Plan, as previously enjoyed, upon their
paying a proportionate part of the expense of keeping same in repair.

*Fig 5.22 The Auction Sale of the Barking Hall Estate on 11th December 1917 - Lot 5, pages 11 & 12, The Woodlands Farm, Badley.
(from the Auctioneers' Catalogue)*

WOODLANDS FARM

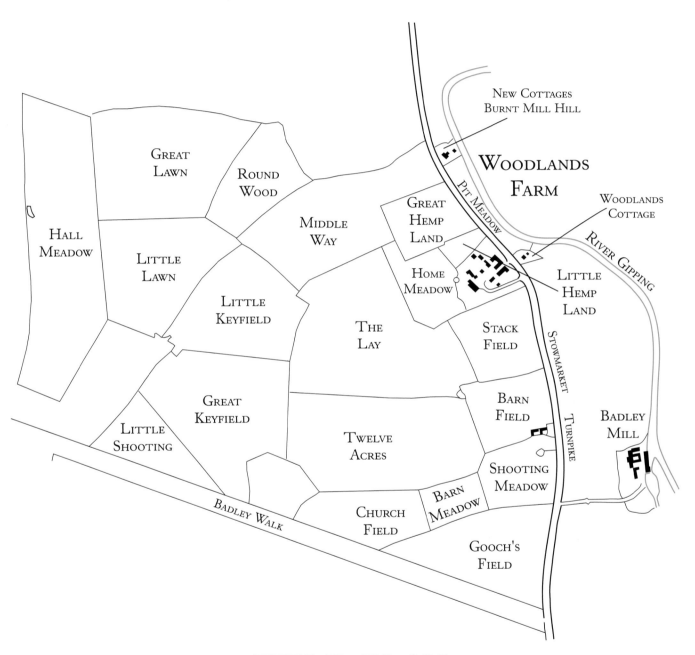

New Cottages
Burnt Mill Hill

WOODLANDS FARM

Woodlands Cottage

Great Lawn

Round Wood

Middle Way

Great Hemp Land

Little Hemp Land

River Gipping

Hall Meadow

Little Lawn

Home Meadow

Little Keyfield

The Lay

Stack Field

Great Keyfield

Twelve Acres

Barn Field

Badley Mill

Little Shooting

Shooting Meadow

Barn Meadow

Church Field

Gooch's Field

Badley Walk

Pit Meadow

Stowmarket Turnpike

FIELD PLAN
BASED ON JOSEPH PENNINGTON'S
1772 SURVEY

Fig 5.23 Woodland Farm field plan.

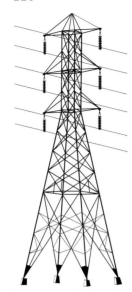

WOODLANDS
substation
TM: 065 568

Historic Note:

The Electric Lighting Act 1882 allowed the Board of Trade to authorise by licence or provisional order the supply of electricity in any area, by any local authority, company or person. It gave local authorities the right to take over the assets of companies after 21 years, later extended to 42 years. The Electricity Act 1926 set up a Central Electricity Board and the National Grid. At Vesting Day, 1 April 1948, all these former undertakings were nationalised.

In Suffolk the use and development of electricity was slower due to the popularity of gas in the area. The Suffolk Electricity Supply Company was started in 1898 by Napier Prentice of Stowmarket. In 1925 its name was changed to the East Anglian Electricity and a Special Order gave powers to develop an area of 294 sq. m. partly in Essex, partly in South West Suffolk. A Parliamentary Bill of 1927 led to the East Anglian Electricity Act which gave powers to supply electricity in Norfolk and Suffolk.

Finborough Hall near Stowmarket was acquired by the East Anglian Electric Supply Co. Ltd in 1936 and was used as the Central Office for the East Anglian, Bedfordshire, Cambridgeshire and Huntingdonshire, Newmarket and Cambridge and Melton electricity companies. At Vesting Day 1948 all these companies were known collectively as Eastern Electricity. *(Source: Suffolk Record Office Ref: IK400/1 Suffolk Electricity Supply Company.)*

In the early 1930's, the East Anglian Electricity Supply Company constructed an electricity supply sub-station adjacent to The Woodlands Farm at Badley (on the Great Hemp Land, see Fig 5.23). To accommodate staff and enable a 24hr presence on site, a house was also constructed there and later a bungalow.

From 1948 until 1978 Great Finborough Hall was the East Anglia Group HQ of the Eastern Electricity Board. Commencing in 1939 the company produced a quarterly magazine *The Finborough Review* (renamed *The Suffolk Sub-Area Review* in 1951). Each site within the company had a correspondent including A.C.E. Woodland. Whilst much of the magazine dealt with staff changes, weddings and deaths, many of whom in respect of the Woodlands related to the Combs part of the site, it nevertheless provides a rich source of genealogical information.

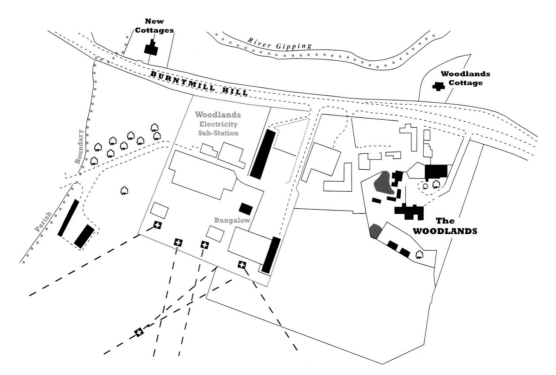

Fig 5.24 Plan showing the location of the Woodlands Sub-station within the Parish of Badley.

Fig 5.25 *This view was taken from within the sub-station in March 1933. The fresh appearance of the concrete driveway and adjacent fences suggest that it was taken soon after the site had opened. Looking north-east across the former A45 road towards Creeting St Peter, the photograph gives a unique view of the Stowmarket Silk Works (now Muntons plc). (Photo courtesy of J Barnard)*

The war-time editions carried a full list of the company staff serving with H.M Forces by depot, those taken prisoners of war and a Roll of Honour for those who lost their lives. These lists are a very sobering read. In the Autumn 1943 edition it was reported that Stowmarket-born Sergeant Robert Leonard Double of No 199 Squadron Royal Air Force, had been awarded the Distinguished Flying Medal. However, in the following Summer's edition it was reported that he had been killed on May 18th 1944 in a flying accident at his base aged 22 years, only ten days after his promotion to Warrant Officer. Robert was the brother of well-known Stowmarket historian and writer, the late Harry Double.

In the October 1954 Suffolk Sub-Area Review, the Woodlands' correspondent welcomed Badley-born Maurice R Sore as a Craft Apprentice.

At the outbreak on WWII the sub-station staff formed a Home Guard Company to protect the installation which was protected during the war years by an electrified fence. The company was disbanded at the end of the war after taking part in the Stowmarket VE thanksgiving day parade and service.

On Thursday 22nd June 1939 the *Stowmarket Recorder & Needham Market, Combs & Stowupland Advertiser* reported :-

"ANTI-GAS DEMONSTRATION AT "WOODLANDS," BADLEY
Exactly what measures would need to be taken in a gas attack emergency were very vividly portrayed at a demonstration which took place in the open at the Woodlands Sub-Station, Badley, of the East Anglian Electric Supply Co Ltd. on Tuesday evening this week."

On the 19th August 1952, Mary Ann Foster, of the Sub-station Badley was buried at Badley, aged 87 (See Appendix A & C).

In May 1954 a new central stores was opened next to the Woodlands sub-station. Although also referred to as The Woodlands, it was in fact within the parish of Combs opposite the entrance to what is now Muntons plc. During WWII this was the site of a black American tented camp, their white counterparts being accommodated on the opposite side of the road at the former Silkworks (now Muntons plc).

An area control (Suffolk Area Control) was later established on the Combs side of the site which at one stage controlled the whole East Anglian Network. In the late 1960's the Eastern Electricity Boards' vehicle workshops were also transferred there from Milton Road, Stowmarket (the site of the current town library) and some of the buildings on the Badley side were used for transformer maintenance amongst others.

The 'Combs side' of the Woodlands site is now closed. One by one its functions were lost or transferred elsewhere, no doubt adversely affected by all the de-mergers and transfers of ownership which have occurred in the industry since it was privatised in December 1990 and in 1998 when the electricity market in England and Wales was opened up to full competition.

The abandonment of a plan to construct a large central office complex on the Combs side (known as the 'Iceni Project') which would have led to the closure of administrative centres in Bury St Edmunds and Ipswich probably dealt the final death-blow.

Part of the former workshop complex is now occupied by electrical contractors Lamva Limited and in June 2005 a planning application was made to develop the remainder of the site for offices and industrial warehousing.

However, the Badley sub-station, now referred to as Stowmarket Grid Sub-station has been largely unaffected and continues to step-down the 132,000 volts intake to 33,000 volts and 11,000 volts respectively for distribution to local sub-stations for further reduction.

Some of the occupants of the house and bungalow which were on the site but have since been demolished were:

1933-40	Walter John (Jack) Barnard (house)
1961	Colin G Haywood (bungalow)
1952-61	J T Foster (cottage)
1966/8	G C Mills (bungalow)

MISCELLANEOUS NOTES:

A.C.E. Woodlands - *Finborough Review* correspondents

1945	Mr. D G. Cole
1950	Mr. R M Taylor
1954	Mr. C. J. Rivers
1957	Mr. Graham C. Lillistone

Eastern Electricity Board - restoration of supplies

In September 1954 the Eastern Electricity Board produced a commemorative booklet which it sent to every member of staff who had been involved in the restoration work following the floods of 1953. One of the recipients was Anthony Hayward, who was based at Badley sub-station.

WOODLANDS COTTAGE
IP6 8RS
TM: 067 569

Technical Description : Situated opposite the Woodlands, a plaster and tiled double-fronted cottage originally comprising of three bedrooms, sitting room, kitchen & pantry, and garden and water pump.

History : This small detached cottage was probably built for agricultural workers employed on the Ashburnham estate and was let with the Woodlands. In 2002/3 a major extension was added to the cottage. Although this has probably more than doubled the size, care over the design has resulted in it already looking part of the original building.

Summary of Tenants/Owners (t/o)

pre 1920	Kerry (son called Wilfred) (t)
1961/70	A E Bloss (t)
1999	Darren Carter (o)
	Emma J Wythe (t)

Fig 5.26 (opposite) Woodlands Cottage before extension.

Fig 5.27 Woodlands Cottage after extension completed in 2004.

MILL FARM
IP6 8RS
TM: 067 569

Fig 5.28 Mill Farm.

Technical Description : A modern detached house, situated next door to Woodlands Cottage.

History : This was built in 1975 as an agricultural dwelling as the farm house for Badley Mill Farm, but now most of the land has been sold off.

Summary of Owners

1975 -   Stephen H & Janet O Farrow

Fig 5.29 Mill House (formerly the Mill Farm House).

MILL HOUSE
(MILL FARM HOUSE)
IP6 8RR
TM: 071 567

house, following the death of Mrs Freshwater (1972), but it was allowed to fall into disrepair. It was unoccupied during the seven years leading up to its purchase by Avril and Anthony Hunt in 1981 when the photographs below were taken (Fig 5.31). They completely restored Mill House, as it is now called and for eight years they ran it as a guest house. It has now reverted back to private accommodation.

During their restoration work, Mr. & Mrs. Hunt discovered the hilt of a sword, concealed between a false wall and a chimney breast on the first floor (Fig 5.30 below). Their find was in good condition, but carried no identiying marks. They took it to Moyses Hall Museum, Bury St Edmunds for examination, where the view was expressed that it dated from 17th century probably originating from the Low Countries and was possibly used against the English during Trade Wars prevailing at that time.

(See entry for Badley Mill for the list of millers & farmers who tenanted or owned the complex.)

Technical Description and History :   A Grade II listed building of 17th century origin, with 18th century alterations, which was extensively renovated in the 1980's. One storey and attics. 3-cell plan, a further cell added to right in 18th century. Timber-framed and plastered, on a plinth of tarred red brick. Gabled plaintiled casement dormers. Casements and panelled entrance door of c.1980. Typical unmoulded 17th century framing with on-edge floor joists. An open fireplace in the hall has a large reused cambered lintel. A 16th century extension to the right has a cellar beneath it, with fine deeply roll-moulded ceiling joists and beams of early 16th century.

They correspond with similar beams above the cross passage at Badley Hall, whose open hall and parlour range was demolished and the components sold off in 1795 (see page 73).

History : *(to be read in conjunction with the history of the mill opposite)* This was originally where the miller and his family lived when Badley Mill and Farm were operational. Mr. Sunshine, a local schoolteacher, bought the Mill Farm

Fig 5.30 The sword hilt found during restoration work.

Fig 5.31 Views of the farm-house prior to renovation in 1981 (photo Mr & Mrs Hunt).

BADLEY MILL LODGE
(formerly BADLEY MILL)
IP6 8RS
TM: 071 567

History : Badley Mill was a water corn mill, its wheel being turned by the water flowing in the River Gipping from Stowmarket. In its later years of operation the mill was used to grind corn for animal feeds.

As Lords of the manor of Badley, the Poley family owned the mill. In those days Badley Mill went by the name of Vaysies (alias Vassyes, Veysies) Mill and went with a 63 acre farm some of which is in Creeting St. Peter. It is believed that the miller's house may have been called the 'Warrens'. When owned by the Poley's, the mill and its farm were leased out to various people as were many of the fields owned by the Poley family in excess of their requirements. When Badley Mill was mentioned in the lease deals, it was described as a messuage called 'Warrens', a water mill called Vaysies Mill, lands called Veysies, a meadow of four acres and a moor or fen called Horse Fenn. On the 1741 map there is a parcel of land called Horse Fen adjacent to the River Gipping, belonging to Badley Bridge farm.

A good mile closer to Stowmarket, the approach to Woodlands Farm from the Combs Ford direction is called Burntmill Hill. Interestingly, William Collier's 1741 manuscript map shows some adjacent land was called 'The Burnt Mill'. (see Fig 5.33 opposite) This is approximately where New Cottages, Burntmill Hill now stand, a convenient location where the Gipping flows close to the turnpike affording easy access. Was this then the site of Vaysies Mill, or even the mill referred to in the Domesday survey?

On Monday 28th March 1833 John Kirby Moore recorded in his diary, "Badley Mill burnt to the ground this morning", and on April 10th , "Dined with Mr. Driver and his brother at 'George Inn', Needham, who came from London to arrange about rebuilding Badley Mill". Mr. Driver, was the Ashburnhams' Steward at the time.

On Jul 2nd he recorded, "Mr. Geo Driver dined and drank tea after looking at Badley new mill and alterations at Mr. Mudd's house on Badley Green". Given that there was no other mill in Badley, he must have been referring to the water mill.

Fig 5.32 Two photographs of Badley Mill before conversion.

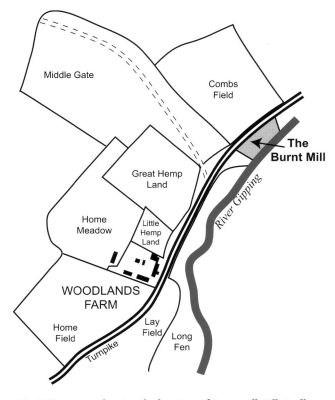

Fig 5.33 a map showing the location of Burntmill Hill, Badley.

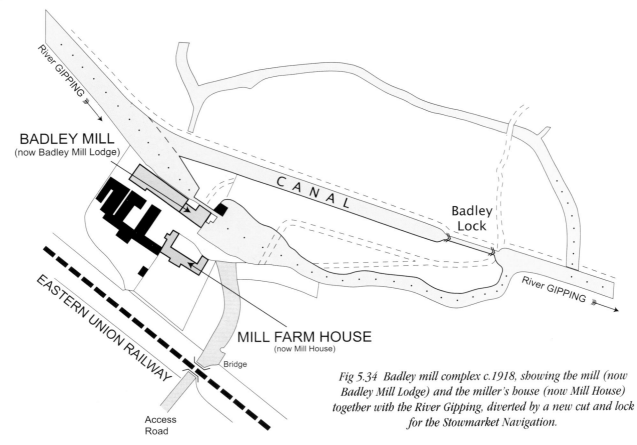

Fig 5.34 Badley mill complex c.1918, showing the mill (now Badley Mill Lodge) and the miller's house (now Mill House) together with the River Gipping, diverted by a new cut and lock for the Stowmarket Navigation.

Fig 5.35 Badley Lock looking upstream.

The mill complex was sold at auction (lot 2) on 12th Dec 1917, to Samuel Willie of Yeovil, Somerset, for £1,700, It was re-auctioned by Woodward & Woodward the following July.

Badley mill was in operation up until the late 1920's when it was owned by Mr. William Freshwater. The mill stopped grinding because the water wheel broke. It was judged to have been destroyed by a company occupying premises in Stowmarket called the Silkworks.

The Silkworks was a large silk processing factory owned by the Bulmer Rayon Company, which used the River Gipping for tipping its liquid waste from its various processes. The chemicals from this waste polluted the river and over the years rotted the wood in the water wheel and eventually the wheel broke.

Between 1925 and 1928 the river was so polluted at Badley Mill that vegetation and fish were destroyed. The smell emanating from the river was so offensive that the premises were ununhabitable from time to time.

In 1931 the Freshwaters successfully took the Silkworks company to court.   The Silkworks was judged to be

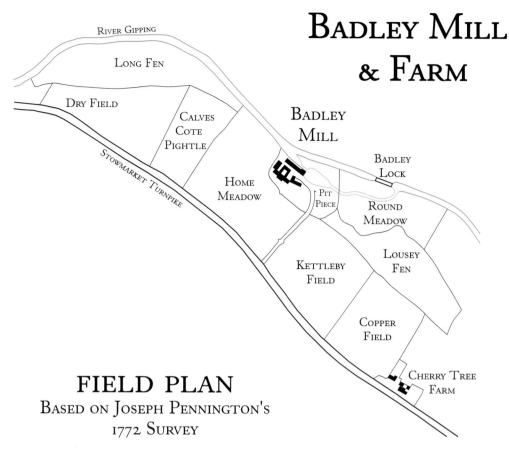

BADLEY MILL & FARM

RIVER GIPPING

LONG FEN

DRY FIELD

CALVES COTE PIGHTLE

STOWMARKET TURNPIKE

BADLEY MILL

BADLEY LOCK

HOME MEADOW

PIT PIECE

ROUND MEADOW

KETTLEBY FIELD

LOUSEY FEN

COPPER FIELD

CHERRY TREE FARM

FIELD PLAN
BASED ON JOSEPH PENNINGTON'S 1772 SURVEY

Fig 5.36 Badley Mill Farm field plan.

responsible for the destruction of the mill's wheel. The court awarded Mr. Freshwater £2,650 compensation, a considerable sum at the time, but unfortunately the Silkworks went into liquidation before his claim could be settled.

A report by the Pure Rivers Society published about 1930, describes in detail the serious state of pollution of the Gipping. It records a public enquiry in Needham Market on 8th August 1928 of the results of this pollution, including fish being destroyed and a smell causing people to vomit.

By the 1933 issue of Kelly's directory, Mrs. Freshwater had established 'Badley Mill Irish Setter Kennels'. The first telephone number for these kennels and the farm was Needham Market 97.

Mr. Freshwater never received his compensation and was faced with the additional burden of having to pay his own legal fees. Subsequently, this situation left him in such a financial position that he was unable to repair the broken wheel.

On 21st July 1939 the local newspaper reported:

"More Pollution In River Gipping
Hundreds of Fish Die at Badley Mill

Another serious pollution has occurred in the River Gipping, this time at Badley Mill. The water became the colour of ink, and there was a strong stench.

For several years the mill pool has escaped pollution. The mill wheel is not in use, and the pool has been a sanctuary and breeding ground for fish. It was the hope of anglers that when pollution was stopped and the river returned to a normal condition these fish would be useful for restocking. But during in the the week-end fish were dying in hundreds in the pool.

A problem faces Mr. Freshwater, who lives at the Mill House, for horses and cows had been drinking from the pool, and, except for a shallow well used for household purposes, there is no other water supply on the farm.

Mrs. Freshwater is a breeder and exhibitor of Irish setters, and her dogs are having to be kept from the river."

Having lost his revenue from the mill, Mr. Freshwater resorted to living off the farm that went with the mill. To this day Badley Mill has not worked since the wheel broke.

Mr Freshwater later died by his own hand and in 1956 the farm land and buildings were sold off.

In 1956 the Mill Farm was purchased by Charles Spenser Farrow (Doveshill Farm), although Mrs Freshwater continued to reside at Mill Farm House along with Miss Lillian Key. The old mill machinery was removed to enable the former mill floor to be repaired. It was subsequently used as a general farm building.

Upon the death of Charles Farrow in 1968, along with Doveshill Farm it passed to his sons Stephen & Richard.

However, following the untimely death of his brother Richard in a road accident on the A14 at Creeting St Mary in 1982, Stephen sold the land to the east of the railway line together with the farm buildings at the Mill.

The mill and outbuildings were purchased by Anthony Beeson who has converted the original mill building into a dwelling which is now known as Badley Mill Lodge.

Fig 5.37 Badley Mill Lodge (Badley Mill) 2002.

Fig 5.38 Another view of the mill taken from the Creeting side of the former Navigation channel.

Summary of Owners and Tenants (o/t) :

1772	Richard Robinson (t)
1830	Widow Jay (t)
1841-1851	Samuel Jay (t)
1858-1874	Henry Wicks (t)
1881-1892	Samuel Southgate (t)
1900-1916	Mary Ann Rose (t)
	(Charles Edward Rose (dob 15/11/08))
	George Thomas Rose
1906-1924	J & E Mudd (t)
1918	Mr Willie of Yeovil (o) bought at auction for £1,700
1922	Alfred Bywater (o)
1924-1956	Mr Wm & Eva Violet Mary Freshwater (o)
1956-1970	Eva V M Freshwater (Mill House only) (t)
	Florence Lillian Key (Mill House only)
1956-1968	Mr & Mrs Charles Spencer Farrow (o)
1968 -1982	Stephen H Farrow (o)
1982 -	Anthony H & Gillian A Beeson (o)

'ROOTS & SHOOTS'
IP6 8RJ
TM: 071 566

Fig 5.39 Roots & Shoots, the popular garden centre situated on the B1113 road mid-way between Combs Ford and Needham Market.

Description & History : In 1984 on an enclosure originally part of Badley Mill Farm called Kettleby Field (see Fig 5.36) situated alongside the old turnpike and adjacent to the driveway to Badley Mill, Alan & Patricia Smith founded what was originally a plants nursery, which has developed over time to become a thriving garden centre business called *'Roots & Shoots'*.

A house and 30,000 square feet of glasshouses were subsequently erected on the site. They take pride in still growing the majority of the plants and the centre now attracts gardeners from all over mid-Suffolk especially in spring and at weekends throughout the year.

Ironically, although this is the most recent development in the parish, it is most likely to be the one, and in most cases, the only location, most know of, or associate, with, Badley!

Website: www.rootsandshootsgc.co.uk.

Figs 5.40 and 5.40a.

Figs 5.41 and 5.41a.

BADLEY WALK

IP6 8RP
TM: 072 564

Description & History :
Now known as Badley Walk, this was once an avenue said to have been lined by elm trees stretching from the front door of Badley Hall to the turnpike (Stowmarket Road). Originally a straight meadow nearly a mile long and forty five yards wide, the Walk leaves the Hall eastwards, crosses Church Green to the north of the church and continues to the road. It is said that a pack road once continued on from this point, crossing the River Gipping (probably at the Mill) forming a road to Creeting Hall and then onto the Norwich Road.

Midway down its length, the Walk passes through a wood called Keyfield (Kyfield, Kyful) or Kyesfield Grove. Mention is made in 1485 that Simon Poley held a parcel of land called Kyesfield. The origins of this name is unknown. At one time three fields also had the same name, but only one, a seven-acre wood, remains today. This wood, which is split symmetrically by the Walk, suggests it was almost certainly man-made. Either planted as decoration for the path at the time the Hall was built, or sculptured from existing woodland to complement it.

The latter seems the more likely when one considers that by Inquisition 3 Henry VII. 327, Henry Poley, the son and heir of Simon and Margaret, already possessed a 'Close called Kyesfield' parcel of Badley Manor, worth 53s. 4d., held by fealty and knight service. The manor was at this time stated to be worth 20 marks and was held by the service of half a knight's fee. (Inquisition 8 Henry VII. 806) (1492)

Tradition relates that Queen Elizabeth I rode along the walk to be entertained by the Poley Squires at the Hall. Her following was said to have included '200 young gentlemen in white velvet on horseback and 300 graver persons in black with gold chains around their necks.'

Although she visited[1] Suffolk several times between 1560 & 1599, there is no documentary evidence to support this visit.

However, Hollingworth's *'History of Stowmarket'* (1844) p131, suggests she may have visited the adjoining parish of Battisford to be entertained by Sir Thomas Gresham (c.1518-1579), a financier, adviser to Queen Elizabeth, and founder of the Royal Exchange.

Fig 5.42 Early photograph of the bungalows at the east end of Badley Walk. (Photo : Maurice Sore)

Fig 5.43 A splendid view of St Mary's Church and Hall viewed from the Walk just beyond Church Green.

White's Suffolk (1855) says of him, "the son of Sir Richard, founded the original Royal Exchange in London, and had the frame of that edifice constructed here upon the common; most of the timber used in the work was grown of this neighbourhood."

With her enormous entourage, it would have made good practical sense for her to have used the convenience of Badley Walk for a mile of easy riding on what was otherwise likely to have been a tiring cross-country journey to Battisford. Was this the source of the Badley story?

Fig 5.44 Sir Thomas Gresham. attributed to Adrian Key C 1565

Elizabethan progresses. It was a very expensive "honour" to entertain Queen Elizabeth and her household. Elizabeth hit on the clever scheme of going on constant "progresses" about the country. Aside from the benefit of bringing her into closer contact with her subjects, she saved a great deal of money by making the nobles with whom she stayed foot the bill for her visit. Many nobles begged off the honour of her stay for fear of bankruptcy. The frequency of the "progresses" of Elizabeth account for the fact that there are so many places today that advertise "Queen Elizabeth slept here". She slept just about everywhere! (Adapted from Elizabethan Life[1]).

Although the Poleys were a wealthy family, faced with the prospect of such expenditure, perhaps they were not too disappointed that the Queen did not call in at the hall after all!

[1]*www.britainexpress.com/History/Elizabethan_life.htm*

THE THREE PHASES OF BADLEY WALK

Today it is possible to divide the Walk into three distinct parts.

a) The section from the Hall to Keyfield Groves is the only part which is still a grassy avenue.

The elm trees were cut down long ago and the elm hedge grown in their place suffers from Dutch elm disease.

b) The next section, from Keyfield Groves to the bungalows, has deliberately been allowed to become overgrown with blackthorn and other trees to form a nature reserve, leaving only a walking track through the middle. In the mid 1990's this piece of the Walk was sold by John Thomas Rose to Maurice Sore, the former having inherited it in 1952.

c) Having remained practically unchanged for centuries, in 1928 Sparrows of Needham Market built six small bungalows at the Stowmarket Road end financed by Edgar Mudd of Creeting who owned Badley Hall at the time.

They were built during the time of the depression to create work for local people. Originally intended for renting out, they are now all privately owned, having been sold to the tenants in 1952 by John Rose for £250 each, with the exception of No 2 which was transferred to Charles Morton of the The Woodlands. In 2002 one of these bungalows was sold for well over £100,000!

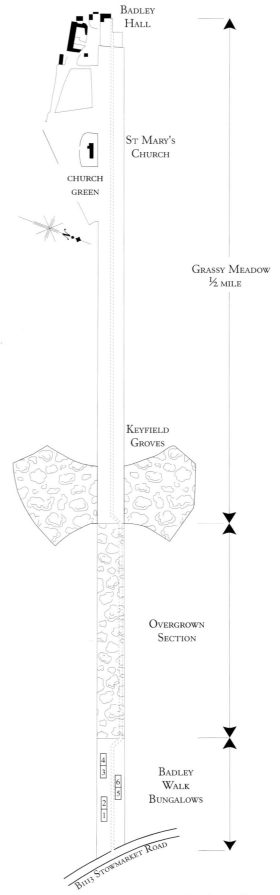

Fig 5.45 The three phases of Badley Walk.

Fig 5.46 Badley Walk bungalows 2002.

Fig 5.46a The overgrown section in summer.

Fig 5.46b (left) Bert Hadley (see page 133) has kindly provided this sketch of the distinctive gates which he recalls were situated at several places in Badley Walk to control livestock. Locations included the junction with the main road and on both sides, halfway along Keyfield Groves, which was fenced off.

SOME OF THE INHABITANTS OF BADLEY WALK
(the date in brackets indicates the year(s) of known occupancy)

1 Badley Walk

(1928)   Hawkins (Harvey?)
(1936)   S Sougate *(see shooting incident page 131)*
(1961-79)   Royal William & Irene Florence Sore
(1999)   Jermy & Sally A Sore

2 Badley Walk

(1930's)   Mr & Mrs Largent
(19--)   Miss Mayne
(19--)   Friend
(1961)   Alfred W & Ivy Mayhew
(1966)   R R Stearne
(1999)   Catherine M Aldis & Tony Farrell
(2002)   Frederick Wm & Ellen Barbara Edwards

3 Badley Walk

(1930's)   Mr & Mrs Aspland
(1950's-92) Cecil George & Ruby Sybil Hadley
(19--)   Manning
(1970)   John Ronald & Rosemary Heather Garnham
(1999)   Paul E & Karen A Manning

4 Badley Walk

(1930's-69) G A & B H M Proctor
(1966)   I Warner
(1989-92)   Colin Russll & Sherry Moss
(1999)   Richard C & Maxine B Clement-Smith

5 Badley Walk

(19--)   Battle
(1943-89)   Luis Andrew & Vera Kathleen Steel *(née Hadley)*
(1999)   Kelvin S & Janitha D Clarke

6 Badley Walk

(1947)   William & Elizabeth Mary Woods (née Fairweather)
(1954-77)   Geo Edward & Nellie Annie Hadley (née Robinson)
(1970)   John Ronald Garnham
(1996)   Nigel J & Teresa J Mann

CHERRY TREE FARM
IP6 8RN
TM: 073 564

Technical Description : A Grade II timber-framed and pebble-dashed smallholding, originally comprising of a double cottage, dates from the mid or late 16th century with 17th century extensions. Of two-cell end-chimney plan, with one storey and attics, it was thatched but now has concrete plaintiled roof, half-hipped at the service end to right. It has gabled casement dormers and there is a 19th century axial chimney of red brick. The windows are late 20th century horizontal sliding sashes with small panes. There is a 20th century entrance porch at cross-passage position, with gabled roof and glazed two-panelled door. Heavy unchamfered first floor joists are exposed in the hall and service room. It has a complete coupled rafter roof. A parlour was added to left beyond the large external chimney, in early or mid 17th century clasped-purlin roof. A short wing behind the service end was added in 17th/18th century.

History : Cherry Tree Farm is not strictly a farm, although in the past it had about 40 acres. Earlier this century the house consisted of two cottages, they fell into disrepair and were later condemned as uninhabitable. In about 1950 the property was bought, renovated and converted into one larger house - see photo next page. Since then it has been further modernised and improved several times bringing it up to the desirable residence that it is today.

The original land which made up Cherry Tree Farm was the plantation opposite the farm house, the land now occupied by 'Roots 'n Shoots' and the meadow (Copper Field) between them and the farm. The latter has since been bought back and is once again part of Cherry Tree Farm.

When the small-holding was sold at auction as part of the Barking Hall Estate in 1917 as Lot 11, it amounted to just over 13 acres comprising of enclosures 135, 146, 147 & 162 on the O.S. map (1904 edition). At the time one of the houses and garden were in the occupation of an under-tenant of Harry Stearn and the other let to an under-tenant of John & Edgar Mudd. It was purchased by a Samuel Willie of South Bank, Yeovil, Somerset, for £610 and sold to Charles Edward Creasey of Trimley within a year.

In 1925 the farm was tenanted by Philip C Hounsfield. Kelly's directory for that year also lists him as the tenant farmer of the Cedars Farm, Needham Road, Combs, trading

Fig 5.47 Cherry Tree farm taken from 'Roots & Shoots'

Fig 5.48 Cherry Tree Farm, described as "recently restored", in the series Pocket Histories of Suffolk Parishes (No. 342 Badley) by Yeoman published in the Suffolk Chronicle and Mercury on February 9th 1934. At this stage it was still a pair of cottages -note the two doors.

as 'Hounsfield Cedars, Stowmarket'. He was the Hon-Sec of the Stowmarket Branch of the National Farmers Union. The Cedars itself was in the occupation of a Miss Smith.

The 1929 directory lists him still farming at both venues, having established a dairy business at the Cedars trading as 'Balfour Grade A Milk Company' telephone number Stowmarket 33. By 1933 and with Miss Smith still living in the Cedars farmhouse, Hounsfield had added a 'Farm and Poultry Alliance' agency to his business portfolio. Although the above telephone number is also listed for this business, the address is given as The Paddock, Combs.

However, he had evidently relinquished the tenancy of Cherry Tree farm, Badley, along with that of the Cedars, Combs to a William Mason by 1932.

Fig 5.49 A surviving Cedars Farm Dairy milk bottle. (Courtesy of The Cedars Hotel)

Fig 5.50 Cherry Tree Farm photographed shortly after conversion in 1950 (Photo: Maurice Sore)

The farmhouse subsequently passed through a succession of owners until November 1978 when it was purchased by John & Eileen Thorpe who developed a successful fire-wood and livery business there, adding a block of six stables and a tack room.

In 1997 they moved into an annexe added to the farmhouse enabling their children and their families to occupy the farmhouse.

In 2003 the farm was purchased by Roger Meacock MRCVS and Julia Walsh as the operating base for their company *Natural Healing Solutions*, which specialises in 'treating animals of all species and people for conditions where a faster healing is desired or there is no other option being provided by conventional veterinary or medical practice.'

In January 2004 ownership changed again and it is now the home of Garry and Lynne Edwards who are re-developing the site to suit their business franchise - Cascade Pools (East Anglia) Ltd., specialist swimming pool consultants and installers. Website: www.cascadepools.co.uk.

Summary of Tenants/Owners (t/o)

1771	Emerson Cornwell (t)
1830	Widow Bedingfield (t)*
1874-1917	J & E Mudd (t)
11th Dec 1917	Samuel Willie (by auction) (£610) (o)
15th Nov 1918	Charles Edward Creasy of Trimley (o) (died 8/8/1923)
	(*Charles Creasy was part of the syndicate which bought the Ashburnham estate at auction the previous year, see page 102*)
8th Aug 1923	Creasey Trustees (o)
1925 -	Philip C Hounsfield (t)
1932	William Mason (t)
	H E Mitton (t)
1936	Walter Fuller (son Fred worked at Doves Hill farm)
4th Dec 1949	Frederick Charles Squire Crockford (o)
26th Oct 1951	Sidney Lancelot Short (o) (died 19/7/1971)
19th Jul 1971	Trustees of S L Short (o)
5th Nov 1971	Wg Cmdr Edward Richard Lacey (o) (died 10/3/1980)
10th Mar 1980	Joan Willis Lacey (widow of above) (o)
9th Dec 1985	Neil Ronald & Christine Mary Brittain (o)
27th Nov 1987	Eileen Marina & John Wm Valentine Thorpe (o)
	Jason & Claire Thorpe
2003	Roger Sidney Meacock MRCVS/Julia Walsh (o)
Jan 2004	Garry & Lynne Edwards (o)

* "does not live at farm nor dependent on it for her maintenance" (Edward Driver, Estate Steward, Survey 1830 - SRO HA1/AB4/2)

At Your Service.
**Everything produced by the
Cow and Hen**

Fig 5.51 Publicity material for Cedars Farm Dairy's 'Grade 'A' Milk', photographed in the rear yard of The Cedars.

Fig 5.52 Cherry Tree farm barn - destroyed by fire in the 1950's. (Photo: Maurice Sore)

Fig 5.53 A view across the back garden of Cherry Tree Farm towards Stowmarket. The prominent tree in the distance is situated on the access road leading to the mill. The field in front is the 'future' site of 'Roots & Shoots' garden centre and to the left of the tree the barn which used to stand in Barn Field on the opposite side of the road is just visible (see Woodland field plan Fig 5.23).

On Thursday 1st July 1936 the *Stowmarket Recorder & Needham Market, Combs & Stowupland Advertiser*, reported - **"Badley Cyclist Injured**

At about 12.15pm Wednesday 1st July, Mr. Walter Fuller of Cherry Tree Farm, Badley, met with an accident when about three quarters of the way down Badley Hill. He appears to have been riding a cycyle and leading another machine when the cycle he was leading came involved with his own. To save himself as he hoped from an acciodent, he let go of the cycle he was leading. The entanglement which followed brought him to the ground. He sustained cuts, severe injuries of the forehead, elbow and knee, and was removed by ambulance to the East Suffolk Hospital . . . . . ."

Cherry Tree Farm was associated with another incident reported in the same newspaper on 20th August 1936 viz

"Sporting Gun Accident at Badley - Two women injured.

At about 8.30 on Thursday evening last, Mr. V. N. Denne, accompanied by Mr. H. Sutton (both of Stowmarket) had been for a rabbit shoot near the Cherry Tree Farm, Badley.

On returning across the field next the highway and at about 60 yards distant, Mr. Denne, who was carrying a double barrell 12-bore gun, proceded to put it off-cock when his foot slipped in the long under-growth and simultaneously on falling to the ground the gun accidently fired.

Hearing cries from the direction of the main Needham Market road and over the hedge intersecting between this higway and the field, both Mr. Denne and his companion at once raced forward and to their dismay discovered the two women who had been conversing on the highway footpath had, apparently, stood in range of the scattering discharge of shot.

Mr. Denne and Mr. Sutton at once hastened off in the formers car back to Stowmarket and quickly returned with Police Inspector J. J. Syrett, Police Constable Ives and Dr. M. C. Hounsfield.

On arrival it was found that shot pellets had lodged in the side of the face, arm and breast on one of the women, **Mrs.** S. Sougate of No 1 The Bungalows, Badley. Her friend, Mrs. H. Last of Church Walk, Stowmaket, had also suffered similarly in the neck . . . .

It was a pure accident and it was most fortunate it did not occur at closer range."

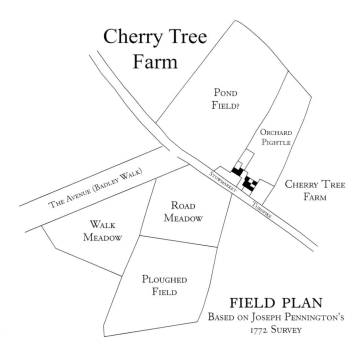

Fig 5.54 Cherry Tree Farm field plan.

DOVESHILL COTTAGE
IP6 8RL
TM: 076 562

Fig 5.55 Doveshill Cottage.

Some were probably hired for a fixed period at Michaelmas (29th Sept) when many tenancies and other agreements were traditionally made, or for example, to assist with the harvest. Whereas skilled horseman were arguably more likely to have been retained for a longer periods. As soon as they lost their job they also lost the use of the tied cottage which usually went with it, forcing them to move on to seek employment and shelter for their family elsewhere.

Technical Description : This cottage, situated on the old Stowmarket turnpike on the crest of Badley Hill is opposite the entrance to Doveshill road which leads to the Church and Hall.

Originally three separate cottages, the right-hand pair contains two bedrooms, sitting room, kitchen and pantry each; the other, one bedroom, sitting room, kitchen and pantry.

History : Until the opening of the Bosmere & Claydon Hundred Union House at Barham in 1766 (see Chapter 2) it appears the cottages were used as the local workhouse to house the parish poor.

In 1917 they were sold with Doveshill Farm as Lot 10, by which time they had long been used as tied cottages occupied by agricultutural worker employed on Doveshill farm.

Some of the families living in the cottages between 1841 and 1901 can be identified in the Census Returns reproduced in Appendix B.

There is evidence that the Rivers family recorded there in the 1891 Census were still living there until at least 1896.

The fact that there was a high turnover of farm labourers in the 1800's is reflected in the Census returns with only few remaining in the parish for the duration of the ten years period.

Many of the tenant farmers also only appear in a single Census.

The lists in Appendix E of persons born in Badley and recorded in other Parishes on other Census dates show that many of those who moved did not travel very far, often only to the next parish.

In 1976 Peter and Barbara Buck bought the cottages and some adjoining land from the Farrow Trust and set about converting the property from three small dilapidated cottages into one luxurious house. An excellent example of the improvements that can be achieved on what was once condemned property *(see photographs page 134)*.

Summary of Tenants/Owners (t/o)

1910 - 17	Frederick Williams (t) *(with farm)*
1917	Samuel Willie, Yeovill, Somerset (o) *(purchased Lot 10 at auction)*
1919 - 34	George Edward Hadley *(Cottage No 1)* (t) [1]
1920's	Frederick Scarff *(Cottage No 2)* (t) [2]
	later Jack Green (t) [3]
	George Mann *(Cottage No 3)* (t) [4]
	Nelson Gosling *(Cottage No 3)* (t) [5]
1951	Charles Spencer Farrow (o)
1961	K J Filby *(Cottage No 1)* (t)
1961-69	W R Roper *(Cottage No 2)* (t)
	V E Allen *(Cottage No 3)* (t)
1965-69	G Rowe *(Cottage No 1)* (t)
1965-66	C H Pettitt *(Cottage No 3)* (t)
1967	H M Tunsley *(Cottage No 3)* (t)
1976	Peter & Barbara Buck (o) *(cottages converted)*

Fig 5.57 George Hadley ploughing at Doveshill in the 1930's.

Fig 5.56 The Hadley family outside No1 Doveshill Cottages on 22nd May 1938. (standing l. to r.) Sidney Ronald*, Cecil George, Vera Kathleen, Bertram Frank* (seated) George Edward & Nellie Annie Mary Hadley (née Robinson) with Jean Margaret* (seated front) (*born at cottage).

Fig 5.58 (below) This delightful photograph was taken on the 25th March 1925 and shows (from l. to r.) George Mann, George Edward Hadley (both of whom lived in Doveshill Cottages) and Joe Fuller who lived in what is now known as Cherry Tree Farm, drilling with a team of horses on Doveshill farm.

(All photographs courtesy of Bert Hadley)

Notes:

1 George Hadley (born at Cotton, Sfk in 1889) was employed at Doveshill Farm, until retiring to Badley Walk in 1954.

Bert Hadley recalls that steam lorries travelling towards Stowmarket and belonging to Quinton's of Needham Market, used to regularly replenish their water supply from a point on the River Bat midway between the two Chain Bridges (i.e. Badley Bridge). Whilst on his way to school on a windy morning in about 1926, he witnessed one of two lorries subsequently stoke-up to negotiate Badley Hill (then much steeper), causing sparks to blow across the road and set the thatch alight on Badley Bridge farm barn which stood parallel to the road. Despite frantic efforts to extinguish the fire the barn was destroyed and when he returned later that day all that remained was a pile of charred timbers and remnants of the thatched roof.

2 The Scarffs had two children Fred and Winifred, neither of whom are believed to have married. Fred Scarff was employed as a roadman by East Suffolk County Council, and was responsible for the road between Badley Bridge and the Woodlands.

3 Jack Green and his wife followed the Scarffs into the middle cottage. They had one son, Norman, whose photograph, along with that of his father, can been seen in Chapter 8 (The Haydons).

4   George Mann & his wife had one son, Stanley, born circa 1919. George also worked at Doveshill Farm.

5   Nelson Gosling, his wife and their daughter Millicent, born circa 1928, later occupied the No 3 cottage (on left-hand side).
(Notes complied from information kindly supplied by Bert Hadley)

The Conversion of Doveshill Cottages

Fig 5.59 The cottages, uninhabited and overgrown by 1975 when these photographs were taken, showing the three separate front entrances and the lean-to extension at the back.

Fig 5.60 The start of building work in 1976. (left) With the front gardens cleared away, the three separate cottages can be more readily seen. (right) The rear lean-to has been demolished and the foundations for the rear extension are in place.

Fig 5.61 (left) The completed rear extension in 1980. (right) An aerial view of the extended cottage and rear garden taken in 1981, with the brow of Badley Hill (B.1113) road in the foreground.

(Photographs courtesy of Peter Buck)

Fig 5.62 Doveshill Cottage from the track leading from Badley church.

DOVESHILL FARMHOUSE
IP6 8RJ
TM: 077 561

Fig 5.63 Doveshill farmhouse.

Technical Description : A post-war bungalow erected on Donkey Meadow, between Doveshill Cottage and the original farmhouse (Doveshill) by Charles Spencer Farrow in 1966.

History : The original farmhouse was renamed Doves Thatch but is now called 'The Dower House' after an earlier name and the bungalow adopted the name of the original Doveshill farm.

The Farrows sold the original Doveshill Farm when they moved into the bungalow in 1966. Upon Charles Farrow's death in 1968, his son Richard took over the bungalow and his mother moved into Needham Market. Richard was tragically killed in a road accident whilst driving an agricultural tractor on the A14 road at Creeting on 11th May 1993 aged 46 years. The bungalow was retained by the family and is currently occupied by his widow. Some of the land originally owned by the family was subsequently put into trust.

Summary of Owners/Occupiers
1966 -1968	Charles Spencer Farrow
1968 - 1993	Richard Charles Farrow
1993 -	Diana F Farrow

The DOWER HOUSE
(formerly DOVES HILL FARM) IP6 8RG
TM: 078 561

Fig 5.58 Doveshill Farm at the time of it's sale in 1918.

Fig 5.59 Doveshill Farm in the 1930's.

Fig 5.60 Doveshill Farm c.1949.

Technical Description : Grade II, late mediaeval core with complex 16th century & 17th century alterations. Mainly of two storeys, the cross-wing also with attics. Timber-framed and plastered. Plaintiled roofs with axial and external end chimneys of red brick. 19th century small-pane casements at first storey, 20th century casements at ground storey.

The wing has small-pane 19th century sashes. Two 20th century boarded entrance doors, both with open gabled plaintiled porches on wooden posts. In the centre of the house is a former open hall of 15th century, or possibly late 14th century. Three mutilated trusses, one with a cambered tie-beam. A post is trenched for a passing-brace, probably indicating reuse from a 13th/14th century building. Tension-braced studwork, each stud having prominent assembly marks.

Fig 5.61 A photograph of the house taken in 2000.

Fig 5.62 This delightful photograph taken outside Doveshill Farm is of the Williams and Richardson families after the wedding of Edmund Josiah Arterton Richardson to Ellen Maria (Goody) Williams at Combs Parish Church on Wednesday July 27th 1910. Back row third from left: Robert Williams next to brother Thomas Williams, extreme right back row is John Rodwell George Williams. Standing left, Atabel Williams (née Steggall). First gent is Harry Williams brother of Robert & Thomas. Front row seated: Edmund James Richardson (with baby), Susannah Jane Richardson (parents of the groom). Extreme right are Frederick Williams (another brother of Robert, Thomas and Harry) next to his wife Jenny (nee Chappell). The best man next to groom is probably John Francis Vincent Ternis? and the bride's maid of honour is probably her sister Alice Jane Williams who both appear as witnesses on the wedding certificate. [Photo and names courtesey of Steve Williams]

A hall window, blocked but complete, has square mullions. Complete coupled-rafter roofs, heavily smoke-blackened. The house was extended to left in 16th century, with widely-spaced studwork with long convex-arched windbraces. A parlour wing was added to right c.1600, with plain framing and good wind-braced side-purlin roof; it was extended rearwards in early 19th century. A further rear wing was added to the service end in 17th century. A date of 1604 is associated with the house; this may relate to the parlour wing extension.

History : Situated near the brow of Badley Hill, this was the original farmhouse at Doveshill. It was renamed Doves Thatch in 1966 when the then owner Charles Farrow transfered the name Doveshill Farm to a new bungalow next door and sold off the farmhouse and garden. It is now called The Dower House after an earlier name.

see Chapter 8 for more information regarding this family's occupancy and further pictures of the farm.

Summary of Tenants/Owners (t/o)

The farm was part of the Crowley/Asburnham Estate between 1735 and 1917.

1772	Joseph Ruffel (t)
1830	Scott Thomas (t)
1841-71	George Hayward (t)
1881	George Hammond (t)
1885-1901	William Fuller (farm baliff) (t)
	Chapman Manning (t)
1900-06	James Hazel (t)
1910-17	Frederick Williams (t)
1922-27	Alfred Bywater (o)
1927-45	Francis Emmanuel Haydon (d. May 1945) (o)
1945-51	John Douglas & Beryl Aggiss Haydon (o)
1951-68	Charles Spencer Farrow (o)
1968-93	Richard Charles Farrow (o) (farmland only)
1969	C Aldous (o) (Doves Thatch only)
	L M Wright (Doves Thatch)
1984-1992	Bradley family
1992 (Aug) -	Stephen & Jill Knell (o) (Dower House only)

DOVESHILL BARN
IP6 8RJ
TM: 078 560

Farmhouse   Granary   Original Barn

Fig 5.63 A photograph of Doveshill Farm from the 1917 sales catalogue showing (l. to r.) Doves Hill farmhouse,
the stable or granary (now known as Doves Barn) and the original Doves Barn on the extreme right (see plan Fig 5.65 next page).

Fig 5.64 Protected only by a rusty corrugated iron roof in the 1990's.

Technical Description : A 2200sq ft (approx) Grade II barn, built c.1600 as a stable range or granary of eight bays; extended to left by two bays in 18th century or early 19th century at which time the original building was converted to a barn. Timber-framed and weatherboarded with a little 18th century plasterwork. Corrugated iron roof, thatched until mid 20th century. A central Midstrey added to the north, and a doorway in the east gable in 20th century. Good quality close-studding with tension stud-bracing.

Tie-beams formerly arch-braced, the braces mainly renewed with knees in 18th/19th century. Good side-purlin roof, the lower tier of purlins butted, and the upper tier wind-braced and clasped with reduced principals. All eight bays of the original building were built with an upper floor which was removed in 18th/19th century, but the centre bay has anomalous early alterations including doorways (later blocked) in each side wall. The two later bays retain an upper floor in poor condition.

History : As for Doveshill farm.

In 1996 it was purchased by Paul Rozier who converted the west end of the barn into a self contained two bedroom brick and flint cottage (Fig 5.66 next page).

In April 1997 planning permission was granted for, *"Conversion of redundant barn and outbuildings to two dwellings, including demolition of later single storey extensions, 20th century Midstrey and outbuildings and erection of garaging, provision of private foul drainage system and use of existing vehicular access (with alterations)."* [Mid-Suffolk District Council Planning Application 971/96].

In 2002 the main barn and cottage, along with 2 acres of land, were offered for sale. The guide price was £300,000.

The cottage was subsequently retained by Mr Rozier and the barn sold to Mr Andrew Mexen for conversion into a family home.

This has presented us with a rare opportunity to witness and record the salvage and re-birth of this ancient parish building which for many years risked being the victim of the next gale.

The completed conversion was purchased by Eleanor de Goni-Parkes in 2003.

Fig 5.64a The barn in the centre of an aerial photograph of Doveshill Farm (Spring 1964).
(Photo: Courtesy of Eleanor de Goni-Parkes) (Copyright: www.skyviewsarchives.com & used with permission.)

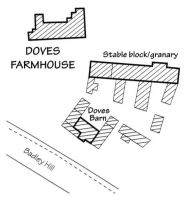

Fig 5.65 Plan showing position of the original barn

Fig 5.66 The western end of the stable block/granary which was converted into a two bedroom brick & flint cottage in the late 1990's.

Fig 5.67 The roof timbers before the removal of the corrugated roof.

Fig 5.68 External resoration December 2002.

Fig 5.69 The roof timbers which originally supported an upper floor and remnants of the partions which divided the bays.

Fig 5.70 General views of the progress of the interior restoration December 2002.

Fig 5.71 January 2003 with the new paintile roof in place and the emerging ground floor extensions.

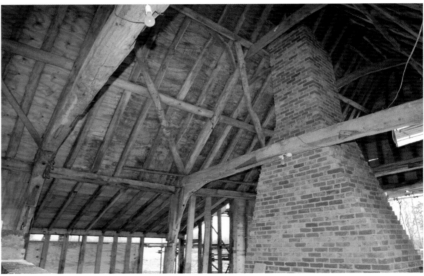

Fig 5.72 January 2003 The freshly-boarded roof, attractive new fireplaces and below left the first two tie-beams which needed replacing.

Fig 5.73 The new south-east elevation.

*Fig 5.74 (above) The family room (left) and (right) a view across the drawing room
towards the Snug showing the open east gallery above.*

Fig 5.75 (above) The kitchen nearing completion and one of the Bedrooms.

Fig 5.76 (top) The view from the east gallery looking towards the west gallery (above, left) the west gallery from the drawing room (above, right) the spiral staircase and ground-floor bathroom entrance.

Fig 5.77 The south elevation showing the completed courtyard.

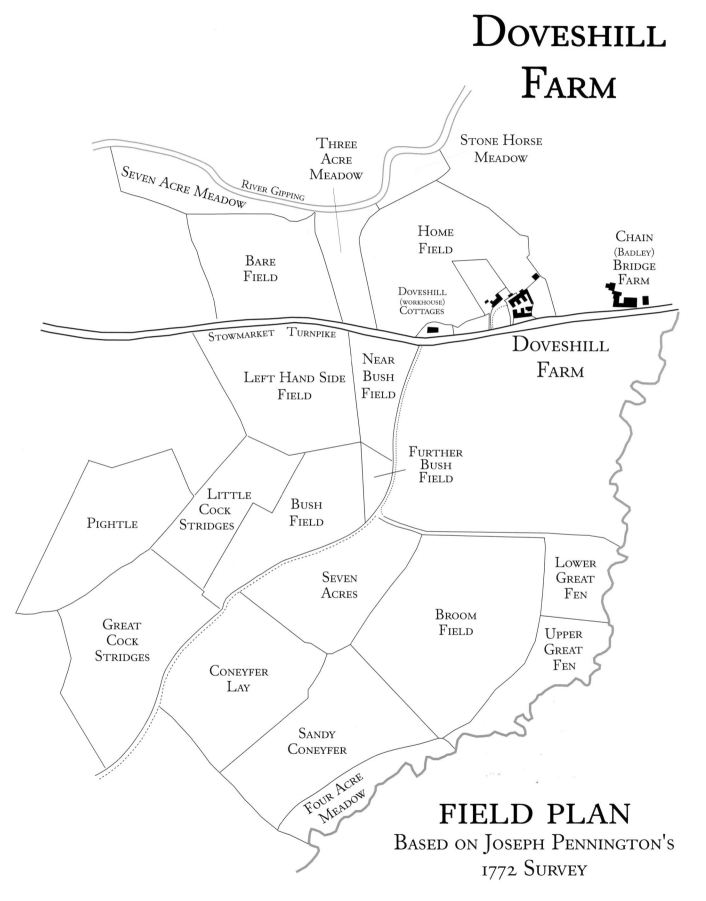

DOVESHILL FARM

STONE HORSE MEADOW

THREE ACRE MEADOW

SEVEN ACRE MEADOW

RIVER GIPPING

HOME FIELD

CHAIN (BADLEY) BRIDGE FARM

BARE FIELD

DOVESHILL (WORKHOUSE) COTTAGES

STOWMARKET TURNPIKE

DOVESHILL FARM

LEFT HAND SIDE FIELD

NEAR BUSH FIELD

FURTHER BUSH FIELD

PIGHTLE

LITTLE COCK STRIDGES

BUSH FIELD

LOWER GREAT FEN

SEVEN ACRES

BROOM FIELD

UPPER GREAT FEN

GREAT COCK STRIDGES

CONEYFER LAY

SANDY CONEYFER

FOUR ACRE MEADOW

FIELD PLAN
BASED ON JOSEPH PENNINGTON'S 1772 SURVEY

Fig 5.78 Doveshill Farm field plan.

THE LAURELS & GRIFFIELDS
Badley Hill IP6 8RJ
TM: 078 560

Fig 5.79 The Laurels (formerly Griffields).

Description & History :   The two modern chalet-bungalows on Doveshill, in-between the former Doveshill and Badley Bridge Farms, were both constructed on behalf of the Beaney family.

The first, *The Laurels* (Fig 5.79 above), was originally called *Griffields* and Peter and Peggy Beaney moved there from the adjacent Badley Bridge Farm in December 1981. Following the death of her husband in 1992, Mrs. Beaney transferred the *Griffields* name to a new chalet-bungalow she had constructed next door in 1995 (Fig 5.80 below).

Since the photograph of The Laurels was taken in 2001, a third garage has been added to the left-hand side.

Summary of Owners

Dec 1981 (new)	Thomas (Peter) & Peggy Beaney (original *Griffields*)
April 1995	Paul & Jacqueline Steady (now *The Laurels*)
April 1995 (new)	Peggy Beaney (the new *Griffields*)

Fig 5.80 Griffields.

BADLEY BRIDGE HOUSE

Badley Bridge Farm (anciently known as Getford Farm)

IP6 8RJ

TM: 079 560

Technical Description : Grade III, late 18th/early 19th century, 'T' plan, two storeys, timber framed, plastered, plaintiles, 3w(s) sashes in flush frames, central glazed-door, pilasters, entablature

History : The farm originally consisted of 111¾ acres plus the house and its garden which are now owned separately, the farm land having been split up and sold off - the water meadows along the river as one lot and the fields by the railway the other. The land across the road now goes with the adjoining piece that was Doveshill land, the farm buildings, originally retained by the owner, have also been sold and one barn has been converted to living accommodation and called Badley Bridge Barn (see page 147).

Until 1969 when Charles Morton sold the farmhouse separately, the property was usually sold together with Ravens Farm which was adjacent to it, but in the Parish of Creeting St Mary.

Summary of Tenants/Owners (t/o)

	Prudence Coleman (wid)
1772	James Christmas (t)
1830	John Kemball (t)
c.1841- July 1869	Thomas Snell Cooper (t)
1885	Labon Southgate (t)
1892-Jan 1917	Abraham Hammond 1892 died Jan 1917 (t)
4 Oct - 11 Dec 1917	Harry Hagon Arnold (o)
12th Dec 1917	A E Fenning (at auction, Lot 13, £2,600) (o)
10th Dec 1918	Robert Dykes Cooper, of Creeting St Mary & Hawks Mill House, Needham Market, miller and corn merchant (o)
1920's	Bilner family
11th Oct 1943	Eric Garnham Hunt (o)
11th Oct 1950	Robert George & Maurice Cyril Meadows, Red House Farm, Rumburgh, nr Halesworth, Sfk. (o)
12th Oct 1953	Maj. Thomas O'Bryen & Elizabeth Yvonne Horsford, Wattisham Castle, Wattisham, Sfk. (o)
6th Oct 1967	Charles & Eileen Morton, Woodlands, Badley (o)
1961-69	G H Lafling (t)
14th Dec 1978	Edward Joseph Garrod, The Lodge, Barking Road, Needham Mkt (outbuildings only) (t)
Apr 1969 - Dec 1981	Thomas Peter B & Peggy Grace Beaney (o)
Dec 1981	Peter and Hedi Marie Clark (o)

Fig 5.81 Badley Bridge Farm.

On WEDNESDAY, September 25th.
At the BRIDGE FARM, BADLEY, Near
Needham Market
WOODWARD and WOODWARD
Will SELL by AUCTION the Live and Dead
FARMING STOCK, comprising:—
5 HORSES, including Chesnut Mare and 2 Chesnut Geldings.
95 Lead of Neat Stock, including 6 Cows.
8 Home-bred Steers and Heifers and Calf.
42 Breeding Sows and Feeding Pigs, and
70 Head of Poultry.
The Dead Stock comprises:—Breasted road waggon, harvest carriage, 3 tumbrils, iron water-cart, McCormick's 5ft. cut binder, Samuelson's 5ft. cut ditto, Samuelson's foot clipper, chaff-cutter, oat and bean mill, 3 ploughs, 3 gangs of harrows, roll, flat iron roll, horse hoe, Smyth's corn drill, horse rake, harness, ladders, troughs and mangers, dairy utensils, and miscellaneous effects, by direction of the Exors. of the late Mr. A. Hammond.
Sale to commence at 2 o'clock punctually.

Fig 5.82 Press advertisement for a farm sale at Bridge farm following the death of the tenant Abraham Hammond in 1917.

BRIDGE FARM BADLEY

At the Bridge Farm, Badley, near Needham Market Station, on Wednesday, Messrs. Woodward and Woodward, by direction of the Exors. of the late Mr. A. Hammond, disposed of the farming stock and effects. Ransomes' iron Y.L. plough sold at £6, a gang of three Bedford harrows at £5 10s, a heavy cylinder flat iron roll (Warren) at £6, a horse hoe frame (Warren,) at £7 5s, Smyth's 8-coulter drill at £12, McCormick's binder at £51, a road waggon at £29, a harvest carriage at £12, and an iron water-cart at £12 10s.

A chesnut gelding made 97gns, and a chesnut mare 44gns. Neat stock sold as follows:—Roan shorthorn cow 37gns, light roan shorthorn cow 34gns, red-and-white polled cow 49gns, light roan shorthorn cow 42gns, white-and-black shorthorn cow 46gns, two home-bred heifers sold at £21 10s each, a home-bred heifer and home-bred steer at £16 10s each. Breeding sows made from £30 to £15 ; four young sows sold at £5 10s per head, and three at £5 2s each. Thirty-one feeding pigs ran up to 80s each, and hens and chickens to 7s 6d each.

The chief buyers were Messrs. A.. Bywater, F. Burton, S. Fulcher, J. and W. Freeman, J. B. Williamson, M. G. Hale, Cornell, F. Williams, C. N. Gooderham, J. Quinton, and others.

Fig 5.83 Press report on the sale.

Fig 5.84 Photograph in auctioneers' catalogue for 1917 sale.

BADLEY BRIDGE FARM

ACREMAN'S MEADOW

FIVE ACRE FEN

HORSE FEN

THREE ACRE FEN

LONG MEADOW

RIVER GIPPING

ALDERCROFT

FIVE ACRE MEADOW

PIT PIECE

SEVEN ACRES

SIX ACRES

EIGHT ACRES

NONSUCH PIECE

CAUSEWAY MEADOW

CALVE PIGHTLE

PEAR TREE PIECE

DOVES HILL FARM

THE CROFT

BADLEY BRIDGE

TURNPIKE

STOWMARKET

GATEFORD MEADOW

BRIDGE FARM

HILL PIGHTLE

THE LAY

GIBBS HILL

GATEFORD FEN

FIELD PLAN
BASED ON JOSEPH PENNINGTON'S 1772 SURVEY

Fig 5.85 Badley Bridge Farm field plan.

BRIDGE BARN
IP6 8RJ
TM: 080 559

Fig 5.86 Badley Bridge Barn prior to conversion (Photos Fig 5.86 and 87: Andrew & Janette Smith).

Fig 5.87 Badley Bridge Barn soon after conversion (above) and with established gardens in 2005 (below).

160mm

64mm

Eric Garnham Hunt owned Bridge Farm, Badley, between Oct 1943 and Oct 1950. In addition to normal farming activities, he established a dairy businesss and this half-pint milk bottle found during the conversion of the Bridge Barn dates from this period.

Fig 5.88 This milk bottle, discovered during the restoration of the barn, is probably the only survivng evidence of Eric Garnham Hunt's Badley milk business.

History : Situated close to Badley bridge, this barn was originally an outbuilding of Bridge Farm and last used as a piggery. The date 1846 written on one of the roof beams probably indicates the construction date.

In 1997, it was purchased separately in a derelict state from Mr. & Mrs C. I. Morton of the Woodlands, Badley and tastefully converted into a family home by the present owners Andrew & Janette Smith.

Summary of Tenants/Owners (t/o)
Pre 1997   as Badley Bridge Farm (page 145)
1997 -   Andrew & Janette Smith (o)

Chapter Six

The
POLEYS
of Badley

The POLEY'S[1] of Badley
(Lords of the Manor of Badley c.1491 -1714)

ARMS:
Or, a lion rampant Sable, collared and chained Or.

MOTTO:
Fortior est qvi se - *"Who is clever than himself"*

THE direct descendants of the Poleys of Badley can be traced through nine generations. In this Chapter, a section, together with the relevant part of the family tree, is devoted to each generation. The founder of each generation is numbered on the tree and in the text to aid identification.

ORIGIN OF THE NAME:

Pool(e), local name meaning pool or tidal stream (Old English); surname found in Somerset - Dorset and also places in Cheshire and Gloucestershire. Also as a first name from the biblical Latin paulus 'small', the name taken by Saul of Tarsus on his conversion; however, not common as a first name in medieval England and oddly unpopular for dedication of churches (save with Peter). Usual pronunciation was Pole or Pool (spelt Poul).

ORIGINS OF THE FAMILY:

Whilst it appears there were already other Poley families established in the County, for example at Yoxford[2], our branch began in the reign of Richard II (1377-99) with the arrival in Suffolk of Thomas Poley(1) who lived at or near Codreth[3], Hertfordshire, aka *Thomas Poley of Walsingham*[4]. Unfortunately it has not been possible to establish his background with clarity.

It has been suggested that his ancestors took their name from Polheye, a town said to have existed in Hertfordshire. The earliest recorded member of the family is possibly Sir Humphrey de Poley, who in the reign of Henry I (1107), bore arms - *Argent, on a bend Gules, three cross crosslets Or.* The Pipe Roll for Essex & Hertfordshire of 2 John (1200) also mentions a Richard de Polhia. From them it is presumed that the above mentioned Thomas Poley was descended.

Exchequer papers at the Public Record Office (Ref: E 40/991, 999 & 1171) refer to a William Poley (1325) & John Poley (1356) both of Buntynford (Hertfordshire). Earlier still, E 40/1172, covering the period 1302-1316, has a William de Poleye witnessing a land grant. Another grant by King Edward III to a Thomas de Poley in 1351 of the Manor of Little Stanbrigge in Hertfordshire could also well refer to the same family.

Thomas married twice. The descendants of his first marriage to Maud(e) (*alias* Alice, in some accounts)[5] Gestringham (1a) (sometimes given as Gislingham) the daughter and heir of John Gestringham, recorded in the *Visitations of Suffolk* as of Stuston, Suffolk, became the lords of the manors of Badley and Columbine. Those of his second marriage to Anne Badwell (1b), the daughter and heir of Thomas Badwell of Boxted, Sfk., succeeded at Boxted, the senior seat (see Chapter Eleven).

Both branches of the family used the same arms i.e. Or, a lion ramp Sa. However, in a manuscript *"De Nobilitate"* Sir Humphrey de Poley, the assumed ancestor of Thomas Poley, bore *"Ar. on a bend Gu. three crosslet Or"* to which was afterwards added *"on a canton Or, a lion ramp Sa"* (Fig 6.2 next page).

This ancient bearing was evidently discontinued and the canton assumed as the coat, but not without dispute. An authentic record recites, *"this bearing noticed as the ancient coat of the Earls of Flanders, by Count Maurice of Nassau, Prince of Orange, and Henry, Earl in the Netherland army, who pretended to descend from the Earl of Flanders, then had some discourse and questions with*

Notes :

1 **Poley:** In documents dated in 1485, Simon Poley of Badley wrote his name Powley and in other instances the family's surname was spelt Powle.

2 **Yoxford:** The Wills of Robert Poley (1558) and Henry (1586) of Yoxford, Sfk., are given in *J J Muskett's Suffolk Manorial Families (1900)* page 238

3 **Codreth:** one of a number of variant names for Cottered, in the Odsey Hundred of Hertfordshire

4 **Thomas of Walsingham:** Thos Walsingham was a Benedictine historian who died c.1422. Although unlikely to be the same person, the Hertfordshire connection and comparable dates make him worthy of note, if only for elimination purposes. He is supposed to have been a native of Walsingham, Norfolk. He was educated at St. Albans Abbey and having become a monk there was made precentor and placed in charge of the scriptorium. Little is known of his life beyond his historical work and the fact that in 1394 he was made Superior of the dependent priory of Wymondham, remaining there until 1409, when he returned to St. Albans. *(Source : The Catholic Encyclopedia)* See also page 153.

5 The Dandy Pedigree (see Appendix G, page 341) adds a third variation to the christian name of Thomas' first wife, that of Matilda.

```
┌─────────────────┐   ┌─────────────────┐   ┌─────────────────┐   ┌─────────────┐
│      - 1a -     │   │      - 1 -      │   │      - 1b -     │   │     iii     │
│ MAUDE (AKA ALICE)│   │  THOMAS POLEY   │   │      Anne       │   │   ABELEYN   │
│   GISLINGHAM    │   │  of Codreth, Herts.│ │    BADWELL      │   │    POLEY    │
│                 │   │  died before May1447│ │ of Boxted Hall, Sfk.│ │  died s.p.  │
└─────────────────┘   └─────────────────┘   └─────────────────┘   └─────────────┘
```

i		ii	iii		iv		i		ii
RICHARD POLEY of Stoke Ash	MARGARET BLYANT of Thorndon	JOHN POLEY 2nd son, ob, s.p.*	ANNE POLEY	NICHOLAS LOVELL Gent	ROSE POLEY		THOMAS POLEY	ALICE ROKEHILL of Wormingford, Essex	ANNE POLEY died s.p.

Fig 6.1 POLEYS of Stoke Ash - FAMILY TREE 1ˢᵗ GENERATION

(Poleys of Boxted)

* recorded in The Visitation of Suffolk 1561 as 'a pryst'

Sir John Poley†, who gave so good satisfaction that it did rightly belong to him, as that they have never after made script touching the same" († of the Boxted branch)

Fig 6.2 The ancient Poley bearing

The Poleys in their different branches were for many generations among the principal gentry of Suffolk.

Separating the two branches (Boxted & Badley) has often proved difficult, when a Poley name is found with little or no supporting information. This is especially so with occurrences at Bury St. Edmunds where both branches of the family appear to have resorted to and London where several of them were married and had property.

Thomas Poley (1) and his first wife Maud resided at Stoke Ash and held the manor of Woodham *or* Woodhall¹. Thomas held his first court there in 21 Rich. III (1397). Their son Richard Poley (2) married Margaret Blyant (2a), the eldest daughter of Simon Blyant from the adjoining manor

of Thorndon, Suffolk. However, it was not until 1451 when another son Simon(3) married Margaret (sometimes refered to as Margery) Alcocke (3a), daughter and coheiress with her sister Elizabeth, of Edmund Alcocke, lord of the manor of Badley, that they gained their first foothold there. (¹ next page)

Simon Poley died on 13th October 1485 at Badley and was buried there. His father-in-law, Edmund Alcocke died six years later in February 1491 and Margaret Poley (née Alcocke) died the following year with her Badley inheritance passing safely on to her son and heir, Henry Poley. Henry's only brother was Edmund, the first in a number of succeeding generations to bear this name and confuse genealogists! *(see Edmund Alcocke's Will Appendix D, page 301)*

The Alcockes, Simon Poley and his wife were all buried at Badley, although the whereabouts of their graves is unknown. Little could they have known that their descendants were to remain lords of the manor of Badley for the next two hundred and fifteen years *(see Chapter 3, page 52)*.

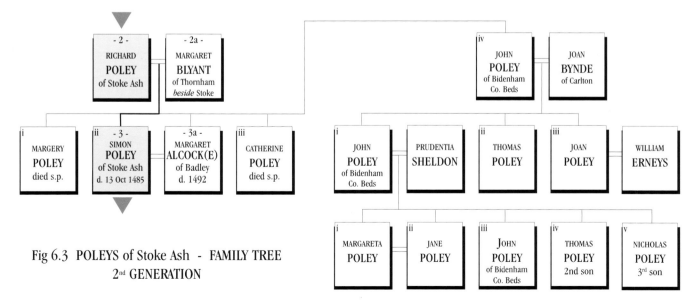

					iv	
- 2 - RICHARD POLEY of Stoke Ash	- 2a - MARGARET BLYANT of Thornham *beside Stoke*				JOHN POLEY of Bidenham Co. Beds	JOAN BYNDE of Carlton

i	ii - 3 -	- 3a -	iii		i		ii	iii	
MARGERY POLEY died s.p.	SIMON POLEY of Stoke Ash d. 13 Oct 1485	MARGARET ALCOCK(E) of Badley d. 1492	CATHERINE POLEY died s.p.		JOHN POLEY of Bidenham Co. Beds	PRUDENTIA SHELDON	THOMAS POLEY	JOAN POLEY	WILLIAM ERNEYS

i	ii	iii	iv	v
MARGARETA POLEY	JANE POLEY	JOHN POLEY of Bidenham Co. Beds	THOMAS POLEY 2nd son	NICHOLAS POLEY 3rd son

Fig 6.3 POLEYS of Stoke Ash - FAMILY TREE 2ⁿᵈ GENERATION

Manor of Woodham (Woodhall) Stoke Ash

The parish of Stok' (Stoke) Ash comprised of two manors Stoke Hall (with Thorpe) and Woodham, later called Woodall.

How Thomas Poley came by the Woodhall manor by 1397 is unclear. Was it by outright purchase or perhaps through his marriage to local spinster Maud Gislingham?

As the table opposite shows, although the Poleys had inherited the Manor of Badley from the Alcockes by 1492, they retained ownership in the Manor of Woodhall, Stoke Ash, which they had already held for nearly 100 years, for a further 148 years. It was sold to accord with the wishes of Edmond Poley (d.1640) to ensure sufficient funds for the legacies and annuities devised in his will *(reproduced Appendix D)* which he feared might not be met by his Badley holdings.

"Therefore my will and mind is, that my Manor of Woodhall in Stoke Ash in the County of Suffolk with all and singular the land and tenements thereunto belonging both free and copy which are called or known by the name of Combes Land or by any other name or names whatsoever with all rights members and appertances belonging or appertaining to the said Manor situate lying extending and being in Stoke Ash aforesaid Thwaite, Thornham, Wickham Skeith or any other town or towns adjoining to them shall be sold within convenient time after my death to raise money for performance of this my will."

Fig 6.5 Wood Hall Farm, Stoke Ash (photo - courtesy Suffolk R.O.)

A Wood Hall farm still exists at Stoke Ash (Map Ref: TM 108699) and this is assumed to be the location or locality of the Poleys former manor house.

Manor of Woodhall, Stoke Ash

A.D.	Reign	Manor held by
1206	8 John	Eustace de Geradville (Gererdeuill) conveyed by fine & carucate and a half of land to Wm de Gerardville
1210	12 John	Wm de Gerardville passed by fine this advowson to the Prior of Eye Thomas de Gerardville
1270	54 Hen III	Wm de Gerardville, son & heir, conveyed the advowson by fine to the Prior of Eye, Sir John Gerardville
1397	21 Rich II	Thomas Poley, 1st Court (dead by May 1447) Richard Poley of Badley Esqr., son & heir Simon Poley Esqr., son & heir (died 1485)
1485	I Hen VII	Henry Poley, Esqr. (died 1487)
1487	3 Hen VII	Edmund Poley (died 1548) (IPM 3 Edw VI 127)
1548	1 Edw VI	John Poley (died 1589)
1589	32 Eliz I	Richard Poley (died 14 Feb 1592)
1592	34 Eliz I	Edmund Poley (died 1640)
1640	15 Chas I	Sir Edmund Poley Knt
1646	21 Chas I	Edmund Hervey Esqr., of Wickham Skeith by purchase for £2,800 on 30th Jan. 1st Court 1648 (died 1664)

Based on 'On the Parish and Parish Church of All Saints, Stoke Ash' by Rev W H Sewell (1874). The same publication gives -
1439 January 21 JOHN POLEY, Rector of Stoke Ash, on the presentation of the Prior and Covent of Eye

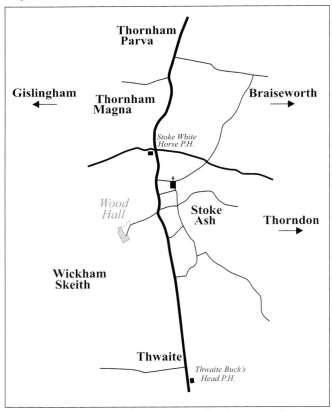

Fig 6.4 Map showing location of Wood Hall Farm, Stoke Ash

The following quitclaim both enlightens and confuses the situation regarding the *first* Thomas Poley's connections with Walsingham, Norfolk.

"To all faithful Christians to whom this present writing comes, Richard Poley of Stoke Assh in the county of Suffolk, gentleman, son and heir of Thomas Poley esquire deceased late of Little Walsyngham in the county of Norfolk, and Alice his wife and Rose Poley daughter of the said Thomas Poley and Anne his wife daughter of Thomas Badwell late of Boxstede in the county of Suffolk esquire deceased Greetings in the eternal Lord. Known you I the aforesaid Richard Poley, and me the aforesaid Rose Poley in my unmarried state and legally empowered have remissed etc to Thomas Poley of Boxstede aforesaid the brother of us the aforesaid Richard Poley and Rose and Alice, the daughter of Gatford Rokell esquire and the heirs of, Thomas Poley of Boxstede our father all right etc which we ever had etc., in the manor of Boxstede, etc., Dated the 8th of May in the 25th year of the reign of King Henry the sixth after the conquest", i.e. 1447. (SRO HA 519/81/13) (Acknowledgement: Anthony Breen for translation.)

Made after the death of their father, the *first* Thomas, it tells us that Richard Poley of Stoke Ash and his unmarried sister Rose, renounced their interest in the manor of Boxted to their younger brother Thomas Poley and his wife Alice (née Rokell). This Thomas was the product of their father's second marriage to Ann Badwell of Boxted.

The manor of Boxted had been owned by Thomas Badwell and passed to his son in law, the *first* Thomas Poley in the right of his wife Anne, the daughter of Thomas Badwell, on his death or possibly at the time of her marriage. The gift may have specified that they, Thomas Poley and Anne, were to hold the manor for the benefit of their children. Following the death of the *first* Thomas Poley, the manor passed to his youngest son Thomas and this could have been contested by his elder brother and sister Richard and Rose.

We should be able to rely on this Mediaeval deed as an accurate source of genealogical information. So, did the *first* Thomas Poley live at Little Walsingham before moving to Stoke Ash, or did he move there upon his marriage to Ann Badwell, only moving to Boxted upon her father's death?

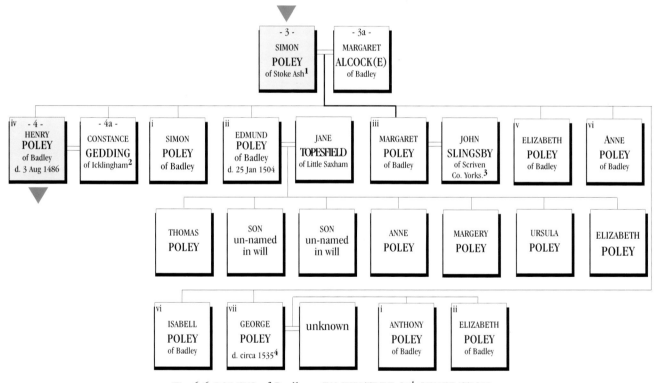

Fig 6.6 POLEYS of Badley - FAMILY TREE 3rd GENERATION

Notes:

1 Died 3rd October 1485 ~ see Chapter 3, page 52.
2 After Henry's death she married John Alleyn, Baron of the Exchequer; of London, Bury St Edmunds and Icklingham and thirdly John Woodhouse.

3 Mortally wounded at the Battle of Flodden Field, Branxton, Northumberland died 16 Sept 1513.
4 Will dated 31 Oct 1535 and proved 28 Mar 1536.

From this time Badley became firmly established as the residence of this branch, although it appears by Inquisition 3 Henry VII. 327, Henry Poley, the son and heir of Simon and Margaret above, already possessed a 'Close called Kyesfield' parcel of Badley Manor, worth 53s. 4d., held by fealty and knight service. The manor was at this time stated to be worth 20 marks and was held by the service of half a knight's fee *(Inquisition 8 Henry VII. 806)(i.e. 1492)*.

Their son and heir Henry Poley (4), the second great grandson of Thomas and Maude Poley, carried the Badley line through to the next generation. He married Constance Geddinge (4a), a daughter and co-heir of William Geddinge (d. 4th Nov. 1457) of Icklingham, Sfk., who was a Lord in Edward IV's reign and the owner of the manor of Little Bradley.

This marriage added Little Bradley to the Poleys portfolio, which was retained by their son and heir *(the second)* Edmund Poley (5) (d. 31st. Dec. 1548) who married Mirabel Garneys (5a) (d. 25th Feb. 1558), the daughter of John Garneys of Kenton, Suffolk.

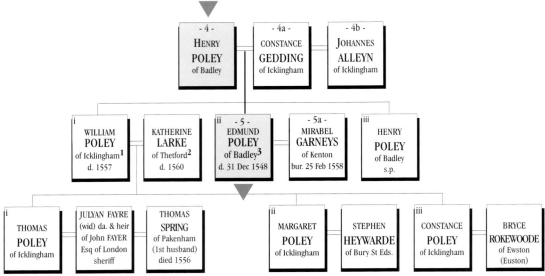

Fig 6.7 POLEYS of Badley and Icklingham - FAMILY TREE 4th GENERATION

Notes:

1 Held the manor of Thamhill in Icklingham. Will dated 3rd October 1540 *(L. Doose. f. 144)*. Reproduced Appendix D, page 287.

2 Will dated 1560 *(L. Paynter. f. 173)*. Proved at Bury St Edmunds 31st January 1560. Executor Thomas Poley (son).

3 Will dated 30th July 1548 *(31 Populwell)*. Reproduced Appendix D, page 301.

In *The Annalls of Ipswche* (Nathaniell Bacon - 1645) published by subscription in 1884, the entry on page 241 appears to refer to Thomas, the son of William and Katherine (née Larke), born 1529. It reads -

"1 Mar: Munday after Palm Sunday [Mar. 19. 1554]
Clement Higham Esqr, one of the Privy Councill to the Queene, and Tho : Pooley Esqr,*(d)* elected Burgesses for this Towne at the next Parli'mt, at Oxenford, 2 Apr: next"

However, despite the fact that all available pedigrees for the Boxted branch of the family indicate there were no Thomas Poleys at the material time, the note accompanying this entry is less sure, viz -

(d) The Family of Pooley or Poley was of Boxsted and Badley, Suff. The authorities quoted give copious pedigrees and notes, but do not distinctly indicate the Tho : Pooley here named. Hervey's Vis. Suff. (Howard) i. 269, &c. Add. MSS, (Davy) 19,145, and (Jermyn) 8213. Harl. 1449, f. 18; ff. 11, 12, 29. Arms : or, a lion ramp. sa.

In his book "*Tudor & Stuart Suffolk*" (2001), Gordon Blackwood, refering to Suffolk puritan gentry joining Lord Leicester's expedition in 1585 to fight for the Protestant cause in the Low Countries, says they were joined by "the veteran West Suffolk Protestant Thomas Poley of Icklingham" (d.1589).

An Epitaph vpon the death of Master Poolies wife of Badly

by James Yates, servingman:
[from The Castell of Courtesie (1582)]

You Dames leaue off your bootlesse teares,
Whose vaine complaintes can do no good,
Since cruell Death hath forc'd your feares,
And stroken such a noble bloud.
And though you waile and weepe your fill,
Yet you can not reuiue your will.
For if high Ioue doth so permit,
That Dreedfull Death shall strike with dart,

It is in vaine to mourne for it,
Sith he can ioy, and he can smart:
He can graunt life, he can graunt death,
He can bereaue each Prince of breath.
This worthie Matron wrapt in clay,
Was wife to Master Pooly she:
Whose noble race for to display,
My witte vnable is I see.

Alas my penne is nothing ryfe,
For to Declare her vertuouse lyfe.
Wherefore twere vaine to pen her praise,
Sith it abrode in world is knowne.
Alas, that death did end her dayes,
And hath her life so ouerthrowne.
Wherefore to mourne, it is in vaine,
Since you no more her can attaine.

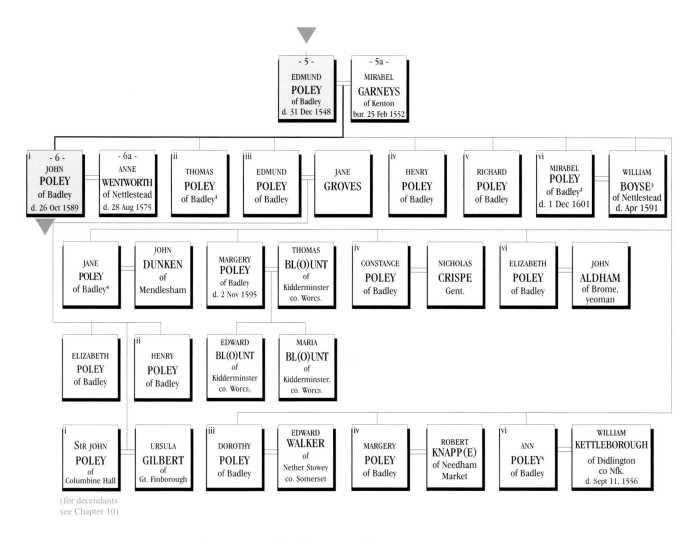

Fig 6.8 POLEYS of Badley - FAMILY TREE 5th GENERATION

Notes:

1. May have been the '*Mr. Thomas Poley was buryed the 5 day of September*' recorded in the register of St Nicholas, Little Saxham in 1597.

2. Mirabel died on 1st December 1601 and was buried in the Chancel at St Mary's, Badley the following day as 'Mrs Boys widdowe' (see Appendix A, page 232).

3. Sometimes written as Bois. See Appendix E, page 319.

4. Said to have been buried at Mendlesham, Sfk., along with her husband in early 1564.

5. This union produced one son William and eight daughters, see page 57 *East Anglian Pedigrees* - Arthur Campling FSA (Harleian Soc. 1945).

Upon the deaths of Edmund and Mirabel, all property passed to their son and heir John Poley (d. 26th Oct. 1589) who married Anne (d. 28th Aug. 1575) the eldest daughter of the Baron, Thomas, 1st. Lord Wentworth of Nettlestead, Suffolk. He evidently sold Little Bradley to John Hunte in 1565.

Their third son *(the third)* Edmund Poley married Jane Groves, the daughter of Thomas Groves. Their son Sir John

Poley was a veteran of the Elizabethan wars and had by 1611 purchased Columbyne Hall, Stowupland from the Earl of Monmouth *(see Chapter Ten)*.

The poem opposite is attributed to amongst others, James Yates, a Suffolk poet who was probably a servant of Henry Reynolds of Belstead. (A marginal note specifies that Mrs Poley was "the sister of my Lady Wentworth").

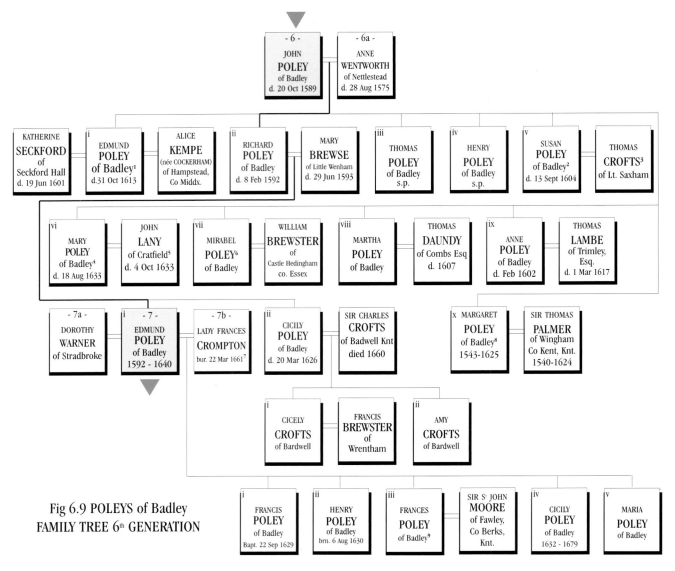

Fig 6.9 POLEYS of Badley
FAMILY TREE 6th GENERATION

Notes:

1 married 2nd wife on 17 Sept. 1601 at Gissing, Nfk. She was the relict of Richard Kempe of Flordon, Nfk. (see Robert Kempe's Will, Appendix D, page 301.
2 For Crofts - read also Croft, Crofte or Croftes.
3 Died at Badley, buried at Lt Saxham on 14 Sept. 1604.
4 Married at Badley on 14th May 1574. This was a double wedding see 6 below.

5 He was Recorder of Ipswich, see page 170.
6 Married at Badley on 14th May 1574. This was a double wedding see 4 above.
7 Lady Frances Crompton née Croftes.
8 See Appendix G, page 333.
9 Married in London by Licence issued by the Bishop of London Dec. 28 1661.

The Annalls of Ipswche (page 373)
"35 El: (Tuesday), 28 August [1593]

mr Edm: Poley shall be retained to be of Councill wth this Towne, and shall have 40s yerely for his fee"

In the notes accompanying this entry it says,
"Son and heir of John Poley, Esq., of Badley. He was admitted at Grays Inn in 1563, and was called to the Bar and became an Ancient in 1574, and Reader in 1587; he died s.p. and was bur. at Badley 31 Oct 1613 ; where there is a monument to him, with insc. in Latin. vid sup. p.241; Harl. 1912. f. 179." (See Chapter 3, Fig 3.62)

The descendency of the manor of Badley continued through John and Ann Poley's son and heir Richard. He married

Mary, the daughter of Sir John Brewse, Knt., of Little Wenham, Suffolk.

Richard Poley died on 14th Feb 1592 and his wife Mary on 29th Jun the following year 1593. Their only son and heir (the fourth) Edmund Poley (Aug 1592 - Sep 1640), married firstly Dorothy Warner, the daughter of Anthony Warner of Stradbroke and Parham, Suffolk on 12th Oct 1613 and secondly Frances Croftes, the 2nd daughter of Sir John Croftes of Little Saxham, Suffolk, who was the widow of Sir John Crompton, Knt., of Skerne, Yorks. (i.e. she was Dame Frances Crompton).

Edmund's only sister Cicily (May 1591 - 20th March 1626) married Sir Charles Croft(e)s, Knt., of Bardwell, Suffolk. The 'Bardwell Croftes' being a branch of the main family seated at Little Saxham *(see Chapter 7)*. They had two daughters Cicely and Amy. Cicely married Francis Brewster of Wrentham. Her mother tragically died giving birth to their third child aged 36, and is buried at Bardwell church where there is a wall monument in her memory (see Fig 6.23).

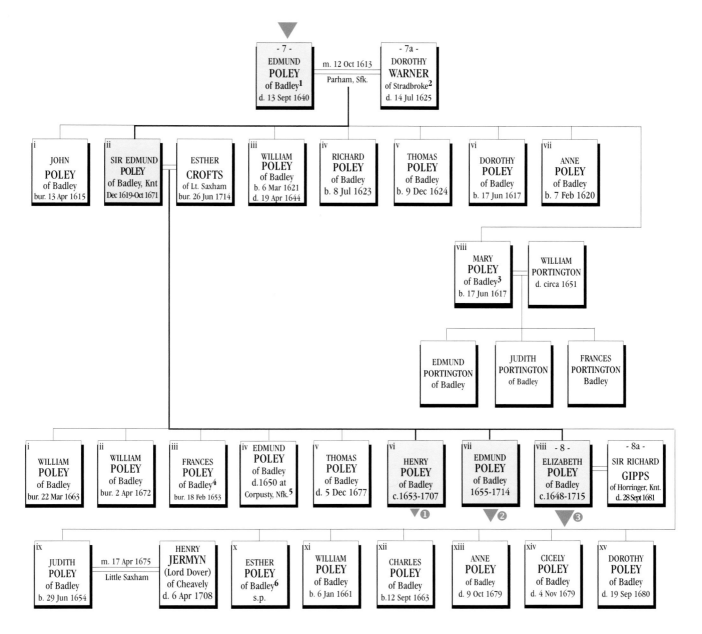

Fig 6.10 POLEYS of Badley - FAMILY TREE 7th GENERATION

Notes:

1 Contributed one horse in 1599 for service of the King in Essex. Was included in a list of 46 Justices of the Peace for Suffolk in Dec 1602.
   (see "*Suffolk in the XVIIth Century ~ The Breviary of Suffolk*" by Robert Reyce (1618), pages 84 and 89.

2 Also of Parham, Suffolk, she was the daughter of Anthony Warner. The Burial Register entry reads, "*1625, Mrs Dorothy Poley wife of Mr Edmund Poley dyed Juli 14th between 2 and 3 in the morning & was buried between 10 & 11 at night*".

3 Born at Marlesford the same day as her sister Dorothy (7v), buried in the chancel at Badley on 11 March 1690 as Mrs.Portington. (see also the Will of her brother Thomas Poley (1677) Appendix D, page 301).

4 Baptised at Little Saxham on 22 September 1629 and buried at there on 18 February 1653.

5 Buried at Corpusty church, Norfolk, small plaque inscribed "Here lyeth the body of Edmund Poley sone of Sr Edmund Poley of Badley in the County of Suffolk Knight etc., Sept. 4 1650 (aged 11 months, 5 days).

6 Buried at Little Saxham 17 March 1657.

There were four other instances of marriage between these two families - see Chapter 7.

Edmund had thirteen children - eight by his first marriage and a further five by his second.

In 1632 it is recorded that Edmund Poley of Badley Hall, held a licence from the Archbishop of Canterbury to eat meat in Lent, provided he gave 6/8d per annum to the poor. The manor succeeded through his son *(the fifth)* Sir Edmund Poley, Knt., (Dec 1619 - Oct 1671) a product of his first marriage to Dorothy Warner.

SIR EDMUND POLEY Knt. (16th Dec 1619 - 22nd Oct 1671)
Sir Edmund was born at Badley Hall, although some accounts say it was at Bury St Edmunds. He was educated at Pembroke College, Camb. (1635) and gained a B.A. there in 1638. The same year he entered Grays Inn, London. In 1640 he inherited Badley from his father and in c.1651 he copied him, in that he also married into the Croft(e)s family of Little Saxham. His bride was Esther Crofts (d. 22 June 1714), the daughter of Sir Henry Crofts. Knt., and heir of William Croftes. The couple produced a grand total of fifteen children - eight males and seven females. Unfortunately their infant mortality was high and with none of the males who survived to adulthood evidently marrying, their eldest daughter Elizabeth, born circa 1648, outlived them all to inherit the manor.

The Civil War 1642-46
From the moment that Charles I raised his standard at Nottingham in August 1642, people throughout the country were forced to choose which side they were on. In Chapter Five of his book *'Tudor and Stuart Suffolk'*, dealing with the first Civil War, Gordon Blackwood discusses 'allegiance and activities' and concludes that during the first Civil War the Suffolk gentry were probably neutral. i.e. the County was neither predominantly Parliamentarian nor Royalist

The Poleys were staunch Catholics and along with most nobles, gentry and about half of all Members of Parliament they supported the Royalist cause. The King's supporters were called *Cavaliers* (see Fig 6.12) because many of them fought on horseback. They were distinguished by their elaborate dress, with lace ruffles, feathers, and velvet, in contrast to the sober attire of the *Roundheads*.

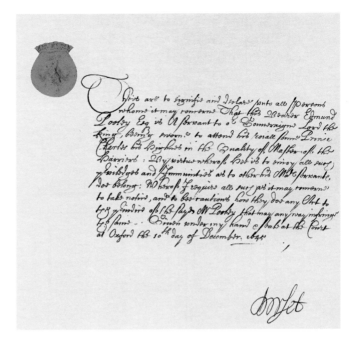

"This are to signifie and declare unto all Persons whom it may concern That this Bearer Edmund Poley Esq is a servante to our Souveraigne Lord the king, beeing sworne to attend his roiall sonne Prince Charles his Highness in the Quality of Master of the Harriers : By virtue whereof Hee is to enioy all such priviledges and Immunities as to other his Majesties servantes doe belong : Whereof I require all such as it may concerne to take notice, and to bee cautious how they doe any Act to the p(re)judice of the sayd Mr Poley that may any way infringe the same. Given under my hand and Seale at the Court at Oxford the 10th day of December 1645

Fig 6.11 Memorandum dated 10th December 1645 signed at the Court at Oxford declaring Sir Edmund Poley of Badley 'Master of the Harriers' to Prince Charles. This and Fig 6.13 are based on monochrome copies provided courtesy of The James Marshall & Marie-Louise Osborn Collection, Beinecke Rare Book & Manuscript Library, Yale University, USA, indicate the status Sir Edmund Poley enjoyed during the reigns of Charles I & II (1625-84).

Fig 6.12 A Cavalier.

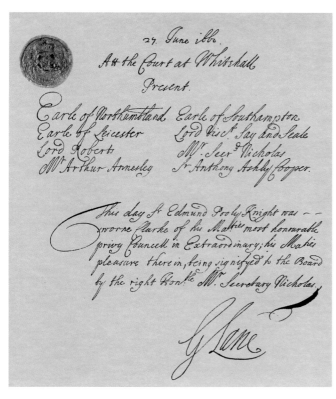

27 June 1660
At the Court at Whitehall
Present

Earle of Northumbland	Earle of Southampton
Earle of Leicester	Lord Visc^t Lay & Seale
Lord Roberts	Mr Secr^y Nicholas
Mr Arthur Annesley	Sr Anthony Ashley Cooper

This day Sr Edmund Pooly Knight was ~ /
sworne Clarke of his Maj^ties most honourable /
privy Councell in Extraordinary; his Maj^ties /
pleasure therein, being signifyed to the Board /
by the right Honble Mr Secretary Nicholas /

G Lane

Fig 6.13 Memorandum dated 27th June 1660 signed at the Court at Whitehall appointing Sir Edmund Poley of Badley 'Clerk Extraordinary of the Privy Council.'

Notes:

Clerks of the Privy Council
The Clerks of the Privy Council were appointed by the Crown and entered office on taking an oath at the council board. In the course of time there came to be a distinction between clerks in ordinary and clerks extraordinary. In the case of clerks in ordinary appointments were embodied in letters patent under the great seal which granted them the office with a salary at the receipt of the exchequer; Clerks Extraordinary, on the other hand, received no patent and no salary.

Clerks Extraordinary 1660-1811
Between 1660 and 1811 there were a varying number of Clerks Extraordinary of the Council. They were appointed by the Crown and admitted in the council in the same manner as the Clerks in Ordinary. The number of extraordinaries was never fixed and fluctuated considerable. Because they were unpaid it is not always possible to establish their periods of service precisely.

(Acknowledgement: Institute of Historical Research)

Edmund fought in the King's army at Oxford and surrendered there, but not before his loyalty had been rewarded with a knighthood on 11th April 1646 (he was the only Badley-based Poley knight).

He was actively involved in politics at a national level. *'The History of Parliament The Houses of Commons* 1660-1690' by Basil Duke Henning 1983 (pages 256-7), provides us with a good insight into Sir Edmund's activities as the member of Parliament for Bury St. Edmunds from 1661 until Oct 1671 (a month before his death).

For example, he was appointed to no less than "169 committees, including the committees on elections and privileges in eight sessions, and acted as teller in seven divisions"; "On 28 March 1670 he reported from committee the bill for repairing Yarmouth pier" and " took a leading role in the bill to prevent frauds in the sale of cattle." The same publication lists his other public offices, viz :

"J.p. Suff. 1643-6, July 1660-d., Sudbury 1664; commr. for oyer and terminer, Norfolk circuit July 1660, assessment, Suff. and Bury St. Edmunds Aug. 1660-9; dep. lt. Suff. c. Aug. 1660-d., commr. for loyal and indigent officers 1662, complaints, Bedford level 1663; sub-commr. for prizes, London 1665-7; searcher of customs, Kent 1667-?d.; receiver of taxes, Norf. and Hunts. 1667-g; commr. for appeals, Bedford level 1668."
Clerk extraordinary to PC by 1660-?d.; commr. for union with Scotland 1670-1."

Continuing to support the Royalist cause while Cromwell's soldiers gradually gained the 'upper-hand' was a very risky business as Sir Edmund was to discover in 1646 when he fell foul of the *Committee for the Sequestration of Delinquents' Estates*, set up in 1643 to confiscate the lands of those who were taking the Royalist side in the Civil War. By wisely confessing his guilt and repledging his loyalty to the Commonwealth, he probably avoided the loss of his estate and was allowed to compound in proportion to his guilt (i.e. he agreed to be assessed a fine in lieu of prosecution).

The Committee's record shows, "Sir Edmund Poley of Badley in Suffolk begs to compound on Oxford articles for his delinquency in bearing arms against the Parliament. Noting that he, Sir Edmund, presented a pass on the 20th June under Fairfax's hand, and took the oath and convenient 7th Sept. 1646. Sir Edmund Poley is fined a tenth of his possessions viz £728. 3rd November 1646. (*State Papers - Committee for Compounding*. Edited by Anne Everett Green, and published under the direction of the Master of the Rolls with the sanction of Her Majesty's Secretary of State. Pt 2, p1475) The fine indicates Sir Edmund's estate was valued at £7,280, a considerable sum of money in 1646 and the equivalent of over a quarter million pounds today. The *"Reports on Delinquents Estates and Fine Levied Thereon"* (PRO SP23) is reproduced in Appendix G, page 333.

Immediately after the Restoration a new Order of Knighthood of the Royal Oak was instituted by Charles II, which soon fell into abeyance. To the ribbon was to be appended a silver medal, with a device of the King in an oak. There were seventeen Suffolk knights of this Order, including Sir Edmund Poley, Knight, who, like most of the others had an estate of £1000 a year (*History of Suffolk* - ChapterXVI - From the Long Parliament to the Revolution J. J. Raven FSA (1895)).

With the majority of his public life seemingly centred on London, it was unlikely Sir Edmund and Lady Poley spent much time at the ancestral home at Badley, which during the late 1630's/early 40's appears to have become partially occupied by Robert (later Sir Robert) Crompton and his wife Catherine (née Holland). Robert was the son of Lady Poley by her first husband Sir John Crompton Knt. and two of their other children Elizabeth and Marie Crompton (see Wills Appendix D, page 301), died at Badley and were buried there in 1635 and 1641 respectively.

Exactly where the Poleys' residence was in London is uncertain. Two of their children Thomas (1677) and Cicely (1679) are recorded in the Badley parish register as having died there. Whitechapel, Middlesex seems likely, although it may have been in Bow. It was quite a surprise to discover them both mentioned in Samuel Pepys' diary, and evidently enjoying a good social life, as the following extracts illustrate :

1664, 24th November (page 6/330)
—*fine gentleman*

"I dined with him, and Mr. Povy with us and Sir Edmd. Pooly, a fine gentleman, and Mr. Chichly;[1] and fine discourse we had and fine talk - being proud to see myself accepted in such company and thought better then I am."

[1]. Pooley was M.P for Bury St. Edmunds and clerk extraordinary to the Privy Council. (This ties in with Fig 6.14 next page)

1665, 1st November (page 6/285)

"At last up, and it being a very foul day for rain and a hideous wind, yet having promised I would go, by water to Erith - and bearing sail, was in danger of oversetting — but made them take down their sail; and

so, cold and wet, got thither as they had ended their dinner. How[ever], I dined well. And after dinner, all on shore, my Lord Brouncker with us, to Mrs. Williams's lodgings, and Sir W Batten, Sir Edmd Pooly and others; and there, it being my Lord's birthday, had everyone a greene riband tied in our hats, very foolishly, and methinks mighty disgracefully for my Lord to have his folly so open to all the world with this woman."

1665, 16th November (page 6/300)

"So I on board my Lord Bruncker, and there he and Sir Edmd Pooly carried me down into the Hold of the India Shipp, and there did show me the greatest wealth lie in confusion that a man can see in the world-pepper scatter [ed] through every chink, you trod upon it; and in cloves and nutmegs, I walked above the knees - whole rooms full - and silk in bales, and boxes of Copperplate, one of which I saw opened."

(To make sense of this, one needs to know that at the time Pepys was one of the principal officers of the navy administration and the 'prize goods' being show were the contents of two captured Dutch ships moored on the River Thames at Erith, Kent, which were in the charge of Lord Brouncker and Sir J. Mennes.)

1665, 19th November (page 6/303)

"Lords day. . . . . . (on board a boat to Erith) "Captain Cocke and other company (the lady not well), and mighty merry we were, Sir Edmd Pooly being very merry, and a right-English gentleman and one of the discontented Cavaliers that thinks their Loyalty is not considered.[2] After dinner, all on shore to . . . . . "

[2]. Pooley (M.P. for Bury St. Edmunds, Suff.) had been forced to compound for his Suffolk estate in 1646. By 1667 at latest he held a clerkship of the Privy Council and several minor fiscal posts. (See page 155 and Appendix G, page 333.)

1665 26th November (page 6/309)

"Lords day. Up, though very late abed, yet before day, to dress myself to go toward Erith - which I would do by land, it being a horrible cold frost to go by water. So borrowed two horses of Mr. Howell and his friend, ... Business done, we to dinner very merry, there being there Sir Edm. Pooly, a very worthy Gentleman."

1665 10th December (page 6/324)

"Lords day. Lay long talking, Hill and I, with great pleasure, and then up; and being ready, walked to Cocke's for some news, but heard none; only, they would have us stay their dinner, and, sent for my wife, who came, and very merry we were - there being Sir Edm. Pooly and Mr. Eveling. Before we had dined comes Mr. Andrews, whom we had sent for to Bow, ..."

1666, 8th August (page 6/240)

"And by and by dinner came up, and then to my sport again, but still honest; and then took coach, and up and down in the country toward Acton, and then toward Chelsy, and so to Westminster, and there set her down where I took her up, with mighty pleasure in her company ; and so I by coach home, and thence to Bow with all the haste I could, to my Lady Pooly's, where my wife was with Mr. Batelier and his sisters; and there I found a noble Supper, and everything exceeding pleasant . . . ."

(The above entry implies the Pooleys were living at Bow.)

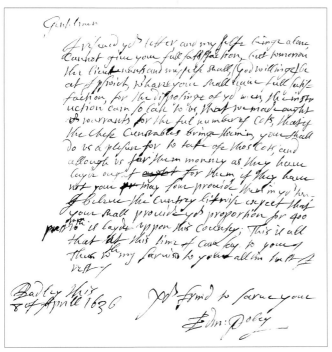

Fig 6.14 A letter (translated below) written by Edmund Poley at Badley on 8th April 1636 to William Moyse and John Barber Bailiffs of Ipswich and Wm Cadge (Cage) and Robert Sparrowe, concerning the raising of money (probably 'Ship Money') or men for military service (SRO: Ipswich Borough Correspondence HD/36/A/114).

Gentlemen

    I received your letter, and myself being alone, cannot give you full satisfaction, but tomorrow the lieutenants and myself shall, (God willing) be at Ipswich, where you shall have full satisfaction, for the disposinge of your men the instruction came so late to us, that we made ought of warrants for the full number of costs that if the Chief Constables bring them in, you shall do us a pleasure for to take off those costs, and allow us for them money as they have laid ought for them if they have not you may four provide then in your turn I believe the country likewise expect that you shall provide your proportion for 400 persons is laid upon this county; That is all that at this time I can say to you of this with my sarvise to you all in haste I v.........

Badley this   Your friend to sarve your
8 of April 1636

                        Edm: Poley

Despite the fact that Sir Edmund was evidently a very busy man in London, he nevertheless still found time to involve himselve in local matters as Fig 6.14 opposite and the below extracts illustrate.

On 8th March 1639, Edward Poley of Stowmarket, whilst appearing to hold the office of Deputy Lieutenant, was signatory to a letter along with Thomas Glemham, George Le Hunte and Roger North, written to the bailiffs of Ipswich, instructing them to have 45 trained men ready equipped for military service at York and elsewhere.
(SRO: *Ipswich Borough Correspondence* HD/36/A/118)

On 4th Feb 1664, Edmund Poley corresponded with [Robert] Clarke the Ipswich Town Clerk, on behalf of a Mark Williams, a Romish recusant of the Stow Hundred, "a poor fellow and not worth a groate", starving in Ipswich goal.
(SRO: *Ipswich Borough Correspondence* HD/36/A/285)

According to the Badley Burial Register (Appendix A, page 241) "*Sr Edmund Poley Knight died at Bury St. Edmunds S^bris 22 and was buried in ye chancel in Badley S^bris 23 1671*".

Compare this with his monument reproduced Chapter 3, Fig 3.77, which gives the date of his death as 12th November 1671, aged 52!

On 22nd November 1676, Sir Edmunds daughter **Elizabeth** married **Richard Gipps** of Little Horringer Hall in Westminister Abbey. He was knighted by **Charles II** at Whitehall in 1682.

Sir Richard died on the 28th September 1681, age 36, and Elizabeth died on 11th November 1715 aged 67 *(see page 170 for illustration on her memorial)*. They had one son Richard and two daughters (see Chapter 7).

Judith Poley, a younger sister, was born on 29th June 1654 and baptised at St. James's, Bury St. Edmunds on 2nd July. She married at Little Saxham church on 17th April 1675, to **Henry Jermyn**, Esq., of Cheveley, 1st. Baron Dover (1636-1708).

He was a prominent figure at the Restoration Court. He was a Roman Catholic in the household of James Duke of York and, on James' accession, began to take part in public affairs.

In 1685 he was raised to the peerage as Baron Dover of Dover and in 1636 became a member of the Privy Council. He followed James into exile in France and was given "Jacobite peerages". After the Battle of the Boyne, where he commanded a troop, Dover was eventually pardoned by William III and spent the rest of his life quietly at his home in Albermarle Buildings near St. James's Park or at his country seat at Cheveley near Newmarket. In 1703 he succeeded his brother as 3rd Baron Jermyn of St. Edmundsbury. He died at Cheveley on 6 April 1708 and his body was taken to Bruges to be buried in the church of the Carmelites.

Judith was also a devout Catholic. Her name appeared amongst the names of Roman Catholics, non-jurors and others who refused to take the oath to King George I, with the annual value of her estates in several counties.

Cambs

Lady Judith, Dowager of Dover of Cheveley Hall	£303 1s 2d

Suffolk

Judith, Lady Dowager Dover	£956 9s 7d

Middlesex

Judith, Lady Dowager Dover of Cheveley, & of Dover St., St. James	£2328 18s

Sir Edmund's youngest son **William Poley**, was born at Badley and baptised there on March 6th 1621. He was admitted to Pembroke College, Cambridge, on January 17th 1638/9 (aged 16), and admitted to Grays Inn, January 23rd 1642/3. According to the Burial Register, he died in April 1644 at Stowmarket aged only 23 years and was buried at Badley on 20th April.

Two of their other sons, who also both died unmarried, are worthy of special note.

HENRY THE LAWYER/POLITICIAN:

Henry Poley was born at Badley in c1653, although there is no record of his baptism there. He was educated at Bury St. Edmunds (probably at the King Edward VI Free Grammar School in Northgate Street). He was admitted to Jesus College, Cambridge on June 6th 1670, where he obtained a Batchelor of Arts degree in 1672/3 and was a Fellow 1673-5. On February 10th 1668/9 he was admitted to Grays Inn, and on March 15th 1672/3 became a member of the Middle Temple. He was Called to the Bar in 1678. He was the son and heir of his father's Badley estate.

As well as being described as "*a cripple and one of the best common lawyers in England*", Henry was also a successful politician being the Member of Parliament for the constituencies of Bury St Edmunds in 1661, the Borough of Eye, Suffolk, 1688, 1690 and Ipswich, Suffolk, 1705 until his death on August 7th 1707, aged 53 years.

His only committee was on the bill for preventing the making of cane chairs and he made no recorded speeches despite his 'extraordinary elocution'.

With his legal and political work centred on London, Henry probably spent little time at Badley Hall.

He died unmarried and in his will (reproduced in Appendix D, page 301) he passed on the Badley estate to his bachelor brother Edmund (the diplomat).

EDMUND THE DIPLOMAT:

Edmund Poley was born at Bury St Edmunds on 14th Dec 1655 and baptised at St. James Church there on 21st. following and not unusually at Badley. After also being educated at the King Edward VI Free Grammer School, in Northgate Street, Bury St. Edmunds, to whose library he donated a book in 1672, he was admitted to Jesus College Cambridge on 15th Oct 1670 (aged 15). He attained a Bachelor of Arts degree in 1674-5, followed by a Master of Arts degree in 1678. He was a Fellow 1675-86.

Spanning the reigns of James II (1684-88), William & Mary (1688-94), William II (1694-1702) and Anne (1701-11), he was the Envoy to the Courts of Sweden (1687), Savoy (Turin, Italy) (1691-96) and Hanover (Germany) 1704-5.

In pursuing a diplomatic career he spent a good deal of time abroad and would rarely have been at Badley Hall.

He was Minister Plenipotentiary to the Germanic states, viz at Ratisbon, in Charles II's reign, and afterwards British Minister at Stockholm under James II. "There is lying on the table a MS. of a mask performed in his honour at Stockholm, in 1687, in which his praises are sung in no mean strain, and special allusion is made to his scientific attainment, in which he was quite cut out Apollo" (Arthur Hervey - Vol III S.I.A.H. 1863).

This was a turbulent time in European politics and Edmund Poley, in the thick of it, must have been regarded as a 'safe pair of hands' to safeguard English interests considering the locations he served the various monarchs.

For example, "In 1686 William had already formed the anti-French coalition to which, after May 1689, he was able to devote English men, money and ships. The League of Augsburg consisted of the Emperor Leopold I, the Kings of Spain and Sweden, the Duke of Savoy and several German princes, including the powerful Electors of Bavaria and Brandenburg. When Louis XIV's dreaded armies invaded and brutally ravaged the Rhenish Palatinate in the autumn of 1688, it was not to be expected that all these states would act with resolution and unanimity. But during the winter the Dutch and the Emperor went to war and William played a key role in negotiating with them and the other Augsburg powers to constitute the first Grand Alliance.

What Europe later knew as 'the Nine Years' War' (1688-97) was in England often, and understandably, called 'King William's War'. Its initial aims were William's own - his long-standing objectives of protecting the Netherlands from France and restricting French expansion elsewhere in order to maintain a balance of power in Europe. But of course the questions of defending the Revolution settlement of the Crown, quelling the Irish rebellion and protecting English trade from a maritime rival now more than the Dutch soon changed its purely continental character."
(*Revolution, War & Politics 1689-1714* - Geoffrey Holmes Chapter 8 Stuart England - Phaidon Press 1986.)

The succession of Queen Anne, who had failed to provide an heir who would survive her, exercised the Government of the day. Under the Act of Succession 1701 they appointed the Hanovrian Dowager Electress Sophia of Hanover, already aged 71 years and a grand-daughter of James I of England, somewhat optimistically to legally succeed her. However, along with Anne she died in 1714 and the crown passed to the first Hanovarian King George I in the same year. (Edmund served at Hanover and Sophia's name appears in his cipher on page 165).

Fortunately many of Edmund's diplomatic papers still survive. Amongst these are the Edmund Poley Papers, which are part of the 'James Marshall and Marie-Louis Osborne Collection' housed in the Beinecke Rare Book Manuscript Library at Yale University, New Haven, Connecticut, USA. These consist of six boxes of correspondence and provide an interesting insight into aspects of English history and foreign policy in the late seventeenth and early eighteenth centuries. The papers span the dates 1645-1707, but the bulk of the material covers the period 1680-1705. For summary of the University's Catalogue see Appendix G, page 333.

Amongst these are introductory letters to the European Courts. Edmund was sent to represent the Crown and not surprisingly, given the volatile political situation prevailing at the time - especially with France, also examples of the cipher use to code dispatches to and from London and containing sensitive political and military information.

Sadly space precludes the reproduction of too much of this fascinating material, but a lengthy letter written by Edmund Poley in 1694 to William Blathwayt, the Secretary for War at Whitehall, is also included in Appendix G, page 333. In it he weighs the pros and cons of continuing his diplomatic career abroad or returning to England. He discusses the adequacy of his allowances, the lack which had caused him to have to "stroted about like a gipsy"! Adding that any improvements which might have been achieved with a "little good husbandry" was very difficult to achieve in Dresden "where good husbandry is not in fashion".

File Ref: SP81/161 at the National Archives, Kew, is a book set of original Edmund Poley letters. I have not read them in full, but amongst other things he describes removing himself to the Hague (Holland) and the considerable difficulties he subsequently experienced trying to obtain a passage to England. The yacht 'Mary' was one of the vessels he hoped to travel on, but they and others were too full of others - army personnel or diplomats such as the Italian Ambassador and his entourage, who completely took all the available space. The wind direction was also unsuitable for weeks! Some contain coded passages using the cipher partially - see Fig 6.18 and 6.19.

On the 18th August 1705 he dictated, "I have so great defluxion fallen upon my right eye, & all that side of my face, that I am unable to write."

Back in England on 9th November 1705 he wrote the paper, "An Account of the Elector and Princes of the House of Brunvic (Brunswick), and of the Dominions which belong to them."

Taken together, Edmund Poley's papers deposited at Yale University, the Public Records Office, Kew, the British Library and elsewhere, provide a fascinating, if not unique, 'coalface' account of an important period in Anglo-European history and all the associated 'wheeling and dealing'.

In Jan 1708/9, Edmund is recorded as having Chambers at Searle's Court, Lincolns Inn.

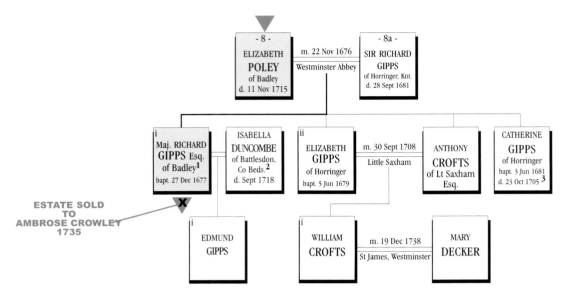

▼

| - 8 - | | - 8a - |
| ELIZABETH **POLEY** of Badley d. 11 Nov 1715 | m. 22 Nov 1676 Westminster Abbey | SIR RICHARD **GIPPS** of Horringer, Knt. d. 28 Sept 1681 |

Fig 6.15 POLEYS of Badley - FAMILY TREE 8th GENERATION.

Notes:

[1] Richard Gipps, Esq., see also Chapter 7.

[2] The Honourable Isabella Gipps, wife of Richard Gipps Esq., was buried at Badley on 27th September 1718, aged about 38 years, having been baptised at Battlesdon on the 31st March 1680. She was the 3rd daughter of William Duncombe Esq., of Battlesdon, co. Bedford and amost certainly a sister of Henrietta Maria Robins (née Duncombe), the wife of Charles Robins of the Middle Temple, London, Esq. She was also buried at Badley (13th February 1728) aged 42 (see Chapter 3, Fig 3.11 and Appendix C, No 65). One would have expected Isabella to have been interred within the church but there is nothing to indicate that she was and in any case there was probably no room to do so by this stage. Unlike her sister Henrietta, who has a wall monument outside on the south wall, surprisingly, given she was the late wife of the Lord of the Manor, there is nothing to indicate where she lays buried.

[3] Catherine was baptised at Horningsherth on 3 Jan 1681. She never married and died at the age of only 23. She is buried in Badley church, see Fig 3.72, Chapter 3.

Fig 6.16 A reproduction of Henry Poley's book label with arms from a collection of texts on 17th Irish Affairs by Sir John Poley. An identical book label except engraved 'Edmund Poley of Badley' and dated 1703 appears in a copy of Brunel's "Voyage d' Espagne" (1667), which also contains his signature on the title page. Both are in the Trinity College Library, Dublin, Ireland. (illustration reproduced courtesy of the Board of Trinity College Dublin)

It appears unlikely that Edmund or his brother Henry spent much time at Badley Hall, preferring to pursue their respect careers abroad or in London. During much of their lifetime and perhaps even before, all or part(s) of the Hall were probably rented out to suitable tenants, the Poleys perhaps reserving just a wing for their own use and that of their extended family. This would explain some of the entries in the parish registers.

Edmund Poley died in his London chambers, unfortunately unmarried, on 16th May 1714. It is said by his own hand *(hanging),* perhaps unable to adapt to the comparatively less glamorous livestyle of a mere 'gentleman' back in England or recurring ill-health. He was buried in the chancel of Badley church on the 21st. May 1714 ∼ the last but one person to be interred within the church (see Chapter 3 for the location).

His will (reproduced Appendix D, page 301) was written 42 days before his death. In it he conveyed Columbine Hall, Stowupland to his nephew Richard Gipps and the reminder of the the Badley estate to his sister Elizabeth Gipps (née Poley).

Sadly, this signalled the end of the 250 years-long association of the Poley family with the manor of Badley. For within 20 years along with Columbine Hall, it was in possession of Ambrose Crowley.

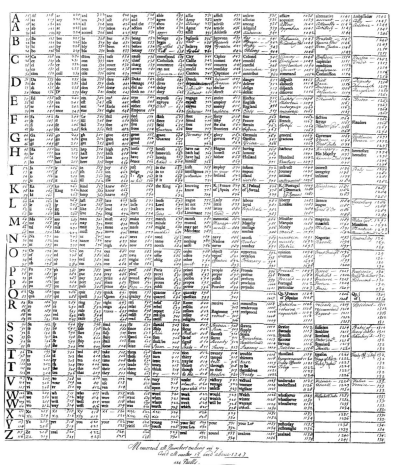

136. dangerous.
137. Mr Ellis.
138. Mr Tucker.
139. Mr Warr.
150. K. of ye Romans.

All between 150 and 200
are Blanks.

200. Emperour
300. French Army in Germany.
350. Empr Army in Italy.
500. Duke of Zelle.

All between 500 and 1000.
are Blanks.

1000. Princess Sophia
1500. Princess of Hatden.
1501. good friends.
1502. fall out.
1503. Inconsequence.
1504. Great importance.

Fig 6.17 Part of a two page hand-written cipher, containing the following note written by Edmund Poley "A private Cipher between me and ye Secretary of State Mr Charles Hedges - given me by him ye 2nd Nov 1703".

A	15	Af	118	ar	220	ard	322	anc	424	age	526	able	629
	16	as	119	ary	221	am	323	act	425	and	528	agree	630
	18	ac	120	an	222	all	324	arm	426	and the	529	abou	631
	19	ab	121	at	223	are	325	ation	428	action	530	after	632
	20	ad	122	ap	224	accord	326	and	429	any	531	appro	633
B	21	Ba	123	bre	225	br	328	but	430	bring	532	besiege	634
	22	be	124	bu	226	ble	329	by the	431	better	533	begin	635
	23	bi	125	by	228	bly	330	been	432	before	534	by what	636
	24	bo	126	bl	229	bla	331	both	433	betray	535	till —	638
C	25	Ca	128	cu	230	ction	332	case	434	cause	536	correspond	639
	26	ce	129	ch	231	con	333	care	435	chief	538	Catholick	646
	28	ci	130	cr	232	can	334	court	436	charg	539	commerce	641
	29	co	131	cl	233	com	335	count	438	crown	540	can not	642
	30	cion	132	coll	234	cile	336	ceive	439	could	541	common —	643

Fig 6.18 (above left) A printed diplomatic cipher book with hand-written entries by Edmund Poley. In the bottom margin he has written, "Memorand all Numbers ending in 7 And all under 15 and above 1343 are Nulls". (above) A close-up of a section of the cipher. (From copies provided courtesy of The James Marshall & Marie-Louise Osborn Collection, Beinecke Rare Book & Manuscript Library, Yale University, USA.)

Further correspondence from this period relating to Edmund Poley's diplomatic career are deposited at the National Archives, Kew and are also summarised in the above Appendix. Copies of some of the papers from these collections have been obtained to illustrate the account within this Chapter.

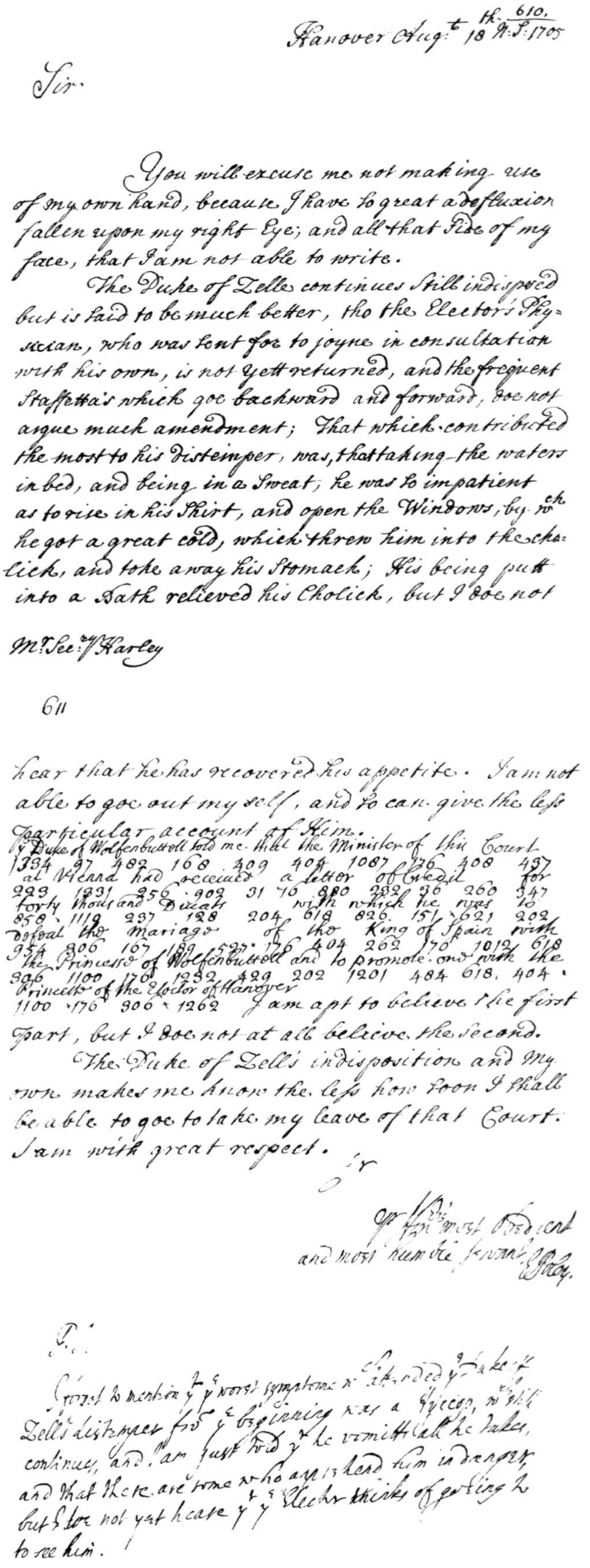

Hanover Aug:^t 18th NS : 1705

Sir

You will excuse me not making use /of my own hand, because I have so great a defluxion /fallen upon my right Eye; and all that side of my /face, that I am not able to write.

The Duke of Zelle continues Still indisposed, /but is said to be much better, tho the Elector's Phy= /sician, who was sent for, to joyne in consultation /with his own, is not yett returned, and the frequent /Staffetta's which goe backward and forward, doe not /argue much amendment; That which contributed /the most to his distemper was, that taking the waters /in bed, and being in a Sweat, he was so impatient /as to rise in his shirt, and open the Windows, by which he got a great cold, which threw him into the cho= /lick, and toke away his Stomack; His being putt /into a Bath relieved his Cholick, but I doe not /

Mr. Sec^{ry}: Harley

611

hear that he has recovered his appetite. I am not /able to goe out myself, and so can give the less /particular account of Him.

Ye Duke of Wolfenbuttoll told me that the Minister of this Court / 1334 97 482 168 409 404 1087 176 408 437 /at Vienna had received a letter of Credit for /223 1331 265 902 31 70 880 232 36 260 347 /forty thousand Ducats with which he was to /858 1119 237 128 204 618 826 151 621 202 /defeat the Mariage of the King of Spain with /954 306 167 189 527 176 404 262 170 1012 618 /the Princess of Wolfenbuttoll and to promote one with the /306 100 176 1232 429 202 1201 484 618 404 /Princesse of the Elector of Hanover /1100 176 306 1262 I am apt to believe the first /part, but I doe not at all believe the second. /

The Duke of Zell's indisposition and my / own makes me know the less how soon I shall / be able to goe to take my leave of that Court. / I am with great respect.
> Sir
> Yr Honorable most obedient
> and most humble servant
> E. Poley

(In Poley's own hand)
Ps

I forget to mention thay ye worst symptom which attended ye Duke of / Zells distemper from ye beginning was a Hyccop, which / continues, and I am just told that he vomitts all he takes / and that there are some who apprehend him in danger, / but I doe not yet heare that ye Elector thinks of going to see him.

Fig 6.19 Edmund Poley's two page letter to Secretary Harley, dated Hanover August 18th 1715. The European politic situation was presumably so volatile, that any sudden change of leadership could affect allegiances and treaties. Consequently envoys were required to report every detail, including any health threats in their correspondence with London. The letter opposite also shows the use of the cipher code and the page numbering system i.e. 610 & 611.

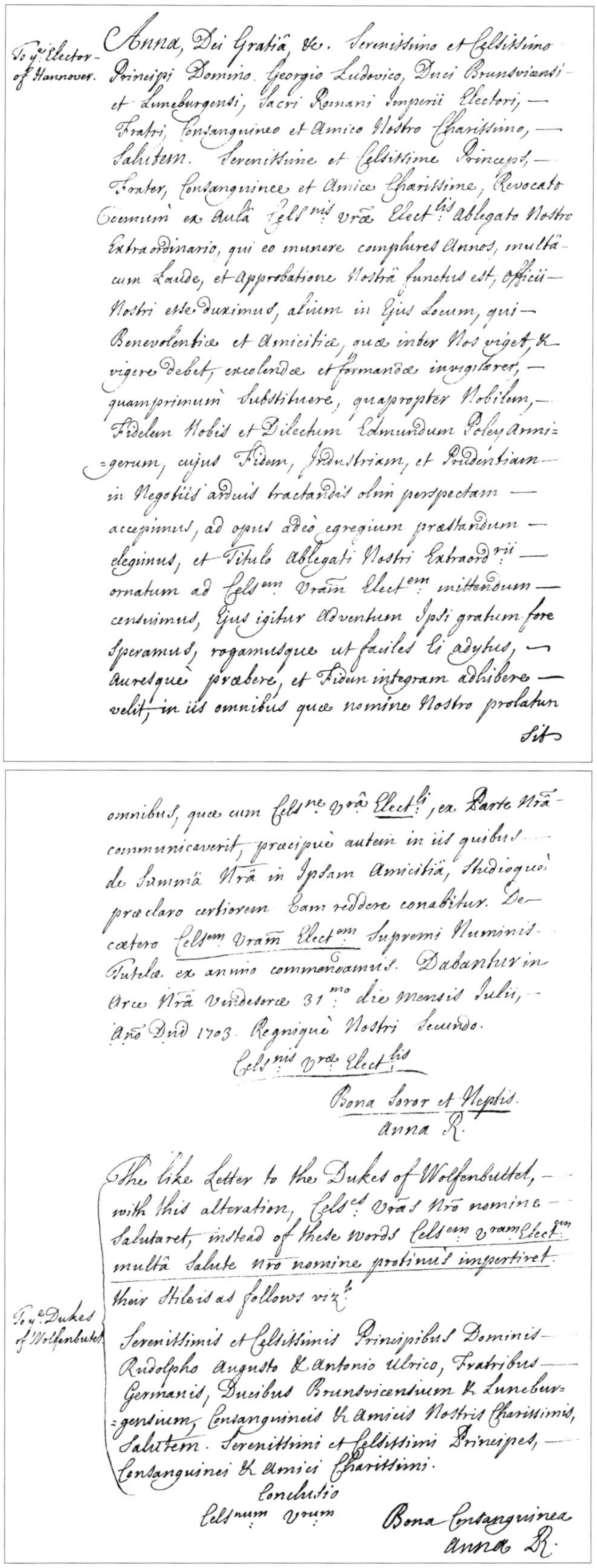

[Fig 6.20 Latin manuscript letter — top left panel. Handwritten text in Latin script headed "Anna, Dei Gratiâ &c. Serenissimo et Celsissimo..." with marginal note "To ye Elector of Hannover."]

[Second manuscript panel — bottom left. Handwritten Latin text with marginal note "To ye Dukes of Wolfenbuttel" and signature "Bona Consanguinea Anna R."]

Fig 6.20 *Two page draft letter in Latin dated 31st July 1703, from Queen Anne "To ye Elector of Hannover" with an amended version "To ye Dukes of Wolfenbuttel" setting out Edmund Poley's diplomatic credentials. 'Elector' in this context refers to any of those princes and Archbishops of the German Empire who had the right to elect the Emperor.*

Hanover 20th May

I am sorry that the first news I have occasion to send you from hence should be so ill as to let you know that yesterday at dinner the Electrice was taken ill with a defluxion which began with much violence and was so troublesome as to oblige her to go to her bed, and it appears to have ended hitherto in what they call here la Rose, but what I suppose we call St Antonies fire, on one side of her face, she still keeps to her bed, but as it is believed that it only proceeds from cold, so it is hoped ye effects of it will not last long.

She is often to blame, If I may be allowed to use ye expression in walking abroad three or four hours in ye evening besides an ill custom which she hath owned to me to have sometimes dressing herself upon the leads *(sic)* of her own apartment and to which this defluxion at present is chiefly attributed which I suppose might affect anybody of less age than she is.

I am with great respect
Sir

Your Honours most Obedient
and most Humble Servant
E. Poley

Fig 6.21 *One of Edmund Poleys diplomatic letters reporting on the health of the Electrice. Source - PRO Calender of State Papers - Charles I (1631-1633).*

Fig 6.22 *Costume of the Nobility & Gentry c.1690, reflecting the type of dress likely to have been worn by Edmund Poley. From prints by Romain de Hooge 1689 & Customes by Myer 1691.*

Other
POLEY
MONUMENTS

The *"Guide to Heraldry in Suffolk Churches"* published by the Suffolk Heraldry Society (1990) lists nineteen Suffolk churches in addition to Badley where the Poley arms [Or a lion ramp Sa (collared and chained Or)], can be found, i.e.

Bardwell	Barrow	Boxted
Combs	Gipping	Groton
Hartest	Horringer	Ickworth
Ipswich St Margaret	Livermere Gt.	Nettlestead
Preston	Sapiston	Saxham Lt.
Stanstead	Stonham Aspal	Thurston

Doubtless there are other Poley related memorials within other churches without heraldic inscriptions.

NOTES :

Bardwell *(SS Peter & Paul)* - there are a number of fine heraldic monuments in this church including two relating to Cecily Poley of Badley, the first wife of Sir Charles Croft(e)s Knt of Bardwell. These both contain fine coloured examples of the arms of Coft(e)s impaling Poley of Badley (Figs 6.23 and 6.24).

Fig 6.24 Barwell church - part of an elaborate wall monument on the left-hand side of the chancel close to the altar, bearing the Crofts arms impaling Poley of Badley.

Fig 6.25 The Heigham monument at Barrow.

Barrow *(All Saints)* - on the south wall of this church there is a rather gaudy heavy mural memorial, by Nicholas Stone, which Gage says, was originally dedicated to Sir John Heigham and his two wives, the second of which was Ann Poley, a daughter of William Poley of Boxted. Hence the prominent 'Poley lion' on the bottom right-hand side of the monument (Fig 6.25 above).

Fig 6.23 Bardwell church, a fine wall monument commemorating Cecily Croftes (née Poley), bearing the arms of Croftes impaling Poley of Badley.

Boxted *(Holy Trinity)* - see Chapter 11

Combs *(St Mary)* - a coloured shield carved on a wood panel in the north aisle - Daundy (Quarterly Az. and Or. in the first quarter a mullet Or.) impaling Poley of Badley, was reported here but can no longer be found. It commemorates Thomas Daundy Esq., of Combs d.1607 who married Martha Poley of Badley who died in 1625.

In the *Proceedings of Suffolk Institute of Archæology & History* Vol 38 (1996) p233, reporting on an excursion to the church in 1993, it states, "Sir John Blois's Church Notes, quoted by D.E.Davy, record lost heraldic glass, mainly with arms of Willoughby family of Parham (successors to Uffords as Lords of manor). The latest recorded shield had Willoughby impaling Jenny, commemorating Sir Christopher Willoughby (1453-1498) and wife Margaret Jenny (d.1515). Their younger son, Robert Willoughby, was Rector of Combs 1500-24." The significance of this is that the same arms were also recorded in the windows of Badley Hall. (Ayse Collection, British Museum) (see illustration Chapter 4, Fig 4.14).

"In the church of Combs, this 12th Sept., 1656, under a marble, lies Thomas Dandy, Esq., who had married Martha, dau., of John Poley of Badley Esq., and of Anne, dau., of Lord Thomas Wentworth, of Nettlested. This Thomas Dandy died about fifty years since. Against the wall in the chancel is nailed a fair plate of brass, for Katherine, dau. of this Thomas. She had been wife to Thomas Sootheby, rector of Combs., 15 years and had borne him viii sons and v daughters. She died in the 32nd year of her age, 1624. Against the wall is a fair monument for Thomas Sotheby, who died the in 63rd year of his age, when he had been rector there for 32 years. His first wife was Katherine, dau., of Thomas Dandy, aforesaid; his second wife was relict of John Crane, of Kings Lynn. Esq — *Reyce*.

On a table against a wall. – The coat of Dandy with Poley, Or a lion rampant Sable. In glass. – Ufford, Sa a cross engrailed Or. The same on the steeple, in stone. Checky, Or and Gu., a fess Ermine. Quarterly, Ufford (as before) and Beke, Gu a cross Moline, empaled with Jenny. Ermine a bend Gu., between two cotices Ermine. Ufford and Beke again impaled – "Or. A lion or beare rumped. With ij tailes Sa. – *Reyce*.
[East Anglian Notes and Queries Vol II p164 - Tree of Family of Dandy]

Dandy brass at Combs Church Suffolk
During the recent work of restoration at Combs Church, a brass measuring 23in. x 6.5ins., which for a great number of years had been hidden from view by late erections, was brought forward. The brass which is now fixed over against the vault commemorates Thomas Dandy, a grandson of Edmund Dandy of Ipswich, which bears the following inscription:-

HIC SEPVLTVS IACET THOMAS DANDY ARMIGER, QVI TEMPORE MORTIS SVE FVIT DOMINVS MANERIJ DE COMBES IN HAC VILLA ET PATRONVS HVIVS ECCLESIE, ET VIR PROBVS ET PRVDENS, ET OBIJT IN FIDE CHRISTIAIANA, DECIMO QVARTO DIE AVGVSTI, IN ANNO INCARNATIONIS DOMINI IESV CHRISTI 1607. IN CVIVS MEMORIAM MARTHA CHARA VXOR EIVS QVE FVIT FILIA VLTIMO GENITA IOHANNIS POLEY DE BADLEY ARMIGERI HOC POSVIT

East Anglian Vol I (Notes and Queries) p.283 (1885-6)

Gipping *(St Nicholas)* - The mediaeval glass in the east window dates from the period between c1494 when Thomas Tyrell of Gipping married Margaret Willoughby d'Ersby and 1513 when he was knighted. Although it was re-set in 1938-9 it is still very jumbled. Shields amongst the surving scattered glass include - Sa. a cross engrailed Or. (Ufford/Willoughby), Or, a lion rampant sable (Poley), Sa. six swallows Arg. (Arundel). Gu. a cross moline Arg. (Beke) and Gu. a fess dancetty Or. between six crosses botonny Or. *(unidentified)* Fig 6.26 below.

Fig 6.26 The scatterd glass in the base of the east window at Gipping Church showing the arms described above.

Groton *(St Bartholomew)*
This church is full of Winthrop memorabilia. John Winthrop of Groton emigrated to New England in 1603, founded Boston and became the first Governor of

Massachusetts. The only Poley arms evident are contained in a faded shield near the top of a south window - Poley *(of Boxted)* quartering **Weller**, impaling Halifax quartering an indecipherable arms.

Hartest *(All Saints)*
The lion here is contained in a brass wall-plaque to the memory of John George Poley (1836-1901) M.A., R.D., J.P., who was rector of the parish for 37 years and probably from the Boxted side of the family (see also Stonham Aspal, page 174).

Horringer *(St Leonard)*
Against the west wall of the north aisle there is a memorial to Sir Richard Gipps which was formerly a ledger slab, set into the floor of the sanctuary.

Upon it there are two carved shields, one of which bears the arms of Gipps Azure, a fess between six etoiles Or, and the other Gipps impaling Poley. Above the inscription is carved the crest of Gipps, Out of a ducal crown Or, two wings expanded Azure, semé d'etoiles of the first. The inscription reads:

> Here Lyeth the body of Sr
> Richard Gipps of Little Hor:
> :ninger inn the county of
> Suffolk, Knight, who marryed
> Elizabeth the eldest daughter
> of Sr Edmund Poley, of Badley
> in the same county, Knight,
> who departed September the
> 28 anno Dom. 1681, in ye
> 36 yeare of his age.

Directly above this there is a large black marble tablet monument to his wife, Dame Elizabeth Gipps (nee Poley of Badley). Above the inscription there is an attractive carved (coloured) lozenge bearing the arms of Gipps impaling Poley of Badley enclosed in an ornmental wreath with an angel's head at the top and a skull at the bottom (Fig 6.27 opposite). The inscription reads:

> Here Lyeth the Body of Dame
> Elizabeth Gipps Relict of Sr Richard
> Gipps of Horrenger fhe Departed
> this Life the 11th day of Novr, 1715 in
> the 67 year of her Age.

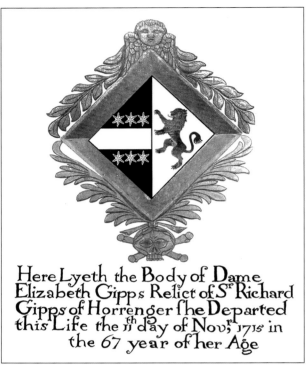

Fig 6.27 Reproduction of Dame Elizabeth Gipps monument with the arms of Gipps of Horringer impaling Poley of Badley.

Ickworth *(St Mary)*
Not visited, but Elizabeth Poley of Boxted married William Harvey of Ickworth. He was buried in the church 2 Nov 1592, and any arms here are likely to relate to the Boxted branch.

Ipswich *(St Margaret)*
John Lany Esq of Cratfield, Recorder of Ipswich, married Mary Poley daughter of John Poley of Badley and Anne eldest daughter of Thomas 1st Lord Wentworth of Nettlestead. He died in 1633 aged 86 and she died on 18 Aug the same year, aged 81.

On the wall of the north aisle there is an elaborate and no doubt costly memorial to them. Unfortunately, like so many others throughout the county, is in need of some sympathetic restoration (Fig 6.28 and 6.29).

The decaying inscription is in Latin (reproduced opposite) and although it acknowledges the Poley and perhaps more significantly the Wentworth ancestry, when I visited the monument in 2001, I was surprsed to discover the arms of neither family were included on the shield.

This apparent conundrum was however solved after consulting the Suffolk Heraldry Society's Booklet 28 which lists the heraldry in St Margaret's church recorded during a county-wide survey conducted between 1978-88 and Some Suffolk Church Notes No XL - St. Margaret, Ipswich by H.W. Birch in the East Anglian Vol IX.

The SHS account appears the more reliable, Birch's description of the heraldry and inscription being eroneous on a number of counts. They record -

Fig 6.28   The Lany/Poley monument in St Margaret's, Ipswich.

"A monument on the wall of the north aisle, with three coloured shields

(i) In the centre Quarterly. 1. Arg. On a bend, between two fleurs-de-lis Gu. A lion passant Arg. **LANY** 2. Or a chevron engrailed Gu. Between three cinquefoils Vert (Az) on a chief Gu a lion passant Or (Arg) **COOKE** of Linstead 3. Gu. A crescent Erm. Within an orle of martlets Or. **BOHUN** 4. Sa nine fleurs-de-lis, three and three Or. (Unidentified)

(ii) At top right corner. Quarterly of four as (i) impaling : Quarterly of nine 1. Or a lion rampant Sa. **POLEY** of Badley 2. Az a fess Or between three birds Arg. legged and beaked Gu. **GESLINGHAM** 3. Arg. A fess between three garbs Gu. **GARDEVILLE** 4. Arg. A chevron engrailed between three griffin's heads erased Arg. **GEDDINGE** 6. Az three chevronels Or. **ASPALL** 7. Arg. A fess between two chevrons Gu. **PECCHE** 8. Quarterly Gu. And Vairy Or. and Vert, over all ab end Arg. **PEVERELL** 9. Arg three chevronels Gu. In dexter chief a mullet for difference **WATERVILLE.**

(iii) *Top left corner* As (ii) Crest : A mermaid proper, crined Or, tailed Vert, holding a mirror in her right hand

Only i) above now remains, the others having apparently disappeared within the past 20 years. Did the 368 year old adhesive finally fail causing them to fall to the ground, or did they suffer some other fate?

Interestingly, the armorial bearings described on the sinister at ii) above closely resemble those illustrated in the shield on page 177 of The Visitation of Suffolk 1664-8, reproduced on the next page (Fig 6.30 overleaf).

The extensive, but faded, Latin inscription reads[1]:

CHRISTIANIS

Viatoribus atq' supremi Candidatis bravii,
Moræ tantillæ luculentum pretium erit, ne nesciant
sacram hanc in Cælos viam dudum præiisse, de CHRISTI
Cathqlicâ in terris Ecclia Qui detritas corporum exuvias
huic tumulo pariter credentes, certijsima sub resur^{r}ectionis
spe, præstolantur D . IESVM de Coelo reducem.

PAR RARVM

Et si restrictim comparentur, atq omnib$_9$ rationibus,
fortean sine pari.

IOANNES	MARIA
FILIVS IOANNIS LANY	FILIA IOANNIS POLEY
De Cratfeild Sudovolgarū generosi iuris Municipalis consultus & huic Municipio Gippovicesi ad aliquot novem (plus minus) lustra à consiliis iuridicis pacisq conservator, in comitatu per XLVIII retrò años.	De Badley Sudovolgaru Armigeri ex Anna vxore quæ primogenita fuif Dñi Thoma Wentworth Baronis de Netlested.

Foedere connubiali feliciter sociati vitam pariter duxerunt
lantam suavem, piam per annos undesexaginta & liberos procrearunt
xv viz: Ioannem, Annam, Bassingbornum, Mariam, Edmundum, Iuditham,
Catherinam, Martham, Dorotheam, Nathanaele, Ianam, Edvardum,
Benjaminvs, Nathanaelem, Fransiscam. Exquorum sex coniogatis
ubi Nepetes XLIX et pronepotes X̄   susi eperant, annorum tandem
bonaec.. existimationis saturi, et migrationem suam in Cælos
iam t..... meditari pariter pieq obeurt.

$$\left. \begin{array}{l} \text{Illa Augusti } \overline{\text{XVII}} \\ \text{Ille Octobris } \overline{\text{III}} \end{array} \right\} \quad 1633 \quad \text{Aetatis suæ} \quad \left\{ \begin{array}{l} \overline{\text{LXXXI}} \\ \overline{\text{LXXXVI}} \end{array} \right\}$$

Iam nihil vosimoramue, viatores christa Agite, Deo sit gloria,
Succlariames, rectà, et vos (ubi dabirur) in cælos' pergite.
Oprimorum Parentum memoræ D. D.
IOANNES primogenitus paterniq' officij professionis, lociq' hæres
BENJAMINVS S. S. Theologiæ professor atq' Aulæ Pembrochianæ
Cantabrigiæ custos

Duo filii superstites

[1] So far as it can be deciphered by a non-Latin scholar!

What a marvellous sight this memorial must have been in 1633 when the heraldry, inscription, marble and gold painted cherub's faces, etc., were all in pristine condition.

Fig 6.29 A close-up of the armorial shield (described at (i) previous page) on the Lany Poley monument.

Fig 6.30 Part of the illustration from page 177 of The Visitation of Suffolk, 1664-8 (see also Chapter 3, Figs 3.80 & 3.84).

Ipswich *(St Margaret)* continued.

To the right of this a wall tablet for Joseph Pooley (1828) and his wife Mary Garway (1825) is somewhat mystifying. It contains the well preserved arms (in colour) of Poley impaling Garway (Arg a pile betw four leopards' faces Gu over all a fess Gu.) (Fig 6.31 opposite) with the motto: *Virtus invicta* and the following inscription:

SACRED

TO THE MEMORY OF **JOSEPH POOLEY** ESQUIRE

ONE OF THE BALIFFS OF THIS BOROUGH ;

WHO TO A ZEALOUS AND ACTIVE DISCHARGE

OF THE DUTIES OF MAGISTRATE,

UNITED THE UNSHAKEN INTEGRITY OF THE MAN,

AND THE UNAFFECTED PIETY OF THE CHRISTIAN.

UNIVERSALLY ESTEEMED AND REGRETTED

HE DEPARTED THIS LIFE DURING HIS BAILIWIC

ON THE 17TH APRIL 1828,

IN THE 69TH YEAR OF HIS AGE.

AND OF **MARY** HIS WIFE, THE DAUGHTER OF

BENJAMIN GARWAY GENT.

WHO DIED DECEMBER 18TH 1825

AGED 71 YEARS

Joseph Pooley was admitted as a Freeman of the Borough of Ipswich in 1781 (by Servitude). But his birth in circa 1759, appears too late for him to have been born to a direct member of the Badley family and there is no record of a Joseph born of the Boxted branch. However, the arms are unmistakably those used by Poley of Badley.

Fig 6.31 Joseph Pooley's monument in St Margaret Ipswich.

He was a Chief Magistrate and Bailiff, who apparenty "had the rare felicity of passing through life without a personal foe". On the 19th April 1828, *The Ipswich Journal* reported Joseph's death and the following week his interment, which was with full Borough honours.

His will (SRO Ref : IC/AA2/114/69) reveals he was a 'wheeler & coachmaker' by profession, he had a brother Samuel, who was a cordwainer at Holbrook and three sons Joseph, George and William.

In 1821 his son George, a clerk, of Ipswich was admitted a Freeman by Patrimony. The sponsor was his father.

Joseph's right to bear the 'Poley' arms, however, remains unresolved.

Livermere Gt. *(St Peter)*
There is a well-preserved and illustrated ledger stone within the sanctuary to Dorothy (née Felton) the wife of Maurice Claxton Esq (d.1687) which states she later married Sr John Poley Knt of Boxted. Hence the inclusion of the Poley arms in the illustation.

Nettlestead *(St Mary)*

Fig 6.32 Wingfield impaling Poley above the entrance porch at Nettlestead Church.

Thomas Wingfield Esq., some time Feodary for Suffolk, and a magistrate, resided in this parish in the time of King Charles. From the family of Wingfield, of Brantham, he died in 1632, was buried in the parish church as was Alice Poley, his second wife, who died in 1629. Her ledger stone bears the arms of Wingfield, impaling Poley. The same arms can be seen over the entrance to the church porch (Fig 6.32).

Despite an earlier association between the Poleys and Wingfields being recorded in the Annals of Ipswich on p.383 *(see next column)*, I cannot be certain which branch of the family this Alice decended from. The inclusion of Edmund in the entry suggests a Badley connection as the Boxted branch did not adopt this forename, whereas the *Visitation of Suffolk 1612* assigns this Alice to Boxted, which is probably correct as this forename was not used for daughters by the Badley branch.

Here lyeth Alice Poley
late wife of Thomas
Wingfield Esqvier who
was buried ther fovth
day of September
Anno Domini
1629

Fig 6.33 The inscription on Alice's ledger stone in Nettlested church.

Fig 6.34 Arms of Wingfield impaling Poley.

38 El: (Friday), [1596]
"Antony Wingfield(a) Edm:Poly, and Humphrey Wingfield(b) have offered in behalfe of the heire of Seckford, to pay 10l yerely for Woodbr: market. And this Towne doth accept thereof, til the heir shall come of age.

a) Probably son and heir of Sir Robt. Wingfield, of Letheringham (p.283), Sheriff of Suff. 39 Eliz. (1596-7) and representative for the County 30 and 31 Eliz. (1588-9); died 29 Sep., 1605, and bur. At Letheringham.

b) Apparently son and heir of Humphrey Wingfield, Esq., of Brantham, Suff. d.1612".

Note also that Edmund of Badley married Katherine Seckford of Seckford Hall (see Fig 6.9 earlier in this Chapter).

Preston *(St Mary)*
There appears to be no genealogical link with the Poleys here. The coloured arms are situated high up in a clerestory window along with those of several other local families and appear to be the result of the enthusiasm for heraldry of local antiquarian Robert Reyce Esq (Author of *The Breviary of Suffolk*, 1618).

Sapiston *(St Andrew)*
In this isolated (now redundant) church, "where no bones of heroes lie!", there is a very well-preserved ledger stone commemorating Jane Croft(e)s, the daughter of William Croft(e)s and Jane (née Poley of Boxted), who was the wife of Thomas Aldham, Gent. It contains no less than six sets of arms, i.e. Croft(e)s impaling Sampson; Croft(e)s impaling Kitson; Aldham impaling Croft(e)s x 2 and Croft(e)s impaling Poley of Badley and Croft(e)s impaling Poley of Boxted in indentical shields at the foot, Fig 6.35 overleaf.

Saxham Lt. *(St Nicholas)*
Along with West Stow, this was the ancestral home of the Crofts family, into which the Poleys married on at least four occasions (see Chapter 7). The church is consequently adorned with Crofts memorials, including Storey's massive monument to Lord & Lady Crofts in the Lucas Chapel. Surprisingly,

Fig 6.35 Croftes impaling Poley in Sapiston church.

however, despite there having been at least three Poley burials here, the only reference now visible to the family appears to be an attractive shield of arms on a south window of the chancel (Fig 6.36 below).

The arms are those of Drury (Arg on a chief Vert two pierced mullets Or.) quartering Harvey (G. on a bend Ar. 3 trefolds slipped Vert.), impaling Poley of Badley, quartering Gislingham (Sa. a fess inter 3 gese close Ar.), Alcock (Ar. 3 cocks inter a chevron ing Sa. combed G.) Gedding (G. a chevron Or, inter 3 eglets' heads), Aspale (Az. 3 chevrons Or, a border Ar.) and Peche (Ar. a fess inter 2 chevrons G.). The arms on the sinister (right) side of this shield are identical to those on the monument to the Poley family in Badley church *(no 23 on the interior plan in Chapter 3)*, and reproduced on the front cover of this book).

Fig 6.36 Poley arms incorporated in stained glass at Little Saxham church.

Stanstead *(St James)*
In this church there is a white marble wall tablet commemorating the Rev. Wm. Weller-Poley MA Rector of Santon, Norfolk, second son of George Weller-Poley of Boxted Hall who died at Brandon on 12th May 1887 aged 72 years. Above the inscription is a well-preserved coloured

shield containing the arms of Poley of Boxted impaling Weller of Tunbridge, Kent (i.e. Weller-Poley).

Stonham Aspal *(Blessed Virgin Mary)*
A fine white marble wall tablet commemorates John George Pooley MA JP, Rector for 37 years, who died there in 1901, aged 65 years, his wife Joan, their three children and and four others, all named with date and place of death. Although the monument is surmounted with a chained black rampant lion, bearing the motto underneath "VENIAT QUNCOMQUE VULT"*(sic)*, this is not the family motto of either the Badley or Boxted Pooleys and the dates of birth appear to be too recent for any of those named to have directly descended from either branch, unless this is the same John George Pooley commemorated in Hartest church, see page 170.

Thurston *(St Peter)*
The only rampant lion found here was contained within a memorial slab on the floor beneath the tower which also contains an unusual brass inscription to George Wickes (1761) and his wife, Alder (1774).

The church guide states that George Wickes was goldsmith to King George III and founder of Garrards, the Crown Jewellers. It also says the College of Arms ruled some years ago that George Wickes had not established his right to the arms carved on this memorial stone. No Poley connection was evident or expected.

———————————

In giving thanks to the Suffolk Heraldry Society for having listed all the Suffolk churches known to have Poley memorials containing heraldry, one is left to ponder whether there are any others without illustrations and what lies elsewhere, given the social status of most of the Poley marriages.

For example:

West Stow *(St Mary)*
Flat stone in the tower - 'to Mrs. Anne Bryers Steiger, the "relict of John Geo Steiger, was a woman of an eminent vertue and exemplary piety" and in memory of her Mrs Cicily Poley laid this stone' *(page 79, West Stow Parish Registers 1558-1850, published by Geo Bold, Church St Woodbridge 1903).*

Wingham, Kent *(St Mary)* - see Appendix G, page 333.

Chapter Seven

Genealogy & Heraldry

the succession of Badley from the Poleys

This Chapter concerns the Manor of Badley the two hundred years after the death of the last direct member of the Poley family and chronicles the succession through the Gipps, Crowley and Asburnham families into individual farm ownership following the 1917 auction.

However, it begins with an explantion of the heraldry on the amorial shield in Badley church Chapter 3, Figs 3.82 and 3.84.

THE reason for the inclusion of the arms of Gestringham (Geslingham/Gislingham), Peche, Aspale and Waterwik (Waterville/ Wateville) with that Poley of Badley, on the crest in Badley church and in the drawing based on the pedigree drawn by Robert Glover in 1579, can be simply explained by marriages. The convergence of these families being best illustrated by the ancestral tree opposite.

In the reign of King Edward III, Sir John Gardeville Knt., is listed in Pages's *Supplement to the Suffolk Traveller*, page 470, as lord of the manor of Winchester in Mendlesham, Suffolk. Of more significance, he also held the manor of Woodhall in Stoke Ash.

The same volume, page 464, has the "lordship of the parish, of Gislingham along with the manor of Rushes, anciently vested in John Geslingham, Esq." Whether he was the same John who subsequently married Maude Gardeville is not clear, but their daughter was Thomas Poley's first wife and their decendants became the Poleys of Badley.

Meanwhile in northwest Suffolk the Geddyng and Aspale families of Lackford were united by marriage, the latter having already absorbed the blood-lines of Peverell, Peche and Waterwik (Wateville).

"In 1561 the arms and crest of Thomas de Aspale were to be seen in the church of Little Thurlow and the arms on the churches of Flempton, Little Bradley and Little Saxham: and also in the house of Mr Poley at Icklingham - MS. Harvey, fol 10.8.7." Page 45, *The History and Antiquities of Suffolk~Thingoe Hundred* by John Gage Esq., (1838).

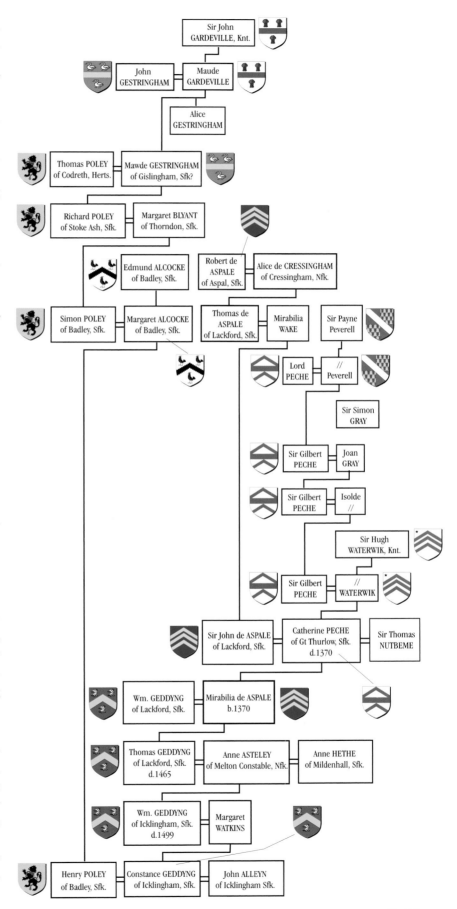

Fig 7.1.

The CROFTES[1] of Little Saxham

(Their connections with the Manor of Badley)

ARMS : Or. three bulls' heads couped, sable

THE foundation stones of Saxham Parva (Little) Hall were laid by Thomas Lucas before he died on 7th July 1531. He had married Elizabeth Kembys and they produced three sons, Jasper, Henry and John and two daughters. Jasper the eldest son acquired the manors of Lackford, Flempton and West Stow through his marriage to Margery, the daughter and heir of Robert Geddyng.

Jasper died during his father's lifetime, leaving amongst other children Thomas. He and his uncle John Lucas, sold their estates in Little Saxham to Sir John Croftes, whose eldest son Thomas married Susan Poley, the daughter of John Poley of Badley, the first of a series of marriages linking the two families (see illustration on next page).

Thomas and Susan had eleven children. Their son William married Jane Poley, a daughter William Poley of Boxted. One of their grandchildren, Frances, a daughter of Sir John Croftes and a great, great grand-daughter, Hester, the daughter of their grandson, Sir Henry Croftes, also married members of the Poley family from the Badley branch.

Frances Croftes was first married to Sir John Compton of Skerne, Yorks., then to Edmund Poley of Badley. By this marriage she had Frances, who was baptised at Lt. Saxham in 1629 and died there in 1654; Henry, who was baptised at Badley in 1630 and died in infancy and Cicely, who was baptised at Badley in 1633 and died unmarried in 1679 (see Chapter 3 for illustrations of their memorials).

Hester Croftes married Edmund Poley's son, also called Edmund (later Sir Edmund). (Edmund's wife Lady Frances Crompton, as she continued to be know, was Hesters Croftes' aunt). It was through this latter marriage that the Badley manor eventually passed to the Gipps of Horringer, by virtue of the marriage of Elizabeth Poley, a daughter of Sir Edmund and Dame Hester Poley, to Sir Richard Gipps of Horringer, all Elizabeth's nine brother having all died without issue (see next section 'Gipps' for further explanation).

The Croftes probably acquired the Manor of Bardwell by grant from the Crown, as parcel of the possession of the dissolved Monastery of St Edmund (although the only one Sir John is attributed to have received was that of West Stow in 1540 for which he paid £497). In 1557 it passed from Sir John Croftes of West Stow to his second son Thomas.

A note in the 'olde' parish register at Little Saxham records:

"Dec 25th 1674 - Ye Lady Poley of Badley, widow, sister to ye Right Hon William Lord Crofts, for ye more decent celebrating of ye sacrament bestowed on this parish a very fair fringed carpet for ye communion table, together with a large damask of cloth and napkin."

Note:
_____

1 *NB. The spelling of the surname of this family varies and can be found as Croft, Crofte, Croftes or Crofts.*

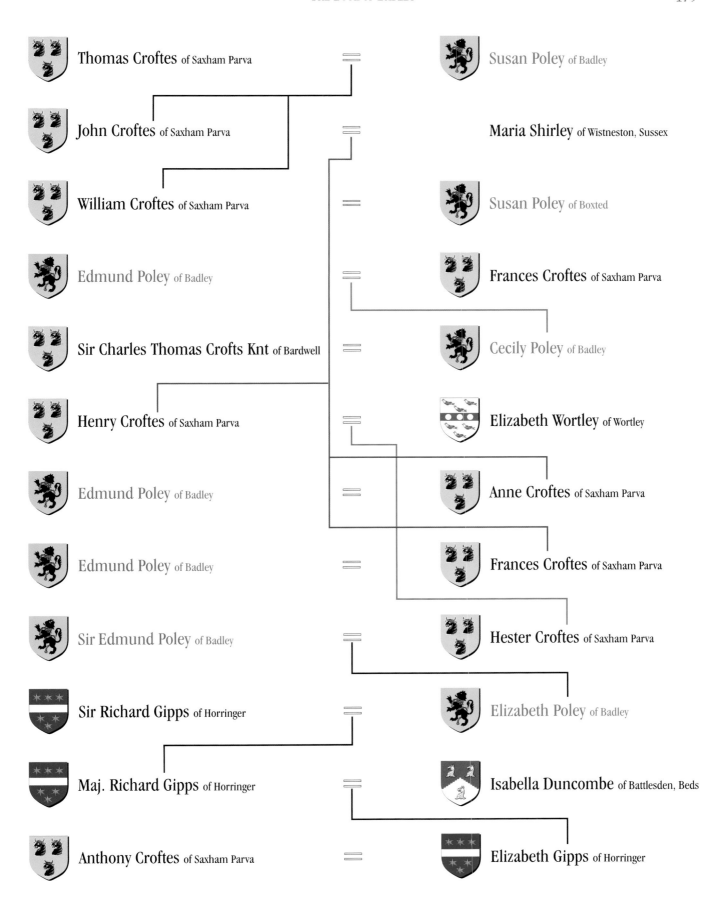

Fig 7.2 Tree showing - (a) the intermarriages between the Croftes of Little Saxham, the Poleys of Boxted and Badley and the Gipps of Horringer; and (b) the reason for the succession of Badley manor from the Poleys to Richard Gipps of Horringer.

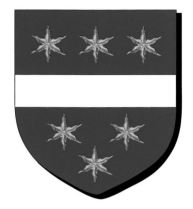

The GIPPS of HORRINGER
(Their connections with the Manor of Badley)

ARMS : Azure; a fess between six estoils, Or.

ELIZABETH Poley, the daughter and heiress of Sir Edmund Poley of Badley married Richard Gipps of Little Horringer Hall in Westminister Abbey in 1676; he being 30 and she 32. (Some accounts say this marriage took place by licence at St Martin in the Fields in November 1676).

According to Gage (p.522), Charles II honoured Lord Croftes with visits to Little Saxham in 1665, 1670 and 1676, conferring the knighthood on Richard Gipps there on 20th Oct 1676.

Elizabeth's father was already dead; her mother, Lady Esther Poley, was the daughter of Sir Henry Croftes of Little Saxham. If Richard's knighthood was conferred at Little Saxham, that visit appears to have ultimately brought him a knighthood and a wife. Sir Richard and Elizabeth had three children all of whom were baptised at Horningsheath (Horringer), viz

1) Richard, baptised on 27th Dec 1677;
2) Elizabeth, baptised on 5th June 1679 and
3) Katherine, baptised on 3rd Jan 1681. She died on 23rd October 1705, aged 23 years, and is buried in the chancel of Badley Church (see memorial No 15 on church plan and Fig 3.28). She was a posthumous child as Sir Richard had died on the 28th of September previous aged 35 years.

Lady Gipps survived him over 35 years dying on the 11th November 1715, aged 67 years. They are both buried at Horringer (see Chapter 6 for details of their monumental inscriptions).

Elizabeth's mother, Lady Poley died at Badley the previous year on 22nd June 1714, where she is buried.

Richard's sister Elizabeth married her cousin Anthony Croftes of Little Saxham on 30th September 1708 and died there on 21st August 1753.

Richard Gipps was an army Major. He is said to have been a brave officer; but was 'basely discharged upon Party-pique[1]'. There is reference to him living at Badley in 1722. He inherited his father's estate at 'Little' Horringer and his mother's estate at Badley. These inheritances ought to have made him a rich man, but as he promptly sold everything perhaps he was not.

He sold the Badley estate to Ambrose Crowley Esq of Barking and it subsequently passed with the Barking Hall estate to the Earl of Ashburnham and Charles Boone Esq., the Member for Castle Rising, who married the two heiresses of the Crowley family.

The Manor of Fornham St Genevieve (or Jenophesa) was acquired by the Gipps family from the Gages of Hengrave Hall. In 1721 Richard Gipps Esq of Badley sold it to Edward Whitaker, Sergeant-at-law.

A Copy of Assignment of Mortgage from the Brent Eleigh Hall Estate records dated 24th March 1731/2 shows Richard Gipps of Badley, Esq., as the only acting executor of Charles Robins[2] of the Middle Temple, London, Esq., concerning a messuage, farm and appurtenances in Lavenham and messuage, farm and appurtenances in Brent Eleigh (SRO [Bury St Edmunds Branch] Catalogue Ref. 1754/1/344).

N.B. Augustine Pages' *'Supplement to the Suffolk Traveller'* (1844) p.566, says that Major Gipps sold the Badley estate to Ambrose Crowley; but Lord Arthur Hervey, in a paper on the Poley family read before the Suffolk Archaeological Institute in Jun 1859 mentions a letter at Boxted written by a Croftes to a Poley in 1726 as saying that Badley passed by inheritance to William Croftes, son of Anthony Croftes, who married Elizabeth Gipps, Major Richard Gipps sister (see Chapter 11 for the contents of this letter).

Notes:

[1] Source: *Antiquitates Suffolciences* by Sir Richard Gipps of Whelnetham.
[2] He was the husband Henrietta Robins who is buried at Badley Church, see Chapter 3, Fig 3.11.

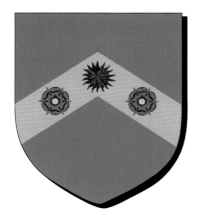

The CROWLEYS of Barking

Owners of the Barking Hall Estate
(which included the The Manors of Badley & Columbine) 1714 - 1754

ARMS : Vert on a chev Or an estoile of sixteen points between two roses Gu.

IN 1715 the Manor of Badley was inherited by Richard Gipps the second, who was a major in the army.

Following the restoration of Charles II, the demand for country houses and agricultural land increased. Men with money, or able to obtain credit, were keen to acquire land, not because it was necessarily a good investment but because it conferred status, influence and power. Many new landowners therefore arrived and most of them were not Suffolk-born. Having succeeded in their chosen fields, they (or their sons) had the money to buy themselves into the landowning gentry or aristocracy.

John Crowley Esqr, Citizen and Alderman of London, lived at East Greenwich and was the only son of iron-master Sir Ambrose Crowley, Knt. He was wealthy, having inherited his father's iron-making business, which included the largest iron-works in Gateshead Co. Durham, manufacturing nails, locks, spades and general iron products, with foundries in the Midlands and warehouses in London and elsewhere. The Crowleys also owned several ships. An indication of the their wealth was demonstrated during the time of John Poley when money was being donated towards the defence of England against the Spanish Armada. Whereas John Poley gave £100, the Crowley family contributed £500.

"The best-known heavy engineering firm of old Gateshead was Hawks, Crawshay & Sons. The firm was started in 1748 by William Hawks at New Greenwich, at the South Shore. Hawks had been a foreman blacksmith at Crowley's works and he named his first factory after Crowley's old premises at Greenwich on the Thames. William Hawks II took control of the firm in 1775 and expanded his premises and trade, foundries were bought and steam introduced. By 1801 the firm produced several kinds of ordnance, anchors, chains, bolts, spades and many other metal products. Government contracts were taken over from the declining firm of Crowley and the stage was set for

Fig 7.3 The faded arms of Crowley quartering Gascoyne (Arg on a pale Sa a demi lucy erect couped Or) on a Crowley monument in Barking Church.

a successful period of trade, helped by the Napoleonic wars and therefore a constant demand for weapons". (From *The History of Gateshead.*)

Although quite able to, John Crowley did not have to buy his way into the 'Suffolk set'. He became part of the Suffolk landowning gentry through his marriage to Theodosia Gascoyne of Enfield, Middlesex, who inherited the Manor of Barking upon her brother's death on 16th October 1714.

John and Theodosia resided at Barking Hall and had six children, two sons and four daughters. On 2nd January 1727 John died at the early age of 39 years and is buried in the family vault in Barking church alongside four of his children. However, during his brief married life he added to the estate various lands in Darmsden, Barking, Hitcham and Buxhall.

Fig 7.4 Barking Hall.

The eldest son Ambrose Crowley Esqr, succeeded his father and added to the estate in 1735 by the purchase from Richard Gipps of the Manors of Badley and Columbine Hall, with lands in Stowupland and Creeting St Mary. He also bought the Manor of Combs from Orlando Bridgeman with lands in Creeting St Olaves.

Sir Ambrose thereby owned practically all of Barking, Badley, Darmsden and much of Combs, Stowupland and Creeting. He was an Alderman of the City of London where he had extensive trading interests.

In 1741 William Collier, a highly spirited artist and gifted draughtsman, was commissioned by Ambrose Crowley to produce a map of his Suffolk estate. The map extends from a point just north of Needham Market to Combs Ford, taking in the whole of the manors of Badley and Combs, farms in the adjoining parishes of Barking, Battisford and the Creetings, as well as detached lands including the Columbyne Hall estate. The effective southern boundary of the map - 'oriented', literally, with west at the top - is the River Gipping (here called the Orwell) and the Ipswich to Stowmarket road. The design of the map gives central place to Badley Hall and Combs Hall and their ornamental grounds. Near the head of the map the arms of Ambrose Crowley are splendidly displayed, though with some artistic licence as to crest and supporters.

The eye is caught immediately, and surely deliberately, by the great double avenue of trees stretching over a mile from Badley Hill to the Hall and beyond to the boundary of Badley Great Park, neatly encircling a large pond (see Chapter 2, Fig 2.6, page 17 and Chapter 4, Fig 4.2, page 71 for examples from this map).

Ambrose Crowley died unmarried on May 22nd 1754, aged 36 years and the Barking Hall Estate passed to his brother John, who died the following year on 15th July 1755 also without issue. The estate ultimately passed through the two surviving sisters, the eldest of whom, Theodosia, married Charles Boone Esqr., M.P. for Castle Rising, Norfolk and Elizabeth, the youngest married the Right Hon. John Ashburnham, 2nd Earl of Ashburnham on 28th June 1756.

Theodosia died on 9th Jan 1756, Elizabeth in 1781 and Charles Boone in 1819, having only had a daughter, who died young. Thus the Barking Hall Estate succeeded to the Earl of Ashburnham.

Crowley Park and Crowley Road in Needham Market serve to remind us of this family's sixty-seven year association with the area, forty-six of which were as Lords of the Manor of Badley.

The south chapel of Barking church is almost filled by a large square pew in which a wooden flooring has been laid, but a large marble tombstone is left uncovered, with this inscription :-

Depositum | lectissimæ fæminæ Annæ Theobald | ex antiqvvs nightingalorvm stemmate | in agro Essex | orivndæ | Roberti Nightingale armig. ex Theodosia | filia Roberti Chester Esqv' Avr' | Unicæ filiæ, | Thomæ Nightingale Baronetti | Germanæ sororis, | Francisci Theobald de Barking in Agro Svf: Arm' | Charissimæ conivgis ; | ex qvo svscepit Franciscvm, Robertvm, Theodosiam, Annam, & Saram, | qvos omnes vna cvm mærente marito reliqvit svper | stites. | Inclyta hæc heroina mvltis eximiisqve dotibvs, | Tvm animi, tvm corporis, plvrifariam perpolita. | Vt formà præstanti ita moribvs sanctissimis, | singvlari integritate & modestià incomparabili | præ cæteris merito spectatà & insigniter lavdata | gravi & divtvrno morbo confecta, firma | in Xto fide & invicta animi patientia, æterno nvmini spiritvm placide reddidit |

Æræ Xtianæ MDCLXIII
Octob' xxv die dominico | Anno Ad cvivs perpetvam

Æatis XXXIII
memorian & in fidei | conivgalis testimonivm mæstissimvs maritvs | hvnc lapidem posvit & devotissime consecravit.

Beneath are incised the arms of Theobald impaling Per pale (erm. & gu.) a rose countercharged, Nightingale. There is tablet on the east wall of this chapel (the three-light Perpendicular window having been filled up) displaying an emblazoned shield - Vert on a chevron or, three roses (or cinquefoils) qu. Crowley; impaling arg. on a pale sa. a conger's head erect (here shown cooped, not erased,) or, Gascoyne. Below is this inscription:

To the memory of John Crowley Esqr of Greenwich in Kent (only son of | Sr Ambrose Crowley Knt.) who died the 2d of January 1727 Aged 39 Years & | is buried in the vault under this isle with four of his children. | He married Theodosia Gascoyne, daughter of the Revd. Doctor Gascoyne, by Ann | daughter of Sr. Fraincis Theobald Knt. and heiress of this manour of Barking, by | whom he had six children, two sons & four daughters. | The eldest son, Ambrose Crowley Esqr. succeeded his father in this estate | of Barking, & added by purchase the manours of Badley, Combs & Collumbine, | He died unmarried May the 22d. 1754 aged 36 years. | John Crowley Esqr. 2nd son died unmarried July 15th 1755 aged 35 years. | Mary, the eldest daughter married the Right Honble Sr. Wm Stanhope, Knt of | the Bath, she died without issue Febry 27th 1746 & is buried at Shelford in | Nottinghamshire, aged 25 years. | Ann the second daughter died Novr. 17th 1734, aged 13 years. Theodosia third daughter & coheiress of her brother's estates married | Charles Boone Esqr by whom she had only one daughter: She died Janry | the 9th 1765 aged 40 years. | Elizabeth the youngest daughter & coheiress of her brother's estates, | now living, married John, Earl of Ashburnham, by whom she had one son & | four daughters. | This monument was erected Novr. the 25th 1771 by Mrs Theodosia Crowley | widow of the said John Crowley Esqr. who survived all her children, and lived | to a great age, an exemplary pattern of virtue and goodness;

blessed with a most | amiable disposition, her constant wish was to make others happy; very generous to | private distress, and very charitable to the poor: no one was more esteemed while | living; or more lamented at her death. She died May the 7th 1782 Aged 89 Years. | (This lady presented the church plate in 1769.)

On the south wall nearby hangs a helmet with gilded visor, and crest on a mount vert a sun in splendour proper, charged with a rose gales.

On the same wall is a tablet with funeral urn carved in low relief, upon which is written:

This monument was erected by | Mrs Theodosia Crowley to the memory | of her affectionate brother, Theobald | Gascoyne Esqr in gratitude for his great | kindness to her in his last will, by which he | left her sole heiress of Barking Hall, the | manour of Barking, and all his | estates therein. He died October the 16th 1714 | aged 26 years, & is buried in the | vault underneath this isle.

The arms of Gascoyne are placed on a shield below. On the opposite wall is another urn-surmounted tablet, with this inscription:

This monument was erected | by a disconsolate husband | to the memory of Theodosia | wife of Charles Boone Esqr | and daughter | of John Crowley Esqr | Alderman of London, by I Theodosia, his wife. | She died the 9th of January 1765 | aged forty years. |
Below is an emblazoned shield, the colouring rather decayed: Az, on a bend-between 6 lioncels (?) or, 3 birds (?) Boone.

The only other inscription to be seen in the church is in the glass of the tower's west window.

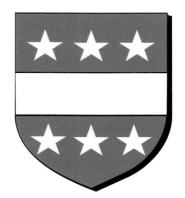

The EARLS of ASHBURNHAM
(Lords of the Manor of Badley 1781-1916)

MOTTO : Le roy et l'estat = The king and the state

ARMS : a fess between six mullets, Ag
Earls coronet. Crest from a ducal coronet Or. an ash tree proper.
Supporters two greyhounds Sa. lined and collared Or.

FOR nearly eight hundred years Ashburnham Place, near Battle, Sussex was the seat of the notable English family, the Lords (later Earls)of Ashburnham.

The family name of Ashburnham or Ashburn descended from Bertram de Ashburnham, who held Dover against William the Conqueror's forces after Hastings, in 1066.

The Administrative History, Ashburnham Family Achive, (East Sussex Record Office Ref: ASH) records, 'The early history of the Ashburnham family may be condensed to the statement that they first emerge as small landowners in the parish of Ashburnham in Sussex towards the close of the twelfth century. With some slight increase in importance they continued there for the next four hundred years, none of their members doing anything sufficiently notorious either for good or ill to find a place in the pages of history. By the time of Queen Elizabeth I the family had become great enough to tempt the heralds to record for them a pedigree fitting to their station and antiquity. Income from the local iron industry and the able administration of their estate enabled the male members of the family to take their place as honest squires, and to fulfil the military and civil obligations which their position demanded'!

As well as the Sussex estate the family, also owned property in Scotland, Dover Street, London W1 (see Fig 7.6), South Wales (Pembry - see below) and of course the Barking Hall Estate in Suffolk from c.1781 to 1917 (see Fig 7.4).

"The Ashburnham Estate papers in the National Library of Wales record, in 1815, the freight of tinplates to Bristol in the sloop 'Eleanor' and her return with timber and iron; also, the carriage of coal to the Tin Mills from the Earl of Ashburnham collieries in Pembrey in 1816". (*Kidwelly Tin Works 1737 to 1914* by W. H. Morris) (mention is also made of the Earl of Ashburnham's canal in Pembrey).

In his Journal (see Chapter 8), John Kirby Moore, the

Fig 7.5 Ashburnham Place, near Battle Sussex.

Steward for the Ashburnham's Suffolk Estate, records travelling to Pembry on Welsh Railway business.

ASHBURNHAM GENEALOGY - succession IN BRIEF

John Ashburnham, (the 1st Lord Ashburnham) was created a Baron on May 30th 1689. On 22nd July 1677, he married Bridget, the daughter and heiress of Walter Vaughan, Esqr. of Brecknockshire. He died on January 22nd 1710, leaving four children:

1 Jane, m. James Haynes Esqr. & died in Aug 1731.
2 Elizabeth, m. a) Robert Cholmondeley, Esq.
   b) Seymour Cholmondeley, Esq. & died 16th Jan 1732.
3 William, (the 2nd Lord) born 20th May 1675 & married Catherine, daughter & heiress of Thomas Taylor, Esqr. of Bedfordshire, but died without issue on 16th June 1710. He was succeeded by his brother -
4 John, (the 3rd Lord & 1st Earl) born 13th March 1687 & created Viscount St. Asaph & Earl Ashburnham by George II on 14th May 1730. He married Mary Butler, the daughter of James, Duke of Ormond on 21st Oct 1710, who died without issue on 12th Jan 1712. He married secondly, Henrietta Stanley, the daughter of William, Earl of Derby (and widow of John Annesley, Earl of Anglesey) and by her, who died on 26th June 1718, had issue,
4a Henrietta Bridget, who died unmarried, August 8, 1732. His Lordship married, thirdly, Jemima de Grey, daughter of Henry, Duke of Kent; who, before she died on 27th July 1731, had
4a Bertram,who died unmarried in 1743 and

4b John, who succeeded to the title on the death his father on the 10th March 1737.

JOHN ASHBURNHAM, (the 2nd Earl), Viscount St. Asaph, Baron Ashburnham, was born on 30th October 1714 and succeeded his father, John, the late Earl, as above.

On 28th June 1756 he married Elizabeth, the daughter of John Crowley Esqr. of Barking, Suffolk, an Alderman of London, and they six children as follows:

1   George, born 2nd Feb 1758, died on 14th Feb following.
2   George, (the 3rd Earl) Viscount St Asaph, born 25th Dec 1760, who married twice. Firstly, on 28th Aug 1784, to Sophia, the third daughter of the Marquis of Bath, by whom he had a two sons, George born 9th October 1785, died 1813; John (1789-1810) and a daughter Elizabeth Sophia, born 17th Sept 1786. Sophia died during childbirth on 9th April 1791.
    He married secondly, on 25th July 1795, Charlotte Percy, eldest daughter of the Earl of Beverley & sister of George, 5th Duke of Northumberland. This marriage produced a further twelve children including Bertram (the 4th Earl) (1797-1878)
3   Henrietta Theodosia, born 8th Nov 1759, died 1847.
4   Jemima Elizabeth, born 1st Jan 1762, who married the Marquis of Graham, (later Duke of Montrose) on 26th Feb 1785, by whom she had a son, born 4th Sept 1786. She died the 18th of the same month, and the child died on 23rd April 1787.
5   Elizabeth Frances, born, on 10th May 1763, died 1854.
6   Theodosia Mary, born 16th June 1765, who married Robert Vyner Esqr. of Gautby in Lincolnshire on 29th May 1788, and died in 1822.

George Ashburnham, (the 3rd Earl) who died on 27th October 1830, left all property in Sussex and Suffolk for the use of his eldest son Bertram, the 4th Earl, in his will dated 26th July 1827 (Proved PCC on 29th December 1830).

Bertram Ashburnham, (the 4th Earl) married Katherine Charlotte the daughter of George Baillie of Jerviswood, Lanarkshire. They produced eleven children including two sons Bertram (the 5th Earl), born 28th Oct 1840 & Thomas (the 6th Earl), born 8th April 1855.

Lady Katherine, Countess of Ashburnham, who died on 6th Feb 1894, and the Honourable Percy Ashburnham, the 4th Earl's brother, who died on 25th Jan 1881, were admitted tenants of the manor of Badley after the death and under the Will of Bertram 4th Earl of Ashburnham who died 22nd June 1878. His title passed to their eldest son Bertram, who attained the age of 21 on 28th Oct 1861.

Fig 7.6 The staircase and cupola at the Ashburnham's elegant late 17th century town house 30 Dover Street, Westminster, London W1.

Fig 7.7 The Ashburnham Coat of Arms.

He married Emily Chaplin but died without issue on 15th Jan 1913. Although the late 4th Earl's fifth son Thomas succeeded as the 6th Earl, his death signalled the end of the Parish of Badley as a single estate, maintained from the Norman conquest of 1066.

Thomas, the 6th Earl of Ashburnham, sold off the 3,450 acre Barking Hall Estate, which included the entire Parish of Badley, to a syndicate in 1916 for £58,000. The estate was finally broken-up when they sold it at auction at Ipswich on Tuesday 11th December 1917 for £73,000 (see Chapter 5).

The 6th Earl married Maria Elizabeth Anderson of Fredericton, New Brunswick and died without issue on 12th May 1924. His heir was his sole surviving sister the Lady Margaret, who was married to John Joseph Bickersteth.

Upon her death in 1953, the estate, including Ashburnham Place, passed to her great-nephew, John Bickersteth, a young clergyman, who gave Ashburnham Place and the surrounding park land to the Ashburnham Christian Trust, who still retain ownership.

There is a hatchment for the late Earl of Ashburnham on the north wall of the nave. Arms: Ashburnham impaling Baillie of Jerviswoode.

The former Gipping Rural District was formed under the East Suffolk Review Order, 1934, by the amalgamation of the Bosmere and Claydon and East Stow Rural Districts.

By Letters Patent dated 25th May, 1951, the Council received a grant of armorial bearings in the following terms :

"Azure semee of Fleurs de lys a Bend wavy Argent between two Ears of Wheat slipped and leaved Or And for the Crest On a Wreath of the Colours On a Mount Vert an Ash 'free proper in the centre and pendent from the branches by a Riband Azure an Escutcheon Sable charged with a Leopard's face Or."

The prevailing colours of blue and white are those of the Blessed Virgin Mary and the Fleur-de-lys is one of Her emblems. The shield is strewn with these as an indication of the great preponderance of parishes dedicated to St. Mary in the district.

The two wheat ears allude to the two former rural districts and the wavy bend represents the River Gipping. The motto, ' Domini est dirigere " means " It is for the Lord to direct." (Gipping Rural District - Official Guide, p.7)

The Ashburnham family's association with the district was depicted by the ash tree on the Council's armorial bearings (Fig 7.8 below).

Fig 7.8 The armorial bearings of the former Gipping Urban District Council.

Fig 7.9 The Needham Market town sign erected beside the main road either side of the town in 1951 incorporates the Ashburnham Coat of Arms. Most who pass them are probably unaware of their significance.

Chapter Eight

Other Notable Badley Families

Several other families have had a long association with Badley. Some of them are included in this account for the part they have played in the history of the parish.

The familes concerned are:

> WOLTON (Badley Hall)
> MUDD (Green Farm & Badley Hall)
> MOORE (Woodlands)
> HAYDON (Doveshill)
> SCOTT (Badley Hall)

Wolton OF BADLEY
(Walton/Woulton/Woolton)

THE Woltons were yeoman farmers who tenanted Badley Hall from the Crowleys. In his book "*A Suffolk Family*" on the history of the Woltons, Eric D Wolton surmises from the various parish records that John Wolton came to Badley from Wyverstone (north of Stowmarket) and by 1801 had moved to Newbourne the birthplace of wife Ann (nee Hyem) of Newbourne Hall, his grandson John's wife.

Major Richard Gipps is recorded as living at the Hall in 1722. He sold it to the Crowley family in 1735, who never lived there, preferring to tenant the property whilst they occupied Barking Hall. The registers and Steward's Surveys indicate that the Woltons were living at farming at Badley Hall between about 1726 and 1779.

Deborah Wolton is said to have been born at Badley Hall on 25th May 1765 and is recorded as having been baptised at St Mary's four days later. There are no marked graves for the Wolton family in Badley churchyard, despite the fact that six Woltons are recorded as having been buried there between 1726 and 1772. viz

Burials :

1726	John Woolton Sept 20th.	
1726	Elizabeth d. of Thomas & Anne Walton Nov 22nd.	
1728	Anne wife of Thomas Walton Oct 19th.	
1737	Alice Woulton widow Feb 15th.	
1739	Alice Wolton Dec 28th.	
1772	Thomas Wolton Dec 26th.	

However, there is a double grave just inside the churchyard, and nearest to the hedge on the immediate right as you pass through the gate, commemorating Jacob and Sara Chandler. This relates to Sarah Chandler (née Wolton) (see baptisms and marriages below), of Stowmarket, who was buried on Feb 12th 1820, aged 84, and her husband Jacob

Chandler who was buried on Jul 13th 1778 (grave number 31 on the graveyard plan in Chapter 3 page 30).

The Baptisms and Marriages:
Baptisms :

1732	John, s. of Thomas & Sarah Wolton, Aug 20th.	
1735	Sarah, d. of Thomas & Sarah Wolton, May 2nd.	
1739	William, s. of Thomas & Sarah Wolton, Nov 18th.	
1761	John, s. of John & Ann Wolton, Dec 1st.	
1764	Thomas, s. of John & Ann Wolton, Feb 29th.	
1765	Deborah, d. of John & Ann Wolton, May 29th.	
1767	Sarah & Thomas, d. & s., of John & Ann Wolton, July 9th.	
1769	William, s. of John & Ann Wolton, Nov 20th.	
1772	Susannah & Jemima, dtrs. of John & Ann Wolton, Nov 17th.	
1775	Higham, s. of John & Ann Wolton, b. 4th Apr 1774, bapt. Jun 10th.	
1779	Charlotte, d. of John & Ann Wolton, Jun 3rd	
1779	James Bead, s. of John & Ann Wolton, Jun 3rd.	

Marriages :

1757	Jacob Chandler of Combs=Sarah Wolton of Badley, both sp. Aug 15th. (Witnesses: Thomas Wolton & John Wood).	
1770	William Wolton of Badley=Susanna Green of Combs, both sp. Lic (Witnesses: Ann Wolton & Jno Wolton) (no date).	

There are no other Wolton marriages, but John Wolton is recorded as a witness to the following marriages:

1761	Samuel Harvey = Ann Francis, both sp. of Badley, May 12th (Witnesses: John Wolton & John Barnard)	
1762	Bass Birch of Gosbeck = Mary Kemble of Badley, both sp., May 7th Lic. (Witnesses: John Wolton & Samuel Scapey)	
1773	John Rainbird = Sarah Hewett, both sp. of Badley, Sep 30th Lic. (Witnesses: John Wolton & Samuel Scapey)	

This indicates that he was a churchwarden or other church official, as Samuel Scapey also appears several more times.

Churchwardens were ex-officio Overseers of the Poor (Poor Law Act 1601) and as noted in Chapter 2, the Woltons served as Overseers and Parish Constable for Badley over a number of years.

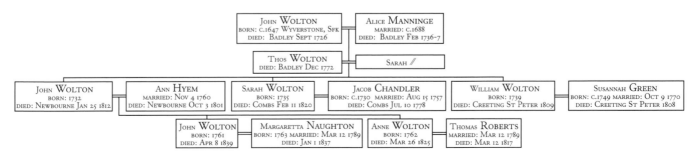

Fig 8.1 The Wolton of Badley - Family Tree (part).

MUDD
OF BADLEY

THE Mudd family has had a long association with Badley, as can be seen from the Parish record extracts below. William Mudd, aged 50, a farmer, was recorded at Badley Hall in the 1841 Census along with his wife Ann and five of their children: Thomas (who succeeded his father at the Hall upon his death in 1856), William, Ann, Frederick and Emily and three servants. Fifty years later Thomas, now aged 67, along with his sister Emily were still living there.

Thomas' brother Frederick was farming the adjacent Badley Green Farm by 1861, and had left there by 1889 judging by a note written that year on the attic wall at Badley Hall which refers to him being a 'late inhabitor' (Fig 8.3 next page).

Baptisms :

1778	Edward, s. of Thomas & Hannah Mudd - Dec 8th.
	Thomas, s. of Thomas & Hannah Mudd - Dec 8th.
	Richard, s. of Thomas & Hannah Mudd - Dec 8th
1786	Susan Elizabeth Mary Ann, d of Thos & Elizabeth Mudd - Mar 16th.
	Richard, s. of Thos & Elizabeth Mudd - Mar 16th.
1807	William, s. of Richard & Ann Mudd, brn. Aug 5th, Bapt. Sep 16th.
	Mary, d. of Richard & Ann Mudd, brn. Aug 5th, Bapt. Sep 16th
	Thomas, s. of Richard & Ann Mudd, brn. Aug 5th, Bapt. Sep 16th.
1809	Thomas, s. of Richard & Ann Mudd - Sep 24th.

Marriages :

1613	Henry Mudd m. Anne Wellam - Nov 1st.
1656	Thomas Mudde m. Elizabeth Painter - Feb 7th.
1666	Margaret Mud of Darmsden, m. Francis Harvie of Coddenham - Sept 25th.
1797	Elizabeth Mudd of Badley, a minor, m. William Simpson of Badley, with consent of her natural mother - Mar 17th.
1800	Robert Mudd of Badley m. Elizabeth Sutton Kemball of Combs - Dec 30th.
1801	Thomas Mudd of Badley m. Lucy Simpson of Badley - Sep 27th.
1799	Richard Mudd of Badley m. Ann Cooper of Badley Jun 5th.
1819	William Mudd, widower of Badley m. Anne Adams of Bedfield - Dec 15th.
1839	Elizabeth Mudd m. George Haywood - Dec 12th.
1848	Ann Maria Mudd m. Robert Mumford - Dec 14th.
1860	Frederick William Mudd m. Mary Smith Cooper Jun 27th.

Burials :

1793	Thomas Mudd, May 21.
1798	Susan Mudd, Nov 22.
1804	John Mudd, Jan 18.
1815	Mary Ann Mudd, Sept 26, aged 31.
1817	Robert Mudd, Feb 14, aged 37.
1817	Elizabeth Mudd, Oct 3, aged 76.
1825	Caroline Mudd, Aug 3, aged 3.
1834	Richard Mudd of Aldham, Mar 21, aged 51.
	William Cupper Mudd, Aug 9, aged 8 months.
1842	Ann Mudd of Darmsden, Aug 23rd, aged 60.
1856	John Mudd of Chevington, Jul 5, aged 48.
1857	William Mudd, Feb 13, aged 68.
1864	Ann Mudd, Aug 15, aged 75.
1866	Clara Mudd, March 14, infant.

The translation of Fig 8.2 next page -
Children of Fred and Mary Mudd
Farmers,
late inhabiters of Badley Green:
Ann E Mudd, Clara Mudd (dead), Mary Mudd
William F Mudd, Frank Mudd, Philip H Mudd
Isabella A Mudd (called Lella), Margaret H Mudd
Caroline J Mudd (called Carrie)
Written by Margaret H Mudd May 3rd 1889

At the time of the 1881 Census two of the children listed above, William F (13) and Frank (12), were boarders at Ballygate Street, Collegiate School, Beccles, Suffolk.

Other Mudds recorded in the same Census as having been born at Badley are:

William Mudd (58) farmer, residing at Willow Marsh, Stoke-by-Nayland (PRO Ref: RG11, Piece 1826, Folio 112, p. 17)
Thomas Mudd (52) farmer, residing a Badley Hall.
(PRO RG11, Piece 1862, Folio 4, p. 2)
Frederick Mudd (50) farmer, residing at Badley Green Farm, with the remainder of the family listed above.
(PRO RG11, Piece 1862, Folio 5, p. 3)

(See Appendix B, page 279, for full listings of the 1841 -1901 Census for Badley.)

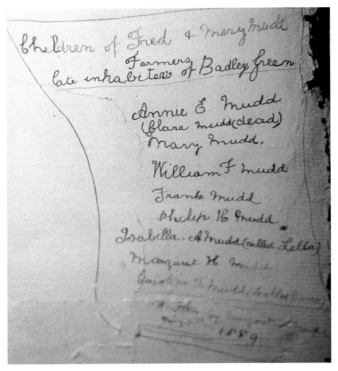

Fig 8.2 A list on an attic wall at Badley Hall recorded by Margaret H Mudd on May 3rd 1889.

Margaret also appears to have written another note (Fig 8.3 below) which reads:

Inhabitants of this House
(The Hall)
Mrs E. Cooper (married)
Mr Thomas Mudd (bachelor)

Thomas was not 'living in sin'! The Mrs E. Cooper referred to was his sister Emily, who had married Alfred Cooper of Combs who died in May 1893.

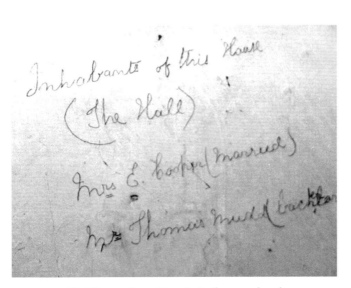

Fig 8.3   Another attic note in the same hand.

Times could be harsh as the following newspaper report illustrates.

Needham Market Petty Sessions
Before Rev J E Schreber (Chairman) & Rev W Simpson

NEGLECTING WORK.

Edward Barrell, labourer, was charged with neglecting his work while in the employ of Mr. Thomas Mudd, farmer, Badley, on the 16th August.

Mr. Mudd said that on the day in question he found the defendant sitting at the bottom of a field. He asked him to go to work, but he went away and did not return.

There was no written agreement. The defendant pleaded guilty and the magistrates committed him to gaol for 14 days.

Extracted from The Stowmarket Courier 2 Sep 1869 page 3, col 5.

On 4th Mar 1909, Edgar Herbert Mudd (known locally as 'Spider Mudd'), of The Grange, Creeting, the tenant of Badley Hall and Badley Green Farms for on 20 years and ancestors for over 20 years unsuccessfully applied to the Earl of Ashburnham for the Agency of the Suffolk Estate "on the lamentable death of Robert Lingwood" (the late Agent).

On 15th November 1918 Edgar Herbert Mudd bought Badley Hall (217 acres). £1,500 was mortgaged.

On 18th Oct 1938 he sold Badley Hall Farm and Badley Green Farm, a total of 440 acres, to William Hunt of Hill House, Needham Market for £3,300 who on the 9th April 1946 sold the Hall Farm to Leonard Scott from Derbyshire in the same year.

On 3rd November 1936, presumaby in failing health, Edgar Mudd assigned power of attorney to Florence Eva Rose, a spinster, of the same address and Charles Edward Rose of Chain House Farm, Needham Market, a farmer. By the following year (1937) he had retired and was living at 35 Queen's Road, Felixstowe, where he died in August 1939 (see obituary report later in this chapter).

The Abstract of Title reveals that in 1936 he owned the following fifteen Mid-Suffolk farms and was, one supposes, by this time a very wealthy individual.

Chain House Farm, Needham Market
Badley Hall Farm, Badley
Green Farm, Badley
Woolney Hall Farm, Creeting St Mary and Earl Stonham
Little College Farm, Creeting St. Mary
Grange Farm, Creeting St. Mary
Poplar Hall Farm, Creeting St. Mary
Whissells Farm, Creeting St. Mary
Hall Farm, Little Stonham
Green Farm, Earl Stonham
Quintons Farm, Earl Stonham
Red House Farm, Stonham
Ulveston Hall Farm, Debenham, Mickfield and Wetheringsett
Oak Tree Farm, Kenton
Suddon Hall Farm, Kenton

Fig 8.4   The large stone slab to the left of the porch, marks the grave of William & Anne Mudd of Badley Hall. It is the grandest of the Mudd memorials and as noted in Chapter 3 (Fig 3.2) it was originally surrounded by an iron railing set into the stone in square lead sheaths, the remains of which are just visible on the left hand side of the photograph.

MUDD MONUMENTAL INSCRIPTIONS at BADLEY CHURCHYARD

(the numbers refer to the grave location on the churchyard plan, Fig 3.12 in Chapter 3)

There are more marked Mudds burials in Badley Churchyard than for any other family.

24.	MUDD W* :	In memory of/ WILLIAM MUDD/ late of Badley Hall/ 7th February 1857/ aged 68 years/ also/ Anne wife of WILIAM MUDD/ who departed this life/ 8th August 1864/ aged 75 years.
28.	MUDD C :	Sacred to the memory of Caroline/ the daughter of/ WILIAM and ANN MUDD/ who died 29th July 1825/ aged 3 years (Footstone : C+M/ 1825).
29.	MUDD R :	In loving memory of/ ROBERT son of/ THOMAS/ and ELIZABETH MUDD/ of Badley/ who departed this life/ February 9th 1817/ aged 37 years (Footstone : R+M/ 1817).
30.	MUDD M A :	Sacred to the memory of/ MARY ANN daughter of/ THOMAS/ and ELIZABETH MUDD/ of Badley/ who departed this life/ September 22nd 1815/ aged 32 years (Footstone : MAM/ 1815).
31.	MUDD J :	In memory of/ John MUDD/ son of/ Thomas MUDD/ late of this Parish/ who departed this life/ the 9th day of January/ 1804.
32.	MUDD T :	Thomas MUDD/ late of this Parish/ 16th August 1793/ aged 48 years.
33.	MUDD E :	In memory/ ELIZABETH/ wife of THOMAS MUDD/ of Badley/ 26th September 1817/ aged 60 years (Footstone : E+M/ 1817).
34.	MUDD R :	Sacred/ to the memory of/ Mr RICHARD MUDD/ of Aldham who/ died March 16th 1834 (Footstone : R+M/ 1834).
41.	MUDD R C :	Erected/ to the memory/ of/ WILLIAM CUPPER MUDD/ infant son of/ WILL and HEPHZIBAH MUDD/ of Stoke by Nayland/ who departed this life/ August 4th 1850. (Footstone : W.C.M./ 1850).
43.	MUDD C :	In memory of/ CLARA infant child of/ FREDERICK and MARY MUDD/ who died March 8th /1866 (Footstone : C+M/ 1866).
50.	MUDD A :	Sacred to the memory of ANN the wife of/ RICHARD MUDD/ who departed this life/ August 13th 1842/ aged 60 years (Footstone : A+M/ 1842).

*See Fig 8.4 above right.

CREETING ST. MARY
Death and Funeral of Mr. Edgar H. Mudd

There were laid to rest in Creeting St. Mary Churchyard yesterday afternoon, the remains of Mr. Edgar Herbert Mudd, who, until about two years ago, had lived all his life in the district, residing for many years at the Grange Farm, Creeting St. Mary.

Mr. Mudd who was 86 years of age, farmed extensively in Creeting St. Mary, Badley and Debenham, removing in 1937 to live at Felixstowe where he died on August 19th after long illness. The deceased was of shrewd business habits, and never sought public life, except for the position of Churchwarden at Creeting St. Mary, which he held for a great number of years up to the time of his removal from the district.

The mourners present were Miss E. Rose, Miss M. A. Rose, Miss G. Rose and Mrs. E. G. Bithrey (nieces), Miss B. H. M. Rose and Mr. E. Rose and Mr. J. T. Rose (great nephews). . . . .

Extract from the *Stowmarket Recorder, and Needham Market, Combs & Stowupland Advertiser*, Thursday, August 24th, 1939, page 5.

Other notes on the Mudd family.

Combs - 16th Aug 1816, William Mudd of Badley, married Sara Robinson.

Moore
OF BADLEY & DARMSDEN

THE Moore family appear to have moved to Badley in 1792, following the marriage of James Moore to Sarah Theobald (alias Medows) by licence at Henley on 7th February.

Sarah was the daughter of John Medows Theobald of Henley Hall, Suffolk, who was High Sheriff for Suffolk in 1787. (He assumed the surname and arms of Theobald in 1774, in pursuance of an Aunt's Will).

The background of James Moore, who was born on 20th November 1765 is presently unknown, but he must have had sufficient social status to marry Sarah Theobald.

Present research suggests he was the son of James Moore a wool merchant in Ipswich born in 1729. This James was married to Sarah daughter of John Brock, but no record has been found of their marriage or their son's christening.

If his father were a wool merchant this would have provided James with the social status he would have undoubtedly required to successfully court John Medows Theobald's daughter.

His name first occurs in the Badley Towne Booke in 1793. On the 17th January the following year, he was sworn in at Ipswich as a Constable of the county.

He was a subscriber of the Barking Association For Prosecuting Persons Guilty of Felony &c., which met half-yearly at the Fox Inn, Barking (see Fig 8.5 opposite).

The Moores lived at The Woodlands, Badley (see Chapter 5), which they tenant-farmed along with the adjoining Holyoak Farm, Combs, a considerable enterprise consisting of 520 acres. In 1871 the Census records 21 men, 3 women and 3 servants employed there. Both farms were part of the Ashburnhams' Suffolk Estate.

They had three children, all born at Badley -
James Meadows Moore, born on the 3rd February 1793.
John Kirby Moore, born on the 28th September 1794.
Sarah Bredell Moore, born on 28th August 1796.

James Moore snr died on 15th June 1831 and his wife Sarah on 5th Oct. 1833. They are both buried in Badley

---

BARKING ASSOCIATION
For Prosecuting Persons Guilty of Felony &c.

Notice is hereby given, That the half yearly Meeting of the Subscribers to this Association, will be held at the Fox, in Barking on Monday, the 15th day of January inst, at the hour of 4 in the afternoon where the Subscribers and all other Persons desirous of becoming Members are requested to attend.

SUBSCRIBERS NAMES
Mr. James Moore   Badley
    John Simpson   "
    Edward Jay   "
    Thomas Scott   "

3rd Jan 1816 } BENJAMIN MORGAN   Treasurer
RICHARD MUDD   Solicitor

Fig 8.5 Reproduction of the advertisement which appeared in the Ipswich Journal on 6th January 1816. Forty subscribers are listed in the notice - only the Badley names are reproduced here.

Churchyard in chevron-shaped tombs which were originally elaborately railed (see grave 51 in Fig 3.12, in Chapter 3).

Their son James Medows Moore never married. In the 1841 Census, aged 45, he is shown as a farmer living at Burnt House Cottage, Darmsden (292) and farming the Pightle (293), Burnt House Field (298) & (302) on the Tithe Map, as well as two strips on the Common Land. He employed two domestic servants Charlotte Chaplin aged 30 and Elizabeth Francis aged 15. He later moved into Darmsden Hall and died there on the 13th April 1855, aged 62. He was buried alongside his parents in Badley on April 21st.

His sister married Joshua Rodwell Esq., of Alderton, Suffolk, at St Mary's Badley on 6th August 1817. They lived at Alderton Hall which is adjacent to the parish church. They had seven children. She died at Chelsea on 28th September 1853, aged 57 and was buried in the vault on the south side of Alderton Church on 4th October.

John Kirby Moore lived with his parents at Badley and took over the tenancy of the two farms when his father died in 1831.

On the 20th December, in the same year, he married Henrietta Pennington at St Nicholas, Godston, Surrey, which was close to her father's home at Leigh Place, Godstone. John and Henrietta lived together at The Woodlands, Badley for the next thirty-five years, until she died, childless, aged 78 years on 8th April 1866 (see Chapter 5, Fig 5.11).

In 1861 Mrs. Moore was in possession of a prayer book printed in 1670 formerly belonging to a Margaret Whitemore of Ludson, Salop.

She was buried in the Moores' family vault in Badley churchyard on 14th April 1866. "The church was filled to overflowing, many could get no nearer than the porch in churchyard. It was estimated that as many as 400 attended". (The Journal of John Kirby Moore of Badley, page 46 - see page 194).

The stained glass east window of Badley Church, designed by the eminent Victorian church architect Frederick Preedy in 1866, is dedicated to her memory.

She was born at Barking on the 5th April 1788, the daughter of Joseph Pennington Esq., and his second wife Henrietta Whitmore of Creeting St Mary. They were married by licence at Creeting All Saints on 12th July 1787.

Joseph's first wife Mary Johnson, was also from Creeting St Mary. He married her there on 23rd January 1776 and she was buried in the churchyard there on 28th November 1784, aged 31 years.

Joseph Pennington was appointed Estate Steward at Barking by the second Earl Ashburnham in 1772 when he was only 22 years old, a position he held close to his death in 1833. JKM undoubtedly met Henrietta through their joint association with the Ashburnhams' Suffolk estate.

"In his first year as Steward, Pennington drew up a fine map of Needham Market and six years later was commissioned to survey Ipswich and produce a town map, becoming noted nationally as a map maker." (*The Manor and Woodlands of Barking* - John Vane 1990).

Prints of *"A Map of Ipswich. In which the Streets, Buildings, Yards &c. Are drawn from an Actual Survey finished 1778. By Joseph Pennington, Land Surveyor"* are available from the Suffolk Record Office. The accompanying note on the reverse states that during his careers he also acted as an Enclosure Commissioner in Derbyshire and further examples of his mapping skills exist for areas of Hampshire and Sussex.

In 1834, aged 40, John Kirby Moore was offered and accepted the Stewardship of the Ashburnhams' Suffolk estate, which by this time had passed to the 4th Earl. He succeeded

Fig 8.6 John Kirby Moore at the age of 70, photographed at William Cobb's Photographic Institute, Ipswich on 22nd July 1864. (Photo courtesy of Nick Balmer)

Edward Driver of Richmond Terrace, London, who held the position for a short time after Joseph Pennington.

Collectively referred to as 'The Barking Hall Estate', John became responsible for administering a holding comprising of Barking Hall and twenty-one mixed farms totalling 3,450 acres. A formidable task and a post he was to hold for 48 years. He probably farmed The Woodland and Holy Oak Farms rent free in lieu of a salary during this period and, judging by the bequests in his Will, amassed a considerable fortune.

With the Ashburnhams only occasionally staying at Barking Hall, their representative JKM was in a position to exercise considerable influence over the tenants. However, there is no evidence to suggest that he was anything but protective towards them, for example, arguing against the Ashburnhams increasing their rents.

We must be grateful to John Kirby Moore for a remarkable 'Journal' he maintained. This diary, commenced on 19th Oct. 1821 and finished on 1st November 1873 - twelve years before his death on 31st October 1885, aged 91.

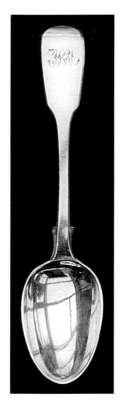

J K M

Fig 8.7 A 1852 silver spoon, part of a dinner service made by George Angel of London and bearing John Kirby Moore's elaborate monogram - enlarged alongside.

Whilst the whereabouts of the original is unknown, a typed copy, said to have been made for a Charles Partridge FSA (see page 5) from the original document, then in the possession of a John Pennington, exists. It is not every-day account, but it gives an intriguing insight into the social and business life of a gentleman farmer of the period, colours in the life of the parish and records many historical facts.

In 2001, in conjunction with the Suffolk Family History Society, I published John Kirby Moore's journal with additional notes and unpublished photographs (ISBN 1 871905 75 3) (see Fig 8.8 opposite).

From the 'Journal' we find that in addition to the Stewardship duties and running his own farms, John was involved in a number of local organisations. He was a Trustee of the 'Stowmarket Navigation', i.e. the Stowmarket - Ipswich canal on the River Gipping (see Chapter 9).

On 5th April 1836 he was elected Vice-Chairman of the Board of Guardians for Bosmere Union whose Union House was situated at Barham.

On several occasions he was required to travel to South Wales to oversee the extension of the railway through the Ashburnhams' 3,300 acre Pembrey estate, which included mining interests.

Along with Thomas Fowler Wood Esq of The Cedars, Combs, he represented Combs as an Acting Guardian of the Stow Union.

He was a member of the Claydon Book Club, established at the Crown Inn, Claydon, for more than a century for the circulation of books and social intercourse, the Suffolk Agricultural Society and the local Conservative Party.

His obvious appreciation of the arts and literature is apparent through his journal. He supported local authors. For example, he was one of the subscribers to *"Poems"* a collection of sixty-one poems by Suffolk romantic poetess **Eliza Acton** (1799-1859) published by R Deck, Ipswich (1826) and *"The History of Stowmarket"* by Rev A G H Hollingsworth, MA., Vicar of Stowmarket with Stowupland, published in 1854.

He was the Churchwarden at St. Mary's Badley for 54 years and according to Kelly's Suffolk Directory he donated an organ to Combs church.

Arguably, he was one of, if not the most important and influential persons in the area during his Stewardship.

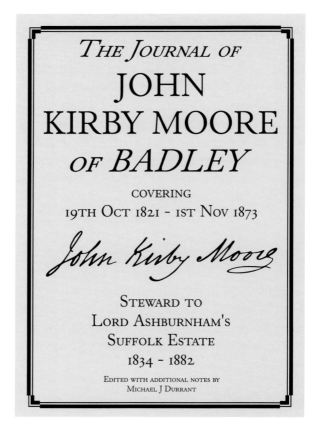

THE JOURNAL OF
JOHN KIRBY MOORE
OF BADLEY

COVERING
19TH OCT 1821 - 1ST NOV 1873

John Kirby Moore

STEWARD TO
LORD ASHBURNHAM'S
SUFFOLK ESTATE
1834 - 1882

EDITED WITH ADDITIONAL NOTES BY
MICHAEL J DURRANT

Fig 8.8 The cover-page of 'The Journal of John Kirby Moore of Badley' published in 2001.

THE IPSWICH JOURNAL.

SATURDAY, JANUARY 27, 1821.

AT a Meeting held on at the Crown Inn, Coddenham, on Thursday, the 11th of January, 1821, for the purpose of considering and adopting a Loyal Address to his Majesty from the Inhabitants of the Hundred of BOSMERE and CLAYDON, the the County of Suffolk.

The **Rev. JOHN LONGE**, in the Chair.

It was resolved unanimously, that the Address now presented to the Meeting, be adopted and signed.

That the Members for the County be requested to transmit the same to the Secretary of State.

To the King's Most Excellent Majesty.

MAY IT PLEASE YOUR MAJESTY,

We, your Majesty's dutiful and loyal subjects, the undersigned Inhabitants of the Hundred of Bosmere and Claydon, in the County of Suffolk, beg to offer to your Majesty the assurance of our dutiful and zealous attachment to your Majesty's Sacred Office and Person.– We feel ourselves called upon at this perilous time to state, that we view with regret and abhorrence measures brought forward and sentiments declared, the tendency of which is to inflame the passions of the unwary and unenlightened part of our fellow countrymen, mislead their judgement, and thus aggravate the difficulties with which we are contending.

We view also with similar feelings of regret and abhorrence, attempts made by the unexampled licentiousness of the press to alienate the affections of your Majesty's subjects from their dutiful allegiance to your Majesty.

But we trust, with unshaken confidence to the laws of our inestimable Constitution, and to the wisdom and justice of Parliament, for the protection of the Altar and the Throne ; and we hope under Divine Providence, your Majesty may long continue to enjoy a prosperous and happy reign over a free and loyal people.

James Moore,	farmer,	Badley
John Kirby Moore,	ditto,	ditto
Wm Mudd,	ditto,	ditto
Thomas Mudd,	ditto,	ditto
Thomas Scott,	ditto,	ditto
Clerk Cooper,	ditto,	ditto
Edward Cooper,	ditto,	ditto
John Kemball,	ditto,	ditto
Charles Davey, J.P.	clk.	Barking
J.W.Pennington,	farmer,	Barking
William Kirby,	clk.	Barham
J. M. Rodwell,	ditto,	ditto
E. Lingwood,	ditto,	Battisford
John M. Theobald, esq. J.P.		Claydon Hall
James Meadows Moore,	farmer,	Darmsden
Charles Broke, K.C.B. Lieut.-Col.		Henley Hall

Fig 8.9 A reproduction of the Loyal Address from the Inhabitants of the Bosmere & Claydon Hundred which appeared on the front page of the Ipswich Journal on Saturday 27th January 1821 (not all names reproduced).

LOYAL ADDRESSES TO THE KING

A great deal of change occurred in the country during latter years of the reign of King George III: mechanization, achieved by the exploitation of coal and steam, a population increase from 7 to 12 million, and the introduction of enclosures and new techniques in agriculture.

Consequential high unemployment and hunger resulted, especially in rural areas, leading to civil unrest. A situation which the King, by this time, confined to Windsor and diplaying symptoms of delirium and delusions caused by porphyria, a hereditary physical illness, was probably oblivious to.

His son, George IV, described by one commentator as a "gifted, educated, artistic profligate" finally inherited his father throne on 29th Jan. 1820, at the age of 57. To the prevailing problems, he added those of his stormy relationship and the attempted divorce of his trollopy Queen, Caroline of Brunswick.

Shortly after the King's accession, the Cato Street Conspiracy was uncovered, the object of which was to murder the Cabinet.

During January 1821 the *Ipswich Journal* carried several Loyal Addresses to the King from various Suffolk Hundred including Bosmere and Claydon on 27th January, which is partially reproduced above, in that only Badley and associated names are preserved.

Both the Moore and Mudd families of Badley along with several other local farmers signed the declaration. One assumes the object was in effect to give moral support to the monarchy and the forces of law and order during what was described as "this perilous time".

John Kirby Moore's long association with his beloved Badley ended with his death at his birth-place The Woodlands, at the age of 91 years on 31st October 1885. He was buried in the family vault in Badley Churchyard on the 4th November.

However, the two large Black pine trees he planted in Badley churchyard on the 4th March 1865 are still growing; the east window in the church; the copious estate correspondence generated during his Stewardship in the Suffolk Record Office and his Journal all serve as a fitting memorial to his contribution to the development and history of Badley.

*Central Suffolk Agricultural Society
Presented by Philip Bennet Esq M.P. to
Mr John Kirby Moore of Badley
for having expended (in proportion to the quantity of
his rental) the greatest sum in Manual Labour
between the 1st July 1846 & the 1st July 1847.*

Journal entry -
1847 : September 30th *(Thursday)*
Agricultural Show at Stowmarket. I obtained Mr. Bennet's
silver cup, given for greatest amount of labour expended in
proportion to rent.

*Fig 8.10 Left, the Philip Bennet Cup, with (above) the inscription,
together with the relevant entry from John Kirby Moore's Journal.
(Photographed by courtesy of Nick Balmer)*

*Fig 8.11 The Moore family vault in Badley churchyard, which was originally surrounded by an ornate iron railing (see Chapter 3, Fig 3.2).
The furthermost stone marks the grave of James Moore and his wife Sarah (née Theobald) and their son James Meadows Moore. The other,
the grave of John Kirby Moore and his wife Henrietta (née Pennington). The chevron stone to the left marks the graves of John Kirby Moore's
nieces, Emily and Mary Jane Pennington of Needham Market. The latter was his constant companion after the death of his wife until his
own death in 1885. For inscriptions see Appendix C, page 297.*

Haydon
OF DOVESHILL

In 1927 Francis Emmanuel (Frank) and Carrie Louise Haydon (née Hammond) left their butchery business in Colchester High Street and took over Doveshill farm. The family farmed there for the next 24 years, initially as the tenants of Alfred Bywater, until they were able to buy the business.

'Frank' was born in Norwich, Norfolk, the son of Edward and Mary Ann Haydon, who are recorded in the 1881 Census for Narborough, Norfolk, as living in the School House, Narford Road, both aged 24. Edward is shown as a School Master and his wife as a School Mistress. Frank was then aged 2 and is listed with two sisters, Florence M., aged 3, born at Norwich and Bertha aged 1, born at Narborough. Edward's mother-in-law, Mary Eliza Potter, aged 51 and his 13 year-old sister in law Edith Cole were also recorded there.

Entry in Kelly's Directory for Norfolk, 1883, p.399-400. Norfolk - Narborough — "Here is a Parochial school of boys & girls, built in 1870; also a Sunday school, partly endowed; Edward Haydon, master".

Twenty years later, in the 1901 Census, Edward and Mary Ann are still living there as a Certificated Schoolmaster and Assistant Mistress, along with their daughters Bertha, now 21 and also an Assistant Mistress and Amy Edith, aged 7 years, born at Narborough.

'Frank' had already left the family home by this time and is recorded in the same Census at The Street, Pulham St Mary Magdalen (Pulham Market), Norfolk, as a journeyman butcher, aged 22, at John Outlaw's butcher's shop.

His wife Carrie was born at Grimston, Norfolk, the eldest of the eight children of Hugh Hunten and Emma E. Hammond (née Polkinhorne). She is recorded in the 1901 Census living with the family at the School House at Grimston, where her father, aged 43, born Harleston, Norfolk, was a Certified Head Teacher and her mother, aged 40, born Litcham, Norfolk, was a Certified Assistant Teacher. Carrie then aged 16, is shown as a Pupil Teacher.

'Frank' and Carrie's five children, who had all been born at Colchester, were Ida Mary, Francis Gordon *(known as Gordon)*, Marjorie *(known as Babs)*, John Douglas and Elizabeth *(known as Betty)*.

Fig 8.12 Francis (Frank) Emmanuel Haydon & Carrie Louise (née Hammond) photographed on their wedding day. (Photo courtesy of Betty Barber née Haydon)

To supplement the pre-war farm income 'Frank' Haydon used to regularly travel to Ipswich by bus to manage the Co-operative Butchery in the Buttermarket operated by Suffolk Farm Producers.

Along with his wife Carrie he was a life-long supporter of St Mary's church, where the latter was a churchwarden (see Chapter 3, page 44). The Haydons were also involved with numerous other local charitable organisations such as the Combs & Badley Nursing Association, whose support was very much appreciated in the final weeks of 'Franks' life whilst suffering from cancer.

Judging from the family photographs kindly provided by Mrs. Elizabeth *(Betty)* Barber *(née Haydon)*, growing up on the farm, especially during harvest, was happy and carefree. However, that all changed as WWII loomed.

Along with scores of other Suffolk families, the Haydons took in a war-time evacuee. His name was Danny (see Fig 8.13 and 8.16).

The family recalls returning to the farm on one occasion to find it had been strafed by a German aircraft, possibly returning from RAF Wattisham. Bullets had entered the dining room under the window and hit the edge of a wooden writing desk.

Fig 8.13 Norman Green (left) from Doveshill cottages and Danny (evacuee) on a Doveshill farm carthorse during the 1944 harvest.

Fig 8.14 A pre-war harvest with young John Haydon on the load and his little sister Betty with eldest sister Ida on the horse.

Fig 8.15 In the stackyard during a pre-war harvest with Jack Green on the wagon with Betty Haydon (wearing school hat) and sister Marjorie (Babs) looking up to brother John just visible on the stack.

Fig 8.16 On the harvest field. (standing l. to r.) Danny (evacuee) and Norman Green* (l.) and (seated l. to r.) Janet Saunders, Ida Saunders (née Haydon), Roger Gordon Saunders & Michael Haydon (Aug 1944) *Norman was the son of Jack Green (see Fig 8.15 below), one of the farmworkers who lived in one of the Doveshill cottages, opposite the track leading to the church (see Chapter 5). (All photos courtesy of Betty Barber née Haydon)

Both the Haydon brothers were involved in the war.

John Douglas Haydon

John joined the Territorial Army in 1939 and became a gunner in the Royal Artillery. Posted to the Middle East he was mentioned in dispatches whilst serving in Tobruk (see newspaper report Fig 8.17 below).

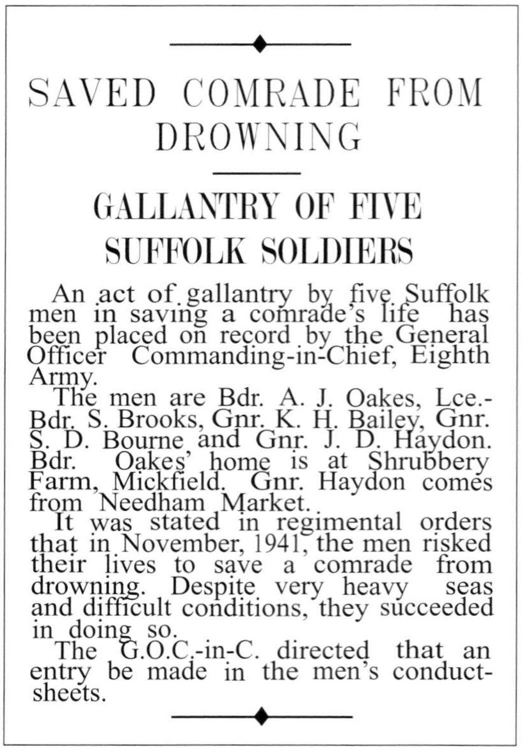

SAVED COMRADE FROM DROWNING

GALLANTRY OF FIVE SUFFOLK SOLDIERS

An act of gallantry by five Suffolk men in saving a comrade's life has been placed on record by the General Officer Commanding-in-Chief, Eighth Army.

The men are Bdr. A. J. Oakes, Lce.-Bdr. S. Brooks, Gnr. K. H. Bailey, Gnr. S. D. Bourne and Gnr. J. D. Haydon. Bdr. Oakes' home is at Shrubbery Farm, Mickfield. Gnr. Haydon comes from Needham Market.

It was stated in regimental orders that in November, 1941, the men risked their lives to save a comrade from drowning. Despite very heavy seas and difficult conditions, they succeeded in doing so.

The G.O.C.-in-C. directed that an entry be made in the men's conduct-sheets.

Fig 8.17 A newspaper report recording John Haydon's heroism.

Fig 8.18 John Douglas Haydon photographed at Cario after three days travelling in the desert without a wash or shave! (Photo courtesy of Betty Barber née Haydon)

Fig 8.19 John and Beryl Aggis Haydon (née Byford) photographed after their wedding. (Photo courtesy of Betty Barber née Haydon)

John's active service also ended at Tobruk, when in June 1942 the town was successfully assulted by the Germans following heavy air attacks. By the evening they had reached the harbour forcing the Tobruk garrison to surrender. John was one of the 30,000 prisoners captured. He became a prisoner of war first in Italy and then Germany until being liberated by the Americans in 1945. In Germany he was forced to work in a steel factory, but, along with his colleagues, did his best to sabotage the work.

He returned to Suffolk in late April 1945, just two weeks before his father died of cancer (buried at Badley on 8th May 1945, aged 65 years).

He took over the running of the farm for his mother and married his fiancée, Beryl Aggis Byford, in her home town, Mile End, Colchester, Essex, in October 1945.

On Christmas day 1949 their son, Brian John, was born at Badley, the only Haydon born in the parish. He was baptised at Badley on June 11th the following year.

Doveshill farm was evidently not well-suited to livestock farming and in 1951, by which time the Haydons had bought the farm, John decided to move the family to Abbey Hall Farm, Buxhall Road, Great Finborough (actually situated in the parish of Buxhall), where their daughter Julia was born.

Although this was a smaller farm it was better suited for him to realise his ambition of maintaining a herd of Friesian cattle.

John eventually sold this farm and the family experienced a completed change of lifestyle by taking over the Post Office Stores in Bramford Road, Ipswich, until retiring to Lockington Road, Stowmarket.

He died at Stowmarket on 7th August 1993, aged 76 years and his ashes were taken to Badley on 13th August. His wife Beryl died in a nursing home close to their daughter Julia's home in Lancashire on 24th April 2004 and her ashes were taken to Badley on 6th May.

Fig 8.20 Sergeant-Pilot 1443638 Francis Gordon Haydon.
(Photo courtesy of Betty Barber née Haydon)

Francis Gordon Haydon

At the outbreak of WWII Francis 'Gordon' was living at Stowmarket with his wife Margery Edna Haydon (née Bell) and their son Michael and working as a fieldsman for the sugar beet industry. He enlisted in the RAF Volunteer Reserves during April 1941 and undertook flying training in Canada under the Empire Air Training Scheme.

Whilst training in England his sister Elizabeth recalls the family receiving a surprise visit from 'Gordon', as he was known, when, accompanied by his instructor he landed a Tiger Moth bi-plane on a large field belonging to the farm known as Cock Hedges (Great Cock Stridges) (see Chapter 5, Fig 5.78) situated to the right of the track leading down to Badley church, to join the family for dinner!

By the time of his posting to No 1 (Coastal) OTU, Sergeant Haydon was a fully qualified pilot. However, he never saw active service as he was tragically killed during a training flight on 9th June 1943.

His resting place is marked by the only military gravestone in Badley churchyard and his name is listed on the memorial gates at Stowmarket. (see Appendix C, page 297).

The circumstances of Sergeant Haydon's death were as follows:

At 11.35pm on 8th June 1943 a Lockheed Hudson Mark I, serial number P5134, piloted by Sergeant Haydon of the Royal Air Force Volunteer Reserve, accompanied by three other crew members, took off from Thornaby-on-Tees aerodrome, near Middlesborough, home to No 1 (Coastal) Operational Training Unit (No 1 OTU). The crew settled into a training sortie which lasted 3 hours 10 minutes, but was to end in disaster.

The aircraft they were using was one of a batch of fifty delivered to the Royal Air Force between March and July 1940 by the Lockheed Aircraft Corp (USA).

At 2.45 am on the 9th June 1943 whilst attempting to land in darkness at Scorton aerodrome near Catterick, Yorkshire, he lost control of the aircraft and it crashed killing all four on board. *(Source: Air Ministry Form 5182, see Fig 8.24 opposite.)*

The No 1 (Coastal) OTU existed to to prepare crews for the arduous duties of operating with RAF Coastal Command which carried our reconnaissance over the sea, protected friendly shipping from enemy air, sea and submarine attacks, anti-submarine patrols and offensive operations against enemy coastal bases and enemy merchant and naval shipping."

(Air crash account based on research by Chris Hearn and used with his permission.)

In 1954, Gordon and Margery's son, Mike Haydon joined Stowmarket builders O Seaman & Son as a student. In the mid-seventies he became a partner in the company and in 1975 its Managing Director.

Fig 8.21 The Lockheed Hudson Mk 1 bomber.

Fig 8.22 Michael Haydon at Doveshill.

Fig 8.23 F G Haydon's gravestone in Badley churchyard.

"He set the claim of duty above desire for happiness.
May his cheerful courage be always our example."

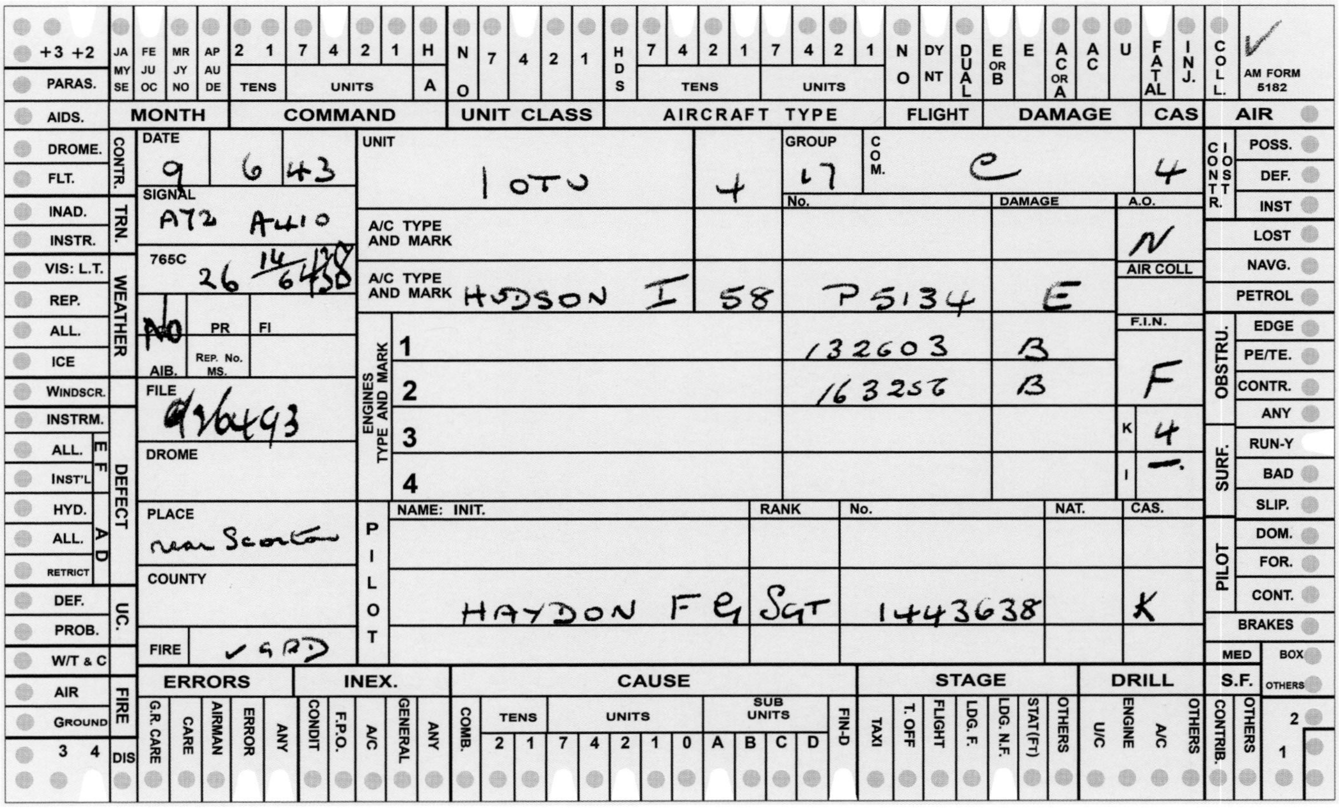

*Fig 8.24 Reproduction of part of
Air Ministry Form 5182.*

Carrie Louise Haydon's mother, Emma Elizabeth Hammond, (the widow of Hugh Hunten Hammond, late of Grimston, Norfolk) died at Doveshill on 6th August 1944, aged 83 and was buried at St Mary's Badley on the 9th.

Carrie Louise Haydon died on July 8th 1981 at a nursing home at Claydon, at the grand old age of 97. Her ashes were brought to Badley Churchyard on 3rd August.

The ashes of her sister, Edith Emma Hammond, aged 87 of Great Ashfield, had been similarly brought there on 31st October 1975, having died on the 12th October.

See Appendix C, page 297, for their Monumental Inscriptions.

Fig 8.25 Francis (Frank) Haydon (left) with a horse-drawn seed-drill in use at Doveshill farm.

Fig 8.26 'Frank' Haydon photographed in his pony and trap outside Doveshill circa 1944/5.

Fig 8.28 Ida Mary Haydon & Leslie Howard Saunders after their wedding at Badley church on 20th June 1936 (see newspaper report Chapter 3).

Fig 8.27 (above) Carrie Louise Haydon outside Doveshill with her mother Emma Elizabeth Hammond in 1936.

Fig 8.29 (opposite) Ida Mary Haydon & Leslie Howard Saunders with their parents outside Doveshill farm on their wedding day. Francis (Frank) & Carrie Haydon are on the left.

Fig 8.30 Doveshill farmhouse circa 1943 with the rambling roses in all their glory and the Haydons' Austin car parked outside.
(All photos courtesy of Betty Barber née Haydon.)

BADLEY WEDDING

Barber—Haydon

The wedding took place at St. Mary's Church, Badley, on Saturday, of Sergt. Edward Barber, Intelligence Corps, on leave from Burma, son of Mr. and Mrs. A. Barber, of Stowmarket, and Miss Betty Haydon, youngest daughter of Mrs. Haydon and the late Mr. F. E. Haydon, of Doveshill, Badley. The bride, who was given away by her brother, Mr. J. D. Haydon, wore an ivory lace dress and

carried a bouquet of red chrysanthemums. Miss Jill Tweed and Miss Janet Saunders (bride's nieces) were in turquoise silk and carried bouquets of chrysanthemums. Sergt.-Pilot S. Caley (groom's cousin) was best man. Mr. T. G. Sharp was at the organ. The Rev. S. S. Shrubbs officiated and the Rev. E. Weir (Congregational, Stowmarket) gave an address. After a reception at Doveshill, Mr. and Mrs. Barber left for London and Cornwall.

Fig 8.31 The text from the local newspaper reporting on Elizabeth 'Betty' Haydon's marriage to Edward Barber at Badley Church on November 10th 1945.

For reports on two further Haydon weddings see Chapter 3, page 47.

INCIDENTS AT DOVESHILL ～ from local newspapers.

MOTOR ACCIDENT AT BADLEY

At about 11.30 on Monday morning last as Mr. Stanley F. Owen of 76 Warwick Avenue, Bedford, was driving an Austin Seven sports motor car from Stowmarket to Ipswich he met with disaster. He was descending the steep hill that leads from Badley to Needham Market, and when within few yards of the farm entrance to Doveshill, his car skidded to its near side; it then ran across the road, turning over on to its side, and finished up by facing in the direction of Stowmarket.

Mr. F. E. Haydon had just emerged from the entrance to his farm, driving a horse with a small wagon attached, and he successfully crossed the road to ascend the hill. Mr. Owen was thrown from the car and rendered unconscious. It is thought that Mr. Owen when nearing the wagon had an idea that he could not pass it and consequently braked, with the result that his car acted in the manner described; within a few feet of where it turned to the offside of the road stands a telegraph post.
THURSDAY, AUGUST 26th, 1937

STACK FIRE AT BADLEY

A stover[1] and some straw stacks were completely destroyed by fire, in the meadow by the cartway that leads to Badley Church, on Thursday last. They were the property of Mr. F. E Haydon of Dove's Hill Farm, Badley.

The Needham Market Fire Brigade attended, but as the nearby pond was empty of water, all the firemen could do was to pull down the stacks and allow them to burn out. There was no danger to other property as the stacks were isolated.
THURSDAY JULY 21st, 1938 (page 1, col. 2)

[1] **stover** i.e. fodder

EYEWITNESS ACCOUNT

BARN FIRE AT BADLEY

Bertram Frank Hadley, the son of George Edward and Nellie Hadley, who was born at Badley Mill in 1919 and moved with his family into Doveshill cottage the following year, recalls that in about 1925/6 he witnessed one of the barns at Bridge Farm catch fire. This was caused by sparks emanating from one of two steam lorries owned by Quintons of Needham Market, who regularly took on water from the river between the two arches at Chain Bridge (Badley Bridge).

See also Chapter 5, Cherry Tree Farm, for a further accident report concerning Badley Hill.

Scott
OF BADLEY HALL

THE Scott family farmed in Derbyshire and on 9th April 1946 Leonard and Emily Frances Scott bought Badley Hall and its associated farmland from William Hunt of Needham Market for £5,600.

They had four children, Leslie, Arthur Blake, Dorothy and Frances.

They were evidently great patrons of St. Mary's Church, serving as churchwardens until their deaths - Emily Frances (1967) and Leonard (1968).

Their work for the church was acknowledge in the Dec. 1967 edition of the Needham Market and Badley Church Magazine as follows:

Mrs. Frances Scott
"The sudden death of Mrs. Scott on November 23rd has underlined for us what all who worship at Badley must have felt and that was her loyalty and constancy in the Church's fellowship and in our little community.

We thank God for her life and example. She will be greatly missed, not least from her place in church Sunday by Sunday - So sudden an end to life so active and full of service to the last comes also great shock to us all and we offer Mr. Scott and their family our sincere sympathy."

And in the Jan. 1968 edition -

"Although the epidemic of foot and mouth disease in the northwest made it unwise for some members of her family to attend the funeral service for Mrs. Frances Scott, it was very much a family occasion when churchgoers and neighbours gathered to express their respect and affection. Canon Shrubbs the Rural Dean as well as Mrs. Scott's son-in-law took part in the service in St. Mary's Church."

Leonard Scott
Sadly within a year, Leonard her husband, had also died and was interred at Badley on October 9th 1968, aged 85 years.

The November issue of the parish magazine reported -

"In the absence of the Vicar on holiday, the service was

Fig 8.32 Dorothy Scott (right) with her mother Emily Frances Scott in the garden at Badley Hall on July 30th 1964.

conducted by the Rural Dean, Canon R. S. Shrubbs, who for many years came to Badley for the Sunday services, and by the Rev. Andrew Hodgson, Mr. Scott's son-in-law (i.e. the husband of Frances Scott).

The members of the congregation of Badley Church extend their sincere sympathy to the members of his family."

Miss Dorothy Scott
Dorothy Scott was buried at Badley on March 7 1968, aged 57 years. The church magazine recorded -

"In a small community such as Badley the loss of one parishioner all too readily leaves a gap in the ranks, which is not easily filled. The sudden death of Dorothy Scott at an early age will be felt by all who worship at St. Mary's Church.

It was rarely that she was absent from her place in Church on Sunday. Week by week she provided the flowers and in a busy and hard-working life she found time to keep a watchful eye on the Church and to attend to a number of things that needed to be done. All of this was done in a quiet and unobtrusive way.

For all these things we shall miss her and we offer our sincere sympathy to all her family."

Arthur Blake Scott
Arthur succeeded at Badley upon the death of Leonard Scott in 1968.

Fig 8.33 A young Arthur Scott taken at a woodcutter competition in Derbyshire before the family moved to Badley

Maintenance and preservation is part and parcel of owning an historic house and Margaret is now engaged in the usual contest with planners and statutory conservation bodies to raise money to conserve one of the most important buildings in the district - the Hall, together with its outbuildings.

Many statutory grants are dependent on recipient being able to match them. Very often this is not possible. Nevertheless, it is hoped the agencies concerned will find ways of providing some financial support, otherwise they will have to bear some of the responsibility for allowing the weather and wood beetles to ultimately take their toll on the hall, destroying unnecessarily 600 years of Suffolk history.

He maintained the family's close support for St. Mary's Church where he was already a Churchwarden. As a member of Badley Parochial Church Council, on 21st March 1969, he was elected their representative to the Diocesan and Rural-deaconal Conferences and to serve on the Synods of the Diocese and Rural Deanery, when these were constituted.

Arthur remained a bachelor and devoted himself to his beloved Badley.

During the latter part of his life the farming operations at the Hall were undertaken by his nephew, Geoffrey Scott.

His niece Elizabeth Margaret Scott, his brother Leslie's daughter and known by everyone as 'Margaret', attended the Hall on a daily basis to cook and clean for him.

He died in August 1997 after a prolonged illness, aged 80, and was interred in the churchyard on 4th September.

In his will, Arthur left Badley Hall to the sitting tenant Geoffrey Scott, maintaining the Scotts' 50 year association with Badley.

Although Geoffrey Scott has subsequently sold off his interest in the estate, his niece Margaret continues to hold the Hall and a proportion of the original farmland along with her beloved Badley cats (thirteen at the last count).

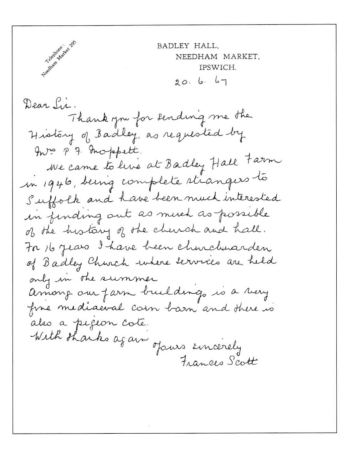

*Fig 8.34 A letter written by Frances Scott, found at the Suffolk Record Office, possibly to thank them for sending a copy of the **Pocket History of Suffolk Parishes No 342 - Badley** - published in the Suffolk Chronicle & Mercury on February 9th 1934.*

Chapter Nine

Notes on

The
Stowmarket Navigation
Company

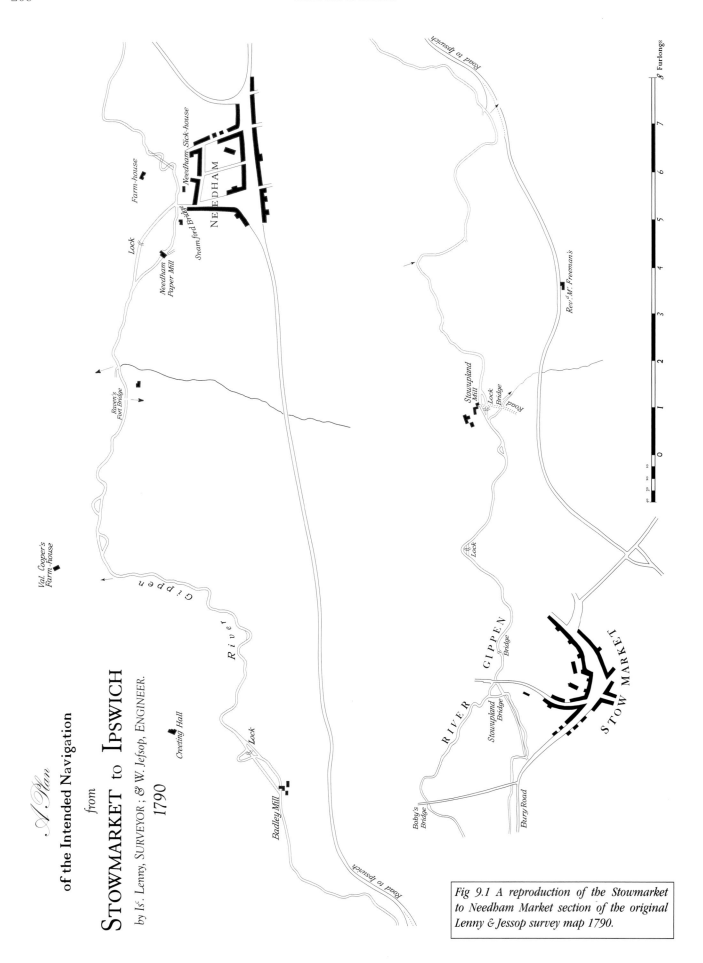

N Plan

of the Intended Navigation

from

STOWMARKET to IPSWICH

by Is. Lenny, SURVEYOR ; & W. Jefsop, ENGINEER.
1790

Fig 9.1 A reproduction of the Stowmarket
to Needham Market section of the original
Lenny & Jessop survey map 1790.

Stowmarket Navigation Co

THE Ipswich & Stowmarket Navigation Act 1790 authorised the establishment of a body of trustees to make and maintain a navigable communication between Stowmarket and Ipswich, a distance of 17 miles.

The Badley parish boundary follows the centre-line of the river Gipping for 1½ miles and includes Badley Lock situated just downstream of Badley Mill, a short section of canal having been constructed upstream towards Stowmarket to by-pass the mill pond.

The first proposal for the construction of the Navigation was in 1719, but Ipswich objected, fearing loss of trade. It was not until 1789 that six local gentlemen with fore-sight realised that because of poor transport, due to badly maintained turnpike roads, the population and industries were dwindling in the Stowmarket area.

They are named in the Act as:
William Woollaston Esq., of Great Finborough, John Wenyeve Esq., of Brittenham (Brettenham), Joshua Grisby, the younger, Esq., of Drinkstone, Roger Walpole Esq., of Beighton (Beyton), Revd Henry Hill of Buxhall and the Revd Henry Jackson Close of Hitcham.

A Parliamentary Bill incorporating them as trustees was passed on April 1st 1790 (Fig 9.2). The Act authorised them to improve the River Gipping, make several artificial cuts and construct a total of sixteen locks. They engaged William Jessop, who employed Isaac Lenny as his surveyor. The relevant part of their survey map is reproduced opposite (Fig 9.1).

(1035)

ANNO TRICESIMO

Georgii III. Regis.

∗ ∗

C A P.   LVII.

An Act for making and maintaining a navigable Communication between *Stowmarket* and *Ipf-wich*, in the County of *Suffolk*.

WHEREAS the making and maintain= Preamble. ing a navigable Communication from Stowupland Bridge, fituate upon the River Gippen, at the Town of Stow-market, to the Town and Port of Ipf-wich, in the County of Suffolk, will render the Conveyance of Corn, Hops, and other Pro-duce of the faid County and Parts adjacent, and of Coal, Timber, Lime, and other Things, lefs expenfive than at prefent, and will in other Refpects be of confider-able Benefit to the Inhabitants of the feveral Towns and Places within the faid County and Parts adjacent, and of publick Utility; but the fame cannot be effected without the Authority of Parliament: May it there-fore pleafe Your Majefty that it may be enacted; and be it enacted by the King's moft Excellent Majefty, by and with the Advice and Confent of the Lords Spi-ritual and Temporal, and Commons, in this prefent Parliament affembled, and by the Authority of the fame,

12 F 2   That

Fig 9.2 Front page - Ipswich & Stowmarket Navigation Act 1790.

T. Prentice & Coˢ· Warehouse   Mʳ· Cowell's Warehouses & Barge, Commerce   Mʳ· Cobbolds Warehouses & Two Barges   T. Prentice & Coˢ·   Mʳ· Cornell's Warehouse   Mʳ· King's Warehouses
One Unloading Salt, Barge Francis (sic)   Barges on the Gipping at 43 Tons Burden   Mary & Emma   Warehouses   by Barge Victoria   & Beyond Prentice & Hewett's Deal Wharf
Gas Chimney

The Quay at Stowmarket, Suffolk. The Foot Bridge Crosses the Head of The Navigable part of The River Gipping   Distance to Ipswich 16 miles by Water & 12 by the Road
Drawn Etched & Published by H. Davy, Globe St. Ipswich Octʳ. 1ˢᵗ, 1838

Fig 9.3 Henry Davy's 1838 sketch of the terminal basin at Stowmarket seen from the wharf in Stowupland Street. This was situated in between the modern-day Stowupland Street and Station Road East road bridges. (The title and notes on Davy's sketch have been reproduced for clarity.)

CONSTRUCTION OF THE NAVIGATION

The Stowmarket end of the Navigation was completed by local contractor John Rennie. He constructed three turf and timber locks between Stowmarket and Needham Market, which was the other main town on the waterway. He advised that further lock structures should be of brick and stone and the additional costs associated with this were raised by a further Parliamentary Bill in 1793. At Stowmarket the terminal basin was just upstream of the present Station Road East road bridge (see Fig 9.3).

The Navigation was completed in 1793 at a total cost £26,263.10s. It was constructed by some 200 navvies - the name given to casual labourers of the time and short for 'navigators'. They were equipped with only picks and shovels. On the 14th September three horse-drawn barges loaded with coal made the 12 mile trip from Ipswich, rising 90 feet through 16 locks of broad construction each 60ft by 10ft. The 35 ton barges had a draught of 3 feet 3 inches. The initial tolls were one penny per ton per mile for cargoes going down to Ipswich, reducing to a halfpenny per ton for the return journey.

TRUSTEES' MEETINGS

The minute books and other records maintained by the Trustees' are held at the Suffolk Record Office (Ref. EM400).

They show that they usually met at the King's Arms Inn, Stowmarket, on a bi-monthly basis and shared responsibility for chairing proceedings. Looking through these accounts along with the bondholders books, the names of new members replacing those who have died or withdrawn can be tracked. Of particular interest John Kirby Moore, gent. of Badley, attended his first meeting on 24th February 1837 and took the chair for the first time on 22th February 1839.

There are many familiar names amongst the Trustees, and nearly all of them are associates of Moore and occur in his Journal - notably the Revd Henry Hill of Buxhall and John George Hart of Stowmarket (see Chapter 8). A copy of the record of one their meetings held at the King's Arms Inn, Stowmarket is reproduced below (Fig 9.4).

It is said that two of the most familiar barges on The Navigation were those used by the dredgers and the carpenters. The former was equipped with a large blade attached to ropes which was towed along the bottom to cut and clear the weeds and the latter usually tied up at one of the locks, which were in constant need of repair.

The most unusual barge was the 'inspection barge', which was loaned from Packard's of Bramford and annually

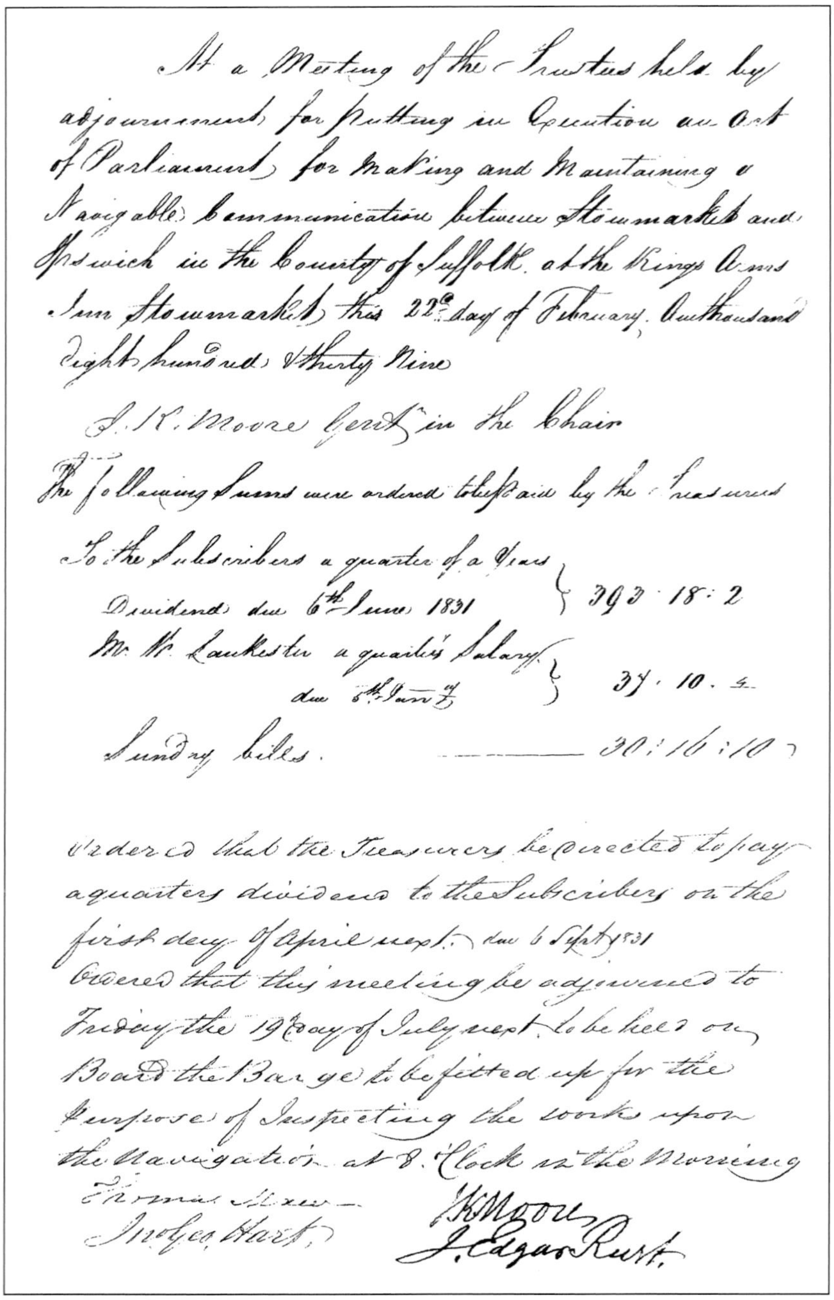
At a Meeting of the Trustees held by adjournment for putting in Execution an Act of Parliament for making and Maintaining a Navigable Communication between Stowmarket and Ipswich in the County of Suffolk at the Kings Arms Inn Stowmarket this 22d day of February One thousand Eight hundred & Thirty Nine

J. K. Moore Gent in the Chair

The following Sums were ordered to be paid by the Treasurer

To the Subscribers a quarter of a Years Dividend due 6th June 1831 } 393 : 18 : 2

Mr W. Lankester a quarter's Salary due 6th Jany } 37 . 10 . –

Sundry bills ——— 30 : 16 : 10

Ordered that the Treasurer be directed to pay a quarters dividend to the Subscribers on the first day of April next due 6 Sept 1831

Ordered that this meeting be adjourned to Friday the 19th day of July next to be held on Board the Barge to be fitted up for the Purpose of Inspecting the works upon the Navigation at 8 o'Clock in the Morning

J. K. Moore

Jno Geo Hart

J. Edgar Rust

Fig 9.4 The Minute Book entry for the Trustees' meeting at the King's Arms Inn, Stowmarket on 22nd February 1839.

toured the river with the trustees on board. As can be seen from the abstract below, the official purpose was to 'inspect the work upon The Navigation', but given they were often accompanied by their wives and were served lunch on board, it was probably an equally important social occasion.

During one such 'inspection' on July 16th 1869 John Kirby Moore recorded in his Journal, *'I went down the Navigation with other Trustees, Mr. Hill etc. in barge - Mr. Lawton and Mr. Prettyman went with us, and others. The barge horse slipped into the river at Sproughton and swam some distance before he was able to get out.'* Apparently residents living alongside the Gipping never failed to turn out and cheer the barge as it passed!

John Kirby Moore continued to attend most of the meetings. His last recorded attendance was a meeting he chaired on 12th July 1881, when he would have been 87 years old.

THE AFFECT OF THE NAVIGATION ON BADLEY

Whether The Navigation brought any direct benefits to Badley is unclear. The preamble in the Navigation Act states that the new canal would *"render the Conveyance of Corn, Hops, and other Produce of the said County and Parts adjacent, and of Coal, Timber, Lime and other Things, less expensive than at present, and will in other Respects be of considerable Benefit to the Inhabitants of the several Towns and Places within the said County and Parts adjacent, and of public utility"* For example, it is not known if any use of it was made by the Ashburnham Estate or their tenant at Badley Mill.

However, the former did received a rent from the Trustees for the use of the towpath created for the purposes of The Navigation. This amounted to £9.15s.0d by the time the estate was sold in 1917.

At least it can be said that the expansion of Stowmarket, which was directly attributed to the canal, did provide the inhabitants of Badley with an alternative sources of employment to agriculture.

THE NAVIGATION IN USE

Initially the boat numbers were in single figures but doubled in the following year. Shipments increased and at the turn of the century over thirty trips were made weekly with coal, slates, manufactured and imported goods upstream, whilst guncotton, beer and agricultural produce were carried on the return run. Manure, by order of the original Act of Parliament, could be carried free of tolls! The return trip took about 16 hours.

Stowmarket certainly prospered after The Navigation opened. Within a few years the population had doubled and new businesses were established by the river. Many of Stowmarket's current industries owe their origins to The Navigation and retain their riverside sites. The I.C.I. paint plant evolved from Prentice's Chemical and Explosives Works and the former Suffolk Iron Foundry is now the main production facility for Bosch-Atco-Qualcast. The town was the largest exporter of malt in the country and Muntons plc still have modern riverside maltings.

Tragedy - in 1841 an iron sailing barge called 'Ironside' lost its skipper William Baker when he was crushed against Creeting Bridge, Needham Market, when he slipped over the side whilst working the barge through.*

In 1842 Stowmarket brewer John Stevens & Co commissioned a barge called 'Gipping' to transport their beer products.* (**Ships & Shipyards of Ipswich 1700-1970* - Hugh Moffat 2002)

THE ARRIVAL OF THE RAILWAY

In 1844 the Eastern Union Railway proposed an extension from Ipswich to Stowmarket along side The Navigation. This now part of the London Inter-City route. Fearing loss of trade, the trustees negotiated for the railway to lease The Navigation and an Act was passed in 1846 allowing the railway company to rent the navigation for 42 years. A clause required the railway company to keep The Navigation in the same condition as it was on the date the Act was passed.

The leasing of the navigation to the railway company was a shrewd financial decision on the part of the Trustees', who received a regular dividend for the next 42 years. However, when the lease came up for renewal in 1888, the railway refused to enter a new agreement for a transport system which was no longer a competitor and from which they derived little income.

Compensation was received from the railway for the bad state of repair of The Navigation; this was as a result of the maintenance clause mentioned earlier - and from 1888 The Navigation Company were running the waterway again.

Fig 9.5 Packard's steam barge 'Trent River' just clearing the Bramford lock and bound upstream for Stowmarket in the 1920's.

The poor state of The Navigation is highlighted in the Minute Book. On 9th June 1879, by which time the meetings were being held at a Bank in Stowmarket, the clerk reported he had made an inspection on 16th September 1878 and in respect of Badley Mill, noted, *"overfall require seeing to - woodwork at lock in bad repair - must be attended to."*

Little seems to have been done, for on the 18th August 1879 another survey at the mill recorded, *'Gate on towing path requires repairing 6 feet of water - upper gates require seeing to - wood work at lock want replacing, as also the paddles, 5 feet 8 inches of water - gate on towing path want seeing to - river very weedy - 4 feet 10 inches of water - gates all along the towing path want seeing to - a 35 ton barge draws 3 feet of water - 5 feet 9 inches - two places on towing path in Badley Pond require seeing to - the horse here refused to go over both places, these were small outlets into the river - 7 feet 4 inches of water - watering places for cattle want mending up - gate on the path require seeing to - a shoal in this pond want removing'.*

Almost two years later at the meeting at the Bank on 27th June 1881 chaired by John Kirby Moore, further depreciation at Badley Mill was reported - *'Southgate - woodwork in bad state- Roadway over bridge past this lock leading to Creeting Green Farm in bad repair and the Bridge quite unsafe for heavy loads - this must be attended to at once.'*

One wonders if John Kirby Moore's vested interest in the navigation compromised his position as the Ashburnhams'

Steward. Unfettered, one would have expected him to pressure the Trustees' to maintain all their property at the mill. Had there been an accident caused by the collapse of one of the Trustees' structures, lawyers would have had a 'field day' given all the reports recording the necessity for urgent repairs.

DECLINE AND CLOSURE

Traffic declined. By 1900 trade on The Navigation to Stowmarket had virtually ceased.

Hopes of a revival, however, still existed as late as 1906 and this was strongly supported by the editor of the local newspaper who published the following article:

Stowmarket Weekly Post
Editorial May 10 1906 p. 4, col. 4
STOWMARKET NAVIGATION

"Once more the question of the advisability of re-opening the river Gipping, at Stowmarket, for traffic has arisen, and upon this occasion there is every probability of the projected navigation between this town and Ipswich being brought to a definite and successful conclusion.

Correspondence between Mr. G. A. Hardy M.P., the New Explosives Co. Ltd., and Messrs. Thomas Prentice and Co., has resulted in this matter again being placed before the Trustees of the Ipswich and Stowmarket Navigation, who met last week to consider the correspondence dealing with the re-opening of the canal. This correspondence was regarded as private, but it can be clearly seen that the writers were all alive to the fact of the great advantage the town would derive from the utilisation of the only waterway for trading purposes.

There is no gain saying the statement that by the re-opening of the river Gipping the trade of Stowmarket would receive an impetus which at the present time would be heartily appreciated by all the inhabitants. It has rightly been said that the river was the main artery of the local trade and in his 'History of Stowmarket', Hollingsworth says that without it commercial life would beat but faintly. Years ago it was a most profitable concern and most useful to the town."

"When the Great Eastern Railway was put down through Stowmarket, however, the river was taken over by the Railway Co., and greatly neglected, until now it is almost in an unnavigable condition and comparatively useless. The Trustees are, however, officially informed that the sum of £2,000 would cover the cost which would have to be entailed in its thorough repair. For this amount the river could be made navigable, and as there is a large demand for barge traffic between Stowmarket and Ipswich it might be converted from a non-paying to a profitable concern.

In 1790 no less than £27,000 was expended upon the Gipping, and it now seems contrary to all reason that for the sake of a thirteenth part of that sum the object upon which such a fortune was spent should continue to remain unremunerative.

From Ipswich to Bramford an extensive river trade is carried on, and there is no earthly reason, beyond that of finding the £2,000, why there should not be an expansion of the trade to Stowmarket. All the local traders testify to the utility of such a scheme for the advancement of Stowmarket industries, which must necessarily benefit from possessing two means of trade exit instead of the one now used.

A meeting of the bond holders of the navigation is shortly to be held, and we hope the business people of the town will take advantage of the opportunity of meeting them and expressing their opinions upon the practicability of the proposed scheme."

On the lower reaches companies such as Edward Packard & Co. Ltd. of Bramford (now Scott Horticulture) continued to use the waterway until the 1920's. They used The Navigation because of difficulties with rail transport. They paid no tolls as they agreed to maintain The Navigation and therefore can be credited with keeping the waterway open for those final years. Fison's and Packard's had their own fleets consisting of steam tugs, such as the 'Trent River' built in by W. H. Orves of Ipswich in 1916, each towing two

barges of about 35 tons capacity (pictured opposite, Fig 9.5). They worked day and night to catch the tides at the Handford sea lock. About 600 tons of fertiliser were shipped daily.

The records of the Trustees show that The Navigation was little used by the turn of the last century and in 1917 they ordered severe cost cutting. As a result the maintenance of the waterway and its features was poor. Unfortunately finances did not improve and on the 16th May 1922 the Trustees resolved to close The Navigation with effect from 3rd June 1922; however some traffic continued.

Eight years passed before the Trustees' met again and agreed to revoke the powers of navigation on the waterway. The Ipswich & Stowmarket Navigation Act Revocation Order was passed 1932 and transferred the responsibility for the river to the East Suffolk Rivers Catchment Board (later the East Suffolk and Norfolk River Board). The Trustees' wound up the business at their final meeting in Ipswich in 1934.

RESTORATION
The Inland Waterways Association, Ipswich Branch, actively promotes the use of the River Gipping for leisure activities.

In the early 1970's they successfully cleared the towpath, which is now a very popular walk at the heart of the Gipping Valley Countryside Project. This is a collaborative venture between Mid-Suffolk District Council, Babergh District Council and Suffolk County Council to conserve the character and enhance the recreational potential of the valley.

They have also been at the forefront of the complete reconstruction of Bosmere Lock, near Needham Lake.

For a sketch of how The Navigation avoided Badley Mill and a photograph of the remains of Badley lock, see Chapter 5, Figs 5.34 and 5.35.

Fig 9.6 Mr. G. Gladding, skipper of the 'Trent River', who claimed to be the only man to take the steam-powered vessel the entire length of The Navigation i.e. Ipswich to Stowmarket. Another Gipping bargemaster who took other barge types through to Stowmarket in the 1890's was Mr. J. W. Hall of Ipswich.

Fig 9.7 This is one of the only 19th century photographs believed to still exist which purports to show one of the Gipping locks. Although opinions differ as to which one, it appears to be the Handford 'Sea' Lock, the last one prior to Ipswich, where the river traffic left the fresh water of the River Gipping and entered the tidal salt water of the River Orwell.

Fig 9.8 A copy of a painting believed to be of the River Gipping, showing a steam tug towing a barge. In the background there is a smoking chimney, said to belong to a cement factory and in the foreground on the left there are young girls on the river bank. (date and artist unknown)

Chapter Ten

Notes on
COLUMBINE
HALL

COLUMBERS   HOTOT   TYRRELL   POLEY

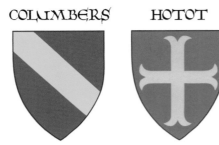

UNTIL 1844 Stowupland was a part of Stowmarket, anciently known as Thorney. To distinguish it from the main manor in Stowmarket/Thorney, a subsidiary manor on the eastern side of the parish was called Thorney Columbers, the second, part of the name commemorating the mediaeval overlords of the manor, the Columbers family of Nether Stowey in Somerset, originally from Colombières near Bayeux in Normandy. The Columbers family also held the manor of Battisford and the manor of Thorney Columbers was held as a dependency of that manor, by service of a quarter of a knight's fee. In time the name was corrupted from Columbers to Columbine.

Columbine Hall is called after Thorney Columbers, a manor of which the Norman family of de Columbers were the feudal overlords. The resident owners, however, were the de Hotot family who held the manor in 1241. The present house was built in about 1390 by Robert le Hotot, a prominent Justice in Suffolk. His great, great grandaughter, Anne, inherited the manor and married Thomas Tyrrell (2nd son of Sir James Tyrrell of Gipping), who supposedly murdered the princes in the Tower in 1455. Their grandson, Thomas Tyrrell, lost Columbine Hall in 1559 through a foreclosed mortgage and it later belonged to Sir Robert Carey, a favourite of Queen Elizabeth I (and believed to be an illegitimate grandson of Henry VIII).

The third Edmund Poley (of Whitechapel, Middx), the 3rd son of Edmund Poley and Mirabel Garneys, married Jane Groves, the daughter of Thomas Groves. Their son Sir John Poley, was a veteran of the Elizabethan wars. He served as a soldier in Spain 1592 and in Ireland where he was knighted by the Earl of Essex at Dublin 1599 (see next page). He married Ursula, the daughter and co-heir of Sir John Gilbert, Knt., of Great Finborough, Suffolk.

On December 6th 1608, whilst living at St Leonard's Bromley adjoining Stratford at Bow, Co. Middx., Sir John acquired the manor of Columbine Hall, which included the manor house and lands in Stowmarket, Stowupland, Newton, Gipping and Onehouse, by Bargain and Sale from

Sir Robert Cary of Hartford Co. York Knt., and Elizabeth his wife, in consideration of £500 paid and £2012.10.0. covenanted to be paid before All Saints 1611. In the agreement it was covenanted that Giles Keble of Newton, yeoman, gave up a lease granted by Sir Robert Cary on 4th October 1608 after Michaelmas (see SRO Ref: HA1/CA/1/2).

Was it Sir John who added the massive brick chimney, built a new staircase and rendered the mediaeval timber frame with pargetting?

Unfortunately the Poleys' association with this fine manor house was comparatively short-lived. Although, during their marriage, John and Ursula produced a total of nine children, six daughters, Peregrina, Elizabeth, Dorothy, Ursula, Mary & Jane and three sons, Henry, Edmond and his heir, John.

"AFFAIRS OF IRELAND" - SIR JOHN POLEY (MS 10837)
No account of Sir John's escapades against the Spanish appear to have survived. However, a manuscript consisting of several texts written by him during his time in Ireland is in the library at The Trinity College, Dublin, Ireland. These texts have been catalogued by the library and are reproduced in Appendix G, page 333.

SIR JOHN POLEY & PAUSEY HALL
About 1560 a house, previously known as Childer House, Pau(w)sey or Pawnsey Hall, was erected on the corner of Finborough Road with Violet Hill Road, Stowmarket (see illustrations overleaf). The Rev A. G. H. Hollingsworth in his *History of Stowmarket* (1844) attributes its construction is to Sir John Poley, but whether or not it was actually built, or owned by him and used as a town house is in my view very doubtful. The construction date of 1660 given in some accounts is incorrect as Sir John died in 1634.

Charles Partridge FSA, in a series of articles on Columbine Hall in the East Anglian Daily Times, also questions Hollingsworth's assertion saying, "The statement of the historian on page 198 is partially erroneous. "In the close

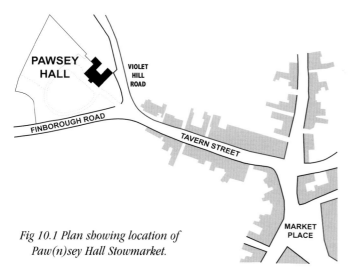

Fig 10.1 Plan showing location of Paw(n)sey Hall Stowmarket.

Fig 10.2 Paw(n)sey Hall. After the death of John Poley it was sold to the Gurdon family and remained in their ownership well into the 19th century. It is referred to by 'Octoginta' the Stowmarket diarist, writing about John Byles of Byles & King & Co, a wealthy local merchant, who was living there with his young wife in 1800.

Another of its noteworthy 19th century tenants was Edward Peter Archer a prominent local business man who was involved with the administration of the Stowmarket Navigation Company and a practising local lawyer.

It then become the town's vicarage for several decades, a practised started by the Revd Hollingsworth who moved there from Milton Road during his ministry 1837-59. It was subsequently used as a school (Hillcroft) and it is currently the Wellington House Nursing Home. (Date of photograph unknown.)

of Sir John's life he removed from 'Columbine Hall to the town, where he erected a house for himself, and J. Poley, Esq., his son, resided in Stowupland in 1665." In the will he is styled: "John Poley, of Collumbine Hall, in the parish of St. Peter's, in Stowmarket." No other house is mentioned, save farmhouses and isolated cottages, and in the inquisition taken after his death at Bury St. Edmunds, 30th October 11th Charles I. (1636), the record is just the same, his son John Poley was then aged 14 years or thereabouts, and all the goods and chattels mentioned are at Columbine Hall. We may take it therefore, that Sir John Poley made it his only Suffolk home, and that he resided there till he died on 14th February 1634."

However, we know that when Sir John purchased the hall from Sir Robert Carey in 1608, the sale included numerous other lands. Hollingsworth must have based his assertion on some fact or other.

Charles Partridge is himself incorrect in relation to Sir John's will which is reproduced in full in Appendix D, as he in fact refers to Pawnsey Hall twice. For example, ". . of all my said manor of Collumbine hall at Thorny Collumbers and all other my lands and of all other my lands messuages and tenements lying in Stowmarket Onehouse Chilton now called by the name of Pawnsey hall."

The *'Abstract of Title relating to Childer Road (Stowmarket) long leaseholds'*, dated 1936, recites the various dealings of the Gurdon family of Assington Hall and their descendants. From it we can extract that John Gurdon, who died in November 1777, inherited a good deal of property in Stowmarket and Chilton, a hamlet of Stowmarket from his father Nathaniel Gurdon Esq., as his heir-at-law.

Fig 10.3 The hall today, showing few signs of external change. (Photo courtesy Steve Williams)

The point being, the property described in the Abstract includes a "capital messuage or tenement with the appurtenances commonly called or known by the name of Childer or Pausey Hall or by whatsoever other name or names then was or were or theretofore had been called..." "AND ALL OTHER the lands tenements and hereditaments of Mary Gurdon purchased by the said Nathaniel Gurdon **deceased of John Pooley theretofore of Combs in the said County of Suffolk Malster and Patience his wife**...."

There is therefore no doubt that Sir John Poley did own property known as Pawnsey Hall in Chilton, but whether this was the premises still standing in Finborough Road is still open to question, especially as the abstract of title refers to a John and Prudience Poley from Combs as opposed to Sir John and Lady Ursula Poley of Columbine Hall. Also is 'Chilton' referred to in the will the same as 'Childer' in the abstract of title?

In his will dated 18 Oct 1634, written in his own hand, in which he says he was, "feeling his own frailty but perfect in memory", Sir John devised the manor to his wife Ursula for life to educate his children, and the messuage and lands late purchased of Edward Balderie of Ipswich, closes called Tye Acres alias Rushie Pightle, Basketts copyhold of Thorney Manor of which Thomas Bendish bart. is lord, grounds heretofore in 3 pieces Great and Little Banyards and Banyards Brooke, Little Gravell Field and other lands to his brother Sir Roger North knt. and cousins Edmund Poley of Badley and Anthony Croftes of Grays Inn Esqs. as trustees to sell, together with £50 p.a. to be paid by Ursula to provide portions of £200 for his 6 daughters and son Edmond at 18; the remainder of the manor to his heir John, with his best horse armour, a guilt Cales bedsted brought out of Spain "the purchase of my sword." His wife was appointed the sole executor and the trustees as supervisors (reproduced page 309, see SRO Ref: HA1/CA/6/8 for Probate copy).

Sir Roger North of Mildenhall Knt., was married to Elizabeth Gilbert, one of Ursula's two elder sisters and was therefore Sir Johns's brother-in law. He died in 1651.

Sir John was succeeded by his widow during the minority of his son, who was aged 14 at the time of his father's death. Lady Ursula Poley died c.1643-6, succeeded by her son John, who died childless and intestate in October 1666.

It appears his brother Edmund, 'of Bury St Edmunds', took over his affairs, but not without controversy.

In HA1/CA/6/11, on 13th February 1667/8 (and apparently without letters of administration), Edmund Poley of Bury St Edmunds Esq., Released to Sir Edmund Poley of Badley Knt., in consideration of £500, the manor of Columbine Hall with the capital messuage and a number of specified properties in Stowmarket and Stowupland. Two days later in HA1/CA/6/12, Sir Edmund then Leases these properties for 1000 years to Edward Barker Esq. and Roger Barnes

gent., both of Bury St Edmunds, as security for the payment of £300 p.a. by Sir Edmund to Edmund Poley of Bury St Edmunds.

This agreement is cancelled on 26th December 1668, by all the properties being Released back to Sir Edmund Poley of Badley, on account of Edmund Poley of Bury St Edmunds being dead (HA1/CA/6/13).

But this tranfer to Sir Edmund Poley did not go unchallenged. Sir John Poley's daughter Mary married John Coleman gent., of Ipswich, who contested it in Chancery Proceedings in 1668. His case was that as the husband of Mary, the only surving member of the family, and the 'next' cousin of both Poley brothers now deceased, he (they) were their natural heirs-at-law and should have inherited the estate, a wish claimed to have been expressed by Edmund (dec) when dying. The action was nevertheless successfully defendend by Sir Edmund Poley and the proceedings were dismissed May 9th 1669 (see HA1/CB/2/1-7 & CB/3/1-2).

On 29th November 1669, Sir Edmund enters into a Mortgage by Lease for 1000 years with Katherine, Anne and Alathea Webbe, all of Elmswell, the daughters of Gardiner Webbe late of Elmswell Esq., for £1700 at 6%, the manor of 'Columbynes' and the capital messuage called Columbine Hall, together with other related properties (listed).

The manor therefore appears to have passed down from John Poley of Columbyne to his brother Edmund Poley of Bury St Edmunds, then on to Sir Edmund Poley of Badley who left it to his son Henry.

Henry died in 1707 without ever having lived at Columbyne Hall. By his will all his real estate (Badley and Columbyne Halls) passed to his brother Edmund, the diplomat, who was also unlikely to have resided there.

Edmund died in 1714, bequeathing Columbyne Hall to his nephew Richard Gipps along with "£300 pounds in ready mony", and the Badley estate to his sister Lady Elizabeth Gipps. (Both wills are reproduced in Appendix D.)

Lady Gipps died on November 11th the following year, enabling her son and heir Richard Gipps to add the Poley's Badley estate to his inheritance (see also Chapter Seven).

In 1735 he sold both manors to Ambrose Crowley Esq of Barking, the son of rich iron merchant John Crowley. The succession to the Earl of Ashburnham in 1756 is described in Chapter 7.

As part of the Ashburnham estate it was let to a succession of farmers, notably the Boby family who are credited with building on the front hall and the Victorian east wing in the 1840's.

John Boby (see Fig 10.6) was evidently an unpopular tenant suffering a series of incendiary fires in 1844. John Kirby Moore records in his journal that a barn was destroyed on 26th March and a large tiled barn and lean-to were burnt on 25th June. On 27th July he notes that Samuel Jacobs, the shepherd, was found guilty of the latter fire and sentenced to transportation.

The sixth Earl sold Columbine Hall and its 240 acres by auction on 30th June 1914. This was three years before the sale of the bulk of the Suffolk estate (See Chapter 5). It was bought for the reserve price of £5000 by the sitting tenant Mr Henry Potter, who had farmed the land for the previous 12 years on a Yearly Tenancy Agreement, at a rental of £249 per Anum. The Potter family left the Hall in the early 1940's.

During WWII evacuees from London were boarded at the hall, which was also used to train members of the Women's

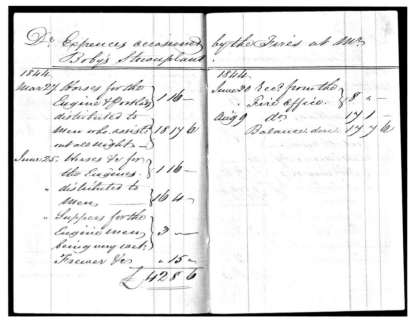

Fig 10.4 The Stowmarket Fire Brigade's expenses account book which shows a deficit of £48 8s 6d for attending the two incendiary fires at Columbine Hall started by Samuel Jacobs.

Land Army and as a testing centre for the Women's Land Army Proficiency Test. For example, on 11th October 1944 a P. Beck hostelled at the hall passed her test (Source: *Land Girls at the Old Rectory* by Irene Grimwood 2000).

In 1951 the Hall was then acquired by the Rednall family, They farmed it until 1993 when the house, with 29 acres of the original manorial lands, was sold to the present owners, Hew Stevenson and Leslie Geddes-Brown. They have restored the house and are now in the process of recreating the garden to a plan devised by the landscape gardener, George Carter, recalling the formal 17th century gardens of Sir John Poley's time.

ESQUIRES. *p.* 244

Pooley. Edmond Pooley of *Collambyne Hall* in the County of *Suffolk Esq;,* is defcended from *Edmond Pooley* Esq;, one of the Readers of *Grayes-Inn,* and a Perfon very Eminent for his learning the Laws in the Reign Queen *Elizabeth.*

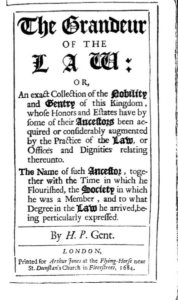

Fig 10.5 The Grandeur of the Law, a 1684 publication, which includes the entry (above right) for Edmond Poley.

HOLLINGSWORTH - some of the other references to Sir John Poley in his *'History of Stowmarket'*:

> **p110, 1623** - Sir John along with Sir Roger North Knt and others appointed by the Chancery Court as a trustee of charity money originally bequeathed by Margaret Gowle in possession of the town of Stowmarket following the suppression of Chantries by Henry VIII & Edward VI. Half of the money was assigned "to making and repairing the high road between Stowemarkett and Ipswiche" and the other was divided between the poor of Stonham and Stow church. The latter to be "expended according to the bequest of this good lady."

An **Edmund Poley Esq**., was also appointed a trustee, but there is no way of telling if this is 'of Badley' or Sir John's son.

In 1653 a new deed of feoffment for this property was made which included J Poley of Stowmarket Esq. (Sir John's son) and Edmund Poley of Badley Esq.

p140, 1618 - Sir John Poley Knt was one of the Overseers of the poor for the 'Upland' of Stowmarket.

p152, 1611 - in a list of persons contributing weeklye to the overseers, "and of the moneye which they have payde unto ye poore people in ye Borowghe of Stowmarket and to ye poore people in ye Uplande in the year last past, viz from xxth day of Aprill 1610 untill xix of April, 1611, beinge 11s weeklye. The contributors names and what they gave weeklye."

Imprimis, Sir John Poley, Knt., listed as paying 11d. Amt. xiiis.

A Mr. Doctor Poley is also listed, but it is not clear who this was.

p156 - "Several knights of ancient families took a lively interest in Stowmarket and some of their signatures appear in the papers. Some of them resided in or adjoining the town : as, (amongst others) Sir Will Poley

In 1602 Robt. Gardiner (Upland) - Wm. Poley - Edw. Poley (and others) - were justices living in Stow Hundred."

As the entries on this page pre-date Sir John Poley's purchase of Columbine Hall in 1608, presumably the Poleys referred to were 'of Badley'.

p159, 1630 - Refers to the 'pinching distress' of the poor during what was a very severe winter and the poor state of church equipment. "Sir John Poley was principally instrumental in assisting the town out of its difficulties. Mr. Edward Pole made them a present of a fat ox at Christmas, and gave them corne to grind into bread for their poor. But as now so then presents were not to be had without 'bere', for money went in bere upon the men to give them drinke when they brought in the befe."

p162, 1642 - "The rates levied for soldiers and the support of the parliamentary war commence thus - "a rate made the 6th June 1642 by Roger Barnes, gent. and J.Brazier, gent. and John Heyward appointed to be seasors with the rest of the inhabitants with the towne for the some of twenty-nine pounde and thirteen shillinge." They then levied on land and goods thus:-

	£.	s.	d.
The Ladye Poley for her own lande 16*l*. per an.	0	7	4
Idem. in goode 150*l*.	0	3	5½
Mrs. Eliz. Poley in goodes 200*l*.	0	4	7
Mrs. Ursula Poley in 200*l*. goodes	0	4	7

Fig 10.6 Mr Boby of Columbine Hall, photographed by W Vick, London Road, Ipswich.

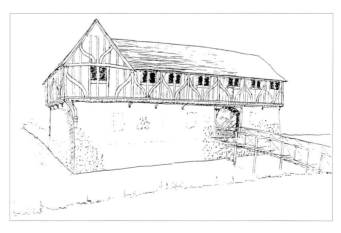

Fig 10.7 The Hall, a reconstruction by John Warren.

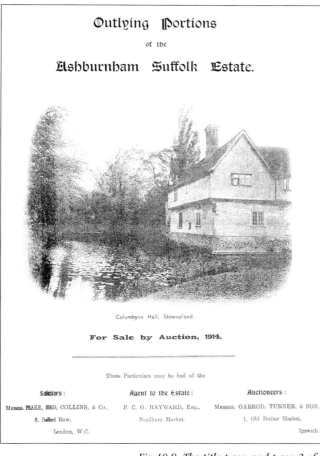

Outlying Portions

of the

Ashburnham Suffolk Estate.

Columbyne Hall, Stowupland.

For Sale by Auction, 1914.

These Particulars may be had of the

Solicitors :	Agent to the Estate :	Auctioneers :
Messrs. PEAKE, BIRD, COLLINS, & Co.,	P. C. G. HAYWARD, Esq.,	Messrs. GARROD, TURNER, & SON,
6, Bedford Row,	Needham Market.	1, Old Butter Market,
London, W.C.		Ipswich.

8

IT NOW COMPRISES

An Old Moated House,

Surrounded by

Fine Old Oak, Elm, Maple, and Whitethorn Trees,

Approached through

An Old FLOWER GARDEN, with Yew, Box, Lombardy Poplar, and Elm Trees.

It is brick and stud and plaster built, with plain tile roof, and has AN OLD RED BRICK CHIMNEY STACK, and contains :—

ENTRANCE HALL ; TWO SITTING ROOMS, respectively 20 ft. by 16 ft. and 15 ft. 6 in. by 13 ft., each 9 ft. 6 in. high ; GARDEN LOBBY ; TWO STOREROOMS, one with old moulded ceiling ; KITCHEN, 18 ft. by 13 ft. by 8 ft. 8 in.; LARGE BACKHOUSE, with brick oven ; DAIRY ; CELLAR ; an Oak Staircase ; Back Staircase ; LANDINGS ; THREE BEDROOMS, respectively 19 ft. by 16 ft. by 9 ft., 21 ft. by 15 ft. by 8 ft., 15 ft. by 14 ft. by 7 ft. 3 in., with carved mantelpiece ; FOUR SMALLER BEDROOMS and ATTICS over the BACKHOUSE.

A Range of brick and tile COAL, WOOD, MEAL, and other OUTHOUSES.

An ORCHARD, with Apple and Walnut Trees.

THE AGRICULTURAL BUILDINGS,

In good order, are chiefly brick pinned, timber and clay built, with tiled, slated, or thatched roofs, with a Cartway between, and comprise :—

West Block.—A TWO-STALL NAG STABLE and GIGHOUSE ; CART STABLE for nine horses, with HAY LOFT over ; HORSE SHED and YARD ; STOCK BARN, with one brick end ; CATTLE SHED and YARD ; FOUR PIGSTYES, with COURTS, SWILLHOUSE and YARD ; PIGGERY and FOWLHOUSE ; a Six-bayed CART LODGE, with LOOSE BOX at end.

East Block.—A CORN BARN, one bay and centre concreted, with lean-to CORN BIN and GRANARY ; NEATHOUSE for nine cows and ROOTHOUSE ; TWO COW SHEDS ; TWO LOOSE BOXES and TWO YARDS.

CORN AND HAY STACKYARDS ; GOOD PONDS OF WATER.

THE LAND

Varies from Mixed Soil to a Heavy Loam, and includes some Good Pastures. It comprises in all by the Ordnance Survey (1904 Edition)

250 ACRES,

Divided as shown by the following

Fig 10.8 The title page and page 3 of Garrod, Turner, & Son's 1914 sales brochure.

Fig 10.9 Old postcards showing two aspects of the Hall, with a modern counterpart.

Columbine Hall - Succession

FEUDAL OVERLORDS (non-resident)

Philip de Columbers 3rd of Nether Stowey, Somerset. Held the manor of Battisford by 1242/3. D.1257 and was succeeded by his son:

Philip de Columbers 4th, d.1272, succeeded by his brother:

John de Columbers, summoned to Parliament 1294, d.1306, succeeded by his son:

Philip de Columbers 5th, summoned to Parliament as a Baron 1314. Died childless in 1342, having sold Battisford to John Salmon, Bishop of Norwich, in 1317/8.

The Bishop of Norwich, the Bishops remained as the overlords of Thorney Columbers until 1535, when it was taken by the Crown.

MESNE LORDS (resident)

John de Hotot (from Huttoft in Lincolnshire?) - held the manor 1242/3.

1326/7 John de Hotot (or le Hotott) - held the manor; taxed 3s 6d in Thorney 1327.

1332/3 Robert le Hotot (Hotoot or Houtot) - d. abt.1346.

1346 Avice Houtot - widow of Robert Houtot.

1346/7 - c.1354/5 Edmund de Saxham (presumably the second husband of Avice Houtot).

by 1377 Robert Hotot - a prominent justice in Suffolk 1381-1399. Probable builder of the existing Columbyne Hall. Dead by 1402, succeeded by his son:

by 1402 John Hotot

1424/5 John Hotot (Hotoft)

1452 John Hotoft - succeeded by his son:

by 1464 Robert Hotoft Esq. - married Joan, the daughter of John Fitz-Ralph Esq. of Pebmarsh, Essex. D.1469, succeeded by his son:

1469 John Hotot Esq. - dead by 1515/6, the last of his family, succeeded by his daughter:

by 1515/6 Anne Hotot - married James Tyrrell (2nd son of Sir James Tyrrell of Gipping) She d. abt.1534, he d. abt.1539.

1534 John Tyrrell Esq. - d. 1557/8, succeeded by his son:

1557/8 Thomas Tyrrell Esq. - lost Columbyne Hall 1559 through a foreclosed mortgage. He is probably the Thomas Tyrrell of London who married Margaret, the daughter of John Howe of Stowmarket.

1559 Thomas Stambridge, merchant of London, mortgagee of Columbine Hall. He sold it on to:

1559 John Gardiner, gent. of London. Gardiner lived at Columbine Hall, but had to fight many law suits against the Tyrrells to retain his property. Died childless 1595/6, succeeded by his widow:

1595/6 Agnes Gardiner (dau. of John Smyth of Cavendish). She remarried Edward Browne of Leiston & died c.1599. Under a deed of settlement designed to prevent the Tyrrells regaining the property, Columbyne Hall passed to a prominent courtier:

c.1599 Sir Robert Carey Knt, a Gentleman of the Privy Chamber (later Earl of Monmouth - younger son of Lord Hunsdon). It is recorded that on 4th Oct 1609, Sir Robert leased 'a capital messuage and site of 'Collobine Hall' alias Thorney Columbers in the parish of Stowe Markett to Giles Keble of Newton, yeoman'.

He sold the property to:

1608 SIR JOHN POLEY (grandson of Edmund Poley of Badley). He served as a soldier in Spain 1592 and in Ireland and was knighted by Robert Devereux, Earl of Essex at Dublin 1599. He died in 1634 and was succeeded by his widow during the minority of his son:

1634 LADY URSULA POLEY (youngest daughter and co-heir of Sir John Gilbert of Gt. Finborough). She died abt.1643-6. She was succeeded by her son:

c.1646 JOHN POLEY Esq. was aged 14 at his father's death, he died childless in 1666. He was buried at Stowmarket on 21st September. His death ended the line of resident lords of the manor as Columbyne Hall passed to his relatives, none of whom who are thought to have resided there.

1714/1735 Major Richard Gipps inherited the Hall from his uncle Edmund Poley who died in 1714 (see Will Appendix D). In 1735 he sold it to:

1735/1754 Ambrose Crowley Esq of Barking Hall (see Chapter 7). Upon his death in 1754 it passed to his brother John, who died the following year and it passed through his sister, Elizabeth, who was married to the Rt Hon. John Ashburnham, who inherited the estate upon her death in 1781.

1781/1914 The Earls of Ashburnham

1914/1927 Henry Potter, (sitting tenant at time of sale)

1927/1941 William John Potter, son of the above

1941 1951 East Suffolk Agricultural Committee

1951/1993 The Rednall family

1993 - Hew Stevenson and Leslie Geddes-Brown

The Poleys of
Columbine Hall
(1608-1668)

*Fig 10.10 Arms of **Poley** (Or. a lion rampant Sa.) impaling **Gilbert** (Az. a chevron engrailed Erm. between three eagles displayed Or.)*

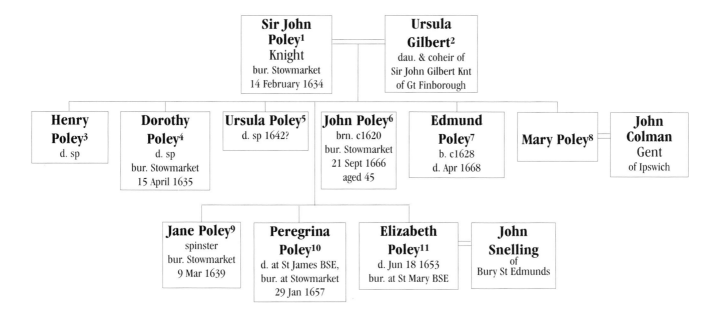

NOTES:
1. Sir John's Will was made in 1634 and is reproduced in Appendix D (page 301).
2. Lady Ursula Poley - no Will or burial at Stowmarket found, but the entry in the Burial Register of St Mary, Bury St Edmunds, "1658, April 3rd. The Honourable the Lady Pooly buried." is thought to refer to her.
3. Henry Poley - very little known, believed to have died young.
4. Dorothy Poley of Stowmarket - Will made 18 Mar 1635, proved 6 November 1636 - Reproduced Appendix D (page 301).
5. Ursula Poley - spinster, little known.
6. John Poley - unmarried, Sir John's heir.
7. Edmund Poley - no record of any marriage, little else know.
8. Mary Poley - probably buried at Ipswich, St Lawrence?
9. Jane Poley - spinster, little known.
10. Peregrina Poley - probably lived at Bury St Edmunds.
11. Elizabeth Poley - lived at Bury St Edmunds. There is a monument to her in the north aisle of St Mary's Church inscribed, "Depositum Lectissimæ Foeminæ Elizabethæ Snelling, ex equestri Familia D'ni Johannis et D'næ Ursulæ Poley, do Stow Mercatu, oriundæ; Quæ Christum p'stolans hic placide obdormit. Obijt decimo octavo die Junij, A'no D'ni 1653," and at the end some verses, with this addition: "Uxori pientissimæ J. Snelling, Moerens superst', P.C." The date is on either side of a shield, bearing within a ducal coronet two arrows in saltire piercing two hearts conjoined. (see p203, *An Architectural and Historical Account of The Church of St Mary, Bury St Edmunds* by Samuel Tymms, F.S.A. (1854)).

For more information relating to Columbine Hall see the Ashburnham Family Archives at the Ipswich Branch of the S.R.O. (Ref: HA1/A8).

Chapter Eleven

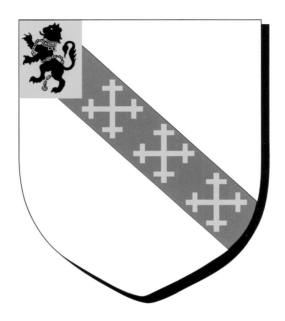

Notes on the Poleys of Boxted

GIVEN that there is sufficient material to compile a separate book on the Boxted Poleys, this chapter is restricted to only a few links about them and the Badley branch of the family.

It has already been established that the Badley and Boxted branches of the Poley family shared a common ancestry. These two small Suffolk parishes have several other things in common.

St Mary's, Badley and Holy Trinity, Boxted (Fig 11.1), can both be rightly described as Poley shrines. The churches are both situated within sight of their 'Poley halls' and both parishes have populations of less than 100 souls. At least the burden of maintaining their church has been lifted from the shoulder of the inhabitants of Badley.

HOLY TRINITY CHURCH

There is no church recorded at Boxted in the Domesday Book (1086). It is believed the current building, situated on a hill to the west of Boxted Hall, may have originally been built as a chapel-of-ease to the adjoining parish of Hartest, with whom it has shared a living since 1224.

On the north side of the chancel a chapel, or *"Burying Place"*, was added by the Poley family, between the deaths of Sir John Poley (d.1629) and Sir William Poley (d.1658).

There are a number of floor stones commemorating various Poleys on the chancel floor, including on the north side, the oldest surviving Poley monument, a palimpset brass - one reusing the reverse of an earlier brass to Richard Poley (1468-1547) and his wife Ann.

On the south side is a tomb chest with rare oak effigies of William Poley (b. 18 Dec. 1587) and Alice his wife (bur. 7 March 1577). He is dressed in armour, with his head on a helmet (Fig 11.2). She has a prayer book with the arms of Poley and Shaa, and rests on a pillow inscribed "BEATI MORTVI QVI IN DOMINO MORIVNTVR" *(Blessed are the dead who die in the Lord)*. A small dog nestles by her feet and there is a date on the left hand side of her head,

A. P. / 1579. / Mar. 7.*

However, it is the granduer of the Poley monuments in their chapel which far exceed those at Badley. An open book and double scroll on the west wall traces the descent of the family from the 14th. to the 20th. centuries (Fig 11.3).

* Given the Register says Alice was buried on the 7th March 1577, one wonders why the date on her efigy is 1579?

Fig 11.1 Holy Trinity Church, Boxted.

Pride of place must go to the magnificent alabaster monuments to Sir John Poley (1558-1638) of Wormegay, Norfolk and his wife Abigail (Fig 11.4).

The inscription describes Sir John as "as man famous for his bravery in arms and for military skills to be reckoned amongst the first commanders" (see full text overleaf). He served under Henry IV of France for three years and King Christian of Denmark for 22 years. Both effigies were erected long after their deaths. Sir John's is late 17th century and attributed to John Bushnell.

Dame Abigail died in 1652, but her monument was not erected until 1725, at the expense of a granddaughter and is believed to be the last English one made of alabaster.

So far no one has been able to explain why Sir John has been sculpted wearing a golden frog earring!

Fig 11.2 The wooden effigies of William & Alice Poley.

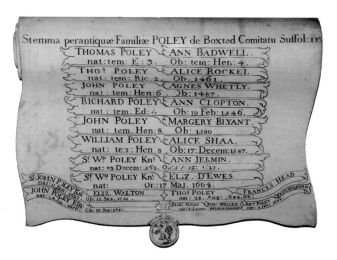

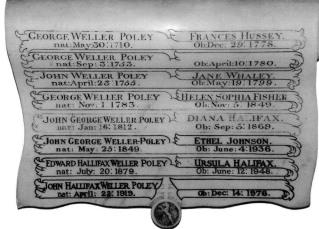

Fig 11.3 The marble 'open books' in the Poley Chapel showing the family genealogy and confirming the common ancestry commencing with Thomas Poley and his 2nd wife Ann Badwell (top left).

Fig 11.4 The impressive alabaster monumemts to Sir John and Dame Abigail Poley in the Poley Chapel.

The inscription below Sir John's figure, which is in Latin, reads :

"Under this marble lies buried, awaiting the second coming of our Lord. Sir John Poley, of Wrongey, in the County of Norfolk, knight; descended from the ancient family of the Poleys of Suffolk, being the second son, and at length heir of Thomas Poley, and grandson of John Poley, of Boxted Hall, in the county of Suffolk, Esq., - a man famous for his bravery in arms, and for military skill to be reckoned amongst the first commanders. For first as captain of English Foot under Henry IVth, King of France, in his wars against the Leaguers, for the space of three years; and afterwards under the standard of Christian, King of Denmark, a; colonel-general, more than twenty years, did he fight with success. With the greatest praise moreover, and reputation for bravery, did he war against the Spaniard, under Elizabeth, Queen of England;

When Cales submitted to, his conq'ring arm, And all Iberia felt the loud alarm.

(continued on next page)

But not only in military virtue and deeds of arms did his praise consist, he excelled too in candour of manners and courteousness of disposition, and on this account was he much beloved both by the above-named Christian, of Denmark, and likewise by James, King of Great Britain; both of whom treated him with familiarity and the greatest kindness. At length our veteran after so much success in foreign wars, now far advanced in year, obtained his discharge, and returned home to his native England, where, at the beginning of the reign of Charles, he passed a tranquil life, blessed with the highest esteem and favour of that monarch, and devoted himself wholly to his God and his king; 'till satisfied with his share of life and fame, he sunk placidly to sleep in the Lord, having passed his eightieth year. He died in his manor of Wrongey, in the year of our Lord 1638".

Fig 11.5 One of several Poley Hatchments.

Fig 11.7 Poley Crests like this one abound in the church. Note the family motto "Fortior Qui Se" is the same as that on the bookplate of Edmund Poley of Badley (Chapter 6, Fig 6.16).

The communion cup at Holy Trinity was donated by John Poley of Boxted. It is described as -

"Cup : silver gilt; the bowl is slightly bell shaped, encircled by a raised moulding. The foot is round.
    Height 7 3/8 inches ; diameter of bowl 4 inches.
    Is inscribed :- *"Ex dono Johannis Poley, Armigeri. Anno Domini, 1708".*

Marks : Britannia; maker's mark, Yo. in quatrefoil (for Edward York, as in Cripps in 1706); court hand N for 1708; lion's head erased. John Poley, of the ancient family of Poley of Boxted Hall, whose fine monuments remain in the church, was probably the second son of Sir John Poley, Knt., M.P. for Sudbury. He was born in 1676, and died s.p."
Suffolk Institute of Archaeology - Church Plate in Suffolk - Deanery of Sudbury by C. R. Manning, F.S.A. p.58 Volume IX, Part I (1895).

Fig 11.6 Poley hatchments in the roof at Holy Trinity Boxted.

BOXTED HALL

The Poleys have occupied a house on the same site at Boxted since the late 14th century. From Figs 11.8 & 9 opposite we can surmise that Boxted Hall has always been a substantial building.

However, the Suffolk Hearth Tax Returns suggest that in 1674 the Badley branch possessed the larger premises -

Sir John Poley	- Boxted in Babergh	22 hearths
The Lady Poley	- Badley in Bosmere	30 hearths

POLEY to WELLER-POLEY

The marriage of Thomas Poley of Codreth, Hertfordshire to Ann Badwell of Boxted, the daughter and heir of Thomas Badwell, Lord of Boxted Manor, during the latter part of the 14th century established the Poleys at Boxted, a position the family have maintain until the present day.

The only significant change during this 600-year association occurred upon the death of John Poley (1676-1757), who was the last Poley at Boxted.

In 1754 he settled the 725-acre estate on his second cousin George Weller the son of Robert Weller and Elizabeth (née Poley) of Tunbridge Wells. John requested that George Weller should take Poley as a second surname, which he appears to have adopted by 1773, commencing the Weller-Poley dynasty, the descendants of whom still occupy the hall today.

MISCELLANEOUS

Thomas Poley of Boxted was involved in a survey of the Muster and Military Defences of the Island of Lothingland in 1584. He was appointed a commissioner along with three others by the Privy Council, (in a period when the fear of a Spanish invasion filled the minds of Englishmen in a momentus year which saw the death of the Duke of Anjou and the murder of William, Prince of Orange,) to make enquiries into the strength of coast defences and as to the disposition and of the inhabitants dwelling in districts where an attempt to land might be made by Parma's troops.

'Sir John Poley, Knt., present as an Alderman (clad in a black gown faced with scarlet velvet) at the election of the Mayor of Sudbury at the Moot Hall on the Market Hill in the first week of the month of April 1665 (7 Charles II).'

Suffolk Institute of Archaeology - Election of the Mayor of Sudbury in 1665 by William Walter Hodson p.11 Volume VIII, Part I (1894).

Fig 11.8 Boxted Hall c.1818.

Fig 11.9 Boxted Hall from the church 2000.

The Ancient Families of Suffolk from Sir Richard Gipps M.S. *(Extract : re the Poleys)*

"POLEY. This very ancient Family of Knts Degree spread itself into several flourishing Branches seated at Boxted Hall in Babergh Hundred, Columbine Hall, in Stowmarket, and at Badley in Bosmere Hundred, Boxted is the elder House, and they have been Knts, successively for many Generations.

Sr John Poley, the last Knt of this Branch, was a Gentleman of a sound understanding, a sincere Heart, and a plain, primitive, and open Behaviour, a loyal subject, and a true Lover of his Country. He was chosen Burgess of Sudbury without his Knowledge, and sat in the Convention against his Inclination; where, in that memorable Debate January 28, 1688 whether the Throne were vacant, he made the following short Speech,

"Mr Speaker.

I am sent hither to do the Church and Cesar right, to vindicate the Doctrines of ye one, and preserve the Majesty of ye other: both which are in Danger from Gentlemens' Arguments on ye Debate of this Day.

Mr Speaker, here is an Affair of ye greatest Weight before us, both as we are Christians and Englishmen ; no less than the deposing a King, whom we have sworn allegiance to. Will our Religion or our Laws, justify such a Proceeding? I know, they will not.

Gentlemen indeed have laid a mighty Stress upon ye original Contract; and urg'd the Vacancy of the Throne from his Majestys Breach of that. But, I hope, we shall not proceed rashly in a matter of such Consequence to us and our Posterity. And therefore I move, that this Debate be adjourn'd, till ye original Contract be produced, and laid upon the table for the Members to peruse, that we may see whether his Majesty has broke it, or no".

After ye Prince and Princess of Orange were declar'd King and Queen contrary to our known Laws, Sr John retir'd to his Seat at Boxted, and never acted in a public Station afterwards ; but liv'd and dy'd, enjoying ye comforts of a private Life and a good Conscience, belov'd and lamented by all who had the Honour to know him.

He left issue one Son. John Poley Esqr. now of Boxted, and one Daughter Elizabeth ; both unmarry'd.

Suffolk Institute of Archaeology - The Ancient Families of Suffolk by Rev Frances Haslewood, F.S.A. - Rector of St Matthew's, Ipswich, p.189-190. Vol. VIII, Part II (1894).

WILLIAM CROFTES LETTER TO GEORGE WELLER-POLEY

Harling
Sept. 8th 1767

"Sir

I received the favour of your letter this morning which I beg leave to assure you gave me great pleasure, as I flatter myself, that by that accidental occurrence, I may be introduced to your acquaintance and that you will do me the honour to look upon me as related to a family for which I have ever had so great a regard.

It is natural, so reasonable, and indeed so necessary in us all, to get the best information we can relating to those from whom we are descended, that there was not any sort of occasion to make the least apology for your application to me upon that subject, especially as the mark for your inquiry to give the last proof of your gratitude, and respect to the memory of your departed friends and relation is so laudable.

My mother was a grand-daughter of Sir Edmund Poley by Lord Croftes sister and her two famous uncles Sir Edmund

and Sir Henry, her aunt Lady Dover, and her only brother Maj. Gipps having all died without issue, I became the heir of that branch of the Poleys, that for so many years resided at Badley; the pedigree, and other papers of my ancestors are consequently come into my hands, but having occasion to carry them to London I can't at present come at them but as soon as I get to town, shall be ready to send them to you in any manner you please to command.

I have the misfortune to be deprived of the use of limbs by hereditary gout that will not permit me to make any visit, or I should most certainly have paid my respects to you at Boxted, and it would have given me a double pleasure in waiting upon you at a place, where I had been so kindly and hospitably received and which my worthy good friend Mr Elves has told me is so much improved by your elegant taste, but if business or amusement should bring you into Norfolk I hope you will be so obliging as to favour me your company at Harling, as it would give me great satisfaction, to pay my compliments to you in person.

John, Sir
your most obedient honourable servant.

Will. Croftes.

As I did not know how to send my
letter by the post, with any certainty,
I hope to excuse the trouble of a messenger

I beg you will excuse the writing as
a weak hand that can scarcely hold
a pen."

NOTES :

a) William Croftes confirms his descendancy from the Poleys of Badley. Although he refers to the Poley brothers Henry and Edmund as "Sirs", there is no evidence to show that either were in fact ever knighted.

b) William Croftes, Esq., died on the 14th November, 1770, at West Harling, Norfolk, in the 60th year of his age. Mary his wife, the daughter of Sir Mathew Decker, Bart., died in 1772.

Source: *(b only) The Gentleman's Magazine Library - English Topography Part VIII (1896) (pages 114-116) West Harling. (1844, Part I.,pp. 153, 154.)*

Chapter Twelve

Miscellany

A check of the Suffolk Archaeological County Sites and Monuments Records (SMR) has revealed that apart from a few metal detected finds, some surface scatters of artefacts found 'field-walking' in the parish and other similiar finds awaiting input into the computerised SMR, the Badley Bowl, featured in this Chapter, remains the most important find within the parish to date.

Not very much recording or field work appears to have taken place in the parish, which probably explains the relatively low number of Badley SMR's. Certainly no evidence has been found to support the suggestion sometimes expressed that present-day Badley is all that remains of a larger village deserted after, for example, a plague.

The Badley Bowl
found at Gateford 1865.

An Ancient Leather Case
is there a Badley connection?

Miscellaneous Finds
metal detection within the parish.

The Badley Triangle
air crashes within the parish.

The Badleybridge Bowl

The following is a summary of 'The Badley (Needham Market) Bowl' by Dr R. H. White, BA, PhD, MIFA (1992).

INTRODUCTION

IN 1865 a group of objects were found at Gateford, Badley Bridge, during the construction of the Stowmarket to Needham Market railway.

"The find appears to have consisted of a Roman vessel full of denarii, a cast copper alloy Byzantine bowl and an unusual enamelled bronze bowl in the hanging bowl tradition.

The associations are unknown, but the latter two objects are probably from grave(s) of the Anglo-Saxon period. The pottery vessel with its hoard need not, however, be associated with the metal bowls. The objects were acquired by a Mr. Maw of Needham Market (the Maws were a local banking family) and were drawn whilst in his possession by Hamlet Watling, who was by all accounts an accomplished artist and antiquarian. The vessels are said to have been disposed of after they 'fell apart' after being drawn, as opposed to when they were discovered, and are only known from these drawings".

The news of the find was first published in 'The Reliquary' by J. R. Allen in 1900. Fortunately Hamlet Whatling's drawing have survived and are reproduced.

The Site

An estate map and survey produced in 1772 by Joseph Pennington (Fig 12.1 opposite) shows James Christmas was the tenant of Badley Bridge farm and amongst his holdings were:

Gateford Meadow	3 acres	2 roods	34 perches
Gateford Fen	4 acres	1 roods	28 perches
Causeway Meadow	4 acres	0 roods	28 perches

A comparison of this map with the relevant section of the 1904 Ordnance Survey map drawn after the construction of the line, shows "that the railway did not go through either Gateford Fen or Meadow, situated to the west of the turnpike, but did pass through Causeway Meadow to the East of the Ipswich to Stowmarket road (Fig 12.2 opposite). The identification of the site with Causeway

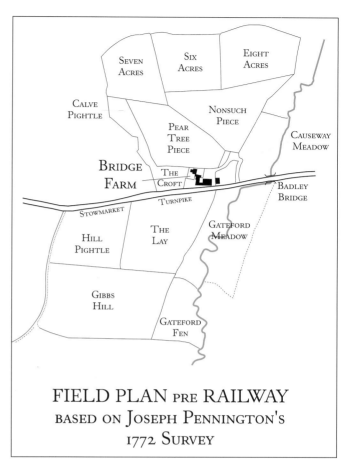

FIELD PLAN PRE RAILWAY
BASED ON JOSEPH PENNINGTON'S
1772 SURVEY

Fig 12.1.

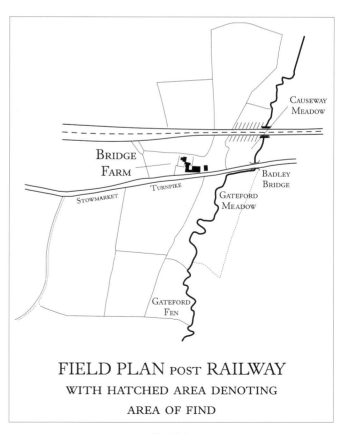

FIELD PLAN POST RAILWAY
WITH HATCHED AREA DENOTING
AREA OF FIND

Fig 12.2.

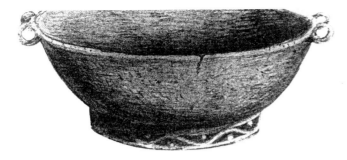

Fig 12.3 Whatling's drawing of the Byzantine bowl.

Fig 12.4 Whatling's drawing of the hanging bowl.

Fig. 12.5 Whatling's drawing of the 'bird' or 'heater' escutcheon (left) with R. H. White's alongside showing the detail of the enamel print.

Meadow seems virtually certain given the proximity of the original site name. The approximate Grid Reference being TM 083559".

Whatling's Drawing

In 1880 the drawing was exhibited at a meeting of the British Archaeological Association. By 1900 it was owned by a Miss Nina Layard of Ipswich and in 1924 it was deposited in the Ipswich Museum by Dr Whitwell of Melton. When R. H. White visited the museum in the early 1990's, only photographs of the drawing were available (Figs 12. 3 and 12.4). "These show the bowls and the enamelled attatchments but not unfortunately the pot and escutcheon ring". He redrew the enamelled prints and escutcheon from these photographs (Figs 12.5 and 12.6).

"The Hanging Bowl is shown in Watling's drawing (Fig. 12.4) as a vessel with two large (c. 78 and 82 mm) circular escutcheons, two 'bird' or 'heater' shaped escutcheons, two suspension rings and an enamelled upright 'band' on top of the vessel. The craftsman thus took two of the heater-shaped escutcheons (not using a third which must originally have been present) and soldered them to the side of the vessel. One of the prints was then soldered onto the base and a rim was formed from an enamelled band which must also have been derived from the broken hanging bowl.

The edge of this strip was covered with a simple copper alloy binding to smooth it over. Finally, a second print was used as a lid, although it seems reasonably clear from the account by Watling that this must have been loose.

The Badleybridge Bowl can be regarded as a unique creation of probably the early 7th. Century, which re-used elements of a broken hanging bowl. The reason for this possible reuse may lie in the function of the vessel after its creation. Metal vessels in Anglo-Saxon graves had two uses: as accessory vessels accompanying inhumations or as containers for cremations.

The latter function is the rarer variety and seems to be linked in time to the later sixth and seventh centuries. Hanging bowls used in this fashion having been discovered at several other locations." It therefore seems likely to have been an *ad hoc* creation which utilised dismembered fragments of a conventional hanging bowl in an inventive and unusual fashion to create a cremation urn.

The circumstances of the Badleybridge find suggest that it would be unlikely that cremated material would have been noted, but in any event, no record of the discovery appears to have been published until 1880, by which time all record of associations would have been lost. Such a conclusion would certainly fit with strong links between post-Roman native craftsmen and the Anglians in the Suffolk region as exemplified by the use of enamel on Anglo-Saxon objects or the use of Germanic motifs on 'Celtic' metalwork.

The possibility that the vessel could have accompanied an inhumation cannot be totally discounted, but the explanation offered here would account for the curious position of Escutcheon 2 as a lid (Fig 12.6), the copper alloy binding strips on the rim and the apparent non-functional nature of the escutcheons".

I am grateful to Dr White for permission to reproduce his text.

For the full text of his re-appraisal paper please see Volume 5, (pp 33-40), *Anglo-Saxon Studies in Archaeology and History*, published by the Oxford University Committee for Archaeology (1992), a copy of which is held in the Lowestoft Branch of the Suffolk Record Office (Ref: 942.01).

Fig. 12.6 R. H. White's drawings of the enamelled basal escutcheon (top) and of the same print used on the loose lid.

The Sweffling Case ~ is there a Badley connection?

Fig 12.7 the Ancient leather case, or bottle case, at St Mary's Church, Sweffling. Size : Height 10ins., Diameter 6ins.

IN the Proceedings of the Suffolk Institute of Archaeology & Natural History, Vol X, Part 3, (1900), the Rev. E. Farrer, F.S.A. discussed the existence of an ancient, elaborately-tooled, leather case, discovered kept in an oak chest at St Mary's church at Sweffling (Fig 12.7).

This summary is included due to the illustrations carved on its surface, all available space being ornamented with scrolls, grotesques and armoral shields. Our interest lies in the five armoral shields carved into the lid, some of which are repeated on the case itself.

The shields on the top cover are:

  i) a lion rampant   ii) a chevron between three mullets
  iii) a cross patonce (or flory?)
  iv) a bend dexter   v) three piles, impaling the same?

Although the charges on the shields are common, it is suggested that their combination could nevertheless help to determine the family of the owner or donor and thereby enable the age of the case to be determined.

Charges i) & ii) are the attraction to us, because they may been seen together on the crest of the large Poley wall monument in Badley church (Chapter 3, Fig 3.84 and the cross patonce singularly in the north window, Fig 3.20.

Due to their abundant usage, the Rev Farrier is reluctant to suggest which family they represent on the case. However,

he acknowledges the use of the rampant lion i) by the Poleys of Boxted and Badley; and the use of charge ii) by the Alcocks. No memtion is made of the cross patonce (charge iii) which it is believed was used by the de Badeles in the 14th century.

It is suggested the case dates from the reign of Edward I or II, that is, 1280 to 1330. This would tie in nicely with the de Badeles, but appears too early for the Poleys and Alcocks, given that the earliest Poley date we have is the arrival of Thomas Poley from Codreth, Hertfordshire in the 15th century.

I'll add my own theory and suggest there is always the possibility that the case is a 15th century reproduction of those known to have existed in Edward's reign.

As to its use, Rev. Farrier suggests that it was *'intended to hold a chalice, or a cup of some kind'.* But he goes on to say, *'but in the early days there would be no need to carry about the chalice belonging to the parish',* and he therefore speculates *'it may have been intended to hold the standing cup belonging to a guild; if so, the hole at the top was made originally for the upstanding knob to pass through. Such a cup might well be, at times, carried about'.*

Although there is doubt, where else can three out of the five charges on the case be found under one church roof other than at St Mary's, Badley?

Miscellaneous Finds ~ within the parish

The following are examples of some of the artifacts found within the parish by means of metal detection. Most of those shown were discovered in the vicinity of Badley Hall or Doveshill Road which leads down to the church.

Fig 12.12 Lead musket balls of varying sizes.

Fig 12.8 Thimbles of various sizes.

Fig 12.9 A bronze token.

Fig 12.13 A lead fishing weight.

Fig 12.10 Lead corn weight used for weighing corn and stamped with a portcullis mark, possibly denoting Harwich.

Fig 12.14 A hand carrying a vase, broken off at the wrist from a larger figurine.

Fig 12.15 A lead loom weight.

Fig 12.11 A selection of buttons.

(All finds courtesy of Neil Little.)

The Badley Triangle? ~ air crashes within the parish

DESPITE its small size (1,050 acres), at least four aircraft have crashed in, or very close to, the Parish, probably due to being located directly under the flight path of RAF Wattisham 2½ miles away!

CRASH ONE :

At 9.24 pm on 12th July 1944, an RAF Avro Lancaster B111 bomber (Fig 12.8 opposite) (ED562) BQ-G, from 550 Sqdn., took off from RAF North Killingholme, near Grimsby, Lincolnshire and joined 377 other Lancaster bombers and 7 Mosquitoes from 1, 5 & 8 Groups to attack rail facilities at Revigny-sur-Ornain, 115 miles west of Paris. Cloud affected the target and only about half the force actually released their bombs.

At 7.20 am on the 13th July, whilst returning to base and over Suffolk, Lancaster BQ-G sustained the failure of an engine and was short of fuel. The aircraft was abandoned in the air by its crew and crashed in the valley between

Fig 12.16 the Avro Lancaster WWII bomber,

Badley Bridge and Green Farm (Map Ref: 523739[1]).

The crash site, a barley field and meadow about ½ mile west of the Needham - Stowmarket road, farmed by Francis Emmanuel Haydon of Doves Farm, Badley, extended over about four acres.

Police Constable 33 Wilfred Barber of Barking became aware of the crash at 7.30 am when the pilot, Pilot Officer J Lord, carrying his parachute, turned up at his police station to report the loss (see his report Fig 12.19). Fortunately the six other crew members, which included the bomb-aimer, Sgt A A A Vass of the RCAF, walked to Somersham police station, all bailed out safely and no one was injured on the ground.

Nine other Lancasters were lost on this raid. The other five crew members were - Flight Engineer Sgt K W C Down, Navigator F/Sgt R Sebaski (RCAF), Wireless Op P/O J Elliott, and Air Gunners Sgt A J Schomberg (RCAF) and Sgt P J Sculley.

Maurice Sore recalls visiting the crash site with his father soon after the occurrence.

I have been unable to established whether or not the wreckage has been completely removed from the crash site.

Note :

[1] this is a 'Modified British System' reference, adopted by the services during WWII and based on the Cassini projection and use of a reference grid. The modern OS Map Ref: equivalent is TM 072 (E) 556 (N).

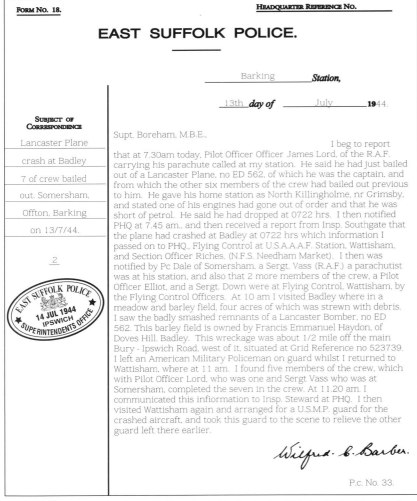

FORM NO. 18.

HEADQUARTER REFERENCE NO.

EAST SUFFOLK POLICE.

Barking **Station,**

13th **day of** July **19**44.

SUBJECT OF CORRESPONDENCE

Lancaster Plane

crash at Badley

7 of crew bailed

out. Somersham.

Offton, Barking

on 13/7/44.

2

[EAST SUFFOLK POLICE stamp: 14 JUL 1944 IPSWICH SUPERINTENDENTS OFFICE]

Supt. Boreham, M.B.E.,

I beg to report that at 7.30am today, Pilot Officer Officer James Lord, of the R.A.F. carrying his parachute called at my station. He said he had just bailed out of a Lancaster Plane, no ED 562, of which he was the captain, and from which the other six members of the crew had bailed out previous to him. He gave his home station as North Killingholme, nr Grimsby, and stated one of his engines had gone out of order and that he was short of petrol. He said he had dropped at 0722 hrs. I then notified PHQ at 7.45 am., and then received a report from Insp. Southgate that the plane had crashed at Badley at 0722 hrs which information I passed on to PHQ., Flying Control at U.S.A.A.A.F. Station, Wattisham, and Section Officer Riches. (N.F.S. Needham Market). I then was notified by Pc Dale of Somersham, a Sergt. Vass (R.A.F.) a parachutist was at his station, and also that 2 more members of the crew, a Pilot Officer Elliot, and a Sergt. Down were at Flying Control, Wattisham, by the Flying Control Officers. At 10 am I visited Badley where in a meadow and barley field, four acres of which was strewn with debris. I saw the badly smashed remnants of a Lancaster Bomber, no ED 562. This barley field is owned by Francis Emmanuel Haydon, of Doves Hill, Badley. This wreckage was about 1/2 mile off the main Bury - Ipswich Road, west of it, situated at Grid Reference no 523739. I left an American Military Policeman on guard whilst I returned to Wattisham, where at 11 am. I found five members of the crew, which with Pilot Officer Lord, who was one and Sergt Vass who was at Somersham, completed the seven in the crew. At 11.20 am. I communicated this information to Insp. Steward at PHQ. I then visited Wattisham again and arranged for a U.S.M.P. guard for the crashed aircraft, and took this guard to the scene to relieve the other guard left there earlier.

Wilfred. E. Barber.

P.c. No. 33.

Fig 12.17 A reproduction of Police Constable Barber's official report of the crash.

CRASH TWO :

This was also a wartime crash. At about 10.50 am on Tuesday 13th March 1945, a United States Army Airforce Republic P47 Thunderbolt single-seater fighter, number 421159, from the 56th Fighter Group based at USAAF Camp, Boxted, near Colchester Essex, crashed at Badley in a meadow adjoining the railway track, about 300 yards south of the Silkworks (Cassini Map Ref: 521753).

The aircraft caught fire after crashing and was completely wrecked, causing slight damage to the railway line. Unfortunately the pilot, No. 0/830584 Lieut. Richard B. Tuttle was fatally injured.

In the police report filed by Police Constable 153 Richard N James of Needham Market it states the aircraft was heard to be in difficulties over Barking and the cock-pit cover was later recovered from a field there, possibly indicating the pilot was attempting to bale-out.

Peter Mayhew who was living at No 1 New Cottage at the time, and still lives there, recalls going to the scene and a subsequent visit by the local policeman to make sure he had not gathered up any souvenirs!

CRASH THREE :

This crash was actually in Creeting and was caused by two Meteor Mk 8 jet fighters, from 257/263 Squadron based at RAF Wattisham touching in mid-air whilst practising for the 1953 Coronation fly-pass.

Both aircraft crashed on the Creeting side of the River Gipping, between the river and Creeting Hall, (roughly in line with Cherry Tree Farm) at Map Refs TM 077568 & TM 076567. However, some of the debris landed in Badley!

CRASH FOUR :

On 29th Sept 1965, a BAe Lighting fighter (XP793) from 111 Sqd. RAF Wattisham crashed near Battisford Hall, narrowly missing farmworkers Edwin Bolton (38) & Robert Worledge (53) both of Church Road, Battisford, having first hit the ground at Hill Field, Badley (close to Badley Green farmhouse).

The pilot Flt Lt Molland ejected safely, landing at Earl Stonham. (See *East Anglian Daily Times*, Thursday 30th September 1965, pp 1 & 7.)

Fig 12.20 The Republic P47 Thunderbolt fighter, together with the emblem of the 56th Fighter Group.

Fig 12.21 The Gloster Meteor Mk8 jet fighter.

Fig 12.22 A BAe Lightning F3 in the colours of the famous 111 Squadron RAF Wattisham.

Appendix A

The
Badley Parish
Registers

NOTES :

All the surviving Badley parish registers are carefully transcribed in this Appendix. They are deposited at the Suffolk Record Office (Ref: FB1) and a fiched copy is available for public use. Current registers are kept at St John the Baptist, Needham Market.

A good deal could be written on the origins and evolution of Parish Registers, but it is sufficient here to record that in 1538 following the Dissolution of the Monastries, Thomas Cromwell ordered parishes to record details of their baptisms, marriages and burials and to purchase a "sure coffer" in which to keep them. However, it was an Order passed in 1597 by Elizabeth I that required them to be kept in book form from 1598 and any earlier records, probably on loose sheets of paper, be copied into them (see next page for details of transfers into the Badley Register Book).

In common with many early registers, Badley's baptisms, marriages and burials are entered in chronological order in the same book, with different events often recorded on the same page. Some of the clerics meticulously maintained 'their' register, whereas others were extremely untidy and their entries muddled. Some entries are now so faded they are sadly indeciferable and it is feared many more are set to follow - due perhaps to the use of cheap or watered down ink!

Until the requirement for printed books, there was no set form for keeping registers. These were gradually introduced with the requirement for printed Marriages registers linked to Lord Hardwicke's Marriage Act of 1754; and books for Baptisms and Burials by the Parochial Registration Act 1812-13) (George Rose's Act) which formalised all entries in the Parish Registers in printed books with every entry of baptism, marriage and burial giving standard information.

Bear in mind, particularly when reading the early entries, that :

Lord Chesterfield's Act 1751-52 - Changed the calendar from Julian to Gregorian. Until then the new year had begun on the 25th March, Lady Day. Thus 1752 began on the 1st Jan 1751/2. The 2nd Sept 1752 was followed by the 14th Sept 1752 to adjust the calendar. So for example, 7th Feb 1666 should be written 7th Feb 1666/7.

age at marriage - the minimum age for a marriage until 1929 was 14 for a male and 12 for a female with parents or guardians consent. From that date the age went up to 16 with the same proviso. It should be noted that in the Sixteenth Century some children were married under 12 (even 5) in the better-off families.

the Poleys of Badley were both Roman Catholics and Royalist. Between 1645 and 1660 some families with these convictions did not have their children baptised because of their disapproval of the changed Rite under the Commonwealth

the Burial in Wool Acts of 1667 & 1678 required all bodies were to be buried in wool only, unless they died from from the Plague (prevalent in Needham Market in 1665) and an affidavit sworn accordingly. The Act was intended to support the woollen trade and the fine for not doing so was £5! (Repealed 1814).

Readers will probably notice that from bequests in Wills (Appendix D) and these register entries that more people were buried in the 'body' and small chancel of St Mary's than have marked graves. Was their grave over-buried by someone considered more important, or are they all still lying undisturbed somewhere beneath the floor, for example Richard Pearch gent., 1737 (page 255, register page 43).

The entries are reproduced in the order in which they occur in the registers. For clarity the year has been added to the beginning of the entry where necessary. Where the book or printed register has a page &/or entry number these are shown in red. The printed parts of registers are reproduced in italics.

The earliest register, the *"Ancient Register of the Parish of Badley"* contains :

Baptisms 1591-1755
Marriages 1597 8/9 - 1753
Burials 1589 - 1742

but there are eleven earlier entries for 1556 -1575.

On the mutilated parchment cover is written:

The Church booke of Badley Renewed
the 29 of September Anno Dom 1589

Written out of the former
Booke October the 25 1613
And thence here continued Per me William Nuttall, Clericum.

Over this, a later hand, has scribbled: [illegible] ye 27th 17(?18) . . . . [illegible].

Turning the book upside-down, on the same cover is written: Badley Hall, Major Richard Gipps 1714.

Besides the covers, this frail old book consists of 27½ leaves. *Burialls* begin on page 1 in 1589: at page 7 *Baptisms* in 1591: at page 15 *Marriages* in 1598-9.

At page 29 is written: "Marriages gathered out of the ould regester booke", followed by five marriages of 1556-1574: at page 31: "Baptisings gathered out of the old register", followed by three baptisms of 1575, 1575, 15 . . .(blank) ; at page 33: "Burialls gathered out of the ould regester booke", followed by three burials of 1575, 1575, 1559-60.

Baptisms end in 1755 at page 46; marriages in 1753 at page 56; burials in 1742 at page 43, for the lower half of leaf 22 (pages 43 and 44) has been cut out. The upper half of page 44 is blank.

By "the ould regester booke," the scribe means that beginning in 1538, made of paper. What a pity he did not copy the whole of it! However, let us remain thankful that so much has survived from this early period - many other Suffolk parishes have not been so lucky.

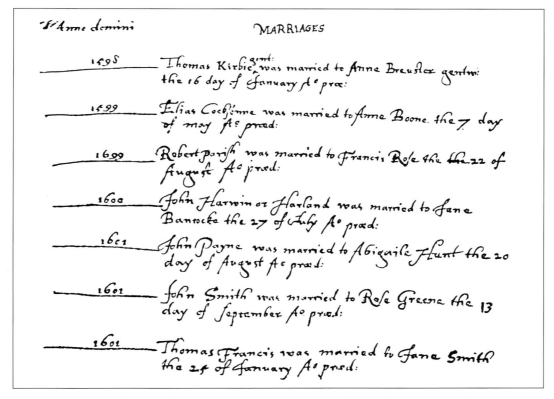

Fig A1 The start of the Marriages in 1598, on page 15 of the earliest Register Book.

(Page 1) BURIALLS

1559/60 Mirable Poolie (died 25 Feb 1558)

1575 William Goodale

1575 Anne Poolie wife of John Poley (died 28 August buried 29 Aug)

1589 John Poley of Badley Esquire Died October 20 in yᵉ 31 yeare of the reigne of Elizabeth I Annᵒ Domini 1589 and lyeth buried in the Chancell of Badley Church

1592 Richard Poley Gent and sonye of John Poley Esq dyed at Little Saxham the 8 daye of February & lyeth buried in the Chancell of Badley Church

1593 Mary Poley the wife of the sayd Richard Poley and ye daughter of Sr John Brewse Knight Dyed at Badley the 29 day of June 1593 and lyeth buried in the Chancell of Badley Church by the sayed Richard

1598 Katherine Goodale the wife of Edmund Goodale buried the 13 day of February Aᵒ Dm

1599 Elizabeth Harland single woman was buried 21 day of May Aᵒ Dm 1599

1599 Edmund Goodale died the 21 day of March and was buried the 22 day of that month 1599 Aᵒ Reyne Elizabeth 42

1600 John Willkinson was buried the 19 day of April 1660 Aᵒ Reyne Elizabeth 43

1600 William Foster was buried the 10 day of June Aᵒ Dm 1600

1601 Katherine Poley wife of Edmund Poley Esquire dyed at Badley 19 day of June Aᵒ Dm and was buried in the Chancell of Badley Church Aᵒ Reyn Elizabeth 43

1601 Mrs Boyse[1] widdowe died the first day of December and was buried in the Chancell of the Church of Badley the second of the same month Anno prædicto[2]

1602 Anne Lambe[3] the wife of Mr Thomas Lambe buried the sixteenth day of Feb. Anno prædicto

1602 Anne Deane the wife of Edward Deane was buried the 16 day of Aprill Anno prædicto

[Written in vertically in the right hand margin, "There appear to have been an ould register booke" from which some marriages, burials and baptisms have been "gathered" the earliest date is 1556 in this book"]

(Page 2) BURIALLS

1603 Jane Harlwin wife of John Harlwin was buried the eighteenth day of Aprill Annᵒ prædicto:

1604 Susan Crofts wife of Thomas Crofts Esquire the eldest daughter of John Poly Esquire and Anne his wife died at Badley the 13th day of September Annᵒ prædicto: and was buried at Saxham

1604 Peter Scrivener the eldest sonne of Ralfe Scrivener gent, died the 7th of December and was buried the same day Annᵒ prædicto:

1604 Ralfe Scrivener the sonne of Peter Scrivener Gent was buried the first day of May Annᵒ prædicto:

605 Elizabeth Balls the wife of Thomas Balls was buried the 3 of November Annᵒ prædicto:

1605 Robert Goodale the sonne of Edmund Goodale and Katherine his wife was buried the 6 day of March Annᵒ prædicto:

1606 Christian Bugge the wife of Robert Bugge was buried the 4 day of November Annᵒ prædicto:

1607 Robert Barker[4] the sonne of Sir Robert Barker Knight and of Susan his Lady was buried the 11 day of September Annᵒ prædicto:

1612 Mary Poly the daughter of John Poly Esquire was buried the 7th of January Annᵒ prædicto:

1613 Edmond Poly Esquire eldest sonne of John Poly Esquire died the last day of October Annᵒ prædicto: And lyeth buried in body of Badley Church

1613 Samuell Spink servant to Mr Poly was buried the 7th day of March annᵒ prædicto: (1613)

1614 Edmund Cowper once servant to Mr Poly was buried the 8 of February Annᵒ prædicto:

1614 Edmund Cowper sonne of Edmund Cowper above sayed was buried the 23 of September annᵒ prædicto:

1615 John Poolie the sonne of Edmund Poolie Esq & Dorothy his wife was buried the 13 day if April Aᵒ præd:

(page 3) BURIALLS

1616 S Ales w. of (from an earlier transcript - now indecipherable)

1617 Edmund Cooper buried 16 Aprill (from an earlier transcript - now indecipherable)

1619 Em Goodall the wife of Edmund Goofdall was buried the 4 day of December

1620 Margett Martin widowe was buried Janʸ 5

Anna Boule daughter of Henry Boule was buried 15 July

1621 Marie Brooke the daughter of Thomas Brooke was buried 7 November

1622 Nicholas Preston sonne of Peter Preston of Mickfield was buried September 10th

1623 Thomas Balls was buried January 6th

Margaret Harlaine yᵉ wife of John Harlain was buried August yᵉ 7th

1625 William Reynolds was buried June 25th

Mrs Dorothy Poley wife of Mr Edmund Poley dyed Juli 14th between 2 and 3 in the morning & was buried between 10 & 11 at night

1616 Thomas Martin of Onehouse servant to Thomas Manning was buried September 4

1628 Francis Buxton yᵉ daughter of Richard Buxton was buried Juli 22

Notes:

[1] Mrs Mirabel Boyse (née Poley) ~ see 5th Generation Family Tree, Chapter 6

[2] 'Annoque praedicto' meaning 'and in the year aforesaid'

[3] Ann Lambe (née Poley) a daughter of John Poley ~ see 6th Generation Family Tree, Chapter 6

[4] Sir Robert Barker knt., was married to Susan Crofts at Little Saxham on 27 Sept 1597 - hence the Badley connection

(Page 4) BURIALLS

1630   Henrie Poley sonne of Edmund Poley and Lady Francis Crompton his wife who died 15th March and was buried ye 17 of ye same month Annº prædicto:
       William Kent servant at Badley Hall & sonne of Thomas Kent dyed Maii 3rd and was buried the following day
1631   Henrie Pulford ye elder was buried August 22 anno prædicto:
       Edmund Beast eldest sonne of Robert Beast was buried August 29 anno prædicto:
1632   John Flint was buried March 4 anno prædicto
       Robert Bray was buried March 24 anno prædicto
1633   Mr Edmund Brewster Esq of Grayes Inne died August 5th & was buried in Badley Church 7th
1635   Francis Pleasants of Badley ye elder was buried Novemb: 4
       William Dove ye elder was buried Novemb: 17
       Mrs Elizabeth Crompton daughter of Sr John Crompton and Lady Frances Crompton his wife was buried Februa: 25 anno prædicto
1636   Anne Pulford wife of Henri Pulford of Badley was Buried at Badley June 25 ann: prædicto
1638   Anne Manning wife of Thomas Manning of Badley was buried Octo 27 anno prædicto
       Elizabeth Whistlecroft widow relict of John Whistlecroft of Earl Stonham was buried Novemb 5th anno præ dicto
       Thomison Pulford widdow of John Pulford was buried Novb 9th anno prædicto

(Page 5) BURIALLS

1638   Mary Beast widdow to Robert Beast was buried January ye sixth
1639   Thomas Pulford was buried March 26
1640   Edmund Poley of Badley Esq was buried Sept 14
       Mrs Marie Snelling gentlewoman to ye Lady Smith was buried January 16
       Thomas Manning was buried January 22
       Cecilie Dove was buried January 27º
1641   Marie Crompton was buried Aprill 14
       Phebe Dove was buried July 4
1643   Robert Buxton was buried January 26
1644   Edmund Goodale was buried the Aprill 2nd
1644   William Poley, gent, second sonne of Edmund Poley of Badley Esquire died at Stowmarket April 19 and was buried at Badley being of age 23 yeare April 20
1645   Susan Balls wife of John Balls was buried December 24
1648   Thomas Edwards servant to ye Ladies Crompton was buried January 23
       Catherine Goodale wife of Edmund Goodale was buried February 14
1649   Mary Balls daughter of John Balls was buried Aprill 23
       Mary Russell widdow to John Russell was buried June 22
       Margaret Coleman wife of Edward Coleman was buried June 22
       John Stookes was buried August 18
       Richard Buxton was buried September 19
       Ales Buxton Widdower was buried September 30

(Page 6) BURIALLS

1650   Henry Raymond wa buried August 11th
1652   John Harlewin was buried August 13th
       Edmund Goodale was buried January 2nd
1653   Elizabeth Sego was buried March 22nd
       Francis Raymond was buried August 19th
1655   Ann Flint was buried January 27th
1656   Isaac Tillot was buried February 15th
       Ann Beast was buried August 24th
1657   Giles Woolfe was buried June 4th
1658   Briers Burges was buried May 15th
       James Clarke was buried August 25th
       Robert Caley was buried March 24th
1659   Edward Sowter was buried April 4th
       Elizabeth Coleman was buried May 3rd
1660   John Lockwood was buried March 29th
1661   The Lady Frances Compton second wife to Edmund Poley of Badley Esq was buried 22 March
1662   Sara Beddow daughter of William Beddow & Alce his wife was buried July 20
       Edward Coleman was buried August 31
1663   John Goodwyn was buried November 11
       William Poley sonne of Sr Edmund Poley was buried March 22
1664   Alce Lambert ye daughter of Richard Lambert & Alce his wife was buried Decemb 11
       Marie Whitecoke ye wife of Thomas Whitecoke was buried March 16

(Page 7) BAPTIZMS

1575   John Lany

1591   Sisly Polye the daughter of Richard Poley Esquire was borne the 23 day of Maye the 34 yeare of the reyne of Queen Elizabeth and was baptized the 25th of the same month Anno p^{r}ædicto

1592   Edmund Polye sonne of the sayd Richard Polye Gent was borne the 25 of Maye in the 35 yeare of the reyne of Queen Elizabeth and was baptized the 28th of the same month Anno p^{r}ædicto

       Marie Cooper the daughter of Edmund Cooper was baptized the 25th day of Sept Anno p^{r}ædicto

       Susan Pulforde the daughter of Henry Pulforde was baptized the 23rd day of January Anno p^{r}ædi:

1594   Edmund Pulforde the sonne of Henry Pulforde was baptized the 6th day of May Anno p^{r}æd:

1596   Anne Flint the daughter of John Flint was baptized the 28 day of June Anno p^{r}æd

1598   Henry Pulforde the sonne of Henry Pulforde was baptized the 15 day of October Anno p^{r}æd

1601   Edmund Harwin the sonne of John Harwin was baptized the 17th day of May

       Thomas Flint the sonne of JohnFlint was baptized the 8th day of Sept. Anno p^{r}ædicto

1602   Stanfeild (Mansfeild) Balls the sonne of Edmund Balls was baptized the 5th day of Aprill Anno p^{r}ædicto

       John Pulforde the sonne of Henry Pulforde was baptized the 12 day of Septemb: Anno p^{r}ædicto

       John Balls the sonne ofThomas Balls was baptized the 23rd day of January Anno p^{r}ædicto

(Page 8) BAPTISINGS

1603   Henry Harwin the soone of John Harlwin was baptized the 18 day of June anno p^{r}æd:

1604   Anne Balles the daughter of Edmund Balles was baptised the 16 day of Aprill Anno p^{r}æd:

       Ralfe Scrivener the sonne of Peter Scrivener gent was baptized the 28 day of Octobe Anno p^{r}æd:

       Ruthe Flint the daughter of John Flint was baptized the last day of December anno p^{r}æd:

       Edmund Kemp the sonne of Roberte Kemp Esq was baptized the 10 day of March A^o p^{r}æd:

1605   Dorothie Pulforde the daughter of Henry Pulforde was baptized the 18 day of August A^o p^{r}æd:

       Edmund Goodale the sonne of Edmund Goodale was baptized the 25 day of August A^o p^{r}æd:

1606   Edmund Balles the sonne of Edmund Balles was baptized the 14 day of October A^o p^{r}æd:

1607   Daniell Balles the sonne of Thomas Balles was baptized the 13 day of August A^o p^{r}æd:

       Cicilie Pulforde the daughter of Henry Pulforde was baptized the 6 day of Octob: A^o p^{r}æd:

       Edwarde Kemp the sonne of Robert Kempe Esq was baptized the 8 day of Novemb: A^o p^{r}æd:

1608   William Flint the sonne of John Flint was baptized the 16 day of June A^o p^{r}æd:

       Thomas Kemp the sonne of Robert Kemp Esq was baptized the 22 of January A^o p^{r}æd:

(Page 9) BAPTISINGS

1609   Marie Balls the daughter of Edmund Balles was baptized the 3rd day of May A^o p^{r}æd:

       Elizabeth Bugge the daughter of James was baptized the 12 day of Decemb: A^o p^{r}æd:

       Marie Crofts the daughter of Charles Crofts gent was baptozed the 6 day of March A^o p^{r}æd:

1610   Frauncis Pulforde the sonne of John Pulforde was baptized the 16 day of September An^o p^{r}æd:

       Thomas Bugge the sonne of Robert Bugge was baptized 15 day of January An^o p^{r}æd:

1611   Thomas Crofts the sonne of Charles Crofts gent was baptized the 24 of February An^o p^{r}æd:

1612   John Harland the sonne of John Harland was baptized the 17 day of May An^o p^{r}æd:

1613   Katherine Balls the daughter of Edmund Balls was baptized the 4 day of Julie A^o p^{r}æd:

1614   Elizabeth Bugge the daughter of Robert Bugge was baptized the 18 day of September A^o p^{r}æd:

       Judith Harland the daughter of John Harland was baptized the 21 day of March A^o p^{r}æd:

1615   John Poolie the sonne of Edmund Poolie Esq and Dorothie his wife was borne and baptized the 12 day of Aprill A^o p^{r}æd:

(Page 10) BAPTISMS

1616   Abraham Knapp the sonne of Abraham (altered to Robert) Knapp was baptized the 9th day of November

1617   Dorothy Poley the daughter of Edm Poley Esq was borne the 17th of June and Baptized the first of July

       Mary Poley the daughter of Edmund Poley was borne at Marlesford the 17th of June and was baptized there the second day of July

1617   Thomas Goodall sonne of Edmund Goodall was baptized ye xxiii of October Anno

1618   Margaret Pleasants the daughter of Francis Pleasants was baptized the 17th day of Jan.

1619   Thomas Webber ye sonne of John Webber was Baptized the 22 of Aprill

       Edmund Poley sonne of Mr Edmund Poley borne ye sixteene day of December and baptized the thirtieth day of ye same month

       Sara Sparrow the daughter of Leonard Sparrow was baptized the fifteenth day of October

1620   Margaret Harwin daughter of John Harwin baptized the xxviii of Decemb:

(Page 11) BAPTISINGS

1620   Alice Webber daughter of John Webber was baptized January ye twentifourth

       Anne Poley daughter of Mr Edmund Poley was borne ye seaventh day of February & baptized ye two & twentieth of ye same month

1621   William Poley ye sonne of Mr Edmind Poley was borne ye sixth of March being After wednesday between two & thre a clock in ye morning & was baptized ye one & twentieth of ye same month

Marye Pleasants ye daughter of Francis Pleasants was borne ye fourteenth day of August & was baptized upon Sunday beinge ye nintenth of ye same month

Marye Brooke ye daughter of Thomas Brooke ye one & twentieth of Octob.

1622 Frauncis Symon ye daughter of William Symon was baptized September ye thirtenth

1623 Richard Poley sonne of Mr Edmind Poley was borne July ye eight & baptized ye twentieth of ye same month

1624 Frauncis Pleasants ye sonne of Francis Plaesants was baptized ye first of May

Thomas Poley sonne of Mr Edmund Poley was borne ye ninth of December being thursday betwen seaven & eight of ye clock at night & was baptized ye one & twentieth of ye same month beinge St Thomas his day

1625 Rose Buxton ye daughter of Richard Buxton was baptized ye ninth of February

Miles Horne ye sonne of Steven Horne cook at Badley Hall was baptized August 22°

(Page 12) BAPTIZMS

1625 Anne Harlwin ye daughter of Jhon Harlwin & Rose his wife was baptized Septe: 8 anno pdicto

1626 Jhon Balls ye sonne of John Balls & Susan his wife was Baptized Janu: 6th being twelthday an: prdicto

1627 Thomas Wellam ye sonne of Thomas Wellam was baptized Junii: 21

Marye Balls ye daughter of John Balls & Susan his wife was baptized Septeb: 5th an: prdicto

Francis Buxton ye Daughter of Richard Buxton was baptized Februa: 5th an: prdicto

1628 Rose Harlwin ye daughter of Jhon Harlwin & Rose his wife was baptized Aprilis 8th Anno prdicto

1629 Elizabeth Wellam ye daughter of Thomas & Ruthhis wife was baptized Janua: 17th anno prdicto

1630 Henrie Poley sonne of Edmund Poley Esq & ye Lady Francis Crompton his wife was borne Augusti sexto (6th) and was baptized decimo quinto anno prdicto (15th August 1630)

1631 John Flint ye sonne of William Flint was baptized the October ye 8th anno prdicto

Edmund Buxton ye sonne of Richard Buxton was baptized Decemb 8th anno prdicto

1632 Ciciley Poley daughter of Edmund Poley Esq and ye Lady Frances Crompton his wife was baptized February 26 anno prdicto

1633 Elizabeth Balls daughter of John Balls was baptized Janua 12 anno prdi:

1637 Thomas Crompton ye sonne of Robert Crompton Esq & Catherine his wife was borne June ye 18 & baptized ye June 29th anno prdicto

Fig A2 - a reproduction of some of the baptismal entries on page 11 of the Register Book.

(Page 13) BAPTIZMS

1637 John Flint sonne of Edmund Flint of Ipswich & Elizabeth his wife was baptized Februa. 18° anno p^rdto

1639 Francis Larwood ye sonne of Jhon Larwood & Rebecca his wife was baptized Aprill: 28

Mathias Flint sonne of Edmund Flint & Elizabeth Flint his wife was baptized Februa 25

1640 Audrie Dove daughter of Mr Will. Dove & Phebe his wife was baptized April 12 anno p^rdicto

1641 Phebe Dove daughter of Mr Will Dove & Phebe his wife was baptized Maii 30th anno p^rdto

Marie Crompton eldest Daughter of Robert Crompton[1] of Badley Esq was baptized August 31

Francis Crompton Daughter of ye a foresaid Robert Crompton borne at ye same byrth was also baptized at ye same time Aug: 31:

1642 Anna Flint daughter of Edmund Flint was baptized June 22

Margaret Dove daughter of Mr William Dove & Phebe his wife was baptized Octob: 8

1643 Catherine Crompton daughter to Sr Robt Crompton Knight was Baptized Septemb 22

John Bets ye sonne of James Bets & Margaret his wife was Baptized Octob 17:

1644 Cicilie Dove daughter of Mr William Dove & Phebe his wife was baptized Maii 19

Ffrancis ye sonne of Henry Raymond & Rose his wife was baptized November 20th

Ffrancis ye sonne of Francis Pleasants & Ellen his wife was baptized Feb: 16

(Page 14) BAPTIZED

1645 John Gooddin sonne of John Gooddin & Rose his wife was baptized ye Octobr 4

William Buxton sonne of William Buxton & Susan his wife was baptized December 6

1645 Stephen Trappet sonne of John Trappet & Mary his wife was baptized December 9

1646 William Dove sonne of William Dove & Phebe his wife was baptized July 4

Mary Raymond daughter of Henry Raymond & Rose his wife was baptized September 13

1647 Francis Gooddin sonne of John Gooddin & Rose his wife was baptized September 15

Sarah Trappet daughter of John Trappet & Mary his wife was baptized February 1

1648 Edward Dove sonne of William Dove & Phebe his wife was baptized August 30

1649 William Cole sonne of William Cole & Mary his wife was baptized Octob^r 17

Frances Norton daughter of Stephen Norton clarke & Audrie his wife was baptized November 20

John Browne sonne of Thomas Browne & Elizabeth his wife was baptized January 1

1650 Edmund Gooddale sonne of Edmund Goodale & Mary his wife was baptized August 5

Phebe Dove daughter of William Dove & Phebe his wife was baptized Octob^r 17

William Gooddin sonne of John Gooddin & Rose his wife was baptized Decemb^r 4

John Norton sonne of Stephen Norton & Audrie his wife was baptized February 18

1651 John Balls sonne of John Balls & Mary his wife was baptized July 24

Henry Younge sonne of Henry Younge & Rose his wife was baptized Decemb^r 14

Mary Browne daughter of Thomas Browne & Elizabeth his wife was baptized Decemb^r 26

Edward Coleman sonne of Edward Coleman & Prudence his wife was baptized February 10

(Page 15) MARRIAGES

Anno domini   Marriages

1598 Thomas Kirbie gent, was Married to Anna Brewster gentlewoman the 16 day of January A° præd:

1599 Elias Cocksonne was married to Anne Boone the 7 day of May A° præd:

1600 Robert Parish was married to Frances Rose the 22 August A° præd:

John Harwin or Harland was married to Jane Bantocke the 27 of July A° præd:

1601 John Payne was married to Abigail Hunt the day of 20 August A° præd:

1602 John Smith was married to Rose Greene the 13 day of September A° præd:

Thomas Francis was married to Jane Smith the 24 of January A° præd:

Thomas Arburte was married to Katherina Westhe the 6 day of Aprill: A° præd:

1604 Edmund Goodale was married to Emma Doane the 16 day of Octobr A° præd:

Thomas Blockett was married to Elizabeth Cooper the 15 day of Noverber A° præd:

Abraham Packe was married to Alice Spincke the 18 day of November A° præd:

1605 Henry Spinnie was married to Alice Harmin the 30 day of May A° præd:

(Page 16) MARRIAGES

Anno domi   Marriages

1605 Thomas Seckforde gent was married to Anne Kirbie gentlewoman, the 8 day of September

Edwarde Deane was married to Clemants Bowall the 13 day of May

1606 Nicholas Hempstone was Married to Anne Neweman the 15 day of June

Charles Crofts gent, was married to Cicilie Poolie gentlewoman, the 17 day of September

1607 Robert Bugge was married to Margaret Balls the 27 day of October

Note:

[1] Richard Crompton was the son of Sr John Crompton of Skerne, Yorks. His mother Frances, the daughter of Sir Henry Crofts of Little Saxham re-married Edmund Poley. Richard was knighted on 12 March 1641-2 inbetween the births of his twin daughters born in 1641 and his third daughter Catherine born in 1643.

1608   Richard Evered gent, was married to Katherine Lang(y) gentlewoman, the 9 day of August
1609   Thomas Sowthbie gent, was married to Katherine Dandy gentlewoman, the 20 day of November
1610   William Barker was married to Pricilla Coulchester the 8 day of July
      William Taylor was married to Mary Shortland the 9 day of October
1611   Richard Wilton gent, was married to Susan Scrivenor gentlewoman, the 18 day of October
1612   Grigory Warner was married to Martha Cooper the 25 day of October
1613   Edmund Poley Gent was married to Dorothy Warner gentlewoman at Parham church the 12 day of Octobr A^o 1613

(Page 17) MARRIAGES

1613   Henry Mudd was married unto Anne Wellam first day of Noverb: A^o præd:
1614   William Princet was married to Elizabeth Baker the 17 day of May. A^o præd:
1615   Thomas Neweman was married to Alice Write the 3 day of Novemb: A^o præd:
1616   Thomas Pepper was married to Elizabeth Leveredge the 2 day of Aprill. A^o præd:
1617   John Cooper was married to Ester Wellam the twentieth of Septemb:
1623   Abraham Holden of Bildeston was married to Anne Parling ye servant at Badley Hall ye 16 of Octbr. A^o præd:
1624   Robert Culham servant at Badley Hall was mnarried to Mary Lambert of Combes Aprill 5th
      John Harlewin of Badley was married to Rose Whitlock of Little Stonham September 14 A^o præd:
      John Balls of Badley was married to Susanna Pulforde daughter of Henry Pulforde of Badley December 13
1625   Robert Jacob ye sonne of Robert Jacob of Creeting St Mary was married to Rose Jacob cum Licentia* decimo tertio (13th) Januari anno præd. (*per licentiam meaning 'by licence')
1627   John Baken of Blakenham was married to Dorothie Boldrow Octbr 27 anno præd: cum Licentiam

(Page 18) MARRIAGES

1628   Francis Raphe of Stowemarket was married to Sara Prettie of Blakenham cum Licentia March 7° anno præd:
      Thomas Baker was married to Katherine Bretland cum Licentia anno p^{r}dict^o April 4th
1631   John Bren of Ipſwich was married to Isabella Balls of Burie St Edmunds Augusti undecimo (11th) anno p^{r}dicto cum Licentiam
      William Morgan of Earle Stanham was married to Sara Goodwyn of Badley Septembris decimo tertio (13th)
1653   Henry Wingfield Gentleman sonne to Harbottle Wingfield of Crowfield Esq. was married to Mrs Dorothy Brewster daughter to Thomas Brewster Gent: of Badley Church cum Licentia Februa: 1° anno p^{r}dicto
1638   Thomas Souter sonne to Henry Souter of Combs was married to Elizabeth Bugg of the parish of Badley Octob: 9th annop^{r}dicto
      Mr Willam Dove of Badley was married to Mrs Pheobe Garnish daughter to Mr Nicholas Garnish of Mickfield Januri: ultimus (31) anno p^{r}dicto
1640   Peter Smith servant at Badley Hall was married to Elizabeth Mayhew servant also there May 12
      Thomas Goodale of Badley was married to Marie Carpenter of Needham Novemb 5th
1641   Thomas Blowers of Badley was married to Martha Felgate of ye same parish May 24th
1644   John Goodwyn was married to Rose Harlwyn of Badley Octob 4th
      John Allen of Petto was married to Dennis Bloomfield of ye same Octob 4th
1648   William Gootrich was married to Dorothie Sugget April 26th

(Page 19) MARRIAGES

1649   James Row was married to Margaret Alexander May 15 1649
      Anthony Morgin was married to Anne Malby August 16 1649
      Edmund Smith was married to Mary Frewer Septemb^r 24 1649
      Thomas Carlow was married to Anne Jacob January 15 1649
1650   Henry Hatch was married to Ales Dove Auguſt 3 1650
      Henry Greene was married to Ffaith Bickers Octob^r 10 1650
      Henry Youngs was married to Rose Raymond Decemb^r 1 1650
1651   John Lockwood was married to Mary (altered to Margaret) Pleasants Octob^r 9 1651
      Thomas Wilchin was married to Mary Greene Octob^r 13 1651
      Thomas Dawes was married to Dorothie Beales January 22 1651
1653   Edward Smie was married to Mary Sugget Aprill 22nd 1653
      Giles Wooplfe was married to Mary Goodale widdow July 4th 1653
1655   Stephen Cooper was married to Joan Clarke March 16th 1655
1656   Thomas Mudde was married to Elizabeth Painter Ffeb: 7th 1656
1658   Robert Denny was married to Rose Parke Auguſt 18th 1658

(Page 20) MARRIAGES

1658   William Rosier was married to Mary Chinery Septemb^r 1st 1658
1659   Robert Argent was married to Susan Hagtree Octob^r 4th 1659
1662   Thomas Whitecake of Needham Market Widdower was married to Marie Woolfe of Badley August 21 1662
      Richard Hatfield alias Maise (sic) of Badley was married to Susan Baker of Combs Octob 13 1662
      Robert Palmer of Needham Market was married to Susan Garnham of ye same their Banns having been 3 severall times published before in ye parish church of Barking, as appears by ye certificate. Octob 18

1663 John Stanford singleman & Susan Goldbold/Godyear (sic) (overwritten) singlewomen both of ye parish of Barking were married November 22

1665 Thomas Whitecake of Badley Widdower was married to Sarah Colchester of Needham of ye parish of Barking single woman Septemb: 11

1666 Francis Harvie of Coddenham widdower was married to Margaret Mud of Darmsden in ye parish of Barking Septemb 25

1667 William Holme & Elizabeth Richmond both of Badly single perſons were married Novemb 17

John Howell widdower & Anne Martin widdow both of Ipſwich were married Julii 16 cum Licentia

1669 Thomas Goode singleman of Ringshall & Margarie Hornie of Combs singlewoman were married Julii 13

Edmund Smyth & Anne Wilson both of Badly singlepersons were married August 17 cum Licentia

(Page 21) BAPTIZINGS

1644 Francis Reamond ye sonne of Henrie Reymond & Rose his wife was baptized Novemb 20th 1644

1650 William ye sonne of William Cole & Marie his wife was baptized Octob 17 1650

1664 Bettie Tildie ye daughter of Richard Lambert & Alce his wife was baptized May 7th 1664

Marie ye daughter of John Balls & Marie his wife was baptized Septeb 24th 1664

Marie ye daughter of William Cocke & Alce his wife was baptized Octob 6th 1664

1665 Thomas ye sonne of William Cock & Alce his wife was baptized Martius (March) 15 1665

William Lambe ye sonne of Richard & Alice his wife was baptized Septemb 11

1667 Elizabeth ye daughter of John Hall & and Elizabeth his wife was baptized Decemb ye first

(written in right-hand side margin) (Elizabeth ye daughter of John Hall & Elizabeth his wife was baptized Novembr 27 1667)

Thomas ye sonne of Richard Lambert & Alce his wife was baptized Februari ye fourth

1669 John ye son of John Hall & Elizabeth his wife was baptized March 13 1669

(Page 22) BAPTIZINGS (Note the following pages are out of sequence in the register book)

1652 Elizabeth Lockwood daughter of John Goodwin and Margaret his wife was baptized August 7th 1652

1652 Stephen Norton sonne of Stephen Norton and Audrie his wife was baptized Septemb^r 14th 1652

1653 Edmund Coleman sonne of Edward Coleman and Prudence his wife was baptized Septemb^r 3rd 1653

Thomas Balls sonne of John Balls and Mary his wife was baptized January 28th 1653

1654 Mary Lockwood daughter of John Lockwood and Margaret his wife was baptized May 27th 1654

Robert Norton sonne of Stephen Norton and Audrie his wife was baptized June 28th 1654

Rose Goodwin daughter of John Goodwin and Rose his wife was baptized Novemb^r 13 1654

Edmund Buxton sonne of Edmund Buxton and Susan his wife was baptized Decemb^r 26th 1654

Elizabeth Dove daughter of William Dove and Phebe his wife was baptized Decemb^r 29th 1654

(Page 23) BAPTIZMS

1655 Francis Burges sonne of Francis Burges and Catherine his wife was baptized Ffebr: 7th 1655

Aster(sic) Coleman sonne of Edward Coleman & Prudence his wife was baptized Ffebr: 27th 1655

1656 Catherine Norton daughter of Stephen and Audrie his wife was baptized Aprill 18th 1656

Ffrancis Balls sonne of John Balls and Mary his wife was baptized May 27th 1656

Margaret Lockwood daughter of John Lockwood and Margaret his wife was baptized May 29th 1656

1657 Briers Burges sonne of Francis Burges and Catherine his wife was baptized Septemb^r 1st 1657

Edward Norton sonne of Stephen Norton and Audrie his wife was baptized Decemb^r 30th 1657

1658 Elizabeth Coleman daughter of Edward Coleman and Prudence his wife was baptized January 10th 1658

William Lockwood sonne of John Lockwood and Margaret his wife was baptized January 27th 1658

Robert Goodwin sonne of John Lockwood and Rose his wife was baptized March 1st 1658

(Page 24) BAPTIZMS

1658 Richard Buxton sonne of Edmund Buxton and Susan his wife was baptized March 24th 1658

1659 William Norton sonne of Stephen Norton and Audrie his wife was baptized August 10th 1659

1660 Catherine Burges daughter of Ffrancis Burges and Catherine his wife was baptized Aprill 22nd 1660

Edmund Balls sonne of John Balls and Mary his wife was baptized August 5th 1660

Richard Lambert sonne of Richard Lambert and Alice his wife was baptized Septemb^r 19th 1660

1661 Joseph Goodwin sonne of John Goodwin and Rose his wife was baptized May 14th 1661

Richard Norton sonne of Stephen Norton & Audrie his wife was baptized Decemb^r 14th 1661

Alce Lambert ye daughter of Richard Lambert alias Sware & Alce his wife was baptized Februi 10

(Page 25) BAPTIZMS

1665 William ye son of Richard Lambert alias Sware & Alce his wife was baptized Octob 12

Sara Shimming ye daughter of Thomas Shimming & Sara his wife was baptized Janua 15

1669 Marie ye daughter of Richard Lambert & Alce his wife was baptized Octob 3rd

Edmund ye son of Edmund Smith & Anne his wife was baptized Junii 28

1670 Marie the daughter of Edmund Buxton & Suſan his wife was baptized Maii 20

1672   Henrie ye son of Edmund Smith & Ann his wife was baptized Junii 7mo
       Thomas ye son of William Coe & Alce his wife was baptized Septemb 15th
1673   Catherine ye daughter of John Hall & Elizabeth his wife was baptized July 20 1673
       John ye son of John Goodwin & Anne his wife was baptized   Decemb 25 1673
       Francis ye son of Francis Courtis & Sufan his wife was baptized Februa: 3 1673
1674   Marie ye daughter of Marie Double was baptized March ye 7th being fourteen years of age ye Michaelmas before
1675   Thomas ye son of Edmund Smith was baptized March ye 28 1674

(Page 26) BAPTIZINGS

1675   Anne ye daughter of John Goodwin & Anne his wife was baptized Noveb ye 14th 1675
       Alce ye daughter of Edmund (sic) Spark & Sufan his wife was baptized Deceb 5 1675
1677   Thomas son of James Winnell & Anne his wife was baptized Auguft 26: 1677
       Alce ye daughter of Alce Wright was baptized Octob: 28 1677
       John ye Son of Francif Courtife & Susan his wife was baptized March ye 24 1677
       Marie ye daughter of John Goodwin and Anne his wife was baptized May Trinity Sunday (*ie Sunday after Whit Sunday*) 1677
1678   Anne ye daughter of John Hall & Elizabeth his wife was baptized June ye 23 1678
1679   Rofe ye daughter of John Goodwin & Anne his wife was born Dec. 25 1679 and baptized Jan: 19th Anno Dñi 1679
1681   Thomas the son of Thomas Balls & Sufan his wife was baptized May 19th 1681
1682   William the Son of John Goodwin & Anne his wife was baptized July 25th 1682
       Edmond the Son of James Hayles & Mary his wife was baptizd July 30th 1682
       Thomas the son of Thomas Balls & Sufan his wife was baptizd Septemb: 15th 1682
1683   Sufan the daughter of Ffrancis Courtife and Sufan his wife was baptized April 1st. 1683
       Edward the Bastard son of Mary Swann was Baptized April 19th. 1683

(Page 27) BURIALLS

1665   Francis Beast singleman was buried September 26 1665.
1666   Charles Poley ye son of Sr Edmund Poley Knight & ye Lady Efter his wife was buried Septemb 12 1666
       Dorothie ye relict of Ifaach Tillet of Badley was buried Novemb 18 1666
1667   Marie ye daughter of John Balls & Marie his wife was buried August 11 1667
       Edmund ye son of John Balls & Marie his wife was buried August 13 1667
       Anne Goulfon singlewoman was buried Aprill 7 1677
1668   Marie Cock ye daughter of William Cock & Alce his wife was buried August 5th 1668
1671   Sr Edmund Poley Knight died at Burie St Edmunds 8^{bris} 22 & was buried in ye chancell in Badley 8^{bris} 23 1671
1672   William Poley ye son of Sr Edmund Poley Knight & ye Lady Hester his wife was buried April ye 2nd in ye chancell
       Sufan ye daughter of Francis Courtise & Sufan his wife was buried Novemb ye 14th 1672
1673   Anne the daughter of Thomas Suggate & Anne his wife was buried Septemb ye 21st 1673

(Page 28) BURIALS

1673   Elizabeth ye wife of Peter Smith was buried Februarie ye 7th 1673
1674   Edward ye Son of Edward Coleman & Prudence his wife was buried March ye 19th 1674
1675   Rofe Harlewin ye widdow of John Harlewin was buried April ye 11 being by computation about ye age of 92 yeares
       Anne Segar singlewoman was buried May ye 16 1675
       Rofe Buxton ye Relict of Richard Buxton was buried Septembr ye 14th 1675
       Edmund Coleman ye son of Edward & Prudence his wife was buried January ye sixth 1675
1677   Thomas Poley ye youngest fon of Edmund Poley Efq died at London Deceb ye 5th & was buried at Badley Decmb: ye eleventh 1677
       John Balls ye son of John Balls was Buried Janua: 23 1677
1677   John Balls father of ye above was buried Februa: 16 1677
1678   Thomas Suggett was buried Sep: 3rd
       Anna Hall was buried Jan: 13th 1678
1679   Francis Burgefs was buried May 5th 1679
       Margaret Lockwood was buried July 30th 1679
       Anne Poley daughter of Edmond Poley Esqr. died Octob 9 and was buried in Badly church Octob: 11th 1679
       Ciclia Poley daughter of Edmond Poley Esqr. died at London Novemb: 4th & was buried in Badley Chancell Novemb: 10th
1680   Dorothy Poley daughter of Edmond Poley Esqr died Septemb: 19th & was buried in Badly Chancell Septemb: 20th. Anno Dñi 1680

(Page 29) MARRIAGES

"Marriages collected out of the ould regester booke" (*written at top of page*)

1574   William Brewster of Castell Hedingham Gent was married unto Mirrable Poolie the Daughter of John Poolie Esq the 14th day of May
       John Lany of Cratfielde Gent: was married to Mary Poolie the daughter of John Poolie Efq. the day yeare and month above fayed

1556	Edwarde Lockwood was married to Joane Cole the daughter of Thomas Cole the 5 day of May A^O fu pradict^O
1560	Charles Bore was married to Alice Rofe daughter to Robert Rofe the 28 of Apriil A^O prad:
	Elis Crampton was married to Margaret Balls daughter of John Balls the 24 of June A^O prad:
1678	Joseph Pooley of Ofton was married to Marie Foreman of Badley Octob ye tenth 1676
1679	Robert Barker of Combes Widdower & Mary Balls of this parifh Widdow were married Sept: 16th. 1679 cum Licèn Comm:
	William Wood of Woodbridge Widdower & Debora Hooker of Stowmarket Widdow were Married at Badly March 15th 1679 cum Licèn Comm:
1682	John Balls Singleman & Sufan Wright Singlewoman both of this parifh were Married Novemb: 28th
1683	Robert Doe of Little Bricet Singleman and Mary Camby of Wefton singlewoman were married June 28th cum Licen Comif:
	George Richardfon of Stowmarket singleman and Rebecca Folkard of the same parifh singlewoman were Married July 17th cum Licèn Comm Dni cancel: vert duo fols

(Page 30)

Top of page and out of sequence -

1639	Faith Jeckerfon (sic) ye daughter of Faith Jeckerfon was baptised ye Aprill 16 1639

BURIALS

1681	Thomas Son of Thomas Balls was buried May 21st 1681
1683	Alice the Wife of William Cock was Buried June 1st 1683
	John the Son of John Balls was buried Novemb: 30th 1683
1685	Robert Tharker (sic) inhabitant last of ye Parish of Podenwick* near Lynn was buryed Novemb: 6th 1685 (* there is no such parish listed near Kings Lynn Norfolk)
1686	Catherine Burgefs the wife of Francis Burgefs was buryed ye 11th of December 1686
	Catherine ye daughter of Sr Henry Crofts of Saxham in Suff. was buryed ye 5th of June 1686
	Thomas and Hester ye son and daughter of Thos. Green : were buryed Ffeb: ye 10th 1686
1687	Frances ye daughter of William Cock (Cook) and Sarah his wife was buryed Aprill 19th 1687
1690	John Goodwin was buried Novemb: 22 1690
1690/1	Mary Portington[1] sister to Sr Edmund Poley was buried in the Chancell March 11th
	Tobias Hawkely was buried March 13th
1691	Alice Cutler was buried Novemb: 6th
169/2	Joseph Goodwin was buried March 6th 1691
1692	Catherine Cutler was buried August 15 1692
1693	Francis Courtis was buried April 28th 1693
	John Thurnwood was buried July 13th 1693
	Jane Fuller was buried October 23rd 1693
1694/5	Mary Thurnwood was buried Feb: 4th 1694/5

(Page 31)
"Baptisings gathered out of the ould register" (written at top of page)

1575	William Raymond ye sonne of Wm Reyment was baptized the 19th of September A^O p^{r}dicto
1575	John Lany sonne of Mr John Lany was baptized September 1st A^O p^{r}dicto
15	Elizabeth Palmer daughter of John Palmer was baptized the 7 of April A^O p^{r}dicto
1622	Frances Simmons ye daughter of . . (blank) . . Simmons was baptized the 13 of September
1624	Francis Pleasants ye sonne of Francis Pleasants was borne Apri: 20th and baptized May 1°

MARRIAGES

1631	Richard Cutting of Needham in ye parish of Barking was married to Eliza Frewer of ye same parish Novemb: 30th Ann^o P^{r}dicto
1669	William Howell clerk Rector of Oteley & Agathe Bright of Creeting St Maria both single perfons were married Octob 19
1671	Nathaniel Chenerie & Marie Kent both single perfons of Ipfwich were married August ye 8
1674	William Rayment of Clare & Rofe Goodwin of Badley both single persons were married July ye first

(Page 32) MARRIAGES

1683	Henry Baskett of this parifh singleman and Alice Suggate of the parifh of Combes singlewoman were married Novemb: 1st. 1683.
	Arthur Colman of Needham Markett Widdower and Hellen Sillett of Stow-upland single woman, were married Feb: 12th. cum Licen: Comiff:
1684	Thomas Foster of this parifh singleman and Mary Foreman of ye same, single woman, were married Novemb: 2nd 1684
1685	John Grey of Needham Markett widdower and Elizabeth Trapnell of Coddenham singlewoman were marryed: June 9th cum Licen: Comiff: 1685
	Richard Thurnwood of Stowupland singleman and Margaret Witherby of Badly singlewoman were married Jan: 24th 1685

---

[1] Mary Portington (née Poley) ~ see 6th Generation Family Tree, Chapter 6

1686   John Suggate of Badley and Amy King of Stowmarkett both single persons were married Aprill 19th 1686:
1694   Geoffrey Curtis and Margaret Sargeant of Ipswich both single persons were married May 5th Cum Licen: Comifs:
1696   William Pettit singleman and Bridget Osborn singlewoman were married May 12th 1696
       Robert Boby, Jane Mary Murten both single persons and of this parish were married October 13th 1696
1698   Wm Blowers and Rachel Moore both single persons and of this parish were married October 15th 1698
       Richard Emerson of Brundish singleman and Mary Grimwade of Creeting All Saints singlewoman were marryed December 15th 1698 cum Licen: Comiff:

(Page 33)

"Burialls gathered out of the ould regester booke" (written on top of page)

1575   William Goodale was buried 12 May A° præd
1575   Mrs Ann Poolie wife of John Poolie Esq was buried the 29 of Aug. A° præd
1552   Marable Poolie widowe late wife of Edmund Pooly was buried 25 of February A° præd.

BAPTISMS

1683   Mary ye daughter of James Haylis and Mary his wife was baptized Novemb: 11th:
1684   Elizabeth ye daughter of John Goodwin and Ann his wife was was baptized Aug: 10th:
       John ye son of Henry Baskett and Allice his wife was baptized February ye 8th:
1685   Thomas ye son of Thomas Foster and Mary his wife was baptized August: 27th:
       Frances ye daughter of William Cock and Sarah his wife was baptized Novemb: 11th:
1686   Thomas and Hester ye son and daughter of Thomas Green and Barbary his wife were baptized June 17
       John ye son of Will: Barton and Frances his wife; was baptized Feb: 4th
       Amy ye daughter of John King and Amy his wife baptized: March ye 9th
1687   Henry ye son of Henry Baskett and Alice his wife was baptized March ye 14th
       Edmund ye son of Tho: Green and Barbary his wife was baptized March ye 18th

(Page 34) BAPTIZMS

1688   George the son of George Thing and Catherine his wife was baptized May ye 13 1688
       Mary ye daughter of Thomas Foster and Mary his wife was baptized Jan: 23
1689   Thomas ye son of John King and Amy his wife was baptized July 18th
1690   Sarah the Daughter of John Sugat and Amy his wife was baptized Aprill 6th
       Thomas ye son of Tho: Green and Barbary his wife was baptized May 12
       Sufanne ye daughter of George Thing and Catherine his wife was baptized May 12.
1690/1   Alice ye daughter of Henry Basket and Alice his wife was Baptized January 4th
1691   James the son of James Cooke and Naomi his wife baptized March 25th
       Mary ye daughter Francis and Susanna Courtis was baptized July 26th
       Edmund ye son of Richard and Mary Buxton was baptized August 4
1692   Prudence ye daughter of Thomas Foster and Mary his wife was baptized April 10th
       Frances ye daughter of George Thing and Katherine his wife was baptized May 7
       Rebecca ye daughter of John King and Amy his wife was baptized May ye 8th
       John ye son of John Suggett and Amy his wife was baptized June 5th

(Page 35) BAPTIZMS

1692   Hester ye daughter ofThomas and Barbary Green was baptized ye 4th day of Sept: 1692
1692/3   Hannah ye daughter of James Cooke and Naomi his wife was baptized March 9th 1692
1693/4   Richard ye son of Richard and Mary Buxton was Baptized February ye 19th
1694   Elizabeth ye daughter of Thomas Green and Barbara his wife was baptized ye 20th day of August 1694
       Mary ye daughter of John Suggett and Amy his wife was baptized January ye 19th 1694
1694/5   Sarah ye daughter of James Cook and Naomi his wife was baptized March ye 13th 1694/5
1695   William ye son of George Thing and Katherine his wife was was baptized May ye 4th
       Elizabeth ye Bastard Daughter of Margar: Pillborough was baptized May 24th 1695
       John ye son of Thomas Ffoster and Mary his wife was baptized July ye 7th 1695

(Page 36) BAPTIZMS

1696   Mary ye daughter of John King and Amy his wife was baptized May 17th 1696
       Elizabeth ye daughter of Arthur Collman and Eleanor his wife was baptized August 2nd 1696
1697   Daniel ye son of James Cook and Naomi his wife was baptized April 6th 1697
       Barbara ye daughter of Thomas and Barbara Greene was baptized April 29th 1697
1698   Sarah the daughter of Thomas and Mary Foster was baptized March 5th 1698
1699   Joseph the son of James Cook and Naomi his wife was baptized May 20th 1699
       Edward ye son Arthur Collman and Eleanor his wife was baptized September 20th 1699
       Robert and Catherine ye son and daughter of Thomas Greene and Barbara his wife were baptized September 14th

1700   Richard ye son of John King and Amy his wife was baptized July 27th 1700
      Anne ye daughter of Thomas Kidd and Anne his wife was baptized October 2nd 1700
1701   Catherine Green ye daughter of Thomas Greene and Barbara his wife was baptized June 12th 1701
1702   Anne ye daughter of Arthur Collman and Eleanor his wife was baptized November 19th 1702
1703   John the son of James Cook and Susanna his wife was baptized May 9th 1703

(Page 37) BAPTIZMS

1703   Samuel the son of Samuel Rungary and Mary his wife was baptized July ye 18th 1703
      Thomas the son of Thomas Kidd and Anne his wife was baptized January 30th 1703
      Martha the daughter of William Blowers and Rachel his wife was baptized March ye 19th 1703
1704   Susanna the daughter of James Cook and Susanna his wife was baptized August 13th 1704
1705   Brice ye son of James Cook and Susanna his wife was baptized October 14th 1705
1706   Esther ye daughter of Arthur Colman and Eleanor his wife was baptized March 31st 1706
      Francis ye son of Francis Southgate and Elizabeth his wife was baptized September 1st 1706
1708   Brice ye son of James Cook and Susanna his wife was baptized July ye 18th 1708
1709   Kebel ye son of James Cook and Susanna his wife was baptized September 18th 1709
1710   Phoebe ye daughter of James Cook and Susanna his wife was baptized December 10th 1710
1711   Francis ye son of Francis Southgate and Elizabeth his wife was baptized April 3rd 1711
1712   Thomas the son of Thomas Green & Anne his wife was baptized October 3rd 1712
      Susanna the daughter of Thomas Southgate and Elizabeth his wife was baptized February 22nd 1712

(Page 38) BAPTIZMS

1714   John the son of Thomas Green & Anne his wife was baptized June 6th 1714
      Hannah the daughter of William Christmas and Mary his wife was baptized March 21st 1714
1715   Mary the daughter of James Cook and Susanna his wife was baptized June 5th 1715
      Sarah ye daughr of Francis Southgate & Elizabeth his wife was baptized June 6th 1715
1716   Edward ye son of Edward Sage & Hannah his wife, was baptized Augst 26th 1716
      Robert the son of John Colman & Susan his wife was baptized Novemb^r 7th 1716
      Cutler the son of Thomas Green and Anne his wife was baptized Novemb^r 16th 1716
      Charles the son of Cherles Hunt & Prudence his wife was baptized January 7th 1716
1717   Henry the son of John Whistle and Mary his wife was baptized July 2nd 1717
      Sarah the base child of Sarah Lockwood was bapt^d July 7th 1717
      Hannah ye daughter of Edward Sage & Hannah his wife was baptized September 15th 1717
1717   Edmund ye son of Thomas Green & Anne his wife was baptized December 1st 1717
      Joseph son of Charles Hunt & Prudence his wife was baptized March 3rd 1717
1718   Thomas ye son of William Christmas & Mary his wife was baptized August ye 10th 1718
      Richard son of John Coleman & Susanna his wife was baptized September ye 5th 1718

(Page 39) BAPTIZMS

1718   John son of Francis Southgate and Elizabeth his wife was baptized Nov: 25th 1718
1719   Prudence daughter of Charles Hunt & Prudence his wife was baptized Dec : 28th 1719
      John son of John Whistle & Mary his wife was baptized Jan: 24th 1719
      Joseph son of Joseph Stammers & Margaret his wife was baptized Jan: 26th 1719
1720   Anne daughter of Thomas Green & Anne his wife was baptized Septr 11th 1720
1721   Margaret daughter of Joseph Stammers & Margaret his wife was baptized Aug ye 6th
      Jeremiah son of John Coleman & Susanna his wife was baptized Aug: 22nd
1722   Catherine daughter of James Mayhew & Mary his wife was baptized June 10th
      Charles son of John Coleman & Susanna his wife was baptized July 1st
      Amy daughter of Wm Xmas & Mary his wife was baptized Jan: 20th 1722
1723   Sheppard son of Joseph Stammers & Margaret his wife was baptized Nov^r: 15th
      Dorcas daughter of Thomas Chandler & his wife was baptized Feb : 16th

(Page 40) BAPTIZMS

1723   James son of James Mayhew & Mary his wife was baptized Ffeb : 28th
1724   Susanna daughter of John Coleman & Susanna his wife was baptized March 18th
1725   Samuel son of Abraham Sougate & Elizabeth his wife was baptized Dec : 28th
      Jan 30th Then Samuel son of Samuel Wakeling & Elizabeth his wife was baptized
1726   Susan daughter of John Mayhew & Mary his wife was baptized May 12th
      Dec 4th Then Thomas son of Wm Bird & Sarah his wife was baptized
1727   September 24 Edward Wakeling son of Samuel & Elizabeth was baptized
      Novr 19th Richard son of James Bloomfield & his wife was baptized
1728   April ye 4th Elizabeth daughter James Mayhew & Mary his wife was baptized
      August 4th John son of John Warren & Frances his wife was baptized
1729   August 31 John son of John Warren & Frances his wife was baptized
      Septr 21 Dorcas daughter of Abraham Sougate & Elizabeth his wife was baptized

Nov 16 Mary daughter of William Bird & Sarah his wife

(Page 41) BURIALS

1723   John Balls of Combs was buried May 8th
         Susanna Haggar was buried Decr 8th

1724   "No Burials this yeare"

1725   Barbara Green widow was buried July 14th
         Samuel infant son of Abraham Sougate & Elizabeth his wife was buried Jan 15th
1726   Mary Buxton widow was buried May 19th
         Anne wife of William Goodwin of Stowmarket was buried May 20th
1726   Edmond Drake labourer was buried August ye 4th
         John Woulton was buried Sept 20th
1727   April 4th Then Amey wife of John Sougate of Creeting St Peter was buried
         Edmund Buxton labourer was buried May 5th
         Augt 8th John Buxton Butcher was buried
         Augt 11th . (blank) . Deekes son of John Deekes was buried
         Augt 13th Sarah Kidd was buried
         Aug 29 Then William Cook aged ninety was buried
         Octr 2nd Edward Wakelin infant was buried
         Nov 22 Elizabeth Walton daughter of Thomas & Mary Anne his wife was buried
         March 3rd Sarah ye wife of John Syer of Wenham was buried
1728   Octr 19th Anne wife of Thomas Walton was buried
         Nov 29th John Warren infant
         Dec 13th Elizabeth Sugate widow

(Page 42) BURIALS

1728   Henrietta Robins wife of Charles Robins of ye Middle Temple, Esq, was buried Feb 13th
1729   May 30th Susanna Cook late of Badley was buried
         June 19th George Thing a labourer
         July 22nd Anne Frewer singlewoman
         March 4th John Warren farmer
1730   May 26th Mary Bird infant
         May 30th James Bloomfield labourer
         June 17th Samuel Wakeling labourer
         Aug^st 20th John Keble labourer
         Aug^st 23th Joseph Bolton servant-man
         Oct^br 27 William Goodwin of Stowmarket Bellfounder
1731   John Sugate senr May 18
         Charles Robins Esq of ye Middle Temple was buried July 16th
         Mary Bird infant Augst 22
1732   Edward Syer son of Edward Syer was buried June 20th
         John Sougate of Brasier Hall in Creeting Septr 29
1732   John Tricker infant March 11th
1734   Robert Goodwin June 9th
         Katherine Thing widow July 2nd
         Ffrancis Groome infant Septr 9th
1736   Ann Goodwin widow aged ninety & upwards April 15
         Balls (or Salls) widow aged 95 March 10th
1737   May 21 Robert Mayhew infant was buried

(Page 43) BURIALS

1739   Decemb^r 22 1737 Then Richard Pearch Gent. was buried in the Chancel under the 1st stone on the left hand going at the altar
1739   Febr 15 Then Alice Woulton widow was buried
         December 28 1739 Alice Wolton was buried
         Septr 18 1739 Ann Green was buried
1740   Edward Bird was buried July 6
         John Kimball was buried Augt 3
         Jonathan Bromley was buried Feb 24

1741   no burials
1742

(remainder of page cut off)

(Page 44)(page blank)

(Page 45) BAPTIZMS

1730   Novr 15 Elizabeth Chandler daughter of Thomas Chandler & Mary his wife was baptized
         John son of William Bird & Sarah his wife & Mary daughter of ye same were baptized May 30th
         Martha daughter of William Lee & Martha his wife was baptized Aug 19th
         Francis son of Francis Groome & Ffrances his wife was baptized Jan 2nd
1732   John son of Thomas Wolton & Sarah his wife was baptized Augst 20th
1733   Deborah & Anne Sougate daughters of Abraham & Elizabeth Sougate were baptized 16 of September
         Thomas Francis Poke son of Francis Poke & Frances his wife was baptized Octb^r 18th
1734   Alice base child of Alice Wright was baptized Jul 26
1735   Sarah daughter of Thomas Wolton & Sarah his wife May 2nd
1736   John son of John Salmon & Rebecca his wife February 10th
1737   Amy daughter of John Dove & Anne his wife was baptized Decr 1st
1738   Mary daughter of John Salmon & Rebecca his wife April 8
                    (written at foot of page in another hand)
1808   Robert Southgate Combs Suffolk 3 *(or B)* 1808

(Page 46) BAPTIZMS

1739   William ye son of Thomas Wolton & Sarah his wife was baptized November ye 10th
1740   Robert son of Samuel & Ann Seapy was bapt^d May 18.
         James son of James & Mary Frost was baptized July 18
         Ann daughter of Mary, Relict of John Kimball was bap^t March 8
1741   Mary daughter of Samuel & Ann Scapy was bapt^d Jany 3
1742   Susanna daughter of James & Mary Frost was bapt^d July 11
1743   Mary the daughter of Samuel Scapy and Ann his wife baptized July 17
1746   Matthere daughter of Daniel Ager & Mary his wife baptized May 11
         Daniel Kimble base child of Mary Kimble baptized January ye 11 1746
1749   Thos Willm base child of Tammisdon Davie was baptized March ye 27th 1749
         Elizabeth the daughter of James Frost & Mary his wife was baptized August ye 20 1749
         Mary and Hanna daughters of Daniel Ager and Mary his wife were baptized Decemb^r ye 31 1749
1755   Sophia daughter of John & Margaret Nicholas was baptized April ye 20 1755
         Saml son of Joseph Ruffels & Ann his wife was baptized August ye 10th *(or 12th)* 1755

(Page 47) BURIALS

1694   Richard ye son of Richard and Mary Buxton was buried Octob: 11th 1694
1695   Elizabeth Smith ye daughter of Rose Rayment was buried April 4th 1695
         Prudence ye wife of Thomas Bankes was buried August 27th 1695
1697   Benjamin Connalt ye son of John Connalt inhabitant of ye parish of Chelsworth was buryed March 17th 1697
1698   John Courtis was buryed July 19th 1698
         Edmund Balls the son of Edmund and Mary Balls was buryed 26th of October 1690
1699   Robert Green the son of Thomas Green and Catherine his wife was buryed 26th Sept 1699
         Mary Suggate ye daughter of John Suggate & Amy his wife buryed Dec 18th 1699
1700   Catherine the daughter of Thomas Green and Catherine his wife was buryed June 21st 1700
         Elizabeth the wife of Thomas Balls of Needham was buryed August 25th 1700
         Naomi the wife of James Cook was buryed October 14th 1700
         Daniel the son of James Cook was buryed October 17th 1700
1701   John the son of George Thing & Catherine his wife was buryed April 12th 1701

(Page 48) BURIALS

1701   John Goodwin the son of William Goodwin and his wife was buryed September 17th 1701
         Edmund Bedwell was buryed November 22nd 1701
1702   Martha King was buryed May ye 19th 1702
         Thomas Foster was buryed June 23rd 1702
         Rose Latham was buryed September 17th 1702
         William Steward was buryed November 17th 1702
1704   Edmund Buxton snr was buryed August 26th 1704
1705   Wm Bromley junr was buryed August 1st 1705
         Catherine ye daughter of Sr Richard Gipps & Dame Elizabeth his wife of Horringer in ye County of Suffolk was buried October 27th 1705
         Brice ye son of James Cook & Susanna his wife was buryed December 7th 1705
1706   Sarah Marjoram was buryed September 4th 1706
         Susanna the daughter of James Cook & Susanna his wife was buryed October 29th 1706
1707   Henry Poley Esq ye son of Sr Edmund Poley K^{nt} and Dame Esther his wife was buried August 15 1707

Robert Welham serv^t to widow Steward was buried September 24th 1707
Amy ye daughter of John Suggate & Amy his wife was buried December 9th 1707

(Page 49) BURIALS

1707 John the son of Thos Kidd of Combes & Anne his wife was buried December 17th 1707
Lucy ye daughter of Arthur Coleman & Eleanor his wife was buried Dec^{br} 17th 1707
1709 Brice ye son of James Cook and Susanna his wife was buried April 8th 1709
Francis ye son of Francis Southgate and Elizabeth his wife was buried June 21st 1709
Elizabeth ye daughter of Wm Goodwin of Stowmarket and his wife was buried October 25th 1709
1710 Thomas Green sen^r was buried November 10th 1710
1710/11 Phoebe the daughter of James Cook and Susanna his wife, an infant, was buried January 14 1710/11
1712 John the son of Thomas Kidd & Anne his wife, an infant, was buried June 24th 1712
1713 William the son of (space) Bromley & his wife, an infant, was buried April 19th 1713
Su/an Buxton widow was buried May 18th 1713
John Goodall was buried July 31st 1713
Mary the wife of Richard Buxton was buried August 17th 1713
Henry Smyth waas buried Septemb^r 13th 1713
Elizabeth Steward was buried Jan^{ry} 24th 1713
1714 Edmund Poley Esq son of Sr Edmund Poley K^{nt} & Dame Esther his wife was buried May 21st 1714
Dame Esther Poley, Relict of Sr Edmund Poley K^{nt} was buried June 26 1714
Mary Curtis was buried Decemb^r 4th 1714
1715 Thomas Balls of Needham was buried May 21st 1715
1716 Edmund Buxton was buried Feb^{ry} 11th 1716
Susanna Curtis widow was buried Feb: 12 1716
Edward ye son of Edwd Sage & Hannah his wife was buried March 22nd 1716

(Page 50) BURIALS

1717 Eleanor, wife of Arthur Colman of Neeham Mark^t was buried May 17th 1717
Mary, wife of Edmund Balls of Needham Mark^t: was buried August 27th 1717
Joseph son of Charles Hunt & Prudence his wife was buried March 24th 1717
1718 The Honourable Isabella Gipps wife of Richard Gipps Esq was buried Sept 27th 1718
Mary Buxton singlewoman was buried Novr ye 1st An præ.
Richard, son of John Coleman & Su/anna his wife was buried September 10th 1718
1719 Thomas Banks widower was buried Aug 13
Hannah Sage wife of Edward Sage was buried Aug 18th
James Cook was buried Oct^{b}r 21st
1720 John Whistle son of John Whistle & Mary his wife was buried July ye 24th
Edmund Green son of Thomas Green & Anne his wife was buried September ye 3rd
Robert Woods singleman was buried Novr 30th
John Whistle husbandman was buried Decr 7th not in Badley, but Barking.
Robert son of John Coleman & Susanna his wife was buried December 10th
1721 Sarah Deekes daughter of John Deekes & Anne his wife was buried April 14th
Richard Buxton was buried May ye 28th
1722 Jeremiah Coleman infant son of John Coleman & Susanna his wife was buried June 28
Francis Southgate labourer was buried Decr 12th
Arthur Collman junr was buried Jan 15th

(Page 51) MARRIAGES

1699 Thomas Kidd of Barrow singleman and Anne Goodwin of this parish singlewoman were married November 7th 1699 cum Licen: officialis
1699 William Davis of Presson singleman and Anne Breakles of this parish singlewoman were married January 17th 1699
1700 John Ottewell singleman and Elizabeth Gouch singlewoman both of Great Finboro were marryed October ye 8th 1700
1700 Thomas Booth of Stowmarket singleman and Elizabeth Blowers of this parish singlewoman were marryed October ye 10th 1700
1700 Richard Jennings of Barking singleman and Sarah Trundle of his parish singlewoman were marryed October ye 10th 1700
1700 Richard Suggate of Combs singleman and Elizabeth Steward of this parish singlewoman were marryed October 16th 1700 cun Licen: Officialis
1700 John Baldry of Benhall singleman and Mary Goodwin of this parish singlewoman were marryed January 7th 1700 cum Licen: officialis Comis Yearii
1700/01 Joseph Birch singleman and Mary Suttle singlewoman both of Stowmarket were marryed March 4th 1700/01
1701 William Mather of Bramford and Anne Swinborne of this parish were marryed April 6th 1701 both single persons cum Licen: Commiff

(Page 52) MARRIAGES

1701   William Norton of St Stephens parish in Norwich singleman and Margaret Bigsby of Stowmarket singlewoman were married April the 20th 1701
John Couzens of this Parish singleman and Rose Goodwyn of ye same singlewoman were married April 21st 1701
James Hunt and Martha Bird both single persons and of ye Parish of Combes were married April 22nd 1701
Thomas Scofield and Frances Denny both single persons and of ye parish of Great Finboro were married October 5th 1701
Thomas Peirson of Ipswich singleman and Ann Biles of Stowmarket singlewoman were married October 21 1701

1702   Daniel Quantel of Bildeston widower and Mary Farthing of Great Finborow widow were married July 20th 1702
Edmund Ship and Ann Gall both single persons and of Great Finborow were married October 4th 1702
Thomas Rosier of Needham and Magdalen Root of Combs were married cum Licencia Commissarii both single persons, Feb: 7th 1702

(Page 53) MARRIAGES

1703   George Munnings of Great Livermere singleman and Mary Breckles of this parish single woman were married October 12th 1703

1704   George Denny and Elizabeth Cooper both of Great Finboro and single persons were married March 28th 1704
John Bugg of Battisford singleman and Susan Alderton of Finboro Magna single woman were married April 16th
William Colchester of Needham widower and Elizabeth Read of the same single woman were married June 18th 1704

1704   William Grimwood of Buxhall singleman and Ann Green of Great Finborrow single woman were married June 20th 1704
Richard Robinson and Frances Walker both single persons of this parish were married October 15th 1704

1705   Wm Baker of Elmsett singleman and Mary Aldersley of Stow-market single woman were married April 15th 1705
(in another hand) not allowed of by ye L Chancellor.

1709   Samuel Robinson of Combes singleman and Susanna Hovel of this parish singlewoman were married October 9th 1709

(Page 54) MARRIAGES

1711   The Reverd Mr Tho Wynnne Rector of Combes & Mrs Alice Sparke of Badley were married November 6th 1711
Thomas Green & Anne Westhroppe both single persons and of ye parish of Badley were married Decr 2nd 1711

1713   Richard Ramplyn of Stow-market singleman & Mary Haxall of this parish were married May 18th 1713

1715   John Whistle & Mary Downing both single persons of ye parish of Badley were married June 6th 1715
John Turner & Lydia Spalding both single persons & of the parish of Badley, were married Septr 30th 1715

1716   Edmund Green & Bridget Westthroppe, both single persons, & of ye parish of Badley, were married Octr 8th 1716

1717   William Thing and Mary Cook both single persons, & of ye parish of Badley, were married Novr 1st 1717

1718   Joseph Stammers & Margaret Sheppard both single persons & both of ye parish of Badley were married Octr 21st 1718 cum Licen: comiss

1719   Thomas Woulton & Ann Cockeral were married Octr 4th being both single persons & both ye parish of Badley
Richard Buxton widow & Mary Foster widow both of ye parish of Badley were married 1719 (no date given)

1727   John Cock & Martha Colcester both single persons & of ye parish of Badley were married April 7th 1727

1730   John Tricker singleman & Margaret Groom singlewoman were married Jany 21st 1730

1732   Philip Broke of Nacton Esq & Mrs Anne Bowes of Bury St Edmunds were married Feb: 1st 1732

1733   Samuel Snewson of Woulton married Martha Carter of Needham both single persons Octo^r 11(18)th 1733

(Page 55) MARRIAGES

1734   Novr 6th then Thomas Burman & Elizabeth Christmas were married

1735   Jan: 19th then Thomas Mully singleman of Langham was married to Alice Wright singlewoman of Badly

1736   May the 13th then Thomas Wright of Stowmarket widower & Elizabeth Rooff singlewoman of Badley were married

1737   John Scofield of Creeting St Mary & Anne Kaly both single persons were married Octb^r 28

1741   John Minter of Hemingstone & Bridget Green of Badley both single persons were married May 7 1741(3 or 5)

1747   Willm Taylor of Badly singleman and Elizabeth Lamberd of Badley single woman was married Sept^t ye 28 1747
James Frost of Badly widdower and Mary Kimble of Badly widow was marryed January ye 19 1747
Willm Juland of Needham widdower and Elizabeth Southgate single woman was married Feb ye 7: 1747

1748   Aprile ye 12 James Cristmas of Badly and Hannah Murrels of the same, widdow, were married
George Lawrence of the parish of St Stephens Ipswich and Sarah Ward of ye parish of Blakenham Parva both single persons were married by Licens aprile ye 21: 1748

1749   Robt Cutting of Needham market and Mary Southgate of Badley both single persons were married April ye 16: 1749

1750   Michel Bremment of Blakenham single man and Mary Wellham single woman was married March ye 7

(Page 56) MARRIAGES

1753   Robt Harvie of Combe single man and Mary Frostwick of Otley was married Aprile ye 16:

------- *END OF REGISTER BOOK* ------

INDEX OF NAMES CONTAINED IN THE PAGES OF THE EARLIEST REGISTER BOOK
Indexed by the vicar by   win M.A., F.S.A.

M.S. INDEX TO BADLEY REGISTERS 1589 - 1900

The original Registers consist of 28 folio parchment leaves numbered 1 - 56. The contents appear to have been collected from two or more books, and the attested leaves to have been copied from the four church copies made under the order of 1597, when the contents of the original paper book were transcribed according to the above mentioned order. The book is contained in a battered parchment cover little remainig of the back leaf. On the front of the cover appears:-

"The Church booke of Badley Renewed etc
* indicates that the name appears more than once upon the page

AGER, Daniel 46*, Hannah 46, Mary 46*
ALDERSLEY, Mary 53
ALDERTON, Susan 53, Thomas 15
ALEXANDER, Margaret 19
ALLEN, Dennis 18, John 18
ARGENT, Robert 20, Susan 20
ARHARTE, Katherine 15
BAKEN, Dorothy 17, John 17
BAKER, Elizabeth 17, Katherine 18, Mary 53, Susan 20, Thomas 18, William 53
BALDRY, John 51, Mary 51
BALLS, Ann 8, Daniel 8, Edmund 7, 8*, 9*, 24, 47*, 50 Elizabeth 2, 12, 47 Francis 23 Isabella 18 John 5*, 7, 12*, 14*, 17, 21, 22, 23, 24, 28*, 29*, 30*, 41 Katherine 9 Manfield 7 Margaret 16, 29 Marie 9, 21* Mary 5, 12, 14, 22, 23, 24, 27*, 29, 47, 50 Susan 5, 12*, 26*, 29 Susannah 17 Thomas 2, 3, 7, 8, 22, 26*, 30*, 47, 49
BANCOCKE, Jane 15
BANK(E)S, Prudence 47, Thomas 47, 50
BARBER, Christian 16 Robert 16
BARKER, Mary 29 Priscilla 16 Robert 2*, 29 Susan 2 William 16
BARTON, Frances 33 John 33 William 33
BASKET(T), Alice 32, 33*, 34* John 33 Henry 32, 33*, 34
BEALES, Dorothy 19
BEAST, Ann 6 Edmund 4 Francis 27 Mary 5 Robert 45
BEDDON, Alice 6 Saxbi 6 William 6
BEDWELL, Edward 48
BETS, James 13, 18 John 13, 18 Margaret 13, 18
BICKERS, Faith 19
BIGSBY, Margaret 52
BIRCH, Joseph 51 Mary 51
BIRD, Edward 43 John 45 Martha 52 Mary 40, 42*, 45 Sarah 40*, 45 Thomas 40 William 40*, 45
BLOCKETT, Elkizabeth 15 Thomas 15
BLO(O)MFIELD, Dennis 18 James 40, 42 Richard 40
BLOWERS, Elizabeth 51 Martha 18, 37 Rachel 32, 37 Thomas 18 William 32, 37
BOBY, Mary 32 Robert 32
BOLDROWE, Dorothy 17
BOLTON, Joseph 42
BOONE, Anne 15
BOOTH, Elizabeth 51 Thomas 51
BORE, Alice 29 Charles 29
BOULE/BOWALL, Anne 3 Henry 3
BOWES, Anne 54
BOYSE, Mistress 1
BRECKLES, Anne 51 Mary 53
BREN, Isabella 18 John 18
BRETLAND, Katherine 18
BREWSE, John 1 Mary 1
BREWSTER, Ann 15, Dorothy 18 Edmund 4 Mirable 29 Thomas 18 William 29
BRICKLES, (see BRECKLES)

BRIGHT, Agatha 31
BROKE, Ann 54 Philip 54
BROMLEY, Jonathan 43 William 48, 49
BROOKE, Marie 3, 11 Thomas 3, 11
BROWNE, Elizabeth 14* John 14 Mary 14 Thomas 14*
BUGG(E), Christian 2 Elizabeth 9, 18 James 9 John 53 Margaret 16 Robert 2, 9*, 16 Susan 53 Thomas 9
BURGES(S), Briers 6, 23 Catherine 23*, 24*, 30, Francis 23*, 24, 28, 30
BUXTON, Alice 5 Edmund 12, 22*, 24, 25, 34, 37, 41, 48, 49 Frances 3, 12 Mary 25, 34, 35, 41, 47, 49, 50, 54 Richard 3, 5, 11, 12*, 24, 28, 34, 35*, 47, 49, 50, 54 Robert 5 Rose 11, 28 Susan 14, 22, 24, 25, 49 William 14*
CALEY, Robert 6
CAMBY, Mary 29
CARLOW, Ann 19 Thomas 19
CARPENTER, Marie 18
CARTER, Martha 54
CHANDLER, Dorcas 39 Elizabeth 45 Mary 45 Thomas 39, 45
CHENERIE, Maria 31 Mary 20 Nathaniel 31
CHENERY, see CHENERIE
CHRISTMAS, Amy 39 Hannah 38, 55 James 55 Mary 38*, 39 Thomas 38 William 38*, 39 (see also XMAS)
CRISMES, see CHRISTMAS
CLARKE, James 6, Joan 19
COE, Alce 21*, 25, 27*, 30 Frances 30
COCK, John 54 Marie 21, 27 Martha 54 Sarah 30 Thomas 21, 25, 27 William 21*, 25, 27*, 30*, 41
COCKEREL, Anne 54
COCKSONNE, Anne 15, Elias 15
COLC(H)ESTER, Elizabeth 53 Martha 54 Priscilla 16 Sarah 20 William 53
COLE, Joane 29 Marie 21 Mary 14 Thomas 29 William 14*, 21*
COLEMAN, Anne 36 Arthur 32, 36*, 37, 49, 50* Aster 23 Charles 39 Edmund 28 Edward 5, 6, 14*, 22*, 23*, 28*, 36 Eleanor 36*, 37, 45, 50 Elizabeth 6, 23, 36 Esther 37 Heken 32 Jeremiah 39, 50 John 38*, 39*, 40, 50* Lucy 49 Margaret 5 Prudence 14, 22, 23*, 28* Richard 38, 50 Robert 38, 59 Susan 38 Susanna 38, 39*, 40*, 50*
COL(L)MAN, see COLEMAN
CONNALT, Benjamin 47 John 47
COOK(E), Brice 37, 48, 49 Daniel 36, 47 Frances 33 Hannah 35 James 34*, 35*, 36*, 37*, 38, 47*, 48*, 49*, 50 John 36 Joseph 36 Kebel 37 Mary 38, 54 Naomi 34, 35*, 36*, 47 Phoebe 37, 49 Sarah 33, 35 Susanna 36, 37*, 38, 42, 48*, 49* William 33
COOPER, Edmund 2*, 3, 7 Elizabeth 15, 53 Esther 17 Joan 19 John 17 Martha 16 Mary 7 Stephen 19
COULAHESTER, see COLCHESTER

LEE,   Martha 45* William 45
LEVEREDGE,   Elizabeth 17
LOCKWOOD,   Edward 29 Elizabeth 22 Joane 29 John 6, 19,
                     22*, 23* Margaret 19, 22*, 23*, 28 Mary 19, 22
                     Sarah 38* William 23
LOVEREDGE,   see LEVEREDGE
MAJOR,   Richard 20 Susan 20
MALBY,   Anne 19
MANNING,   Anne 4 Thomas 3, 4 5
MARJORAM,   Sarah 48
MARTIN,   Ann 20 Margett 3 Thomas 3
MATHER,   Anne 51 William 51
MAYHEW,   Catherine 39 Elizabeth 18, 40 James 39, 40*
                     Mary 39, 40* Robert 42 Susan 40
MINTER,   Bridget 55 John 55
MOOR,   Rachel 32
MORGAN,   Anne 19 Anthony 19 Sarah 18 William 18
MORGIN,   see MORGAN
MUD(D),   Ann 17 Elizabeth 19 Henry 17 Margery 20
                     Thomas 19
MULLY,   Alice 55 Thomas 55
MUNNINGS,   George 53 Mary 53
MURRELS,   Hannah 55
MURTEN,   Mary 32
NEWMAN,   Alice 17 Anne 16 Thomas 17
NICHOLAS,   John 46 Margaret 46 Sophia 46
NORTON,   Audrie 14*, 22, 23*, 24* Catherine 23 Edward
                     23 Frances 14 John 14 Margaret 52 Richard 24
                     Robert 22 Stephen 14*, 22*, 23*, 24* William
                     24, 52
OSBORN,   Bridget 32
OTTEWELL,   Elizabeth 51 John 51
PACKE,   Abraham 15 Alice 15
PAINTER,   Elizabeth 19
PALMER,   Elizabeth 31 John 31 Robert 20 Sarah 20
PARISH,   Frances 15 Robert 15
PARKE,   Rose 19
PAYNE,   Abigail 15 John 15
PEARCH,   Richard 43
PEIRSON,   Ann 52 Thomas 52
PEPPER,   Elizabeth 17 Thomas 17
PETTIT,   Bridget 32 William 32
PILLBOROUGH,   Elizabeth 35 Margar 35
PLE(A)SANTS,   Ellen 13 Francis 4, 10, 11*, 13*, 31*
POKE,   Frances 45 Francis 45 Margaret 10 Mary 11,
                     19 Thomas 45*
POLEY,   Ann 2, 11, 28, 33 Charles 27 Cicilie 7, 12, 16, 28
                     Dorothia 16 Dorothy 2, 3, 9, 10, 28 Edmund 1,
                     1, 2*, 3, 5*, 6*, 7, 9, 10*, 11* 12*, 16, 27*, 28*, 30,
                     32, 48, 49   Ester 27, 48, 49
                     Frances 4, 6, 12* Henry 4, 12, 48
                     Hester 27 John 1*, 2*, 9, 29*, 33 Joseph 29
                     Katherine 1 Marie 29 Mary 1, 2, 10, 29, 30
                     Mirable 29, 33 Mr 2* Richard 1*, 7*, 11 Susan 2
                     Thomas 11, 28 William 5, 6, 11, 27
POLY,   see POLEY
POLYE,   see POLEY
POOLIE,   see POLEY
POOLY,   see POLEY
PORTINGTON,   Mary 30
PRESTON,   Nicholas 3 Peter 3
PRETTIE,   Sara 18
PRINCET,   Elizabeth 17 William 17
PUL(L)FORD(E),   Ann 4, 7 Cicilie 8 Dorothy 8 Edmund 7 Francis
                     9 Henry 4, 7*, 8*, 17 John 4, 7, 9 Susan 7
                     Susanna 17 Thomas 5 Thomison 4
QUANTAL,   Daniel 52 Mary 52
RAMPLYN,   Mary 54 Richard 54
RAPHE,   Francis 18 Sarah 18
RAYMENT,   Elizabeth 47 Francis 6, 13, 21 Henry 6, 13, 14,
                     21 Mary 14 Rose 23, 24, 21, 31, 47 Smith

                     47 William 31
RAYMOND,   see RAYMENT
REYMOND,   see RAYMENT
READ,   Elizabeth 53
REYNOLDS,   John 31 William 3, 31
REYNOULD,   see REYNOLDS
RICHARDSON,   George 29 Rebecca 29
RICHMOND,   Elizabeth 20, 34
ROBINS,   Charles 42* Henrietta 42
ROBINSON,   Frances 53 Riachard 53 Samuel 53 Susanna 53
ROOFF,   Giles 19 Mary
ROOLFE,   see ROOFF
ROOT,   Magdalen 50
ROSE,   Alice 29 Frances 15 Robert 29
ROSIER,   Magdalen 52 Mary 20 Thomas 52 William 20
ROWE,   James 19 Margaret 19
RUNGARY,   Mary 37 Samuel 37*
SAGE,   Edward 38*, 49*, 50 Hannah 38*, 49, 50
SALLS,   Widow 42
SALMON,   John 45* Mary 45 Rebecca 45*
SEAPY,   Ann 46* Mary 46* Robert 46 Samuel 46*
SCOFIELD,   Ann 55 Frances 52 John 55 Thomas 52
SCRIVENOR,   Peter 2*, 7 Ralph 2*, 7 Susan 16
SEAGO,   Anne 28 Elizabeth 6
SECKFORD,   Ann 16 Thomas 16
SEGAR,   see SEAGO
SERGEANT,   Margaret 32
SHEPPARD,   Margaret 54
SHIMMING,   Sara 25* Thomas 25
SHIP,   Anne 52 Edmund 52
SHORLAND,   Martha 16
SILLETT,   Helen 32
SIMMON,   Frances 31 Francis 11 William 11
SMIE,   Edward 19 Mary 19
SMITH,   Anne 20, 25* Edmund 19, 20, 25* Elizabeth 18,
                     28, 47 Henry 25, 49 Jannne 15 John 15 Lady
                     5 Peter 18, 28 Rose 15 Thomas 25
SMYTH,   see SMITH
SNELLING,   Mary 5, 19
SNEWSON,   Martha 54 Samuel 54
SORTER,   Edward 6 Elizabeth 18 Henry 18 Thomas 18
SOUGATE,   Abraham 40*, 41, 45 Amy 41 Ann 45 Deborah
                     45 Dorcas 40 Elizabeth 37*, 38, 39, 40*, 41*,
                     45, 49, 55 Francis 37*, 38, 39, 49*, 50 John 39,
                     41, 42 Robert 45 Sanmuel 40, 41 Sarah 38
                     Susanna 37
SOUTHEBIE,   Katherine 16 Thomas 16
SOUTHGATE,   see SOUGATE
SOWTER,   see SORTER
SPALDING,   Lydia 54
SPARK(E),   Alice 26, 54 Edmund 26 Susan 26
SPARROWE,   Leonard 10 Sara 10
SPINCKE,   Alice 15 Samuel 2
SPINK,   see SPINCKE
SPINNIE,   Alice 15 Henry 15
STAMMERS,   Joseph 39*, 54 Margaret 39*, 54 Sheppard 39
STANFORD,   John 20 Susan 20
STEWARD,   Elizabeth 49, 51 widow 48 William 48
STOOKES,   John 5
SUG(G)AT(E),   Alice 32 Amy 32, 34*, 35, 47, 48* Ann
                     27* Dorothy 18 Elizabeth 51 John 32, 34*, 35,
                     47, 48 Mary 19, 35, 47 Richard 51 Sarah 34
                     Thomas 27, 28
SUGGATE,
SUGGET(T),
SUGGITT,
SUGGUT,
SUTTLE,   Mary 51
SWANN,   Edward 26 Mary 26
SWARE,   see LAMBERT
SWARI   see LAMBERT

SWINBORNE,   Anne 51
SYER,   Edward 42* John 41 Sarah 41
SYMON,   see SIMMON
TAYLOR,   Martha 16 William 16
THARKER,   Robert 30
THING,   Catherine 34*, 35, 42, 47 Frances 34 George 34*, 35, 42, 47 John 47 Mary 54 Susan 34 William 35, 54
THURMWOOD, John 30 Margaret 32 Mary 30 Richard 32
THURNWOOD, see THURMWOOD
TILLET,   Dorothy 27 Isaac 6*, 27
TILLOT,   see TILLET
TRAPNELL,   Elizabeth 32
TRAPPET,   John 14* Mary 14* Sarah 14 Stephen 14
TRICKER,   John 42, 54 Margaret 54
TRUNDLE,   Sarah 51
TURNER,   John 54 Lydia 54
WAGGER,   Susanna 41
WAKELIN(G),   Edward 40, 41 Elizabeth 40* Samuel 40*, 42
WALKER,   Frances 53
WALTON,   Anne 41* Elizabeth 41 Thomas 41*
WARD,   Sarah 55
WARNER,   Dorothia 16 Gregory 16 Martha 16
WARREN,   Frances 40* John 40*, 41, 42
WEBBER,   Alice 11 John 10, 11 Thomas 10
WELHAM,   Ann 17 Elizabeth 12 Ester 17 Robert 48 Ruth 12 Thomas 12*, 46
WELL(H)AM,   see WELHAM

WESTE,   Katherine 15
WESTHE,   see WESTE
WESTHROPPE,   Ann 54 Bridget 54
WHILCHIN,
WHISTLE,   Henry 38 John 38, 39*, 50*, 54 Mary 38, 39, 50, 54
WHISTLE-CROFT,   Elizabeth 4 John 4
WHITECAKE,   Mary 6, 20 Sarah 6 Thomas 6, 20*
WHITECOKE,   see WHITECAKE
WHITLOCK,   Rose 17
WILCHIN,   see WHILCHIN
WILLKENSON,   John 1
WILSON,   Ann 20
WILTON,   Richard 16 Susan 16
WINGFIELD,   Dorothy 18 Henry 18
WINNELL,   Anne 26 James 26 Thomas 26
WITHERBY,   Margaret 32
WOLTON,   Alice 43* Anne 54 John 41, 45 Sarah 45*, 46 Thomas 45*, 46, 54 William 46
WOOD(S),   Debora 29 Robert 50 William 29
WOOLFE,   Giles 6 Marie 20
WOOLTON,   see WOLTON & WALTON
WOULTON,   see WOLTON & WALTON
WRIGHT,   Alice 17, 45*, 55 Alce 26* Susan 29
WRITE,   se WRIGHT
WYNNE,   Alice 54 Thomas 54
YOUNG(E),   Henry 14*, 19 Rose 14, 19

BADLEY REGISTER 1756

Baptisms
1756

1756 Daniel son James & Mary Frost July 25
1757 Mary daugt of Rachel Page baseborn Jany 23

Burials 1756

1756 Mary Elliott April 29
1757 Samuel Hunt Jany 11th

Baptism 1757 None

Burials None

Baptisms 1758 None

Burials None

Baptism 1759

1759 Sarah d of Henry & Sarah Thorpe June 10th
1759 Rachel Page d of Rachel baseborn June 17th
1759 Joseph s of Joseph & Ann Ruffles Jany 1st

Burials 1759

1759 Cousins, Rose widow Octr 3
      Keeble, Ann Decr 16
      Elliott, Sarah Decr 16

1760 Baptisms none

1760 Burials none

1761
Baptisms

1761 John Wolton s of John Wolton Decr 1
1762 Anne Ruffle d of Joseph & Ann Jany 25

Burials

1761 Philip Lee Nov 24th

Burials

1762 Thomas Green Jany 9th

1762 No Baptisms

Burials 1673

1763 Edward Cornish May 28

Baptisms none

Baptisms 1764

1764 Thomas Wolton s of John & Ann Febr 29th

Burials 1674 none

Baptisms 1765

1765 Deborah Wolton d of John & Ann May 29th
      Mary Dove d of Charles & Mary Novr 14th
      Elizabeth Collins d of Frances & Susan Dec 12
      Elizth Codd d of Fleetwood & Elizth Feby 18

Burials 1765 none

Baptisms 1766 none

Baptizms 1767

1767 Fleetwood Codd s of Fleetwood & Elizth March28th
William Stevens & Hannah s & d of John & Hannah
May 10th

Burials 1766 *(out of order)*

1766 Elizabeth Thorpe Nov^r: 9
Ann Bird Decr 6th
William Bird Decr 8

Baptisms 1767

1767 Ann Ruffles d of Joseph & Ann June 9
1767 Sarah Wolton and Thomas d & s of John & Ann July 9

Burials none

Baptisms 1768

1768 Mary d of Fleetwood & Elizth Codd May 29th
Frances d of Francis & Hannah Collins Octr 21
1769 William s of Joseph & Ann Ruffles March 24

Burials none

Baptisms 1769 (cont)

1769 William Wolton s of John & Ann Novbr 20th
1770 John & James Gladwin s of John & Mary Gladwell Apr 15

Burials 1769 none
1770 Baptisms none

Burials 1770

1770 Edmund Green June 22

Baptisms 1771

1771 Benjamin Ruffles s of Joseph & Anne Aug 1st
1772 Benjamin Gladwell s of John & Mary March 1st

Burials 1772

1772 William Lee July 8

Baptisms 1772

1772 Benjamin s of John & Mary March 1st (this is a
duplicate entry)
Thomas Stevens s of John & Martha Octr 11th
Susannah & Jemima Wolton ds of John & Anne Novbr
17th

Burials 1772

1772 Thomas Wolton Decr 26th

1773

1773 James Christmas March 13

1774 Baptisms none

Burials 1775

1775 John Salmon Febr 3

1775 to 1776
Baptisms

1775 Higham Wolton s of John Wolton & Ann born 4th
April 1774 baptized June 10th

1777 Baptisms

1777 John Archer s of John & Mary March 2nd
Isaac Stevens s of s of John & Martha May 15(8)th
John Gladwell s of John & Mary May 15(8)th

Burials 1777 none

1778 Baptisms

1778 Edward Mudd s of Thos & Hannah Dec_r 8
1778 Thomas Mudd s of Thos & Hannah Decr 8
1778 Richard Mudd s of Thos & Hannah Decr 8
Burials 1778

1778 Mary Dow June 7
1778 Jacob Chandler July 13

1779 Baptisms

1779 Charlotte Wolton d of John & Ann June 3rd
1779 James Bead Wolton s of John & Ann June 3rd
1779 William Gladwell s of John & Mary Sepr 27
1779 Elizth Gladwell d of John & Mary Novr 27

Burials 1779

1779 Eleanor Cooper Augt 5

Baptisms 1780

1780 John Scott s of John & Elizth born 25th Novr 1772,
3rd June
Burials 1780

1780 Francis Collins Novr 8
1781

1781 Mary Bromley from Needham April 4

Baptisms 1781

1781 Susan d of John & Mary Gladwell Decr 2nd

Burials none

Baptisms 1782 none   Burials 1782 none

Baptisms 1783 none

Baptizms 1784

1784 Matilda Simpson d of John & Amy March 9th
arah d of John & Mary Gladwell April 10
Elizth d of John & Mary Fairs July 18
Thomas Clark & Ann Cooper s & d of Clark & Esther
Cooper Octr 3

1784 Burials none

1785 Baptisms none

1785 Burials none

Baptisms 1786

1786 Charlotte d of John & Mary Gladwell March 16
Susan Elizabeth Mary Ann & Richard son and daughters
of Thos & Elizth Mudd March 16

1786 Burials none

1787 Baptisms none

1788 Burials none   1788 Baptisms none
Baptisms 1789 none

1790

1790 Susan Archer d of Jonathan & Susan Febr 14 1790

Burials 1790 none

Baptisms 1790

1790 Maria Baker d of Wm & Mary Baker May 23(5)

Burials 1790

1790 Samuel Denny Augt 23

Baptisms 1791 none   Burials 1791 none
Baptisms 1792 none   Burials 1792 none

Baptisms 1793

1793 William Baker s of Wm & Mary July 28th
Elizabeth Lee d of John & Elizth Oct 13th
James Medows Moore born Feb ye 3 1793 s of James &
Sarah Nov 20th

1794
1794 Robert Archer s of Jonathan & Susan Feby 9th

Burials 1793

1793 Thos Mudd May 21st

Burials 1794 none

Baptisms 1794

1794 John Kirby Moore brn Sept 28th 1794 s of James &
Sarah Decr 2

Burials 1794 none
Burials 1795 none

1795 Elizabeth Simpson March 19th

1795 Baptisms none
1796 Baptisms none

1796 Samuel Cooper s of John & Mary Jany 3

Burials 1975

1795 Samuel Cooper May 6

Baptisms 1796

1796 Elizth Archer d of John & Susan Aug 21

Baptisms 1797 none
Burials 1796

1796 Mary Baker Decr 21
1797 William Baker Jan 8
John Baker Jan 8
William Bird Jany 29

Baptisms 1797

1797 Joseph Baker s of Wm & Mary Augst 27
Sarah Bredell Moore d of James & Sarah born August
28th 1797 Novr 8

Elizabeth Simpson d of Wm & Elizabeth (no date given)
Burials 1797 & 1798 none

Baptisms 1798

1798 William s of Wm & Mary Haggar May 2

1799 none

Burials 1798

1798 Susan Mudd Novr 22

Burials 1799

1799 William Simpson Feby 2

1799 Baptisms

1799 Thomas Archer s of Jonathan & Susan Archer June 11
Sarah Tokelove Jay d of Edward & Sarah Novr 26
Charlotte Baker d of Wm & Ann Decr 8
1800 William Youngs s of Danl & Elizth March2
Sarah Haggar d of James & Mary March 9th
Elizabeth & Mary Ann Simpson daughters of William
& Elizh Oct 3

Burials 1779 none

Burials 1800

1800 Abraham Webster Simpson Feb 9

Baptisms 1801

1801 Ann Tokelove Jay d of Edward & Sarah born June 3rd
1808 July 16th Martha Stevens d of Isaac & Elizabeth Decr 6th

1801 Burials none

1802
1802 Simon Haggar son of James & Mary Feby 28

Burials 1802

1802 Abraham Simpson from Harwich Novr 11th
Sarah Simpson Novr 18th

Baptisms 1803

1803 Hannah Stevens d of Isaac & Elizabeth June 1st
Samuel Turning Jay s of Edward & Sarah born Sepbr 1st
John Archer s of Jonathan & Susan Novr 6th

Burials 1803

1803 William Stevens Augst 21st
Clark Cooper Septbr 18th

Baptisms 1804

1804 John Haggar s of James & Mary Haggar Jany 8
Isaac Stevens s of Isaac & Elizabeth July 1st
Samuel Turner(sic) Jay s of Edward & Sarah July 10th

Burials 1804

1804 John Mudd Jany 18th

Baptisms 1805

1805 John Gladdele s of John & Elizabeth Feby ye 4th
Edward Jay s of Edward & Sarah born 12th Novr 1804
March 3rd

Burials 1805 none

Baptisms 1806

1806 Mary d of Jonathan & Mary Archer June 8th

Burials 1806 none

Baptisms 1807

1807 Joseph s of Joseph & Mary Haggar born Jan ye 5th baptized Jan ye 25th

Ann d of John & Sarah Kimball born July 13th 1801, Sep^{br} 16th

Esther d of John & Sarah Kimball born Feb ye 4th 1803, Sep^{br} 16th

William s of Richard & Ann Mudd born Augst 5th 1804, Sep^{br} 16th

Mary d of Richard & Ann Mudd born March 10th 1806, Sep^{br} 16th

Thomas s of Richard & Ann Mudd born June 26th, baptized Sep^{br} 16th

1807 Burials none

1808 Baptisms none

Burials 1808

1808 John Stevens April 25th

Baptisms 1809

1809 John Mudd s of Richard Mudd & Ann Mudd bapt Sepbr 24th 1809

George s of James & Mary Haggar Novr 19th 1809

Burials 1809

1809 Benjamin Gladell January 11th

END OF REGISTER

MARRIAGES (Start of Printed Register)

The Registers of Badley in the County of Suffolk (handwritten at top of page)

(The Year 1754) Page 1

1754 1. Josph Ruffels *of* [*this*] parish single man *and* Ann Southgate *of* [*this*] parish spinster *were* Married *in this* [Church] *by* [Licence] *this* 3rd *Day of* December *in the Year One Thousand* seven *Hundred and* fifty four *by me* Sam^{el} Uvedale [curate]. *In the Prefence of* Robt Cutting & John Webb

1755 2 Sam^{el} Baker *of* [*the*] Parish of Creeting St Mary *and* Elizabeth Day *of* [*this*] parish *were* Married *in this* [Church] *by* [Banns] *this* 5th *Day of* Nov^{br} *in the Year One Thousand* seven *Hundred and* fifty five *by me* Samuel Uvedale [curate]. *In the Prefence of* Robt Parker & John Wood

1756 3. Willm Cutbert widower *of* [*this*] Parish, of Badley in the County of Suffolk *and* Elizabeth Rands spinster *of* [*the*] same *were* Married *in this* [Church] *by* [Banns] *this* 11th *Day of* Octb^r *in the Year One Thousand* seven *Hundred and* fifty six *by me* Sam^{el} Uvedale [curate]. *In the Prefence of* Bridget Keeble & The mark of John Banks (sic)

1757 4. Jacob Chandler singleman *of* [*the*] Parish of Combs in the County of Suffolk *and* Sarah Wolton spinster *of* [*this*] parish *were* Married *in this* [Church] *by* [Licence] *this* 15th *Day of* August *in the Year One Thousand* seven *Hundred and* fifty seven *by me* Sam^{el} Uvedale [curate]. *In the Prefence of* Thos Wolton & John Wood

(The Year 1761) Page 2

1761 5. Samuel Harvey *of* [*this*] Parish single man *and* Ann Frances *of* [*the*] same spinster *were* Married *in this* [Church] *by* [Banns] *this* 12th *Day of* May *in the Year One Thousand* seven *Hundred and* sixty one *by me* Amrose Uvedale [curate]. *In the Prefence of* John Wolton & John Barnard

1762 6. Bass Birch *of* [*the*] Parish of Gosbeck single man *and* Mary Kemble *of* [*this*] Parish spinster *were* Married *in this* [Church] *by* [Licence] *this* 17th *Day of* May *in the Year One Thousand* seven *Hundred and* sixty two *by me* Ambrose Uvedale [curate]. *In the Prefence of* John Wolton & Samuel Scapey

Next two entries on page blank

(The Year 1764) Page 3

1764 7. Willm Keeble *of* [*the*] Parish of Hitcham widower *and* Eliz^{bth} Bird *of* [*the*] same spinster *were* Married *in this* [Church] *by* [Licence] *this* 12th *Day of* Augst *in the Year One Thousand* seven *Hundred and* sixty four *by me* Amb^{se} Uvedale [curate]. *In the Prefence of* Jo Ruffell & Samel Scapey

1764 -_{th} Robt How *of* [*this*] parish single man *and* Elizbth Squirell *of* [*this*] Parish spinster *were* Married *in this* [Church] *by* [Licence] *the* 4th *Day of* Sept^{br} *in the Year One Thousand* seven *Hundred and* sixty four *by me* Amb^{se} Uvedale [curate]. *In the Prefence of* Hen^{ry} Thorpe (x) & Sarah Choett (x)

1770 9. Stephen Nunn *of* [*the*] Parish of Combs single man *and* Susanna Harvey *of* [*this*] Parish single woman *were* Married *in this* [Church] *by* [Banns] *this* 9th *Day of* Augst *in the Year One Thousand* seven *Hundred and* seventy *by me* Amb^{se} Uvedale [curate]. *In the Prefence of* Susanna Green & Tho Sougate

1770 9. William Wolton *of* [*this*] Parish singleman *and* Susanna Green *of* [*the*] Parish of Combe spinster *were* Married *in this* [Church] *by* [Licence] *this* 9th *Day of* Oct^o *in the Year One Thousand* seven *Hundred and* seventy *by me* Amb^{se} Uvedale [curate]. *In the Prefence of* Ann Wolton & Jno Wolton

(The Year 1773) Page 4 (NB entry numbers are incorrect as a result of a mistake on the previous page - they start at 10 & should start at 11)

1774 10. John Rainbird *of* [*this*] Parish singleman *and* Sarah Hewett *of* [*the*] same single woman *were Married in this* [Church] *by* [Licence] *this* thirtieth *Day of* September *in the Year One Thousand* seven *Hundred and* seventy three *by me* Edward Griffith [curate]. *In the Prefence of* John Wolton & Sam^{el} Scapey

1774 11. John Lambert *of* [*this*] parish singleman *and* Sarah Peck *of* [*the*] same, singlewoman *were Married in this* [Church] *by* [Banns] *this* tenth *Day of* Octoberr *in the Year One Thousand* seven *Hundred and* seventy four *by me* Edwd Griffiths [curate]. *In the Prefence of* Robt Beales, Ann Wolton & John Boggis's (x)

1774 12. Philip Webb *of* [*this*] Parish singleman *and* Elizabeth Grey singlewoman *of* [*the*] Parish of Hemingston in this County *were Married in this* [Church] *by* [Licence] *this* twelfth *Day of* October *in the Year One Thousand* seven *Hundred and* seventy four *by me* Edward Griffiths [curate]. *In the Prefence of* William Major & Robert Beales

1778 13. James Ellis *of* [*this*] Parish singleman *and* Sarah Rose *of* [*this*] Parish singlewoman *were Married in this* [Church] *by* [Banns] *this* 17th *Day of* March *in the Year One Thousand* seven *Hundred and* seventy eight *by me* Thos Naylor [curate]. *In the Prefence of* Robert Beales & Webber Scales

(The Year 1779) Page 5 (NB the entry numbers seem to have been abandoned)

1779 -. Henry Edwards *of* [*the*] Parish of Barham Batchelor *and* Ann Scapey *of* [*this*] Parish *were Married in this* [Church] *by* [Licence] *this* 12th *Day of* October *in the Year One Thousand* seven *Hundred and* seventy nine *by me* Amb^{se} Uvedale [curate]. *In the Prefence of* Robt Scapey & Robert Beales

1782 -. Thos Turner *of* [*the*] Parish of Barking widower *and* Mary Scapey *of* [*the*] Parish spinster *were Married in this* [Church] *by* [Licence] *the* 14th *Day of* Feb^{ry} *in the Year One Thousand* seven *Hundred and* eighty two *by me* Amb^{se} Uvedale [curate]. *In the Prefence of* Mary Scapey & Samuel Turner

1787 -. Robert Smith *of* [*the*] Parish of Batisford Batchelor *and* Mary Cooper *of* [*this*] Parish spinster *were Married in this* [Church] *by* [Licence] *this* 18th *Day of* September *in the Year One Thousand* seven *Hundred and* eighty seven *by me* Amb^{se} Uvedale [curate]. *In the Prefence of* Samnuel Cooper & Robert Beales

1789 -. Samuel Cooper *of* [*this*] Parish Batchelor *and* Mary Simpson *of* [*the*] same spinster *were Married in this* [Church] *by* [Licence] *this* 24th *Day of* Febr^{yr} *in the Year One Thousand* severn *Hundred and* eighty nine *by me* Amb^{se} Uvedale [curate]. *In the Prefence of* John Simpson, Amy Simpson & Elizabeth Simpson

(The Year 1791) Page 6

1791 18. John Gladwin *of* [*this*] Parish Batchelor *and* Hannah Roberts *of* [*this*] Parish singlewoman *were Married in this* [Church] *by* [Banns] *this* 15th *Day of* February *in the Year One Thousand* seven *Hundred and* 91 *by me* W C Uvedale [curate]. *In the Prefence of* Robt Scapey & Robert Beales

1791 19. Robt Craske *of* [*the*] Parish of Drinkston Batchelor *and* Elizabeth Scott *of* [*this*] Parish spinster *were Married in this* [Church] *by* [Licence] *this* sixth *Day of* Oct^{br} *in the Year One Thousand* seven *Hundred and* ninety one *by me* Amb^{se} Uvedale [curate]. *In the Prefence of* Jno Scott & Thomas Scott

1795 20. John Woodward *of* [*the*] Parish of Barking Batchelor & Amey Simpson spinster *of* [*this*] Parish *were Married in this* [Church] *by* [Licence] *this* 18th *Day of* November *in the Year One Thousand* seven *Hundred and* 95 *by me* W C Uvedale [curate]. *In the Prefence of* John Simpson, Susannah Simpson & Lucy Simpson

1797 21. William Simpson *of* [*this*] Parish Batchelor *and* Elizabeth Mudd *of* [*this*] parish spinster a minor *were Married in this* [Church] *by* [Licence] with consent of her natural mother *this* 17th *Day of* March *in the Year One Thousand* seven *Hundred and* 97 *by me* W C Uvedale [curate]. *In the Prefence of* Lucy Simpson, Mary Mudd, Edwd Mudd, Thos Mudd & RobertMudd

(The Year 1797) Page 7

1797 22. James Stokes *of* [*this*] Parish batchelor *and* Hannah How spinster *of* [*the*] Parish of Old Newton *were Married in this* [   ] *by* [   ] *this*   *Day of*   *in the Year One Thousand*   *Hundred and*   *by me*   [   ]. *In the Prefence of*
(The remainder of this entry was left blank & presumably the marriage did not take place)

1797 22. John Turner *of* [*the*] Parish of Pettaugh in this County *and* Theodosia Scott spinster *of* [*this*] parish *were Married in this* [Church] *by* [Licence] *this* 24th *Day of* October *in the Year One Thousand* seven *Hundred and* ninety seven *by me* W C Uvedale [curate]. *In the Prefence of* Elizabeth Borley & Jno Scott

1798 23. Edward Jay *of* [*this*] Parish Batchelor *and* Sarah Emmerson spinster of the Parish of Barking *were Married in this* [Church] *by* [Licence] *this* 20th *Day of* November *in the Year One Thousand* seven *Hundred and* 98 *by me* W C Uvedale [curate]. *In the Prefence of* Sarah Eagle, & Maria Eagle & Thos Emerson

1799 24. John Kemball *of* [*the*] Parish of Combs Batchelor *and* Sarah Cooper *of* [*this*] Parish spinster *were Married in this* [Church] *by* [Licence] *this* seventeenth *Day of* May *in the Year One Thousand* seven *Hundred and* ninety nine *by me* Amb^{se} Uvedale [curate]. *In the Prefence of* Robert Mudd & Ann Cooper

(The Year 1800) Page 8

1800 25. Robert Mudd *of* [*this*] Parish Batchelor *and* Elizabeth Sutton Kemball *of* [*the*] Parish of Combs *were Married in this* [Church] *by* [Licence] *this* 30th *Day of* December *in the Year One Thousand* eight *Hundred by me* W C Uvedale [curate]. *In the Prefence of* Mary Mudd & Lucy Simpson

1801 26. Thomas Mudd *of* [*this*] Parish Batchelor *and* Lucy Simpson spinster *of* [*the*] same *were Married in this* [Church] *by* [Licence] *this* 27th *Day of* September *in the Year One Thousand* eight *Hundred and* one *by me* W C Uvedale [curate]. *In the Prefence of* John Simpson & Susanna Simpson

1802 27. Thomas Cooper *of* [*this*] Parish Batchelor & Elizabeth Plummer spinster *of* [*the*] Parish of Drinkston *were Married in this* [Church] *by* [Licence] *this* 11th *Day of* November *in the Year One Thousand* eight *Hundred and* two *by me* W C Uvedale [curate]. *In the Prefence of* Ann Cooper & Clark Cooper

1804 28. Richard Mudd of [this] Parish singleman and Ann Cooper of [the] same single woman were Married in this [Church] by [Licence] this 5th Day of June in the Year One Thousand eight Hundred and four by me Ambse Uvedale [curate]. In the Prefence of John Kemball, Mary Ann Mudd & Susan Mudd

(The Year 1804) Page 9

1804 29. Benjn Kerridge of [the] Parish of Bramford Batchelor and Matilda Sympson of [this] Parish spinster were Married in this [Church] by [Licence] this second Day of July in the Year One Thousand eight Hundred and four by me Ambse Uvedale [curate]. In the Prefence of T Pyman, Susanna Simpson & John Simpson

1804 30. James Welham of [the] Parish of Hawleigh Batchelor and Susanna Simpson of [this] parish spinster were Married in this [Church] by [Licence] this 7th Day of November in the Year One Thousand eight Hundred and four by me W C Uvedale [curate]. In the Prefence of Susan Welham, John Simpson & T Pyman

1806 31. Frederick Cock of [the] Parish of West Creeting & Elizabeth Neave singlewoman of [this] Parish were Married in this [Church] by [Banns] this 10th Day of July in the Year One Thousand eight Hundred and six by me W C Uvedale [curate]. In the Prefence of Joseph Haddock & Ann Eagle

1806 32. Samuel Deaves of [this] Parish singleman & Sarah Gladdel of [this] singlewoman were Married in this Church] by [Banns] this fourteenth Day of October in the Year One Thousand eight Hundred and six by me Wm Aldrich [Minister]. In the Prefence of John Gladdel (x) & Thos Southgate

(The Year 1808) Page 10

1808 33. Thomas Southgate of [the] Parish of Combs singleman and Susan Gladdell of [this] Parish spinster were Married in this [Church] by [Banns] this 26th Day of December in the Year One Thousand eight Hundred and eight by me W C Uvedale [curate]. In the Prefence of John Gladdell (x) & Thos Purkes (x)

1812 34. William Baker minor & Batchelor of [this] Parish and Susan Smith spinster of [this] Parish were Married in this [Church] by [Banns] with consent of parent, this 21st Day of June in the Year One Thousand eight Hundred and twelve by me James Wood [curate]. In the Prefence of Daniel Young (x) & Elizabeth Young (x)

Remainder of page blank & the records continue in new revised printed register

Page 1

MARRIAGES folemized in the Parifh of Badley in the County of Suffolk in the Year 1817

1817 1. Josuha Rodwell of the Parish of Alderton singleman and Sarah Moore of this Parifh single woman were married in this Church by Licence with Confent of Parents this sixth Day of August in the Year One thousand eight hundred and seventeen By me Wm Kirby Minister This Marriage was solemized between us - Josuha Rodwell/Sarah Bredell Moore In the Prefence of Sarah Moore, Frances Rodwell & A M Rodwell

1819 2. William Miller of the Parish of Battisford singleman and Elizabeth Simpson of this Parifh singlewoman were married in this Church by Licence with Confent of - this tenth Day of March in the Year One thousand eight hundred and nineteen By me James Wood Curate This Marriage was solemized between us - William Millerl/Elizabeth Simpson In the Prefence of Wm Mudd & Susan Kemball

1819 3. Samuel Youngs of this Parish a Batchelor and Sarah Garnham of this Parifh spinster were married in this Church by Banns with Confent of Parents this fifteenth Day of November in the Year One thousand eight hundred and nineteen By me Chrisr. Lawson Curate This Marriage was solemized between us - Samuel Youngs (x)/Sarah Garnham (x) In the Prefence of Daniel Youngs (x) & Mary Wright

Page 2

1819 4. William Mudd of this Parish widower and Anne Adams of the Parifh of Bedfield spinster were married in this Church by Licence with Confent of Parents this fifteenth Day of December in the Year One thousand eight hundred and nineteen By me Chrisr Lawson Curate This Marriage was solemized between us - William Mudd/Ann Adams In the Prefence of William Miller & Mary Ann Simpson

1820 5. Robert Berry of the Parish of Yaxley in this County batchelor and Rachel Archer of this Parifh spinster were married in this Church by Banns with Confent of Parents this seventeenth Day of March in the Year One thousand eight hundred and twenty By me Chrisr Lawson Curate This Marriage was solemized between us - Robert Berry/Rachel Archer In the Prefence of William Smith & Charlote Archer

1820 6. Daniel Young of this Parish a Batchelor and Mary Jeffrey of this Parifh spinster were married in this Church by Banns with Confent of Parents this twelfth Day of October in the Year One thousand eight hundred and twenty By me Chrisr. Lawson Curate This Marriage was solemized between us - Daniel Youngs (x)/Mary Jeffrey (x) In the Prefence of Jeremiah Jeffry (x), Martha Leader (x) & Elizabeth Jeffrey (x)

Page 3

1821 7. Joseph Raffe of this Parish singleman and Charlotte Archer of this Parifh single woman were married in this Church by Banns with Confent of - this twentieth Day of March in the Year One thousand eight hundred and twenty one By me Charles Davey Curate This Marriage was solemized between us - Joseph Raffe/Charlotte Archer In the Prefence of Thomas Archer (x) & Ann Archer

1825 8. John Archer of this Parish single man and Susan Abbott of this Parifh single woman were married in this Church by Banns with Confent of - this eleventh Day of November in the Year One thousand eight hundred and twenty five By me Charles Davy Perp Curate This Marriage was solemized between us - John Archer (x)/Susan Abbott (x) In the Prefence of Mary Archer (x), Thomas Archer (x) & John Southgate

1827 9. William Archer of this Parish single man and Elizabeth Gardiner* of the Parifh of Old Newton were married in this Church by Licence with Confent of Parents this seventh Day of September in the Year One thousand eight hundred and twenty seven By me Charles Davy Perp Curate This Marriage was solemized between us - William Archer)/Elizabeth Gardiner In the Prefence of Tho Archer (x), Mary Buckingham, Ann Archer & J Raffe *note in register - 'further licences spelt Gardner'

Page 4

1827 10. Henry Ellis Batchelor *of* the *Parish of* Creeting St Peter *and* Esther Kemball spinster *of* this *Parifh were married in this* Church *by* Licence *with Confent of* - *this* twenty eight *Day of* November *in the Year One thousand eight hundred and* twenty seven *By me* Charles Davy Perp Curate *This Marriage was solemized between us* - Henry Ellis/Esther Kemball *In the Prefence of* Charles Coe, Susan Coe & John Kemball

1828 11. John Knights widower *of* this *Parish and* Ann Brett single woman *of the Parifh of* Stowmarket *were married in this* Church *by* Banns *with Confent of* - *this* fifth *Day of* September *in the Year One thousand eight hundred and* twenty eight *By me* Charles Davy Perp Curate *This Marriage was solemized between us* - John Knight/Ann Brett (x) *In the Prefence of* Judith Tricker & William Tricker (x)

1828 12. Theodore Banyard *of the Parish of* Stowmarket single man *and* Ann Archer spinster *of* this *Parifh* single woman *were married in this* Church *by* Banns *with Confent of* - *this* twenty first *Day of* November *in the Year One thousand eight hundred and* twenty eight *By me* Charles Davy Perp Curate *This Marriage was solemized between us* - Theodore Banyard/Ann Archer *In the Prefence of* Louiza Dennis (x) & Robert Howlett

Page 5

1829 13. Elisha Groom *of the Parish of* Combs single man *and* Ann Rozier single woman *of* this *Parifh were married in this* Church *by* Banns *with Confent of* - *this* nineteenth *Day of* October *in the Year One thousand eight hundred and* twenty nine *By me* Charles Davy Perp Curate *This Marriage was solemized between us* - Elisha Groom (x)/Ann Rozier (x) *In the Prefence of* Kezia Rozier & John Southgate

1831 14. John Wilding *of the Parish of* Sproughton single man *and* Sarah James *of* this *Parifh* single woman *were married in this* Church *by* Banns *with Confent of* - *this* thirteenth *Day of* Septemb^r *in the Year One thousand eight hundred and* thirty one *By me* Charles Davy Perp Curate *This Marriage was solemized between us* - John Wilding/Sarah James (x) *In the Prefence of* Elizabeth James (x) & Jno List (x)

1831 15. John Jewers *of the Parish of* Drinkstone single man *and* Mary Lusher *of* this *Parifh* single woman *were married in this* Church *by* Licence *with Confent of* - *this* sixth *Day of* October *in the Year One thousand eight hundred and* thirty one *By me* Charles Davy Perp Curate *This Marriage was solemized between us* - John Jewers/Mary Lusher *In the Prefence of* Thos Scott, Robert Lusher & H Hunt

1834 16. James Archer *of* this *Parish* single man *and* Elizabeth Brett *of* this *Parifh* single woman *were married in this* Church *by* Banns *with Confent of* - *this* fourteentht *Day of* October *in the Year One thousand eight hundred and* thirty four *By me* Thos Nunn Off^g Mnst^r *This Marriage was solemized between us* - James Archer/Elizabeth Brett *In the Prefence of* Edward Brett & Susan Brett

No further entries

START OF NEW STYLE PRINTED REGISTER

(Landscape, two entries per page) (NB This register is not the original and appears to have been copied by a single hand. The Rank of Profession of the couple, their place of residence and their father's name, rank or profession, along with the name of the officiating minister, the signatures (or mark) of the couple and the names of the witnesses are all blank)

Page 1 - *Marriage solemnized at* the Parish Church *in the Parish of* Badley *in the* County of Suffolk

Page 1

| 1838 | 1. | 24th November | William James, Full Age, Singleman & | Harriott Hagger, Full Age, Single |
| 1839 | 2. | 12th December | George Hayward, Full Age, Single Man & | Elizabeth Mudd, Full Age, Single |

Page 2

| 1842 | 3. | 25th December | John Archer, Full Age, Widower & | Caroline Barrett, Full Age, Singlewoman |
| 1847 | 4. | 5th September | John Buckle, of Full Age, Batchelor & | Sarah Salter, of Full Age, Spinster |

Page 3

| 1847 | 5. | 12th December | Robert Manby, of Full Age, Batchelor & | Elizabeth Hill, Minor, Spinster |
| 1848 | 6. | 14th December | Robert Mumford, Full Age, Batchelor & | Ann Maria Mudd, Full Age, Spinster |

Page 4

| 1850 | 7. | 20th July | Joseph Buckle, Full Age, Single & | Harriet Copping, Full Age, Single |
| 1852 | 8. | 9th May | Samuel Copping, Full Age, Single & | Ann Theobald, Full Age, Single |

Page 5

| 1853 | 9. | 31st September | John Barker Johnson, Full Age, Widower & | Anne Maria Mumford, Full Age, Widow |
| 1855 | 10. | 29th May | John Wright, of Full Age Batchelor & | Mary Ann Bugg, 19, Spinster |

Page 6

| 1855 | 11. | 6th November | James Bugg, Full Age, Single & | Sarah Lambert, 19, Single |
| 1860 | 12. | 27th June | Frederick William Mudd, Full Age, Single & | Mary Smith Cooper, Full Age, Single |

Page 7

| 1865 | 13. | 21st July | Aaron Snowdon, Full, Single & | Sophia Palmer, Full, Single |
| 1865 | 14. | 8th November | Charles Parker, Full, Single & | Thunza Pretty, Full, Single |

Page 8

| 1866 | 15. | 4th November | William Bloomfield, Widower & | Caroline Archer, Widow |
| 1867 | 16. | 11th June | John Brame, 19, Single & | Mary Hitchcock, 17, Single |

Page 9

| 1867 | 17. | 27th November | William Martin, Single & | Matilda Lloyd, Single |
| 1867 | 18. | 25th December | Walter Eslea, 22, Single & | Amy Archer, 19, Single |

Page 10
| 1870 | 19. | 13th August | Frederick Doughty, Full, Widower & | Emily Kersey, Full, Spinster |
| 1873 | 20. | 24th September | Frederick Thomas Kent, Full, Batchelor & | Mary Anne Hayward, Full, Spinster |

Page 11
| 1877 | 21. | 25th October | Eliajar Buxton, of full age, Batchelor & | Mary Ann James, of full age, Spinster |
| 1889 | 22. | 10th September | Frederick Hammond, 21, Batchelor & | Ruth Boone, 26, Spinster |

Page 12
| 1892 | 23. | 17th December | John Copeland, 30, Batchelor & | Emma Elizabeth Emmerson, 24, Spinster |
| 1894 | 24. | 13th August | Henry James King, 22 Batchelor & | Harriet Matilda Southgate, 18, Spinster |

Page 13
| 1894 | 25. | 24th December | William Joseph Day, 22, Batchelor & | Kate Copeland, 23, Spinster |
| 1896 | 26. | 14th November | Arthur Sharman, 22, Batchelor & | Emma Brown, 25, Spinster |

Page 14
| 1897 | 27. | 17th November | Henry Hammond, 27, Batchelor & | Harriett Kate Mayhew, 27, Spinster |
| 1898 | 28. | 15th January | Herbert Wm Scopes Underwood, 46, Batchelor & | Charlotte Francis, 46, Widow |

Page 15
| 1899 | 29. | 26th April | John Freeman, 24, Batchelor & | Alice Hammond, 24, Spinster |
| 1899 | 30. | 13th August | James Palmer, 60, Widower & | Esther Andrews, 36, Spinster |

Page 16
| 1900 | 31. | 26th December | William Andrews, 39, Batchelor & | Jesse Emma Oxborrow, 27, Spinster |
| 1905 | 32. | 30th September | Horace Whiting, 24, Batchelor & | Sophia Mayhew, 29, Spinster |

Page 27
| 1909 | 33. | 7 July | Samuel Fulcher, 31, Batchelor & | Anna Hammond, 37, Spinster |
| 1914 | 34. | 6 November | George Lockwood, 22, Batchelor & | Jane Gertrude Meakings, 30, Spinster |

Page 28
| 1915 | 35. | 16 August | Henry Killick, 25, Batchelor & | Dulcie Selina Pooley, 24, Spinster |
| 1920 | 24. | March | Frederick William Lockwood, 23, Batchelor & | Lily Lockwood, 24, Spinster |

Page 29
| 1921 | 37. | 17 September | Bertie Albert Mayhew, 28, Batchelor & | Althea Ethel Ansell, 30, Widow |
| 1929 | 38. | 13 July | Reginald Kerridge, 21, Batchelor & | Ada Amelia Langent, 19, Spinster |

Page 30
| 1936 | 39. | 20 June | Leslie Howard Saunders, 28, Batchelor & | Ida Mary Haydon, 25, Spinster |
| 1942 | 40. | 12 September | Ernest Henry Rampley, 28, Batchelor & | Doris May Bugg, 23, Spinster |

Page 31
| 1945 | 41. | 10 November | Edward Amos Barber, 22, Batchelor & | Elizabeth Elinor Haydon, 21, Spinster |
| 1951 | 42. | 4 September | Frederick Charles S. Crockford, 32, Batchelor & | Peggy Doreen Smith, 26, Spinster |

Page 32
| 43 | | end of dummy register |

Book 2

Page 1
| 1954 | 1. | 11 September | Ronald Arthur Rampley, 26, Batchelor & | Margaret Joyce Canham, 18, Spinster |
| 1955 | 2. | 4 June | Barry Alan R. J. Firman, 21, Batchelor & | Jean Margaret Hadley, 21, Spinster |

Page 2
| 1967 | 3. | 23 September | David Whatling, 24, Batchelor & | Pauline Anne Steel, 20, Spinster |
| 1973 | 4. | 29 September | Timothy William Moore, 27, Batchelor & | Susan Frances Tweed, 29, Spinster |

Register Closed as Church was declared redundant on 28 Oct 1986

START OF BAPTIZSMS IN PRINTED BOOK

BAPTISMS folemized in the Parifh of Badley in the County of Suffolk in the Year 1813

Page 1
1813	1.Jany 24th	John son of	John & Sarah	Kemball	of Badley	husbandman	James Wood Curate
1814	2.March 6th	Harriett daughtr of	William & Susan	Baker	of Badley	labourer	James Wood Curate
1815	3.May 28th	Susanna daughtr of	James & Sarah	Buckle	of Badley	labourer	James Wood Curate
1815	4. Novr 5th	John son of	William & Susan	Baker	of Badley	labourer	J H Sisly (sic) Minister
1816	5.Octr 13	Elizabeth daughtr of	Elizabeth & Benjamin	Copping	of Badley	labourer	James Wood Curate

Year	No.	Date	Child	Parents	Surname	Abode	Occupation	Minister
1817	6.	June 8th	William son of	Mary & Robert	Abbott	of Badley	labourer	James Wood Curate
1817	7.	July 3rd	Thomas son of (Priv: bapt born March 13th 1817 rec. into church Sept 14th 1817)	James & Sarah	Buckle	of Badley	labourer	James Wood Curate
1817	8.	Sepr 25th	William son of (Priv: bapt. born Sepr 25th 1814 recd into Ch: Octr 12th 1817)	Shadrack & Martha	James	of Badley	labourer	James Wood Curate

Page 2

Year	No.	Date	Child	Parents	Surname	Abode	Occupation	Minister
1817	9.	Octr 12th	Shadrach son of (born Feb 1817)	Sharach & Martha	James	of Badley	labourer	James Wood Curate
1818	10.	April 19th	Charlotte daught of (born March 16th 1818)	Benjamin & Elizabeth	Copping	of Badley	labourer	James Wood Curate
1819	11.	Aug 22nd	Matilda daughtr of (Priv: bapt. born Augst 19th 1816 recd into Church Jany 12th 1819)	Thomas & Lucy	Mudd	of Badley	farmer	Rev Mr Ward of Haughley & James Wood Curate
1819	12.	Novbr 22nd	Lucy daughter of (Priv: bapt. born Novbr 19th 1818 rec into Church Jany 12th 1819)	Thomas & Lucy	Mudd	of Badley	farmer	James Wood Curate
1819	13.	Decbr 17th	James son of	James & Sarah	Buckle	of Badley	labourer	Chr Lawson Curate
1820	14.	Novbr 26th	Daniel son of	William & Matilda	Dalinger	of Badley	labourer	Charles Davy Curate
1821	15.	March 18th	Elizabeth daughtr of (born March 14th)	William & Ann	Mudd	of Badley	farmer	Charles Davy P. Curate
1821	16.	June 24th	Charlotte daughtr of	Joseph & Sarah	Baker	of Badley	labourer	Charles Davy P. Curate

Page 3

Year	No.	Date	Child	Parents	Surname	Abode	Occupation	Minister
1822	17.	July 17th	Caroline daughtr of (born June 28th)	William & Ann	Mudd	of Badley	yeoman	Charles Davy P. Curate
1823	18.	Jany 5th	John son of (born July 5th 1822)	James & Sarah	Buckle	of Badley	labourer	Charles Davy P. Curate
1824	19.	Febry 8th	William son of	Joseph & Sarah	Baker	of Badley	labourer	Charles Davy P. Curate
1824	20.	Febry 29th	Thomas Adams s. of	William & Ann	Mudd	of Badley	yeoman	Charles Davy P. Curate
1825	21.	Febry 9th	Joseph son of	James & Sarah	Buckle	of Badley	labourer	Charles Davy P. Curate
1825	22.	July 24	Meshack daughtr of	Shadrach & Martha	James	of Badley	labourer	C Davy Curate
1825	23.	July 24	Abednego son of	Shadrach & Martha	James	of Badley	labourer	C Davy Curate
1826	24.	Jany 22	William son of	William & Ann	Mudd	of Badley	yeoman	C Davy Curate

Page 4

Year	No.	Date	Child	Parents	Surname	Abode	Occupation	Minister
1826	25.	June 18th	Sarah Ann daughtr of	Joseph & Sarah	Baker	of Badley	labourer	Charles Davy P. Curate
1827	26.	April 15th	Ann Maria daughtr of	William & Ann	Mudd	of Badley	yeoman	Charles Davy P. Curate
1827	27.	Augst 26th	John son of	John & Susan	Archer	of Badley	labourer	Charles Davy P. Curate
1829	28.	Jany 9th	Esther Ann daughtr of (born August 16th 1827)	Henry & Esther	Ellis	of Badley	yeoman	Charles Davy P. Curate
1829	29.	April 5th	Susanna daughtr of	Joseph & Sarah	Baker	of Badley	labourer	Charles Davy P. Curate
1829	30.	May 24	Frederick Wm s. of	William & Ann	Mudd	of Badley	yeoman	Charles Davy P. Curate
1829	31.	Novbr 1st	Richard Gardener s. of (born Sept 21st 1813)	Edward & Sarah	Jay	of Badley	miller	Charles Davy P. Curate
1830	32.	May 2nd	James son of	Willm & Martha	Dalenger	of Badley	labourer	Charles Davy P. Curate

Page 5

Year	No.	Date	Child	Parents	Surname	Abode	Occupation	Minister
1830	33.	Augst 15th	Esther Ann daughtr of	Henry & Esther	Ellis	Coddenham	brewer	Robert Longe Off. Minister
1830	34.	Sept 19th	Anna Maria	John & Susanna	Archer	Badley	labourer	
1832	35.	April 29th	George	William & Martha	Dallenger	Badley	labourer	
1832	36.	Sept 16th	Emily	William & Ann	Mudd	Badley	farmer	
1833	37.	April 21st	Matilda	Joseph & Sarah	Baker	Badley	labourer	
1833	38.	July 17th	Caroline Sarah (Jan 20th 1831)	John & Caroline	Kemball	Badley	farmer	
1833	39.	July 17th	John Clarke (Sept 16th 1832)	John & Caroline	Kemball	Badley	farmer	
1833	40.	July 17th	Henry John Ellis	John & Caroline	Kemball	Badley	farmer	

Page 6

Year	No.	Date	Child	Parents	Surname	Abode	Occupation	Minister
1834	41.	Feb 16th	George	John & Sarah	Archer	Badley	labourer	
1835	42.	May 10th	Sarah	John & Caroline	Kemball	Badley	farmer	
1835	43.	Oct 4th	Ann (born Mar 13 1834)	John & Caroline	Kemball	Badley	farmer	
1835	44.	May 22nd	Mary Ann	Stephen & Mary Ann	Bugg	Badley	labourer	
1836	45.	July 24th	Anne	John & Anne	Choat	Badley	labourer	
1836	46.	July 24th	Maria	John & Anne	Choat	Badley	labourer	
1837	47.	Feb 26th	Susan brn. May 1836	John & Susan	Archer	Badley	labourer	
1837	48.	Feb 26th	Robert 9 1/2 years	Shadrach & Martha	James	Badley	labourer	

Page 7

Year	No.	Date	Child	Parents	Surname	Abode	Occupation	Minister
1837	49.	July 30th	Sophie	Charles Manley & Charlotte	Burcham	Badley	farmer	
1837	50.	Oct 5th	Mary Smith	Thomas Snell & Mary Ann	Cooper	Badley	farmer	

1837	51. Oct 21st	Robert	John & Susan	Archer	Badley	labourer	
1839	52 Feb 17th	Mary Anne	Thomas & Charlotte	Barrell	Badley	labourer	
1839	53. July 5th	Thomas Philip	Thomas Snell & Mary Ann	Cooper	Badley	farmer	
1841	54. Mar 9th	Frederick	George & Elizabeth	Hayward	Badley	farmer	
1841	55. Mar 9th	Elizabeth Hicks	Thomas Snell & Mary Ann	Cooper	Badley	farmer	
1843	56. Mar 5th	Elizabeth	Caroline	Barrell	Badley		
Page 8							
1843	57. Aug 9th	George	George & Elizabeth	Hayward	Badley	farmer	
1844	58. Jun 18th	Elizabeth	George & Elizabeth	Hayward	Badley	farmer	
1844	59. Aug 18th	Jane	John & Caroline	Archer	Badley	labourer	
1846	60. Aug 2nd	Hannah	Benjamin & Hanna	Hill	Badley	labourer	
1846	61. Aug 24th	Mary Ann	George & Elizabeth	Hayward	Badley	farmer	
1847	62. May 2nd	Susan 16 yrs old	John & Elizabeth	Gladwell	Barking	labourer	
1847	63. Aug 29th	Alfred base:born	Eliza	Copping	Badley	labourers daughter	
1847	64. Oct 24th	Frederick	Benjamin & Hannah	Hill	Badley	labourer	
Page 9							
1848	65. Nov 28th	William	George & Elizabeth	Hayward	Badley	farmer	
1851	66. Aug 24th	Amy	John & Caroline	Archer	Badley	labourer	
1852	67. April 23rd	Emily	George & Elizabeth	Hayward	Badley	farmer	
1852	68. April 23rd	Horace	George & Elizabeth	Hayward	Badley	farmer	
1853	69. June 12th	Eliza	John & Caroline	Archer	Badley	labourer	
1858	70. June 18th	Alice	George & Elizabeth	Hayward	Badley	farmer	
1858	71. June 18th	Caroline	George & Elizabeth	Hayward	Badley	farmer	
1858	72. June 18th	Thomas	George & Elizabeth	Hayward	Badley	farmer	
Page 10							
1859	73. April 10th	Catherine	George & Elizabeth	Hayward	Badley	farmer	
1859	74. June 12th	Robert	Meshach & Elizabeth	James	Badley	labourer	
1859	75. June 12th	Eliza Martha	Meshach & Elizabeth	James	Badley	labourer	
1859	76. June 12th	Elizabeth Maria	Meshach & Elizabeth	James	Badley	labourer	
1859	77. June 12th	Mary Ann	Meshach & Elizabeth	James	Badley	labourer	
1861	78. June 5th	Annie Elizabeth	Frederick Wm & Mary Smith	Mudd	Badley	farmer	
1861	79. June 13th	Clara	George & Elizabeth	Hayward	Badley	farmer	
1863	80. June 28th	John	Isaac & Jane	Copeland	Badley	labourer	
Page 11							
1863	81. July 10th	Mary	Frederick Wm & Mary Smith	Mudd	Badley	farmer	
1863	82. July 12th	Walter	Meshach & Elizabeth	James	Badley	labourer	
1863	83. July 12th	Eleanor Amelia	George & Lucy	James	Badley	labourer	
1863	84. July 12th	Alfred	Edward & Maria	James	Badley	bourer	
1863	85. July 12th	George Edward	Edward & Maria	James	Badley	labourer	
1863	86. July 12th	Anna Maria	Edward & Maria	James	Badley	labourer	
	87. & 88.	blank					
1864	89. Dec 25th	Harry	Isaac & Jane	Copeland	Badley	labourer	
	90. to 96.	blank					
1865	97. April 30th	Mary	George & Elizabeth	Mounts	Badley	labourer	
1865	98. April 30th	Emma	George & Elizabeth	Mounts	Badley	labourer	
1865	99. April 30th	William	George & Elizabeth	Mounts	Badley	labourer	
1865	100. Nov 8th	Clara	Frederick Wm & Mary Smith	Mudd	Badley	farmer	
1866	101. Dec 25th	Eliza	Isaac & Jane	Copeland	Badley	labourer	
	102 to 104	blank					
1867	105. Aug 25th	Eliza	William & Eliza	Bloomfield	Badley	labourer	
1867	106. Aug 25th	Anne	William & Eliza	Bloomfield	Badley	labourer	
1867	107. Aug 25th	Richard	William & Eliza	Bloomfield	Badley	labourer	
1867	108. Aug 25th	James	William & Eliza	Bloomfield	Badley	labourer	
1868	109. Feb 2nd	Wm Frederick	Frederick Wm & Mary Smith	Mudd	Badley	farmer	
1868	110. June 7th	Frederick	Abraham & Sarah	Hammond	Badley	labourer	
1868	111. Oct 11th	Emma	Isaac & Jane	Copeland	Badley	labourer	
1869	112. May 9th	Anna (adult)	Robert	Land	Badley	domestic servant	
1869	113. May 9th	George (adult)	George & Sarah	Berry	Badley	labourer	
1869	114. May 23rd	Anna Maria	George & Sarah	Berry	Badley	labourer	
1869	115. May 23rd	James	George & Sarah	Berry	Badley	labourer	
1869	116. may 23rd	Samual	George & Sarah	Berry	Badley	labourer	
1869	117. May 23rd	Tom ?	George & Sarah	Berry	Badley	labourer	
1869	118. May 23rd	Sarah	George & Sarah	Berry	Badley	labourer	
1870	119. May 8th	Henry	Abraham & Sarah	Hammond	Badley	labourer	
1870	120. July 3rd	Frank	Frederick Wm & Mary Smith	Mudd	Badley	farmer	
1871	121. June 11th	Kate	Isaac & Jane	Copeland	Badley	labourer	

Year	No.	Date	Name	Parents	Surname	Place	Occupation
1872	122.	April 28th	Anna	Abraham & Sarah	Hammond	Badley	labourer
1872	123.	May 26th	Herbert	George & Sarah	Berry	Badley	labourer
1873	124.	April 11th	Philip Hicks	Frederick Wm & Mary Smith	Mudd	Badley	farmer
1874	125.	July 29th	Mary Ann	Isaac & Jane	Copeland	Badley	labourer
1874	126.	Nov 24th	Alice	Abraham & Sarah	Hammond	Badley	labourer
1875	127.	Aug 15th (brn. Feb 2 1874)	Isobella Adams	Frederick Wm & Mary Smith	Mudd	Badley	farmer
1876	128.	May 28th (b. Apr 21 1873?)	Ellen Lambert Berry	Charles & Sarah	Lambert Berry	Creeting London	labourer domestic servant
1876	129.	May 28th	Eliza (b. Nov 8 1875)	Isaac & Jane	Copeland	Badley	labourer
1876	130	Nov 26th	Margaret Henrietta (b. Feb 1 1876)	Frederick Wm & Mary Smith	Mudd	Badley	farmer
1877	131.	April 29th	Sarah (b. Jan 2 1877)	Abraham & Sarah	Hammond	Badley	labourer
1878	132.	May 12th	Helen (b. Aug 25 1877)	Isaac & Jane	Copeland	Badley	labourer
1878	133.	June 23rd (b. Mar 11 1858)	Iefrie ? daughter	Robert & Mary	Brown	Isleworth Mdx	bootmaker
1879	134.	April 16th (brn. Mar 13 1879)	Caroline Theobolds	Frederick Wm & Mary Smith	Mudd	Badley	farmer
1879	135.	Oct 12th	William (b. Aug 17 1879)	Isaac & Jane	Copeland	Badley	labourer
1881	136.	April 17th	Alice (brn. Mar 4 1881)	Isaac & Jane	Copeland	Badley	labourer
1882	137.	June 4th	Arthur Laban	Laban & Charlotte	Southgate	Badley	farmer
1882	138.	June 4th	Thomas Charles	Isaac & Jane	Copeland	Badley	labourer
1882	139.	June 4th	Alfred Ernest	Alfred & Betsy	James	Badley	labourer
1882	140.	June 18th	Fanny	Edward & Maria	James	Needham	labourer
1882	141.	June 18th	Letitia	Edward & Maria	James	Badley	labourer
1882	142.	June 18th	Emma	George & Mary Ann	Scarff	Needham	gamekeeper
1882	143	Dec 24th	George William	William Thomas & Mary Ann	Fuller	Ipswich	merchant
1882	144.	Dec 24th	Maude Ellen	George & Caroline	Palmer	Badley	labourer
1882	145.	Dec 24th	Kate Rose	George & Caroline	Palmer	Badley	labourer
1884	146.	June 15th	Oliver? Frederick	Frederick & Emma	Robinson	Combs	labourer
1884	147.	Aug 3rd	Ellen	Isaac & Jane	Copeland	Badley	labourer
1884	148.	Nov 2nd	Thomas Decimus	Laban & Charlotte	Southgate	Badley	farmer
1884	149.	Nov 2nd	Edith Florence	Alfred & Betsy	James	Badley	labourer
1886	150.	July 4th	Jeremiah William	Walter & Rose	Rivers	Badley	labourer
1886	151.	July 4th	Walter Charles	Walter & Rose	Rivers	Badley	labourer
1887	152.	Aug 10th	Albert Victor	Laban & Charlotte	Southgate	Badley	farmer
1888	153.	April 12th	Alice Florence	Walter & Rose Anna	Rivers	Badley	labourer
1890	154.	Feb 2nd	Frederick Bertram	Frederick & Ruth	Hammond	Needham Mkt	labourer
1890	155.	June 29th	Martin (adult)	Martin & Sarah	Wright	Stowmarket	labourer
1890	156.	July 6th	Edward Stanley	Alfred & Betsy	James	Badley	labourer
1890	157.	Jul 6th	Robert Daniel	Alfred & Betsy	James	Badley	labourer
1890	158.	July 6th	Albert	Samuel & Sarah	Death	Badley	labourer
1890	159.	July 6th	Arthur	Samuel & Sarah	Death	Badley	labourer
1890	160.	Aug 17th	Clara Kathleen	Walter & Rose Anna	Rivers	Badley	labourer
1890	161.	Aug 17th	Charles William	Frederick William & Emily	Lockwood	Badley	labourer
1891	162.	Mar 1st	Muriel Gertrude	Frederick & Ruth	Hammond	Creeting St. Mary	labourer
1892	163.	June 19th	Amy Ellen	John & Mary Ann	Robinson	Badley	labourer
1892	164.	Jun 19th	George	Frederick William & Emily	Lockwood	Badley	labourer
1892	165.	July 3rd	Ebenezer Frank	Ebenezer George & Laura	Rose	Combs	soldier
1893	166.	Dec 17th	Dorothy Annie	John & Elizabeth	Copeland	Badley	labourer
1894	167.	June 17th	Percy James	Alice Mary	Southgate	Badley	single woman
	168.		error corrected as 169				
1895	169.	Feb 24th	Eva Matilda May	Henry James & Harriet Matilda	King	Elmswell	coal porter
1895	170.	March 17th	Edwin Archer	Alfred & Betsy	James	Badley	labourer
1895	171.	March 17th	Ella Marian	Frederick & Ruth	Hammond	Needham Mkt	labourer
1895	172.	April 6th	Dora Gladys	William & Ellen	Souter	Badley	labourer
1895	173.	June 30th	Rose Victoria May	Walter & Rose Hannah	Rivers	Badley	labourer
1896	174.	June 20th	Lilly	Frederick William & Emily	Lockwood	Badley	labourer
1897	175.	April 4th	Rose May	Arthur & Emma	Sharman	Badley	labourer
1899	176.	Aug 3rd	Louisa Violet	John & Mary	Mayhew	Badley	labourer
1899	177.	Oct 9th	Hilda Bessie	Arthur & Emma	Shaw	Badley	labourer
1899	178.	Oct 9th	Annie Jane	Sophia	Mayhew	Badley	single woman
1900	179.	May 6th	Frederick Spencer	Frederick William & Emily	Lockwood	Badley	labourer
1901	180.	June 19th	Annie	Thomas & Ellen	Kemp	Badley	labourer
1901	181.	June 9th	Charles Edward	Walter John & Mary Alice	Firman	Badley	labourer
1901	182.	July 24th	Elsie Mabel	John & Mary	Mayhew	Badley	labourer

Year	No.	Date	Forename(s)	Parents Forenames	Surname	Abode	Father Occupation
1902	183.	July 13th	Frederick William	Frederick William & Emily	Lockwood	Badley	labourer
1902	184.	July 13th	Gertrude Alice	William & Jessie Emma	Andrews	Badley	labourer
1902	185.	Aug 24th	Stanley William	Jane	Rose	Ipswich	not married
1904	186.	April 17th	Alfred William	John & Mary	Mayhew	Badley	labourer
1905	187.	July 9th	Cecil John	John & Mary	Mayhew	Badley	labourer
1906	188.	March 10th	William Raynor	William Edward & Emma	Firman	Badley	labourer
1907	189.	Dec 1st	Ruby Sybil	Edward & Emma	Firman	Badley	labourer
1907	190.	Dec 1st	Reginald Ray	Edward & Emma	Firman	Badley	labourer
1908	191.		Cyril Stanley	Charles & Florence	Firman	Badley	labourer
1908	192.		Charles William	William & Jessie	Andrews	Badley	labourer
1909	193.	July 15th	Isobel Alice Florence	Charles & Florence Elizabeth	Firman	Badley	labourer
1910	194.	Sept 10th	Edith Annie Edna	Charles & Florence Elizabeth	Firman	Badley	labourer
1912	195.	Aug 11th	Russell James	James & Annie	Mayhew	Badley	labourer
1912	196.	Aug 11th	Leonard Thomas	James & Annie	Mayhew	Badley	labourer

Year	No.	Date	Date Brn.	Forename(s)	Parents Forenames	Surname	Abode	Father Occupation
1912	197.	Aug 12th	Jul 20 1909	Dudley	William Edward & Emma	Firman	Badley	labourer
1912	198.	Oct 6th	Aug 20 1912	Russell George	Charles & Florence Eliz.	Firman	Badley	labourer
1913	199.	May 25th	Dec 14 1912	Albert Samuel	William & Jessie Emma	Andrews	Badley	labourer
1913	200.	May 25th	Apr 15 1912	Ivy May	William John & Annie	Hales	Badley	carter
1913	201.	Sep 21st	Aug 26 1913	Clifford	Edward William & Emma	Firman	Badley	labourer
1913	202.	Nov 2nd	Sept 27 1913	Percy Walter	Charles & Florence	Firman	Badley	labourer
1914	203.	June 28th	Jun 5 1914	Evellyne Maud	Willim John & Mary Ann	Hales	Badley	carter
1915	204.	Oct 17th	Jun 8 1915	Bertram John	Charles & Florence	Firman	Badley	labourer
1915	205.	Oct 17th	Aug 9 1915	Florence	George & Jane Gertrude	Lockwood	Badley	labourer
1918	206.	June 30th	May 20 1918	Florence	William Alfred & Agnes	Catchpole	Badley	labourer
1918	207.	Aug 11th	Jun 15 1918	Albert James	Mary Ann	Hales	Badley	----
1930	208.	June 8th	Feb 28 1930	David Charles	Charles William & Ellen May	Lockwood	Badley	horseman
1930	209.	June 15th	Apr 12 1930	Joyce Muriel	Reginald & Ada	Kerridge	Badley	lorry driver
1932	210.	Jul 24th	Jun 14 1932	Jean Margaret	Edwin Alfred & Evelyn	Burman	Badley	railway employee
1933	211.	May 21st	Mar 29 1933	Peter Alan	Charles William & Ellen May	Lockwood	Badley	horseman
1933	212.	May 21st	Jun 30 1930	Peggy June	William John & Clara	Neeve	Badley Hall	horseman
1935	213.	June 2nd	Apr 18 1935	Arthur William	Frederick William & Lily	Lockwood	Badley Green	horseman
1935	214.	June 9th	May 9 1935	Thomas Frank	Thomas & Agnes Ruth	Dobson	Badley	labourer
1936	215.	Sep 13th	Aug 3 1936	Dennis? George	Thomas & Agnes Ruth	Dobson	Badley	labourer
1938	216.	June 12th	Feb 11 1938	Maurice Royal	Royal Wm & Irene Florence	Sore	Badley	electric worker
1938	217.	Aug 25th	Sept 29 1937	Doreen Joyce	Thomas & Agnes Ruth	Dobson	Badley	labourer
1939	218.	Sep 17th	Jul 11 1939	Hazel Mary	Cecil George & Ruby Sybil	Hadley	Badley	motor driver
1939	219.	Sept 24th	Jun 25 1939	Raymond William	Royal Wm & Irene Florence	Sore	Badley	labourer
1943	220.	June 20th	May 12 1943	Margaret Gillian	Luis Andrew Charles & Vera Kathleen	Steel	Badley	tinsmith
1944	221.	July 9th	Feb 9 1944	Roger Gordon	Leslie Howard & Ida May	Saunders	Stowmarket	lands officer
1947	222.	July 27th	Feb 18 1947	Rosemary Heather	Cecil George & Ruby Sybil	Hadley	Badley	chemist
1947	223.	July 27th	May 29 1947	Geoffrey Graham	Royal Wm & Irene Florence	Sore	Badley	maintenance worker
1947	224.	July 27th	Jun 25 1947	Pauline Anne	Luis Andrew Charles & Vera Kathleen	Steel	Badley	tinsmith
1947	225.	Oct 5th	Sep 1 1947	Terence Allen	George Arthur & Beatrice	Proctor	Badley	ICI worker
1949	226.	May 15th	Dec 4 1948	Laraine	Ronald Arthur & Peggy	Brighty	Needham Mkt	commercial traveller
1950	227.	May 28th	Dec 25 1949	Frederick Arthur	Edwin & Eunice Vera	Hollis	Green Fm Cott.	farmer
1950	228.	June 11th	Dec 25 1949	Brian John	John Douglas & Beryl Aggiss	Haydon	Doveshill	farmer
1952	229.	March 23rd	Jan 10 1952	Valerie Eileen	Charles Ian & Eileen Winifred	Morton	Woodlands	farmer
1953	230.	June 21st	Oct 27 1952	Philip	Claude & Bertha Kathleen	Hayward	Badley Green	electrician
1955	231.	Oct	Aug 5 1955	Eric Charles	Charles Ian & Eileen Winifred	Morton	Woodlands	farmer
1956	232.	April 6th	Dec 10 1955	Martin Christopher	Thouroud O'Bryan & Eliz. Yvonne	Horsford	Bridge Farm	farmer
1957	233.	Aug 11th		Andrew	Claude & Bertha Kathleen	Hayward	Harleston Grn	electrician
1959	234.	Aug 16th		Veronica Carol	Royal Wm & Irene Florence	Sore	Badley	chargehand
1963	235.	Sep 23rd		Philip William	Peter John & Margaret Rose	Mayhew	New Cottages	
1964	236.	Sep 6th	Jun 13 1964	Jeus Henrick	John & Kirsten Jugeborg	Christensen	Green Farm	farmer
1964	237.	Sep 6th	Jul 19 1964	Penelope Heather	Donald & Barbara Jenifer	Black	6 Uvedale Gdns NM.	journalist
1965	238.	June 13th	Apr 13 1965	Jeremy	Maurice Royal & Cynthia Joan	Sore	29 St Mary's Gdns.	service rep.
1966	239.	May 22nd	Sep 1 1964	Tracey Ann	David John & Josephine Ann	Stone	5 Coronation Glebe	
1966	240.	May 22nd	Oct 22 1965	Julie	David John & Josephine Ann	Stone	Ringshall	motor engineer
1969	241.	Sep 14th	Apr 3 1969	Richard David	David & Hazel Jennifer	Hughes	7 Freehold Rd.	oxygen tester
1969	242.	Oct 26th	Sept 21 1969	Richard	Maurice Royal & Cynthia Joan	Sore	82/84 High St. NM.	carpenter
1970	243.	Oct 18th	Aug 6 1970	Darin John	John Ronald & Rosemary Heather	Garnham	3 Badley Walk,	digger driver
1971	244.	Sep 12th	May 23 1971	Joanne	David & Pauline Anne	Whatling	19 Woolmers Cl.	local gov. officer
1971	245.	Sept 12th	Jul 6 1971	Nicola Jane	David & Hazel Jennifer	Hughes	7 Freehold Rd.	lorry driver
1976	246.	July 18th		Simon Charles	David & Hazel Jennifer	Hughes	7 Foxglove NM.	lorry driver
1990	247.	March 11th	21 Sep 1989	Ryan George	Colin Russell & Sherry	Moss	4 Badley Walk	engineer
1992	248.	31 May 31st	4 Feb 1992	Megan Hannah	Colin Russell & Sherry	Moss	4 Badley Walk	welder

PRINTED BURIALS REGISTER

BURIALS in the Parish of Badley *in the County of* Suffolk *in the Year* 1815

Page 1

1815	1.	Sept 26th	Mary Ann Mudd	of Badley	age 31 yrs	James Wood Curate
1817	2.	Jany 23rd	John Gladwell	of Badley	age 28 yrs	James Wood Curate
1817	3.	Febry 14th	Robert Mudd	of Badley	age 37 yrs	James Wood Curate
1817	4.	Febry 15th	William Simpson	of Badley	age 41 yrs	James Wood Curate
1817	5.	August 24th	Mary Gladwell	of Badley	age 76 yrs	James Wood Curate
1817	6.	October 3rd	Elizabeth Mudd	of Badley	age 60 yrs	James Wood Curate
1818	7.	August 17th	George Abbot	of Badley	age 6 yrs	James Wood Curate
1820	8.	Febry 12th	Sarah Chandler	of StowMarket	age 84 yrs	Cr Lawson Curate

Page 2

1820	9.	Febry 27th	Mary Cooper	of Needham Mkt	age 52 yrs	
1820	10.	August 14th	Esther Cooper	of Badley	age 78 yrs	
1821	11.	June 10th	Charlotte Baker	of Badley	age 22 yrs	
1822	12.	July 12th	Edward Jay	of Badley	age 56 yrs	
1825	13.	March 4th	Martha Amy Woodward	of Needham Mkt	age 19 mo	
1825	14.	March 1st	Mary Pyman (Woodward)	of Needham Mkt	age 55 yrs	
1825	15.	August 3rd	Caroline Mudd	of Badley	age 3 yrs	
1826	16.	Febry 12th	Abednigo James	of Badley	age 8 mo	

Page 3

1827	17.	April 27th	Clark Cooper	of Badley	age 90 yrs	Charles Davey Perpetual Curate
1830	18.	Jany 1st	Daniel Youngs	of Badley	age 56 yrs	Charles Davey Perpetual Curate
1831	19.	May 27th	Ann Tokelove Jay	of Badley	age 25 yrs	Charles Davey Perpetual Curate
1831	20.	June 21st	James Moore, Gent.	of Badley	age 66 yrs	Charles Davey Perpetual Curate
1831	21.	Sept 14th	John Simpson	of Cotton	age 23 yrs	Charles Davey Perpetual Curate
1831	22.	Octbr 30th	Anne Abbott	of Badley	age 78 yrs	Wm Roberts Officiating Minister
1832	23.	July 11th	Elizabeth Roper	of Cotton	age 52 yrs	Robert Longe Officiating Minister
1832	24.	Novbr 28th	John Kembal	of Badley	age 52 yrs	Charles Davey Perpetual Curate

Page 4

1833	25.	Augst 15th	Elizabeth James	of Badley	age 25 yrs	Charles Davey Perpetual Curate
1833	26.	Octbr 11th	Sarah Moore	of Badley	age 77 yrs	Robert Longe Curate
1834	27.	March 21st	Richard Mudd	of Aldham	age 51 yrs	Charles Davey Perpetual Curate
1834	28.	June 8th	Matilda Baker	of Badley	age 2 yrs	Charles Davey Perpetual Curate
1834	29.	Novbr 20th	Susanna Baker	of Badley	age 5 yrs	Charles Davey Perpetual Curate
1835	30.	June 2nd	Sarah Kemball	of Badley	age 5 wks	G A Paske Officiating Minister
1836	31.	June 26th	James Dallinger	of Badley	age 6 yrs	G A Paske Officiating Minister
1836	32.	Novbr 17th	Mary Ann Simpson	of Bedfield	age 36 yrs	Edwd Paske Officiating Minister

Page 5

1837/8	33.	Febry 5th	Ann Gladwell	of Combs	age 74 yrs	Charles Rawlins Officiating Minister
1839	34.	Jany 20th	Sarah Baker	of Combs	age 43 yrs	C Hill PC
1839	35.	June 13th	Mary Baker	of Badley	age 84 yrs	C Hill PC
1840	36.	Decbr 11th	Thomas Pyman	of Needham	age 70 yrs	Edwd Paske Officiating Minister
1841	37.	Febry 26th	Amy Archer	of Badley	infant	C Hill PC
1841	38.	March 14th	Susan Archer	of Badley	age 33 yrs	C Hill PC
1841	39.	Novbr 8th	Frederick Hayward	of Badley	infant	C Hill PC
1842	40.	May 8th	James Gladwell	of Combs	age 72 yrs	C Hill PC

Page 6

1842	41.	May 13th	Elizabeth Hill?	of Badley	age 63 yrs	C Hill PC
1842	42.	June 14th	John Choet	of Badley	age 33 yrs	C Hill PC
1842	43.	July 12th	Edwd Cooper	of Needham	age 72 yrs	Edwd Paske Officiating Minister
1842	44.	Augst 23rd	Ann Mudd	of Darmsden	age 60 yrs	Charles Green Officiating Minister
1843	45.	May 16th	Sarah Ann Baker	of Badley	age 16 yrs	J M Pyke Officiating Minister
1843	46.	Jun 10th	Thomas Barrell	of Badley	age 7 yrs	C Hill Perp: Cur:
1843	47.	July 2nd	Mary Ann Barrell	of Badley	age 4 yrs	C Hill Perp: Cur:
1845	48.	Novbr 7th	John Choet	of Badley	age 78 yrs	J M Pyke Officiating Minister

Page 7

1847	49.	August 22nd	William Copping	of Badley	age 24 yrs	Frederich Wm Freeman Curate
1848	50.	June 13th	Alfred Copping	of Badley	age 1yr 9 mo	Frederich Wm Freeman Curate
1850	51.	Augst 9th	William Cuffer Mudd	of Badley	age 8 mo	Copinger Hill Perp. Curate
1850	52.	Sept 28th	Robert Mumford	of Combs	age 41 yrs	Copinger Hill Perp. Curate

1857	53.	Febry 19th	Sarah Jay	of Badley	age 74	Copinger Hill
1853	54.	June 26th	Eliza Archer	of Badley	age 11 wks	Copinger Hill Perp. Cur:
1855	55.	April 21st	James Medows Moore	of Darmsden	age 62 yrs	Copinger Hill Perp. Cur:
1856	56.	March 17th	William Hayward	of Badley	age 7 yrs	J M Pyke

Page 8

1856	57.	July 5th	John Mudd	of Chevington	age 48 yrs	G A Paske Officiating Minister
1856	58.	Sept 28th	Benjamin Coppin	of Badley	age 62 yrs	C Hill Per: Cur:
1857	59.	Febry 13th	William Mudd	of Badley	age 68 yrs	C Hill Per: Cur:
1857	60.	April 15th	George James	of Badley	age 2yr 8 mo	Henry Eaton Officiating Minister
1858	61.	March 7th	Elizabeth Copping	of Needham	age 78 yrs	William Tipton Officiating Minister
1858	62.	August 1st	Mary Abbott	of Needham	age 78 yrs	C Hill Perp Cur:
1858	63.	Sept 17th	John Archer	of Badley	age 54 yrs	C Hill Perp Cur:
1859	64.	May 16th	Ellen Mather	of Badley	age 57 yrs	Thos Da(u)nn Officiating Minister

Page 9

1863	65.	Sept 2nd	Elizabeth Blomfield	of Badley	age 47 yrs	Copinger Hill
1864	66.	Jany 23rd	Henry Mounts	of Badley	infant	Copinger Hill
1864	67.	July 31st	Shadrach James	of Badley	age 90 yrs	James Brown Officiating Minister
1864	68.	Augst 15th	Ann Mudd	of Badley	age 75 yrs	J M Pryke Officiating Minister
1865	69.	April 20th	Elizabeth Hicks Manistre	Creeting St Mary	age 24 yrs	Copinger Hill
1866	70.	March 14th	Clara Mudd	of Badley	infant	Copinger Hill
1866	71.	March 25th	William Dallinger	of Badley	age 80 yrs	Copinger Hill
1866	72.	April 14th	Henrietta Moore	of Badley	age 77 yrs	Copinger Hill

Page 10

1867	73.	Decbr 3rd	Elizabeth Mary Manistre	Creeting St Mary	age 2½ yrs	Henry Hill Officiating Minister
1868	74.	May 10th	Eliza Copeland	of Badley	age 1 yr 8 mo	Copinger Hill Pl. Cur.
1869	75.	Augst 4th	Thomas Snell Cooper	of Badley	age 62 yrs	Copinger Hill Vicar
1870	76.	May 6th	Robert Copeland	of Badley	age 8 yrs	John R Heawood Officiating Minister
1871	77.	April 2nd	James Berry	of Badley	age 8 yrs	John R Heawood Vicar
1874	78.	June 30th	Isaac Welham	of Badley	age 25 yrs	Wm M Townsend Officiating Minister
1874	79.	Sept 27th	Susan Parker	of Badley	age 68 yrs	A P Davies Officiating Minister
1876	80.	Jany 30th	Robert James	of Badley	age 19 yrs	H J Curry

Page 11

1876	81.	Febry 23rd	Mary Snell Cooper	of Badley	age 63 yrs	W L Eliot Officiating Minister
1877	82.	March 8th	Elizabeth Crisp	of Badley	age 83 yrs	H J Curry
1879	83.	August 21st	Benjamin Hill	of Needham	age 80 yrs	H J Curry
1879	84.	August 27th	Martha James	of Badley	age 95 yrs	H J Curry
1881	85.	April 3rd	Alice Copeland	of Badley	age 7 wks	H J Curry
1881	86.	Decbr 31st	Sarah Hammond[1]	of Badley	age 4 yrs	H J Curry
1882	87.	Jany 17th	Helena Copeland	of Badley	age 4 yrs	H J Curry
1882	88.	August 30th	George Berry	of Badley	age 52 yrs	H J Curry

Page 12

1884	89.	Jany 26th	Caroline Bloomfield	of Badley	age 62 yrs	Wm Baillee Hamilton R. of Combs
1884	90.	Decbr 27	Samual Parker	of Needham	age 77 yrs	Francis John Wright Girling Curate
1885	91.	Novbr 4th	John Kirby Moore	of Badley	age 91 yrs	Willam Baillie Hamilton Vicar
1886	92.	Augst 4th	Walter Charles Rivers	of Badley	age 3 mo	Francis John Wright Girling Curate
1888	93.	Augst 21st	Edith Ellen Souter	of Badley	age 23 mo	Arthur Baillie Hamilton Vicar
1889	94.	April 25th	Alice Florence Rivers	of Badley	age 13 mo	Francis John Wright Girling Curate
1890	95.	May 21st	Martha Dallinger	of Badley	age 89 yrs	Francis John Wright Girling Curate
1891	96.	Jany 9th	Emily Robinson	of Badley	age 14 yrs	Francis John Wright Girling Curate

Page 13

1891	97.	June 8th	Edward Stanley James	of Badley	age 13 mo	Francis John Wright Girling MA Curate
1893	98.	June 1st	Alfred Jacob Cooper	of Stowmarket	age 69 yrs	Francis John Wright Girling MA Curate
1897	99.	March 18th	Emily Cooper	of Needham	age 65 yrs	W J Knighton Vicar
1897	100.	May 30th	Robert Daniel James?	of Badley	age 7 yrs	W J Knighton Vicar
1897	101.	Novbr 8th	Susan Palmer	of Badley	age 72 yrs	C E Lowe Rector of Combs
1898	102.	March 12th	William Bloomfield	of Badley	age 75 yrs	W J Knighton Vicar
1898	103.	Novbr 14th	Sarah Death	of Badley	age 61 yrs	C E Lowe Rector of Combs
1900	104.	June 14th	Fredk Spencer Lockwood	of Badley	age 3 mo	W J Knighton Vicar

Page 14

1901	105.	Augst 8th	Emily Pennington	of Needham	age 71 yrs	
1902	106.	June 25th	Mary Jane Pennington	of Needham	age 77 yrs	

---

[1]Sarah Hammond, daughter of Abraham, a horseman, aged 4, died accidently as a result of swallowing a stud at Badley on 27th December 1881

1902	107.	Augst 21st	Elsie Mabel Mayhew	of Badley	age 7 yrs
1911	108.	May 16th	Unknown	unknown	age about 35 yrs
1917	109.	Jany 5th	Sarah Tydeman Hammond	of Badley	age 80 yrs
1917	110.	Jany 26th	Abraham Hammond	of Badley	age 82 yrs
1927	111.	April 14th	George Francis Webb	of The Green Badley	age 37 yrs
1928	112.	Sept 6th	Ellen Birch	of Badley Hall	age 66 yrs

Page 15

1934	113.	Octbr 15th	Russell Wm Lockwood	of Badley	age 12 mo
1938	114.	May 25th	Emily Lockwood	of Badley	age 74 yrs
1943	115.	June 13th	Francis Gordon Haydon	of Badley (RAF)	age 31 yrs
1944	116.	August 9th	Emma Elizabeth Hammond	of Doves Hill Badley	age 83 yrs
1945	117.	May 8th	Francis Emmanuel Haydon	of Doveshill Farm	age 65 yrs
1947	118.	Jany 29th	William Woods	of 6 Bungalows Badley	age 80 yrs
1947	119.	Novbr 13th	Frederick Hollis	of Green Fm Badley	age 64 yrs
1948	120.	April 29th	Charles Morton	of Woodlands Farm Badley	age 73 yrs

Page 16

1950	121.	Novbr 13th	Frederick Wm Lockwood	of Green Cottage	age 83 yrs
1952	122.	August 19th	Mary Ann Foster	of Substation Badley	age 87 yrs
1967	123.	Novbr 28th	Emily Frances Scott	of Badley Hall	age 82 yrs
1968	124.	Octbr 9th	Leonard Scott	of Badley Hall	age 86 yrs
1968	125.	Octbr 31st	Charles Spencer Farrow	of Doves Hill Farm	age 58 yrs
1969	126.	March 7th	Dorothy Scott	of Badley Hall	age 57 yrs
1969	127.	Sept 23rd	Nellie Annie Mary Hadley	of Bungalows	age 79 yrs
1972	128.	Sept 26th	Eva Violet Mary Freshwater	of 15 Shrimpling Close Combs	age 79 yrs

Page 17

1975	129.	Octbr 31st	Edith Emma Hammond (ashes)	of Great Ashfield	age 87 yrs
1977	130.	April 9th	George Edward Hadley	of Badley Walk	age 87 yrs
1977	131.	Novbr 15th	Janet Dawson (ashes)	of Murray Rd Ipswich	age 85 yrs
1979	132.	June 6th	Royal William Sore	of Badley Walk	age 67 yrs
1981	133.	August 3rd	Carrie Louise Haydon (ashes)	of Great Horkesley	age 97 yrs
1982	134.	Febry 19th	Frances Hodgson	of 12 Brook St. Heage Derby	age 67 yrs
1982	135.	August 6th	Vera Kathleen Steel	of 5 Badley Walk	age 66 yrs
1987	136.	Decbr 18th	Ethel Mabel Wood	of Doveshill Cottage	age 94 yrs

Page 18

1989	137.	Jany 17th	Florence Lilian Key	of 11 Shrimpling Close, Combs	age 91 yrs
1989	138.	August 31st	Dorothy Watkins	of Thropton Cott Lt London	age 87 yrs
1989	139.	Decbr 20th	Luis Andrew Steel	of 5 Badley Walk	age 82 yrs
1991	140.	Decbr 30th	Andrew Hodgson (priest)	10 Brook St. Heage Derby	age 78 yrs
1992	141.	Octbr 9th	Cecil George Hadley	3 Badley Walk	age 81 yrs
1993	142.	May 20th	Richard Charles Farrow	Doveshill Farm	age 46 yrs
1997	143.	Sept 1st	Irene Florence Sore	Chilton Meadows, Stowmarket	age 78 yrs
1997	144.	Sept 4th	Arthur Blake Scott	Badley Hall	age 80 yrs

PRINTED BANNS OF MARRIAGE BOOK

(The Year 1754) (Page 1)

1. *Banns of marriages between* John Elsing of the Parish of Combs in ye County of Suffolk Wid. *and* Elizabeth Squirrel of this Parish Spinster *were publifhed on the three Sundays underwritten :* That is to fay, *On Sunday, the* 15th *of Sept* 1754 *by me* Saml. Uvedale Curate *On Sunday, the* 22nd *of Sept* 1754 *by me* Saml. Uvedale Curate *On Sunday, the* 29th *of Sept* 1754 *by me* Saml. Uvedale Curate

1755

2. *Banns of marriages between* Saml Baker of the Parish of Creeting St Mary in ye County of Suffolk Single man *and* Elizabeth Day of this Parish of Badley Spinster *were publifhed on the three Sundays underwritten :* That is to fay, *On Sunday, the* 28th *of Sept* 1755 *by me* Saml. Uvedale Curate *On Sunday, the* 5th *of Sept* 1755 *by me* Saml. Uvedale Curate *On Sunday, the* 12th *of Sept* 1755 *by me* Saml. Uvedale Curate

1756

3. *Banns of marriages between* Willm Cutbert of this Parish of Badley in the County of Suffolk Widower *and* Elizabeth Elizabeth Rands of the same Spinster *were publifhed on the three Sundays underwritten :* That is to fay, *On Sunday, the* 19th *of Sept* 1756 *by me* Saml. Uvedale Curate *On Sunday, the* 26th *of Sept* 1756 *by me* Saml. Uvedale Curate *On Sunday, the* 3rd *of Oct* 1756 *by me* Saml. Uvedale Curate

1758

4. *Banns of marriages between* Benjamin Felgate of this Parish Single man *and* Sarah Fryatt of the Parish of Swilland in ye County of Suffolk Spinster *were publifhed on the three Sundays underwritten :* That is to fay, *On Sunday, the* 9th *of April* 1758 *by me* Saml. Uvedale Curate *On Sunday, the* 16th *of April* 1758 *by me* Saml. Uvedale Curate *On Sunday, the* 23rd *of April* 1758 *by me* Saml. Uvedale Curate

(The Year 1797)   **Page**

Banns of Marriage between *James Stokes of the parish Batchelor* and *Hannah How spinster of the parish of Old Newton* were publifhed on the three Sundays underwritten :

That is to fay, On Sunday, the *10*   *Sept by W C Uvedale Curate*
On Sunday, the *17*   *Sept by A Uvedale Curate*
On Sunday, the *24*   *by W C Uvedale Curate*

1790

Banns of Marriage between *William Gladwin of the parish Batchelor* and *Sarah Pollard spinster of the parish of Buxhall* were publifhed on the three Sundays underwritten :

That is to fay, On Sunday, the *4*
On Sunday, the *11*   *Nov by W C Uvedale Curate*
On Sunday, the *18*

Fig A An extract from the top of Page 3 of the printed Badley Banns Register.

5. Banns of marriages between Samuel Harris single man *and* Ann Francis spinster, both of this Parish *were publifhed on the three Sundays underwritten :* That is to fay, On Sunday, the 26th ofApril 1758by me James Sherwood   On Sunday, the 3rd of May 1758 by me James Sherwood   On Sunday, the 10th of May 1758 by me James Sherwood

The Year 1770) (Page 2)

6. Banns of marriages between Stephen Nunn of y[e] Parish of Combs *and* Susan Harvey of this Parish *were publifhed on the three Sundays underwritten :* That is to fay, On Sunday, the 22nd of July 1770 by me Saml. Uvedale Curate   On Sunday, the 29th of July 1770 by me Saml. Uvedale Curate   On Sunday, the 5rd of Aug 1770 by me Saml. Uvedale Curate

7. Banns of marriages between John Lambert of this Parish Singleman *and* Sarah Peck singlewoman of the same *were publifhed on the three Sundays underwritten :* That is to fay, On Sunday, the eleventh Day of Sept 1774   On Sunday, the eighteenth Day of Sept 1774   On Sunday, the second of October 1774

8. Banns of marriages between James Ellis of this Parish Single man *and* Sarah Rose of this Parish Single woman *were publifhed on the three Sundays underwritten :* That is to fay, On Sunday, the 22nd of February 1778 by me Thos Naylor Curate   On Sunday, the 1st of March 1778   On Sunday, the 8th of March 1778 by me Thos Naylor Curate

9. Banns of marriages between Stephen Bumpstead of this Parish Batchelor *and* Mary Brett *were publifhed on the three Sundays underwritten :* That is to fay, On Sunday, the Sept[r] the 19 by Thos Naylor Curate   On Sunday, the Sept[r] the 26th by A Uvedale Curate   On Sunday, the 3rd of Octo[r] 1758 by Thos Naylor Curate

10. Banns of marriages between Thos Dallinger of this Parish Batchelor *and* Mary Banyard of the Parish of Creeting All Saints *were publifhed on the three Sundays underwritten :* That is to fay, On Sunday, the 7th of Sept[r] 1758 by me A Uvedale   On Sunday, the 14th of Sept[r] 1758 by me W[m] Uvedale Curate   On Sunday, the 21st of Sept[r] 1758 by me A Uvedale

(The Year 1797) (Page 3)

11. Banns of marriages between James Stokes of this Parish Batchelor *and* Hannah How spinster of the Parish of Old Newton *were publifhed on the three Sundays underwritten :* That is to fay, On Sunday, the 10th of Sept[r] 1797 by W C Uvedale Curate   On Sunday, the 17th of Sept[r] 1797 by A Uvedale Curate   On Sunday, the 24th of Sept[r] 1797 by W C Uvedale Curate

1798
12. Banns of marriages between William Gladwin of this Parish Batchelor *and* Sarah Pollard spinster of the Parish of Buxhall *were publifhed on the three Sundays underwritten :* That is to fay, On Sunday, the 4 of Nov 1798 by W C Uvedale Curate   On Sunday, the 11 of Nov 1798 by W C Uvedale Curate   On Sunday, the 18 of Nov 1798 by W C Uvedale Curate

1800

13. *Banns of marriages between* Richard Andrews single man of this parish *and* Sarah Pyman spinster of Stowupland *were publifhed on the three Sundays underwritten :* That is to fay, On Sunday, the 7 Septr 1800 W C Uvedale Curate   On Sunday, the 14 Septr 1800 W C Uvedale Curate   On Sunday, the 21 Septr 1800 W C Uvedale Curate

14. *Banns of marriages between* Isaac Stevens of this parish Batchelor of *and* Elizabeth Baskett spinster of the Parish of Creeting All Saints *were publifhed on the three Sundays underwritten :* That is to fay, On Sunday, the 21 Septr 1800 by W C Uvedale Curate   On Sunday, the 28 Septr 1800 by W C Uvedale Curate   On Sunday, the 5th October 1800 by W C Uvedale Curate

1805

15. *Banns of marriages between* James Hill singleman of this Parish *and* Elizabeth Brown spinster of the Parish of Coddenham *were publifhed on the three Sundays underwritten :* That is to fay, On Sunday, the 12 May 1805 by C Davy Curate   On Sunday, the 19 May 1805 by Amb^se Uvedale Curate   On Sunday, the 26 May 1805 by Amb^se Uvedale Curate

(The Year 1806) (Page 4)

16. *Banns of marriages between* Frederick Cock singleman of this parish *and* Elizabeth Neave single woman of the Parish of West Creeting *were publifhed on the three Sundays underwritten :* That is to fay, On Sunday, the 22nd June 1806 W C Uvedale Curate   On Sunday, the 19th June 1806 W C Uvedale Curate   On Sunday, the 6rd July 1806 W C Uvedale Curate

17. *Banns of marriages between* Samuel Deaves of this Parish single man *and* Sarah Gladdel Spinster of this Parish *were publifhed on the three Sundays underwritten :* That is to fay, On Sunday, the 21st of Septr 1806 by me William Taylor Minister   On Sunday, the 28th of Septr 1806 by me William Taylor Minister   On Sunday, the 5th of Octb^r 1806 by me William Taylor Minister

The Year 1807

18. *Banns of marriages between* Thomas Garrard singleman of the parish of Barking *and* Mary Randle single woman of this Parish *were publifhed on the three Sundays underwritten :* That is to fay, On Sunday, the 15th June 1807 by me Robt? Marriott Curate   On Sunday, the 22nd June 1807 by me Robt Marriott Curate   On Sunday, the 29th July 1807 by me Robt ? Marriott Curate

The Year 1808

19. *Banns of marriages between* Thomas Southgate of the parish of Combs *and* Susan Gladdell spinster of this Parish *were publifhed on the three Sundays underwritten :* That is to fay, On Sunday, the 11th Dec 1808 by me Robt? Marriott Curate   On Sunday, the 18th Dec 1808 by me Robt? Marriott Curate   On Sunday, the 25th Dec 1808 by me Robt? Marriott Curate

The Years 1812

20. *Banns of marriages between* William Baker of this Parish Batchelor *and* Susan Smith Spinster of the same *were publifhed on the three Sundays underwritten :* That is to fay, On Sunday, the 31st of May^r 1812 by me James Wood Curate   On Sunday, the 7 of June^r 1812 by me James Wood Curate   On Sunday, the 14 of June 1812 by me James Wood Curate

(The Year 1812) (Page 4)

21. *Banns of marriages between* Richard Jackman Batchelor of this Parish *and* Mary Harvey of the Parish of Combs Spinster *were publifhed on the three Sundays underwritten :* That is to fay, On Sunday, the 4th of October 1812 by me James Wood Curate   On Sunday, the 11th of October 1812 by me James Wood Curate   On Sunday, the 18th of October 1812 by me James Wood Curate

NO FURTHER ENTRIES IN REGISTER

SUDDEN DEATHS

Although Inquests were held into the two following sudden deaths at Badley, the persons concerned were evidently buried elsewhere:

Samuel Death, farm labourer, aged 45 years, accidently killed as a result of falling from a waggon at Badley on 4th August 1882

Joseph Wardle, an erector, aged 44 years, accidently killed as a result of injuries sustained by being struck by a railway engine at Badley on 16th March 1885

Appendix B

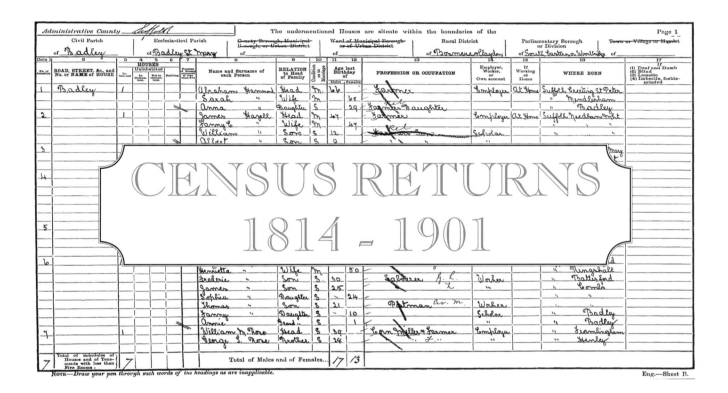

No. of Schedule	ROAD, STREET, &c. and No. or NAME of HOUSE	HOUSES			Number...	Name and Surname of each Person	RELATION to Head of Family	Condition as to Marriage	Age last Birthday		PROFESSION OR OCCUPATION	Employer, Worker, or Own account	If Working at Home	WHERE BORN	(1) Deaf and Dumb (2) Blind (3) Lunatic (4) Imbecile, feeble-minded
		In-habited	Un-inhabited	Building					Males	Females					
1	Badley	1				Abraham Hammond	Head	M	66		Farmer	Employer	At Home	Suffolk Cretting St Peter	
						Sarah "	Wife	M		65				" Mendlesham	
						Anna "	Daughter	S		29	Farmers Daughter			" Badley	
2		1				James Hazell	Head	M	44		Farmer	Employer	At Home	Suffolk Needham Mkt	
						Fanny C "	Wife	M		44				" "	
						William "	Son	S	12		Scholar			" "	
						Albert "	Son	S	9					" Mary	
						Henrietta "	Wife	M		50				" Ringshall	
						Fredric "	Son	S	30		Labourer G.L.	Worker		" Battisford	
						James "	Son	S	25			"		" Combs	
						Sophia "	Daughter	S		24				" "	
						Thomas "	Son	S	21		Platman Ag.M.	Worker		" "	
						Fanny "	Daughter	S		10		Scholar		" Badley	
						Annie "	Grand "	S		1				" Badley	
7		1				William M Rose	Head	S	39		Corn Miller & Farmer	Employer		" Framlingham	
						George L. Rose	Brother	S	26		" F.			" Henley	
7	Total of Schedules of Houses and of Tenements with less than Five Rooms	7				Total of Males and of Females...			17	13					

NOTE—Draw your pen through such words of the headings as are inapplicable.

Eng.—Sheet B.

NOTES:

Ever since the Domesday Survey (1085) governments have periodically held a census to collect population data. These were generally numerical counts until 1841, when the names, age and county of birth of all individuals were recorded for the first time. Since then a National Census has taken place every ten years and the data is released into the public domain on the first working day the year following the year in which the returns become 100 years old. i.e. 1901 Census was released on 1st January 2002.

The Census data in this Appendix has been abstracted from the returns held on microfilm at the Suffolk Record Office and the Family Records Centre, London.

Although the Census forms have tended to vary slightly over the seven decades listed, a standardised 'form' has been used for this presentation.

The enumerators were locally recruited and listed the occupants they found in each household in the order in which they visited them. Whilst they are undoubtedly a great source of information for genealogists, they have to be viewed with the usual caution. Villagers, who may have been illiterate, may not always have been able to accurately answer the questions put to them concerning their age and place of birth and some may have deliberately provided false information. Coupled with the fact that many of the enumerators struggled to understand the 'age formula' devised for the 1841 Census and consequently incorrectly recorded these.

Disappointingly, few of the returns for Badley were completed in full, for e.g. the location of the premises visited is either not stated or simply referred to as 'cottage' or 'near Turnpike' etc., frustrating identification.

However, perhaps we can surmise an enumerator would start on the turnpike (now the B.1113 road) at the Needham Market end of the parish and work his way to the boundary with Combs, before he travelled down the track towards Badley Hall. This would provide the sequence - Badley Bridge (or Chain Bridge) Farm, Doveshill Farm, the three workhouse cottages (opposite the track to the church), two cottages (now Cherry Tree Farm), Badley Mill, Woodlands Farm, Badley Hall, Green Farm, Green Farm cottages (2), and Badley Hall cottages (2)(situated in Badley Lane) i.e. 15 households. The increase to 18 households recorded in the 1891 & 1901 returns can be explained by the construction of Woodlands Cottage and New Cottages at Burnt Mill Hill and the occasional practice of two families sharing the Badley Hall.

Consequently, and notwithstanding the random order some enumerators evidently toured the hamlet to complete their task, it has still been possible to identify the location of most of the households with a fair degree of certainty and add this to the entry in red.

As the graph below shows, with the exception of the 1861 count, Badley's population has remained remarkably stable over the 70 years spanned by the Census, some families residing there a lifetime. A footnote to the 1861 Census states, "The decrease in population in most of the parishes of the Bosmere District is attributed to migration to the manufacturing districts."

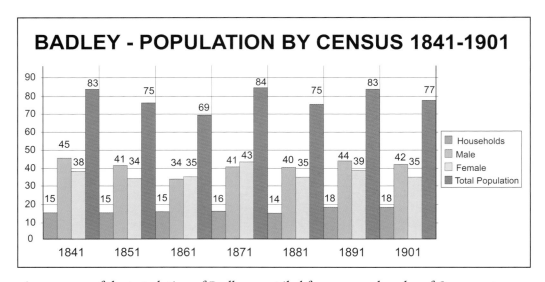

A summary of the population of Badley compiled from seven decades of Census returns.

1841

NOTES : Taken on Sunday 6/7 June - includes every person in each house that night, and anyone absent due to return to the house in the morning. Only surnames & first Christian names were recorded. The exact age of children up to 14 was recorded, the ages of all others were given in five year groups i.e. 15 to 19 incl. are shown as 15, 20 to 24 as 20 & so on. 'Where born' was restricted to 'Yes' or 'No', i.e. in this instance, where you born in Suffolk, and all those enumerated where.

Place	Name & Surname of Person who abode in the house on the night of	Relation to head of Family	Condition	Age of Male	Age of Female	Rank Profession or Occupation	Where Born
1	Thomas COOPER			30		Farmer	
	Mary Ann COOPER				30		
	Mary COOPER				3		
	Thomas COOPER			3			Chain Bridge Farm?
	Elizabeth COOPER				5mths		
	Catherine BAKER				15	Female Servant	
	Eliza PEARSON				13	Female Servant	
	Charles SCOPES			15		Male Servant	
2	George HAYWARD			25		Farmer	
	Elizabeth HAYWARD				20		
	Frederick HAYWARD			5mths			Doveshill Farm?
	John COPPIN			12		Male Servant	
	Mary GINN				15	Female Servant	
	Elizabeth MILLER				13	Female Servant	
3	William JAMES			25		Ag. Lab.	
	Harriott JAMES				30		Workhouse Cottage Doveshill
	Elizabeth MOORE				30	Ind.	
	Samuel MOORE			5			
4	James HILL			70		Ag. Lab.	
	Elizabeth HILL				60		
	Eliza HILL				?8		Workhouse Cottage Doveshill
	Joseph BAKER			40			
	Ann BAKER				15		
5	John CHOAT			30		Ag. Lab.	
	Ann CHOAT				30		
	Samuel CHOAT			9			
	Ann CHOAT				7		Workhouse Cottage Doveshill
	Maria CHOAT				5		
	John CHOAT			2			
	Charles CHOAT			4mths			
6	Shadrach JAMES			60		Ag. Lab.	
	Martha JAMES				55		Cottage now Cherry Tree Farm
	Meshach JAMES			20			
	Robert JAMES			14		Wheelwright's Apprentice	
7	Samuel PARKER			35		Ag. Lab.	Cottage now Cherry Tree Farm
	Susan PARKER				30		
8	Sarah JAY				60	Ind.	
	Samuel JAY			35		Miller	
	John DENNY				15	Miller's Apprentice	
	Sarah BRIDGEMAN				15	Ind.	Badley Mill
	Thomas JENNINGS			25		Male Servant	
	Elizabeth LAWRENCE				20	Female Servant	
	Eliza LONGE				14	Female Servant	
9	Kirby MOORE			45		Farmer	
	Henrietta MOORE				45		
	Dinah NUNN				20	Female Servant	The Woodlands
	Susan WOLLARD				20	Female Servant	
	William PARKER			20		Male Servant	

1841 cont.

Hall (10)	William MUDD			50		Farmer	
	Ann MUDD				45		
	Thomas MUDD			15			
	William MUDD			15			
	Ann MUDD				13		Badley Hall
	Frederick MUDD			12			
	Emily MUDD				9		
	Abraham BALDWIN			15		Male Servant	
	John ARCHER			19		Male Servant	
	Jemima PIKE				15	Female Servant	
11	Robert ABBOTT			55		Ag. Lab.	
	Mary ABBOTT				50		Green Farm?
	Alfred BARRELL			15		Male Servant	
12	Stephen BUGG			30		Ag. Lab.	
	Mary BUGG				30		Badley Hall Cottage
	Stephen BUGG			8			Badley Lane
	James BUGG			7			nr Moats Tye?
	Mary BUGG				5		
13	William DALLENGER			50		Ag. Lab.	
	Martha DALLENGER				40		Badley Hall Cottage
	Daniel DALLENGER			20			Badley Lane
	George DALLENGER			9			nr Moats Tye?
14	John PARKER			30		Ag. Lab.	
	Maria ARCHER				10		
	George ARCHER			7			
	Susan ARCHER				5		Green Farm Cottage
	Robert ARCHER			3			Badley Green?
	Thomas ARCHER			40			
	John ARCHER			17			
15	Thomas BARRELL			30		Ag. Lab.	
	Charlotte BARRELL				35		
	Henry BARRELL			14			Green Farm Cottage
	Caroline BARRELL				7		Badley Green?
	Thomas BARRELL			5			
	Mary Ann BARRELL				2		

Summary for 1841:
    No of Households = 15
    No of Males = 45
    No of Females = 38

                    Total Population = 83

1851

NOTES : Taken on 31 March for night of 30/31 - this was the first Census to record actual ages and places of birth. Unless otherwise stated, all births occurred within Suffolk.

Place	Name & Surname of Person who abode in the house on the night of	Relation to head of Family	Condition	Age of Male	Age of Female	Rank Profession or Occupation	Where Born
(1) Badley Bridge Farm	Thomas Snell COOPER	Head	Mar	44		Farmer : 113 acres, employing	Hadleigh
	Mary COOPER	Wife	Mar		39	5 men & 1 boy	Mdx. Hoxton
	Thomas PHILIP	Servant	U/Mar	19		Scholar	Badley
	Elizabeth HICKS	Servant	U/Mar		10		Badley
	Sarah PENN	Servant	U/Mar		18	House Servant	East Bergholt
(2) Turnpike Doveshill Farm	George HAYWARD	Head	Mar	35		Farmer : 260 acres, employing	Ringshall
	Elizabeth HAYWARD	Wife	Mar		30	12 men	Badley
	George HAYWARD	Son	U/Mar	8		Scholar	Badley
	Elizabeth HAYWARD	Dau	U/Mar		6		Badley
	Mary Ann HAYWARD	Dau	U/Mar		4		Badley
	William HAYWARD	Son	U/Mar	2			Badley
	Emily HAYWARD	Dau	U/Mar		6mths		Badley
	Mary WRIGHT	Servant	U/Mar		24	Dairy Servant	Stowupland
	Harriet PARKER	Servant	U/Mar		24	House Servant	Copdock
	John LEE	Servant	U/Mar	14		Backhouse Servant	Battisford
(3) Doveshill Workhouse	William JAMES	Head	Mar	36		Ag. Lab.	Finborough
	Harriet JAMES	Wife	Mar		43		Creeting St Mary
(4) Doveshill Workhouse	Ann CHOAT	Widower	U/Mar		41	Labourers wife. Pauper	Rattlesden
	John CHOAT	Son	U/Mar	12			Badley
	Isaac CHOAT	Son	U/Mar	10			Badley
(5) Doveshill Workhouse	Benjamin HILL	Head	Mar	50		Ag. Lab.	Coddenham
	Hannah HILL	Wife	Mar		49		Barham
	John HILL	Son	U/Mar	15			Combs
	Anna HILL	Dau	U/Mar		6		Badley
	Frederick HILL	Son	U/Mar	3			Badley
(6) Near Turnpike	Shadrach JAMES	Head	Mar	73		Ag. Lab.	Hitcham
	Martha JAMES	Wife	Mar		65	Cottage, now Cherry Tree Farm	Nfk. Brockdish
	Robert JAMES	Son	U/Mar	23		Carpenter	Badley
(7) near Moats Tye Hall Cottage	Benjamin COPPIN	Head	Mar	64		Ag. Lab.	Swilland
	Elizabeth COPPIN	Wife	Mar		66		Crowfield
	John COPPIN	Son	U/Mar	26		Ag. Lab.	Willisham
	Samuel COPPIN	Son	U/Mar	24		Ag. Lab.	Willisham
(8) Near Turnpike The Woodlands	John Kirby MOORE	Head	Mar	56		Farmer : 515 acres employing	Badley
	Henrietta MOORE	Wife	Mar.		60	22 men & 7 youths	Barking
	Abraham SUTTON	Servant	U/Mar	40		Farm Servant	Combs
	Charlotte COPPING	Servant	U/Mar		21	House Servant	Helmingstone
	Sarah PIZZEY	Servant	U/Mar		21	House Servant	Barking
(9) Badley Mill	Samuel JAY	Head	Mar	47		Miller	Badley
	Ann JAY	Wife	Mar		41		Badley
	Samuel Turner JAY	Son		9		Scholar	Badley
	Thomas Nunn JAY	Son		5		Scholar	Badley
	James SMITH	Messenger		51		Messenger	Gls. Bristol
	Robert HILLS	Servant		32		Servant	Creeting
	Frances OSBORNE	Servant			27	Dairy Servant	Gosbeck
(10) Badley Hall	William MUDD	Head	Mar	62		Farmer : 412 acres employing	Badley
	Ann MUDD	Wife	Mar		58	16 men	Bredfield
	Frederick MUDD	Son	U/Mar	21			Badley
	Emily MUDD	Dau	U/Mar		18		Badley
	Sarah TUCKER	Servant	U/Mar		22	House Servant	Stowupland
	Hannah ?	Servant	U/Mar		17	House Servant	Combs
	Robert PILBROUGH	Servant	U/Mar	19		Farm Servant	Battisford
	John SNOWDEN	Servant	U/Mar	20		Farm Servant	Creeting
	George DAVEY	Servant	U/Mar	14		Farm Servant	Combs

1851 cont.

(11) *Green Farm*	Robert ABBOTT	Head	Mar	70		Farm Baliff		Willisham
	Mary ABBOTT	Wife	Mar		70			Monks Eleigh
	William NUNN	Servant	U/Mar	20		Farm Servant		Barham
(12) Badley Green nr Moats Tye	Stephen BUGG	Head	Mar	40		Ag. Lab.		Barking
	Mary BUGG	Wife	Mar		42			Stowmarket
	Stephen BUGG	Son	U/Mar	19		Ag. Lab.	*Hall Cottage*	Barking
	James BUGG	Son	U/Mar	17		Ag. Lab.	*Badley Lane*	Barking
	Mary BUGG	Dau	U/Mar		15			Badley
	William BUGG	Son	U/Mar	2				Badley
(13)	William DALLENGER	Head	Mar	65		Ag. Lab.	*Hall Cottage*	Burgh
	Martha DALLENGER	Wife	Mar		50		*Badley Lane*	Creeting St Peter
	George DALLENGER	Son	U/Mar	19		Ag. Lab.		Badley
(14)	John ARCHER	Head	Mar	46		Ag. Lab.		Badley
	Caroline ARCHER	Wife	Mar		33			Needham Mkt
	George ARCHER	Son	U/Mar	17		Ag. Lab.		Badley
	Susan ARCHER	Dau	U/Mar		14		*Green Farm Cottage*	Badley
	Robert ARCHER	Son	U/Mar	13		Ag. Lab.	*Badley Green?*	Badley
	Elizabeth ARCHER	Dau	U/Mar		8			Badley
	Jane ARCHER	Dau	U/Mar		6			Badley
(15)	Samuel PARKER	Head	Mar	42		Ag. Lab.	*Cottage now*	Creeting
	Susan PARKER	Wife	Mar		45		*Cherry Tree Farm*	Hintlesham

Summary for 1851:

    No of Households = 15

    No of Males = 41

    No of Females = 34

               Total Population = 75

1861

NOTES : Taken on 8 April for night of 7/8 April - Unless otherwise stated, all births occurred within Suffolk.

Place	Name & Surname of Person who abode in the house on the night of	Relation to head of Family	Condition	Age of Male	Age of Female	Rank Profession or Occupation	Where Born
(1) Doveshill Farmhouse	George HAYWARD	Head	Mar	46		Farmer: 260 acres employing 9 men & 2 boys	Ringshall
	Elizabeth HAYWARD	Wife	Mar		40		Badley
	George HAYWARD	Son	U/Mar	18			Badley
	Elizabeth HAYWARD	Dau	U/Mar		16		Badley
	Mary Ann HAYWARD	Dau	U/Mar		14		Badley
	Emily HAYWARD	Dau	U/Mar		10		Badley
	Horace HAYWARD	Son	U/Mar	9			Badley
	Alice HAYWARD	Dau	U/Mar		7		Badley
	Caroline HAYWARD	Dau	U/Mar		5		Badley
	Thomas HAYWARD	Son	U/Mar	3			Badley
	Catherine HAYWARD	Dau	U/Mar		2		Badley
	Clara HAYWARD	Dau	U/Mar		5mths		Badley
	Mary PRENTICE	Servant	U/Mar		18	House Servant	Battisford
(2) 2 Workhouse Cottages Doveshill	William BLOOMFIELD	Head	Mar	38		Labourer	Badley
	Eliza BLOOMFIELD	Wife	Mar		44		Badley
	George Coppin BLOOMFIELD	Son	U/Mar	16		Labourer	Wattisham?
	Frederick BLOOMFIELD	Son	U/Mar	11		Scholar	Combs
	James BLOOMFIELD	Son	U/Mar	9		Scholar	Combs
	Robert BLOOMFIELD	Son	U/Mar	7		Scholar	Combs
	Ann BLOOMFIELD	Dau	U/Mar		2		Badley
(3) Badley Hall	Thomas MUDD	Head	Mar	35		Farmer: 340 acres employing 10 men & 3 boys	Badley
	Ann MUDD	Wife	Mar		64		Bedfield
	Isaac COPELAND	Servant	Mar	28		Farm Servant	Buxhall
	Jane COPELAND	Servant	Mar		23	House Servant	Wattisham
	John SNOWDEN	Shepherd	U/Mar	30		Shepherd	Creeting All Saints
(4) Badley Lane Cottage	Caroline ARCHER	Head	Widower		39	Pauper	Needham Mkt.
	Robert ARCHER	Son	U/Mar	23		Labourer	Badley
	Elizabeth ARCHER	Dau	U/Mar		19	*Green Farm Cottage, off Badley Lane*	Badley
	Jane ARCHER	Dau	U/Mar		17		Badley
	Amayus ARCHER	Son	U/Mar	10		Scholar	Badley
(5) Cottage	William DALLENGER	Head	Mar	75		Labourer *Badley Hall Cottage, near Moats Tye*	Burgh
	Martha DALLENGER	Wife	Mar		60		Creeting St Peter
(6) Cottage	Stephen BUGG	Head	Mar	50		Labourer *Badley Hall Cottage, near Moats Tye*	Stowmarket
	Mary Ann BUGG	Wife	Mar		58		Stowmarket
	William BUGG	Son	U/Mar	12		Scholar	Badley
(7) Green Farm	Frederick MUDD	Head	Mar	30		Farmer: 211 acres employing 7 men & 3 boys	Badley
	Mary Smith MUDD	Wife	Mar		23		Badley
	Sarah CUTTING	Servant	U/Mar		19	General Servant	Stowupland
	John CUTTING	Servant	U/Mar	21		Groom	Stowupland
(8) Chain Bridge Farm	Thomas Snell COOPER	Head	Mar	54		Farmer: 110 acres employing 4 men & 1 boy	Hadleigh
	Mary COOPER	Wife	Mar		49		Mdx. London
	Thomas Philip COOPER	Son	U/Mar	21		Grocer	Badley
	Eliza THURLOW	Servant	U/Mar		18	Dairy Maid	Crowfield
(9) Workhouse Cottage Doveshill	Henry BARRELL	Head	Mar	33		Labourer	Needham Mkt.
	Maria BARRELL	Wife	Mar		32		Buxhall
	Frederick BARRELL	Son	U/Mar				Combs
(10) Workhouse Cottage Doveshill	Edward JAMES	Head	Mar	40		Labourer	Darmsden
	Anna Maria JAMES	Wife	Mar		30		Badley
	Alfred JAMES	Son	U/Mar	2			Badley
	George JAMES	Son	U/Mar	11mths			Badley

1861 cont.

(11) Cottage	Samuel PARKER	Head	Mar	52		Groom	Creeting
	Susan PARKER	Wife	Mar		53	Cottage, now Cherry Tree Farm	Hintlesham
	John PARKER	Lodger	U/Mar	60		Pauper	Creeting
(12) Cottage	Shadrach JAMES	Head	Mar	86		Labourer Cottage,	Hitcham
	Martha JAMES	Wife	Mar		76	now Cherry Tree Farm	Nfk. Brundish
(13) Workhouse Cottage Doveshill	Meshach JAMES	Head	Mar	39		Labourer	Badley
	Elizabeth JAMES	Wife	Mar		42		Battisford
	Frederick JAMES	Son	U/Mar		12	Scholar	Combs
	Elizabeth JAMES	Dau	U/Mar		18	Labourer	Combs
(14) Farmhouse The Woodlands	John Kirby MOORE	Head	Mar	66		Farmer: 515 acres employing 19 men & 4 boys	Badley
	Henrietta MOORE	Wife	Mar		69		Barking
	Margaret RODWELL	Visitor	U/Mar		30	Visitor	Alderton
	Thursa PRITTY	Servant	U/Mar		47	Cook	Framsden
	Caroline GINN	Servant	U/Mar		21	House Maid	Debenham
	Abraham SUTTON	Servant	U/Mar	52		House Servant	Combs
(15) Watermill House Badley Mill	Henry WICKS	Head	Mar	51		Miller	Tunstall
	Sarah WICKS	Wife	Mar		47		Ringshall
	Robert WICKS	Brother	U/Mar	57			Tunstall
	Harriet MILES	Servant	U/Mar		20	Servant	Mendlesham
	Emma LAFLIN	Servant	U/Mar		15	Servant	Ringshall

Summary for 1861:
> No of Households = 15
> No of Males = 34
> No of Females = 35

Total Population = 69

1861 Cenus Footnote - Badley:

The decrease in population in most of the parishes of the Bosmere District is attributed to migration to the manufacturing districts.

1871

NOTES : Taken on 3 April for night of 2/3 April - Unfortunately the Enumerator has failed to complete the form, consequently where each family were living and some of their occupations are omitted, which is a pity. Unless otherwise stated, all births are within Suffolk.

Place	Name & Surname of Person who abode in the house on the night of	Relation to head of Family	Condition	Age of Male	Age of Female	Rank Profession or Occupation	Where Born
(1) Badley Road	Elizabeth MANISTER	Head	Mar		25	Wife of Civil Engineer	Badley
	Kate MANISTER	Dau			2	*Chain Bridge Farm*	Creeting St Mary
	Henrietta MANISTER	Dau			1		Creeting St Mary
	Emma SMITH	Servant			17	General Servant	Kenton
(2) Badley Road Doveshill Farm	George HAYWARD	Head	Mar	56		Farmer: 387 acres employing 30 men & 2 boys	Ringshall
	Elizabeth HAYWARD	Wife	Mar		49	Farmer's Wife	Badley
	Mary Ann HAYWARD	Dau	U/Mar		22	Farmer's Daughter	Badley
	Emily HAYWARD	Dau	U/Mar		20	Farmer's Daughter	Badley
	Horace HAYWARD	Son	U/Mar	19		Farmer's Son	Badley
	Alice HAYWARD	Dau	U/Mar		17	Farmer's Daughter	Badley
	Caroline HAYWARD	Dau	U/Mar		15	Farmer's Daughter	Badley
	Thomas HAYWARD	Son	U/Mar	13		Farmer's Son	Badley
	Catherine HAYWARD	Dau	U/Mar		11	Farmer's Daughter	Badley
	Clara HAYWARD	Dau	U/Mar		10	Farmer's Daughter	Badley
	Sarah BERRY	Servant	U/Mar		17	Dairy Servant	Laxfield
	Martha CLARKE	Servant	U/Mar		15	Servant Domestic	Needham Mkt.
(3) Cottage	Samuel BALDWIN	Head	Mar	55		Farm Labourer *Workhouse Cottage*	Combs
	Susan BALDWIN	Wife	Mar		50		Finborough
	Frederick BALDWIN	Son	U/Mar	18		Farm Labourer	Creeting St Mary
(4) Cottage	Meshach JAMES	Head	Mar	50		Ag. Lab.	Badley
	Elizabeth JAMES	Wife	Mar		52	*Workhouse Cottage*	Battisford
	Robert JAMES	Son	U/Mar	14		Ag. Lab	Combs
	Walter JAMES	Son	U/Mar	8			Badley
(5) Cottage	Edward JAMES	Head	Mar	51		Farm Labourer	Darmsden
	Ann M JAMES	Wife	Mar		40		Badley
	Alfred JAMES	Son	U/Mar	12			Badley
	George JAMES	Son	U/Mar	10			Badley
	Ann M JAMES	Dau	U/Mar		9	*Workhouse Cottage*	Badley
	Emma JAMES	Dau	U/Mar		7		Badley
	Alice JAMES	Dau	U/Mar		5		Badley
	Fanny JAMES	Dau	U/Mar		4		Badley
	Lettice JAMES	Dau	U/Mar		1.10mths		Badley
(6) Cottage	Martha JAMES	Head	Widower	87		*Cottage, now Cherry Tree Farm*	Nfk. Brundish
	Maria JAMES	Dau			65		Finborough
(7) Cottage	Samuel PARKER	Head	Mar	60		*Cottage, now Cherry Tree Farm*	Creeting St Mary
	Susan PARKER	Wife	Mar		65		Hintlesham
(8) Badley Mill	Henry WICKS	Head	Mar	61		Miller: employing 3 men & Farmer: 60 acres employing 2 men & 3 boys	Tunstall
	Sarah WICKS	Wife	Mar		57		Ringshall
	Robert WICKS	Brother	U/Mar	69		Labourer	Tunstall
	Henry FAIRWEATHER	Nephew	U/Mar	18		Miller	Framlingham
	Emma LAFLIN	Niece	U/Mar		25		Ringshall
	William SHELDRAKE	Servant	U/Mar	20		Carter	Kenton
(9) Cottage	Abraham HAMMOND	Head	Mar	36		Ag. Lab.	Creeting St Peter
	Sarah J HAMMOND	Wife	Mar		35		Hintlesham
	George HAMMOND	Son	U/Mar	5			Stowmarket
	Frederick HAMMOND	Son	U/Mar	3			Badley
	Henry HAMMOND	Son	U/Mar	1			Badley

1871 cont.

(10)	John MOORE	Head	Widower	74		Farmer: 520 acres employing 21 men & 3 women	Badley
The Woodlands	Mary Jane PENNINGTON	Dec'd's wife's sister	U/Mar.	40		Underwriter's Daughter	Sry, Camberwell
	Ann PRITHE	Servant	U/Mar.		38	Domestic Servant Cook	Earl Stonham
	Rebbeca CUMMOULD	Servant	U/Mar.		32	Domestic Servant Housemaid	Combs
	George WOLLARD	Servant	U/Mar.	16		Groom	Barking
(11)	Thomas MUDD	Head		45		Farmer: 336 acres employing 9 men & 5 boys	Badley
Badley Hall	George FRANCIS	Servant	Mar.	49		Farm Servant	Creeting All Saints
	Sarah FRANCIS	Servant	Mar.		47	Housekeeper	Westerfield
	John SNOWDEN	Shepherd	U/Mar.	40		Shepherd	Creeting All Saints
(12)	Frederick W MUDD	Head	Mar.	39		Farmer: 211 acres employing 7 men & 2 boys	Badley
Green Farm	Mary Ann MUDD	Wife	Mar.		32		Badley
	William F MUDD	Son	U/Mar.	3			Badley
	Frank MUDD	Son	U/Mar.	2			Badley
	Ellen RUSH	Servant	U/Mar.		26	General Servant Domestic	Creeting St Peter
	Sarah PROCTER	Servant	U/Mar.		16	Nurse Maid Domestic	Onehouse
(13)	William BLOOMFIELD	Head	Mar.	48		Farm Labourer	Combs
	Caroline BLOOMFIELD	Wife	Mar.		48		Needham Mkt.
Cottage	Frederick BLOOMFIELD	Son	U/Mar.	21		Farm Labourer	Combs
	James BLOOMFIELD	Son	U/Mar.	13		*Green Farm Cottage, off Badley Lane?*	Combs
	Richard BLOOMFIELD	Son	U/Mar.	12			Combs
	Ann BLOOMFIELD	Dau.	U/Mar.		6		Badley
	Eliza BLOOMFIELD	Dau.	U/Mar.		9		Badley
(14)	Isaac COPELAND	Head	Mar.	36		Ag. Lab.	Wattisham
	Sarah COPELAND	Wife	Mar.		32		Buxhall
Cottage	John COPELAND	Son	U/Mar.	8		*Green Farm Cottage, off Badley Lane?*	Badley
	Henry COPELAND	Son	U/Mar.	6			Badley
	Emma COPELAND	Dau.	U/Mar.		2mths		Badley
	Isaac WELHAM	Lodger	U/Mar.	20		Ag. Lab.	Buxhall
	Ann BATTLE	Nurse	Mar.		49	Nurse	Combs
(15)	George BERRY	Head	Mar.	41		Farm Labourer	Laxfield
	Sarah BERRY	Wife	Mar.		39		Laxfield
Cottage	George BERRY		U/Mar.	18		Ag. Lab. *Badley Hall Cottage, near Moats Tye?*	Laxfield
	Ann M BERRY		U/Mar.		11		Laxfield
	Samuel BERRY		U/Mar.	4			Badley
	Thomas BERRY		U/Mar.	2			Badley
(16)	Martha DALINGER	Head	Widower		70	*Badley Hall Cottage, near Moats Tye?*	Creeting St Peter
Cottage	William DALINGER	Grandson	U/Mar.	7mths			Creeting St Peter

Summary for 1871:
    No of Households = 16
    No of Males = 41
    No of Females = 43

                    Total Population = 84

1881

NOTES : Taken on 4 April for night of 3/4 April -

Place	Name & Surname of Person who abode in the house on the night of	Relation to head of Family	Condition	Age of Male	Age of Female	Rank Profession or Occupation	Where Born
(1) Stowmarket Road Bridge Farm	Labon SOUTHGATE	Head	Mar	38		Farmer: 110 acres employing 7 men & 1 boy	Barking
	Charlotte SOUTHGATE	Wife	Mar		37		Barking
	Emily SOUTHGATE	Dau.	U/Mar		9	Scholar	Barking
	Ruth SOUTHGATE	Dau.	U/Mar		8	Scholar	Barking
	Eliza SOUTHGATE	Dau.	U/Mar		5	Scholar	Barking
	Robert SOUTHGATE	Son	U/Mar	3			Barking
	George SOUTHGATE	Son	U/Mar	2			Barking
(2) Stowmarket Road Doveshill Farm	George HAMMOND	Head	Mar	66		Farmer: 315 acres employing 8 men & 4 boys	Ringshall
	Elizabeth HAMMOND	Wife	Mar		60		Badley
	Emily HAMMOND	Dau	U/Mar		29		Badley
	Alice HAMMOND	Dau	U/Mar		26		Badley
	Caroline HAMMOND	Dau	U/Mar		24		Badley
	Thomas HAMMOND	Son	U/Mar	22			Badley
	Kate HAMMOND	Dau	U/Mar		20		Badley
	Clara HAMMOND	Dau	U/Mar		18		Badley
	Rosa FULLER	Servant	U/Mar		18	General Servant Domestic	Creeting St Mary
(3) Stowmarket Rd	Meshach JAMES	Head	Mar	60		Ag. Lab. Battisford *Workhouse Cottage Doveshill*	Badley
	Elizabeth JAMES	Wife	Mar		61		
(4) Stowmarket Road	Edward JAMES	Head	Mar	61		Ag. Lab. *Workhouse Cottage Doveshill*	Darmsden
	Ann Maria JAMES	Wife	Mar		50		Badley
	Alfred JAMES	Son	U/Mar	22		Miller's Carter	Badley
	George C JAMES	Son	U/Mar	20		Miller's Carter	Badley
	Fanny JAMES	Dau	U/Mar		18	Domestic	Badley
	Letitia JAMES	Dau	U/Mar		11	Scholar	Badley
(5) Stowmarket Road	Samuel BALDWIN	Head	Mar	60		Farm Labourer *Workhouse Cottage Doveshill*	Combs
	Susan BALDWIN	Wife	Mar		54		Finborough
	Frederick BALDWIN	Son	U/Mar	27		Farm Labourer	Creeting St Mary
(6) Badley Mill	Samuel SOUTHGATE	Head	Mar	56		Miller & Farmer: 60 acres employing 2 millers, 1 lad & 4 labourers	Combs
	Emma SOUTHGATE	Wife	Mar		42	Miller & Farmers wife	Nfk. Bressingham
	Abraham SOUTHGATE	Nephew	U/Mar	22		Miller	Combs
	Alice SAMBOLLS	Servant	U/Mar		16	General Servant Domestic	
	William NUNN	Servant	U/Mar	17		Farm Servant (Miller)	Finborough
(7) The Woodlands	John Kirby MOORE	Head	Widower	86		Farmer: 490 acres employing 15 labs, 2 boys & 3 women	Badley
	Mary Jane PENNINGTON	Niece	U/Mar		56	Underwriters Daughter	Sry. Camberwell
	Mary Jane BUGG	Servant	U/Mar		22	Cook Domestic	Harkstead
	Robert HAMMOND	Servant	U/Mar	41		Groom	Creeting St Peter
	Eliza GLADWELL	Servant	U/Mar		21	Housemaid	Badley
(8) Badley Hall	Thomas MUDD	Head	Widower	57		Farmer: 337 acres employing 9 labs & 1 shepherd	Badley
	John SNOWDEN	Servant	U/Mar	48		Shepherd	Nacton
	George FRANCIS	Servant	Mar	59		Farm Labourer	Barking
	Sarah FRANCIS	Servant	Mar		57	Domestic Servant	Westerfield

1881 cont.

(9)	Frederick MUDD	Head	Mar	50		Farmer: 212 acres employing 7 men & 1 boy	Badley
	Mary Smith MUDD	Wife	Mar		42	Farmer's wife	Badley
Green Farm	Mary MUDD	Dau	U/Mar		17		Badley
	Philip Hicks MUDD	Son	U/Mar	8		Scholar	Badley
	Isabella A MUDD	Dau	U/Mar		7	Scholar	Badley
	Margaret H MUDD	Dau	U/Mar		5		Badley
	Caroline F MUDD	Dau	U/Mar		2		Badley
	Rosa JACKAMAN	Servant	U/Mar		20	General Servant Domestic	Battisford
(10)	George BERRY	Head	Mar	50		Ag. Lab.	Laxfield
	Sarah BERRY	Wife	Mar		49		Laxfield
	Samuel BERRY	Son	U/Mar	14		Ag. Lab. *Badley Hall Cottage, near Moats Tye?*	Badley
	Thomas BERRY	Son	U/Mar	11		Scholar	Badley
	Herbert BERRY	Son	U/Mar	9		Scholar	Badley
(11)	Isaac COPELAND	Head	Mar	48		Farm Labourer	Wattisham
	Jane COPELAND	Wife	Mar		39		Buxhall
	John COPELAND	Son	U/Mar	18			Badley
	Emma COPELAND	Dau	U/Mar		17	Scholar	Badley
	Kate COPELAND	Dau	U/Mar		10	Scholar	Badley
	Anne COPELAND	Dau	U/Mar		8	Scholar	Badley
	Eliza COPELAND	Dau	U/Mar		5	Scholar	Badley
	Ellen COPELAND	Dau	U/Mar		3	*Green Farm Cottage, off Badley Lane?*	Badley
	Willie COPELAND	Son	U/Mar	1			Badley
	Alice COPELAND	Dau	U/Mar		4mths		Badley
(12)	Martha DALLINGER	Head	Widower		80	Pauper *Badley Hall Cottage, nr Moats Tye?*	Creeting
	Daniel DALLINGER	Son	Son	60		Farm Labourer	Badley
(13)	William BLOOMFIELD	Head	Mar	55		Farm Labourer	Combs
	Caroline BLOOMFIELD	Wife	Mar		57	*Green Farm Cottage, off Badley Lane?*	Needham Mkt
	Richard BLOOMFIELD	Son	U/Mar	25		Farm Labourer	Combs
(14)	Abraham HAMMOND	Head	Mar	45		Farm Labourer	Creeting St Peter
	Sarah HAMMOND	Wife	Mar		44		Mendlesham
	George HAMMOND	Son	U/Mar	15		Farm Labourer	Stowmarket
	Frederick R HAMMOND	Son	U/Mar	13		Scholar	Badley
	Henry HAMMOND	Son	U/Mar	11		Scholar *Cottage, now Cherry Tree Farm?*	Badley
	Anna HAMMOND	Dau	U/Mar		9	Scholar	Badley
	Alice HAMMOND	Dau	U/Mar		6	Scholar	Badley
	Sarah HAMMOND	Dau	U/Mar		4	Scholar	Badley

Summary for 1881:

No of Households = 14

No of Males = 40

No of Females = 35

Total Population = 75

1891

NOTES : Taken on 6 April for night of 5/6 April - one would have hoped that as the Census became 'more recent' the Enumerators would include more not less detail as to the location of the premises they visited. Unfortunately this has not been the case and it therefore very difficult to deduce which cottages the agricultural workers were living in. Unless otherwise stated, all births occurred within Suffolk.

Place	Name & Surname of Person who abode in the house on the night of	Relation to head of Family	Condition	Age of Male	Age of Female	Rank Profession or Occupation	Where Born
1	William LOCKWOOD	Head	Marr	23		Agricultural Labourer	Creeting St Peter
	Emily LOCKWOOD	Wife	Marr		29		Creeting St Peter
	Charles LOCKWOOD	Son	U/Marr	9mths		*Badley Hall Cott nr Moats Tye?*	Badley
2	William BLOOMFIELD	Head	Widow	69		Agricultural Labourer	Combs
	Eliza PIKE	Wid	Widow		76		Battisford *Green Farm Cottage, off Badley Lane?*
3	Benjamin MAYHEW	Head	Marr	43		Agricultural Labourer	Battisford
	Henrietta MAYHEW	Wife	Marr		41		Ringshall
	May Jane MAYHEW	Dau	U/Marr	21			Essex, Dedham
	Frederick MAYHEW	Son	U/Marr	20		Agricultural Labourer	Battisford
	John MAYHEW	Son	U/Marr	17		Agricultural Labourer	Combs
	James MAYHEW	Son	U/Marr	16		Agricultural Labourer	Combs
	Sophia MAYHEW	Dau	U/Marr		14		Combs
	Thomas MAYHEW	Son	U/Marr	10			Combs
	Fanny MAYHEW	Dau	U/Marr		8mths		Badley
4	Daniel DALLENGER	Head	Marr	70		Agricultural Labourer	Badley *Badley Hall Cott nr Moats Tye?*
5	Issac COPELAND	Head	Marr	51		Agricultural Labourer	Hitcham
	Jane COPELAND	Wife	Marr		50		Badley
	John COPELAND	Son	U/Marr	28		Agricultural Labourer	Buxhall *Green Farm Cottage, off Badley Lane?*
	William COPELAND	Son	U/Marr	11		Agricultural Labourer	Badley
	Charles COPELAND	Son	U/Marr	9			Badley
	Ellen COPELAND	Dau	U/Marr		7		Badley
6	William SOUTER	Head	Marr	25		Agricultural Labourer	Mendham
	Nellie SOUTER	Wife	Marr		28		Stowmarket
7	Charles SOUTER	Head	Marr	52		Agricultural Labourer	Mendham
	Louisa SOUTER	Wife	Marr		47		St Peter South Elmham
	James SOUTER	Son	U/Marr	23		Agricultural Labourer	Mendham
	John SOUTER	Son	U/Marr	18		Agricultural Labourer	Mendham
	Frederick SOUTER	Son	U/Marr	15		Agricultural Labourer	Mendham
	Susanna SOUTER	Dau	U/Marr		13	Mothers Helper Domestic	Mendham
	Mary SOUTER	Dau	U/Marr		2	Scholar	Mendham
	Florence L SOUTER	Dau	U/Marr		7	Scholar	Mendham
8	William ROBINSON	Head	Marr	55		Agricultural Labourer	Stowupland
	Mary Ann ROBINSON	Wife	Marr		57		Needham Market
	William ROBINSON	Son	U/Marr	17		Groom	Stowupland
	Alexis ROBINSON	Son	U/Marr	13			Stowupland
	Grace ROBINSON	Dau	U/Marr		10	Scholar	Stowupland
	Amy Ellen ROBINSON	Dau	U/Marr		6	Scholar	Stowupland
9 The Woodlands	Edwin STEARN	Head		58		Farmer	Stowupland
	Sarah Emily STEARN	Dau	U/Marr		22		Stowupland
	Laura STEARN	Dau	U/Marr		21		Stowupland
	Roland STEARN	Son	U/Marr	18			Stowupland
	Sydney STEARN	Son	U/Marr	16		Apprentice Chemist	Stowupland
	Margaret STEARN	Dau.	U/Marr		10		Stowupland
	Jane GOODERHAM	Servant	U/Marr		16	Housemaid	Stowmarket
	Anna BEALES	Servant	U/Marr		15	Dairymaid	Bramford
10 Badley Mill	Samuel SOUTHGATE	Head	Marr	66		Miller and Farmer	Combs
	Emma SOUTHGATE	Wife	Marr		52		Nfk. Bressingham
	Eva SOUTHGATE	Visitor	U/Marr		6	Scholar	Stutton
	John SOUTHGATE	Nephew	U/Marr	24		Miller	Crowfield
	Kate PALMER	Servant	U/Marr		13	Domestic Servant	Battisford

1891 cont.

11	Sarah DEATH	Widow	Widow		50		Combs
	William ANDREWS	Son	U/Marr	29		Agricultural Labourer	Combs
	Alfred DEATH	Son	U/Marr	16		Agricultural Labourer	Battisford
	Albert DEATH	Son	U/Marr	13		Agricultural Labourer	Battisford
	Arthur DEATH	Son	U/Marr	11		Agricultural Labourer	Battisford
12	James PALMER	Head	Marr	57		Agricultural Labourer	Battisford
	Susan PALMER	Wife	Marr		66		Preston
13	George PALMER	Head	Marr			Agricultural Labourer	Ringshall
	William E PALMER	Son	U/Marr			Agricultural Labourer	Battisford
	Alice DEATH	H/keeper	U/Marr		20	Domestic Servant	Battisford
14	Walter RIVERS	Head	Marr	28		Agricultural Labourer	Needham Market
	Rose A RIVERS	Wife	Marr		26		Creeting St Mary
	Annie E RIVERS	Dau.			6		Badley
	William J RIVERS	Son		4			Badley
	Clara R RIVERS	Dau			9mths	Badley	
15	William FULLER	Head	Marr	51		Farm Baliff _Green Farm?_	Crowfield
	Maria FULLER	Wife	Marr		40		Crowfield
16	Abraham HAMMOND	Head		55		Farmer	Creeting St Peter
	Sarah HAMMOND	Wife			56		Mendlesham
Bridge Farm	Henry HAMMOND	Son		21		Farmer's son	Badley
	Anna HAMMOND	Dau			19		Badley
	Alice HAMMOND	Dau			16		Badley
17	Thomas MUDD	Head	Widow	67		Farmer	Badley
Badley Hall	Emily COOPER	Sister				Housekeeper Domestic	Badley
	John SNOWDEN	Shepherd		60		Shepherd	Creeting
18	Alfred JAMES	Head	Marr	32		Agricultural Labourer	Badley
	Betsy JAMES	Wife			36		Blakenham
	Alfred E JAMES	Son		9			Creeting St Mary
	Edith E JAMES	Dau			6		Badley
	Albert JAMES	Son		5			Badley
	Grace A JAMES	Dau			3		Badley
	Edward L JAMES	Son		?mths			Badley
	Robert J JAMES	Son		?mths			Badley

Summary for 1891:

No of Households = 18
No of Males = 44
No of Females = 39

Total Population = 83

1901

NOTES : Taken on 31 March - unfortunately the Enumerator has again failed to indicate on the return exactly where each family were living. Unless otherwise stated all births occurred within Suffolk.

No of Schedule	ROAD, STREET, &c & No. or NAME of HOUSE	In-habited	Name and Surname of each Person	RELATION to Head of Family	Condition as to Marriage	Age last Birthday of Male	Age last Birthday of Female	PROFESSION OR OCCUPATION	Employer, Worker, or Own Account	If Working at Home	WHERE BORN
1	Badley Bridge Farm	1	Abraham Hammond	Head	M	66		Farmer	Employee	At Home	Creeting St Peter
			Sarah Hammond	Wife	M		65				Mendlesham
			Anna Hammond	Dau	S		29	Farmers Daughter			Badley
2	Doveshill Farm	1	James Hazell	Head	M	47		Farmer	Employee	At Home	Needham Market
			Fanny E Hazell	Wife	M		47				Needham Market
			William Hazell	Son	S	12		Farmers Son	Scholar		Needham Market
			Albert Hazell	Son	S	9		Farmers Son	Scholar		
3	Workhouse Cottage Doveshill	1	James Bugg	Head	Wdr	69					Creeting St Peter
			James Bugg	Son	S	29		Horseman on Farm	Worker		Needham Market
			Henry Bugg	G. son	S	5			Scholar		Needham Market
4	Workhouse Cottage Doveshill	1	William E Stammers	Head	M	55		Horseman on Farm	Worker		Alpheaton
			Hephiziba Stammers	Wife	M		38				Battisford
			Kathleen Stammers	Dau	S		9		Scholar		Badley
			Herbert Stammers	Son	S	8			Scholar		Badley
			Maud Stammers	Dau	S		7		Scholar		Badley
			Rose Stammers	Dau	S		1		Scholar		Badley
5	Workhouse Cottage Doveshill	1	William Andrews	Head	M	39		Stockman on Farm	Worker		Combs
			Jessie E Andrews	Wife	M		27				Framsden
			Adela Oxborrow	St. Dau	S		5			Scholar	Battisford
			Albert Death	Bro	S	23		Stockman on Farm	Worker		Battisford
6	Cottage, now Cherry Tree Farm	1	Benjamin Mayhew	Head	M	53		Labourer	Worker		Battisford
			Henrietta Mayhew	Wife	M		50				Ringshall
			Frederic Mayhew	Son	S	30		Labourer	Worker		Battisford
			James Mayhew	Son	S	25		Labourer	Worker		Combs
	Cottage, now Cherry Tree Farm		Sophia Mayhew	Dau	S		24				Combs
			Thomas Mayhew	Son	S	21		Postman	Worker		Combs
			Fanny Mayhew	Dau	S		10		Scholar		Badley
			Annie Mayhew	G. Dau			1		Scholar		Badley
7	Badley Mill	1	William M Rose	Head	S	39		Corn Miller & Farmer		Employee	Framlingham
			George S Rose	Bro	S	28		Corn Miller & Farmer		Employee	Henley
			Maud E Rose	Sister	S		24				Sproughton
			Ethel G Rose	Sister	S		16				Sproughton
			Frederck Neale	Visitor	S	17					Saxmundham
8		1	Ellen Kemp	Wife	M		29				Thorndon
			Frank Kemp	Son	S	4					Stowupland
			Annie Kemp	Dau	S		3mths				Badley
9		1	Alfred Manning	Head	M	36		Yardman on Farm	Worker		Haughley
			Mary Manning	Wife	M		33				Wetherden
			Alfred Manning	Son	S	11			Scholar		Stowmarket
			Ernest Manning	Son	S	7			Scholar		Stowmarket
			Harry Manning	Son	S	5			Scholar		Stowmarket
10		1	Charles Souter	Head	M	62		Horseman on Farm	Worker		Mendlesham
			Louisa Souter	Wife	M		57				Bungay
			Susanna Souter	Dau	S		22	Housemaid Domestic			Mendham
11		1	John Mayhew	Head	M	27					Combs
			Mary Mayhew	Wife	M		24				Rushmere
			Louisa Mayhew	Dau	S		2				Badley
			Mabel Mayhew	Dau	S		5mths				Badley
12	The Woodlands	1	Edwin Stearn	Head	M	65		Farmer	Employee		Stowupland
			Margaret Stearn	Dau	S		20	Farmers Daughter			Stowupland
			Harry Stearn	Son	S	34		Grocer	Own Account		Stowupland
			Emma Turner	Serv	S		16	Dairy Servant			Haughley
			Daisy Manning	Serv	S		15	House Servant			Haughley

1901 cont.

No of Schedule	ROAD, STREET, &c & No. or NAME of HOUSE	In-habited	Name and Surname of each Person	RELATION to Head of Family	Condition as to Marriage	Age last Birthday of Male	Age last Birthday of Female	PROFESSION OR OCCUPATION	Employer, Worker, or Own Account	If Working at Home	WHERE BORN
13		1	Isaac Reynolds	Head	M	65		Retired Farmer	Own Account		Combs
			Susan E Reynolds	Wife	M		63				Creeting St Peter
14		1	John Brown	Head	M	58		Stockman on Farm	Worker		Barham
			Mary A Brown	Wife	M		58				Creeting All Saints
			James Brown	Son	S	29		Horseman on Farm			Creeting All Saints
15		1	William Parker	Head	M	37		Horseman on Farm			Combs
			Jane Parker	Wife	M		33				Stowmarket
			Arthur Parker	Son	S	11		Scholar			Combs
			Daisy Parker	Dau	S		9	Scholar			Combs
			Henry Parker	Son	S	6		Scholar			Combs
			Beatrice Parker	Dau	S		4				Combs
			Gustave Parker	Son	S	1					Badley
16		1	John Firman	Head	M	27		Horseman on Farm			Creeting St Peter
			Mary Firman	Wife	M		26				Creeting St Peter
			David Firman	Son	S	3					Creeting St Peter
			Ernest Firman	Son	S	2					Creeting St Peter
			Charlie Firman	Son	S	3mths					Badley Green
17	Green Farm Cottage	1	William Lockwood	Head	M	33		Farm Baliff	Worker		Creeting St Peter
			Emily Lockwood	Wife	M		37				Creeting St Peter
			Charles Lockwood	Son	S	10		Scholar			Badley
			George Lockwood	Son	S	9		Scholar			Badley
			Lilly Lockwood	Dau	S		5	Scholar			Badley
18		1	James Palmer	Head	M	67		Labourer on Farm	Worker		Battisford
			Esther Palmer	Wife	M		49				Battisford

End of the Ecclesiatical Parish of Badley

Summary for 1901:
No of Households = 18
No of Males = 42
No of Females = 35

Total Population = 77

1871, 1881, 1891 & 1901 Census

The release via the Internet of an increasing number of 19th century National Census records has made it possible to easily track the dispersal of the Badley born after they left the parish. Created from the above Census years, the following lists show all the persons recorded as having being born at Badley and living elsewhere in the County unless otherwise stated. However, whilst compiling this relatively short list I discovered there were a number of mistakes within these indexes when compared against the enumerator's original forms - re-enforcing the genealogist's maxim, to always check back to source material whenever possible. Where it has been possible to positively identify married women by their maiden name this has been added.

1871

Ambrose, Amy	45	w.	Poslingford[1]
Ames, Susanna	37	w.	Stowmarket
Archer, James	52	h.	Stowmarket
Armstrong, Abner	12	s.	Bury St Edmunds (St Mary)
Armstrong, Maria	34	w.	Bury St Edmunds (St Mary)
Baker, William	85	h.	Grundisburgh
Banyard, Ann	65	w.	Stowmarket
Barnard, Thomas	30	lo.	Ipswich St Nicholas
Beideman, Charlotte	50	w.	Combs
Berry, Robert	48	h.	Preston next Faversham, Kent
Buckle, Susannah	46	si.	Combs
Buckle, Thomas	42	h.	Creeting St Mary
Bugg, George	11	s.	Baylham
Bugg, James	38	h.	Creeting St Mary
Bugg, William	22	s.	Battisford
Burcham, Charles	35	h.	Twickenham, Middlesex
Chinnery, Jane	25	w.	Chatham, Kent
Choat, W John	33	h.	Camberwell, London
Clark, James	46	h.	Wanstead, Essex
Cooker, Eliza	60	h.	Grundisburgh
Cooper, Emily	33	w.	Badwell Ash
Cooper, Thomas P	31	as.	Beccles
Copeland, Emma	2	v.	Buxhall
Coppin, Samuel	43	h.	Ipswich St Matthew
Daking, Matilda	52	w.	Bentley
Dallenger, Daniel	50	lo.	Stowmarket
Dallenger, William	51	h.	Needham Market
Dallenger, George	39	h.	Needham Market
Dowton, Henry	35	h.	Stourbridge, Worcestershire
Garnham, John	57	h.	Tranmere, Cheshire
Gowing, Susanna	35	w.	Aldham
Hagger, Charlotte	51	w.	Ipswich St Margaret
Hagger, William	74	h.	Dedham, Essex
Hayward, George	27	h.	Harleston
Hill, Frank	23	h.	Bramford
Hill, John	35	h.	Ipswich St Clement
James, Robert	45	h.	St Pancras, London
James, Shadrach	54	h.	Creeting All Saints
Jay, Eliza Ann	22	d.	Ipswich St Margaret
Jay, Samuel	37	h.	St James, Westminster, London
Jay, Samuel Turner	67	h.	Ipswich St Margaret
Jay, Thomas Nunn	25	s.	Ipswich St Margaret
Mount, Emma	7	d.	Needham Market
Mount, William	5	s.	Needham Market
Mudd, Annie E	9	p.	Stowmarket
Mudd, Mary	7	p.	Stowmarket
Mudd, William	42	h.	Stoke by Nayland
Mulley, Anna	26	w.	Bramford
Potter, Ann	40	w.	Ipswich St Margaret
Simpson, Matilda	48	sil.	Gestingthorpe, Essex
Stevens, Isaac	68	h.	Creeting St Mary
Vince, Marianne	60	sil.	Bentley
Wicher, Robert	32	h.	Stowmarket
Willar, George	50	h.	Lambeth, London
Wotton, Samuel	90	f.	Newbourn
Wright, Mary A	35	w.	Stowmarket
Youngs, Samuel	71	h.	Combs

[1] the Census says 'born at Badley Hall'

1881

Ames, Susan (45) h. Regent Street Cottage, Stowmarket (née Archer?)

Archer, James (62) h. Childer Road, Stowmarket, bricklayer

Archer, John (51) Hill Street Bufferland (West Side) Pembroke, Wales, labourer

Archer, Joseph (54) lo. 29 George Street, Shelton, Staffs. labourer (lodger)

Archer, Robert (42) h. 5 Spring Row Cotage, Stowmarket, general labourer

Armstrong, Maria (44) Six Bell PH 49 Angel Hill, Bury St Eds., w. of John (51) Lic Victualler

Arthur, Ann (55) h. 37 Little Pulteney Street, Westminster, Middx, milliner

Banyard, Ann (75) h. Violet Hill, Stowmarket, bricklayers widow (née Kimball?)

Berry, Robert h. (59) Preston Street, Preston next Faversham, Kent, gardener

Bloomfield, Eliza (19) Ipswich Street, Stowmarket, a gen se. for Alexander Curdling (32) draper

Brett (née Baker), Charlotte (60) Hadleigh Road Combs, w. of William Bridgman (61) farm lab.

Buckle, Susan (60) Moats Tye, Combs, w. of Samuel Buckle (57) agricultural lab.

Bugg, James (48) h. Ravens Bridge Cottage, Creeting St Mary, agricultural lab.

Bugg, William (37) h. Battisford, farm labourer

Burcham, Charles (43) h. 33 High Street, Weston Super Mare, Som. hatter hosier etc[1]

Chinery (née Archer), Jane (37) The Green, Stowupland, w. of John (44) chemical lab. (Mf)

Choat, John 42 & Susannah (44) his wife, 21 Lisford Street, Camberwell, Surrey

Clarke, Ann (57) 5 Prospect Street, Ipswich, w. of Robert (59) lab. at manure works

Cooper, Eliza (71) h. Grundisburgh

Cooper, Emily (40) h. Lime Tree Place, Stowmarket, retired farmers wife

Cooper, Thomas Philip (41) h. St Matthew Street, Ipswich, grocer

Copeland, Henry (16) 1 South View, South Sea Road, Croydon, Surrey, brewers lab.

Copping, Samuel (50) h. The Harp, Ipswich, Beer House keeper

Cox, Thomas (40) lo. 39 Holliday, Birmingham, War. Bricklayers lab.

Daking (née Mudd), Matilda (66) Bentley Lodge, Bentley, w. of Robert (60) farmer[1]

Dallinger, George (49) h. High Street, Barking, railway platelayer

Dallinger, William (61) h. High Street, Barking, agricultural lab.

Elliston, Mary A. (60) Ebbs Green. Lawshall, w. of Henry (39) a Head Carrier

Eslea, Amy (29) Tavern Street, Stowmarket, w. of Walter 37) malsters lab. (née Archer?)

Garnham, Henry (28) h. 5 Church Street, Lambeth, Surrey, private policeman

Goddard, Sarah (32) East Stockwell Street, Colchester, Essex. w. of David (42) stone sawer

Gowing, Susanna (50) Elmsett w. of John A Gowing (44) a retired farmer

Hayward, George (37) h. Old Farm House, Creeting All Saints, gentleman

Hill, Frederick (33) (head) Bramford Works, Bramford, general labourer

James, Alice (15) Bury Street, Stowmarket, se. (gen) for Wm Tydeman (52) furniture broker

James, Shadrack (64) h. Creeting All Saints, agricultural labourer

Jay, Thomas Nunn (34) h. Caldwell Hall Road, Caldwell Villa, Ipswich, coal merchant

Kemble, John (48) 9 Bull Inn, St Martin in the Fields, Middx. greengrocer

Kent, Mary Ann (32) Town Farm House, Little Stonham, w. of Frederic (35) farmer

Lambert, Ellen (7) 1 South View, South Sea Rd, Croydon, Surrey, d. of Chas E (28) brewers drayman

Moore, Harriett (46) 351 Goswell Road, Clerkenwell Middx. w. of George (47) hosier

Morter, Caroline (50) 26 Club Road, Bethnal Green, Middx. w. of Henry (54) ivory turner (née Kemball?)

Mount, Emma (20) Raily Hotel, Park Lane, Tottenham, Middx. general domestic servant

Mount, William (16) High Street, Barking, agricultural lab., s. of George (49) railway platelayer

Mudd, Frank (12) bo. Ballygate Street, Collegiate School, Beccles

Mudd, William (58) h. Willow Marsh, Stoke-by-Nayland, farmer

Mudd, William F (13) bo. (boarder) Ballygate Street, Collegiate School, Beccles

Mulley, Ann (45) 9 Wapping Road Shadwell, Middx. w. of Samuel (46) corn miller

Mulley, Anna (36) Westbourne, Ipswich, w. of William (42) general labourer

Smith, William (47) h. Tannery Road, Combs, tannery labourer

Terry, Elizabeth (31) Collinson Cottage, Teddington, Middx. w. of Henry (27) head gardener

Webster, Eliza A (32) St Helens, Ipswich, w. of Albert Webster (36) Innkeeper

KEY:

h. = head	w. = wife	s. = son	d. = daughter	se. = servant
si. = sister	v. = visitor	sil. = sister-in -law	snil. = son-in -law	lo. = lodger
bo. = boarder	f. = father	p. = pupil	as. = assistant	

1891

Archer, George	58	f.	Fulham, London	
Archer, James	82	h.	Stowmarket	
Archer, Robert	51	h.	Stowmarket	
Armstrong, Maria	54	h.	Bury St Edmunds (St Mary)	
Banyard, Ann	85	h.	Stowmarket (née Archer?)	
Berry, Thomas	21	snil.	Croydon, Surrey	
Bloomfield, Frederick	37	h.	Weeley, Essex	
Bridgman, Charlotta	71	w.	Great Finborough	
Buckle, John	66	h.	Needham Market	
Bugg, William	42	h.	Creeting St Peter	
Chapman, Eliza	27	w.	Hulme, Lancashire	
Chinery, Jane	48	w.	Stowmarket	
Choat, John	52	h.	Camberwell, London	
Clarke, Ann	66	w.	Ipswich St Matthew	
Cooper, Thomas P	51	h.	Ipswich St Matthew	
Copeland, Ann	19	se.	Stowmarket	
Copeland, Eliza	17	se.	Stowmarket	
Copeland, Harry	26	h.	Woodbridge	
Dallenger, George	59	h.	Barking	
Dallenger, William	72	h.	Needham Market	
Easler, Walter	52	h.	Stowmarket	
Hammond, Frederick	23	h.	Creeting St Mary	
Hayward, Alice	37	d.	Creeting All Saints	
Hayward, Caroline	35	d.	Creeting All Saints	
Hayward, Catherine	28		Orford, Suffolk	
Hayward, Emily	40	d.	Creeting All Saints	
Hayward, Horace	39	h.	Creeting St Mary	
Hill, Frederick	43	h.	Bramford	
James, Alice	25	se.	Ipswich St Margaret	
James, Ann M	29	se.	Ipswich St Matthew	
James, Anna Maria	60	se.	Coddenham	
James, Emma	27	se.	Shenfield, Essex	
James, George E	30	h.	Ramsey, Essex	
James, Letitia	21	se.	Ipswich St Matthew	
James, Meshach	69	h.	Creeting St Mary	
James, Shadrack	74	h.	Creeting All Saints	
James, Walter	28	lo.	St Margaret & St John the Evangelist Westminster	
Jay, Thomas N	45	h.	Ipswich St Margaret	
Jennings, Kate C	20	se.	Ipswich St Margaret	
Lambert, Ellen	17	se.	Croydon, Surrey	
Manister, Elizabeth	46	w.	Wonersh, Surrey	
May, Susan	53	w.	Stowmarket	
Meakings, Sarah	48	w.	Islington, London	
Moore, Harriett	56	w.	Clerkenwell, London	
Mudd, Annie E	26	d.	Stonham Aspall	
Mudd, Caroline T	12	d.	Stonham Aspall	
Mudd, Frank	22	s.	Stonham Aspall	
Mudd, Frederick W	46	h.	Stonham Aspall	
Mudd, Isabella A	17	d.	Stonham Aspall	
Mudd, Margaret H	15	d.	Stonham Aspall	
Mudd, Mary	23	d.	Stonham Aspall	
Mudd, Mary Smith	52	w.	Stonham Aspall (née Cooper)	
Mudd, Philip H	18	s.	Stonham Aspall	
Mulley, Anna	46	w.	Ipswich St Matthew	
Pizzey, Sarah	50	w.	St Paul Deptford, London	
Ruffles, Rosetta J	19	se.	Streatham, London	
Sheppard, Fanny	23	w.	Mickfield	
Southgate, Albert	3	s.	Stowupland	
Southgate, Arthur	9	s.	Stowupland	
Southgate, Thomas	7	s.	Stowupland	
Wyard, Emma	23	w.	Ipswich St Matthew	

1901

Ames, Ann M	39	d.	Ipswich Stoke St Mary	
Archer, Robert	63	h.	Stowmarket	Labourer chemical works
Armstrong, Maria	64	h.	Bury St Edmunds	
Battle, Annie	28		Combs	
Berry, Samuel	33	bo.	Croydon, Surrey	Navvy
Berry, Thomas	31	h.	Croydon	Brewer's drayman
Bloomfield, Frederick	46	h.	Adleigh, Essex	Horseman on farm
Brooks, Emma	37	w.	Rickmansworth, Herts.	
Bugg, James	67	br.	Milden	
Bugg, William	52	h.	Milden	Farm baliff/stockman
Chinery, Jane	56	h.	Stowmarket	Timekeeper (née Archer)
Clay, Caroline	47	w.	Bury St Edmunds	
Cooper, Thomas	61	h.	Felixstowe	Retired tea merchant
Copeland, Charles	18	v.	Ipswich St Matthew	General labourer
Copeland, Ellen	17	se.	Stowmarket	Housemaid
Copeland, Harry	36	h.	Woodbridge	Coachman domestic
Copeland, John	38	h.	Combs	Ordinary agricultural lab.
Currey, Arthur	21	se.	St George, Hanover Sq., London	
Dallenger, Daniel	80	h.	Stowmarket	General labourer retired
Dallenger, William	81	h.	Barking	
Dawson, John	13	v.	Lambeth, London	
Day, Kate	30	w.	Washbrook	(née Manister?)
Easles, Amy	53	w.	Stowmarket	(née Archer)
Freeman, Alice	26	w.	Creeting St Mary	
Game, Annie	26	w.	Creeting St Mary	
Hammond, Dorothy	30	w.	Creeting St Mary	
Hammond, Frederick	23	h.	Creeting St Mary	Ordinary agricultural lab.
Hayward, Alice	49	go.	Milton Lilborne, Wilts.	Governess
Hayward, Clara	30	v.	Sundridge, Kent	Living on own means
Hayward, Emily	50	ni.	Barking	
Hayward, Horace	50	h.	Creeting St Mary	Farmer
Holden, Eva Mildred	6	d.	Stoke by Nayland	
James, Albert	15	s.	Gosbeck	Yardman on farm
James, Alfred	42	h.	Gosbeck	Horseman on farm
James, Alice	35	n.	Ipswich St Nicholas	Monthly nurse
James, Ann M	70	h.	Ipswich Stoke St Mary	
James, Edwin A	7	s.	Gosbeck	
James, Florence	16	se.	Willesden, Middx.	Domestic servant
James, George E	40	h.	Benhall	
James, Grace E	13	se.	Coddenham	General servant domestic
James, Leitia	31	bo.	Ipswich St Matthew	
James, Walter	39	h.	Waltham Holy Cross, Essex	Metropolitan Police Insp.
Jay, Thomas N	55	h.	Ipswich St Margaret	Cab proprietor
Kent, Mary Ann	51	w.	Sundridge, Kent	(née Hayward)
Kent, Thomas G	25	s.	Sundridge, Kent	Farmer's son
Malley, Annie	56		Ipswich St Matthew	Laundress
Mercer, Ellen	27	w.	Croydon, Surrey	
Moy, Susan	64	w.	Stowmarket (née Archer)	
Mudd, Annie	32	h.	Ipswich St Margaret	Schoolmistress
Mudd, Caroline L	21	si.	Ipswich St Margaret	
Mudd, Frederick	71	f.	Ipswich St Margaret	Retired Farmer
Mudd, Margaret H	24		Derby	Probationer nurse
Mudd, Mary	32	si.	Ipswich St Margaret	Schoolmistress
Mudd, Philip	27	bo.	Portsmouth, Hants.	Schoolmaster
Mudd, Thomas	78	h.	Barking	
Mudd, William	33	bo.	Erith, Kent	Draper's manager
Mulley, Annie	56	w.	Ipswich St Matthew	
Rivers, Clara	11	d.	Creeting St Mary	Attending school
Rivers, Rose	5	d.	Creeting St Mary	Attends school
Rivers, William	15	s.	Creeting St Mary	Carrier's help
Roberts, Ethel	1	d.	Combs	
Sawyer, Ellen	30		Rushmere St Andrew	
Sharman Hilda	1	d.	Nacton	
Sharman, Rosie	4	d.	Nacton	
Sillett, Louisa	17		Orford	
Souter, Dora G	6	d.	Combs	
Southgate, Albert C	13	s.	Chelmondiston	At school
Southgate, Arthur	19	s.	Chelmondiston	Groom on farm
Southgate, George	21	s.	Chelmondiston	
Southgate, Thomas	17	s.	Chelmondiston	Postman
Steggnel, Eliza	25	w.	Stowmarket	
Terry, Elizabeth	57	w.	Fulwood, Lancs.	(née Hayward?)
Turner, Alice	4	d.	Creeting St Mary	
Webster, Eliza Ann	51	w.	Ipswich St Margaret	Living on own means
Wyard, Emma	32	w.	Ipswich St Matthew	

KEY:

h. = head	w. = wife	s. = son	d. = daughter
se. = servant	si. = sister	sil. = sister-in -law	v. = visitor
snil. = son-in-law	lo. = lodger	bo. = boarder	f. = father
p. = pupil	as. = assistant		

Appendix C

St Mary's Churchyard Badley

Monumental Inscriptions

NOTES

As noted in Chapter 3 and illustrated by Fig 3.12, less than a quarter of those buried in the churchyard now have a marked grave.

Although there have been 448 recorded burials since 1589, there are now only 65 monuments in the churchyard, commemorating 85 persons. 32 of these relate to 20th & 21st century burials.

With the exception of one or two on the left of the pathway, all the inscription have been freshly transcribed. For those, which were too faded to read properly, I have incorporated a transcription recorded approximately 100 years ago obtained from the Suffolk Record Office.

MONUMENTS TO THE LEFT OF THE PATHWAY (South -west corner) (see plan Chapter 3, Fig 3.12)
(each line of the inscription is separated by '/')

1.	HAYWARD W	:	Sacred to the memory of WILLIAM third son of GEORGE /and ELIZABETH HAYWARD /of this Parish /11th March 1856 / aged 7 years (F/stone : WH)
2.	MUMFORD R	:	To the memory of /ROBERT MUMFORD /(late of Combs) /who departed this life Sept 23 1850.
3.	CLARK P	:	PETER CLARKE /1936-1999 (Died on 27th March 1999, buried on 1st April 1999
4.	ROSE J T	:	JOHN THOMAS /ROSE /30.4.1910 - 13.9.1999 / God is the strength / of my heart and my / portion forever
5.	WELHAM I	:	In loving remembrance /of /ISSAC WELHAM /who departed this life /June 28th 1874 /aged 25 years. (F/stone : I+W)
6.	HAMMOND E	:	In /most loving memory of /EMMA ELIZABETH /widow of /HUGH HUNTEN HAMMOND /late of Grimston, Norfolk
	HAMMOND E E	:	/who died August 6th 1944 /in the 84th year of her age /chosen of God and precious /also of /EDITH EMMA HAMMOND /died October 12th 1975 /aged 87 years.
7.	HAYDON F G[1]	:	(Military grave - RAF) 1443638 Sergeant /F G HAYDON /Pilot /Royal Air Force /9th June 1943, age 31 /He set the claim of duty /above desire for happiness /may his cheerful courage /be always our example. (i.e Francis Gordon Haydon)
8.	HAYDON J D	:	In /loving memory of /my beloved husband /JOHN DOUGLAS HAYDON /who died 7th August 1993 /Aged 76 years.
	HAYDON B A		And in memory of /BERYL AGGIS HAYDON / loving wife, mother and grandmother /1st April 1916 - 24th April 2004.
9.	HAYDON F E	:	In /loving memory of /my beloved husband /FRANCIS EMMANUEL HAYDON /who died May 4th 1945 /aged 65 years
	HAYDON C L		/The strife is o'er /also /CARRIE LOUISE HAYDON /passed away July 8th 1981 /aged 97 years.
10.	HOLLIS F	:	In loving memory of /beloved husband and father /FREDERICK HOLLIS /who fell asleep 9th Nov 1947 /aged 64 years.
11.	FOSTER M A	:	In /loving memory of /our dear mother /MARY ANN FOSTER /died 15th August 1952 /aged 87 years /Gone but not forgotten.
12.	MORTON C	:	In /loving memory /of /CHARLES MORTON /who died April 26th 1948 /aged 73 /Thy will be done (At foot) Also his
	MORTON B W		beloved wife /BARBARA WADDELL MORTON /who died Sept 18th 1954 /aged 65 years.
13.	SCOTT E F	:	In /loving memory of /EMILY FRANCES /SCOTT /1985 - 1967.
14.	SCOTT L	:	In /loving memory of /LEONARD SCOTT /1881 - 1968.
15.	FARROW C	:	In /affectionate /memory of /a dear husband /father and grandpa /CHARLES S. FARROW /who died 20th Oct 1968 /aged 58 years.
16.	WATKINS D	:	DOROTHY WATKINS /1902-1989 /a Geordie /at home in /Little London.
17.	FARROW R C	:	In everlasting memory of /a devoted husband /and father /RICHARD CHARLES FARROW /28th January 1947 /11th May 1993 /aged 46 years.
18.	SORE R W	:	In loving memory /of ROYAL WILLIAM /SORE /died 30th May 1975 /in his 68th year /and his beloved wife IRENE F.
	SORE I F L		L. SORE /died 21st Aug 1997 /aged 78 years.
19.	SCOTT D	:	In /loving memory of /DOROTHY SCOTT /died 4th March 1969 /Aged 58 /much loved mother /of GEOFFREY /Rest in Peace
20.	HODGSON F	:	Sacred /to the memory of /FRANCES HODGSON /1914 - 1982 /also her husband /ANDREW 1913 - 1991
	HODGSON A		
21.	HADLEY N A M	:	In /loving memory /of /a dear wife and mother /NELLIE A. M. HADLEY /who died 18th Sept 1969 /in her 80th
	HADLEY G E		year /forever with the lord /GEORGE EDWARD /HADLEY /passed away 4th April 1977 /aged 87 years /Reunited with mother
22.	HADLEY R	:	In /loving memory of /a dear wife /mother and grandmother /RUBY HADLEY /29.9.1907 - 11.12.1973 /also a dear
	HADLEY C		husband /father and grandfather /CECIL HADLEY /1.4.1911 - 4.10.1992 /Reunited.
23.	STEEL V K	:	In /loving memory /of /a dear wife /mother and grandmother /VERA K. STEEL /died 2nd Aug 1982 /aged 66 /dearly
	STEEL L A C		loved - sadly missed /also a dear father and grandfather /LUIS A. C. STEEL /died 14th December 1989 /dearly loved - sadly missed.
24.	WOOD E M	:	To the /dear memory of /a beloved mother /and grandma /ETHEL MABEL WOOD /devoted wife of THOMAS PERCY /who passed peacefully /into rest /12 December 1987 /aged 96 years.

25.	MUDD W MUDD A	:	In memory of /WILLIAM MUDD /late of Badley Hall /7th February 1857 /aged 68 years /also /ANNE wife of WILLIAM MUDD /who departed this life /8th August 1864 /aged 75 years.
26.	BUCK B M	:	In loving memory /of /BABARA MARY BUCK /'Bub' /who died 16th January 2001 /aged 81years /a devoted wife, mum, /grandma & great grandma /Always in our thoughts
27.	MANISTRE E	:	In memory of /ELIZABETH wife of J W MANISTRE of Creeting St Mary /daughter of M. T. S. COOPER of this Parish /who entered into rest on the 15th April 1865 /be thou faithful unto death /and I will give thee the crown of life.
28.	COOPER M S COOPER T S	:	Sacred to the memory of /MARY wife of THOMAS SNELL COOPER late of this Parish who died 16th February 1876 aged 64 years. Sacred to the memory of /THOMAS SNELL COOPER /late of the Bridge Farm in this Parish /who departed this life /July 30th 1869 /aged 62.
29.	SCOTT A B	:	In / memory of / ARTHUR BLAKE SCOTT /of / Badley Hall / 16th August 1917 - 27th August 1997

MONUMENTS TO THE LEFT OF PATHWAY. (South-east corner)

30.	THORPE J W V	:	John THORPE (Temporary small wooden cross to mark ashes) (Died 1999)(close to porch and south wall)
31.	CHANDLER J CHANDLER S	:	(Double headstone) In memory of /JACOB CHANDLER /who /departed this life /July 10th 1778 /aged 48 years /also SARAH CHANDLER /who /departed this life /February 11th 1820 /aged 84 years (Double footstone : S+C /1820 & J+C /1778)
32.	MUDD C	:	Sacred to the memory of CAROLINE /the daughter of /WILLIAM and ANN MUDD /who died 29th July 1825 /aged 3 years (Footstone : C+M /1825)
33.	MUDD R[2]	:	In loving memory of /ROBERT son of /THOMAS /and ELIZABETH MUDD /of Badley /who departed this life / February 9th 1817 /aged 37 years. (Footstone : R+M /1817)
34.	MUDD M A	:	Sacred to the memory of /MARY ANN daughter of /THOMAS /and ELIZABETH MUDD /of Badley /who departed this life /September 22nd 1815 /aged 32 years (Footstone : MAM /1815)
35.	MUDD J	:	In memory of /JOHN MUDD /son of /THOMAS MUDD /late of this Parish /who departed this life /the 9th day of January /1804.
36.	MUDD T	:	THOMAS MUDD /late of this Parish /16th August 1793 /aged 48 years
37.	MUDD E	:	In memory /ELIZABETH /wife of THOMAS MUDD /of Badley /26th September 1817 /aged 60 years (Footstone : E+M /1817)
38.	MUDD R	:	Sacred /to the memory of /Mr RICHARD MUDD /of Aldham who /died March 16th 1834 (Footstone : R+M /1834)
39.	FREWER A	:	ANN FREWER /19th July 1729 /aged 21 years
40.	GOODWIN A	:	..... / memory of ANN /wife of W GOODWIN / who died 10 May 1726 /aged 89 years
41.	GOODWIN J[3]	:	Here lieth the body /of JOHN GOODWIN /died the 14th of /November 1690 /aged 46. (Footstone : J+G / ...)
42.	SMITH H	:	Mr HENRY SMITH /20th September 1713 /aged 41 years
43.	PENNINGTON PENNINGTON	: :	In memory of /MARY JANE PENNINGTON /born 6th March 1825 died 21st June 1902. In memory of /EMILY PENNINGTON /late of Needham Market /born 21st May 1830 died 4th August 1901.
44.	WOODS W	:	In /loving memory of /a devoted husband and father /WILLIAM WOODS /who died 25th Jan 1947 /aged 80 years.
45.	MUDD R C	:	Erected /to the memory /of /WILLIAM CUPPER MUDD /infant son of /WILL and HEPHZIBAH MUDD /of Stoke by Nayland /who departed this life /August 4th 1850. (Footstone : W.C.M. /1850)
46.	HAYWARD F	:	Erected /to the memory of /FREDERICK HAYWARD /the infant son of /GEORGE and /ELIZABETH HAYWARD /who died / November 1841. (Footstone : F+H /1842)
47.	MUDD C	:	In memory of /CLARA infant child of /FREDERICK and MARY MUDD /who died March 8th /1866. (Footstone : C+M /1866)
48.	ROPER E	:	In memory of /ELIZABETH wife of /ROBERT ROPER /who departed this life /July 7th 1832 /aged 55 years. (Footstone : E+R /1832)

Fig 1[1]

Fig 2[3]

NOTES:

[1] F G HAYDON : This airman's death is recorded on the Memorial Gates, Finborough Road, Stowmarket, on a bronze plaque "IN HONOURED MEMORY OF THOSE OF THIS TOWN WHO FELL IN THE SECOND WORLD WAR 1939 - 1945". Born at Badley, he was married and lived at Stowmarket. (Fig 1 above).

[2] R MUDD : In 1923 Charles Partridge recorded this headstone as being 'alongside the south wall of the nave', adding , "I remember him well. As children we went picking primroses in his wood. As far as I can recollect, he is the only person born in the eighteenth century (28 Sept 1784) whom I ever saw."

[3] J GOODWIN : Dated 10th November 1690, this is the oldest marked grave in the churchyard (Fig 2 above).

49. SEAPY S	:	SAMUEL /SEAPY /late of this parish /who departed this life /the 30 March 1744 /aged 58 years (Footstone : S+S /1744)
50. MOORE J	:	JAMES MOORE of this Parish /who died June 15th 1831 aged 66 years /Also of SARAH his wife daughter of /JOHN
MOORE S	:	MEDOWS THEOBALD of Henly Hall in this County /who died October 5th 1855 aged 76 years. In memory of JAMES
MOORE J M	:	MEADOWS MOORE son of /JAMES and SARAH MOORE /who died April 13th 1855 aged 62 years. In
MOORE H	:	memory of HENRIETTA wife of /JOHN KIRBY MOORE of this Parish the daughter of JOSEPH PENNINGTON of
MOORE J K	:	Godstone in the County of Surrey /who died April 8th 1866 aged 77 years. In memory of /JOHN KIRBY MOORE /54 years Churchwarden of this parish /who died October 31st 1885 /aged 91 years
51. COOPER S	:	SAMUEL son of CLARK and ESTHER COOPER /1st May 1795 /aged 30 /MARY wife of SAMUEL COOPER /daughter
COOPER M	:	of JOHN and AMEY SIMPSON /15th February 1820 /aged 52 (Footstone : M+C /1820 & S+C /1795)
52. COOPER C	:	Sacred /to the memory of /CLARK COOPER /aged 22 years /who accidently lost his life /September 15th 1805 /in the service of a friend /whom he voluntarily offered /to asist in concluding /his harvest. (Footstone : C+C /1805)
53. COOPER C	:	CLARK COOPER /of this Parish /20th April 1827 /aged 90 /ESTHER wife of CLARK COOPER /10th August 1820
COOPER E	:	/ aged 78 years (Double footstone : EC+CC /1820 1827)
54. MUDD A	:	Sacred to the memory of Ann the wife of /RICHARD MUDD /who departed this life /August 13th 1842 /aged 60 years. (Footstone : A+M /1842)
55. PYMAN A	:	In memory of /AMEY PYMAN /wife of THO PYMAN /of Needham Market /who died /5th March1825 /aged 55 /Know
PYMAN T	:	I................the Lord /Mr. THOMAS PYMAN /Died 6th December 1840 /aged 71 years
56. SIMPSON W	:	In memory of /WILLIAM, son of /JOHN SIMPSON /and Amy his wife /who departed this life /February 9th 1817 /aged 41 years. (Footstone : W+S)
57. SIMPSON A	:	Abraham son of JOHN and AMEY SIMPSON /8th November 1802 /aged 28 years /SARAH wife of the above /daughter
SIMPSON S	:	of WEBSTER & ABIGAIL ADAMS /14th November 1802, aged 23 years
58. SIMPSON E	:	ELIZABETH daughter of JOHN and AMEY SIMPSON /24th March 1795 aged 24 (Footstone : E+S)
59. JAY A T	:	Sacred /to the memory of /ANNE TOKELOVE JAY /the surviving daughter of /EDWARD and SARAH JAY /of this Parish /who departed this life /the 23rd of May 1831 /Aged 50 years. (Footstone : ATJ /1831)
60. JAY E	:	Sacred /to the memory of /EDWARD JAY /late of this Parish /13th July 1822 /aged 56 years (Footstone : ... /...)
61. HAMMOND A	:	In /loving memory of /ABRAHAM HAMMOND /who died January /1917 /aged 82 years /Also of /SARAH HAMMOND
HAMMOND S	:	/wife of the above /who died December 31 /1916 /aged 80 years /In thy presence is fulfillness of joy.
62. HAMMOND S	:	In /memory of /SARAH /the dear child of /ABRAHAM and SARAH HAMMOND /of this Parish /died Dec 27 1881 /aged 4 years /The Lord gave and the Lord haith /taken away blessed be the name /of the Lord
63. FRESHWATER	:	EVA VIOLET MARY FRESHWATER /September 23 1972 /Rest in Peace.
64. KEY F L	:	FLORENCE LILIAN KEY /January 6th 1987 /Peace Perfect Peace.
65. ROBINS H[1]	:	Tablet on south wall - (now indeciferable) but from an transcript made on 12 July 1873: HENRIETTA MARIA, wife of CHARLES ROBINS /of ye Middle Temple Esq., and daughter /of WILLIAM DUNCOMBE of Battlesden /in ye County of Bedford /lyeth here /she died ye 5th of February 1728 in ye 42 year of her age. (Arms: per pale argent and sable, two flanches and three fleurs de lis all counterchanged [ROBINS?] impaling per chevron engrailed gules & argent 3 tallbots, heads erased counterchanged [DUNCOMBE]) (reproduced Chapter 3, Fig 3.11).

NOTE:

[1] Maj Richard Gipps, Esq.,who had inherited the manor of Badley from the Poleys, was married to Isabella Duncombe, who is presumed to be Henrietta's sister. Henrietta probably spent a lot of her time at Badley while her lawyer husband was working from his chambers in London, which would explain why she was buried at Badley (see also Chapter 6, Note [2], page 164).

Appendix D

Some Badley Wills
&
Inqusition Post Mortems

WILLS :

There is a good selection of wills at the Suffolk Record Office, (mainly in the Ashburnham Family Archives (HA1)) and in the National Archives (PCC Wills available online) relating to the Poleys or Badley.

Many of these wills still have tantalising fragments of their seals attached, but unfortunately those that remains are understandably very brittle and too fragile to copy.

In this Appendix some of the examples selected are reproduced in full, whereas others have been summarised. Those written in the 15th and 16th centuries give an interesting insight into the type and location of property bequeathed as well as old English usage.

The earliest, relating to Edmund Alcocke (1491), is quite specific and important in this account on Badley, as it provides the evidence of the accession of the Manor from Roger Mortimer through to the Poleys. As discussed in Chapter 3, I also believe it clarifies the location of the Badley Chantry.

The will of Elizabeth Garneys (1537) is a pleasure to read. Although she resided at Kenton, her will, like that of her husband William (1525) (39 Bodfelde), is Badley-related. Whether she was actually "buryed in the churche of Badley, before our ladye's aulter, by my sonne William, and a marble stone to be layde over me" in accordance with her wish is unclear. If she was, the memorial is certainly not there now. It may, of course, have had to make way for the later Poley-related memorials we find there today.

At the end of his will Edmund Poley (1640) apologises to his wife for not leaving her as much as she probably expected and asks her, "not to take it unkindlie that I did not more for her, she deserving soe much from me, I would gladly have donne it, if my state would have permitted it."

The wills of the bachelor brothers Henry (1704) and Edmund Poley (1714) are short and simple and both written in their own hand. They were the last males in the Badley/Poley dynasty and show the transfer of the main estate, firstly from one to the other and then onto their sister, Elizabeth Gipps (née Poley).

The Will marked * is summarised from *"Wills from The Archdeaconry of Suffolk 1637-1640"* by M E Allen & N R Evans (1986).

The size of the bequeaths in some of these wills shows that the Poleys' possessed great wealth. Some sources suggest that for example a £1 bequeathed in 1491 is the equivalent of over £550 now; £500 bequeathed in 1671 is the equivalent of over £52,000 and £400 bequeathed in 1714 is the equivalent of over £39,000.

INQUISITIONS POST MORTEM :

TENANTS who held land directly from the Crown were known as tenants in chief. On the death of a tenant in chief, an enquiry was held by the **escheator** of the county concerned. These enquiries are known as **inquisitions post mortem** (IPM's) and detail the land held by the tenant at the time of his death, by what rents and services this land was held and the name and age of the next heir - the oldest son, if they had one. Many tenants in chief were also manorial lords so IPM's will often include details of manors. This procedure continued to operate until Knight Service, which was its basis, fell into disuse and was finally abolished in 1662.

The two records reproduced below for **Henry Poley** (1487) and **Edmund Alcocke** (1492) from the *Inquisition Post Mortem* calendars 1352-150 commence with a writ date. These refer to The Writ of Diem Clausit Extremum (*'he has closed his last day'*) i.e. the date it was issued by the Court of Chancery to the escheator, instructing him to make the inquisition. Sometimes the escheator acted without a writ.

IPM's are held at the Public Record Office, Kew. The main series are those in C 132-142. There are transcripts in E 149-150 and WARD 7. The principal finding aids are:

Calendar of Inquisitions Miscellaneous, Henry III to VII (London 1916-1968) Calendar of Inquisitions Post Mortem, Henry III to IV & VII (London 1898-1989) List & Indexes XXII, XXVI, XXXII, XXXIII Index of Inquisitions Post Mortem, Henry VIII to Charles I

They can be a useful resource for genealogists as

- they include details of the next heir;
- they may assist in tracing the descent of manors &
- they contain the names of the local jurors.

Inquisition Post Mortem

Henry Poley of Badley, Suffolk (1487)

Writ: 9 Oct 3 Hen VII : Inq. the last day but one of October, 3 HenVII (1487)
Jurors: William Spryngwell, Thomas Russell, Nicholas Lesse, John Smalwode, Thomas Bullyannt, William Lely, William Tutwey, John Philpot, John Lese, Thomas Gelyot, Richard Barker & John Chilter.

He died 3 Aug., 2 Hen VII seised of the undermentioned close in fee. Edmond Poley, aged 2 and more, is his son and heir.

SUFF : A close called 'Kyesfield' in Badle, parcel of the Manor of Badle, worth 53s 4d., held of Cicely, Duchess of York, as of the Honour of Clare by Knight service.

Edmund Alcok of Badley, 'gentilman' (1491)

Writ: 24 May 7 Henry VII : Inq. Saturday the eve of St Simon & St Jude the Apostles, 8 Henry VII (1491)
Jurors : Geoffrey Bergham, William Geffrey, John Wymbyll, Henry Ottley, Roger Hamlyn, Ralph Baker, Thomas Perkyn, John Man, William Grenegres, Thomas Ryngbell, Richard Brane, Walter Deye & Robert Balhed.

He died on St Valentine's day last, seised of the undermentioned manner and land in fee. Elizabeth, wife of Roger Roookwode esq, aged 30 and more, his daughter, and Edmund Poley, aged 6 and more, his cousin, viz son of Henry Poley, son of Margery Poley, late wife of Simon Poley deceased, his other daughter, are his next heirs

SUFF : Manor of Badley Halle in Badley, Needham and Combs, with 20 marks, held of Cicely Duchess of York, as of the honour of Clare, by service of ½ of a Knights' fee.

Forty Acres of land and 40a. pasture in Badley, with 5 marks, held of the said Duchess, as of the said Honour, by fealty and 4d. yearly, for all service.

Wills

IN DATE ORDER

Edmund Rafeman als Alcoke, Gent. of Badley, Suffolk, Gentleman (10 Feb 1491)

IN the name of god amen the 10th day of February 1491, I Edmund Rafeman also known as Edmund Alcoke of Badley in the diocese of Norwich gentleman being of sound mind and memory yet sick in body make my testament in this manner.
First I bequeath my soul to god almighty to the blessed virgin Mary and to all the saints my body to be buried in the churchyard where ever it pleases god. Item I bequeath to the high altar of the parish church of Badley for tithes forgotten 6s 8d. Item I bequeath to the fabric of the same church of Badley 40s. Item I bequeath to the high altar of the parish church of Combs 6s 8d. Item I bequeath to the high altar of the parish church of Battisford 3s 4d. Item I bequeath to the high altar of the parish church of Ringshall 3s 4d. Item I bequeath to the repair of the parish church of Little Finborough 3s 4d. Item I bequeath to the house of the Franciscan [minor?] friars of Ipswich 10s. I bequeath to the convent of the same place to sing for my soul 10s. Item I bequeath to the convent of Dominican friars of Ipswich 10s. Item I bequeath to Brother Nicholas to sing for my soul 10s. Item I bequeath to the convent of Carmelite friars to sing for me 10s. Item I bequeath to an honest priest who will sing for my soul in the parish church of Badley aforesaid for my soul & for the souls of my ancestors and for the soul of Richard Schyrlocke my uncle, my wives Beatrice and Isabel, and all my friends and benefactors until the end and term of 5 years immediately following after my death, 10 marks lawful money of England coming from my lands lately purchased by me as appears below and one messuage by me newly built called Prestshows with garden and orchard ajoining the same as now enclosed rendering therefore to the chief lords of the fee 12d per annum. Item I will that my heirs are always to choose the said priest provided always that if my heirs do not find an honest priest for nine months [?] then I will that the house bequeathed to the said priest and the said money be expended by my heirs to the repair and sustenance of my chapel there and the said priest's house. And if for all no priest will have it then I will that the Master of the College of Metyngham who then is to have it and for the time being have the said 10 marks of silver until my heir does have an honest priest. Item I will that Edmund Poley senior have half my manor of Badley lately purchased and recovered from Robert Mortymer until my heir come to his legal age so that with the farm thereof he can provide for his sisters viz. Margaret, Elizabeth, Anna and Isabella at marriage. Item I will that the said Edmund Poley have all my lands and tenements on the south side of Badley that are held in fee simple to him and his heirs in perpetuity rendering therefore annually to my said presbytery from the said lands in part payment of the said 10 marks, 40s lawful money of England until the end of 5 years aforesaid. Item I will that the said Edmund Poley senior to have all my lands and tenements purchased by me in Combs and Battisford to hold to him and his heirs for ever rendering therefore annually to the said presbytery 53s 4d lawful money of England in part payment of the said 10 marks as above. And if it happens that the said Edmund his heirs and assigns default in payment of the said 7 marks in part or in full in any of the 5 years then all the foresaid lands and tenements in Badley, Combs and Battisford are to be sold by my executors as for my heirs and the money thereby coming to be fully disposed in good works for me and my benefactors. Item I will that Roger Rookwood esquire have all my land and tenements in Badley to the north with one water mill leading from Combs Ford towards Needham to hold to him, his heirs and assigns for ever rendering therefore annually to my said presbytery for the time being or to the College of Metyngham as above 40s in part payment of the said 10 marks and if happens that Roger, his heirs or assigns default in payment of the said 40s in part or in full in any year of the said 5 years then my executors are to sell the said lands and tenements and use the money fully in works of charity and improvement viz. in Badley aforesaid wherever most necessary. Item I will that Richard Cowper and his wife to have the tenement in which they dwell with all its appurtenances lying between the lane leading from the gate of Mattystye towards Combs church and from that church towards Denndye excepting one tenement called Cagges with its appurtenances lately purchased from John Roschbroke. Item I will that John Skypwyth have all that my messuage called Bottler with its appurtenances lying in Badley for the term of his life and after his decease to remain as above. Item I will that the farm of the Lyme Kylne in Needham be first used for the repair of the church of Badley manor there and the house of the said priest in the same if it is necessary or given to the poor [?] for the king's tenth and fifteenth whenever it happens. Item I require all my cofeoffees and my heirs always to deliver their estate of and in all my lands and tenements following the tenor of this my last will. The residue of all my goods not before bequeathed I bequeath to the disposition of my executors to dispose for the salvation of my soul as it appears most pleasing to god whom I ordain make and constitute Edmund Poley gentleman and William Bunttyng of Nedeham aforesaid. I appoint Roger Rokewood esquire to be supervisor. In witness Richard Cowper, John Cordye, John Skypwyth and others. Given at the day place and year above written.   [Probate at Ipswich 22nd May 1492]

NOTE: *This is an important will as it establishes the correct location of the Chantry. That is, within Badley Church and not in the grounds of the Hall shown on the Ordnance Survey map; and it refers to a water mill* "leading from Combs Ford towards Needham". *Was this on the site of the one referred to in Domesday or on the site of what we now refer to as Badley Mill?*

Edmund Poley, of Badley, Gentilman (25 July 1504)

IN the name of god Amen. The xxv Daye of the moneth of July, In the yere of oure lord god MDIV. I, Edmond Poley, Gentilman, being in good mynd, bequeith my Soule vnto Almighty god, and to oure blessed Lady saint Mary, and to all the Blessed company of heven, and my body to be buried in the church of Badley. Also, I gif to the high alter of Badley for my tithes forgotten vjs. viijd. Item, I gif vnto the Reparacion of the chirch of Badley xiijs. iiijd. Item, I gyf vnto the chirch of saint Mary Cretyng, vis. viijd. Item, I gif vnto the chirch of Blakynh'm of the Water, vjs. viijd. Item, I will haue a preest to sing for my Soule in the chirch of Badley a yere, and he to haue for his s'uice, vjs. viijd. Item, I gif to Jane my Wif, my tenement called Coterells, With alle other Landes, medues, and pastures longing vnto the same in Combys, Heigh'm, and litell ffynberrers and grete ffynberrers, both free and Copy, for terms of hir lif. And after my Wifs decesse, to remayne to myn heirs accordyng to the Will of my fader. Also, I will that Jane my Wif, have my tenementes called Notcroft, and Neutonfeld, lying in Berkyng and cretyng, till my secund Son be of the age of xxii yeres, and then I will that he shall entre into the said lands and ten'ts, To have to him, his heires, and assignees for euir. Also, I will that Jane my Wif, have my tenement called Mersshys, and a feld called Oxlands, and a medewe lying by the Ryvers side, late John Aylmer, being in Basfords, till my iiide son Thomas Poley be of th age of xxii yeres, and then he to entre to have it to him, his heirs and assignees for euirmore. And if it happe one of the ii yonger sonnes for to dye affore they com to the Age of xxii yeres Then every of them to he others heire in fourme aforesaid. And if it hap' bothe of them to dye affore the said age of xxii yeres, Than I will all their partes to be

sold by myn Executours, and the money thereof comyng evenly for to be deuided amonge my daught's then being alyve. Item, I Will and bequeith vnto eche of my daught's, that is to says, Anne, Margery, Vrsula and Elizabeth, xxti m'rks apece, at the daye of theire mariage, orells thage of xxti yeres. And if any of them dye within the age, then I will that they being alyve shalle diuide the same money betwene them. Also, I bequeith vnto my eldest Son my second pece of silu', to be deliu'ed vnto him at th' age of xx^{tie} yeres. And to eche of my other children beside ii spones of siluer at the same age to be deliuered vnto them. Also, I bequeith vnto my Wif xxli in Cornys in Whete and Barly, and What other Corne that she will have. Also, I will that all such lands as my fader hath assigned to be sold being in Stoke for the mariage of my sister to be sold by myn Executours to the p'forma'cion of my fader's will. Also, I will that Jane my Wif have the Indentures of cretyng and Blakenh'm, and seint Rob'ts in the Wode, as long as she kepeth hir sole; And aft'that to Remayne to my broder Thomas Poley. And Executours of this my present testament I ordeyne and make the said Jane, my Wif, and Thomas Poley, my broder, vnto Whom for his labour I gif xls. And Maist' Richard Wenford I make ou'vseer of the same, vnto whom I gif for his labors iiii mrks. Thise being Witnesse, John Purser, Clerk, p'son of Badley, Thomas Ralyns, and John Tanner, with others.
[EDMUND POLEY PCC 25 Holgrave 1504. Proved: 14 February 1504]

𝕰liʒabeth 𝕲arneys, of 𝕶enton (18 𝔐arch 1537)

𝕴 Elizabeth Garneys, wydowe, late the wife of John Garnes of Kenton, Esquier, the xviij daye of Marche, 1537, do make and ordeigne this my last will, as here followythe. Furst I bequeth my soule to almighty god, to our Ladye Sainte Marye, and to all the celestyall companye in hevyne ; and my bodye to be buryed in the churche of Badley, before our ladye's aulter, by my sonne William, and a marble stone to be layde over me. I bequeth to my sonne Roberte a goblett of syluer, wt a couer pcell gilte, a counter poynte wrought wt butterflyes, and, xxvis viijd for a gowne. lso I giue to my doughter yn lawe his wif my brode dyaper clothe (and) to my sonne Roberte's doughter fyve poundes. I give Margarett, my sonne Roberte's doughter, xlj to hir maryagge. To John Garneys my graundchylde a standinge cuppe gilt. To my sonne Thomas Garneys twentye poundes ; also a siluer salte wt a couer pcell gilte & six siluer spones wt sharpe knoppes. To my doughter Grymston a gilt goblett and three angell nobles. To my doughter Powley, my doughter Cotten, my doughter Wyseman, my doughter Agnes, nonne of Brosyard, my sonne Powley [and to] Margerye Poley my graundchild. I give tenne poundes to be bestowyd on repayrynge on the highe waye betwyxte Nedeham markett and Stowe. The Residewe of my goodes to be distrybuted by myne executours for the wealthe of my soule, whome I ordeyne my sonne in lawe Edmonde Poley, John Garneys my graundechilde and Thomas Garneys my sonne.
[ELIZABETH GARNEYS PCC 13 Crumwell 1537. Proved May 1539]

𝖂illiam 𝕻oley, of 𝕴cklingham, 𝕾uffolk, 𝕲entleman (3 𝕺ct 1540)

𝕴 N the name of god Amen. I Willyam Poley of Icklingham in the county of Suff. gentleman beinge in feythfull mynde thanks be to god the iijde daye of Octobre in the yere of our most dreade sovereign Lorde 1540, make and order this my presente Testament & last will in maner and forme followinge ffirst I commende my Sowle to god almightye and to our Ladye St. Marye and to all the companye of heaven and my wretched bodye to be buryed in holye Sepulture Itm I revoke anull and dysable all my other Testaments will or wills of myne by me made or wrytten before the date and daye of the present Testament and last will. Item I bequethe to Katheryne my wife all our sylver plate & stuff with all utensills & hostillamentts of howsholde which was hyrs before I maryed hyr or at any tyme synce we were maryed beyinge myne at my departynge this present lyfe. It I gyve & bequeath to the sayd Katheryne my wyfe all hyr Juells & Ryngs xcept I gyve and bequeth unto my mother Constance Aleyn one golde rynge for a remembraunce desyrynge hyr to be good to my sayd wyfe and to my chyldren in my steade and absince and that yt will please my sayd mother to be good unto my sone Thomas Poleye that he maye have all suche Legacyes & bequests as my graundfather Willyam Geddynge Esquier did gyve unto me as iiij ewes goynge in his flocke in Icklingham aforesayd and ij fether bedds. It. I gyve & bequethe to Katheryne my sayde wyfe all my shepe & lambes aswell hogge shepe as all other kynde of shepe. And also I gyve & bequeth to the sayd Katheryne my wyfe the Lease & ferme I bought of Mr. George Rows Upon this condicon that my sayde wyfe shall quarterlye paye unto Thomas Poley my sone durynge my terme in this sayde Lease & fferme yf my sayde wyfe shall lyve so longe iiij nobles sterlynge & the sayde Thomas Poley shall have goynge & pasturynge yerelye one c ewes goynge in William ffyrmags flocke & one hundred ewes goynge in John Bollings flocke & one c wethers goynge and pasturynge in harlyngs flocke and half an hundred yonge shepe goynge in Robert ffyrmages flocke & all this I gyve hym to fynde hym in chauns & Courte. It I will that yf my wyfe Katheryne departe this present lyfe before my lease be under that then I will my said son Thomas to have them during my terme and yeres & then his two Systers Constance & Margaret everye of them to have half c goynge in the flocke of Willym ffymage John Bollynge harlings and Robt. ffyrmages so longe as my leases shall endure. It. I bequeth unto Thomas my sone at such at such tyme as Katheryne my sayde wyfe shall depart this present lyfe all my flocke of shepe xcept my said daughters to have in everye flocke that they shall have goynge & pasturynge half an c shepe. It. I gyve & bequeth to Constance my daughter xl^{li.} sterlynge. It. I gyve & bequeth to Margaret my daughter xl^{li} sterlynge to be payd them at their maryage or ells at xxij yeres of age yf they marrye not before that age & yf any of my sayde daughters descease before the age of xxij yeres & before they doe marrye then I will the other daughter shall have hyr parte that shall hapt to be decease & yf both my sayde daughters depart this present lyfe before they be maryd & before thage of xxij then I will y^t Thomas Poley my sone shall have both theyr parts. And I gyve & bequeth to Thomas Poley my sone one hundred pounde to be payd hym at xxiiij yeres of age or at hyr maryage yf that he marrye before. Itm yf Thomas my sone departe thys present lyfe & be not payd hys c^{li} then I will it to be equallye devyded betwene hys ij Systers Constance and Margaret or to one of them yf the other be departed thys present lyfe. Item I gyve and bequeth to Thomas my sone a sylver Bowle with the coverynge & a dosen sylver spones. Item I bequeth to Constance my daughter half a dosen sylver spones & a sylver bowle Item I bequeth to Margaret my daughter half a dosen sylver spones & a sylver bowle. It. I gyve and bequeth to my brother Edmunde Poleye my best gowne. Item I will that an honest pryest synge for my father's sowle my mothers sowle & my grande fathers sowle with all christian sowles one holl yore next after my departynge assone as it maye be done convenyently. Item I gyve & bequeth to the reparacion of all Saynets churche in Icklyngham xxs. The Resydewe of all my goods & Cattells not bequethed I doe gyve & bequeth to Katheryne my sayd wyf whom I orden and matte myne Executrice of this my Testament & last will. In wytness whereof I have wrytten this my Testament & last will with myne owne hande & sealed with my seale the day & yere above sayd. It. I gyve & bequeth to the churche of all Saincts in icklingham my whyte Cope. By me Willyam Poley.
[Proved at Bury St. Edmund's the 6th day of September, A.D. 1557]   *L. Doose. f 144.*

The old English in this will is a joy to read. The "hogge shepe" mentioned in this will refers to young wether sheep so called because much care is required in bringing them up when young.

Edmund Poley, of Badley, Esquire (30 July 1548)

In the name of god Amen I Edmond Poley of Badley in the Countie of Suff / Esquye in good p(er)fyk mynde the 30th day of July in the yere of our lorde god a Thowsand / fyve hundreth fourty and Eight And in the second yere of the reign of o(u)r sovereigne / Lord Edward the sixe by the grace of god kinge of England France and Ireland / defend(e)r of the faithe and in the supreme hedd of the Church of England and Ireland / do make and ordayne this my last will and testament as foloweth First I bequeath my / soule to Almightie god my body to be buryd in the church of Badley. First I bequeathe / unto myrable Poley my wyf that my parte of the maner of Badley lying in Sowthe / fylde of the kinges highe wayes leading from Stowemarket unto nedeham with all my / Landes and tenements belonging unto my pate of the foresaid man(e)r of Badley lying and / being in the p(ar)isshes of Badley Combes and Batsworth in the saidCountie of Suff for / terme of her lyfe. Item I give unto Edmond Poley my sonne foure marks of good and / Lawfull mony of England to be paid out of my maner of Bradley in the foresaid Countie / for terme of his lyfe. Item I give unto henry Poley my sonne foure m(ar)kes of good & lawfull / money of England to be paide oute of the foresaid maner of Bradley and in the countie / to fulfill and p(er)forme this my last will and testament thensedewe of my maner of / Bradley be unto thuse of this my last will and testament for the spane and terme of fyve / yeres ymmediatly after my deceas. Item I give unto my wyf 12 of the best mylche neate / Item I give her 8 of my two yeryinges Item I give her 8 of my yeryinges Item I / give her Ten Ewes and Ten hogge lambes Item I give her Fortie Combe malt / Twentie Combe of wheat and eight combe mystlen Item I give unto John Poley / my sonne two trussing beddes two pillowes two bolsters two payre of sheets two payre of / blanketts two coverlett(es) belonging unto the same beddes Item I give hym my standing Cuppe / whiche my mother gave unto me. Also I do give unto my daughter in lawe Anne poley my / Cuppe with a Cover which hath my Armys in yt. It(e)m I give unto Jane Poley my daughter / and Myabyll Poley my daughter and to eche of theym Fourty mark(es) of laufull money of / England at the day of there mariages 20 mark(es) And thother 20 m(a)rks that day 12 mo(n)ths / next ensuyng ther mariag(es) Provided always that my two daughters Jane and myrable / do not mary afore the yere of our lorde 1552 yeres then I will that myn Exucutors do / paye unto eyther of them fourtye mark(es) ymmediatly after the saide yere of o(u)r lorde god a / 1552 yeres to dispose at their own will(es) Item I give unto Custaune Cryspe my / daughter Syx pound(es) so that two sufficient suerties wilbe bound for hym to leave my saide / daughter his wyfe after his deatyhe worthe Ten pound(es) of laufull money of England / Item I give unto Richard Poley my sonne Ten Pounds Item I give unto Myrable my / daughter a Cowe Item I give unto John Poley my sonne the forme in Badley whiche I have / by lease of my Cosyn Rocwoode and now in thoccupying of walter Watlond gentima(n) Item I / give unto ev(er)y one of my grandchildren being my godchildren 3s 4d if it wilbe borne of / my goodes Item I will that myn Executor and myn Executors do paye my debts Receave / my debts and fulfill this my last will and testament The residue of my plate and stuf of / household not bequeathed this my last will fulfilled and my debt(es) paid I do give unto mywyf / whom I make myn Executrix And john Poley and Thomas Poley my sonnes I do make / myn Executors This being witness of this my will and testament whose names do / followe Robert Knoppe Robert Williams clerke And Thomas Aldryche

John Pooley, of Badley, Esquire (18 August 1586)

In the name of god Amen I John / Pooley of Badley in the countie of Suff Esquire beinge of good and perfect remembraunce / Laude and prayse be therefore given to Allmightie god remembering the uncerteyntie of this life / and that Deathe is moste certeyneto all men do make and ordeyne this my laste will and testam(en)t / the eightene daye of Auguste in the nyne and twentithe yere of the raigne of our soueraign / Ladie Elizabeth by the grace of god of England France and Ireland Quene defender of / the faith etc in manner and forme followinge Firste and principallye I Commende my soule to / the mercye of Allmightie god hopinge and firmelie beleevinge o be saued by and thoroughe / the meritt(es) only of oure Lorde and Savioure Jesus Christe and my bodie I will to be honestlye / and decentlye buryed in the churche of Badley aforesayed. Touchinge toe Disposic(i)on of my land(es) / Tenement(es) goodes and chatells I will as folowethe First I give unto Richard Pooley and / Thomas Pooley my sonnes to either of them one rente chardge of tenne poundes a peece to be taken / yssuinge and goinge out of all my free landes tenement(es) and hereditament(es) that I purchased / of my cosin Edmonde wiseman to have and perceyve unto them seuerallie and yerely duringe / theire naturall lives at two Feastes in the yere that is to saye at the Feaste of the Annunciac(i)on / of the blessed virgin Marye and Sainte Michaell the Archangell by even portions. And I / will that yf one of them dye that the other shall have the whol twentie pounds a yere / duringe his naturall life. Item I give unto my sonne Edmonde Pooley and to his heires for / ever all my Mannors Landes tenement(es) and hereditament(es) whatsoever as well Freehouldes / as coppie and custumarye hould(es) Item I give unto every one of my daughters namely / Susan Croftes Margaret Palmer Mary Lanye Anne Lambe and Martha Daundye and / allso to my daughter in lawe Katherine Pooley Fower poundes a peece to buye eache of / them a / peece of plate for a rememberaunce of me. And I will the saied severall sonnes shalbe payed / unto them within halfe a yeere after my decease. Item I give and bequeathe toevery on of / my godchildren beinge my grandchyldren tenne pounde a peece to be paid unto them as / they shall severallie accomplishe the age of one and twentie yeres. And yf yt shall happen / any of them to dye before they shall have receyved the saied Legacy then I will that the / parte of hym so dyinge shalbe equallie devyded amongeste his Brothers and Sisters th(a)t / shalbe lyving at suche tyme as he so deade should have accomplished the age of one and / twentie yeres Item I give and bequeathe unto John Pooley John Boyes and John Crispe / my god children Fyve poundes a peece to be paied unto them within one Yere next after my / decease. Allso I do give unto Thomas Aldrich *John Goodale* my godchildren tenne / shillinges a peece and to Edmonde Cowper the sexton Edmond Cowper the Sawer and Rob(er)t / Bugge tenne shillinges a peece. Item I will that every one of my sonne Edmonde Pooley Etc / houshoulde servint(es) shall have five shillinges *&* eighte pence a peece to be paied untothem / within one monthe after my decease. Item I give to the reparac(i)on of Badley churche / Twentie shillinges to the poore people of Needham market twentie shilling(es) And / allso to the poore people of Stowemarket twentie shilling(es) Item I give to my sonne Thom(a)s / Pooley tenne pounes The residue of all my goodes and chattells not bequeathed {my debt(es)} / and legaceys beinge firste paied and performed and my Funeralle dischardged. I give / wholly to my sonne Edmond Pooley whome I do make one of my Executors of this my / present testamente and my sonne Richard Pooley my other Executor to whom for hys / paines therein to be taken I do give Five poundes. And I do ordeyne and appoynte / my sonne in Lawe John Lanye Supravisor of this my testament and laste will and I / do give him for his paynes therein to be taken Fyve poundes In witnesse whereof I / have to this present witnesse beinge my testament and laste will put my hande and seale the daye / and / yere first above written John Pooley Reade and published in the presence of Thomas Lambe and / Richard Grymston

A Schedule annexed to my last will / Item I do give unto Martha Lanye my grandchilde Fortie poundes of money to be delyvered by my Executore or Assiance into the handes of Mr John Layne / my sonne in Lawe or to my daughter / his wife to the use of the sayed Martha Layne within six weekes next after my decease. And yf / it shall fortune the sayed Martha Layne to dye before the saied money be due unto her then I / will the saied Legacy of Fortie pounde(s) be equally devyded amongeste her sisters nowe my / grandchildren then beinge alive. Item I do give unto John Kyrspe [sic] my godsonne Five poundes / Item I do give unto Thomas Kyrspe Five poundes Item I do give to Tobye Kirspe Five poundes / All which summes of money thus bequeathed unto the foresaied three brothers John Thomas / and Tobie my Nepheues I will be delyvered unto them within one quarter of a yere next after / my decease And yf it shall fortune any of the saied bretheren to dye before the saied money / shall be due unto hym or them. I will then thesaied Legacy be equallye devyded unto the / Survivor or Survivors of the saied Bretheren at the daye before mencyoned. Written with / myne owne hande the tenthe daye of June a thousande Fyve hundred and eighte

Richard Poley, of Badley, Gentleman (1st September 1592)

IN the name of god etc. I Richarde Poley of ~ / Badley in the County of Suff gent being god be thanked sounde in bodye and of perfecte ~ / Rememberaunce doe make my Last will and testament in mannor following First I doe betake and / bequeathe my Sowle into the handes of Almighty god by Whose mercye in Jesus Christ I / trust onely to be saved. Item I doe give and bequeathe unto Marye my Welbeloved wyfe all my / bedding Linnen plate apparell Jewells and all my other stuff whatsoever within my Lodging / at Badley aforesaid {excepte my Bootes the hanging of my Chamber and my graven armo(u)r / Item I doe further give unto my saide wyfe my Chaine of goulde and two hundred mark(es) in / money whereof twenty poundes to be paide unto her within one month after my decease, And / the Rest within one yeare after that or sooner {yf my Executors maye conveniently doe it} Item / I doe give and bequeathe unto Cicely my daughter Five hundred poundes to be paide unto her at / the daye of her mar[r]iage Item I doe give unto Edmund my sonne Fowre hundred poundes to / be paid unto him within six months after my his mar[r]iage {yf he maryeth not before he com(m)eth / to the age of one and twenty yeares} And if he maryeth before Then my Will is that the / saide money shall not be paide unto him before he com(m)eth to the saide age excepte my Executor / shall for his preferment soe cause to paye it before. And if my daughter Cicely shall happen / to dye before her mar[r]iage. Then I doe give and bequeathe her porc(i)on of five hundred pounds / unto my saide sonne to be paide unto him at the time before Limited. And if it shall happen / that my saide sonne doe dye before he maryeth. Then my Will is that my saide daughter shall / have the saide som(m)e of Fowre hundreth poundes to the nearest of her porc(i)on and to be paide / unto her at the daye of her mar[r]iage. And if it please god that they bothe dye before they come / to be mar[r]ied Then I doe give and bequeath the saide som(m)e of nine hundred ponds in manner / following. First I doe give unto my brother Mr Thomas Poley {if he be then Living} One ~ / hundred poundes Item I doe give unto my sisters children five hudred poundes to be distibuted / amonge them according to the discreac(i)on of my Brother Mr Edmund Poley as he shall / thincke them to have most neede of releife And the rest of the saide money and other goods whiche / I shall or maye have at the time of my deceasee not before or hereafter bequeathed I doe give / unto my saide brother Mr Edmund Poley. Item I doe give unto every one of my Sisters / that shall be Living at my decease Forty shilling(es) to buye them a Ringe withall and forty shilling(es) / to my sister Poley. Item I doe give unto my brother Mr Thomas Poley thee pounds six shilling(es) / eighte pence and my white gelding. Item I doe give unto my neece Anne Brewster tenne pound(es) / And my nephewe William Crofts three pounds six shilling(es) eighte pence. Item I doe give unto / my brother Mr Edmond Poley three pounds six shilling(es) eighte pence to make him a Ringe I doe / Further give unto him all my Bookes and the hanging(es) in my Chamber I doe give unto my godsonnes / and nephewes Beniamyn Lany Edmund Lam and John Dandy every of them three pounds six / shilling(es) eighte pence. I doe give unto my Brother and sister Wingfeild either of them Twenty / shilling(es) to buye them a Ringe, And Twenty shilling(es) to my Brother Mr Giles Bru(e)z I doe / give unto Henry Copeland my Servaunt Forty shilling(es) yf he happen to serve me at the time / of my deathe} And tenne shilling(es) to Anne Winter my maide yf she happen to serve me at the time of / my deathe I doe further give unto my saide servaunt Henry Copeland suche a sute of apparell / as my wyfe shall thinck fitt to bestowe uppon him Item I doe give unto every one of my brother / Mr Edmond Poleys servaunts that shall serve him ordinarily in householde at the time of my deathe / six shilling(es) eighte pence Item I doe give unto the poore of Badley and other townes adioyning ~~ / Twenty nobles to be distributed at the discrec(i)on of my Executors Item I doe give and appointe / further to be paide unto my saide wyfe forty markes by yeare for the bringing upp of my Children / And if one of them happen to dye Then my meaning is that there shalbe but twenty markes ~ / allowed unto her And when my sonne shall come to yeares fitt to be putt to schoole I doe desyre / and appointe my saide Brother Mr Edmund Poley to take the tuic(i)on and government of him / And towards his bringing upp to defaulte twenty markes owte of the saide Forty markes before / allowed to my saide wyfe Item I doe will and appointe that my Lande in Essex whiche I / boughte of my cosen Mr Henry Kirbye shalbe soulde by my Executors towards the performaunce / of this my Will within some further convenyent times as he shall thinck fitt Item I doe appoynte / my welbeloved brother Mr Edmond Poley to be the Executor of this my Last will and testament / And if my saide Brother my Executor doe happen to dye before this my Will be performed / Then I doe appointe Marye my wyfe my Loving cosen Mr Richard Kempe of Florden and my / Loving brother Mr John Lany to be my Executor And in witnesse of this my Last will and testament written / with my owne hande I have sett my hande and seale unto the same the first daye of September 1592 / And in the fowre and thirtieth yeare of the Reigne of our Soveraigne Ladye Elizabeth by the grace of god of England / France and Ireland Quene defender of the faithe etc.   Richard Poley

We Thomas Crofte of Litle Saxham in the Couny of Suff Esquyre / Susan Crofte wyfe of the same Thomas and Marye Poley of Badley in the saide County widowe late / wyfe of Richard Poley of Badley aforesaide gent deceased doe rectifye by this present writing unto all / persons unto whome it shall apperteyne that the saide late Richard Poley being of good and perfect rememberaunce / And the sixte daye of February nowe last past will be worde of mouthe. That whereas by his Last will he / hade bequeathed unto Cicely Poley his daughter thre hundred pound(es) of Lawfull English money And unto / Edmond Poley his sonne Foure hundred poundes of Lyke money. That for so muche as he did nowe / certeinly understand the saide Marye his wyfe to be conceived with childe and that it was a Christian care for / everyman to provide for his children. Therefore he did will that the childe wherewith she was conceived / weare it sonne or daughter shoulde have one hundred and Fifty pounde out of the porc(i)on of Five hundred / poundes given to Cicely his daughter And also one hundred and Fifty poundes owte of the porc(i)on of foure / hundred poundes given to his saide sonne Edmund Poley. And that if the saide Childe shoulde happen to / dye That the porc(i)ons of the saide Cicely and Edmond first above menc(i)oned shoulde contynue and be as / before they should have bene. Amd that the saide Richard dyed at Saxham aforesaide the Eighte daye of / February then next ensewing In Testimonye whereof wee the saide Thomas Susan and Marye have / hereunto subcribed our names the eightenthe daye of Maye <158> 1593 Thomas Crofte Susan Crofte / Marye Poley

Edmond Pooley, of Badley, Suffolk, Esquire (15 June 1607)

MADE 15 June 1607 (in my own hand), to be buried in Badley Church amongst my ancestors. Upon the marriage of Cicely POLEY, my niece, with Charles CROFTS, son and heir apparent of Charles CROFTS, Esq.; I have covenanted to pay Charles CROFTS in consideration of the sd marriage the sum of £1,000 of which I have already paid £700. To my exors all my messuages and lands etc. on the left hand of the common roadway leading from Stowmarket to Needham Market, Suffolk, for the term of 15 years to the end that they will pay to Charles CROFTS £300. Alice, my wife, shall have during her life all such lands, messuages etc. as before her marriage to me or at any times since, I have conveyed to her from time to time. plus her dower with licence to fell timber as necessary but not otherwise. Edmond POLEY my nephew and heir, at 21 shall take the meadow called Gosley Meadow and the close called Gosseley Close, and the close called Samplees queache (sic) which I purchased of brother DUNDYE, and the close commonly called the Lodge Close, purchased of my cousin John KNAPP late of Ipswich, dec'd, and of Martha his wife, and the 16 acres of land and pasture, which I purchased of Thomas LEWGER, gent. lying in Oxland and Stoneyland in full recompense and satisfaction of all legacies of money bequeathed unto him by his father and mother. To nephew Edmund the wardship of his own body which I purchased of the Queen and that he should have the benefit of his own marriage, but executors have the government and education of him during his minority. To Edmund and Cicely all jewels and rings, chain of gold plate household stuff and goods from their parents wills. To Alice all plate and goods which I had by reason of our marriage and six pairs of best sheets, plus pillowbearers plus ten pairs of the coarser sort, all beds, coffers, pictures, tapestries etc., used in named chambers. Corn and grain etc., Use of everything at Badley Hall during her life or until she leaves. To Edmund BREWSTER my nephew for his life, my messuage and the lands in Combes, now or late in the occupation of the widow COOPER and William KYNGE, and also my lands in Combes now in the occupation of John COOPER. To the sd Edmund BREWSTER, and to Thomas William and Edward BREWSTER my nephews & brothers of the sd Edmund BREWSTER, £20 apiece. To everyone of my sisters as shall be living at the time of my decease 20/- apiece. To my son in law Robert KEMPE Esq. and to Dorothy his wife, 20/- apiece, and to my nephew Thomas SECKFORD and Ann his wife 20/- apiece, and to my nephew Henry SECKFORD his brother, the like sum, and to my nephew Edmund POLEY all my rings and seals of arms, and to my nephew Charles CROFTS and Cicely his wife 20/-. To my nephews and godchildren Edmund DENDLEY, Edward LACEY, Edmund LAMBE, £5 apiece; and to my niece Katherine LANEY, my first wife's goddaughter*, £10; to my niece Winifred LAMBE £20. To Johane SPYNKE a poor woman who served me and my father long, 30/- a year during her life, and to Samuel SPYNKE her son, if he shall be in my service at my death 53/4d. To the poor of Badley 10/- ; to the poor of Stoke Ash 20/- ; to the poor of Battisford 20/- ; to the poor of Combs 30/- ; to the poor of Needham £3; to the poor of Stow Town 50/-. To my cousin Mr. John BOYS my term and interest in the portion of the tythes in Elmsett. To my cousin Sir John POLEY, Knight, son of my uncle Edmund POLEY dec'd, £30 and 40/- for a ring Alice, my wife, exix. My son-in-law Robert KEMPE Esq. and my nephew Edward BREWSTER exors. My nephew Sir John CROFTS, Kt. and my brother in law John LACYE Esq., Supervisors. No witnesses. [EDMUND POLEY PCC 107 Capell 15 June 1607. Proved: 29 Nov 1613 by Alice POLEY (nee Cockram), relict and exix.]

NOTES: *Edmond Pooley was the nephew of Margaret Pooley who married Robert Knapp, Cicely was Edmund's sister.*
* *She was Katherine SECKFORD See Kempe family tree next page*

Robert Kempe, of Gissing, Norfolk, Esquire (1613).

TO be buried in my chapel, at Gissing. Poor of Gissing, Diss, Dicklburgh, Bruston, East Ruston, Shephanger. To the churchwardens at Flordon. £3.6. 8d. for a silver Communion Cup. Eldest son Robert KEMPE all my lands at Gissing. Second son John KEMPE £40 a year. Third son Richard KEMPE* £40 a year to issue out of my manor of Burnells in East Ruston. Fourth son Arthur KEMPE £40 a year. Fifth son Edmund KEMPE £40 a year. Sixth son Edward KEMPE £40 a year. Seventh son Thomas KEMPE £40 a year. Wife Dorothy KEMPE to have the use of these annuities until sons reach 21. 1,000 marks to daughter Dorothy at 18 or on marriage. 1,000 marks to daughter Elizabeth at 18 or marriage. Eldest son Robert still under 21. To father-in-law Edmund POLEY Esq. best gelding. To mother-in-law Mistress Alice POLEY a gold ring. Witnesses: John KETTILBOROWE, Jeremy CORBAULD, Thomas SPINKE. Exix: wife Dorothy.
[ROBERT KEMPE PCC 46 Capell 20 Nov 1612. Proved: 5 May 1613 by Dorothy KEMPE (nee HARRIS), relict.]

NOTES:
Later Secretary and Governor of Virginia. Edmund Poley of Badley married Catherine Seckford of Seckford Woodbridge. She died in 1601 and in 1606 he married Alice Kempe (nee Cockram), the widow of Richard Kemp, of Gissing, Norfolk. The testator Robert Kempe above, was Alice's son by her first marriage to Richard Kempe. See family tree below:

KEMPE *family tree (part)*

Richard Kempe of Gissing Nfk 1541-1600	Alice Cockram of Hampstead Middx	Edmund Poley of Badley Sfk 1544-1613 osp	Catherine Seckford of Seckford Sfk d. 1601
Dorothy Harris d.1626	Robert Kempe of Gissing Nfk 1567-1613		

Edmond Brewster, of Grays Inn, London (1633)

TO be buried in that parish where I die. To the poor of that parish I give £5. Whereas I stand seised of the moiety of a wood called The Great and Little Birchetts, near Dedham, Essex, which I purchased of John TREYLMAN and Thomas NEWSON, for which there is a yearly rent of £4.10.8d. and which moiety contains 90 acres. I do give it to my cousin Edmond POLEY of Badley, Suffolk, Esq. for 21 years commencing immediately after my death, so that by the sale of the fellable wood, he may be able to perform this my will. The reversion to my niece Mrs Mary CAGE, the wife of Anthony CAGE, Esq. and to her heirs and assigns forever, to whom the other moiety of the sd wood belongs. On the marriage of my sd niece I paid to her husband over and above the sum of £1,400 part of the personal estate belonging to her, the sum of £400 which was in recompense of such free and copyhold lands belonging to her and lying intermixed amongst the lands then and now belonging to her cousin Captain SECKFORD. To my brother Edward BREWSTER £300. To my nephew Thomas BREWSTER, the eldest son of my dec'd brother, Mr. William BREWSTER, £200, £100 whereof to be employed for binding him apprentice, either to some merchant or other good trade in London, and the other £100 to be paid to him when his apprenticeship shall expire or at 21 and further for the maintenance of the poor in the Almshouse in Woodbridge, Suffolk, called Seckford's Almshouses whereupon I had disbursed £100 before the sd lease was made during the minority of my nephew Thomas SECKFORD dec'd. To my godson Thomas POLEY the youngest son of my cousin Edmond POLEY of Badley, Esq.* the counter standing in my chamber in his father's house at Badley, and my bed, bedding, etc. To my good and worthy friend Sir Gilbert GERRARD Bart. £40 and to his wife £10. My cousin, the Lady CROMPTON now wife my sd cousin Poley £20. My servant Myles EDWARDS the tenement, orchard and ground in two closes in Harrow-on-theHill, Middlesex, and my lease thereof from the Governors of the Free Grammar School in Harrow afsd founded by John LYON, dec'd and such of my wearing apparel and linen and my bed and bedding in my lodging chamber, and my man's chamber at Gray's Inn, and my chests, trunks, press, desks and cupboards, chairs, stools, etc. and that gelding whereon he usually rides. My cousin Edmond POLEY of Badley, Esq., exor. No witnesses.

[EDMOND BREWSTER PCC 95 Russell 10 April 1633. Proved: 6 Nov 1633 by Edmond POLEY]

*Notes: * The testator's mother Mirable POLEY was sister of Richard POLEY of Badley, whose son Edmond, 1592-1640 was the father of the Thomas referred to here. Her eldest brother, also Edmond POLEY, 1544-1613 (PCC 107 Capell) married as his first wife Katherine SECKFORD, the aunt of Sir Thomas SECKFORD. She died in 1610. The testator evidently died at Badley and judging by the bequest to his godson Thomas Poley, he was living at the Hall either as the guest or tenant of the Poleys. In accordance with his wish was buried there (in the church) - see Chapter 3, memorial No 3.*

Sir John Poley, of St Peters, Stowmarket, Knight (1634)

IN the name of God Amen, The / Eighteenth daie of October in the yeare of our Lord God one thousand six hundred / thirtie and fower and in the tenth yeare of the raigne of our Sov(er)aigne Lord Kinge / Charles of England Scotland France and Irelan defender of the faith etc. I John Poley / of Collumbine hall in the parish of St Peters in Stowm(ar)ket and in the dioces of ~ ~ / Norw(i)ch knowing the uncertainety of mans life and feeling my owne frailty, yet perfect in / memory I thanke my god I doe hereby provide to dispose of such estate as God hath lent me in / this world whereby I might leave peace behinde mee as it hath pleased God to finish this my / desire in peace And therefore hereby I make and declare and publish this my last will and testament / Revokeing all former wills and draftes of will or writings to any such purpose in maner and / forme following, desiring it maie be beneficially expounded according to my true meaninge / Inprimis my body I comend to Christian buriall And in token of my assured faith in Christ / my Saviour, that I shall rise agine to life everlasting, by his meritts and passion suffered / for me Secondly in respect of the true love I beare to Ursula my loving and welbeloved wife / I doe give and bequeath unto her. All that my Mannor and mannorhouse and lands whatsoever to the / same belonging called Cullimbine hall al(ia)s Thorny Collumbers with all rents services, profitt(es) of Court(es) / Comons, wast grounds, Fishings and other appurtenances whatsoever to the same belonging And alsoe one / Capitall messuage with all the lands, thereunto belonging conteyning by estimac(i)on five and forty acres / more or lesse, except and allwaies reserved all timber and tymber trees now growing in the lands of ~ / Collumbine aforesaid, or the lands in Stow, one house or any other townes scituate lying and being in / Stowe Stowupland aforesaid. This Capitall messuage and the lands aforesaid lying in Stowmarkett ~ / Chilton or any other Townes next adioyninge were sometymes one Thomas Smithes Clerke ~ / deceased and now lately named or called by the name of Pawnsey hall with all and singular there / appurtenances whatsoever to the same belonging and all and singular other my lands tenement(es) and / hereditaments whatsoever scituate laying and being in the parish or parishes of Stowm(ar)ket Stowupland / Dagworth Newton Gipping one house Chilton or elsewhere in the said County of Suff All that my / lands and messuage lately purchased of Edward Baldry of Ipsw(i)ch and all the perticuler closes of ~ / land meadow and pasture hereafter p(ar)ticularly named and expressed, only excepted and foreprized that / is to saie, All that Close now or heretofore called and known by the name or names of Tye acres / or the rushes pightle conteyning five acres more or lesse And all that Close called Basketts beinge / Copiehold of the mannor of Thorny. The lord thereof is Thomas Bendish Barronett and all those / ground heretofore lying in three peeces, and now or heretofore called great Banyards, Banyards / Brooke and little Banyards conteyning together eighteen acres more or lesse, All that Close / now or heretofore called the litle Gravellfeild together with that part of dovehouse Pitle now or lately laid *in* to the same, conteyning togethe eighteen acres more or lesse All that meadowe / now or heretofore called kitke Gravellfeild meadow, conteyning seaven acres and a halfe more or / lesse, All that meadow lying in the nether end of litle Gravellfeild conteyning five acres more / or lesse, All that close now or heretofore called Great Gravellfeild conteyning thirtie acres more or lesse / and all those two closes now or heretofore called dulls conteyning together twentie fower acres / more or less All w(i)th premisses for p(ar)ticulerly before name and intended to be excepted & foreprized / are now together with the said messuage and lands lately purchased of the said Edward Baldry p(ar)te / also of what is intended to be excepted and foreprized now in the tenure and occupac(i)on of / Lancaster or his assignes, and also further excepted and foreprized one litle meadow lying at Dagworth / bridge conteyning three roods and twelve p(er)ches more or lesse now in the tenure and occupac(i)on of ~ / Rob(er)t Jennery or his assignes, and alsoe one pightle late in the tenure of John Hubberd conteyning five / acres three roods and thirtie five perches more or lesse To have and to hold my said mannors lands ~ / Tenements and hereditaments with all and singular theire appurtenances {except as is before excepted} / unto her the said Ursula for and during her naturall life and in recompence of her dowry & thirds / and for and towards her better maintenance and livelyhood after my death and for and toward the ~ ~ / educac(i)on and bring*ing* up of my sonne and heire John Poley Esq(uir)e untill he shall attaine <to> his age of ~ / Eighteen yeares. And for and towards the maintenance and educac(i)on of all other my Children ~ / untill their severall ages of eighteene yeares or daies of marriage or porc(i)ons hereafter by me

/ bequeathed unto them shall or ought to be paid them, she the said Ursula my wife yearly payinge / out of the yearly rents and profitts of the premissed after my death untill my sonne and heire shall or / might accomplish his age of eighteen yeares <or daies of marriage> unto my loving brother Sir / Roger North knight and my loving Cosins Edmund Poley of Badly and Anthony Croftes of ~ / Grayes Inn Esquire, the som(m)e of fiftie pounds of currant English money yearly on the feast / daie of St Michaell the archangell, and the annunciac(i)on of the blessed Virgin Mary or within / twentie and eight daies next after by even and equall porc(i)ons And after my sonne and heire shall / accomplish his age of eighteen yeares, paying yearely unto him in like maner the *like* som(m)e of fiftie / pounds during her naturall life for his livelyhood and maintenance wherew(i)th I devise him to be fully / content during the life of his said mother. Item I doe give and bequeath unto my said loving brother / Sir Roger North knight and my said Cosin Edmund Poley of Badly hall and Anthony Croftes of / Grayes Inn Esquire All that my messuage, and those my lands formerly excepted lately purchased / of the beforenamed Edward Baldery And also all those other my lands meadows and pastures <before> / before p(ar)ticularly named and excepted and menc(i)oned and entended to be excepted and to be toge- / -ther w(i)th the said messuages and lands purchased of the said Edward Baldrie in the tenure and / occupac(i)on of the said ~~~ Lancaster or his assignes And alsoe all that litle meadow / lying at Dagworth Bridge formerly also excepted now in the tenure or occupac(i)on of <the said> / Rob(er)te Jennerie and also all that pightle now in mine owne occupac(i)on formerly also excepted / and foreprized and menc(i)oned to be sometyme in the occupac(i)on of one John Read And alsoe all / that pightle called Jenneries pightle formerlie also excepted and foreprized and menc(i)oned to / be sometimes in the tenure of one John Hubberd To have and to hold the same and every part and / parcell hereof with theire and every of theire appurtenances by the names and contents before / expressed, or by what other name or names soever the same be now called and knowne and of / what other content or contents soever the same be unto them the said Sir Roger North knight / and Edmund Poley and Anthony Crofts of Grayes Inne Esquires and theire heires & assignes / for ever To the end that they or the survivor of them within convenient tyme after my death / shall or maie sell the same and every part thereof to the best value the same can be sold for, And my / will and minde is, and my hartie desire and request unto them is That they will take care to ~ / preserve and imploy the monies which shalbe raised by the sale thereof together with the fiftie / pounds yearly which I have appointed my wife to pay them untill my sonne and heire shall ~ / accomplish his age of eighteene yeares out of the profitts and rents of my Mannor and other my / lands devised to my said wife during her life for the payment of the severall porc(i)ons of two / hundred pounds apeece to each of my six daughters now living and of the like som(m)e and porc(i)on ~ / of two hundred pounds unto my sonne Edmund being my youngest child now alos living. At / theire severall ages of eighteene yeares, if they shall live to attaine that age And for and towards / some help of maintenance unto them in the meane tyme in theire education, and for some help / of their mother therein, in such maner as my said brother Sir Roger North knight and my / said Cosins Edmund Poley and Anthony Crofts aforesaid Esquries in theire Judgments and / discrec(i)ons shall thinke fitt, and if any surplusage shall happen to be raised more then will satisfie / and paie the said porc(i)ons of two hundred pounds apeece to my younger children either by the sale of / the said lands soe appoynted to be sold or by the death of any of my younger Children before theire / ages of eighteene yeares or before theire said porc(i)ons shalbe paid unto them then my will and ~ / minde is That such surplusage shalbe inployed for the benefitt of my sonne and heire and payed / over unto him at his age of one and twentie yeares. And if he shall happen to die before then <the> / to his said brother my sonne Edmund at his like age and if they *both* shall <both> happen to die before / such theire ages Then to be equallie devided mong such of my daughters as shalbe then living / Item I doe give and bequeath unto my said sonne and heire John Poley and to his heires for ev(er) / The reverc(i)on and remainder of all my said Mannor of Collumbine hall al(ia)s Thorny Collumbers / and of all other my lands and of all other my lands messuage and tenements lyinge in ~ / Stowmarkett Onehouse Chilton, now called by the name of Paunsehall, and of all other / my lands formerly given to his said mother for her life desiring and requiring him in Gods / name to be a good and loving brother to all his sisters, and a dutifull sonne unto his mother / And further remembrance of my love to him and carefor him I doe further give unto him / my best house armour and sword To the end he maie remeber that it was my Cover in battaile / and that God gave it me to leave *it* <to> him for the service of God and his Country / And I doe alsoe give him my guilt Cales bedsteed w(hi)ch I b*r*ought out of Spayne the purchase / of my sword and silke quilt coverlett for the same guilt bedsteed w(hi)ch I wrought with my ~ / owne hands for a covering for it, and the bedd, blankett(es) and furniture thereto belonging To the / end he maie remember I was not idle in peace Item all the rest of my moveable goods plate / household stuffe Cattell and stocke whatsoever I give and bequeath unto my said l;oving wife ~ / Whom I nominate to be the sole executor of this my last will and testam(en)t. Revoking all former / wills made by me And my desire is that if she shall live to see any my daughters married That / then she will bestowe upon every of them a bedsteed and bedd furnished and for *her* my said loveing wives / assistance, and the good of my Children whom I leave in gods peace and commend to his good ~~ / blessing nominate and appoint my said laving brother Sir Roger North knight and my said / loving Cisins Edmund Poley and Anthomy Crofts of Grays Inn Esquires my Supervisors of / this my will delivering theire care and paines to advise and divert my wife with theire best help and / Councell for the better performance of this my will for the good and comfort of herselfe and her / poore Children And in wintnes hereof I have unto this my will conteyned in three sheete of ~~ / paper and a halfe written with my owne hand whereunto I have left my hand to every leafe and / to the last my hand and seale this eighteenth daie of October in the said Tenth year of the raigne / of o(u)r Soveraigne lord King Charles of England etc Anno Dm One thousand six hundred / thirtie fower John Poley declared and published for the last will and testament of the said / Sir John Poley In the presence of us whose names are underwritten the eighteenth daie of / August 1634 Roger North Edmund Poley Robert Copinger.

[Proved : London 29th April 1635]

In his will, Sir John makes several reference to Pawnsey Hall in Chilton, see Chapter 10.

𝔇orothy 𝔓ooley, of 𝔖towmarket, 𝔖pinster 19 𝔐arch 1635/36

COMMENDS soul to God trusting through Jesus Christ to rise again to eternal life. I give the poor of Stowupland 40s to be distibuted at discretion of minister and churchwardens, and the like sum of 40s, to poor of borough of Stowmarket to be distributed as aforesaid. The money to be paid by my ex'trix within 3 weeks of my burial. To Dame Ursula Poolye widow, my dear mother, £20 which I desire her to accept as a token of my humble duty and thankfulness to her. To my eldest sister Elizabeth £60, to my sisters Ursula, Jane, Mary and Peregrina £20 each. To my elder brother John £10 and to my younger brother Edmund £20. These legacies are to be paid to my mother and such of my sisters as are of age within 12 months of my decease, and the others are to retain in hands of my ex'trix until legatees come to full age. I make my dear sister Elizabeth sole ex'trix and I bequeath to her whatever belongs to me and is unbequeathed. Supervisors: my loving friends Mr Edmund Poolye of Badley esquire and Mr James Tyrell of Gipping esquire. Wit. Thomas Young, Simon Woodey. [Proved : Bury 6 November 1636 by Thomas Eden. Ex'trix took oath before Thomas Young, vicar of Stowmarket.]

This was one of the daughters of Sir John Poley of Columbine Hall

Elizabeth Crompton, of Badley, Suffolk, Singlewoman (8th February 1635)

IN the name of God Amen / I Ms Elizabeth Crompton of Badley in the Countie of Suff Singlewoman / being sicke in body, but (praysed be God) of goode and perfect memorie / doe make this my last will, and testament in manner, and forme following / First I give and bequeath my soule into the hands of Almightie God my creator / with hope of free pardon, and remission of all my sinnes in Jesus Christ my / Redeemer, next my bodie to be buried in the Parish Church where it shall / please God to call mee, as for my personal estate I bequeate it as following / viz: Impris I give and bequeate unto my deere and loving Mother the / Lady Crompton the summe of fiftie pounds Item I give unto my lovinge / Brother Robert Crompton Esq. the sum of Threescore pounds and besides fortie / pounds which is owing him, the totall being a hundred pounds Item I give / unto my deere Uncle Anthonie Crofts Esq. the summe of tenn pounds Item / I do give unto my Sister Mrs Dorothie Poley, Francis Poley and Cicilia Poley / to either of them the summe of tenn pounde These severall legacies to be paid within / six moneths after my decease Item I give unto my loving Sister Mrs Katherine ~ / Crompton my clocke [cloak] Item I do nominate my deare Sister Ms Marie Crompton / my sole Executrix of this my last will and testament bestowing the residue of my estate / upon her desiring her to see this my will successfully performed. In witness wereof I / have hereunto sett my hand and seale this Eight day of February In the Eleventh / year of our Soveraign King Charles over England etc Anno Dmi one Thousand / six hundred thirty five. Elizabeth Crompton Sealed published and delivered in the / presence of Edm Poley Thos Westhroppe

[35 Pile: Proved : London 16th June 1636 by sister Mary Crompton]

(This was one of the unmarried daughters of Lady Frances Crompton's first marriage to Sir John Crompton Knt., of Skerne, Yorkshire, who was living at Badley Hall.)

Edmund Poley, of Badley, Suffolk, Esquire (8 June 1640)

IN the name of god Amen I Edmund Poley of Badley in the County of Suff esquire, being nowe god be thanked in good and perfect health and memory and well knowing both the certainty and uncertainty of death to all men, doe for the better setling of that temporall estate both reall and personall wherwith god Allmightie of his mercy and goodnes to me hath blessed me in this worlde, doe make and ordaine this my last will and testament in manner and forme following and doe further revoake all wills hereby formerly by me made. First com(m)ending my soule by prayer unto god Allmightie my Creator Steadfastlie hoping and believing by faith in the incarnc(i)on and passion of Christ Jesus my most mercifull Redeemer, and by his onely merritt and mediac(i)on to be saved. I doe direct my bodie to be buried in the Chancel of Badley Church as neare the bodie of my deare and late deceased wife as maie be with convenience, and my grave to be covered with a faire gravestone in such decent manner as shall seeme fitt to my Executor hereafter named. Item I doe give and bequeath unto my sonne and heire Edmund Poley my Mannor of Badley with the right(es) members and appurtenances thereof, and all Rent(es) services and and appurtencenances to the same belonging or appertayning And alsoe all other mymessuages tenem(ent)s Farmes, land(es) pastures, meadows wood(es) and woodmound(es) and other hereditament(es) whatsoever both free and Coppie, scituate, lying, extending and being in and into the Townes, parishes, field(es) and precinct(es) of Badley aforesaid, Battisforde Combes, Barking, Needham either of the Creating(es) or in any other Towne or Townes next adioyning or any of them together with the Reverc(i)on and Reverc(i)ons, Remainder and Remainders of the same, and of every part and parcill thereof. I doe hereby give and bequeath my said Mannor and all other my land(es) tenement(es) and hereditament(es) before menc(i)oned both free and Coppie unto my said sonne and heire Edmund Poley and his heires for ever. And whereas I have heretofore grannted by certaine writing(es) or deed(es) under my hand and seale thereby grannting unto my three younger sonnes certaine severall Annuities or rent charges during their naturall lives yssuing and going out of my Mannor and Lands aforesaid I doe desire and direct my said sonne and heire to pay the same according as I have thereby sev(er)ally gran(n)ted the same in and by the said writing(es) or deed(es). Item I doe give and bequeath unto my nowe loving and welbeloved wife Dame Frances Crompton all her wearing apparell lynnen and Jewells and ornament(es) for her person and all the Boxes Chest(es) Trunnk(es) Cupbord(es) deskes Caskitt(es) and Caremuett(es) (sic) wherein they are usually laid and kept, onely I give and bequeath unto my daughter Dorothy one pearle Chaine which was her mothers. And alsoe I give and bequeath unto my said wife my Coach and Coach horses, and two other Nagg(es) fitt for servant(es) to be appointed her by my Executors. Also I doe give unto her twentie Combs wheate, and fortie Combs Malt; And for and concerning all other my good(es) and chattels whatsoever whereof I shalle possessed or whereto I shall or maie be intitled at my death, I doe devise and beaqueath the same in manner and forme following, First for all my outward stocks of Corne Cattell grasse, haie, tillage, horses, sheepe and implament(es) for husbandry whatsoever. I doe give and bequeath the same wholie to my Executor here after named to be by him sould for and toward(es) the performance of this my will. And for all my inward stocke of plate, pewter, brasse and for all my hanging(es) chaires, stooles, formes, tables, picures, bedstead(es), bedd(es) with all furniture whatsoever belonging unto them wherewith my parlore or any other the lower or upper chambers and roomes of my house are furnished or adorned and all of my fine and course lynnen either for bedd or boards, and my wollen stuffe or silken stuffe whatsoever for the furniture of any my lodging(es) and Chambers of my house, and all other my househoulde stuffe of what kinde or nature soever, not formerly bequeathed to my wife or hereafter to any other my will and mynd is that the one halfe or moitie thereof shalbe sould by my said Executor for and toward(es) the performance of this my will, to which ende and purpose I doe hereby give and bequeath the one halfe or moitie thereof to my said Executor to be by him sould. And the other moitie or halfe thereof I doe give unto my said Executor and his assignes for ever therewith to contayn and remain in my man(n)or house com(m)only called Badley hall. And my desire and will is that my wife soe long as she shall live and contynue to Keepe house there shall have the Custody possession and use of these good(es) and utensills for houshould stuffe which shalbe sett out out for the moitie and half devised to my said Execuor and his assignes as aforesaid, she giving my Executor secuitie to prsent them the best she canne in the using of them, and to leant them soe preserved to him whenever she shall either give over to keepe the house there her selfe, or shall depart this transient life. And I doe desire and direct to have a perfect Inventory indented made of the goods soe to be left in the possession and use of my said wife, one part thereof to be subscribed by her and to remaine with my Executor, and the other to be subscribed by him and to remaine with her that thereby the number qualitie kinde and value of the said good(es) maie be manifested and app(a)rent. Item I doe give and bequeath unto my daughters Dorothy Poley and Anne Poley my daughter by my first wife, and unto Frances Poley and Sisley Poley my daughter by my nowe wife the sum(m)e of five hundred pound(es) a peece, and unto my daughter Mary Poley the sum(m)e of fower hundred pound(es) for their severall porc(i)ons and advancements from me, to be paid unto them at their severall ages of one and twenty yeares, or severall daies of their marriages which shall first happen, if my *said* daughter shall marry with the consent of my nowe wife, or my Executor, or my supervisor to this my will hereafter named or any two of them. And my will and meaning is that my Executor shall pay yearly to every of my every said daughters the sam(m)e of twentie pound(es) a peece toward(es) their maintenance and bringing upp untill they accomplish their severall ages of fowerteene yeares, then my meaning is that my Executors shall pay unto every of them the sum(m)e of thirie pound(es) a peece yearly untill they shall marry or the porc(i)ons togrowe due as aforesaid. And my further will and minde is, that my younger sonne shall either of them have allowed out of the proffitt(es) of my said land(es) from the time of my death untill their severall ages of sixteene yeares, at which ages the severeall Annuities I have granted them out of my said Mannor and land(es) are to com(m)ence, the sum(m)e of twenty pound(es) yearly for their educac(i)on and maintenance. And for that I conceive that the proffitt(es) of my said Mannor and land(es) and my personall estate formerly devise to my said sonne and heire may fall out to be much to litle, both to pay my debt(es) and to raise the porc(i)ons and legacies before bequeathed for my younger children, especially if I should happen to dye during the minoritie of my sonne and heire, in respect of the charge it would then be to compound for the Wardshipp of my heire and such part of my Mannor and land(es) as will then belong to his Maiestie during his nonage As also in respect of the Joynture to my wife, and Annuities to my younger sonnes wherewith my Mannor and land(es) stand charged. Therefore my will and mynde is that my Mannor of Woodhall in Stoake Ashe in the Countie of Suff with all and singular the Land(es) and tenem(en)t(es) thereto belonging both free and Coppie which are called or knowen by the name of Combes Land(es) or by any other name or names whatsoever with all right(es) members and appurtenances belonging or appertayning to the said Mannor scituate lying and being in Stoake Ashe aforsaide Thwaite, Thornham, Wickhamsleith or any other Towne or Townes adioining to them shalbe sould within convenient tyme after my death to raise moneyes for perfrmances of this my will. And therefore I doe herby for that purpose give devise and bequeath the said Mannor of Woodhall, and all the said Land(es)s and Tenement(es) both free and Coppie with all and singular their appurtenances scituate lying and being in Stoake Ashe aforesaid or in any the Townes or parishes last before named or within the field(es) or perimet(es) of the same. And the Reverc(i)on and Reverc(i)ons Remainder and Remainders of the same and every part and parcell thereof unto S(i)r Henry Crofte of litle Saxham in the said County of Suff knight, and Francis Warner of Parham in the said Countie esquire. To have and to hould the same, and every part and parcell thereof with their appurtenances to them and their heires for ever, desiring them earnestlie so soone as shalbe convenient after my death for the better and more certaine performance of this my will in all thing(es) to make sale of all or soe much of the premisses as wilbe needefull to raise moneys to enable my Executor thereto. And if any surplusage shalbe upon the sale thereof more then will performe this my will. I doe give and bequeath the same unto my said sonne and heire Edmund Poley and his assignes. But if my said sonne and heire shall by his marriage porc(i)on or otherwise satisfie and pay all such porc(i)on and porc(i)ons to my said daughter as is given and devised in and by this my last will and testament, then I desire and direct the said S(i)r Henry Croft(es) and Francis Warner and the heires of them to assurt and convey by good Conveyance upon my said sonne and heire and his heires who I wish and desire maie be enabled by his marriage porc(i)on or otherwise to satisfie my said daughter their porc(i)ons and their severall Annuities or yearly payment(es) which I have in this my will given them for their educac(i)on and maintenance untill their saide severall porc(i)ons shall growe due, and thereupon have the whole land(es) Conveyed and assured unto him and his heires by the said S(i)r Henry Croft(es) and Francis Warner and their heires. And my will and meaning is that the severall Annuities or yearly payment(es) given unto my saide daughter for and toward(es) their maintenance and educac(i)on shalbe paid out of the said Land(es) soe devised to be sould untill their said severall porc(i)ons shall growe due as aforesaid. Item I doe give and bequeath unto my said sonne Edmund Poley all my bookes and Counter and other boxes in my Clossett or Studdy. And also my will and meaning is, that if it shall not be thought fitt by my Executor to make sale of the one halfe or moitie of my good(es) formerly by me devised to be sould, then I give and bequeath them unto my said Executor to remaine in my manc(i)on house com(m)only called Badleyhall. And my desire and will is, that my wife soe long as she shall contynue to keepe house there shall have the Custodie possession and use of those good(es) and utensills of householdstuffe she giving my Executor such surritie to preserve them the best she canne in the using of them as she shall give for the other moitie and halfe formerly bequeathed unto her, and to leave and deliver them soe preserved to him whenever she shall leave housekeeping there or shall depart this transitorie life, or when my said Executor shall happen to marry and keepe house And I doe desire and direct my said Executor to pay unto my sonne Thomas Poley the sum(m)e of tenne pound(es) given and devised unto him by the last will and testament of Edmund Brewster esquire deceased. Item I doe give and bequeath unto my loving cosen S(i)r Thomas Glemham knight, to my loving sonne in lawe Robert Crompton esquire to John Wentworth esquire, to my loving daughter in lawe M^s Mary Crompton to every of them the sum(m)e of five pound(es) a peece. Item I doe give and bequeath unto Francis Raymond the sum(m)e of tenne pound(es) and a suit of my apparell to be appointed him by my Executor if he shall serve me at the time of my decease. Item I doe give and bequeath unto Francis Burgis the sum(m)e of five pound(es) if he shall serve me at the time of my decease. Item doe give and bequeath unto the Towne of Badley, Combe Stowe, Battisford Needham, Creating St Maries and Stoake Ashe in the said County of Suff the sum(m)e of forty marks to be distributed by myne Executor as he shall seeme fitt. And my will and mynde is that the legacies given as aforesaid shalbe paid within halfe a yeare after my decease or sooner if my Executor shall seeme fitt. Item I doe nominate constitute and ordaine Edmund Poley my sonne and heire sole Executor of this my last will and testament unto whom I doe give all my good(es) C[h]attells and and chattells of what kinde or nature soever, not heretofore given and demise for and toward(es) the performance of this my will. And I doe hereby nominate and appoint S(i)r Henry Crofte of litle Saxham in the said Countie of Suff knight, and Francis Warner of Parham in the said Countie of Suff esquire supervisors of this my last will and testament earnestly, desiring them to be Assistant unto my said Executors in the performance of this my will, and in the good and godly educac(i)on and bringing upp of my children and God I hope will requite them for it; And for their paines therein I doe give and bequeath unto them the sum(m)e of twentie pound(es) a peece. In wittnes whereof I have hereunto sett my hand and seale; the eight daie of June Anno Dmi 1640. And in the sixteenth yeare of the Raigne of our Soveraigne Lord Charles by the grace of god of England Scotland France and Ireland king Defender of the faith etc. Edm(und) Poley. sealed publishe and declared in the presence of Will(ia)m Cole, Isaac Tillott, signed Ed(mun)d Eastis. I doe intreat my deare and loving wife not to take it unkindlie that I did not more for her, she deserving soe much from me, I would gladly have donne it, if my state would have permitted it. I doe likewise intreat her to have a care of my children by her, as also of those by my first wife especially my daughters, soe farr as they may not be chargeable to her. And I charge both sonnes and daughters to be dutifull to her as they hope for god(es) blessing. Edm(und) Poley. [Edmund Poley PCC 133 Coventry 1640. Proved: 20 Oct by Edmund Poley]

By this will the Poleys' long association and ownership of the Manor of Woodhall, Stoke Ash is brought to an end, being sold to accord with the wishes of Edmund's will to ensure sufficient funds for the legacies and annuities devised, which he feared might not be met by his Badley and other holdings. The apology to his wife at the end of the will is worthy of note.

Thomas Mannyng, of Badley, Yeoman 15 November 1640*

Brother was George. Amongst bequests - to Wm, Richard & Thomas Poley, three younger sons of Edmund Poley Esq., deceased, 20s. each to buy them a ring. To Dorothy, Mary, Ann, Frances & Cicely Poley five of the said Edmund Poley's daughters, 20s. each to buy them a ring.
[Proved : Ipswich 17 March 1640]

Marie Crompton, of Badley, Suffolk, Singlewoman (2nd December 1641)

IN the name of God Amen I Marie / Crompton of Badley in the County of Suff Singlewoman weake in body / yet in perfect memorie. I give God thankes doe make this my last will and testament / this second day of December one thousand six hundred thirtie and eight Anno ~/Dmi decimo quarto I doe com(m)end my self to God calling to yeeld my soule to god / that gave yt and my body to the earth from whence yt had beginning hoping and / with a true faith beleeving that in and through the merrit(es) and mercies of / Jesus Christ my Saviour and Redeemer both soule and body shall by him be raised / and united together again And by him p(re)sented in a more glorious manner unto my / heavenly Father in whose safe protecc(i)on I rest humbly entreating my dear and / most loveing mother Frances Lady Crompton whom I make my sole executrix of / this my last will and testament to see my body decently buried in the parish / church where yt it shall please my mercifull god to take to him self my soule / and separate yt for a little while from this earthly tabernacle; I do give unto / the Minister of God whoe shall preach at my buriall twenty shillings and I / request my deare mother to paye to him and to the Church all other duties to /them belonging. Item I give and bequeath all my goods money Debt(es) and / Chattles other than such som(m)e or sum(m)es of money menc(i)oned herein and by this my / last will given by me as legacies humbly requesting my said mother and / executrix to whome I give them to pay out of my estate my debt(es) & legacies / and to accept the residue as a token of my true love and dutifulness to her / Item I give and bequeath unto my dear and loveing father Edmond Poley Esq / ten pounds. It(em) I give <and bequeath> unto my deare and loveing Uncle Anthony / Crofte Esq. ten pounds as a token of my thankfulness to him for his care of me and / my estate. It(em) I give unto my deare and loveing Aunt Alice Lady Smith / twenty pounds as a token of my love and thankfullness to her. It(em) I give unto my / loveing brother Henry Crompton fyftie pounds Item I do give unto my loving brothers / Charles Crompton Edward Crompton Frances Crompton and Anthony Crompton / to every of them ten pounds a peece It(e)m I give to my loveing sister Francis Poo-ley / ten pounds over and above the money given her by my Sister Elizabeth Crompton / deceased Item I give unto my said sister Cicely Pooley fiftie pounds over and above / the money given her by my said sister Elizabeth to be put out for her by my / said executrix to be payed unto her together with the benefitt and encrease thereof / at her day of marriage or when shee shall attaine to the age of one and twenty / yeares which shall first happen And yf my said sister Cicely shall happen to dye / before her marriage or her age of one and twentie years then my will is that the / said £50 with the benefitt and increase thereof shalbe paide to my said sister ~ / Francis Pooley at her day of marriage or her age of one and twentie years w(hi)ch / shall first happen.And yf my said sisters Francis and Cicily shall both happen / to dye before their marriage or age of one and twenty years Then my will is / that w(i)thin three moneths next after their decease the said £50 with increase and / benefitt thereof to the day of the decease of the longer liver of them shalbe paid / to my said executrix It(em) I give and bequeath unto my deare and loving sister M^S / Katherine Crompton my Amodys [Amethyst] Ring. It(e)m I give unto my loveing sister Dorothie / Pooley my watch. It(em) I give unto my loveing sister Mary Pooley my silver pott. It(em) I / give unto my loving sister Anne Pooley five silver spoons. It(em) I give unto my / loveing sister Elizabeth Holland a plaine gould Ring. Item I give to my / very good friend Mr Thomas Brewster 20s. to buy him a Ring. It(em) I give to my / Mayd w(hi)ch shalbe with me at the tyme of my death five pounds & such of my / wearing lynen as my executrix shall thinke fitt It(em) I give and bequeath unto my deaer and loveing brother Robert Crompton Esq the som(m)e of five hundred pounds All / w(hi)ch said legacies I define and humbly request my executor to paie six moneths / after my decease And I doe request my said executrix to take care of my / sister Cicily her legacies Thus haveing setled my estate I pray god to bless me / in my life in my death and to endowe me and all my frends with his heavenly grace / and blessing(es). And now takeing my leave of all my friends in confirmac(i)on of / this my last will and testament I have hereunder sett my hand and seale and published this my last will and testament in the presence Mary Crompton / Sealed delivered and published in the presence of Tho(mas) Brewster Jo(hn) Heigham ~ / Mary Snelling. (*Probatum proved in London 1st May 1641*)   (*This was the other unmarried daughter from Lady Frances Crompton's first marriage.*)

Isaack Tillett, of Badley, Yeoman (20th December 1656)

BE it rembred that upon the one and twentyeth day of December / in the yeare of our Lord one thousand six hundred fifty and six Isaack Tillot / late of Badley in the Countie of Suff yeoman deceased being the sickly and ill of the disease on the sickness whereof he dyed, but sound of minde and / memory did call in or cause to be called in, into the room of his house / in Badley aforesaid where he then lay first one Thomas Love being his / friend (and neighbour) and Ann Cooke his maid servant and upon their coming in / he said he know not how long tyme he had had to live And therefore desired / them both to take notice that he had then an intent to make and declare / his last will and testament by word of mouth touching such estate as the Lord / had bestowed on him in this world And then he did declare and pronounce / his will and meaning to be in theise words or the same in effect following / That is to say I do give to Dorothy my wife all my goods chattles and / household stuffe Lease lande bond bills and booke debts and whatever else / I have belonging to me To hold to her and her heires forever And I / doe appoint her my said wife and Robert Richmond my brother in law / executors of this my last will and doe give unto him the said Robert five pounde/ for his paines to be taken therein There being then and there present at / the uttering and declaring thereof as aforesaid the above named Thomas / Love and Ann Cooke who in Testimonie of the truth of the promises / have hereunto sett and subscribed their for present And shall / and will for all tymes for the future be ready to affirm and answer the / same for truth upon theire corporall oathes if thereunto required, / Tho: Love The mark of Ann Cooke

This Will was proved at London before the Judges for probate / of wills and granting of Administration lawfully authorised the Tenth / day of March in the yeare of our Lord one thousand six hundred fifty six / English style by the oathes of Dorothy Tillott his relict and Robert Richmond / joynt Executors named in the said will to Administration was Committed / of all and singular the goods Chattles and Debts of the said deceased / they being first sworne by Commission truely to Administer.

Sir Edmund Poley, of Badley, Suffolk, Knight (20th October 1665)

IN the name of God Amen I Edmund Poley of Badley in the County of Suffolk Knight, being in perfect health and memory for which I bless God, but considering the great uncertainty of life especially these infections and mortall times, I make and sign this my last will and testament in manner and form following. First I recommend my soul to Almighty God most humbly imploring his most infinite mercy in the pardoning and forgiving my manifold and grievous sins and offences and the afterward salvation of my soul through the merritt and mediac(i)on of my only saviour Jesus Christ and direct my body to be buried in the chancel of the Parish Church at Badley aforesaid if I shall happen to die nearwhereabouts so as it may be performed without trouble and thought Next my Will and desire is that my dear wife shall hold and enjoy all those lands which I have settled upon her for a jointure during her natural life without any disturbance whatsoever. Item I doth give unto my daughter Elizabeth Poley the sum of five hundred pounds to be paid her at her day of marriage or her age of one and twenty years whichever shall first happen. Item I doth give unto my daughter Judith Poley the like sum of five hundred pounds to be paid her at her day of marriage or her age of one and twenty years whichever shall first happen AND Whereas my dear wife is at present nourished with Child of which blessed God in her own time she may be happily delivered, in case the said child shall prove a daughter I doth give unto that daughter the like sum of five hundred pounds to be paid her at her day of marriage or her age of one and twenty years whichever shall first happen Now in regard the severall sums of money hereby before given to my said daughters, and the severall debts to which I owe (the payment whereof I do hereby direct and appoint by my Executrix hereinafter named) can in no way be paid and discharged without the sales of some of my lands for the doing thereof. I do hereby therefore for that end and purpose Will and devise all my lands and tenements situated and lying in Badley aforesaid Combs, Battisford, Barking and Needham in the County of Suffolk or in any other towne to them or any of them near adjoining (which are not in jointure with my said dear wife) unto my Executrix hereafter named for the sale of all or such parts thereof as shall be judged fitting for the payment of my just debts and the several portions and legacies in this my last will given and I do hereby give full power and authority to my Executrix for the selling thereof at the best price can be gotten for the same, and out of those monies arising upon such sale shall in the first place to pay such of my debts for which for which any of my lands are or stand charged, And in the next place to pay all the residue of my inst debts and this being performed, then my Will and meaning is that the residue of the money arising upon such sale be put out upon good scrutiny for the paying and discharging the several portions herein given to my said daughters at their several ages and days aforesaid. And my Will and meaning is, that the interest and profit arising for the loan of such money so put out as before as aforesaid shall be equally expended for and towards the maintenance and education of all the children I have by my dear wife as well "sonnes and daughters" during the life of my said dear wife or until the time of payment of such portions aforesaid which shall first happen. But in case my dear wife should happen to die before the time of payment of such portions as aforesaid, then I do direct and appoint that the respective profit for the interest or loan of such respective portions should be paid to such of my daughters only as the said portions are herein before given and I devise for their several and respective maintenance until such portions shall be due and paid to them respectively at the times aforesaid But as to these severall portions thus given to my severall daughters as aforesaid my Will and meaning is that if any of my daughters shall happen to depart this life unmarried, and before they shall accomplish the age of one and twenty years then my Will and meaning is that the portion hereby given to such daughter so dying before the time of payment hereby before limited shall be given and paid, and paid to my sonne and heir Henry Poley and the heirs of his body in case he has any such heirs but if not then to my next oldest sonne who shall be then living. Item I do give and bequeath unto my sone and heir Henry Poley and to his heirs for ever. All that my manor of Badley aforesaid, and all the Lands Tenements and Hereditaments thereunto belonging which are now in Joynture to my dear wife with all the rights and appurtenances belonging to the same and contained in the jointure aforesaid, willing and intending nevertheless that the Manor and lands hereby given to my said son and heire Henry Poley shall be subject and liable to the payment of the several annuities and rent charges of Forty pounds yearly to every one of my younger sones. Viz Edmund Poley, Charles Poley, and the child my wife is now of, in case it proves a son, which several yearly annuities of forty pounds I do hereby give to every one of my said sonnes the said severall annuities of Forty pounds annually to continue to each of my said sons for and during their naturall lives respectively, and to be paid to every of vthem every half year at our Lady day and Michaelmas day by even and equal portions the said payments to commence on such of the said days as shall first happen after the death of my dear wife. The which said Annuity I doe hereby direct and appoint my said son and heir aforesaid to pay his several brothers respectively as is aforesaid directed, out of the Rents issued and profit of the Manor and lands herein before given to my said son and heir And in case my said son and heir should fail to pay the said Annuities so as is aforesaid. Then I do hereby authorize and impower all and every one of my said younger sons to whom the said Annuity during their respective lives are herein before given, to enter into such Manor and Lands and take distresses for all or such of the said Annuities as shall be behind and unpaid, and to sell the said distresses, and to return the surplus after due satisfaction to themselves of what was so behind and unpaid. And also the charges of taking such distress, to the owner of such goods as were distressed. Item I do give unto my sisiter Ann Poley the sum of Twenty Pounds. Item I do give unto my servant Edmond Smith if he serves me at the time of my death all my cloathes, and one years wages. Item I do direct and appoint that my Excutrix hereafter named should make use of the assistance and advice of my two cousins Benjamin Cutler and John Sothby (sic) Esq in the enforcement of this my Will and especially in the selling, of such Lands as shall be thought fit to be sold for the performance thereof And I doth make hereby the said Benjamin Cutler and John Sothby supervisors of this my last Will and Testament. And for their care and pains to them do give to each of them as a kind remembrance of me the sum of Ten pounds a year, further I do direct and appoint that in case there remain to any of the London tenements vested hereto in my Executrix for favour for the performance of this my last Will and Testament be unsold or that by God's blessing my debts and legacies and portions or any part of them comes otherwise to be paid and satisfied then by sale thereof That then my Executrix hereafter named shall settle and convey by all due and requisites made all or so much of the said lands as remained unsold upon my sonne and heir and his heirs for ever. Lastly I do hereby nominate and appoint my most Dearly Beloved wife Dame Hester Poley the sole Executrix of this my last Will and Testament revoking all former Wills whatsoever In Witness whereof I have here unto set my hand and seal the five and twentieth day of October in the year of our Lord 1665. Edmund Poley Signed, sealed and declared to be my last Will and Testament in the presence of Stephen Moore, Thomas Poley, Edmund Smith. This will all written by my own hand, and is contained in four sheets of paper, and hath these words entered in it in the first sheete and Tenants (sic) at the beginning of the forth line by the bottom of the leafe [thereof] in the third line of the second leafe, and the yearely in the fifth line of the third leafe on sheet. Edmund Poley.

[Proved 7th March 1673]

Thomas Poley, of St Martin in the Fields, co Middlesex, Gent (2nd Nov 1677)

IN the name of God Amen I Thomas Poley of the Parish of St Martin in the Fields in the County of Middlesex gent being sick in Body but of sound and perfect mind and memory Blessed be God for if And knowing the uncertainty of this transitory life and that all flesh must yield unto death whensoever it shall please God to call do make and ordain this my last Will and Testament in manner and form following that is to say Frst and principally I commend my Soul to Almighty God to make hoping and assuredly believing through the Merits and mediac(i)on of Jesus Christ my only Saviour and Redeemer to obtain free Pardon and Absolution of all my Sins and after this life has ended to enjoy everlasting Bliss and happiness And my body to the earth to be buried in such Christion like manner as my Executors hereinafter named shall judge most meet and convenient And concerning those wordly Goods which it hath pleased God to send me I give and dispose of the same in manner and form following, (viz) I give unto my sister Mrs Mary Portington the Relict of Mr William Portington the sum of three hundred pounds Item I give unto her son my nephew Mr Edmund Portington one hundred pounds Item I give unto her daughters my Nieces M^S Judith and M^S Frances Portington two hundred and fifty pounds apiece (that is) five hundred pounds to be divided equally between them Item I give to my Sister Anne Poley two hundred pounds Item I give to my Sister Dame Frances More wife of Sir John More two hundred pounds As for my Sister Dorothy and my Sister Cicily Poley they need not Gift of mine, howbeit I give and bequeath unto each of them twenty pounds apiece as a Token of my Love Item I give unto my Nephew Henry Poley Esquire son of Sir Edmund Poley knight deceased two hundred pounds Item I give unto my Nephew Mr Edmund Poley son of *Sir Edmund Poley* knight deceased one hundred pounds And I do further give unto them two Mr Henry and Mr Edmund Poley to be equally divided between them the Assets of my Annuity of forty pounds per Annum left me by my Father be the same three hundred pounds more or less if they think good to require it or not, that the money in discharge of these Assests, do arise and be paid out of the Lands Rents charged with the Annuity aforesaid Item I give unto Mr John Heath at the greene Man in Canon Street London five pounds And if there be anything of my Estate left more that what is bequeathed already I give the same unto my two nieces Mrs Judith and Mrs Frances Portington to be equally divided between them And I do hereby revoke and make void all former Wills constituting and appointing my Sister Dame Frances More and my Nephew Henry Poley aforesaid joint executors of this my last Will and Testament which is contained in two sheets of paper tied together with a black ribbon In witness whereof this Second day of November being All Souls I have to both the sheets set my hand and Seal in the twenty-ninth year of King Charles the second Anno Domini One thousand six-hundred seventie seven I desire fortie shillings may be given to Mr Samuel Bridge Minister of Alresford in Essex by Colchester and late Elmsted thereby. Thomas Poley. Signed Sealed and published in the presence of Edm B Godfrey : John Jones : The mark of Anne West.

[Proved in London 17th December 1677]

Henry Poley, of Badley, Suffolk, Esquire (10 August 1704)

THIS is the Last Will and Testament of me the said Henry Poley of Badley in the County of Suffolk Esq made and written with my own hand this tenth day of August One thousand Seven hundred and four. Imprimis I give unto the Lady Poley my dear mother the sum of ffive hundred pounds as Testimony of my Duty and affection to her.

Item I give unto my Lord Dover and to my Dear sister the Lady Dover ffifty Guineas apiece to buy them Mourning. Item I give unto my Dear Sister the Lady Gipps ffive hundred pounds. Item I give unto her two Daughters Elizabeth and Catherine Gipps two thousand pounds apiece. Item I give unto my nephew Richard Gipps Esqr ffifty Guineas to buy him a horse or what else he likes best. Item I give unto Mr William Chichley youngest Son of of my Lady Chichley ffive hundred pounds. Item I give unto Charles Robins my clerk two hundred pounds to help to advance him in the world. Item I give unto my Servant Paul Devall the sum of one hundred pounds. Item I give unto my Serving Boy John Sidwell thirty pounds to bind him an apprentice. Item I give unto every one of my Servants that shall be Living with me at the time of my Death one years Wages over and besides what shall be then due to them. Item all the rest and residue of my reall and personal Estate whatsoever my Debts ffuneral and Legacyes being first paid I give and devise to my Dear Brother Edmund Poley Esqr whom I make my Sole Executor of this my Last Will & Testament and my Will and desire is that my Legacys herein before given be paid within one year after my decease or as soon as moneys can be gotten in for the Payment of the same and in testimoney that this is my last Will and Testament I have hereunder sett my hand and Seal the day and year first above written. Henry Poley.

Signed Sealed and published by the said Testator as and for his last Will and Testament in the presence of us who have by his desire and in his presence Subscribed our Names as Witnesses hereinto. Tho Felton, Paul Devall, John Sidwell.

[Probate granted to Edmund POLEY (brother) 22 August 1707]

Anthony Croftes, of Badley, Suffolk, Gentlemen (15th September 1712)

IN the name of God Amen / I Anthony Crofts of Badley in the County of Suffolk Gentleman ~ / being at this time in perfect mind and memory do make this my ~ / last will & testament in manner and form following ~~ / revoking all others by me made and first I commend my Soul into / the hands of Almighty God my maker hoping that through the / merits of my only Saviour Jesus Christ it shall enjoy everlasting ~ / happiness I do hereby give and bequeath to my Nephew Mr ~ / Charles Crofts the sum of five hundred pounds I do also give / to my Nephew Mr Henry Crofts the sum of five hundred ~~ / pounds I do also give to my Maire Crofts fifty pounds And I do ~ / hereby give to my sister M^S Ann Crofts fifty pounds And I do ~~ / hereby give to the Lady Poley of Badley in the County of Suffolk ~~ / the sum of One hundred pounds and I give to the poor of the ~ / Parish of Little Saxham in the County of Suffolk the sum of twenty / pounds and I give to the poor of the parish of Badley in the County / of Suffolk the sum of Ten pounds and I do hereby give to the ~ / poor of the parish of WestStow in the County of Suffolk the sum of Ten pounds And lastly I do hereby nominate and appoint ~~ / my Nephew Mr Anthony Crofts my sole Executor of this my last / Will and Testament and when all the above legacies and all my ~ / debts are paid I do hereby give and bequeath all I have in the ~ / world to my above named Executor Mr Anthony Crofts In ~~~ / Witness whereof I have this day set my hand being the ~~~ / fifteenth day of September in the year of our Lord God One ~~/ Thousand Seven Hundred and Twelve Anthony Crofts ~~

Appeared personally Thomas Stisted of Ipswich in the / County of Suffolk Gentleman and being sworn on the holy ~~~~ / Evangalists did dispose as followeth viz. that he knew and was ~ / ...... well acquainted with Mr Anthony Crofts late of Badley ~ / in the County of Suffolk Gentleman deceased for about seven ~ / years before his death And the deponent hjath seen him ~ / write and hath received diverse letters from him the said Mr ~ / Crofts deceased by reason whereof he became very well aquainted / with his manner and Character of handwriting And says that ~ / he having now seen and perused the Will hereunto annexed ~~ / beginning thus In the name of God Amen I Anthony Crofts of ~ / Badley in the County of Suffolk Gentleman and ending thus In ~ / Witness whereof I have this day set my hand being the ~ / fifteenth day of September in the year of our Lord God One / Thousand seven hundred and twelve Does verily believe ~ / the same to be totally wrote and subscribed by him the said ~ / Anthony Crofts deceased Tho Stisted 3rd day of March 1713 /

Appeared personally James Chambers of the parish / of Saint Dunstan in the West London Goldsmith and being ~/ Sworn on the holy Evangalist did depose as followeth viz: that he knew and / was well acquainted with Mr Anthony Crofts late of Badley in the / County of Suffolk Gentleman deceased for about fifteen years ~~ / before his death and that this deponent hath often received diverse / letters from him the said Mr Crofts deceased by reason whereof ~ / he became very well acquainted with his manner and character / of handwriting And says that having now seen and perused / the Will hereunto annexed beginning thus In the name of God / Amen I Anthony Crofts of Badley in the County of Suffolk Gentleman / and ending thus In Witness whereunto I have this day set my hand / being the fifteenth day of September in the year of our Lord / God One thousand seven hundred and twelve does verily ~~ / believe the same to be totally wrote and subscribed by him the ~ / said Anthony Crofts deceased. James Chambers 3rd March / 1713

Fig D1 Part of Edmund Poley's short handwritten will made only 42 days before committing suicide on May 16th 1714. Note the memorandum in the margin in which he verifies a correction in line five. The original Will is in the S.R.O. Ref: HA1/DA1/7/9.

Edmund Poley, of Badley, Esquire (1st April 1714)

THIS is the last Will and Testament of me Edmund Poley Esquire of Badley in the County of Suffolke made / and written with my own hand the third day of April One ~ / Thousand Seven Hundred and fourteen. Imprimis I give unto my dear / Mother the Lady Poley the summe of four hundred pounds as / a mark of my duty and affection to her Item I give unto my dear / sister the Lady Dover the summe of fifty guineas to buy her ~ / mourning. Item I give unto my nephew Richard Gipps my Estate / of Columbine Hall and five hundred pounds besides in ready mony. / Item I give unto my niece Mrs Crofts the summe of one hundred / guineas to buy her mourning. Item I give unto Jesus College ~ / where I had my education one hundred pound. Item I give unto / John Olbeith (sic) my servant the summe of fifty pounds. Item I give / unto all my Servants who shall be with me at the time of my death / a years wages over and besides what shall be then owed to them / Item all the rest and residue of my reall and personal Estate ~ / my debts and legacyes being first paid I give and devise unto my dear sister the Lady Gipps who I make my sole executor of this my last Will and Testament and I will and desire is that my Legacyes herein given be paid within one year after my decease or as soon as money can be gotten for payment of the same and in Testimony that this is my last Will and Testament I have hereunto sett my hand and Seal the day and year above written. Edm. Poley.

Signed Sealed and published by the said Testator as and for his last Will and Testament in the presence of us who have by his desire and in his presence Subscribed our Names as Witnesses hereinto. Charles Robins, J Aldrich jun, Samuel Goodwin

Notes : *Edmund was last direct surviving male of the Poleys' Badley dynasty. His mother Dame Hester Poley (née Croftes) died 37 days later on 22nd June 1714, His sister Judith Poley married Henry Jermyn who was created Lord Dover in 1685. Lady Gipps is Edmund's sister Elizabeth Poley married to Richard Gipps snr.. The wording of Edmund's will is almost identical (apart from the bequests) to that drawn up by his barrister brother Henry on the previous page. As he was his brother's executor, perhaps he copied the format!*

Robert Scapy, of Badley, Suffolk, Gentleman (17th January 1790)

THIS is the last Will / and Testament of me Robert Scapy of Badley in / the County of Suffolk Gentleman first I direct that all / my accounts as executor of the last Will and Testament / of Thomas Emerson the Younger late of Barham in the / said County Gentleman deceased and also of the last Will / and Testament of Thomas Emerson the Elder of Coddenham in the said ~ / County Gentleman deceased together with all my Just ~ / Debts funeral expenses and Charges of proving this my Will / be fully paid and satisfied Item I given and devise unto / my dear sister Ann the wife of Henry Edwards of Sutton / in the said County farmer all that my Messuages or Tenement farm Lands and premises both freehold ~ / and copyhold situate lying and being in Stow Upland in the / said County or in some other Parish or place next or next adjoining thereto which I some time since purchased of / Brampton Gurdon Dillingham Esquire and now in the / Occupation of William Pearle or his undertenants To / hold to her the said Ann Edwards for and during the / Term of her natural Life And from and immediately after / the decease of my said Sister Ann I do give and devise / the said farm Land and Premises unto Henry Edwards ~ / the son of the said Henry and Ann Edwards and to / his heirs forever But my Will and Mind is and I do / hereby charge the said Messuages or Tenement farm / Lands and Premises so devised to my Sister Ann ~ / and Nephew Henry Edwards as aforesaid with the Payment / of One Annuity or thear Yearly Rent Charge of fifty / pounds to my dear mother Ann Scapy for and during ~ / the Term of her natural Life to be paid by four equal / quarterly payments in every year the first payment / thereof to be made at the expiration of Three Months / next after my decease And also with the payment of / one other Annuity or thear Yearly Rent Charge of / Ten Pounds to my Aunt Mary the Wife of the said / Thomas Emerson the Elder to be paid in like manner / Also I give and bequeath unto Samuel Turner and / Mary Turner the children of my late Sister Mary the / wife of Thomas Turner Three Hundred pounds each To be /paid them on their severally arriving at the age of / twenty one years But in case either of them shall happen / to depart this Life under the said Age of Twenty one / years and without lawful issue Then I do bequeath the / said Legacy of him or her so dying to the survivor of / them and in case of the death of both of them the / said children of my late sister Mary under such / Age and without issue as aforesaid I do give and bequeath / the said several Sums of Three hundred pounds unto / my said Nephew Henry Edwards to be paid him at / his Age of Twenty one years But in the mean ~ / time and until the said Samuel Turner and Mary Turner / shall respectively arrive at their age of Twenty / one years I do hereby authorise and empower my ~ / Executors after named to place out the Legacies ~ / given to them or one of them as aforesaid Upon Covenant / or other permanent Security And the Interest and Proceed / thereof to be applied for and towards their education / and advancement in Life at the discretion of my / Executors herein after named Also I give and bequeath / to my Aunt Mary the wife of John Scott deceased ~ / the sum of Ten shillings and six pence to be paid / her quarterly for and during the Term of her natural / Life Also to such of the first Cousins of my late / father as shall be living at the time of my ~ / decease the sum of Three pounds to be paid them ~ / within six months after my deceased and I do hereby / nominate and appoint my brother in Law the said Henry / Edwards and my friend Jonathan Abbott the Younger / of Needham Market Executors of this my said Will / and Guardians to the _____ Children of the said Thomas / Emerson the Younger And I do give and bequeath to each / of them the sum of Forty pounds for their trouble / in the performance of their several Trusts hereby in / them reposed And all the Rest Residue and Remainder / of my Real and Personal Estate of what nature ~ / or kind soever and wheresoever I give devise and ~ / bequeath unto my Brother in Law the said Henry ~ /Edwards his Heirs Executors and Administrators and / lastly I do hereby revoke all former and other Wills ~ / by me heretofore made and I do declare this to be my / last Will sand Testament In Witness whereof I have / to this my said Will contained in three sheets of / paper to the two first set my hand and to this last / sheet thereof my hand and Seal this seventeeth day / of January one thousand seven hundred and ninety / Robt. Scapy Signed Sealed published and declared by / the said Robert Scapy the testator as and for / his last Will and Testament in the presence of us who / in his presence at his request and in the presence / of each other have hereunto subscribed Our names / as Witnesses the Words " an A..." between the eighteenth / and nineteenth Lines of the first Sheet hereof ~ / being first interlined J Thomson - Nath[l]. Bucke and Rich[d] Mudd.

This Will was proved at London the seventh day of June in the Year of Our Lord One thousand seven hundred and ninety one before the Right Honourable Sir William Wynne Knight_____ Portor of Laws Master Keeper or Commissary of the Perogative Court of Canterbury lawfully constituted by the Oaths of Henry. Edwards and Jonathan Abbott the Younger the Executors named in ths said Will to whom Admon was granted of all and singular the Goods Chattels and Credits of the deceased having been first sworn by commission duly to administer.

OTHER BADLEY-RELATED WILLS FROM THE CALENDAR OF WILLS RELATING TO THE COUNTY OF SUFFOLK PROVED IN THE PREROGATIVE COURT OF CANTERBURY BETWEEN 1383 & 1675

(Unless otherwise stated, all testators are "of Badley")

1407	Shepheard, John	R2/252; A/6/3/6
1460	Tomner, John	R2/59a
1486	Vessy Robert	R3/35
1501	Rush, John	R4/23
1504	Poley, Edmund, Gent	25 Holgrave*
1525	Garneys, William, All Hallows Bredstrete London & Badley, Sfk	39 Bodfelde
1537	Garneys, Elizabeth	13 Crumwell*
1549	Poley, Edmond	31 Populwell*
1568	Allam, Faith	R22/213 : W20/156
1570	Cowper, Edmund	R28/181 : W21/117
1584	Poley, Edmund, 30th Jul	
1587	Tuumer, Edmund, yeoman	
1587	Poley, John, 18th Aug, and codicil of 10th Jun 1588	*
1588	Goodwyn, John, yeoman	
1590	Poley, John, Esquire	32 Drury
1592	Poley, Richard, 1st Sep	*
1593	Poley, Mary, 13th Jun	
1593	Poley, Mary, widow	21 Dixy
1593	Poley, Richard, Gent	45 Nevell
1596	Harwyn, John, yeoman	R36/204 ; W34/105
1601	Poley, Jane, of Whitechapel Co. Middx	
1607	Poley, Edmond, 15th Jun	*
1613	Poley, Edmund, Esq	107 Capell
1615	Cooper, Edward	A6/3/11
1617	Spynnie, Alice, widow	R50/77 ; W53/61
1617	Cooper, Edmund, husbandman	R48/9 : W51/4
1620	Marten, Margaret, widow	R53/157;W56/102
1620	Bowle, Ann, spinster	R53/124 : W56/84
1622	Balls, Thomas, yeoman	W58/75
1632	Beast, Robert, cooper	W68/20
1632	Flint, John yeoman	W68/44
1635	Dow(e), William, eld, yeoman	W71/128
1635	Poley, Sir John of Columbine Hall	39 Sadler (pr. Apr 29 by relict Dame Ursula Poley)*
1636	Beast, Edmund, yeoman	R60/208 ; W67/133
1636	Crompton, Elizabeth, spinster	35 Pile (pr. Jun 16 by sister Mary Crompton)*
1640	Poley, Edmund Esq	133 Coventry (pr. Oct 20 by son Edmund Poley)*
1640	Manning, Thomas, yeo	W78/119
1641	Crompton, Mary, spinster	50 Evelyn (pr. May 21 by mother Frances Crompton)
1648	Harlewyne, Thomas, tailor	
1649	Buxton, Richard, yeoman	W87/5
1649/50	Goodwyn, John, cordwainer	
1652	Harlewin, John, yeoman	W88/52
1653	Harlewyn (Harlwine), Thomas	387 Brent (pr. Jun 11 by brother Henry Harlewyn)
1654	Seagoe, Elizabeth	1654/465
1654	Raymond, Francis, bachelor	1654/168
1655	Poley, Edmund, 25th Oct	
1657	Tillet, Isaac, yeoman	1657/95*
1658	Clarke, James, yeoman	1658/685
1662	Coleman, Edward, yeoman	R69/77 ; W92/142
1666	Tyllott, Dorothy, widow	W90/139
1674	Lockwood, Prudence	R72/83;W104/105
1675	Coleman, Edmond, yeoman	R72/183 ; W105/100

* reproduced in this Appendix

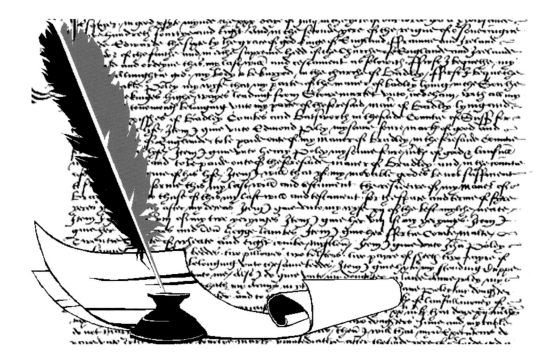

Miscellaneous Returns & References relating to Badley

SUFFOLK IN 1327 - SUBSIDY RETURN FOR SUFFOLK A.D.1327

List of men's names under the township in which they had their taxable property, followed by the amount of tax they had to pay.

VILLATA DE BATISFORDE CUM BADLEY

	s.	d.
De Roberto be Badele	ix	viii
" Johanne de Stanefelde	ix	ii
" Sampson de Badele	ii	
" Johanne le Marechal	iiii	
" Willmo Chek	ii	
" Johanne Bateman	xii	
William de Batisforde	iiii	
Thoma Haruy		xii
Thoma Jordon	ii	
De Ricardo Marechal	ii	vi
Michaele de Badele	xii	
Richardo Sewalle		xv
Magistro Hospital de Batisford	v	

	s.	d.
Roberto le Marechal	xviii	
Willmo de Bosco		xii
Richardo de Cruce	xii	
Episcopo Norwycense	viii	
Johanne Doble		xv
Richardo Alfred		ix
Isolda le Donnere	xv	
Waltero Tyde		xviii
Gilberto de Pheipe	xii	
Roberto de Gretforde	xii	
Roberto Bucher		xii
Prob. Summa [etc.]	lxiii	x

Suffolk Green Books No IX, Vol II, page 17, Bosmere Hundred

RETURN FOR SUFFOLK OF THOSE WHO PAID THE SUBSIDY (EXTRACT OF)
granted to Henry VIII in the 15th year of his reign

1523				
Badley	Edmond Poley (£20)	£1.	0s.	0d.
Stanstede	John Poley, gent (£4)	£0.	5s.	0d.
1524	Edmond Poley, gent., in landes £20	£1.	0s.	0d.
	William Lucas, in movabis £1. 45s 0d.	£0.	0s.	7d.
	Roger Vessy, in movabis £10	£0.	5s.	0d.
	Andrew Cook, Robert Goodhalle, William Leyham,			
	Agnes Crane[1], wedowe, eche of them in movabis £2.	£0.	4s.	0d.
	Robert Green, in movabis £1. 6s 8d.	£0.	0s.	8d.
	Robert Draper, Edmund Burges, John Panter, in movabis eche £1	£0.	1s.	6d.

RETURN FOR SUFFOLK FOR A SUBSIDY GRANTED IN 1566

1568					
Badley	-	John Poley, gent, £17 in landes	£1.	2s.	8d.
	-	Thomas Aldreth, £2 in landes	£0.	2s.	8d.
	-	William Goodall, £4 in goodes	£0.	3s.	4d.
	-	Robert Goodall, £4 in goodes	£0.	3s.	4d.
	-	William Colchester, £3 in goodes	£0.	2s.	6d.
Combs	-	Edmund Poley, £4 in landes	£0.	5s.	4d.
	-	Alys Pol, widdow, £1 in landes	£0.	1s.	4d.
Icklingham		Thomas Poley, esq, £30 in landes	£2.	0s.	0d.
Ewston	-	Gyelles Poley, gent, £8 in movables	£0.	6s.	8d.

[1] This Agnes Crane, widow, is thought to have been a member of the Cranes of Chilton family, near Sudbury, as opposed to Chilton, near Stowmarket. See S.I.A.H., Vol. XX p.89 (1930)

MUSTER ROLLS - ABLE MEN OF SUFFOLK

Muster Rolls of the Territorials in Tudor times

During the reigns of the Tudor Sovereigns several musters of the male population were made at various intervals, when occasion demanded it, to ascertain what military forces were available for the service of the Crown. They were made in pursuance of orders from the Sovereign and Privy Council and there is no reference to them on the Statute Book except the Act in 1557/8 which concerns itself mostly with penalties to be inflicted on those who absented themselves.

Among the Stowe MSS. in the British Museum there is a paper which gives the method of procedure in 1522, which was as follows:- The King appointed Commissioners for every hundred, and these Commissioners charged the chief Constables of the hundred, who in their turn gave orders to the constables of each parish in the hundred to appear on a certain day with certificates in writing of the names of all the men above 16 years of age dwelling in each town, village, and hamlet. All these were to appear before the Commissioner "furnished and appareled in their best arraye for the warre, that is to saye with bowes, arrowes, bills, harnes, or any other weapon, artillery, or harnes for the warre, which they or anye of them have."

It seems that from the able men between the ages of 16 and 60 a selection was made and those so selected were drilled to some extent and put through some kind of training. In the return for the franchise of Bury St Ednmunds in 1573, a **Thos. Polye** was recorded as a Captain along with a Thomas Crofts.

Antony Poley is listed as having harnes in the seid towne of Westowe, where he is also shown as a Bylmen. (presumably this means had possession of a 'bill' - a pike or halberd with a narrow hooked blade - OE for sword)

William Poley, gent, the brother of **Edmund of Badley**, is listed at Iklyngham. Under the section "Here after folowe the namys of all them that have horse or harneys, withyn the Towne of Iklyngham according unto the statute" it is also noted he "haith too harneys, to holbeerds, to swords, and to daggers."

(extracted from *Muster Rolls* - SIA Vol XV [1913] p.114)

1638
BADLEY

Edm: Poley, esq.	Roberte Crompton, esq.	Edm: Pooley, jr.	Fr: Raymond
William Hartstonge	Fr: Burgis	Isaack Tillet	William Petham
Edm: Eustate	Peter Dunt	Jo: Dale	Edm: Denny
Ric: Johnson	Anth: Belton	Jo: Larwood	Martine Seaman
Gregory Felton	Edm: Goodale	Thomas Goddard	William Keriside
William Frauncis	William Dove, gent.	Thomas Wallis	Theop: Glanfeild
Edw: Colman	Thomas Blowes	Fr: Beaste	James Pettet
Ric: Buxton	Jo: Balls	Roberte Kidman	

TOTAL : 31
(Jo: Harwyn, constable)

SUFFOLK SHIP-MONEY RETURNS 1639-40

The introduction of Ship-Money in 1634 was one of the means resorted to by Charles I to replenish his treasury during the period when he was attempting to carry on the Government without Parliament. In Suffolk this tax fell mainly on the landowners

Tax on their land was levied so that each leet paid forty pence for every pound and vils comprising the leet were assessed according to the proportional amount of land each contained.

BADLEY - 28th Mar 1640

Pooley, Edm. Esq	£2. 2s. 4d.	Dove, Wm	£1. 6s. 1½d.
Mannyng, Thos	£1. 1s. 0d.	Coleman, Edw	£0. 15s. 1½d
Buxton, Rich	£0. 9s. 7½d.	Gooddale, Edm	£0. 6s. 2¼d.
Buxton, Robt	£0. 2s. 9d.	Flynt, Anne, wid.	£0. 2s. 9d.
Harwyn, Jn	£0. 6s. 10½d.	Balls, Jn	£0. 16s. 6d.
Pleasance, Margt. wid.	£0. 2s. 9d.	Martyn, Rich	£0. 4s. 9¾d.
Codling, Edm	£0. 3s. 9½d.	Cooper, Jn	£0. 4s. 1½d.
Lockwood, Wm	£0. 0s. 8d.		

(Edw Coleman : *constable*)

SUFFOLK HEARTH TAXES - RETURNS 1662-1689

The Hearth Tax was introduced in England and Wales by the government of Charles II in 1662 at a time of serious fiscal emergency. The original Act of Parliament was revised in 1663 and 1664 and collection continued until the tax was finally repealed by William and Mary in 1689. Under the terms of the grant, each liable householder was to pay one shilling for each hearth within their property for each collection of the tax. The tax was payable by people whose house was worth more than 20s a year and who contributed to local church and poor rates. Large numbers of people were exempt from paying the tax. Those individuals who were not liable to pay for reasons of poverty were required to obtain a certificate of exemption from the parish clergyman, churchwardens and overseers of the poor, countersigned by two Justices of the Peace. As a result, the hearth tax assessments cannot be considered to provide anything approaching a comprehensive census of the population. Payments were due twice annually, at Michaelmas (29 September) and Lady Day (25 March), starting at Michaelmas 1662. However, the administration of the tax was extremely complex and assessment and collection methods changed radically over time. As a result, the majority of the surviving documents relate to the periods when the tax was administered directly by royal officials, who returned their records to the Exchequer, namely the periods 1662-1666 and 1669-1674. Outside these periods, the collection of the tax was 'farmed out' to private tax collectors, who paid a fixed sum to the government in return for the privilege of collecting the tax. These farmers were not required to send their assessments into the Exchequer, although a few returns from these periods do survive. *(Source: Summarised from 'National Archives, Domestic Records Information Leaflet 32')*

These returns provides further compelling evidence for the original grandeur of Badley Hall, placing it 17th out of the 55 returns made (Hengrave Hall returned the most hearths with 55). They also show that the Poleys' Badley seat was larger than that of the senior branch of the family resident at Boxted.

Boxted in Babergh	-	Sir John Poley	22 hearths
Badley in Bosmere	-	**Sir Edmund Poley**	**30 hearths**

The Hearth Tax was very unpopular and many people demolished hearths in order to avoid paying it.

1664 *(E179/257/12 PRO 1664, document not dated)*

Pooley, Edmond knt	30 hearths	*(1)* (Ar) *(Badley Hall)*
Balls, John	3 hearths	*(2)*
Goodwin, wid	3 hearths	*(3)*
Lambert, Richard	2 hearths	*(4)*
Holloborough, Thomas	2 hearths	*(5)* clerk
Younge, Henry	2 hearths	*(6)*
Buxton, Edmond	2 hearths	*(7)*
Cocke, Willm	3 hearths	*(8)*
Thurmood, John	2 hearths	*(9)*
Burgis, wid	1 hearth	*(10)*
Whitecake, Thomas	2 hearths	*(11)*
Wood, Wm	4 hearths	*(12)*
Colman, wid	3 hearths	*(13)*
Lockwood, Margarett wid	1 hearth	*(14)* *(Exemption certificate)*
Beast, Francis	1 hearth	*(15)* *(Exemption certificate)*
TOTAL =	**61 hearths**	

1666 *(E179/183/616 part 4 1666 Lady Day paper book)* (Walking Order)

Poley, Edm knight	30 hearths	*(1) (Badley Hall)*
Bankes, Thomas	3 hearths	*(2)* Ids
Wood, Willm	4 hearths	*(3)*
Hall, John	2 hearths	*(4)*
Burges, Mr	1 hearth	*(5)*
Thrumwoods, Jon	2 hearths	*(6)*
Cooke, William	3 hearths	*(7)*
Burton, Edm	2 hearths	*(8)*
Youngs, Henry Mr	2 hearths	*(9)* Ids
Lambert, Rich	2 hearths	*(10)*
Balls, John	3 hearths	*(11)*
Goodinge, Willm	3 hearths	*(12)*
Lockwood, wid	1 hearth	*(13)* Arrears poor
Holborough, Thom	2 hearths	*(14)* Arrears poor empty
TOTALS =	**60 hearths**	

Rec £2.15.00; ds 2; poor 3

1669 *(E179/257/17 Not dated, Geo Key, collector 1669)*

Poley, Edm Sir	30 hearths	*(1) (Badley Hall)*
Hall, Jo	2 hearths	*(2)*
Burgis, Mrs	1 hearth	*(3)*
During, Walter	2 hearths	*(4)*
Cock, Will	3 hearths	*(5)*
Buxton, Edm	2 hearths	*(6)*
Smith, Edm	2 hearths	*(7)*
Balls, Jo	3 hearths	*(8)*
Banks, Tho	2 hearths	*(9)*
Wood, Will	3 hearths	*(10)*
Goodwin, wid	3 hearths	*(11)*
Lambert, Rich	2 hearths	*(12)*
Bull, Jo	2 hearths	*(13)*
1 more rec collection	1 hearth	*(14)*
Goodwin, Jo constable	-	*(15)*
TOTAL =	**58 hearths**	

1674

Pooly, The Lady	30 hearths	*(1) (Badley Hall)*
Smyth, Edm	3 hearths	*(2)*
Wood, William	4 hearths	*(3)*
Hall, Jo (2)		*(4)*
Burgis, Mr (1)	3 hearths	*(5)*
Furman, Jo	2 hearths	*(6)*
Cooke, William	3 hearths	*(7)*
Buckson, Edm	2 hearths	*(8)*
Balls, Jo	3 hearths	*(9)*
Boules, Thomas	3 hearths	*(10)*
Goodinge, wid	3 hearths	*(11)*
Lambert, Ri (2)		*(12)*
Bull, Jo (2)	4 hearths	*(13)*
TOTAL =	**60 hearths**	

(1664, 1666 & 1669 transcriptions courtesy of Desmond & Shelagh Herring and Brian A Southgate)

POLL BOOKS

These books were concerned with elections and voters in county and Parliamentary elections. They show how the persons elligible voted in an election.

1710 - **Suffolk Poll Book - 18th October at Ipswich**
Candidates: Sir Thomas Harmer, Bt. (H), Sir Robert Davers, Bt. (D) & Sir Philip Parker, Bt. (P).

Badley	Edmund Poley, Esq	H, D
	Henry Sage	H, D
Boxted	John Poley, Esq	H, D

1727 - **Suffolk Poll Book - 30th August**
Candidates: Sir William Barker (B) & Sir Jermyn Daves (D).

Badley	Issac Peek	B, D
	Richard Gipps, Esq	B, D

1790 - Poll - 29th/30th June
Candidates: Sir John Rouse, Bt. (R), Sir Thomas Charles Bunbury, Bt. (B) & Sir Gerald William Vanneck, Bt. (V)

Badley	**Freeholds in**
Robert Scapey	Stowupland
John Scott	Stowmarket
Jon Simpson	Monks Eleigh

LAY SUBSIDIES (EXCHEQUER) SUFFOLK
Hundred of Lackford - 2, 3 Edw 6

William Poley	goods	iiij^{li}	v^{li}

(1540)

Constance Aleyn for hur lond & tents	xx^{s}	
William Poley for his movabulls	xl^{s}	

William Poley held Manor of Thwamhill (i.e. Lords) 6 Hen 6 (147*) died 3P & M 1556

8 Eliz (1566)

Thomas Poley Esquier, land	xxx$^{l:}$	xj^{s}

MISCELLANEOUS REFERENCES TO INHABITANTS OF BADLEY

1239 : *Fine* : Hugh de Badelee *v.* Alan de Hulm in Badele. (24 Hen III)

1239 : *Fine* : Thomas son of Geoffrey *v.* Geoffrey de Baddel in Baddel (24 Hen III)

1316 : *Grant* : by James Mandyon to William of Badley, messuages with apperrences as inclosed within certain bound in Badley, which Gilbert Mandyon and Lucia his wife acquired abutting on to the way from Stowmarket to Ipswich. Sunday after BMV Assump 10 Edward son of Edward (22nd October 1316). Witness : John of the Bridge

1331/2 : *Fine* : John Alcok & Simon his son *v.* John del Hegh Chaplin in Weybrede (6 Edw III)

1331/2 : *Fine* : Robert de Batesford & Cecilia his wife & William and John, his sons *v.* William de Batesford & Johanna his wife in Battesford, Badele, Berkyng, Ryngesele & Combes. (6 Edw III)

1334 : *Grant* : by Peter, clerk of Elmsete, to Robert de Gretforde of Badley and Matilda his wife of all the moveables which he has of the gift of Robert of Badley. Sat. Barnab. ap 8, Edward III (11th June 1334)

1356/7 : *Fine* : Alan Hautboys, parson of Cokefield church and John de Stanfield *v.* Robert de Batesford & Mable his wife in Battisford, Ryngefeld & Badelee.

1364/5 :   *Fine* : Philip Deneys *v*. John Deneys and Thomas Colette & Katherine his wife of two parts of the manor of Badele. (39 Edw III)

1398 :   *Fine* : William Burgate Knt, John Hobert Clk., William Cloutyng, John Glemham, John Lynge, and William Lampet *v*. Thomas Poley & Matilda his wife of the Manors of Swartesham & Gyslynghames. (22 Rich III)

1434 :   *Fine* : Edmund Neve chaplin, John Furbusshour chaplin, and William Bret chaplin *v*. Henry Alcock and Elizabeth his wife in Badle (13-15 Hen VI)

1446 :   *Feoffment* : by John Neve, of Stowemarket [co. Suff.], to Edmund Alcok, of Badlee [Badley, co. Suff.], "armiger," and Matthew Gerlyng, of Needham Market [co. Suff.], of lands in Badlee. Witn.: John Resshbrook, John Heggeman, John Austyn, etc. Dat. at Badlee, 2 May, 24 Hen. VI. [1446]. Lat. Seal.

1657 :   *Lease* : John Goodwin of Badley to Fras. Huggin of Ipswich, lands called Hemingston Read in Barham. (Ashburnham Collection SRO Ref: HA1/46)

1662 :   *Will* : Probate copy of Will 14th Oct 12 Car II, of Edward Coleman of Badley, yeo., devising his house where Mary Wolfe, widow, dwells in Badley and land to Prudence his wife, for life, then Edward his son, the messuages where John King dwells and lands purchased of Robert Small, Tavernor Field and Tavernor Land in Combs. Henry Young of Badley, supervisor, and Frances Burge of Badley proved Archdeaconry of Suffolk, 2nd September 1662

1662 :   *Indenture* : by which Edmund Poley of Badley, Esq., John Lany of Ipswich, Esq., and Thomas Daundy (Dandye) of Bury St Edmunds, gent., convenant that Dandye shall suffer recovery of the use of himself and his heirs, the manor of Combs and its appurtences. 10th Oct. 36 Eliz. (1594) (Ashburnham Collection SRO Ref: HA1/EA/2/2)

1663 :   *Indenture* : by which Edward Coleman of Badley, yeo., and Margaret his wife, late Margaret Beast, widow, covenant to levy a fine to John Harland of Badley, yeo. and John Balls of the same, yeo., of the share of three freehold messuages called Lowdhams, Adgors and St Johns, and lands part copyhold of Combs, being formerly of Thomas Pattle of Combs, yeo. 28th September 1636) (Ashburnham Collection SRO Ref: HA1/EA/43)

From the IVEAGH MANUSCRIPTS - PHILIPS COLLECTION

FEOFFMENT (1322)

i) Ralph Attewode of Parva Helynham (Helmingham?) ii) Robert de Gretford
(i) to (ii) and heirs of his body lawfully begotten, all lands and tenements in Balele with which (ii) formerly enffeoffed (i); to hold of chief lords of fee for accustomed services in default of such issue, remainder to Gilbert de Pheipe. Given at Balele, Monday after feast of St Denis. 16 Edw. II. Witnesses: William de Badele, Robert de Badele, John de Thewic, James Herin, John Batemen, Robert le Hotot, John le Mareschal and others. (latin; 1 seal) (SRO Ref : HD/1538/121/1)

FEOFFMENT (1395)

i) Joan Vincent, widow of Simon Vincent of Badalee ii) John Bateman and his wife Margery of the same John Cokerel of Oxford, William Hunting of Needham Market, Hugh Pyn of Needham
(i) to (ii) all her lands & tenements in Badalee which she lately purchased jointly with her late husband of John Rodyngg & John Pykerke; to hold of chief lords of fee for accustomed services. Warranty clause. Witnesses: John Pykerke, Michael Yve, John Trunmere, Thomas Cokesegh, Robert Fysshere of Needham and others. Given at Badalee Tuesday the feast of St Mark. 19 Ric II (25 Apr 1395) (latin; 1 seal) (SRO Ref : HD/1538/1212/2)

??? (1410)

the heirs to occupy, administer and keep the Manor of Badele, with all goods and chattles, moveable and irremoveable and to receive all monies. Given 10th June. 11 Hen IV (latin: 3 seals) (1 armorial incomplete another fragmentary) (on two tags another tag presumably with two seals missing) (SRO Ref : HD/15312/1/3 (check))

GRANT (1437)

i) Edmund Alcoke *alias* Rafman of Badley; ii) Sir Thomas Tuddenham, Knight, Sir Joseph Heuenyngham, Knight, Thomas Mauncellsen of Nettlestede (Nettlestead) John Lauerok, Robert Gloson and John Martyn of Needham Market.
(i) to (ii) all his goods and chattles moveable and immoveable living or dead in Suffolk or elsewhere in England. Witnesses: Thomas Greene of Cretyng (Creeting), John Leyng' of Basford (Battisford), William Wrangyll, William Boteller', John Demner of Badley & others. Given at Badley Monday the Nativity of St John the Baptist. 15 Hen VI (24th Jun) (latin; 1 seal) (SRO Ref : HD/1538/12 121/4)

FEOFFMENT (1475)

i) Simon Poley of Badley; ii) Edmund Alcocke; iii) John Bakk' senior, William Byntyng, John Sele, John Meller
(i) to (ii) Messauge with land belonging to it in Badley, lately of Michael Bateman of Badley which (i) lately had together with John Coke and Matthew Gerlyng, both now deceased by gift of John Sefrey and John Norman; to hold of chief lords of fee for accustomed services. Also (i) ? (ii) their attorneys to deliver seisin. Witnesses: Thomas Treker senior, of John Cobb of Combys, John Dey, William Austen, Robert Bole and others. Given at Badley 12th November 15 Edw IV (latin; seal & tag missing) (SRO Ref : HD/1538/121/5)

FEOFFMENT (1603/4)

Evidences of title - Feoffment by William Payne of Stowmarket, tailor to Thomas Balles of Badley, carpenter, of tenement (boundaries specified) in Stowmarket, for £24. - ref. HD 1538/368/1 - date: 6 Jan 1603/4

DEPOSTIONS

Volume containing the following original depositions relating to crimes committed in Suffolk. Depositions of John Roberson of Combs and John Dow of Badley, gamekeepers, re assault on J.R. by William Peake and William Reeve of West Creeting, allegedly snaring hares on manor of Combs - ref. HD 1538/43/31 - date: n.d

CONDITION OF THE ARCHDEACONRIES OF SUFFOLK & SUDBURY IN THE YEAR 1603.

Yaxley

Mr Egidius Polye, Vicarius, dicit.

Ae lm. the somber of Comunicantes are about — c.

Ae 2m. et 3m. theare are men recusantes Seaven, and women recusantes Eleaven, and theis doo not receyve the holie Comunion, there are no other.

Ae 4m. he hath but this poor Vicaredge of Vaxley.

Ae 5m. et 6m. theare is an Impropriation, indued wth the sayed Vicaredge, the Vicaredge valued in his Mat^{tie} Book at vj^{li} vj^{s} vj^{d} the personage impropriate to his knowledge not valued theare.

Ae 7m. his Mat^{tie} booth patron and proprietarye.

Above reproduced from p27, Vol. XI, Part 1, *Suffolk Institute of Archæology & Natural History* (1901).

This *Egidus* (Latin for Giles) appears to be the same Gyles Poolie referred to in the Visitation of Suffolk 1561, who was the third son of John Poley of Boxted. He married Alice Tenderlove at Boxted in 1554 and was inducted to the vicarage at Yaxlie on 27 September 1570 and later instituted as Rector of Thornham Magna on 27 July 1573. Although this entry concerns a member of the Boxted branch of the family, it is included as it relates to a period when the Badley branch were still lords of the manor of Woodhall in nearby Stoke Ash.

EXCHEQUER RECORD :

Liber Feodorum: The Book of Fees commonly called *Testa de Nevill** (1198-1293)

De feodis honoris de Clare Galfr' de Baddele tent unu feod' milit' in BADELE de eode   (290b - 326)

(* The origins of this document are unclear some believe it be the Return of Abel Moyfey Esq., Deputy King's Remembrancer)

SUFFOLK NOTES & MUSTER - *Miss E Bell*

Taxation of Ipswich for the Welsh War in 1282

p.17 **Idonea de Badele** in caseis 10*s.*, in pecunia 8*s.*, in jocalibus 2*s.*, in utensilibus 4*s.*

Summa	one-thirteenth
£0. 24*s*. 0*d*.	10½*d*.

CHURCHWARDEN & OVERSEERS AT BADLEY
From the Badley Towne Bookes

Churchwarden & Overseer of the Poore were elected from within the Parish to serve the whole year or from Easter to Michaelmas/Michaelmas to Easter

Date	Churchwarden	Overseer	Date	Churchwarden	Overseer
1669	William Holmes	William Wood	1685	William Cock	Thomas Banks
1670	Walter Durbdon	John Balls	1686/7	John Goodwin	
1671		Edmund Smith	1688		William Cock
1672		Thomas Banks	1689		William Cock
1673	John Goodrum	William Lock	1690	Thomas Green	
1674	John Goodrum	Walter Durdbon	1691	Thomas Green	
1676	Edmund Smith	Richard Lambert	1692		James Cook
1677	William Cock	Thomas Balls	1693		James Cook
1678	John Goodwin	(check)	1694	William Stannard	
1679		Thomas Banks	1695		James Cook
1680	William Cock	John Barker	1696		William Cock
1681	Wiliam Cock	John Barker	1697		William Stannard
1682	William Barton		1698		William Stannard
1683	Edmond Buxton	Thomas Banks	1699		James Cook
1684	Thomas Balls	John Goodwin	1700		James Cook *(continued overleaf)*

Date	Churchwarden	Overseer	Date	Churchwarden	Overseer
1701		James Cook	1725		John Deeks/Diggs
1702		John Sougate	1726		
1703		John Goodrun	1727		John Wolton
1704		William Cock	1728		
1705		Edmund Buxton	1729		John Deeks/Diggs
1706		William Boahams	1730		John Groom
1707		James Cook	1731		Richard Robinson
1708		William Blowors	1732		Richard Robinson
1709		John Sougate	1733		Richard Gipps Esq
1710		John Sougate		William Christmas	Thomas Poke
1711		John Woughton	1734		Thomas Wolton
1712		John Woughton	1735		Thomas Wolton
1713		James Cork			Abraham Southgate
1714		William Blougs	1736	William Christmas	
1715		William Cork	1737		Thos & Jno Wolton
1716		William Grismos	1738	William Christmas	Edmund Groom
1717			1739	William Christmas	Edmund Groom
1718		William Blouoss	1740	Abraham Southgate	Richard Robson
1719		William Blouoss	1741	Abraham Southgate	Samuel Seapey
1720		William Blouoss	1741	William Kedington	William Christmas
1721		John Wolton	1742		
1722		John Wolton	1743		
1723		John Wolton	1744		Thomas Wolton
1724		John Coleman			

SUFFOLK RETURNS FROM THE CENSUS OF RELIGIOUS WORSHIP OF 1851

A unique census of places of worship took place on the same day as the decennial population census (Sunday 30 March 1851). *(National Archives Classification HO 129)* Some of the questions asked were: how many free and other (appropriated) sittings each place had; what was the estimated number of attendants (general congregation and children) in the morning, afternoon, and evening of 30 March, with the average number over a period of months. Questions were also asked regarding the buildings in which the congregations met. The filling out the forms of the religious census was left to the clergy; as a result not all census returns were completed. In 1997 the Suffolk Records Society published a transcription of the Suffolk Returns, which fortunately includes those for St Mary, Badley *(HO 129/220 - Bosmere)*, reproduced below.

"509 BADLEY   [population 74]   [Area. 1050a]
PARISH CHURCH. *Endowed* with £40. *Sittings* free 30, others 26. *Present* morning 23 Average (12 months) mornings 24; afternoon 28; No scholars. *Signed* Coppinger Hill, Perpetual Curate, Buxhall. (41) Scattered parish said to be mostly owned by Earl of Ashburnham. Single duty. Holy Communion four times a year; average of 12 to 14 communicants. Perpetual Curate Licensed 1838; J.P. Some Independants."

(Adapted from the Editor's Introduction: The Census and How It Was Taken in Suffolk and entry 509, page 94. *'Suffolk Returns from the Census of Religious Worship 1851'*, published by the Suffolk Records Society 1997).

SOME BADLEY INHABITANTS MARRIED ELSEWHERE

At St Mary, COMBS

27 Sep 1607	Thomas Everson	married	Ann Bugg (of Badley)
11 Oct 1779	Stephen Bumstead (of Badley)	married	Mary Brett (of Combs)
30 May 1803	George Turner (of Badley)	married	Mary Wetherstead (of Combs)
3 Mar 1811	William Kemball (of Badley)	married	Susan Mudd (of Badley) (by Lic.)
19 Oct 1812	Richard Jackaman (of Badley)	married	Mary Harvey (of Combs)
16 Aug 1816	William Mudd s.(of Badley)	married	Sarah Robinson s. aged 20 (of Combs) (by Lic.)
27 Jul 1910	Edmund J A Richardson	married	Ellen Maria Williams (of Badley)

At St Mary, BARKING

1657	Lionel Bugby (of Badley)	married	Mary Richerson (of Needham Market)
16th May 1813	Geo English (of Badley)	married	Eliza Tydeman (of Needham Market)
25th May 1817	William Chapman	married	Mary Ann Cockerill (of Badley)
17th Dec 1825	Benjamin Coleman	married	Ann Kemball (of Badley)

At St James, BURY ST EDMUNDS

26	1716	Edward Sage (of Badley)	married	Hannah Cooke (of Badley) (By Lic.)
11 Oct 1730		William Lee s. yeo. aged 29 (of Battisford)	married	Martha Crismas s w, aged 24 (of Badley) (By Lic.)
01 May 1742		Abraham Southgate s. aged 23 (of Badley)	married	Ann Jacob s. aged 22 (of Combs) (By Lic.)

At St Mary, BURY ST EDMUNDS

| 25 Aug 1731 | Francis Groome s. yeo. aged 28 (of Badley) | married | Frances Warren s. (of Badley) (by Lic.) |

At BURY ST EDMUNDS *(location unknown)*

| 01 Oct 1714 | Jas. Gladdell s. yeo. aged 23 (of Badley) | married | Elizh. Avis s. aged 22 (of Rougham) (By Lic.) |

At King Charles the Martyr, SHELLAND

| 26 Sep 1809 | Thos. Scott s. (of Badley) | married | Mary Lusher s. (of Shelland) (by Lic.) |

At SS Peter & Paul, STOWMARKET

| 20 May 1831 | Jn. Kemble s. (of Badley) | married | Carol Ungless s. (of Stowmarket) (by Lic.) |

ELECTORAL ROLE 1873 & 1875

Bosmere & Claydon

No 11 Needham Market

Parish or Township of Badley

Voters in respect of property, including tenant occupiers at a rent of £50 and upwards

6177	**Hayward**, George	Badley	Farm as occupier	Dove's Hill
6178	**Hayward**, Horace	Badley	Farm as occupier	Near turnpike road
6179	**Heawood**, John Richard Rev	Combs	Freehold benefice	Perpetual curate of Badley
6180	**Moor**, John Kirby	Badley	Farm as occupier	Near turnpike road
1681	**Mudd**, Frederick	Badley	Farm as occupier	Badley Green
1682	**Mudd**, Thomas	Badley	Farm as occupier	Badley Hall
1683	**Wicks**, Henry	Badley	Farm as occupier & mill as occupier	Badley Mill, near Eastern Union Railway

---

LACKFORD

"The advowson of the rectory belonged to Bury Abbey; Edward Lord North, obtained a grant of it in the 3d year of the reign of Philip and Mary, of whom John Drury, of Rougham, purchased it, and sold it to John Poley of Icklingham, of whom Sir Thomas Kytson bought it, ..."

WEST STOW

The chancel contains several gravestones, formerly inlaid with brass plates, one only remains with a Latin inscription, which has been thus translated :

Halyfax produced me. Cambridge taught me.
Suffolk heard me. Angina (pectoris) carried me off, now
The tomb holds my body ; Christ my soul.
My name was William Bois. He died on the 22d
of April,1591. Farewell Reader. Meditate often
on that saying of Tertullian
The Resurrection of the dead
Is the confidence of Christians

Mr. Bois was educated at St. Michael's Hall, now Trinity College, Cambridge. He first settled at Nettlestead, near Hadleigh, where he took a farm and lived a layman ; here he married a gentlewoman of ancient descent, eminent for religion and virtue, as appears by the following testimony, written in a Common Prayer Book:– "This was my Mother's Book ; my good Mother's Book. Hir Name was first **Mirable Poolye** ; and then afterwards Mirable Bois : being so called by the Name of hir Husband, my Father, William Bois : who lived in the Ministry divers Years, and was buried at a Village, not above four Miles from S. Edmond's-Bury, called West-Stow, where he had been Pastour, & remained so 'till the Time of his Death. My Mother over-lived my Father about ten Years, For being much alike in Years when they married, my Father died Anno Ætatis suœ lxviij° and my Mother lxxviij° plus minus. She had read the Bible over twelve Times, and the Book of Martyrs twice ; besides other Bookes, not a few."

In the early part of Queen Elizabeth's reign, Mr. Bois took the cure of Elmsett, and, on the death of the incumbent, was presented, by the Lord Keeper to the living, and soon after to that of West Stow, by his brother, Mr. Pooley ; . . . ."

Paraphrased from *"A Concise Description of Bury St Edmunds and Its Environs"*, page 335, published by subscription (1827).

LOCAL ADS DIRECTORIES OF STOWMARKET, NEEDHAM MARKET, MID-SUFFOLK - BADLEY ENTRIES:

1961

Allen V E	3 Doves Hill Cottage
Bloss A E	Woodlands Cottages
Brown G W	Badley Lane
Crysell C H	New Cottage
Farrow C S	Doveshill Farm
Filby K J	1 Doves Cottage
Foster J T	Cottage Woodlands Sub-Station
Freshwater E M	Badley Mill
Hadley C G	3 Badley Walk
Hadley G E	6 Badley Walk
Haward C G	Bungalow Woodlands Sub-Station
Laffling G H	Badley Bridge Farm
Mundell H C	Badley Green Farm Cottages
Pettitt C H	3 Doveshill
Proctor G A	4 Badley Walk
Roper W R	2 Badley Hill Cottage
Rowe G	1 Doveshill Cottage
Scott A B	Badley Hall
Short S L	Cherry Tree Farm
Sore R W	1 Badley Walk
Steel L A C	5 Badley Walk
Vale D H	Scott's Cottage Badley Lane

1965

Bloss A E	Woodlands Cottages
Crysell C H	New Cottage
Farrow C S	Doveshill Farm
Freshwater E M	Mill House
Hadley C G	2 Badley Walk
Hadley G E	6 Badley Walk
Key F L	Mill House
Laffling G H	Badley Bridge Farm
Mayhew B J	New Cottage
Morton C I	The Woodlands
Mundell H C	Badley Green Farm Cottages
Pettitt C H	3 Doveshill
Proctor G A	4 Badley Walk
Roper W R	2 Badley Hill Cottage
Rowe G	1 Doveshill Cottage
Scott A B	Badley Hall
Short S L	Cherry Tree Farm
Sore R W	1 Badley Walk
Steel L A C	5 Badley Walk
Vale D H	Scott's Cottage Badley Lane

1966

Bloss A E*	Woodlands Cottages
Crysell C H	New Cottage
Farrow C S	Doveshill Farm
Freshwater E M	Mill House
Hadley C G	3 Badley Walk
Hadley G E	6 Badley Walk
Key F L	Mill House
Laffling G H	Badley Bridge Farm
Mayhew P J	New Cottage
Mills G C	Woodlands Bungalow
Morton C I	The Woodlands
Mundell H C	Badley Green Farm Cottages

Pettitt C H	3 Doveshill
Proctor B H M	4 Badley Walk
Roper W R	2 Badley Hill Cottage
Rowe G	1 Doveshill Cottage
Scott A B	Badley Hall
Short S L	Cherry Tree Farm
Sore R W	1 Badley Walk
Stearne R R	2 Badley Walk
Steel L A C	5 Badley Walk
Warner I	4 Badley Walk

1967/68

Bloss A E*	Woodlands Cottages
Crysell C H	New Cottage
Farrow C S	Doveshill Farm
Freshwater E M	Mill House
Hadley C G	3 Badley Walk
Hadley G E	6 Badley Walk
Key F L	Mill House
Laffling G H	Badley Bridge Farm
Mayhew P J	New Cottage
Mills G C	Woodlands Bungalow
Morton C I	The Woodlands
Mundell H C	Badley Green Farm Cotage
Proctor B H M	4 Badley Walk
Roper W R	2 Badley Hill Cottage
Rowe G	1 Doveshill Cottage
Scott A B	Badley Hall
Short S L	Cherry Tree Farm
Sore R W	1 Badley Walk
Sterne R R	2 Badley Walk
Steel L A C	5 Badley Walk
Tansley H M	3 Doveshill Cottage

1969/70

Aldous C	Doves Thatch
Bloss A E	Woodlands Cottages
Crysell C H	New Cottage
Farrow C S	Doveshill Farm
Freshwater E M	Mill House
Hadley C G	3 Badley Walk
Hadley G E	6 Badley Walk
Key F L	Mill House
Laffling G H	Badley Bridge Farm
Mayhew P J	New Cottage
Morton C I	The Woodlands
Proctor T A	4 Badley Walk
Roper W R	2 Badley Hill Cottage
Rowe G	1 Doveshill Cottage
Scott A B	Badley Hall
Short S L	Cherry Tree Farm
Sore R W	1 Badley Walk
Sterne R R	2 Badley Walk
Steel L A C	5 Badley Walk
Wright L M	Doves Thatch

A mistake in the 1966 & this directory gives this as Badley A E!

Appendix F

ORDERS IN COUNCIL
Parish of Badley

A.

This is a reproduction of the entry which appeared in the London Gazette on page 5430 on Tuesday 14th August 1928. This Order in Council amalgamated the benefices of Badley and Needham Market, but preserved their individual Parish status.

At the Court at *Buckingham Palace*, the
14th day of *August*, 1928
PRESENT,
The KING's Most Excellent Majesty in
Council.

WHEREAS the Ecclesiastical Commissioners for England have, in pursuance of the Union of Benefices Measure, 1923, duly prepared, and laid before His Majesty in Council, a scheme bearing date the 26th day of July, 1928, in the words and figures following, that is to say:—

" We, the Ecclesiastical Commissioners for England, acting in pursuance of the Union of Benefices Measure, 1923, have prepared, and now humbly lay before Your Majesty in Council, the following Scheme for effecting the union of the Benefice (being a Vicarage) of Badley and the Benefice (being a Vicarage) of Needham Market, both of which Benefices are situate in the County of Suffolk and in the Diocese of Saint Edmundsbury and Ipswich:

" Whereas Commissioners appointed at our request by the Right Reverend Walter Godfrey, Bishop of Saint Edmundsbury and Ipswich, pursuant to the provisions of the said Union of Benefices Measure, 1923, to inquire into and report upon the union of the said two Benefices of Badley and Needham Market duly made their Report to the said Bishop of Saint Edmundsbury and Ipswich and therein recommended the union of the said two Benefices and the terms for effecting the union, and the said Bishop of Saint Edmundsbury and Ipswich signified in writing his approval of the said Report :

" And whereas we, the said Ecclesiastical Commissioners for England, have pre-pared this Scheme for the union of the said two Benefices based upon the terms recommended in the said Report :

" And whereas the said Benefice of Needham Market is now full, the Reverend William George Hargrave Thomas being the present Incumbent thereof and the said Benefice of Badley is at present vacant :

Numb. 33412　　　　　　　　　　**5427**

The London Gazette.

Published by Authority.

The Gazette is registered at the General Post Office for transmission by Inland Post as a newspaper. The postage rate to places within the United Kingdom, for each copy, is one penny for the first 6 ozs., and an additional half-penny for each subsequent 6 ozs. or part thereof. For places abroad the rate is a half-penny for every 2 ozs., except in the case of Canada, to which the Canadian Magazine Postage rate applies.

** *For Table of Contents, see last page.*

TUESDAY, 14 AUGUST, 1928.

" And whereas only one Parsonage House will be left standing or remaining within or belonging to the United Benefice when the union which is hereinafter recommended and proposed shall take effect namely the Parsonage House belonging to the said Benefice of Needham Market :

" And whereas the interest of the Patron of the said Benefice of Badley is so small that the share of the Patronage of the United Benefice which upon a fair and just apportionment would be assignable in respect of his interest would in our opinion be negligible :

" Now, therefore, we the said Ecclesiastical Commissioners for England, with the consent of the said Walter Godfrey, Bishop of Saint Edmundsbury and Ipswich (in testimony whereof he has signed this Scheme), do humbly recommend and propose to Your Majesty as follows, that is to say:—

" 1. That the said Benefice of Badley and the said Benefice of Needham Market shall be permanently united together and form one Benefice with Cure of Souls under the style of ' The United Benefice of Needham Market with Badley ' but the Parishes of the said Benefices shall continue distinct in all respects.

" 2. That if upon the day when any Order of Your Majesty in Council ratifying this Scheme shall be published in the London Gazette both of the said two Benefices shall be vacant the union of the same two Benefices

shall take effect forthwith ; and if one only of the said two Benefices shall be then vacant the said union shall take effect upon the next avoidance of the other of the said two Benefices; and if neither of the said two Benefices be then vacant the said union shall take effect upon the next avoidance of that one of the said two Benefices which shall last be avoided after the date of the publication in the London Gazette of any Order of Your Majesty in Council ratifying this Scheme.

" 3. That upon the said union taking effect the Parsonage House at present belonging to the said Benefice of Needham Market shall become and be the house of residence for the Incumbent of the United Benefice.

" 4. That after the said union has taken effect the Patronage of the United Benefice shall belong wholly to the Patron of the said Benefice of Needham Market.

"Provided always that nothing herein contained shall prevent us from recommending and proposing any other measures relating to the matters aforesaid, or any of them, in accordance with the provisions of the said National Assembly of the Church of England, or of any Act of Parliament."

And whereas drafts of the said Scheme have been duly published in accordance with the provisions of said Union of Benefices Measure, 1923 and Notices have been transmitted to the persons or bodies entitled under the same Measure to receive

Notice requiring any objections to such draft Scheme to be stated or transmitted in writing to the said Ecclesiastical Commissioners within the time prescribed in the Statutory Rules applicable to proceedings under the said Union of Benefices Measure, 1923 :

And whereas the prescribed time has elapsed and no such objections have been so stated or transmitted to the said Ecclesiastical Commissioners :

And whereas public notice of the certification to His Majesty in Council of the said Scheme and the consent thereto in writing of the Bishop of Saint Edmundsbury and Ipswich has been duly given in the manner and within the time prescribed in the Statutory Rules aforesaid :

And whereas the said Scheme has been approved by His Majesty in Council :

Now, therefore, His Majesty, by and with the advice of His said Council, is pleased hereby to affirm the said Scheme and to order that the Benefices therein recommended to be united shall be united to the extent and for the purposes recommended in the said Scheme and further to order and direct that the said Scheme and every part thereof shall be effectual in law immediately from and after the date when this Order shall have been duly published in the London Gazette pursuant to the said Measure.

And His Majesty, by and with the like advice, is pleased hereby to direct that this Order be forthwith registered by the Registrar of the Diocese of Saint Edmundsbury and Ipswich.

M. P. A. Hankey

B.

This is a reproduction of the wording of the Order in Council dated 5th June 1986, which amalgamated the parish of Badley with that of Needham Market to form the new parish of 'Needham Market with Badley' and declared the church of St Mary Badley redundant from the 1st July 1986.

At the Court at Buckingham Palace

THE 5TH DAY OF JUNE 1986

PRESENT,

THE QUEEN'S MOST EXCELLENT MAJESTY
IN COUNCIL

Whereas the Church Commissioners have duly submitted for confirmation by Her Majesty in Council the Scheme which is set out in the Schedule to this Order:

And whereas the provisions of the Pastoral Measures 1983 relating to the preparation and submission of the said Scheme have been duly compiled with:

Now, therefore, Her Majesty, by and with the advice of Her Privy Council, is pleased hereby to confirm the said Scheme.

Gl de Deney

SCHEDULE

PASTORAL SCHEME

This Scheme is made by the Church Commissioners this 28th day of May 1986 in pursuance of the Pastoral Measure, 1983, the Right Reverend Eric, Bishop of Dunwich, duly appointed in that behalf pursuant to section B of the Church of England (Miscellaneous Provisions) Measure 1983, having consented thereto.

Union of Parishes

1.   The parish of Needham Market and the parish of Badley, being the parishes which comprise the area of the benefices of Needham Market with Badley in the diocese of Saint Edmundsbury and Ipswich, shall be united to create a new parish which shall be named "The parish of Needham Market with Badley".

Parish church

2.   The parish church of the parish of Needham Market shall be the parish church of the new parish.

Archdeaconry and deanery

3.   The new parish shall belong to the archdeaconry of Ipswich and the deanery of Bosmere.

Declaration of redundancy

4.   (1)   The parish church of the parish of Badley (hereinafterreferred to as "the redundant building") shall be declared redundant by this Scheme.

(2)   The marriage register books appertaining to the redundant building shall be dealt with in accordance with section 62 of the Marriage Act 1949 and, subject to any provisions of the Parochial Registers and Records Measure 1978 that apply thereto and any direction thereunder,any other register books and records of the redundant building which remain in parochial custody shall be transferred to the new parish church of the new parish.

Vesting of the redundant building and its contents

5.   The Redundant Churches Fund (hereinafter referred to as "the Fund") shall be responsible for the care and maintenance of the redundant building.

6.   (1)   The contents of the redundant building, excluding the plate used fot the purpose of Holy Communion, shall vest in the Fund which shall be responsible for their care and maintenance.

(2)   The said plate shall be transferred to the parish church of the new parish.

7.   The following rights shall vest in the Fund to enable it to perform its functions:

(a)   the right of the Fund and all persons authorised by it to pass and repass on foot over and along the pathways in the churchyard leading to the redundant building, subject to the Fund keeping the said pathways in repair;

(b)   the right of the Fund to the passage of soil, water, electricity, gas and telecommunication services (if any) through the sewers, drains, pipes, wire and cable (hereinafter together called "the services") now laid under, upon or above the said churchyard;

(c)   the right of the Fund and all persons authorised by it upon reasonable prior notice in writing to the parocial church council of the new parish, or without notice in emergency, to enter, with or without vehicles, equipment and apparatus upon such parts of the said churchyard as may be necessary for the purposes of inspecting, repairing and maintaining the redundant building and the services subject to the person exercising such right causing as little damage as possible to the said churchyard and any graves, tombstones, monuments and memorials therein, and subject to the Fund making good any damage so caused to the reasonable satisfaction of the said parochial church council or other the person for the time being responsible for the care and maintenance of the said churchyard; and

(d)   all other rights and easements over land other than the said churchyard appertaining or reputed to appertain to the redundant building (in common with all others entitled to the like rights).

Coming into operation of this Scheme

8.   This Scheme shall come into operation upon the first day of the month following the date of any Order of Her Majesty in Council confirming this Scheme.

Appendix G

PRO

UNIVERSITY
OF
DUBLIN

YALE
UNIVERSITY

Other
POLEY & BADLEY
Sources

NOTES:

A surprising number of Badley and Poley-related documents survive in various repositories around the world in addition to those in the Ashburnham Collection at the Suffolk Record Office (HA/1 & HA/2).

However, it has to be said that the bulk of these other papers relate to the correspondence of diplomat Edmund Poley (1655-1714).

A section of these and a few of the others, with a short description are included in this appendix, from the catalogues of the following repositories:

1. The National Archives (PRO), Kew, Richmond, Surrey TW9 4DU.
2. The British Library, 96 Euston Road, London, NW1 2DB.
3. Yale University, New Haven, Connecticut 06520 USA.
4. Trinity College Library, College Street, Dublin 2.

A thumbnail sketch, compiled from various Internet sources, of the three of the politicians with whom Edmund Poley, the diplomat, regularly exchanged correspondence are given below:

WILLIAM BLATHWAYT (1649?-1717) was a successful civil servant, who acted as William III's Secretary at War and Secretary of State. He entered public life as clerk in the embassy of Sir William Temple at The Hague, 1668-72. He served as secretary to the Earl of Conway, Secretary of State for the Northern Department, 1681-83, and purchased the office of Secretary at War in August 1683.

His offices were renewed by William III in 1689 and from 1692-1701 he attended William during his campaigns in the Low Countries. Between 1693 and 1710 Blathwayt represented the constituency of Bath in the House of Commons. Although his offices were renewed again with the accession of Queen Anne, he gradually lost them during her reign. He was dismissed as Secretary at War in 1704, from the Board of Trade in 1707 and lost his seat in Parliament in 1710. He was married Mary Wynter of Dyrham Park, Gloucestershire and died there on August 16th 1717. The house and grounds are now owned by the National Trust.

GEORGE STEPNEY (1663-1707) was one of the most remarkable men of the end of the seventeenth century. He was considered one of the eight poets worthy of emulation, while 'no Englishman ever understood the affairs of Germany so well, and few Germans better.'

Born at Westminster and educated there, transferring to Cambridge at nineteen. His qualifications suited him to foreign employments. In 1692 he was sent envoy to the elector of Brandenburgh; in 1693 to the imperial court; in 1694 to the elector of Saxony; in 1696 to the electors of Mentz and Cologne, and the congress at Frankfurt; in 1698 a second time to Brandenburgh; in 1699 to the king of Poland; in 1701 again to the emperor; and in 1706, to the states general. In 1697 he was made one of the commissioners of trade. He died aged 44, and is buried in Westminster Abbey. He was the sitter in 3 portraits exhibited at the National Portrait Gallery and his biography, *George Stepney, 1663-1707, Diplomat and Poet* by Susan Spens MBE was published in 1977.

HEDGES, Sir CHARLES (d. 1714), lawyer and politician. He was returned as M.P. for Orford in Suffolk in 1698, but unseated by an election committee confirmed by the House of Commons by a majority of one vote. He was sworn as Secretary of State and a Privy Councillor on 5 November 1700. He attended the Queen to Bath in August 1702, and for a short time (April to May 1704) he was declared the sole secretary, both home and foreign. During 1705 the Whigs constantly endeavoured to eject him from office to make room for the Earl of Sunderland. The Queen eventually agreed on 3 December 1706, but it was stipulated that Hedges should be appointed to the judgeship of the Prerogative Court of Canterbury. He was mentioned as the third plenipotentiary to negotiate the Treaty of Utrecht, but it never passed beyond rumour.

1. - <u>THE NATIONAL ARCHIVES, KEW, LONDON</u>

EXAMPLES OF REFERENCES TO BADLEY AND THE POLEYS INCLUDING DIPLOMATIC CORRESPONDENCE BETWEEN
EDMUND POLEY AND LONDON SUPPLEMENTING THOSE DEPOSITED AT YALE UNIVERSITY USA.
(using the National Archives Internet 'on-line' search facility PROCAT)

KEY :

E references   =   records of the Exchequer & its related bodies with those of the Office of First Fruits & Tenths, & the Court of Augmentations

SP references   =   records assembled by the State Paper Office, including papers of the Secretatry of State up to 1782

DL references   =   records of the Duchy of Lancaster

PRO Reference	Title/Scope and Content
IA.3117	Grant by William, son of Geoffrey de Baddele, to the canons of the Apostles Peter & and Paul, of Ipswich, for 10s. yearly rent Brokes, and the fee from which it issues, in frank almoin. Witnesses :- John Rolland, Warin de Gudeleford, Thomas Manser, and others (named).
A.3425	Grant by William, son of Geoffrey de Badele to the canons of the Apostles Peter and Paul of Ipswich, of 13s. yearly rent in Brokes, and the land from which it issues, in frank almoin, for the Souls of himself and Beatrice his wife, &c. Witnesses :- Adam de Ulmo, Warin de Gutheleford, Thomas Manser, and others (named). Portion of Seal.
A. 3426	Grant, by Geoffrey de Badele, knight, to the same, for 40s., of 15 acres of his fee in Brokes, in the field called "Aldegate", and yearly rents of 8d. and 6d. and 4 hens, to hold to them in all things as witnessed by the Grant of John Testepin, paying 3s. yearly. Witnesses :- William Godeskalc and Mathew de Porta, bailiffs of Ipswich, and others (named). Equestrian Seal.
A.3441	Grant by Geoffrey de Badeleia, son of Robert de Badeleia, to Roger de Badleleia, his uncle, of a moiety of Hageneford mill, paying half a marc yearly. Witnesses :- Bartholomew de Glanvill, William de Creppinge, and others (named).
A.3442	Release by Thomas de Porta to John son of Hugh de Badele, for 11 marcs, of all his right in one marc yearly, rent from Haveneford mill, which he formerly bought of the said John. Witnesses :- Mathew de Porta & Hugh Lyv, bailiffs in Ipswich & others (named). Seal. *(August 40 Henry III (1255))*
E 44149	(1)Assignment of title by Peter Scrivener, son and heir of Rauff Scrivener, gent, and Leonard Caston of Ipswich, Suff, gent, to Edmund Pooley of Badley, Suff, Christopher Cole of East Bergholt, Suff, Mathew Scrivener and Nicholas Scrivener, two other sons of the said Rauff Scrivener; concerning Cockfield Wood and the Manor of Cockfield in Witnesham, Suff *(dated 44 Eliz 1 Aug 21)*
	(2) Covenant to stand seized between Raphe Scrivener, of Little Belstead, Suff, of the one part, and Edmund Poley of Badley, Suff, esq, and Peter Scrivener, son and heir of the aforesaid Raphe, of the other part; concerning the manors of Bridgeplace and Newhall, the tenement called Pyppes in Coddenham, and Chylde Mylne in Baylham and Coddenham, Suff *(dated 44 Eliz 1 Aug 23)*
E 321/43/178	[The king] v. Edmund Poley Answer: lands given for the finding of a priest in Badley, [Suff]
DL 26/8	The King to Ann lady Seckford of Seckford Hall, Anthony Felton knight of Playford (Plaiford), Edmund Poley, of Badley (Badly), Henry Seckford of Seckford Hall Edmund Brewster of Badle esquires, all co. Suffolk: Lease indented for the minority of Thomas son and heir of Thomas Seckford knight whose inheritance it is, of lands (described) called St Mary's Close, co. *(16 Dec 8 Jas I [1610])*
DL 27/298	Indented Grant by Elizabeth I, of the wardship of Thomas Seckford, son and heir of Charles to Mary Seckford, his mother, Anthony Wyngesfield of Hetheringham, Edmund Pooley of Badley, and Humphrey Wingefield, all of Suffolk. Schedule of lands in wardship attached: Felixstowe Priory, messuages in St. *(34 Eliz I)*
SP 46/124/fo 5	William Rygges to Mr. Hanbye: Has allowed Mr. Poley £4 paid by him to Sir George Throamerton for his fee as steward of the lands late of Balsall commandery for 1545-6; Seint Johns. *(5 July 1547)*
SP 81/161	Edmund Poley *(1704 Mar - 1705 Nov)*
SP 84/47	Sir Jn. Poley to Burghley *(1593 Oct 9)* (reproduced next page)
SP 84/47	Note of horses lost by Sir J. Poley in Dutch service. *(1593 Dec)* (see next page)
SP 84/48	Sir Jn. Poley to Burghley *(1594 Jan 11)*
SP 90/3	Tilson to [Richard] Warr, [Undersecretary of State]. Swedish ambassador's public audience. Frederick I's travels. Death of the Emperor. Personal greetings. PS: Rumour about Poley's future. *(1705 May 12 Berlin)*
SP 105/54	To Blathwayt. Reflects, at great length, upon his own future, i.e. his prospects and expectations. Wishes to remain in the foreign service, at least for the duration of the war by the end of which he 'may have better pretensions to some moderate, but lasting settlement at home' (page 344).
SP 105/54	To [Edmond] Poley First four paras identical with those of the foregoing letter to Dr Montague (see f.44, ante) as indicated by the heading in Stepney's hand: 'Mr Poley. Taken out of the foregoing letter as farre [as] my life is concern'd mark'd X'. Requests information on the 'manners of living at Ratisbone and what manners I must take to legitimate & introduce myself there'. *(1694 July 17/27 Dresden)*
SP 105/54	To Vernon. Asks him to examine his registers at the Office and find out 'with what letters Mr Poley was equipt when he went for Ratisbone'. From what Egar wrote him [two years ago], it does not seem that Poley did have credentials, but perhaps Etheredge did. *(1694 July 17/27 Dresden)*
SP 105/54	To Egar. Refers to his letter to Poley (see f.45v, ante) which he encloses with the request to forward it, after reading it, to Poley if the latter has gone to the country. Should Vernon speak to him about the matter, he, Stepney, knows that Egar will forget nothing that may be to his advantage. *(1694 July 17/27 Dresden)*
SP 105/58	[Edmund] Poley [English envoy extraordinary Savoy] to Stepney. Acknowledges letter of Jan. 11/21. Gives, apparently on request, an account of the effective strength of the allied forces in Savoy. Imperial troops should be 20,000, but are at a guess 16,000; Bavarians should be 3,000 but are about 2,300; Savoy troops should be 12-13,000; English between 3 and 4,000. *(1693 Feb 4/14 Turin)*
SP 105/82	From Charles Montnue. Introduces bearer who is going to Edmund Poley [envoy to Sweden] as chaplain and desires some information on Hamburg. Endorsed by Stepney. *(1687 Nov 3/13 n.p.)*

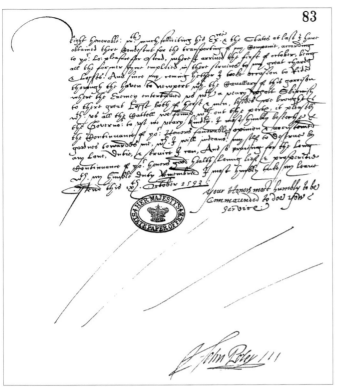

Fig G.1 SP84/47/83 Sir John Poley Knt note to Burghley

Fig G.2 SP84/74/201 Note of horses lost by Sir John Poley in Dutch service

TRANSLATION:

Right honourable w(i)th much solliciting his Ex(ecut)rix & the States at last I have/ obtained there Condesent for the transporting of my Companie, according/ to yo(u)r. Lo(rd): pleasure for Ostend, where I arrived the first of October, being/ all the former by me emploied in there services to my great chardg/ & losses. And since my coming hither I took occasion to ride/ through the haven of Newport with the Cavallary of this garrison/ where the enemy entertained us w(i)th a veary whott skirmish/ to there great losse, both of horse and men besides we bought/ w(i)th us all the chattles we found without the porte, it pleaseth/ the Govenor to use me veary kindly, I most humbly beseeche I/ the Continuance of yo(u)r: Honours favourable opinion & very fond/ goodness towards me, w(hi)ch I will indeavo(u)r my all to deserve by/ my love, Untie, & service I can, And so praising for the long/ Continuance of yo(u)r honours good health, long life & prosperitie/ w(i)th my humble duty Remember I most humbly take my leave/ Thens this ixth October 1593.

Your Honors most humbly to be
commanded to does your
service:

Sir John Poley

TRANSLATION:

A note of suche horses as Sr John Poley hath lost at divers services in y(e) Low Countries between ye xj[th] Octobre 1589 and y(e) xy[th] of Octobre 1592:

At the overthroe of the Convoy between Antwerp and Rosendale in Decembre - 1589	3
At the taking in of Bredawe(?) in January 1589 lost	3
During the camp before Gramer, hale Crevicuer(?) & Steneburghen in Aprell & May 89 lost	6
At the camp before Deventer & Zutphen in June July & August 89 lost	5
In the journey to Gronning, Delphes Jlt, and Frisekind through in May & June -90 lost	7
At the Overthrow of the Duke of Parma his horse in ye Betonoe, in July & August -90 lost	5
At the seigh of the Betowe in Aprill 92	4
At the seigh of Nentham in May -92	8
At the seigh of Stenwirk in Maye -92	3
At the seigh of Couerden in June & July -92	6

fiftie horses:

A note What ye some amounteth 50:
unto:

Fiftye horses; every house according to her ma(s)te(r) paye at £2-5s x men..to be passed in muster - 4 monthes without check, amounteth unto the some of iiij li. *(i.e. £450)*

Most humbly beseeching your honor to consider, of the great chardg I have bin at in/ reinforcing my Company for the losses I have had in her majesties service in these p(ar)tes, that it/ may stand wth your honored good liking my wherk may be forborne, ow on hundred & tenne/ poundes to be restoored unto me, which hath bin by the Maurchantes yearly taken out of the paye I pertyne from them by the space of this 4 yeares which cometh unto/ £450 my & the On any other consideration to be had for my Releif such as yo(ur) Lo(rd) shall/ think fitt to allow me: And to for the interest of your honors good health and/ prosperitie I pray unto god almightie:

NB. Although I originally thought the above documents referred to Sir John Poley, knight, of Columbine Hall, I now believe they may in fact related to Sir John Poley (1558-1638) of Wormegay, Norfolk, *id est.* of the Boxted branch. See Chapter 6, page 150 (col. 2) and Chapter 11, pages 226/7.

2. - THE BRITISH LIBRARY, LONDON

EXAMPLES OF MISCELLANEOUS REFERENCES TO BADLEY AND THE POLEYS INCLUDING DIPLOMATIC CORRESPONDENCE BETWEEN
EDMUND POLEY AND LONDON SUPPLEMENTING THOSE DEPOSITED AT THE PRO & YALE UNIVERSITY USA.

(using the British Library's Internet 'on-line' Public Catalogue (BLPC) search facility)

32,483, 32,484. RUBBINGS of sepulchral brasses and inscriptions in the county of Suffolk; collected by David Elisha Davy, the Suffolk historian. In two solander cases. Arranged under the Hundreds of the County:- 32,483. Bosmere and Claydon. ff. 75-92.

Extract: 37407. ORIGINAL LETTERS relating to political affairs from British Envoys and others abroad, addressed, with three exceptions, to George Stepney, as secretary to the Hon. John Johnston, Envoy at Berlin, and as Envoy to various European Courts; 1691-1706. They belong to the collection of Stepney Papers

Extract: 41834-41841. MIDDLETON PAPERS. Vols. XXXII-XXXIX. Letters from Edmond Poley and Sir George Etherege, Residents at Ratisbon, to successive Secretaries of State, 1682-1688. Other letters of Poley, Feb. 1681- May 1683, are in Add. MSS. 37986, 37987. Of those of Etherege, a certain number (e.g. Add. M

Extract: 41831. MIDDLETON PAPERS. Vol. XXIX (ff. 243) Letters to successive Secretaries of State from British representatives at Stockholm, viz: (a) from Jo[hn] Robinson, [Bishop of London 1714] 4 Apr. 1683-6 Jul 1687. ff. 1-116;b) from Edm[ond] Poley, 3/13 Jun 1687-10 Oct. 1688. ff. 117-243.

Extract: Stowe 241 Vol. 1. (ff. 243) 1688-1712. 1. J[oseph] Addison, [Under Secretary of State] to [Erasmus] Lewis, [Under Secretary of State] [Menin in W. Flanders] 26 July, 1706. f. 71. 2.Charles Boyle, 4th Earl of] O[rrery,Ambassador to the Netherlands] to [William North, 6th Baron North & 2nd Baron Grey; 28

Extract: 21,551. ORIGINAL letters and drafts relating to political affairs, chiefly addressed to George Stepney, English Minister at Vienna and other Courts; 1690-1706: 1. [Daniel Finch] Earl of Nottingham, Secretary of State, to [the Hon. John] Johnston, Envoy at Berlin; 12 Aug. 1690, f. 1. 2. H[ugh] Greg,

Extract: 61147. BLENHEIM PAPERS. Vol. XLVII (ff. 238) Letters from: — 1) James Cresset, Envoy at Hanover, chiefly in the form of notes appended to copies of his letters to Sir Charles Hedges; 1702-1707. ff. 1-14b. 2) Sir Rowland Gwynne, Resident at Hanover; 1704-1709. ff. 15- 51b. 3) Edmund Poley, Envoy at H

Extract: POLEY PAPERS 45731. LETTERS addressed (with two exceptions) to Edmond Poley, Envoy at Stockholm, by (among others) Sir Peter Wyche, Resident at Hamburg, & by John Cooke, Richard Warre, & Dr. Owen Wynne, Under-Secretaries of State; 28 Sept. 1688-19 Mar. 168,8/9. Included are several unsigned news

Extract: 40138. PEDIGREE, in Latin, of the Poley family, of Badley,.co. Suffolk, with arms in colour. Compiled in l579 for Edmund Poley, Esquire, by Robert Glover, Somerset Herald, it is in general agreement with the pedigree given in Add. MS. 5523, f. 68 b, and was continued to 1724 by Philip Jones, York Herald, in order to Show the descent of the Gipps family, of Horninger [Horningsheath], co. Suffolk. Copy, 19th cent. Linen roll; 10 ft. 6.1/2 in. x 2 ft. xix cent. Presented by Sir Charles Hercules Read.

Extract: 37986, 37987. BLATHWAYT CORRESPONENCE. Vols. VIII. IX. (ff. 329, 326) Letters of Edmund Poley, Envoy at Berlin, Frankfort, Ratisbon, etc. to the same; 8 Feb. 1681, O.S. 10 May, 1683, O.S. Two volumes. Vol. I. 8 Feb. 1681, O.S.29 Mar. 1682, O.S. Vol. II. 1 April, 1682, O.S.10 May, 1683, O.S. Prefixed

Extract: Lansdowne 1160. folio. An Account of the Elector and Princes of the House of Brunsvic, and of the dominions which belong to them: by Mr. Poley. Transcribed from the Paper- office Whitehall, 9 Feb. 1767, by desire of the Earl of Shelburne.

Extract: Eg. 3683. BULSTRODE PAPERS. Vol. VI (ff. 180) (1) Edmund Poley, Envoy at Berlin, Frankfurt, and Regensburg; 1680- 1685. Cf. Add. MSS. 37986, 37987. ff. 1-147b. (2) Sir John Lytcott, Ambassador at Rome; 1688-1689. ff. 148-178b. (3) Draft of a letter from Bulstrode; n.d. f. 179. (4) Five Latin elegiac

Extract: 72482. TRUMBULL PAPERS. Vol. CCXLI (ff. 168) 1. ff. 1-53v. Letters from Sir Leoline Jenkins, as Secretary of State, to Richard Graham, 1st Viscount Preston, as Ambassador in Paris; 1682-1683. Including (f. 34) one from Edmund Poley, 5/15 April 1683. Partly in cipher and some in a clerk's hand signed

Extract: 75305. Althorp Papers. Vol. v. Letterbook containing letters from Edmund Poley, English Resident at Ratisbon, to Robert Spencer, 2nd Earl of Sunderland, & Sidney Godolphin, afterwards 1st Earl of Godolphin, as Secretaries of State, including a few of their letters to Poley & enclosed diplomatic

45731. POLEY PAPERS. Letters addressed (with two exceptions) to Edmond Poley, Envoy at Stockholm, by (among others) Sir Peter Wyche, Resident at Hamburg, & by John Cooke, Richard Warre, & Dr. Owen Wynne, Under-Secretaries of State; 28 Sept. 1688-19 Mar. 168,8/9. These include several unsigned newsletters. The names of the writers are given in the Index to the present Catalogue. The letters are concerned for the most part with events of the Revolution of 1688; for other related material see the Middleton Papers, Add. MSS. 41803-41842. Poley's own embassy records are in the Royal Library, Stockholm (cf. Historisk Tidskrift, Stockholm, 1946, pp. 55-56). Paper; ff. 127. Folio. 1688-1689. Presented by Lt.-Col. T. C. L. Rivis, D.S.O., R.A.S.C.

All the following relate to Edmund Poley except where shown

41823 ff. 81, 83, 97, 97b, 100, 104,	Resident at Ratisbon, etc Correspondence with successive Secs. of State 1682-1688 " " "
15892 f. 153	Letter to the Earl of Rochester 1683
39246 f. 3	Letter to the Lord Lieut. of co. Suff. 1665 Copy
39245 ff. 174, 178 b, 179	Letters to the captains of trained bands, etc., in co. Suff. 1638, 1639
33597 f. 38	Particulars of lands [in Norfolk ?] purchased from T. Dandie 1594
37407	Envoy at Berlin Letter to G. Stepney 1704
37986 passim Add. 37987	Envoy at Berlin Letters to the Earl of Conway and W. Blathwayt, etc. 1681-1683
28915 ff. 148, 168, 195 etc,	Envoy to Hanover, Zell & Wolfenbüttel Letters to J. Ellis 1704, 1705
35104 ff. 3-77 b passim	Envoy to Hanover, Zell, & Wolfenbüttel Letters to, when Envoy at Brandenburg, from Lord Conway 1681-1682
38696 f. 55	Envoy to Turin Letter to the Marquis de St. Thomas 1692. Fr. Copy
36662 ff. 164, 233	Envoy to Turin Letters to Sir W. D. Colt 1691
56245 ff. 90-91v	Diplomatist Letter to Lord Conway 1682 Imperf
64950 f. 115	Diplomatist Letter to Sir R. Bulstrode 1682
Eg. 3683 ff. 1-147b	Diplomatist Letters to Sir R. Bulstrode 1680-1685
Eg. 3723 A	Poley (Henry) M.P.; of Badley Owned 1703 *(armorial bookplate f. 1b*)*
39245 f.28b	Poley (John) Sir. Letter to Sir H.Glemham 1615. Copy

3. - <u>YALE UNIVERSITY, NEW HAVEN, CONNECTICUT, USA.</u>

BEINECKE RARE BOOK AND MANUSCRIPT LIBRARY - JAMES MARSHALL & MARIE-LOUIS OSBORN COLLECTION

EDMUND POLEY PAPERS
by Bruce P Stark, New Haven, Connecticut, May 1991 (updated Jan 1998)

DESCRIPTION OF THE PAPERS *(summarised)*

The Edmund Poley Papers consist of six boxes of correspondence and related diplomatic papers documenting aspects of English history and foreign policy in the late seventeenth and early eighteenth centuries. The papers span the dates 1645-1707, but the bulk of the material covers the period 1680-1705.

Series I, *Correspondence (Boxes 1-3)*, primarily contains letters sent to Poley by cabinet officers, undersecretaries of state, and clerks at Whitehall, with a smaller quantity of letters from English diplomats in Europe and copies of letters of European monarchs, diplomats, and soldiers. The correspondence covers four distinct periods of Edmund Poley's career. The first major section contains letters written between October 1680 and January 1685, when Poley was an English resident at Berlin, Frankfurt-am-Main, and Ratisborn (Regensburg). The second group of letters, written while Poley was in Stockholm, begins July 1687 and continues to December 1688. Another group of letters covers the period of his service at the court of Savoy in Turin from October 1691-November 1696, while the January 1704-October 1705 letters concern the time that Poley was at the court of Hanover.

The letters of the clerks and secretaries often contain detailed information on English politics, events abroad, news from London, and life at the court of Charles II, including such subjects as the King's difficulties with Parliament, the Titus Oates affair, the exclusion crisis, the Rye House Plot, and the reform of city charters in order to make municipal governments more amenable to the wishes of the crown. The Prince of Hanover, the future George I and unsuccessful suitor for the hand of Princess Anne, was described in a letter of December 28, 1680 as "a well accomplished Prince not 20 years old."

This first group of letters ends in January 1685, and the correspondence does not resume until July 1687, when Poley had taken up his post in Stockholm. The correspondence for 1691-96, when Poley represented William and Mary at

the court of Savoy, includes letters from English correspondents such as the Earl of Nottingham, Secretary of State for the Southern Department, 1689-93; Blathwayt; David Eger; Richard Warre, civil secretary to Blathwayt; and Robert Yard, plus letters from English diplomats like Sir Paul Rycaut (Hamburg) and Alexander Stanhope (Madrid). It also contains a series of letters from Poley to Nottingham (1691-92) describing events at the court and campaigns against the French in the Italian theatre of the War of the Grand Alliance.

The final group of letters covers the period January 1704-October 1705. Almost two-thirds of these were written between January and April 1704, in the critical months before the great allied victory at Blenheim in the War of the Spanish Succession. Poley, posted to the court of Hanover, received numerous letters from English correspondents John Ellis, first clerk in the Northern Office, John Tucker, and Richard Warre; from Adam Cardonnel, secretary in attendance to the Duke of Marlborough; and from diplomats William Aglionby (Zurich), Charles Davenant (Frankfurt), Richard Hill (Turin), John Robinson (Danzig), Alexander Stanhope (The Hague), George Stepney (The Hague), Thomas Strafford, Earl Raby (Berlin), George Tilson (Berlin), James Vernon (Copenhagen), and Baron Whitworth (Vienna). Their letters concern affairs in England, the Dutch Republic, the German States, and the Empire prior to the 1704 campaign.

The 1705 letters discuss such topics as the poor health of Edmund Poley's brother Henry, the death of the Queen of Prussia, parliamentary elections, and Poley's departure from Hanover.

Series II *Related Papers (Boxes 4-6)*, contains a variety of chronologically arranged documents. The two earliest, dated 1645 and 1660, appoint Edmund Poley, father of the diplomat, "Master of the Harriers" to Prince Charles and clerk of the Privy Council and the 1703 credentials of Poley to the court of Hanover, plus diplomatic memorials and drafts of conventions and treaties.

Series II. Related Papers *(summarised i.e. some folders omitted)*
2.0' (3 boxes) Dates: 1645-1707

Box	Folder		Date
4	170	Appointment of Edmund Poley as Master of the Harriers to Prince Charles	1645 Dec 10
	171	Appointment of Edmund Poley as Clerk of Privy Council	1660 Jun 27
	175	Princes of the Empire, Queries about (in French)	[1681 Feb]
	176	Credential of the Sieur de Bourgonville, French envoy to Wuerttemberg (copy in French in Poley's hand)	1682 Feb 4
	180	Conolusium Collegy Electoralis (in Latin)	1682 Dec 12
	181	Allowance for Edmund Poley of £3 per day	
	186	Charles II: Answer to memorial of Arnaut Van Citters	1684 Mar 25
	187	Memorial of Count Franz Sigismund Thun-Hohenstein to Charles II (copy in French)	1684 Jul 20/30
	189	"Catalogue of the Nobility and Principal Gentry Said to be in Arms with the Prince of Orange & in Severall other Parts of England"	[1688 Dec]
	190	Diplomatic credentials for Edmund Poley to the court of Savoy (in French)	1692
	191	Memorial of military supplies needed to undertake siege of Pinerolo (in Italian)	[1692 Jul 28]
	192	Guarantee of treaty between two branches of the House of Brunswick-Lueneburg (in Latin)	1695 May 2
	194	Memorial of Comte de Mansfeld concerning neutrality of Italy (in French)	[1696 Oct?]
	195	Draft of articles of peace between France and Savoy (in Italian)	[1696]
	196	Draft of article of proposed peace in Italy (in Latin & French)	1696 Nov 20
5	197	Answer of court of Vienna to proposed treaties of Westphalia and Nijmegen (in Latin)	[1696]
	198	List of letters to and from Savoy [1696] Inscription for triumphal arch to honor Georg Ludwig, Elector of Hanover, and Wilhelm, Duke of Celle (in Latin)	1700
	200	Convention between the Queen of Great Britain and Elector and Duke of Brunswick-Lueneburg (in French)	1702 Jun 21
	204	Diplomatic credentials for Edmund Poley to the court of Hannover (in Latin)	1703 Jul 31
	205	Private cipher between Edmund Poley and the Secretary of State (photo copy)	1702 Nov 2
	206	"Treaty with the House of Lunebourg for 10,000 Men" (in French)	1703 Dec 13/24
	208	List of French officers taken prisoner at Blenheim (in French, in Poley's hand)	1704 Aug
	209	List of English officers killed and wounded at Batttle of Hochstadt	1704 Aug
	211	Credentials of Edmund Poley from Elector of Hanover	1705 Sep 14
		Settlement of estate of Henry Poley (RE-PRODUCED PAGE 6)	1707 Aug 27
		"Cypher between Earl of Nottingham and Mr. Poley"	n.d.

LIST OF CORRESPONDENTS

The Yale listing also gives an alphabetical list of the ninety-three correspondents together with the dates for the letters listed. Notable amongst whom are :

Anne, Queen of Great Britain (1665-1714) : 1705 Mar 9, Jun 17

Dover, Lady : 1705 Mar 12 (*alias Judith Poley, Edmund's sister*)

George I, King of Great Britain (1660-1717) : 1700 Jul 2

Leopold I, Holy Roman Emperor (1640-1705) : 1695 Sep 10

Marlborough, John Churchill, First Duke of (1650-1722) : 1704 Jul 4

Poley, Henry (1653-1707) : 1692 Feb 19: 1704 Mar 25; 1705 Jan 6, Apr 3 (*this was Edmund's brother*)

Victor Amadeus I, King of Sardinia (1666-1723) : numerous between 1692 Apr & 1696 Nov

William III, King of England (1650-1702) : 1692 Jun 11, 12, Sept 11: 1693 May 5/15, Jul 20, Oct 25; 1696 Jun 29, Jul 15/25

BEINECKE RARE BOOK AND MANUSCRIPT LIBRARY - YALE UNIVERSITY, USA - JAMES MARSHALL & MARIE-LOUIS OSBORN COLLECTION

WILLIAM BLATHWAYT PAPERS
by Bruce P Stark, New Haven, Connecticut, May 1991 (updated Jan 1998)

POLEY, EDMUND, 1655-1714

139 **17 ALS to William Blathwayt, Turin** (1692 Apr 5 - May 21/31)
Writing as envoy extraordinary to the Court of Savoy about military preparations against the French, his need of payment in order to afford an audience, & his efforts to raise money for the Duke of Schomberg & three French Reformed regiments. Accompanied by a copy of his letter to the Marquis of St. Thomas, 1692 May 30, the first minister to the Duke.
1. Great Britain--Foreign relations-Savoy.
2. Great Britain. Army.
3. Schomberg, Charles Schomberg, 2nd Duke of, 1645-1693.
4. St. Thomas, Marquis de.
5. Victor Amadeus 1, King of Sardinia, 1666-1732.
6. Grand Alliance, War of the, 1689-1697.

140 **9 ALS to William Blathwayt, Turin** (1692 Jun 3 - 18/28)
Reporting allied preparations in the campaign in support of the Vaudois against the French & the drawn-out negotiations to get an edict for the re-establishment of the Vaudois. Accompanied by Poley's memorial to the Duke of Savoy, 1692 Jun 4, & his letter to the Marquis de St. Thomas, 1692 Jun 19. Enclosed in the letter of Jun 3 are answers of the Marquis de St. Thomas to Poley's memorial of May 26 & other letters.
1. Great Britain--Foreign relations-Savoy.
2. Great Britain. Army.
3. St. Thomas, Marquis de.
4. Victor Amadeus I, King of Sardinia, 1666-1732.
5. Waldenses--Piedmont.
6. Grand Alliance, War of the, 1689-1697.

10 ALS to William Blathwayt, Turin (1692 Jul 1-29)
Reporting the irresolution of the Court of Savoy in pressing the military campaign against the French & in publishing the edict for the re-establishment of the Vaudois.
1. Great Britain--Foreign relations-Savoy.
2. Waldenses --Piedmont.
3. Grand Alliance, War of the, 16891697.

141 **11 ALS to William Blathwayt, Turin** (1692 Aug 2-30)
Reporting the advance of the allied troops, including Schomberg's regiment, into France.
1. Great Britain. Army.
2. Schomberg, Charles Schomberg, 2nd Duke of, 16451693.
3. Grand Alliance, War of the, 1689-1697.

16 ALS to William Blathwayt, Turin (1692 Sep 2 - Nov 4)
Sending news of military engagements involving allied troops and of their retreat to winter quarters, & insisting that his offer to resign his post be presented to the King without prior reference to Lord Nottingham. Accompanied by a project of the defensive alliance between the Duke of Savoy & the Protestant Cantons, agreed at Baden 1690 Jun 3, by the project of an edict to be published for the re-establishment of the Vaudois, & by a schedule of pay for the Duke of Savoy's army.
1. Nottingham, Daniel Finch, 2nd Earl of, 1647-1730.
2. Great Britain. Army.
3. Savoy (Duchy) Treaties, etc., 1675-1730 (Victor Amadeus I).
4. Waldenses--Piedmont. 5. Victor Amadeus I, King of Sardinia, 16661732.

142 **16 ALS to William Blathwayt, Turin** (1693 Apr 1/11- Jun 6)
Sending news of allied military preparations during his last two months before being recalled as Envoy to the Court of Savoy. His last audience with the Duke of Savoy took place on 1693 Jun 4.
1. Great Britain--Foreign relations-Savoy.
2. Grand Alliance, War of the, 1689-1697.
Memorandum of cypher used by Poley in his diplomatic correspondence: contemporary [1692] ms. (copy) (see Chapter 6)
1. Cyphers (see Chapter 6).

4. - TRINITY COLLEGE, DUBLIN, IRELAND

TRINITY COLLEGE LIBRARY - MANUSCRIPTS DEPARTMENT

AFFAIRS OF IRELAND - SIR JOHN POLEY, KNT.
(TCD MS 10837)

This manuscript, consisting of several texts by Sir John Poley, is in library at The Trinity College, Dublin, Ireland and is catalogued as follows.

Title :	Several texts / by Sir John Poley
Author :	Poley, John. d.?1638
Description :	ix, 49p ; 300 x 204mm
Notes :	Trinity College (Dublin, Ireland). Library MS 10837

Marginalia occur in pp.4-21, 27, 38-41 and these refer often to other pages of the work (here termed folium/folia). Deletions occur e.g. on p.34 the last two and a half lines of the main text. Corrections in the text occur esp. in pp.46-47 where Poley substitutes 'Poley' for 'I'. Catchwords on nearly every page (i.e. on 4-20, 23, 30-33, 44-48). Previous paginations i-iii, 1-48 but it is partly incorrect and a new pagination from 41-49 has been imposed. The old pagination 1-40 (possibly with the page 40bis) may be contempoary (and near contemporary).

Sir John Poley, d.?1638; colonel; cashiered and discharged 27 March 1598; knighted 12 July 1599; signatory of the 'Declaration touching the defeat at Armagh'. — Pages iii, and 2-34. Untitled discourse (the beginning of the main text on p.4): The first of my Lord of Essex arivell in Ireland hee punished ... is as followeth. His Lordshipp with the Councell ... P.iii has [To the Reader] God inlighten the Reader's vnderstandinge... — P.2 has a summary: A breuiate or sume of my followinge Discours for which I suffer ... — P.3. Further summary comments. — P.22 A new beginning in the text: 'Sir John Poley Provided to give ...'. — P.26. A new beginning in the text: 'Questions collected out of the former Discours ...' — P.30. A new beginning in the text: 'The Discours of Poleys Imployment by my Lo: of Essex commaunde: ...' These last three can be taken as new texts.

Pp.35-37 are blank pages. — Pp.38-41. Copies of letters, three by Poley, one by Mountjoy, one by Sir Robert Gardener, one by the Lord Lieutenant the Earl of Devonshire, one from the Chancery (Dublin) 1598-1603, and undated. —

Pp.iv-ix. A map, now in two parts, or two related maps: one (?being the right side of the original map, and made up of two pieces of paper pasted together), showing a hilly area beside the Blackwater River, and near Blackwater Fort, surrounded by woods, one battle formation labelled 'vang[u]ard overthro[w]n', with red wash for an area of ?bloodshed and of gunpowder on fire; and the other (?being the left side of the original map), showing an area near 'Ardmaugh church' and [RC] chapel and another ecclesiastical site

(this labelled ?'Campse') with six gable ends each having a cross above it, the city not shown, both parts showing battle formations of soldiers mostly labelled R(eare), but some labelled B(attaile), and two labelled V(anguard). Both maps are in green and blue washes, with ink for trees and one part or map (iv-vii) is folded and guarded-out, the other (viii) is guarded; ix is blank. So far as can be judged without disbinding the damaged left edge of page v matches the damaged right edge of page viii, though not with the same top and bottom line. To match therefore would require that these both should be pieces of a larger map cut down to the format of the size of Sir John Poley's writing paper or of its present binding.

Pp.42-43 (inserted during binding or re-sewing) Reasons to induce ous[=us] to the contracte ... This inserted sheet is oversize, and partly folded over; has a brief on the verso, i.e. on p.43. — Pp.44-49. A new discours sett donne by (?Collonell deleted and Sir John, abbreviated, written instead and above) Poley the same night They made there Retreat to Ardmaugh after the defeat of the vang[u]ard.

Purchased at Christies' auction 'Valuable English and continental books from the Bute library' [from the library of the Marquesses of Bute, specifically of the 6th Marquess deceased] on 15 March 1995 (lot 332, on p.200 of the catalogue).

Red straight-grained morocco leather, blind roll and stamp, spine has four raised sections over binding strings, gilt labelling on spine AFFAIRS OF IRELAND. SIR JOHN POLEY. M.S.S. (19th cent. binding); on the back board, crudely stuck on, a recent label marked in pencil: 'G B STABLES/LORD BUTE'S ROOM/2'. Book label with arms on front flyleaf: 'Henry Poley of Badley (Suffolk) 1703'; also on front flyleaf in pencil 'MS 147' (probably altered from 146, ?Marquess of Bute's library number, as ?also the 'F4' on p.i, ?old shelf number). P.iii has 'C', perhaps a classification.

Citation : The manuscript was previously described in Historical Manuscripts Commission third report (MSS of the Marquess of Bute), p.203. The second short text on page 3 is largely published in Christies' catalogue, op cit infra, p.200. In the calendar of State papers for the years 1598-1600 Poley is referred to being spelt as Pooley. The description in Christies' catalogue of the auction gives fuller information on some sections of the text and says: 'written 30 years after' the event(s).

Subject :	Ireland - History - 17th century Uniform
Title :	TCD MS 10837
Location :	Manuscripts Department
Call Number :	TCD MS 10837

(See Chapter 6, p164, Fig 6.16 for illustration of book label.)

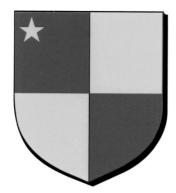

5. - THE DANDY (OR DAUNDY) PEDIGREE

A pedigree probably drawn up about the end of the 16C, authenticated by Ralph Brooke (1553-1625) York Herald and entered in the *Visitation of Suffolk* by John Raven in 1612.

Consisting of eleven sheets of paper pasted together to measure 9' 6" x 2' 2½" (2895 x 675), this document contains sixteen generations of the Dandy family and some of its alliances.

"This manuscript pedigree is of value both as a genealogical and heraldic record. For the genealogist it provides a number of descents which gives a lead to family alliances perhaps not otherwise easily ascertainable, and at the same time emphasises that close connexion between many families in a relatively small area."

Francis W. Steer, F.S.A., *The Dandy Pedigree*, p133, S.I.A.H. Vol XXVII Part 3 (1957).

Within the 141 references contained within the chart, represented diagramatically opposite, the Poleys are mentioned no less than 14 times, viz:

45.   Poley. Arms: *Or a lion rampant sable.*

52.   Poley the father of Thomas Poley of Codreth in Hartfordshire. Arms: No 45 impaling [blank].

58.   Matilda daughter and heyre of John Geslingham Esqr the first Wyffe of Thomas Poley.

59.   Thomas Poley of Codreth in the Countie of Hartford Esqr married two Wyves. Arms: 45 impaling Geslingham as in 51.

60.   Anne daughter & heyre of Thomas Badwell of Boxsted in Suff' Esqr second wyffe of Thomas Poley had yssue.
      Arms: *Sable a chevron engrailed or between three pierced mullets argent.*

65.   Richard Poley Esqr sonne & heyre married Margret the eldest daughter of Simon Bliant of

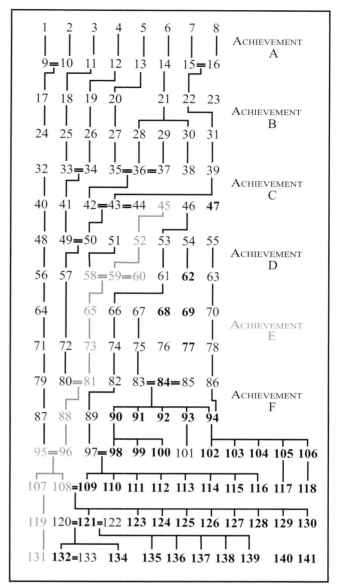

Fig G.3 The Dandy Pedigree key chart based on F.W. Steer's article. The numbers in red show the position of the Poley family and those in bold refer to members of the Dandy family.

Thornham next Stoke Esqr Suff'. Arms: 45 impaling *Gules three lozenges conjoined in fess ermine between three marlets argent.*

73.   Simon Poley sonne & heyre married Margerie daughter & coheyre of Edmund Alcock of Badley in Suff' Esqr he died AO1485 [rest gone]. Arms: 45 impaling *Argent a chevron engrailed between three cocks sable armed crested and wattled gules.*

81.   Henrie Poley Knt sonne & heyre of Simon Poley died AO [blank] and is buried at [blank] he was the first husband of Const'. Arms: 45 impaling 3.

88.   Edmund Poley of Badley in Suff' married Mirabell the daughtr of John Garnish of Kenton in Suff' Esqr & of Elizabeth Sullyard his Wiffe he died AO1548.

95.   Ann the daughter of Sir Thomas lord Wentworth

barron of Wentworth died AO 1575 and is buried at Badley.

96. John Poley of Badley in the Countie of Suff' Esqr sonne and heyre of Edmund died in A0 1589 and is buried at Badley.

107. Richard Poley married Marie daughter of Sir John Brewse of Henham (? recte Wenham) in Suff': he died A0 1592: his wife died A0 1593, bothe buried at Badley. Arms: 45 with *a crescent gules in the dexter chief for difference, impaling Argent semee of crosses crosslet and a lion rampant gules crowned or.*

108. Martha the daughter of John Poley of Bad' in Suff' Esquire and of Ann Wentworth his Wiffe died the 15 of December ?1603 and is buried at Combes.

119. ?Edward Poley sonne and heyre of Richard and heyre of his uncle Edmund married Dorothie daughter of Anthony Warner of Stradbrooke in Suff' Esq. Arms; 45 impaling *Or a bend engrailed between six roses gules, seeded of the field barbed vert.*

131. Poley [rest gone]. Arms: 45 impaling [blank].

Notes:

the original spelling has been retained, words omitted in the original or lost through flaking etc., are indicated by the use of square brackets thus [ ].

No 81 - this is the only instance where Henry is referred to as a Knight and may be a mistake

No 88 - this is usually 'Garneys of Kenton'

No 107 - this should be Wenham, Suff'

No 119 - should be Edmund and not Edward

"ACHIEVEMENT E.
Quarterly, 1, Or a lion rampant sable: 2, Azure a fess or between three birds Argent beaked & membered gules: 3, Argent, a fess between three garbs gules: 4, Argent a chevron engrailed between three cocks sable, beaked legged and wattled gules: 5, Argent a chevron between three pierced mullets sable: 6, Argent a cross sable: 7, Gules a chevron or between three griffins' heads erased argent: 8, Azure three chevrons or: 9, Argent a fess between two chevrons gules: 10, Quarterly gules, and vair or and vert, over all a bendlet argent: 11, Argent three chevrons gules, in the dexter chief a mullet sable for difference.

Crest: *On a wreath or and sable a lion rampant sable collared and chained or.*

Mantling: *Argent and gules.*

This is the quartred Coat and Crest of Poley of Badley in Suff' Esqr the first is borne by the name of Poley, the second by the name of Geslingham: the third by the name of Bar . . . : the forth by the name of Alcock: the fift by the name of [blank]: the sixt by the name of [gone]: the seventh by the name of Gedding : the eight by the name of Aspall : the nynth by the name of [gone]: the tenth by the name of Peverell: the eleventh by the name of Watvyle."

These arms are a combination of those contained above monument 23 in Badley church and reproduced on the front cover and those illustrated in the Visitation of Suffolk 1664-8 reproduced in Chapter 6, page 64. The missing quarterings above are as follows:

3rd   Gardeville
5th   Badwell of Boxted as described in 60 on chart
6th   de Badley of Badley
9th   Peche

The great disappointment with this manuscript is the loss of the information relating to the "father of Thomas Poley of Codreth in Hartfordshire" - entry 52 on the chart. Had the impalement been preserved the ancestors of the Thomas Poley responsible for introducing the family name to Badley and Boxted may well have been positively identified.

Although only the Poley names had been reproduced here, there are many very familiar family names contained within the other entries to support Mr Steers' contention of close local inter-family ties, something equally applicable to the Poley marriages.

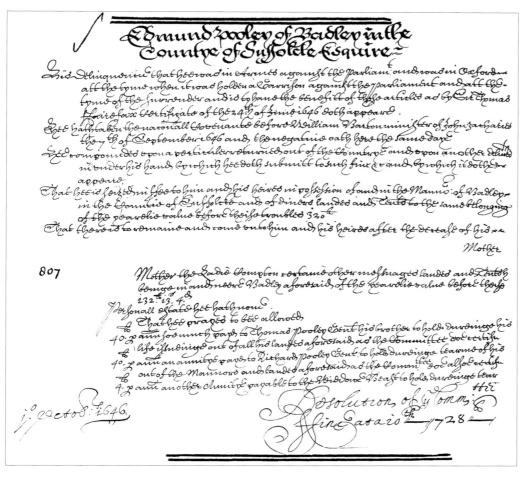

Fig G.4 (Top) Sir Edmund Poley's entry in the "Royalist Composition Papers. Entries of Reports on Delinquents Estates and Fines Leived Thereon" [PRO Ref: SP 23] & (below) a translation.

Edmund Pooley of Badley in the County of Suffolk Esquire

THIS delinquent that he rose in Arms against the parliament and rose in Oxfordshire at the time when it rose holden a Garrison against the parliament and at the time of the surrender and is to have the benefit of those articles as by Sir Thomas Fairfax certificate of the 24th of June 1646 doth approve.

HE has taken the national covenant before William Barton minister of John Zachariah the 7th of September 1646 and the negative oath here the same day.

HE compounded upon a particular returned out of the country and upon another delivered in under his hands by which he doth submit to such fine etc and by which it doth appear.

THAT he is seized in fee to him and his heirs in possession of and in the Manor of Badley in the County of Suffolk and of divers landes and tenements to the same belonging of the yearly value before these troubles 320*l*.

THAT there is to remain and come unto him and his heirs after the decease of his mother the Lady Crompton certain other messuages landes and tenements being in and near Badley aforesaid of the yearlie value before these troubles 232*l* 13*s* 4*d*.

PERSONAL estate he hath none.

THAT he prayed to be allowed

   to

40*l* per annum so much payed to Thomas Pooley Gent his brother to hold during his life issuing out of all his lands aforesaid as the Committee doth certify

   to

40*l per* annum an annuity payed to Richard Pooley Gent to hold during terme and of his [life?] out of the Manors and lands aforesaid as the Committee doth also certify

   to

4*l per* annum another charity payable to the Widdoe Beast to hold during term

1st October 1646   Resolution of ye Committee

                                   Fine at a 20th — 728*l* —

MOVES and POSTINGS

Page 335 lists the documents deposited at the The National Archives, Kew, concerning Edmund Poley, the diplomat. Reproduced below is a lengthy letter, which Poley himself describes as 'tedious', written to William Blathwayt, the Secretary of War to King William III from Dresden in 1694. In it he discusses whether his future should remain abroad or at home.

It is contained in a handwritten book of letters (Ref: SP105/54) which appear to have been made at the time, presumably as an 'office copy' and is therefore not his own hand. The clerk's spelling is not consistent and words are frequently abbreviated. The latter, for example, ye for the, yr for your, wt for with and wch for which, have been removed. However, the spelling/meaning of a few words are still doubtful.

Although Poley was evidently staying at Dresden when this letter was written, this was during the time he was serving at the Court of Savoy in Turin (i.e. Oct 1691-Nov 1696).

To Mr. Blathwayt, Secretary of War   Dresden 10/20 July 1694

Honble Sir

I have the honour of your letter of the 5th instant; N.S.I whereby I perceived instead of being weary of the constant addresses I make to you, you are pleased to look forward to what may become of me hereafter, and take care of me both ways 1st that I may appear at Ratisbonne in the best manner if it be my lot to remove hither, 2nd that I may be provided for at home, if I think it my interest to return.

You may easily imagine Sir, how sensibly I am touched by a such kind offer and consequently that I can not but resolve to cast myself entirely into your hands, leaving to your guidance of my fate, which has been prosperous ever since you have been pleased to make it some part of your care, I must therefore entreat you for the future to look on me as none of my own master, but one who is ready to embrace any proposals you can offer, being assured your choice cannot be perfectly good since your prudence and will whence it proceeds are our such. However for this once I take the liberty you allow me of weighing all considerations, and shall range my arguments on both sides (as Count Kinsky used to do) without knowing which conclusion to come to.

To speak first in general, I have put my hand to the phloug (plough) and I am unwilling to take it off again, I mean I have overcome all the difficulties that a man can meet with all who is employed in Germany, having their language, being used to their customs and ways of living having the honour to be personally known to most of the Chief Princes of the empire and no stranger to their civil interests and principal ministers; and consequently whatever we call business is nothing now but pastime to me: being therefore thus fitted for forraine (foreign) employment, I think it most advisable to stick by me, and will flatter myself that His Majesty's service may suffer less in my hands than in any other man's who is to come fresh out of England and to begin with that I am already acquainted with having been abroad before the Revolution, having been employed during the course of the Ware (war); which makes me the more willing to santer about until we may see the end of it; By which time I may have better pretensions to some moderate, but lasting settlement at home, which such patrons as are disposed to promote my poor interest will have leisure enough to look and procure for me.

About a year ago Mr. Montaque writ me word I was once upon the tapis to be sent Envoy to Sweden and Mr. Vernon hinted some such thing, as you will observe of his letter XtoR you may please to remark from my answer XtoR my thoughts then were much the same with yours now; no impression; To which purpose you will remember I have expressed myself more than once in my letters to you; But the advice Mr. Vernon gave me in his reply No 3 send so very cordial and just that all from the time I have laid aside all thoughts of returning so soon as I have them fancied, especially after the council you was pleased to give me soon after, whereof I add an extract No 4.

To speak to the point of present interest, I must confess I have been no considerable gainer by a forraign (foreign) employment, which I can neither attribute to the narrowness of His Majesty's allowance (which thro' your favour has been made plentiful enough) or to any extravagance of my own, which I cannot upbraid myself with; But you know Sir, for those 2 years (I have set up for myself) I have stroted about like a gipsy, which has hindered me from making those advantages I might have done, with a little good husbandry. If I had been first, and settled in any station, where my expenses could have been regulated. At Berlin and Vienna this was impossible because my stay in either of these places was but uncertain, & in Saxony it has been much more practicable by your inconstant humour and the late Elector by the doubtfully prospect we had what might be the issue of our negotiations; Besides Dresden is a place where good husbandry is not in fashion and where (in the circumstances I was under) I could not but live up to the height of my allowance for several considerations which I have formerly hinted and need not now repeat, so that after having balanced my accounts, I can assure you upon my conscience I have not pocketed 50tt in 9 months service here: But to help out, I shall venture to hedge into my Bill of Extrarier, which is now upon your anvil a very odd article, (for treats and extraordinary expenses, which I could not but be at in Saxony - - 100tt) which I hope Duke Schrewsbury will have the good nature to let slip, especially since I have been lucky in concluding my business, & since the King has not been pleased to gratify me in my pretensions. Besides at partimo re bene gesta I expect a present from the Elector in plate or jewels to the value of 500 dollars (not so much as merchants are allowed for exchange or provision) after the rate of half p cent for m/100k. I have paid to the chest of war and the mt/vz more which have allowed me to distribute among the Ministers.

This has been the advantage of my employment in Saxony and it is much as I proposed to myself thou I must confess it has been hard enough got when I consider what uneasiness I at first lay under before I could surmount the malicious insinuations of Schönin's party against me and the wild humour of the late Elector but the happiness of Savino concluded with success makes amends for those hardships and now God has given us an Elector, who loves to live easy with all mankind, as who as to my particular (both while he was Duke and since he is become Elector) always used me with marks of kindness and behind my back has frequently expressed himself so favourable in speaking to the King of me, that I have reason to be more than satisfied. The same thing I may say of all the Privy Councillors, and officers of the Court, who have since February (when I begun to talk high) have treated me in all respects as they have done Baron Benebourg and Mr. Ham, thou otherwise I could not challenge those civilities being in an inferior character, which now & then made me at a loss how to behave myself. To avoid being an amphibious animal, & not to be overshadowed by Mr. Ham who (being a Dutchman and a creature to ld l**) was but too apt to be impertinent, & to speak truth, in hopes of laying up 40 p diem (for in effect, had I been Envoy, my expenses would not have been much more than they are now) I solicited upon the renewal of my credentials, that my character & allowances might be increased, not so much that I mattered the former there, as I did the latter, being assured if I had once the good fortune of passing the Seals for 5tt a day, & I should be entertained on the same foot all the time I should be abroad; Whereby I might have laid in a good provision for a rainy day; & I thought His Majesty might have judged an Envoy as necessary between the two Electors of Saxony & Brandenburgh, as with the several branches of the House of Lueneburgh, and being I am the only Englishman who had a full knowledge of these Courts, I easily flattered myself I should be your man you Sir (for whose kind endeavours I stand ever obliged know best on which rock this project miscarried; which however does not discourage me, when I reflect from which beginnings I came, how little I have served, & how high I have raised myself by your favour in the little time what I have had your honour to appear. To which consideration if I add up the comfortable assurances No 5 which Duke Shrewsburgh (at great good man, whom God, by the means of Councillor Montague Mr. Blathwayt and Mr. Vernon, has raised up to be my patron likewise) gives that I am not yet arrived at my Ne plus autre I see no cause why I should not be perfectly satisfied with my present condition, and continue in the road in which I am so fairly advanced.

The rather since my good fortune has given me also a constant patron in the Treasury, who never lets slip any opportunity of doing me good; which leaves me no reason to complain of irregular payments as the rest of our distressed Ministers do but too frequently.

To sum up which I had been saying; the thoughts of the luck I have I have had hither to, the sense of my being well at present, the hopes of having still better fortune hereafter and the assurance that I shall meet to with regular payments make me willing to renew my lease of wandering, and wherever I am sent, from Muscovy to the Mogul, is all alike to me, so the King be served, and I find my Count. It is true after having frequented the Vienna, Dresden and Berlin, (the greatest courts of Germany) Ratisbonne may seem but a civil banishment, where the August assembly is so much debased, that little remains but Pedantry and Chicane; But I do not propose by going thither to polish my parts in any more than Sir Ellen Apsley went to Ireland to learn the language; Queren da pecnia primum, for which a place is the most proper. Mr. Vernon (who spent some time there) having assured me 2 years ago, when I was first named for that station, that he never saw anywhere more frugality and cheapness; & whereas I am to appear there as it were precariously & without a character, the King having nothing to say in the diette, I may live very plentifully, and yet sink 300tt yearly out of my salary; which I cannot promise myself in England in consideration of the job I had done here, which is the best merits I have to allege. Next thou the consideration of Drs be a little barbarians, they have their merits as well as other people; and the laws and constitutions of the Empire, with the pretensions of the several members (which are worth knowing) are best to be learned there, by one in my circumstances, who shall pass for homme sans consequence I have ingress and regress without ceremony, frequent promiscuously all persons with an indifferent familiarity, and squeeze out of every one separately all he is good for. Thirdly when we come to talk seriously of a peace, great part of the scene will lie at Ratisbone, or elsewhere if the diette should chance to be removed to another place. For though this probable the main points will be discussed at the Hague, Aix la chapelle, or some such place, to be chosen by the Allyes (allies) for the conference of their Plenipotentiaries; yet the joint assembly which represents the Empire will certainly have their part, in these deliberations; so that the post will not be altogether a sine cure which is a comfort, to one who proposes to do something for a livelihood, and would not be contented to eat the bread of idleness Fourthly If a Negotiation of Peace with Turehs (sic) should be set on foot at Ratisbone I am at hand to fall down to Vienna if my Lord Lexington go on to try; or maybe used as a Mercury between him and Lord Padgett, if they want a fellow who is always ready to run the risk where he hopes to be useful.

Those are my thoughts of Ratisbone, and the advantages to be made of the station; where I shall be contended to make my ordinary residence on the terms I am now, and in the same circumstances as Mr. Poley, and Sir George Etherage were there, the only two (as I know of) ever employed by England in these assemblies; the first under King Charles I while the armistice was treatino, & the other under King James in the beginning of his reign: I suppose they had the general title of Minister only, and might have had some letter of recommendation, whereby they were legitimated as public persons included under the laws of the nations; otherwise I cannot think any Minister would communicate with them they passimo at that time for no better than spies and their masters being suspected to be no friends to the Empire; but I may hope to be conversed with more freely, Since this since His Majesty is known to be a strict ally with the Empire and with most of the Princes who have their representatives at the diette. However to be perfectly informed with methods these gentlemen observe, I had written this evening to Mr. Vernon, to examine by the book in the office with letters they had, a to whom; as likewise to Mr. Poley, desiring him to inform me out of his papers, how he governed himself in several other respects and that no time may be lost I have entreated them to send you a duplicate of their letters to me for your information likewise. All that I know of Sir G Etherage (with whom I should have gone, but that gentle Knight bilked me, as he used to do his creditors) is that he was all allowed 300tt for his equipage which all the town knew, for (by the same token) he lost his money at play the day after he received it; If I have the good fortune to have a the like favour shown me, I hope I shall make a much better use of it: For I will always have such an equipage ready that at a week's warning I may set out on any errand in the neighbourhood which His Majesty's service shall require as to Prince Lewis, to the circle of Suabia & Franconia, and to the Elector of Saxony twice a year when the Terms of Subsidies are to be paid: For I hope, now I have had the luck of concluding the Treaty, none else may take from me the agreeable office of giving out, since it is most of natural that I should nurse my own child; and I have comported myself in such a manner, that I shall not be ashamed to appear again at this Court; where I have found the Prince gracious, and the Ministers friendly; with which last, I shall have still a greater interest, when I have dealt out their gratifications. For these reasons I humbly offer, if His Majesty be pleased, upon with Count Friezen shall represent, to confer the Garter on his Elected Highness, that I may have the honour of presenting it, or at least be joined in commission with him that does, since I assisted in the like ceremony at Berlin: and what ever present, His Majesty may send the Elector in return of the seven Polish horses which Count Friezen has carried to the King, I hope I may have the honour of delivering it; which services create an interest that some time may be of advantage to the Master; as well as a as profitable and honourable accident to who is employed. But these are projects only which may, and may not be granted: and whereas the best foreign employments are not freeholds, but subject to many casualties and encumbrances, I have not so absolutely set my heart upon them, but a moderate being a present and a prospect of further advantage and a lasting settlement at home (as you say) would easily tempt me to throw up; since the design of by wandering is only to deserve thereby some resting place hereafter, where I may live in ease and comfort with my relations, to whom I had been long a stranger: I am perfectly of your mind, that a good foundation is difficult; and on the other hand must close with the hint you gave that often transplanting gives no good root, and my friends may not be always at my side.

By what I've said, you will observe Sir, I am a trimmer who knows not yet his own mind, being not able to guess of what nature may be the proposals you would make; whereof I entreat you will be pleased to explain yourself a little more, not only to me, but also to Mr. Montague and to Mr. Vernon, to whom I shall take the liberty of representing the overtures you are pleased to make, and send them copies of this long answer. I hope what I do will not displaced displease you, since I am persuaded both are persons for whom you have great consideration; as you know Sir, I owe to the good offices of these two my first happiness of being recommended to favour, so I make it a matter of conscience and duty not to dispose of my self in a concern on which your welfare of my life is to depend, without first having their approbation and consent.

In the meantime it is with great pleasure I find it King may be persuaded to let me take a step to Flanders a to give him an account of the Court of Saxony, and then I may take my choice of either for going to Ratisbone or disposing of myself, otherwise, The opportunities will be very favourable; I have no more, to do here but to exchange the Ratification (which is long a coming) and to gratify the Ministers. It is uncertain as yet how the Elector may dispose of himself; The interview with Brandenburgh is no more discoursed of; but sometimes in his frolics the Elector talks of running lost to his army as soon as the ceremonies of homage is over in all places; the truth is, he knows not his own mind, but takes his resolutions at an minutes warning. Our business being at an end, all the foreign Ministers are preparing to be gone: Baron Beneburgh will have his audience of Conge in a day or two, and Mr. Ham will soon be returning to Berlin, but without taking a recreditive, being willing to keep his footing here, & to come over as often as any business offers, or any payments are to be made, which will not be till Michaelmas. I therefore beg you to dispose His Majesty to let me lay myself at his feet in this vacancy; and when I get to Flanders I flatter myself, after four years that I had been left abroad, I may be allowed three weeks a month to pass in to the England to visit my friends, and look after some small concerns, which for which will be of great comfort and used to may if I am to return again to Germany: besides I shall be at hand to quicken the Treasury that the payment of our second terms of subsidies may not be so long as it was last and they may get as it was last this here as it was last in; and they may get back to Leipzig and again by Michaelmas for which it is the beginning of October, and in the meantime I have a discreet youth with me and who may stay here and keep up the correspondence to learn know what becomes of me.

In your favour of the 11th inst. (which is to come to hand as I am closing this), you say Mr. Lexington may give me a rendezvous to be informed of the Court of Vienna; If I should meet him any of the Courts of Lueneburgh, I shall have made half my journey to Flanders; where therefore you shall know his Majesty's pleasure, of giving the leave to see him or not, I beg a copy of your orders may be sent under a covert to Mr. Crefiet, since is likely they may find me with him at one of his stations. I have reason to beg your pardon for this tedious letter, and shall be ever with all duty and respect.

Honourable Sir,
Your obedient servant

E Poley

Indenture (settlement of estate of Henry Poley 1707 - OSB MSS1 Box 6 Folder 219)

To all Christian People to whom those present shall come **Edmond Poley** of Badley in the County of Suffolk Esquire Sole Executor of the last Will and Testament of his late Brother Henry Poley of Lincolns Inn in the County of Middx. Esquire Deceased Anthony Crofts of Badley aforesaid Esquire and Ann Crofts of Bury St. Edmunds in the County of Suffolk aforesaid widower send greetings whereas by Indenture of seven parts bearing Date the seven and twentieth day of June last past before the Date of those presents and made or mentioned to be made between Richard Overman of Thavies Inn in the County of Middx Gentleman Administrator of James Wainwright late Citizen and Haberdasher of London deceased of the first part of Sir Joseph Wolfe Knight Administrator of the Goods and Chattells Rights and Credits of Sir John Wolfe late of London Knight deceased of the second part Sir William Leman of Northaw in the County of Hartford Barrister Son and Heir of Mansell Leman deceased (who was the only Son of Sir William Leman late of Northaw aforesaid in the County aforesaid Barrister deceased) and John Leman of Northaw aforesaid in the County aforesaid Esquire Surviving Trustee of the said Sir William Leman the Grandfather of the third part Dame Mary Leman Widow Relict and Executrix of the said Sir William Leman the Grandfather deceased of the fourth part the said Henry Poley of the fifth part the said Anthony Crofts of the sixth part and the said Ann Crofts of the seventh part writing as therein is writed the said Richard Overman in Consideration of ten shillings to him paid by the said Henry Poley did (by the disertion and appointment of the said Dame Mary Leman and Sir William Leman testified as therein) assign transfer and set over unto the said Henry Poley all that the Manor or Lordship of Barnes with the Rights Members and Appurtenances thereof in the Parish of St. Buttolph without Aldgate London and in the parish of St Buttolph without Aldgate St. Mary Matfellon alias White Chapel and Stebbunheath alias Stepney in the County of Middx and all Messuages Houses Tenements and Hereditaments therein particularly mentioned in the said several parishes or any of them **To Hold** for the residue of a certain term of three hundred years therein mentioned and writing as therein is further writed in Consideration of three thousand and eight hundred pounds to the said Sir Joseph Wolfe paid by the said Henry Poley and of five shillings apeice to the said Sir William Leman and John Leman paid by the said Anthony Crofts the said Sir Joseph Wolfe did (by direction of the said Sir William Leman and Henry Poley (testified as therein) assign and set over and the said Sir William Leman and John Leman did ratify confirm unto the said Anthony Crofts several parcels of Ground called Goodmans fields alias Leman fields situate in the parish of St. Mary Matfellon alias White Chapel in the said County of Middx therein particularly mentioned To hold for the Residue of a certain term of one thousand years therein mentioned and the said John Leman for the consideration aforesaid and of five shillings to him paid by the said Ann Crofts did (by the direction and appointment of the said Lady Leman, Sir William Leman and Henry Poley (testified as therein) assign and set over and the said Sir William Leman did ratify and confirm unto the said Ann Crofts all that the Manor of Barnes commonly called Goodmans fields and all and singular other premises therein mentioned with their appurtenances To hold for all the Residue and Remainder of a certain term of one hundred years therein mentioned for which the said Indenture is contained a proviso for Redemption of all and singular the said promises upon payment by the said Sr. William Leman and John Leman their or either of their Heirs Executors Administrators or assigns unto the said Henry Poley his Executors Administrators or assigns of the full sum of three thousand nine hundred and ninety pounds as therein is mentioned as in and by the said in part writed Indenture (Relation thereunto being had) now at large may appear Now we the said Edmund Poley Anthony Crofts and Ann Crofts doe hereby for our own selves our Heirs Executors and Administrators Respectively declare and agree to and with each other of us that the sum of two thousand pounds and four hundred pounds part of the said sum of three thousand eight hundred pounds so lent and advanced to the said Sir William Leman as aforesaid was and is part of the sum of six thousand pounds belonging to the said Anthony Crofts as Surviving Trustee mentioned and appointed in Reign of his late Majesty King Charles the second made upon the marriage of the said Ann Crofts with William Crofts late of Saxham in the said County of Suffolk Esquire Her late Husband deceased and that the said sum of two thousand and four hundred pounds together with the Interest thereof during the Continuance of this present Mortgage is to go and be applied to such and the same Uses Trusts and confidences as are mentioned limited and appointed in and by the said Indenture of and concerning the said six thousand pounds and not otherwise and we do hereby further declare and agree that the sum of fourteen hundred pounds residue and reminder of the sum of three thousand eight hundred pounds was the proper money of the said Henry Poley deceased and is now the money of the said Edmund Poley as Executor to the said Henry Poley and that the names of the said Henry Poley and of us the said Anthony Crofts and Ann Crofts in the said several Securities were and are made of use of and the said several terms of years assigned to the said Henry Poley and to us the said Anthony Crofts and Ann Crofts respectively as aforesaid in trust only and for securing the said several sums of two thousand and four hundred pounds and fourteen hundred pounds severally as aforesaid and to and for no other uses trusts or confidences whatsoever **In Witness** whereof we have hereunto set our hands and seals this twenty seventh day of August in the year of our Lord God one thousand seven hundred and seven and in the sixth year of the Reign of our Sovereign Lady Ann by Grace of God of Great Britain France and Ireland Queen Defender of the faith etc.

Sealed and delivered by the above named
Edmund Poley in the presence of
Charles Robins
Paul Devall

Sealed and delivered by the above named
Anthony Crofts in the presence of
Tho. Wynne
John Glanvios

Sealed and delivered by the above named
Ann Croft in the presence of
John Turner
Thomas Casbell

Edmond ⬭ *Poley*

Anthony ⬭ *Crofts*

Ann ⬭ *Crofts*

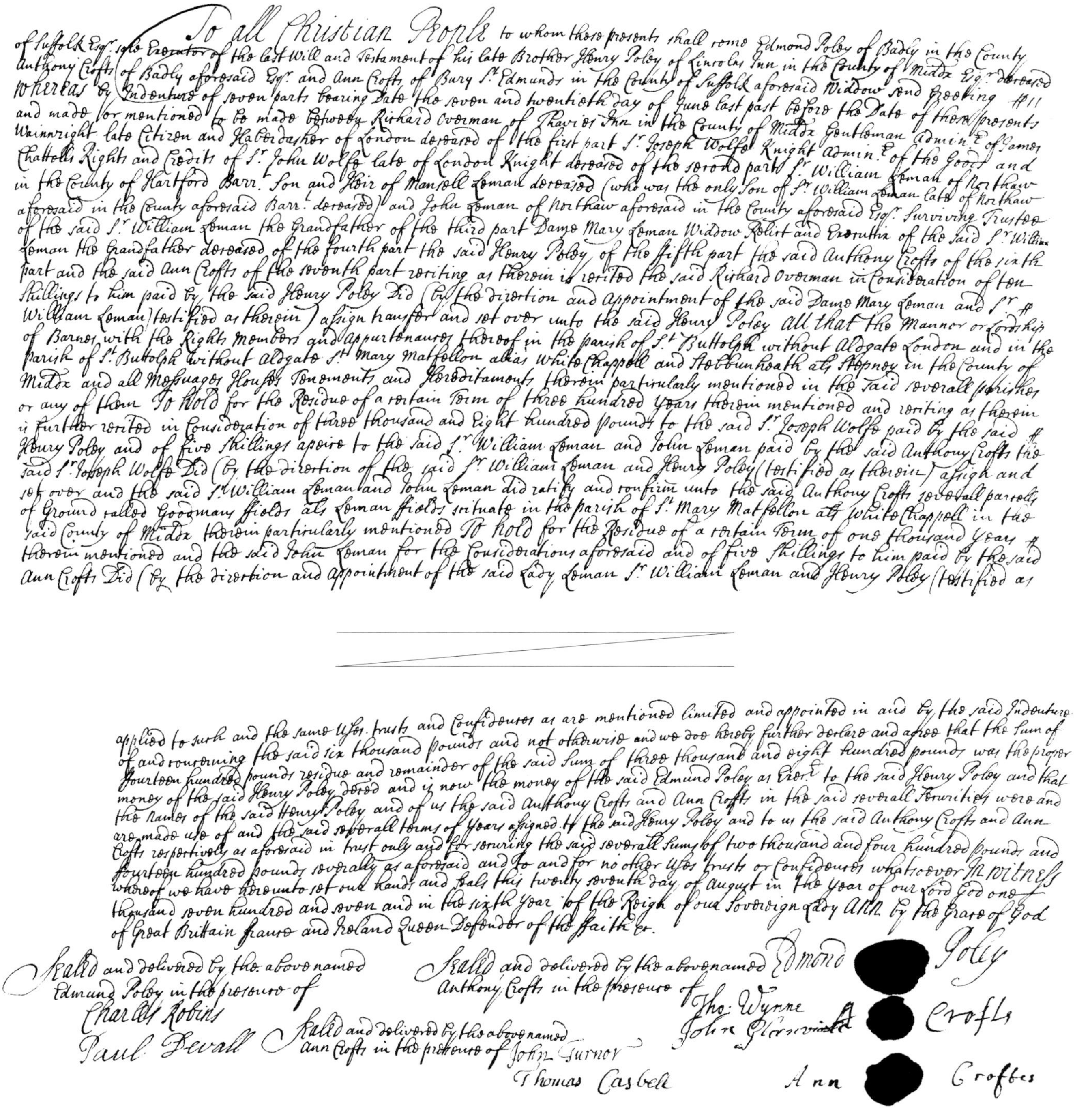

To all Christian People to whom these presents shall come Edmond Poley of Badly in the County of Suffolk Esqr sole Executor of the last Will and Testament of his late Brother Henry Poley of Lincolns Inn in the County of Midx Esqr deceased Anthony Crofts of Badly aforesaid Esqr. and Ann Crofts of Bury St Edmunds in the County of Suffolk aforesaid Widow send Greeting Whereas by Indenture of seven parts bearing date the seven and twentieth day of June last past before the date of these presents and made (or mentioned to be made) between Richard Overman of Thavies Inn in the County of Midx Gentleman Administr of James Wainwright late Citizen and Haberdasher of London deceased of the first part St Joseph Wolfe Knight Administr of the Goods and Chattells Rights and Credits of St John Wolfe late of London Knight deceased of the second part St William Leman of Northaw in the County of Hartford Barr. Son and Heir of Mansell Leman deceased (who was the only Son of St William Leman late of Northaw aforesaid in the County aforesaid Barr. deceased) and John Leman of Northaw aforesaid in the County aforesaid Esqr Surviving Trustee of the said St William Leman the Grandfather of the third part Dame Mary Leman Widow, Robert and Bertha of the said St William Leman the Grandfather deceased of the fourth part the said Henry Poley of the fifth part the said Anthony Crofts of the sixth part and the said Ann Crofts of the seventh part writing as therein is writed the said Richard Overman in consideration of ten Shillings to him paid by the said Henry Poley did (by the direction and appointment of the said Dame Mary Leman and Sr William Leman) testified as therein) assign transfer and set over unto the said Henry Poley All that the Mannor or Lordship of Barnes with the Rights members and appurtenances thereof in the parish of St Buttolph without Aldgate London and in the parish of St Buttolph without Aldgate St Mary Matfellon alias White Chappell and Stebunheath alt Stepney in the County of Midx and all Messuages Houses Tenements and Hereditaments therein particularly mentioned in the said severall parishes or any of them To Hold for the Residue of a certain Term of three hundred Years therein mentioned and writing as therein is further writed in Consideration of three thousand and eight hundred pounds to the said Sr Joseph Wolfe paid by the said Henry Poley and of five Shillings apeice to the said Sr William Leman and John Leman paid by the said Anthony Crofts the said Sr Joseph Wolfe did (by the direction of the said Sr William Leman and Henry Poley) testified as therein) assign and set over and the said Sr William Leman and John Leman did ratify and confirm unto the said Anthony Crofts severall parcells of Ground called Goodmans fields als Leman fields situate in the parish of St Mary Matfellon alt White Chappell in the said County of Midx therein particularly mentioned To Hold for the Residue of a certain Term of one thousand Years therein mentioned and the said John Leman for the Considerations aforesaid and of five Shillings to him paid by the said Ann Crofts did (by the direction and appointment of the said Lady Leman Sr William Leman and Henry Poley) testified as

applied to such and the same Uses, trusts and Confidences as are mentioned limited and appointed in and by the said Indenture of and concerning the said six thousand pounds and not otherwise and we doe hereby further declare and agree that the sum of fourteen hundred pounds residue and remainder of the said Sum of three thousand and eight hundred pounds was the proper money of the said Henry Poley deced and is now the money of the said Edmund Poley as Exor to the said Henry Poley and that the names of the said Henry Poley and of us the said Anthony Crofts and Ann Crofts in the said severall Securities were and are made use of and the said severall terms of Years assigned to the said Henry Poley and to us the said Anthony Crofts and Ann Crofts respectively as aforesaid in trust only and for securing the said severall Sums of two thousand and four hundred pounds and fourteen hundred pounds severally as aforesaid and to and for no other Uses trust or Confidences whatsoever In Witness whereof we have hereunto set our hands and seals this twenty seventh day of August in the year of our Lord God one thousand seven hundred and seven and in the sixth year of the Reign of our Sovereign Lady Ann by the Grace of God of Great Britain France and Ireland Queen Defender of the faith &c.

Sealed and delivered by the abovenamed
Edmund Poley in the presence of
Charles Robins
Paul Devall

Sealed and delivered by the abovenamed
Ann Crofts in the presence of John Turnor
Thomas Casbeh

Sealed and delivered by the abovenamed
Anthony Crofts in the presence of
Tho: Wynne
John Glanvill

Edmond Poley

A Crofts

Ann Croftes

Fig G.5 Part of the Indenture reproduced in full opposite, relating to the settlement of Henry Poley's estate.
(Reproduced courtesy of The James Marshall and Marie-Louise Osborn Collection
Beinecke Rare Book and Manuscript Library, Yale University, CT, USA.)

Notes
on the marriage of
MARGARET POLEY of Badley
to
Sir THOMAS PALMER Knt., of
Wingham, Kent

Fig G.6 Arms of Palmer of Wingham, Kent *(Or two bars gules, each charged with three trefoils)* impaling Poley of Badley *(Or, a lion rampant sable collared and chained or).*

Sir Thomas Palmer of Wingham in East Kent (eldest son of Sr Henry was borne 1540). His Father left him a Ward of about 17 yeares old (as may be seene in the Rolles of that Court) & in the 4th of Elizab. he came of age. He was high Sheriffe of Kent in the 37th of the said Queene. King James made him Gentleman of His Privy Chamber and in the 19 yeare of his Reyne Baronett viz[t] imediatly following S[r] Lewis Watson (afterwards Lord Rockingham) & just before S[r] Richard Roberts since Lord Roberts which is the 151st or as tis in Bakers Catalogue the 141st in number. He was eminent for his hospitality having kept 60 open Christmasses with his Lady without ever breaking up House. He died the 7th of Jan. 1625 in the 85th yeare of his age and was buried in his own Church where there is a very faire marble monument erected to his memory mentioning most of these Particulars (Fig G.7 opposite).

Margaret wife to Sr Thomas Palmer aforesaid was Daughter of John Poley of Badley Esq[r] Head of that very excellent & antient Family in Suffolke. Her mother was daughter to the Lord Wentworth Treasurer or Comptroler of the Household to Hen. 8, so that she was descended from, & makes her Posterity allied to many noble families, as to the Nevils, Chenyes, Barcleys, Lovelaces, Benetts &c. She was borne 1543 & having lived with much repute in her Countrey & happinesse with her Husband for 62 yeares, she soon followed him & is buried with him at Wingham She died in Aug[t] 1626 in the 83 yeare of her age.

(Miscellanea Genealogica Et Heraldica, p.108)

Monumental Inscription

To the
Memory of Sir
Thomas Palmer of
Wingham Knight & Baronet
and of Dame Margaret his wife
daugliter of John Poley of Badly Es[r]
of that auntient Fameley in the County of Sovthfolke
This Place was the Seate of his inheritance but not of his Dissent be
inge lineally extracted from the Howse of
Angmering in the County of Svssex
God crown'd him with y[e] blessinge of a
longe & prosperous life and augment
ed it with y[e] comforte of a virtuous
and pious Wife wth whose belou'd Societie
hee was enricht 62 yeares
The threades of theyr liues were euenly
Spunn they liu'd in Concord died in peace
his Period was 85 ⎫
           ⎬ yeares.
hers of 83 ⎭
They were Beloou'd of their Neighbours
Lamented by their Friends Honored by
their Children & Mist by y[e] Poore for
whose sakes they neuer brake up howse
in this Place for yeares Thus liu'd
they happely and died Christianly
hee the 7th of Janyary
she the Avgvst following
Anno 1625
They had
issue Six Sonnes
& fiue Daughters
where of
John—Mabell ⎫
Henry—Marie ⎬ died young.
John—Francis ⎭
Sir Thomas Palmer Knight
(father to Sir Thomas Palmer
Baronet now liuing) died be
fore his Father and lyes allso
heere interred
S[r] Roger Palmer Knight
of the bath was Cupbearer to y[e]
Princes Henry and Charles
and now master of the Howshowld to
Kinge Charles
James Palmer of the bedchamber
to King James of blessed memory
Jane first married to Sir William
Meredith Knight and after to the
Lord Vaughan
Margaret married to Richard
Amhvrst Eq[r] Seriant at Law
these last 4 are yet liuing
Anno 1627.

Fig G.7 The inscription on the memorial to Sir Thomas Palmer Knt.,and Dame Margaret (née Poley) his wife in the Collegiate Church of St Mary the Virgin, Wingham, Kent.

Index

This simple keyword index, arranged alphabetically, lists over 4000 selected names, places and events etc.
(Surnames are in bold type and places are in capitals)